16

DISCARD

APR 9 2009

LIKEWISE

The High School Comic Chronicles of

ARIEL SCHRAG

A Touchstone Book
Published by Simon & Schuster
New York   London   Toronto   Sydney

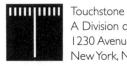

Touchstone
A Division of Simon & Schuster, Inc.
1230 Avenue of the Americas
New York, NY 10020

Certain names and identifying characteristics have been changed.

First Touchstone trade paperback edition April 2009

TOUCHSTONE and colophon are registered trademarks of Simon & Schuster, Inc.

For information about special discounts for bulk purchases,
please contact Simon & Schuster Special Sales at
1-866-506-1949 or business@simonandschuster.com.

The Simon & Schuster Speakers Bureau can bring authors to your live event.
For more information or to book an event contact
the Simon & Schuster Speakers Bureau at 1-866-248-3049
or visit our website at www.simonspeakers.com.

Manufactured in the United States of America

10 9 8 7 6 5 4 3 2 1

Library of Congress Cataloging-in-Publication Data is available.

ISBN-13: 978-1-4165-5237-6
ISBN-10: 1-4165-5237-5

Portions of this work were previously published, in serial, by SLG Publishing.

For
Ms. Stahl

Likewise is based on my senior year of high school. It was
written between June 1998 and August 1999, the year after I graduated.

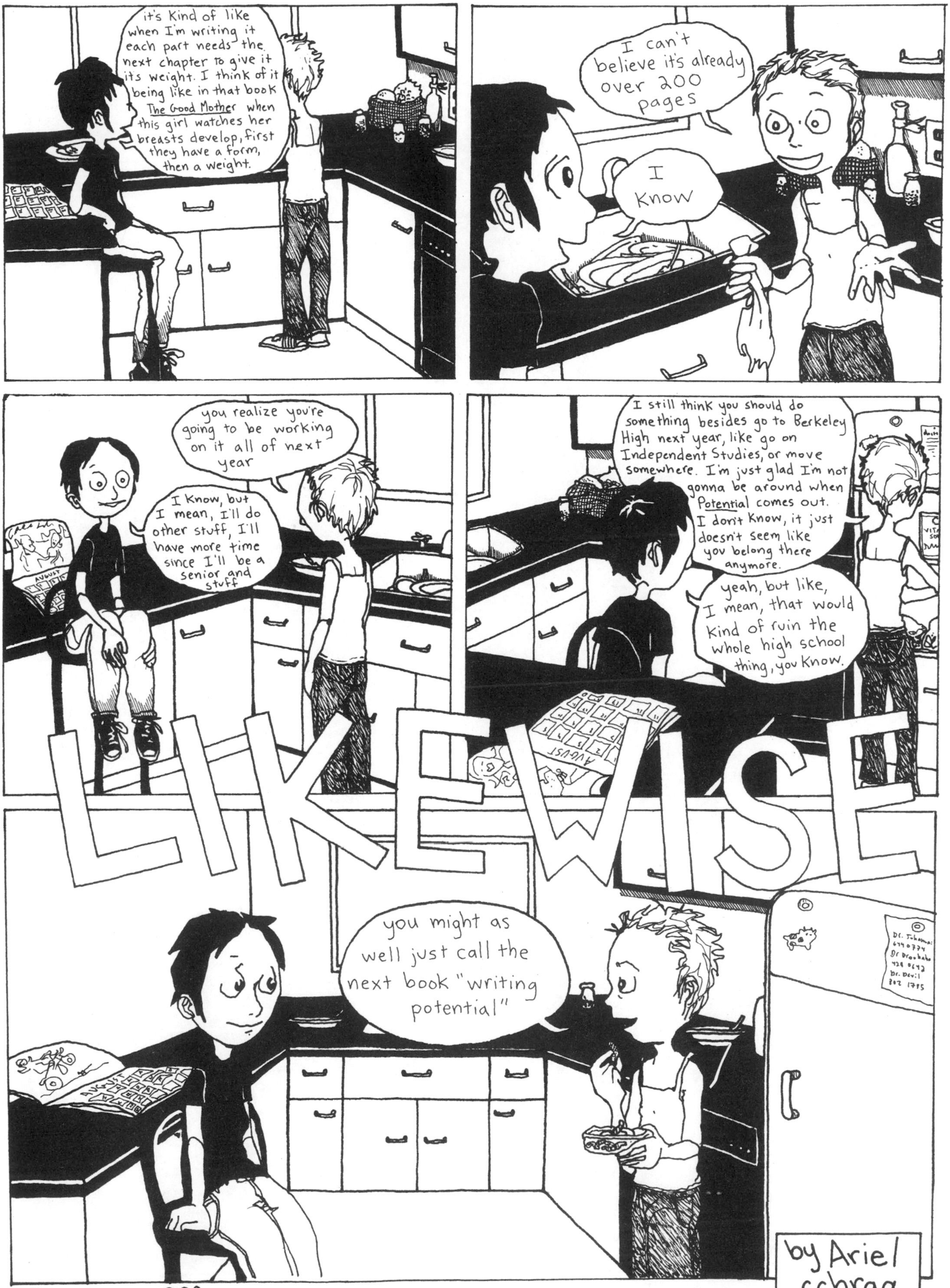

it's Kind of like when I'm writing it each part needs the next chapter to give it its weight. I think of it being like in that book The Good Mother when this girl watches her breasts develop, first they have a form, then a weight.
I can't believe it's already over 200 pages
I Know
you realize you're going to be working on it all of next year
I Know, but I mean, I'll do other stuff, I'll have more time since I'll be a senior and stuff
I still think you should do something besides go to Berkeley High next year, like go on Independent Studies, or move somewhere. I'm just glad I'm not gonna be around when Potential comes out. I don't Know, it just doesn't seem like you belong there anymore.
yeah, but like, I mean, that would Kind of ruin the whole high school thing, you Know.
LIKEWISE
you might as well just call the next book "writing potential"
by Ariel schrag

© summer 1998

I

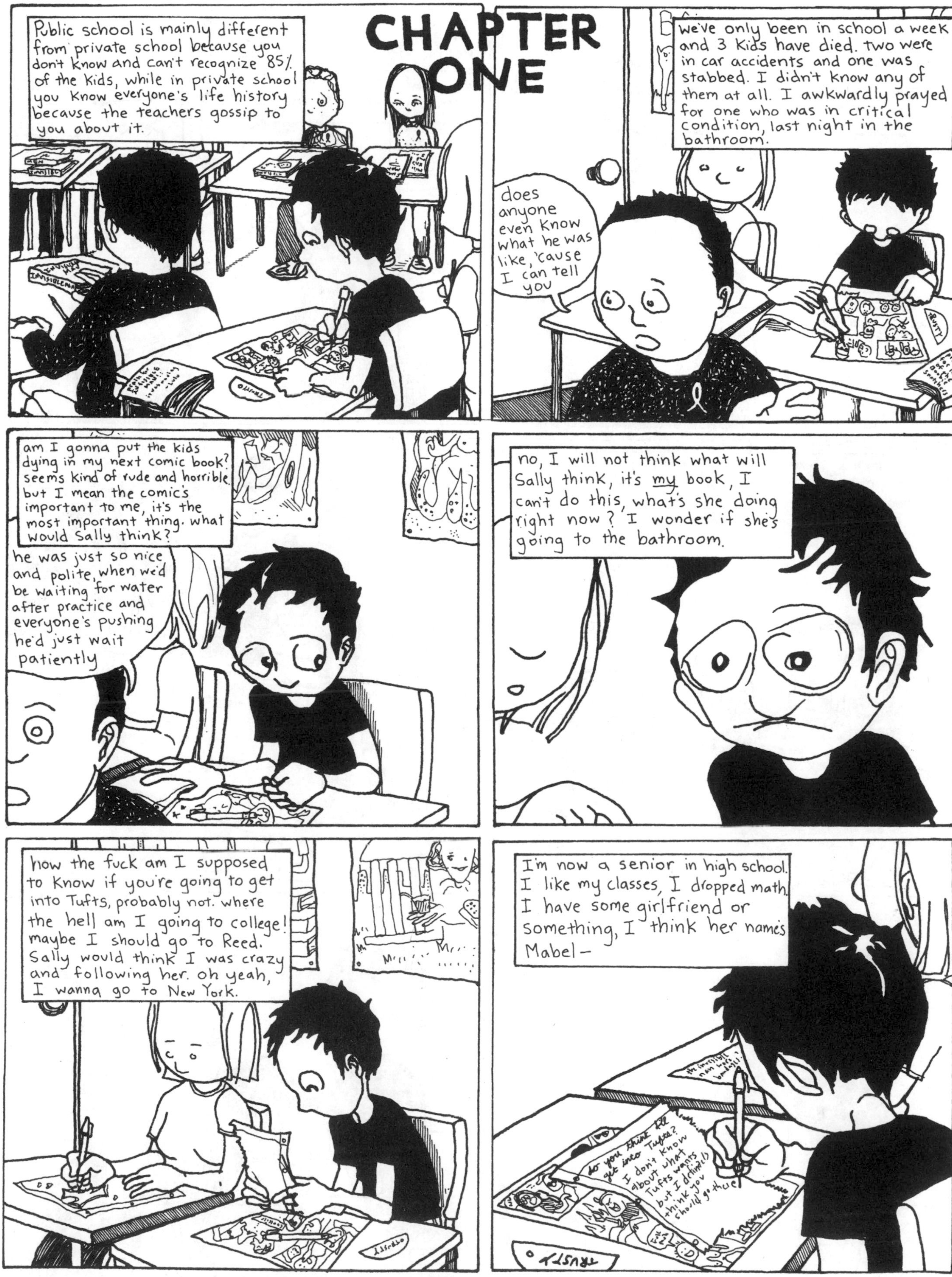
CHAPTER ONE
Public school is mainly different from private school because you don't know and can't recognize 85% of the kids, while in private school you know everyone's life history because the teachers gossip to you about it.
We've only been in school a week and 3 kids have died. two were in car accidents and one was stabbed. I didn't know any of them at all. I awkwardly prayed for one who was in critical condition, last night in the bathroom.
does anyone even know what he was like, 'cause I can tell you
am I gonna put the kids dying in my next comic book? seems kind of rude and horrible. but I mean the comic's important to me, it's the most important thing. what would Sally think?
he was just so nice and polite, when we'd be waiting for water after practice and everyone's pushing he'd just wait patiently
no, I will not think what will Sally think, it's my book, I can't do this, what's she doing right now? I wonder if she's going to the bathroom.
how the fuck am I supposed to know if you're going to get into Tufts, probably not. where the hell am I going to college! maybe I should go to Reed. Sally would think I was crazy and following her. oh yeah, I wanna go to New York.
I'm now a senior in high school. I like my classes, I dropped math. I have some girlfriend or something, I think her name's Mabel –
do you think I'll get into Tufts?
I don't know about what Tufts wants but I definitely think you should go there
TRUSTY

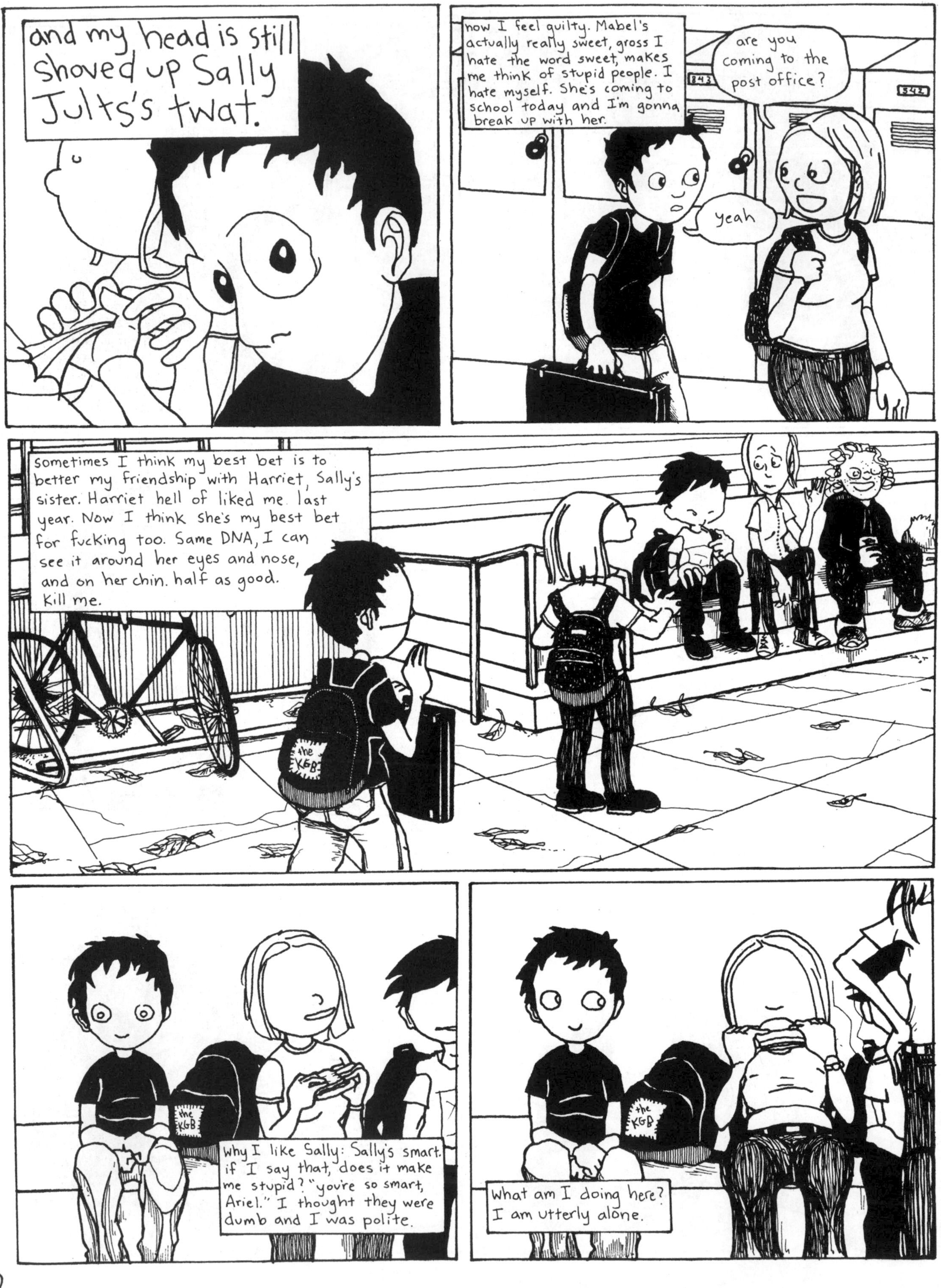
and my head is still shoved up Sally Jults's twat.
now I feel guilty. Mabel's actually really sweet, gross I hate the word sweet, makes me think of stupid people. I hate myself. She's coming to school today and I'm gonna break up with her.
are you coming to the post office?
yeah
sometimes I think my best bet is to better my friendship with Harriet, Sally's sister. Harriet hell of liked me last year. Now I think she's my best bet for fucking too. Same DNA, I can see it around her eyes and nose, and on her chin. half as good. Kill me.
the KGB
the KGB
Why I like Sally: Sally's smart. if I say that, does it make me stupid? "you're so smart, Ariel." I thought they were dumb and I was polite.
the KGB
What am I doing here? I am utterly alone.

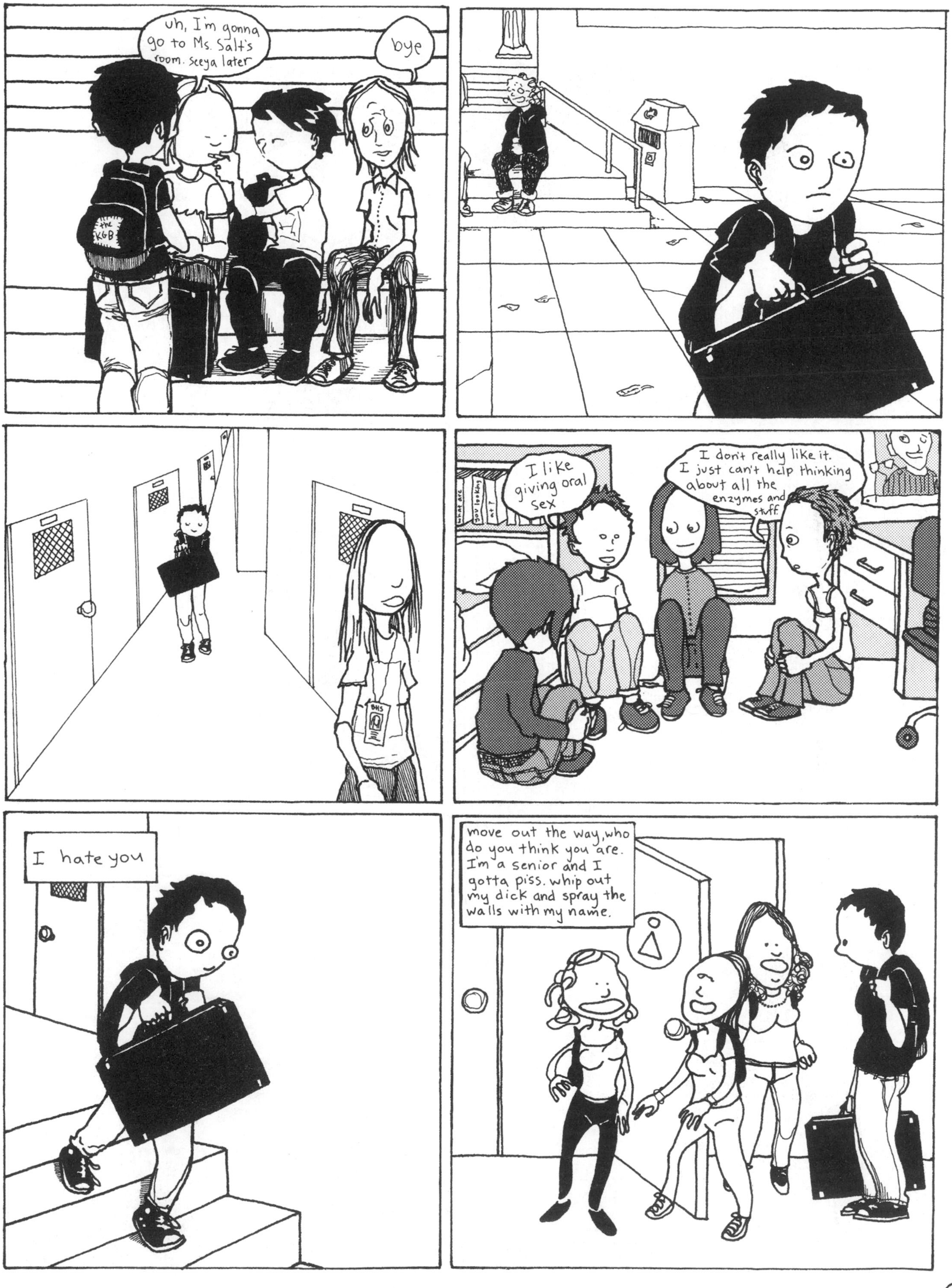
uh, I'm gonna go to Ms. Salt's room. seeya later
bye
I like giving oral sex
I don't really like it. I just can't help thinking about all the enzymes and stuff.
I hate you
move out the way, who do you think you are. I'm a senior and I gotta piss. whip out my dick and spray the walls with my name.

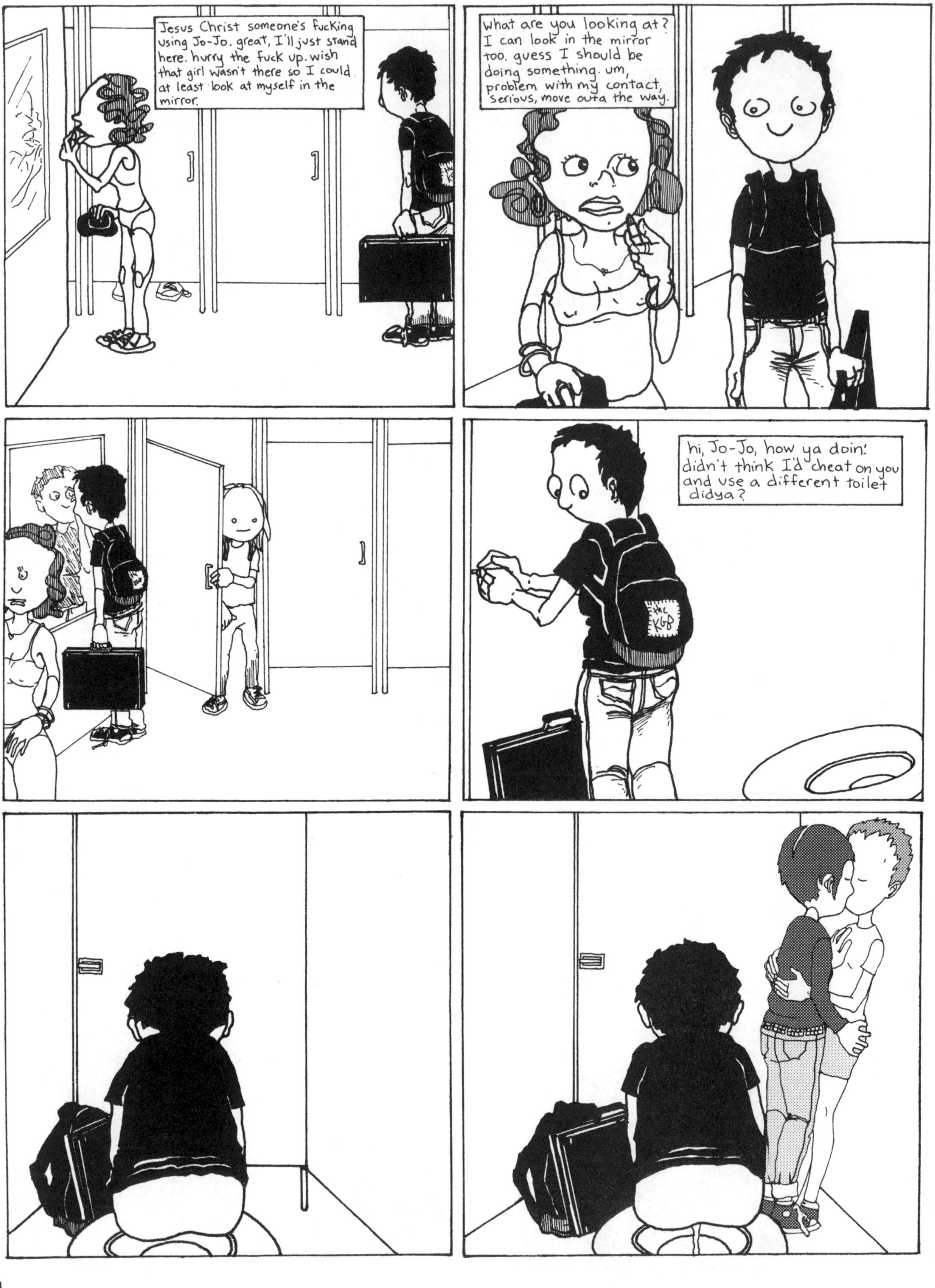
Jesus Christ someone's fucking using Jo-Jo. great, I'll just stand here. hurry the fuck up. wish that girl wasn't there so I could at least look at myself in the mirror.
What are you looking at? I can look in the mirror too. guess I should be doing something. um, problem with my contact, serious, move outa the way.
the KGB
hi, Jo-Jo, how ya doin! didn't think I'd cheat on you and use a different toilet didya?

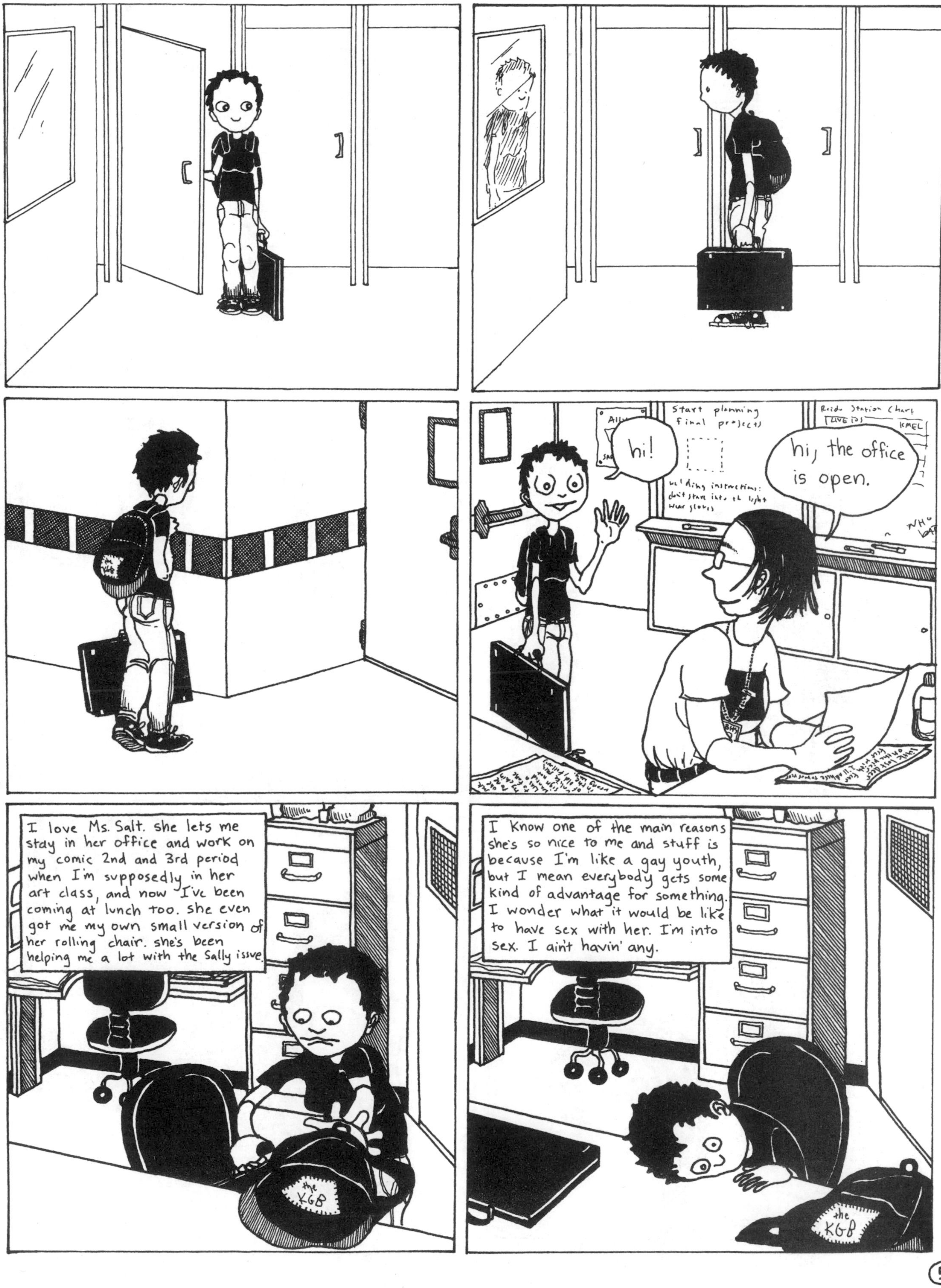
hi!
hi, the office is open.
I love Ms. Salt. she lets me stay in her office and work on my comic 2nd and 3rd period when I'm supposedly in her art class, and now I've been coming at lunch too. she even got me my own small version of her rolling chair. she's been helping me a lot with the Sally issue.
I know one of the main reasons she's so nice to me and stuff is because I'm like a gay youth, but I mean everybody gets some kind of advantage for something. I wonder what it would be like to have sex with her. I'm into sex. I ain't havin' any.

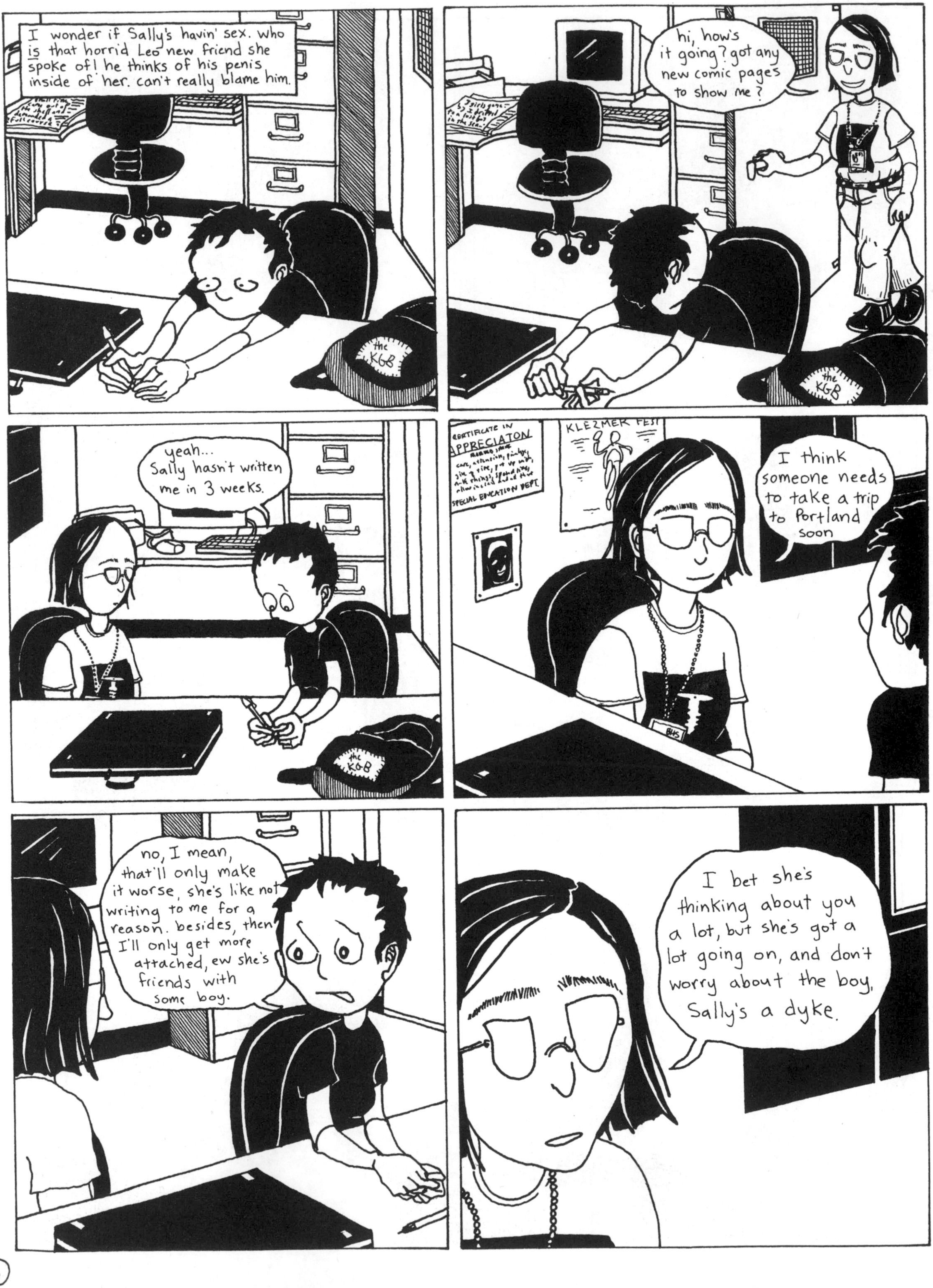

I wonder if Sally's havin' sex. who is that horrid Leo new friend she spoke of! he thinks of his penis inside of her. can't really blame him.
the KGB
hi, how's it going? got any new comic pages to show me?
the KGB
yeah... Sally hasn't written me in 3 weeks.
the KGB
CERTIFICATE IN APPRECIATON
SPECIAL EDUCATION DEPT.
KLEZMER FEST
I think someone needs to take a trip to Portland soon
no, I mean, that'll only make it worse, she's like not writing to me for a reason. besides, then I'll only get more attached, ew she's friends with some boy.
I bet she's thinking about you a lot, but she's got a lot going on, and don't worry about the boy, Sally's a dyke.

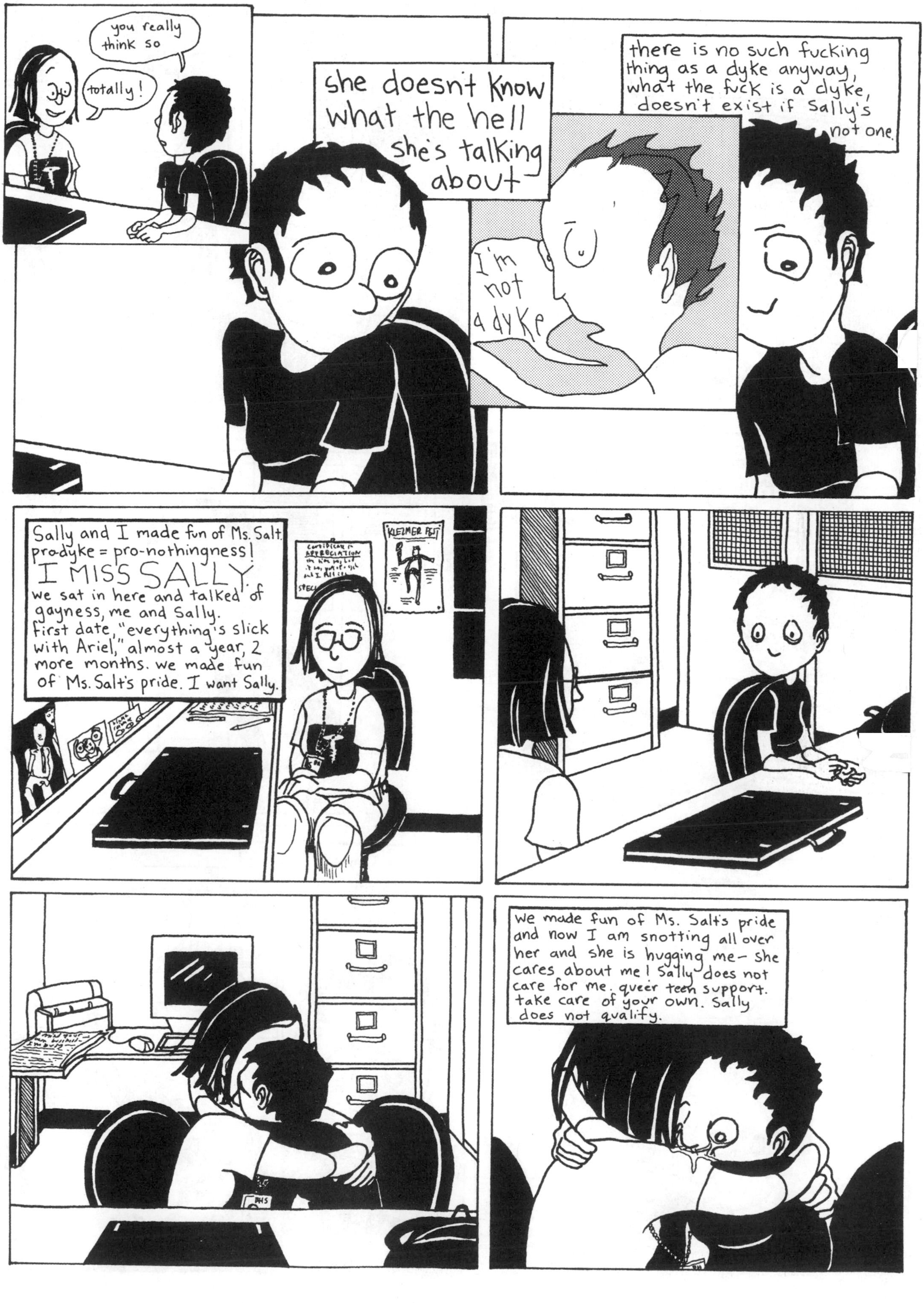

you really think so
totally!
she doesn't know what the hell she's talking about
I'm not a dyke
there is no such fucking thing as a dyke anyway, what the fuck is a dyke, doesn't exist if Sally's not one.
Sally and I made fun of Ms. Salt. prodyke = pro-nothingness! I MISS SALLY. we sat in here and talked of gayness, me and Sally. first date, "everything's slick with Ariel," almost a year, 2 more months. we made fun of Ms. Salt's pride. I want Sally.
KLEZMER FEST
We made fun of Ms. Salt's pride and now I am snotting all over her and she is hugging me— she cares about me! Sally does not care for me. queer teen support. take care of your own. Sally does not qualify.

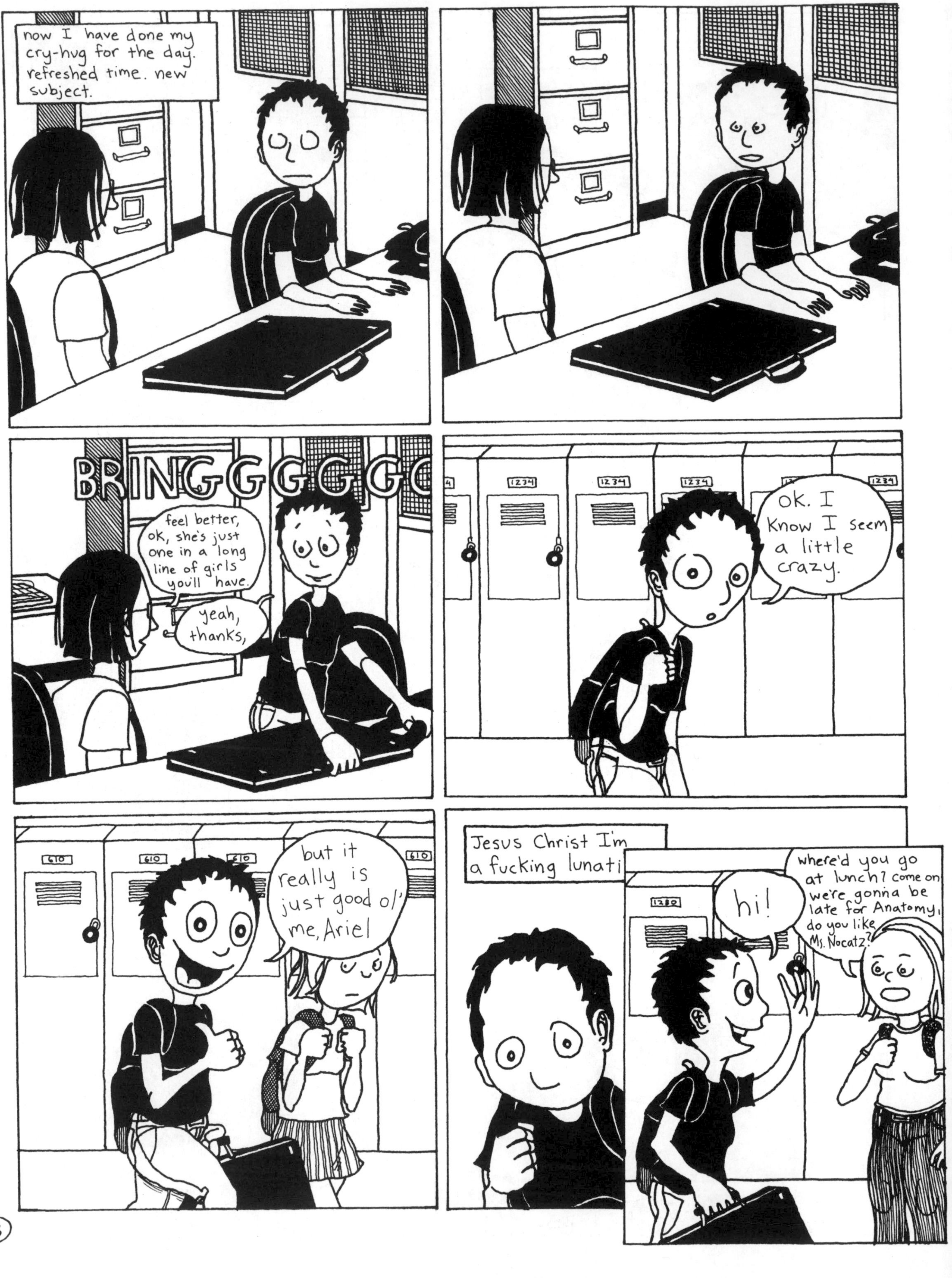
now I have done my cry-hug for the day. refreshed time. new subject.
BRINGGGGGG
feel better, ok, she's just one in a long line of girls you'll have.
yeah, thanks,
ok. I know I seem a little crazy.
but it really is just good ol' me, Ariel
Jesus Christ I'm a fucking lunati
hi!
where'd you go at lunch? come on we're gonna be late for Anatomy, do you like Ms. Nocatz?

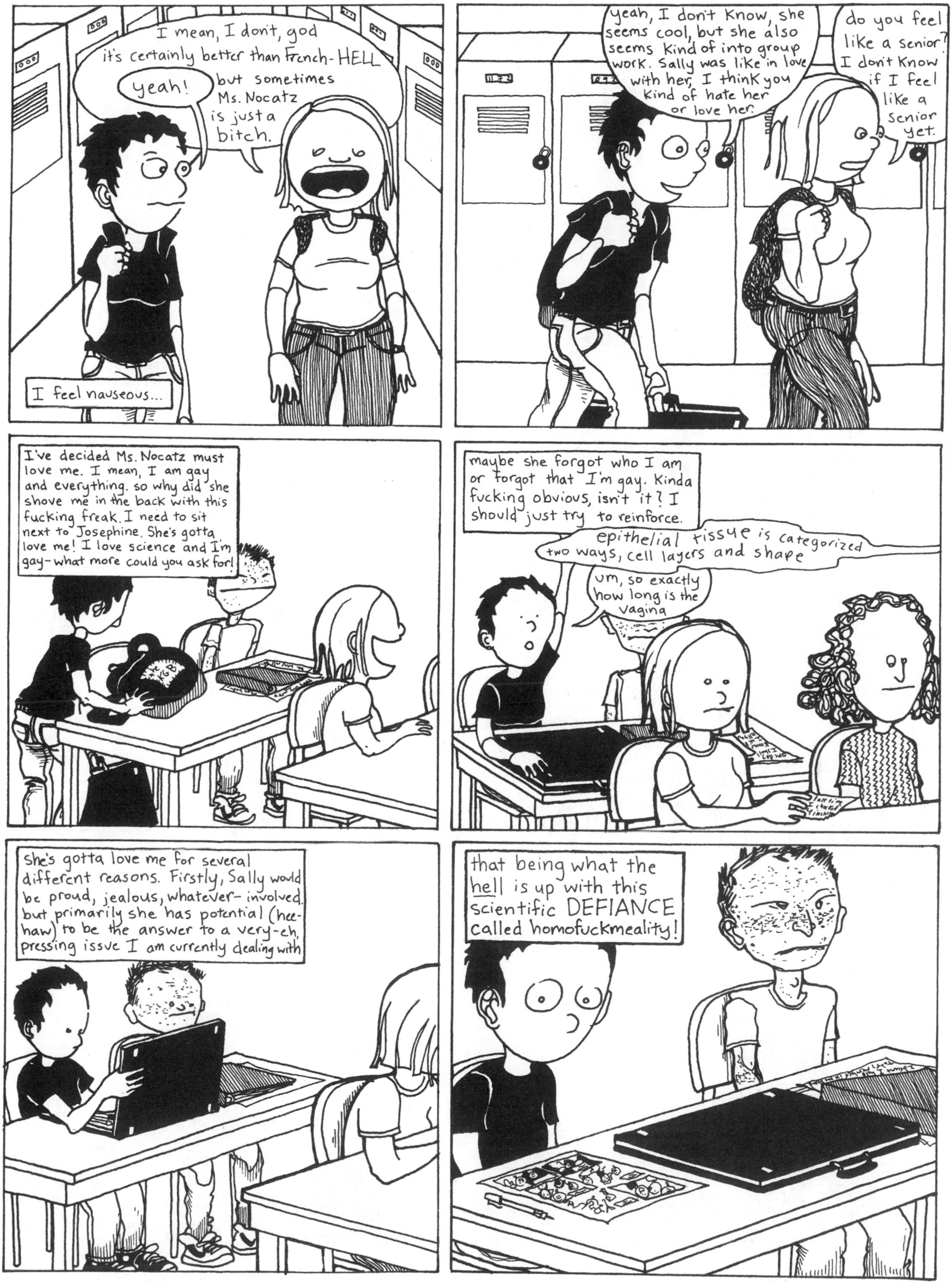
I mean, I don't, god it's certainly better than French- HELL
yeah!
but sometimes Ms. Nocatz is just a bitch.
I feel nauseous...
yeah, I don't know, she seems cool, but she also seems kind of into group work. Sally was like in love with her, I think you kind of hate her or love her.
do you feel like a senior? I don't know if I feel like a senior yet.
I've decided Ms. Nocatz must love me. I mean, I am gay and everything. so why did she shove me in the back with this fucking freak. I need to sit next to Josephine. She's gotta love me! I love science and I'm gay- what more could you ask for!
maybe she forgot who I am or forgot that I'm gay. Kinda fucking obvious, isn't it? I should just try to reinforce.
epithelial tissue is categorized two ways, cell layers and shape
um, so exactly how long is the vagina
she's gotta love me for several different reasons. Firstly, Sally would be proud, jealous, whatever- involved. but primarily she has potential (hee-haw) to be the answer to a very-eh, pressing issue I am currently dealing with
that being what the hell is up with this scientific DEFIANCE called homofuckmeality!

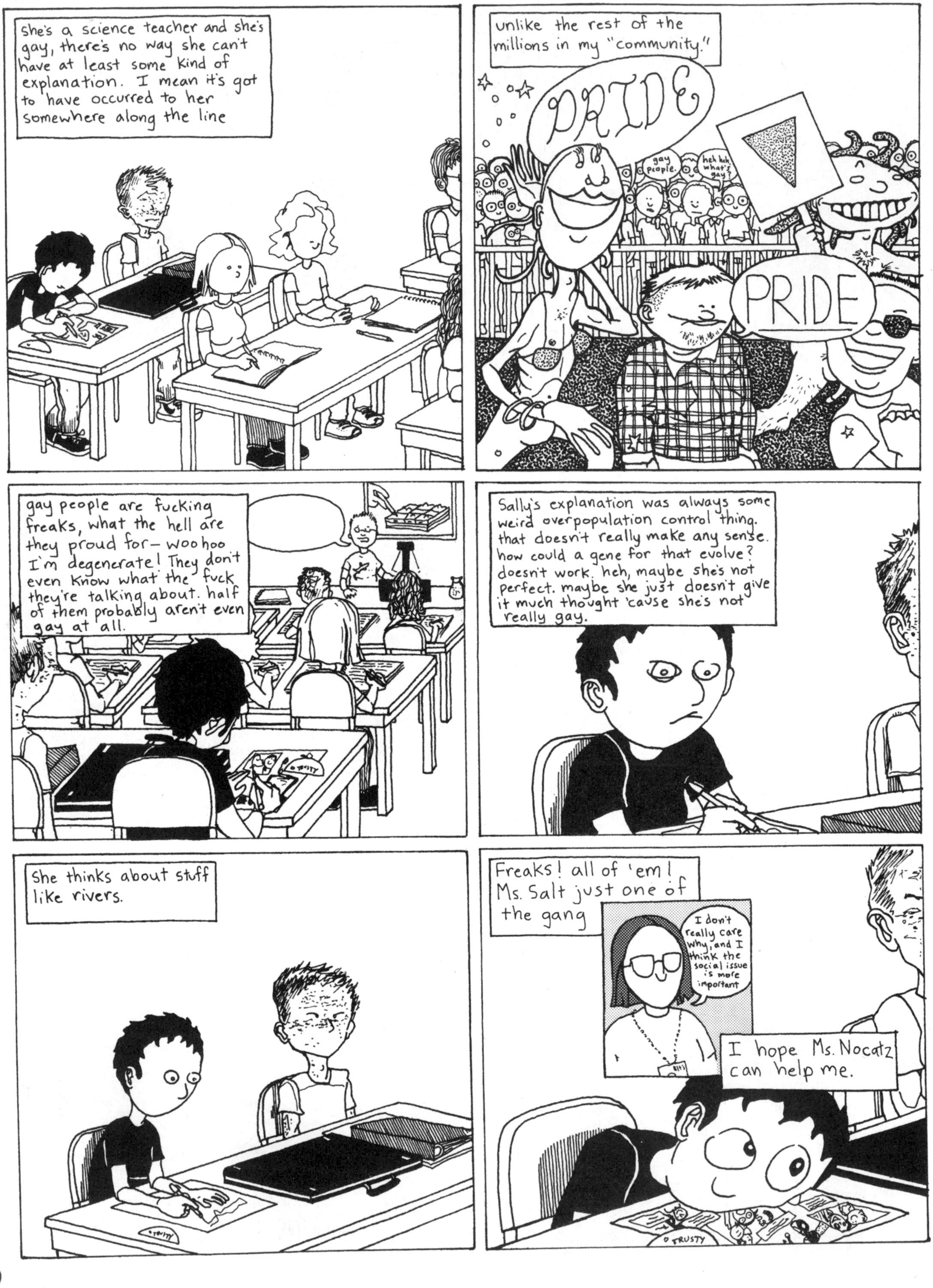
she's a science teacher and she's gay, there's no way she can't have at least some kind of explanation. I mean it's got to have occurred to her somewhere along the line
unlike the rest of the millions in my "community."
PRIDE
gay people.
heh heh, what's gay?
PRIDE
gay people are fucking freaks, what the hell are they proud for— woo hoo I'm degenerate! They don't even know what the fuck they're talking about. half of them probably aren't even gay at all.
Sally's explanation was always some weird overpopulation control thing. that doesn't really make any sense. how could a gene for that evolve? doesn't work. heh, maybe she's not perfect. maybe she just doesn't give it much thought 'cause she's not really gay.
She thinks about stuff like rivers.
Freaks! all of 'em! Ms. Salt just one of the gang
I don't really care why, and I think the social issue is more important
I hope Ms. Nocatz can help me.

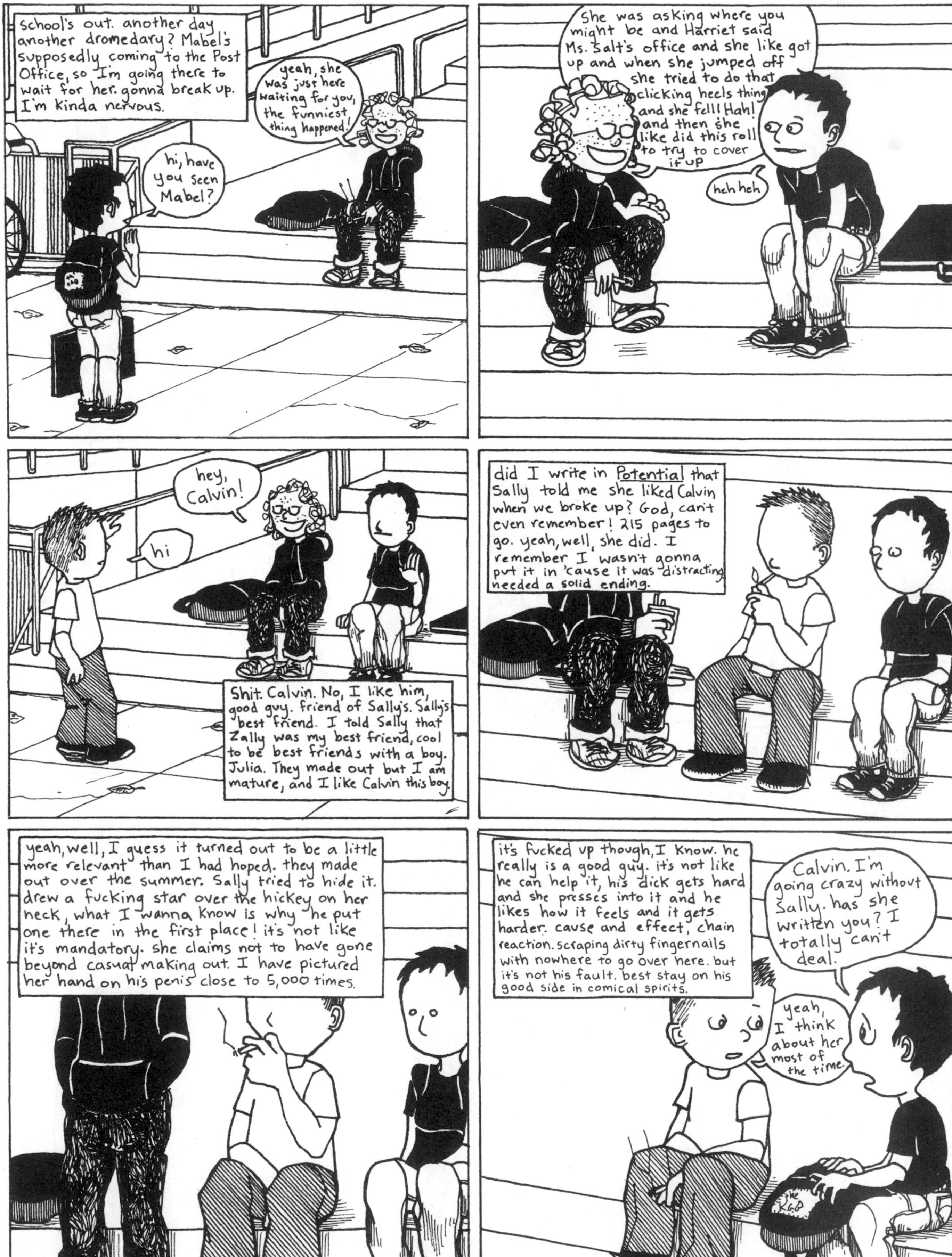
school's out. another day another dromedary? Mabel's supposedly coming to the Post Office, so I'm going there to wait for her. gonna break up. I'm kinda nervous.
hi, have you seen Mabel?
yeah, she was just here waiting for you, the funniest thing happened!
She was asking where you might be and Harriet said Ms. Salt's office and she like got up and when she jumped off she tried to do that clicking heels thing and she fell! Hah! and then she like did this roll to try to cover it up
heh heh
hey, Calvin!
hi
Shit. Calvin. No, I like him, good guy. friend of Sally's. Sally's best friend. I told Sally that Zally was my best friend, cool to be best friends with a boy. Julia. They made out but I am mature, and I like Calvin this boy.
did I write in Potential that Sally told me she liked Calvin when we broke up? God, can't even remember! 215 pages to go. yeah, well, she did. I remember I wasn't gonna put it in 'cause it was distracting needed a solid ending.
yeah, well, I guess it turned out to be a little more relevant than I had hoped. they made out over the summer. Sally tried to hide it. drew a fucking star over the hickey on her neck, what I wanna know is why he put one there in the first place! it's not like it's mandatory. she claims not to have gone beyond casual making out. I have pictured her hand on his penis close to 5,000 times.
it's fucked up though, I know. he really is a good guy. it's not like he can help it, his dick gets hard and she presses into it and he likes how it feels and it gets harder. cause and effect, chain reaction. scraping dirty fingernails with nowhere to go over here. but it's not his fault. best stay on his good side in comical spirits.
Calvin. I'm going crazy without Sally. has she written you? I totally can't deal.
yeah, I think about her most of the time.

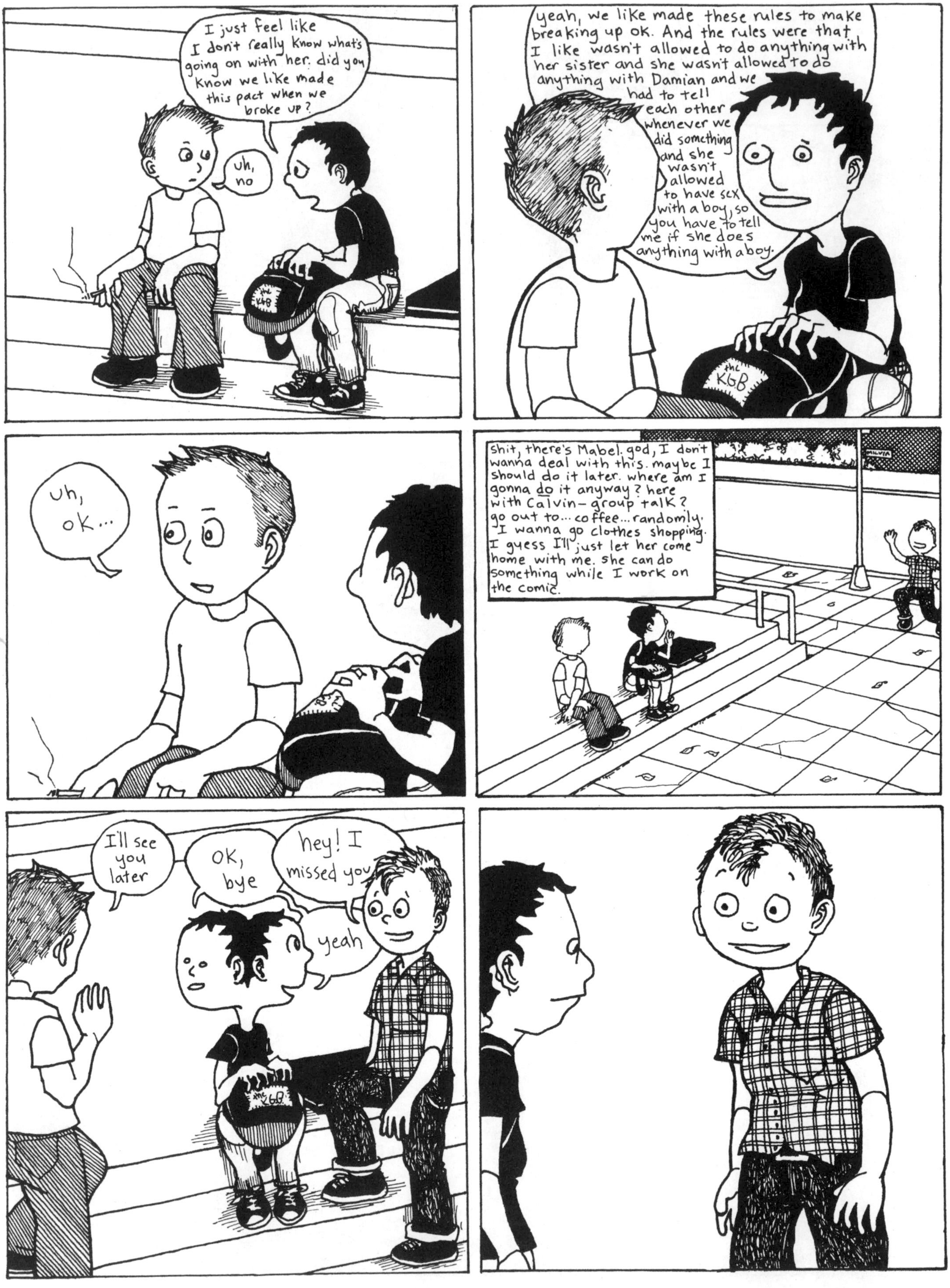

I just feel like I don't really know what's going on with her. did you know we like made this pact when we broke up?
uh, no
yeah, we like made these rules to make breaking up ok. And the rules were that I like wasn't allowed to do anything with her sister and she wasn't allowed to do anything with Damian and we had to tell each other whenever we did something and she wasn't allowed to have sex with a boy, so you have to tell me if she does anything with a boy.
the KGB
uh, ok...
shit, there's Mabel. god, I don't wanna deal with this. maybe I should do it later. where am I gonna do it anyway? here with Calvin- group talk? go out to... coffee... randomly. I wanna go clothes shopping. I guess I'll just let her come home with me. she can do something while I work on the comic.
I'll see you later
OK, bye
hey! I missed you
yeah

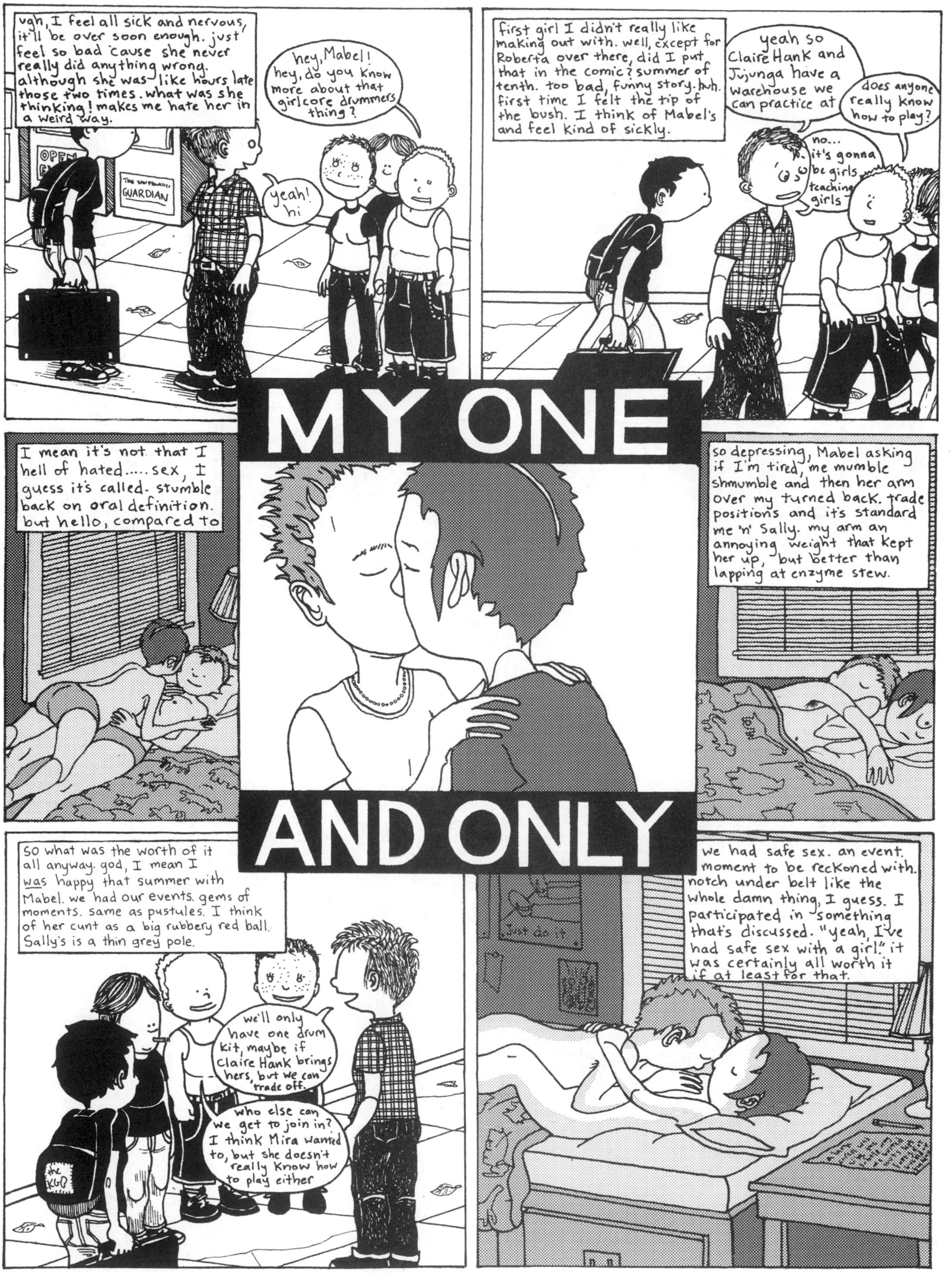

ugh, I feel all sick and nervous, it'll be over soon enough. just feel so bad 'cause she never really did anything wrong. although she was like hours late those two times. what was she thinking! makes me hate her in a weird way.
hey, Mabel! hey, do you know more about that girlcore drummers thing?
yeah! hi
OPEN
GUARDIAN
first girl I didn't really like making out with. well, except for Roberta over there, did I put that in the comic? summer of tenth. too bad, funny story. huh. first time I felt the tip of the bush. I think of Mabel's and feel kind of sickly.
yeah so Claire Hank and Jujunga have a warehouse we can practice at
does anyone really know how to play?
no... it's gonna be girls teaching girls
MY ONE
AND ONLY
I mean it's not that I hell of hated..... sex, I guess it's called. stumble back on oral definition. but hello, compared to
so depressing, Mabel asking if I'm tired, me mumble shmumble and then her arm over my turned back. trade positions and it's standard me 'n' Sally. my arm an annoying weight that kept her up, but better than lapping at enzyme stew.
so what was the worth of it all anyway. god, I mean I was happy that summer with Mabel. we had our events. gems of moments. same as pustules. I think of her cunt as a big rubbery red ball. Sally's is a thin grey pole.
we'll only have one drum kit, maybe if Claire Hank brings hers, but we can trade off.
who else can we get to join in? I think Mira wanted to, but she doesn't really know how to play either
we had safe sex. an event. moment to be reckoned with. notch under belt like the whole damn thing, I guess. I participated in something that's discussed. "yeah, I've had safe sex with a girl." it was certainly all worth it if at least for that.
Just do it

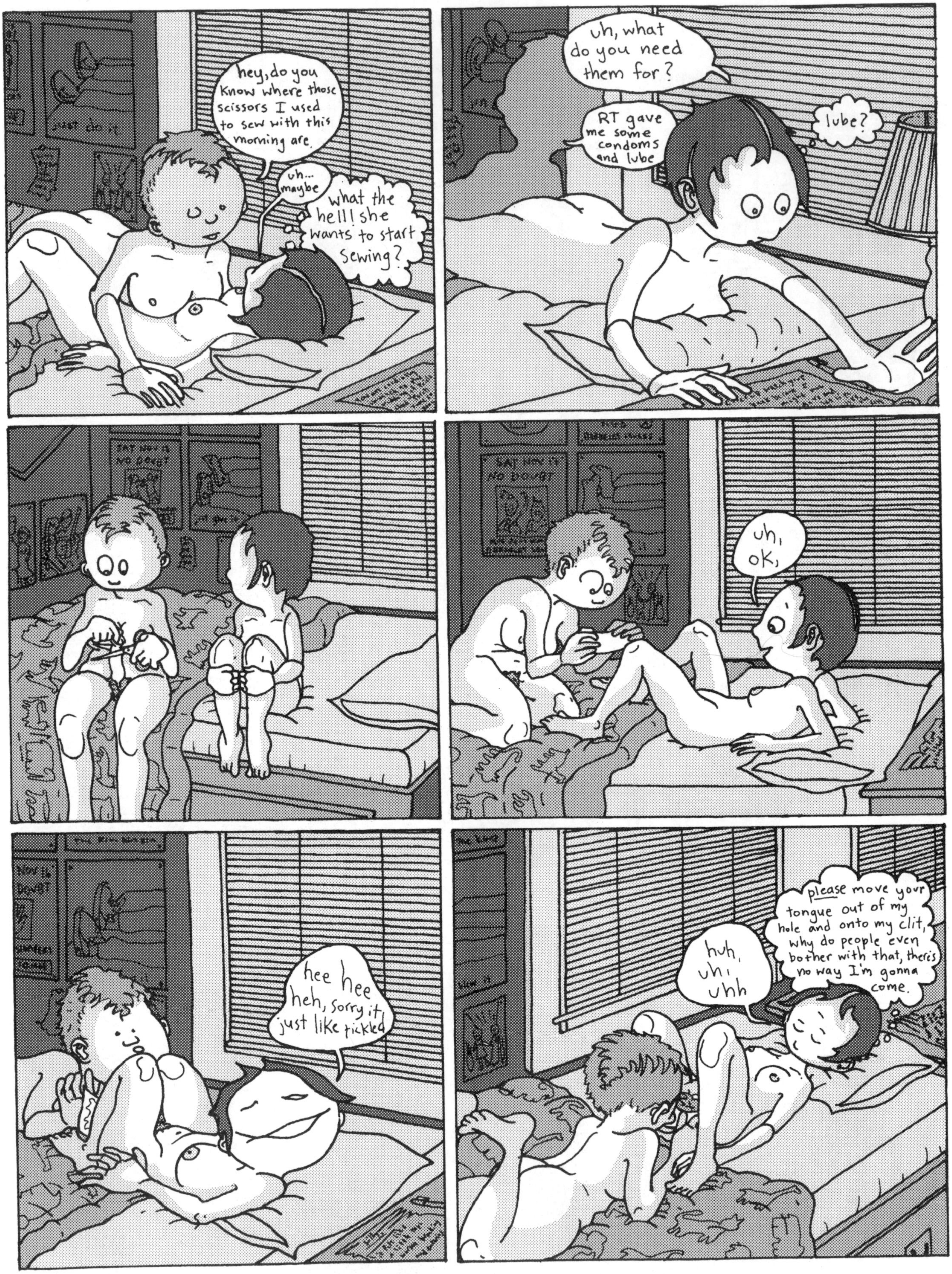
hey, do you Know where those scissors I used to sew with this morning are.
uh... maybe
what the hell! she wants to start sewing?
uh, what do you need them for?
RT gave me some condoms and lube
lube?
uh, ok,
hee hee heh, sorry it just like tickled
huh, uh, uhh
please move your tongue out of my hole and onto my clit, why do people even bother with that, there's no way I'm gonna come.

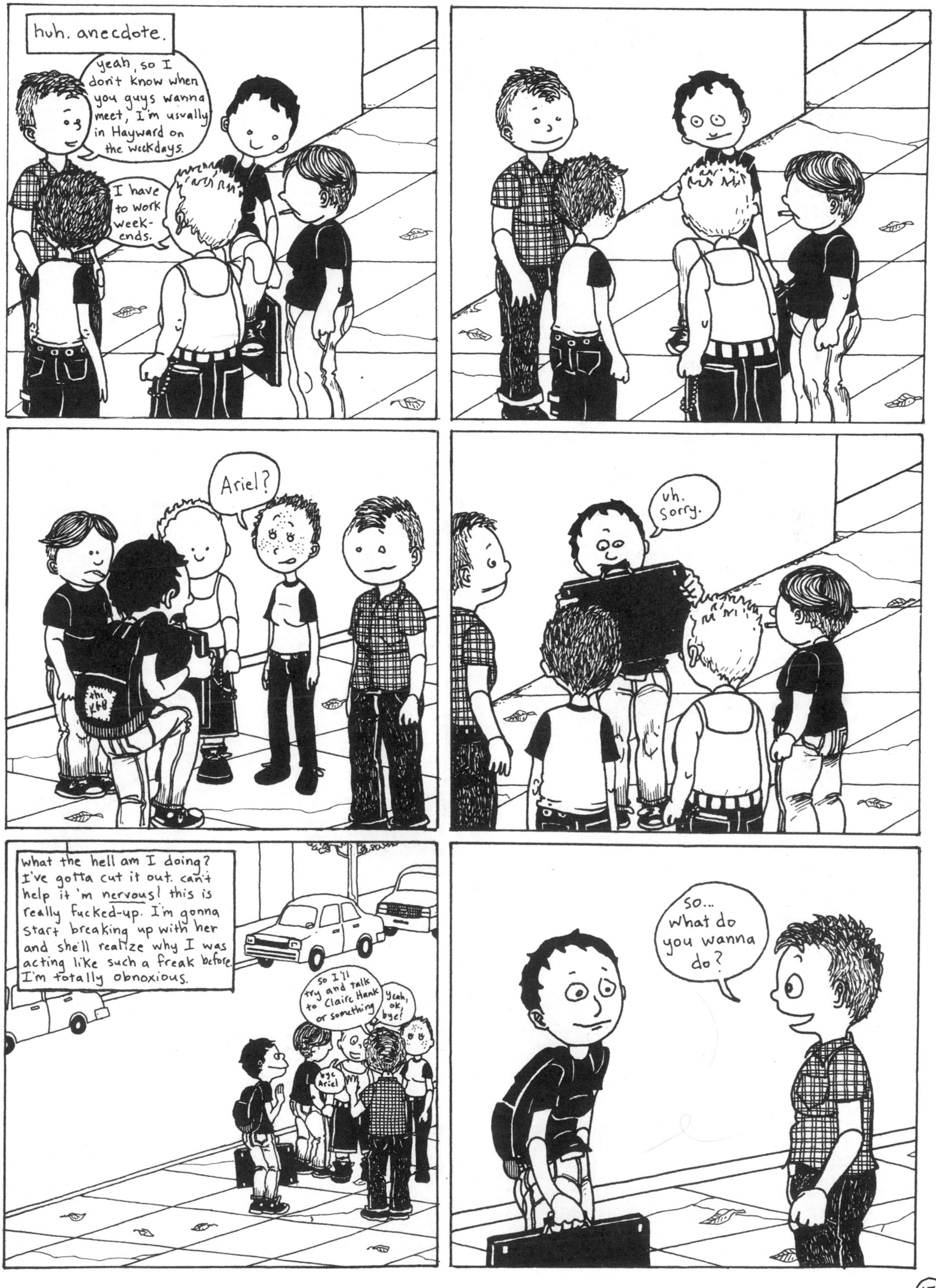
huh. anecdote.
yeah, so I don't know when you guys wanna meet, I'm usually in Hayward on the weekdays.
I have to work week-ends.
Ariel?
uh. sorry.
what the hell am I doing? I've gotta cut it out. can't help it 'm nervous! this is really fucked-up. I'm gonna start breaking up with her and she'll realize why I was acting like such a freak before. I'm totally obnoxious.
So I'll try and talk to Claire Hank or something
Yeah, ok, bye!
bye Ariel
so... what do you wanna do?

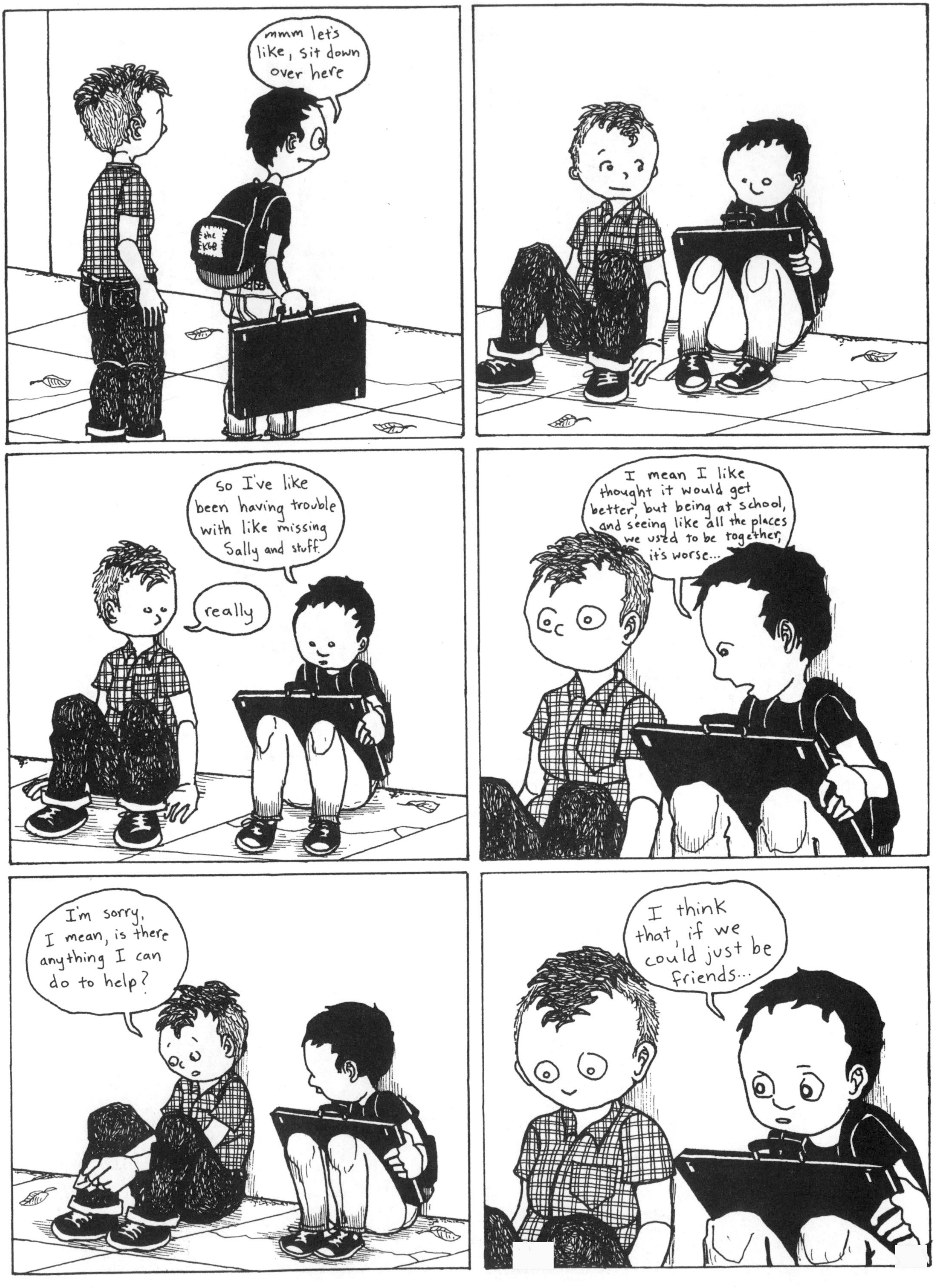
mmm let's like, sit down over here
so I've like been having trouble with like missing Sally and stuff.
really
I mean I like thought it would get better, but being at school, and seeing like all the places we used to be together, it's worse...
I'm sorry, I mean, is there anything I can do to help?
I think that, if we could just be friends...

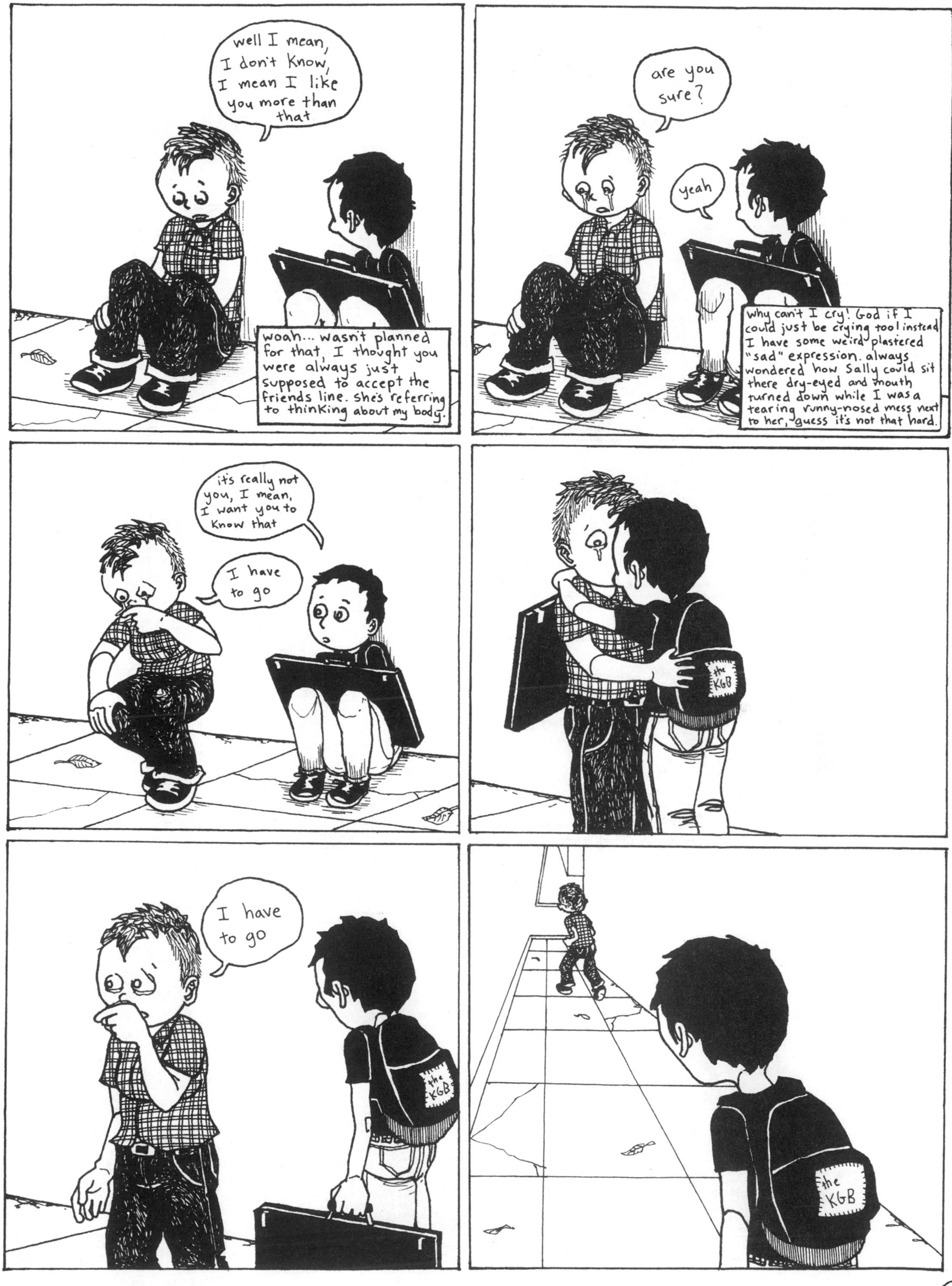

well I mean, I don't know, I mean I like you more than that
woah... wasn't planned for that, I thought you were always just supposed to accept the friends line. she's referring to thinking about my body.
are you sure?
yeah
why can't I cry! God if I could just be crying too! instead I have some weird plastered "sad" expression. always wondered how Sally could sit there dry-eyed and mouth turned down while I was a tearing runny-nosed mess next to her, guess it's not that hard.
it's really not you, I mean, I want you to know that
I have to go
the KGB
I have to go
the KGB
the KGB

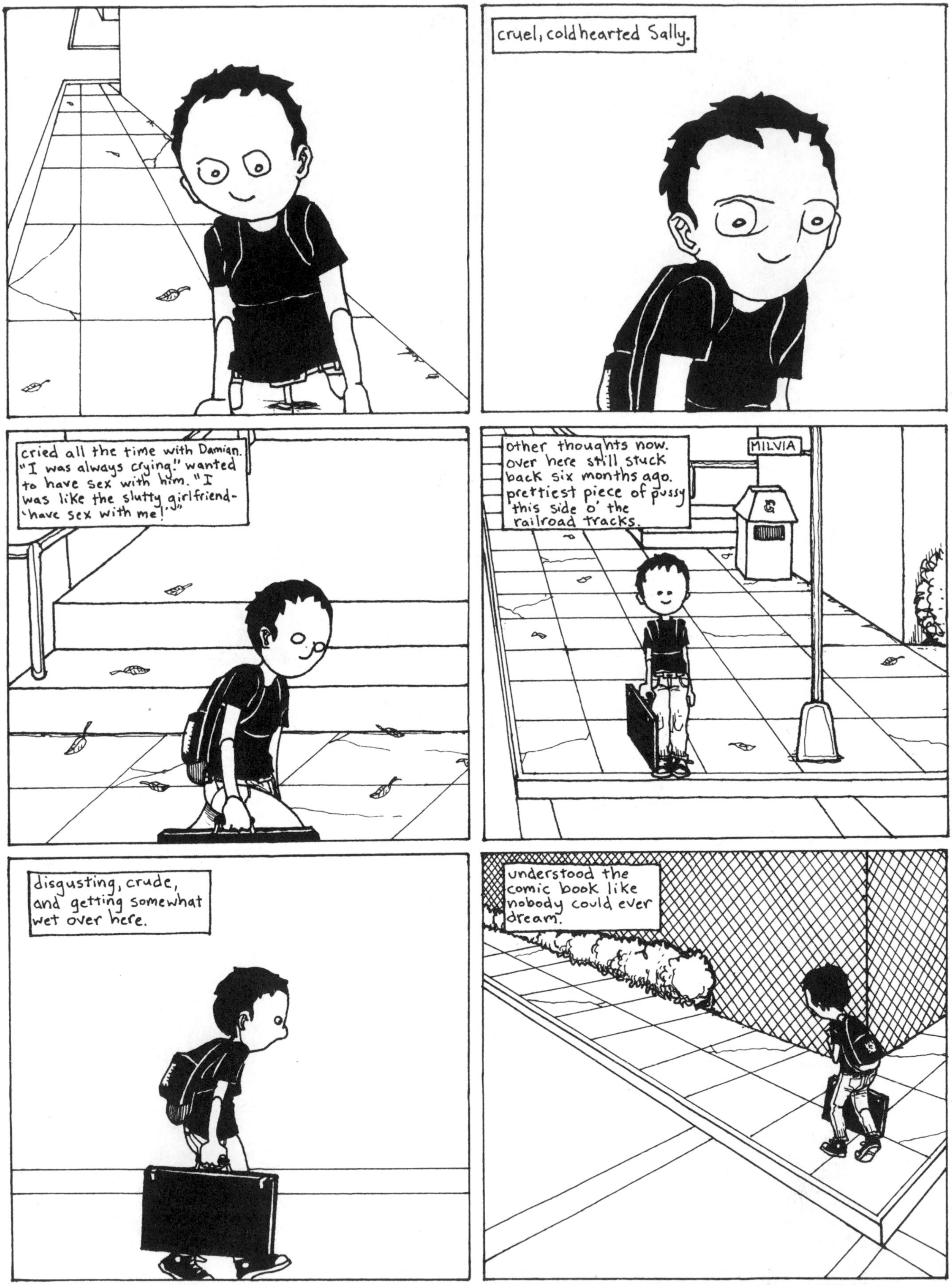
cruel, coldhearted Sally.
cried all the time with Damian. "I was always crying." wanted to have sex with him. "I was like the slutty girlfriend- 'have sex with me!'"
other thoughts now. over here still stuck back six months ago. prettiest piece of pussy this side o' the railroad tracks.
MILVIA
disgusting, crude, and getting somewhat wet over here.
understood the comic book like nobody could ever dream.

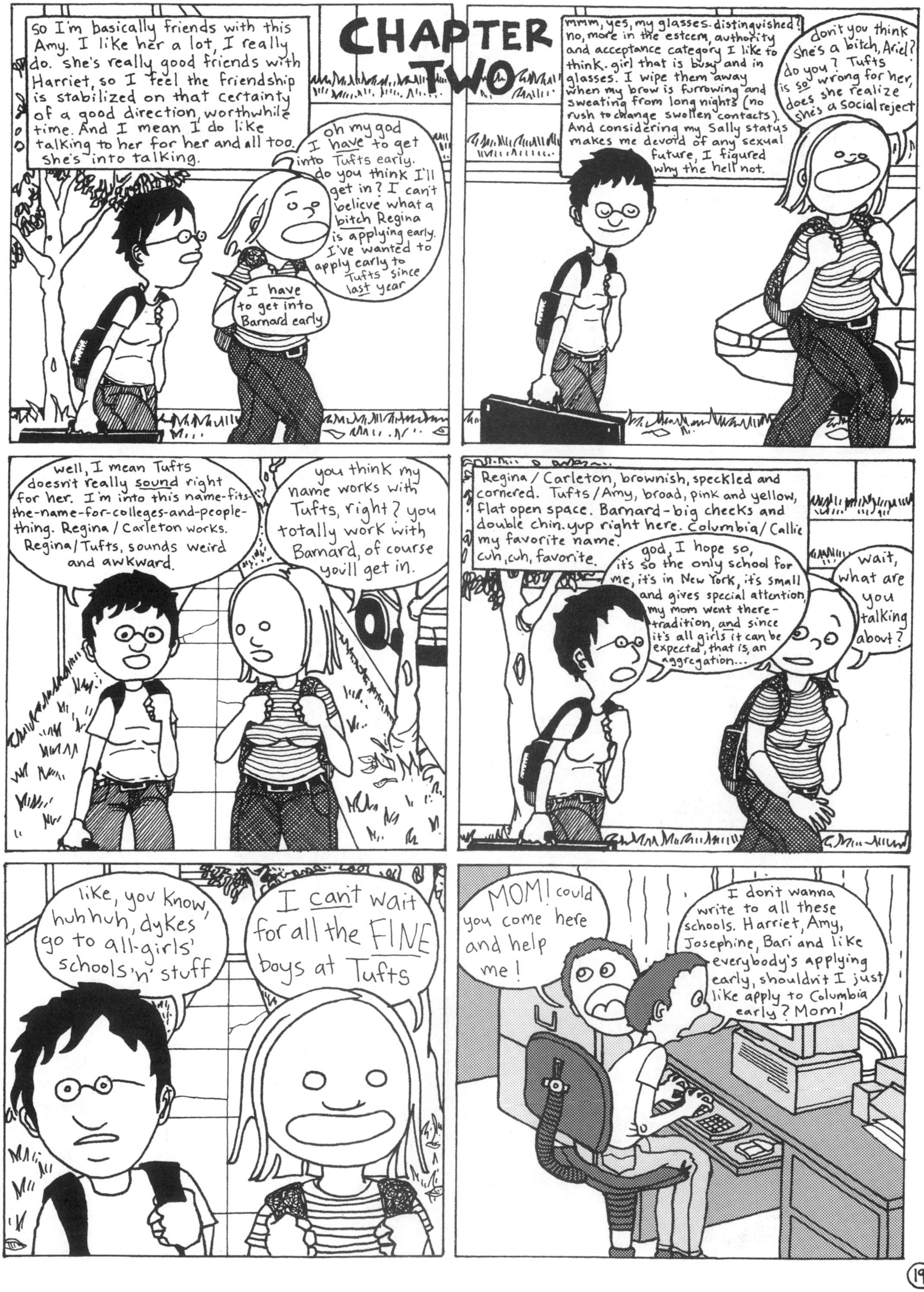
CHAPTER TWO
so I'm basically friends with this Amy. I like her a lot, I really do. she's really good friends with Harriet, so I feel the friendship is stabilized on that certainty of a good direction, worthwhile time. And I mean I do like talking to her for her and all too. she's into talking.
oh my god I have to get into Tufts early. do you think I'll get in? I can't believe what a bitch Regina is applying early. I've wanted to apply early to Tufts since last year
I have to get into Barnard early
mmm, yes, my glasses-distinguished? no, more in the esteem, authority and acceptance category I like to think. girl that is busy and in glasses. I wipe them away when my brow is furrowing and sweating from long nights (no rush to change swollen contacts). And considering my Sally status makes me devoid of any sexual future, I figured why the hell not.
don't you think she's a bitch, Ariel? do you? Tufts is so wrong for her, does she realize she's a social reject
well, I mean Tufts doesn't really sound right for her. I'm into this name-fits-the-name-for-colleges-and-people-thing. Regina / Carleton works. Regina/Tufts, sounds weird and awkward.
you think my name works with Tufts, right? you totally work with Barnard, of course you'll get in.
Regina / Carleton, brownish, speckled and cornered. Tufts / Amy, broad, pink and yellow, flat open space. Barnard - big cheeks and double chin. yup right here. Columbia / Callie my favorite name. cuh, cuh, favorite.
god, I hope so, it's so the only school for me, it's in New York, it's small and gives special attention, my mom went there-tradition, and since it's all girls it can be expected, that is, an aggregation...
wait, what are you talking about?
like, you know, huh huh, dykes go to all-girls' schools 'n' stuff
I can't wait for all the FINE boys at Tufts
MOM! could you come here and help me!
I don't wanna write to all these schools. Harriet, Amy, Josephine, Bari and like everybody's applying early, shouldn't I just like apply to Columbia early? Mom!

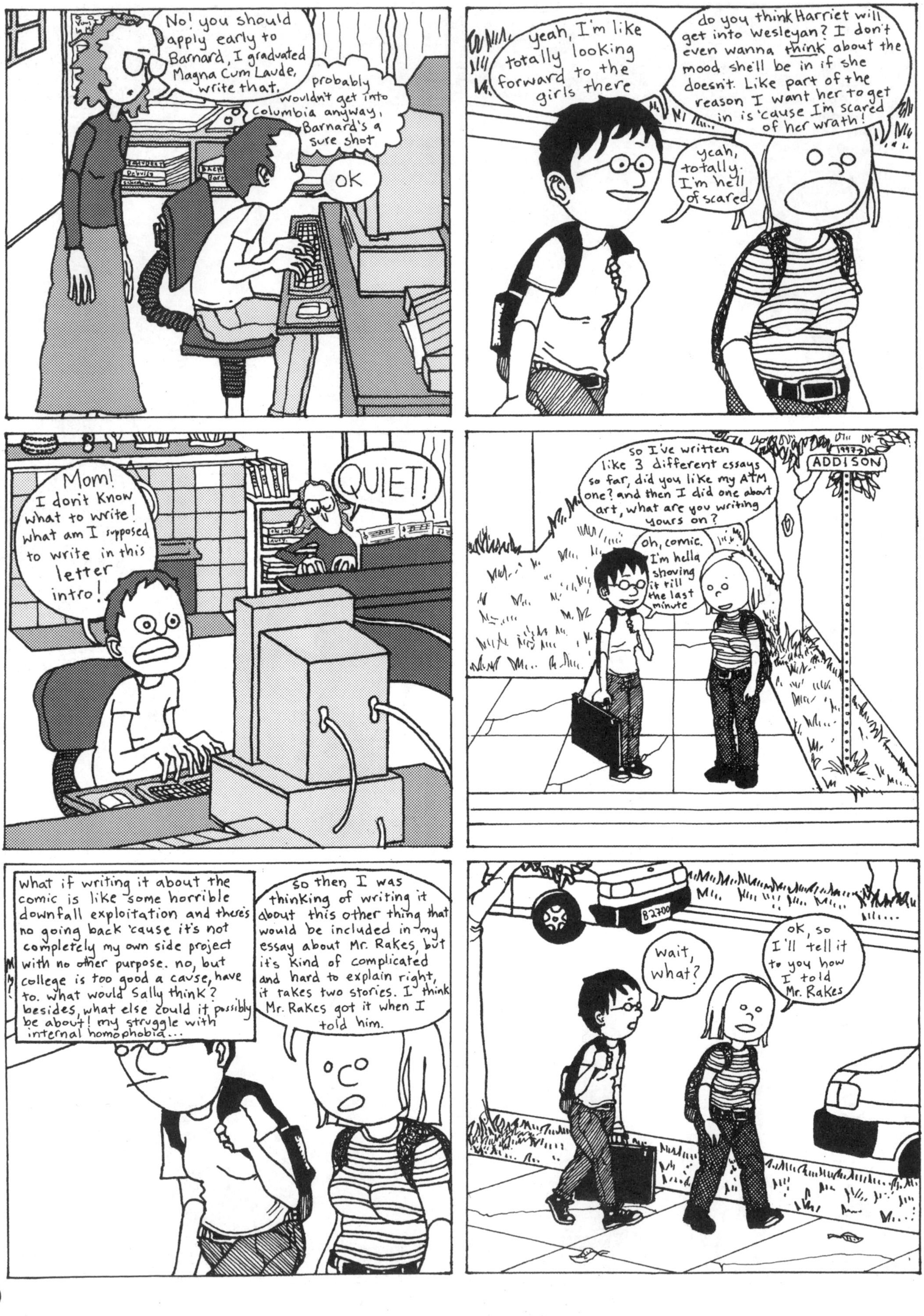

No! you should apply early to Barnard, I graduated Magna Cum Laude, write that.
probably wouldn't get into Columbia anyway, Barnard's a sure shot
OK
yeah, I'm like totally looking forward to the girls there
do you think Harriet will get into Wesleyan? I don't even wanna think about the mood she'll be in if she doesn't. Like part of the reason I want her to get in is 'cause I'm scared of her wrath!
yeah, totally. I'm hell of scared.
Mom! I don't Know what to write! what am I supposed to write in this letter intro!
QUIET!
ADDISON
so I've written like 3 different essays so far, did you like my ATM one? and then I did one about art, what are you writing yours on?
oh, comic. I'm hella shoving it till the last minute
what if writing it about the comic is like some horrible downfall exploitation and there's no going back 'cause it's not completely my own side project with no other purpose. no, but college is too good a cause, have to. what would Sally think? besides, what else could it possibly be about! my struggle with internal homophobia...
so then I was thinking of writing it about this other thing that would be included in my essay about Mr. Rakes, but it's kind of complicated and hard to explain right, it takes two stories. I think Mr. Rakes got it when I told him.
wait, what?
ok, so I'll tell it to you how I told Mr. Rakes

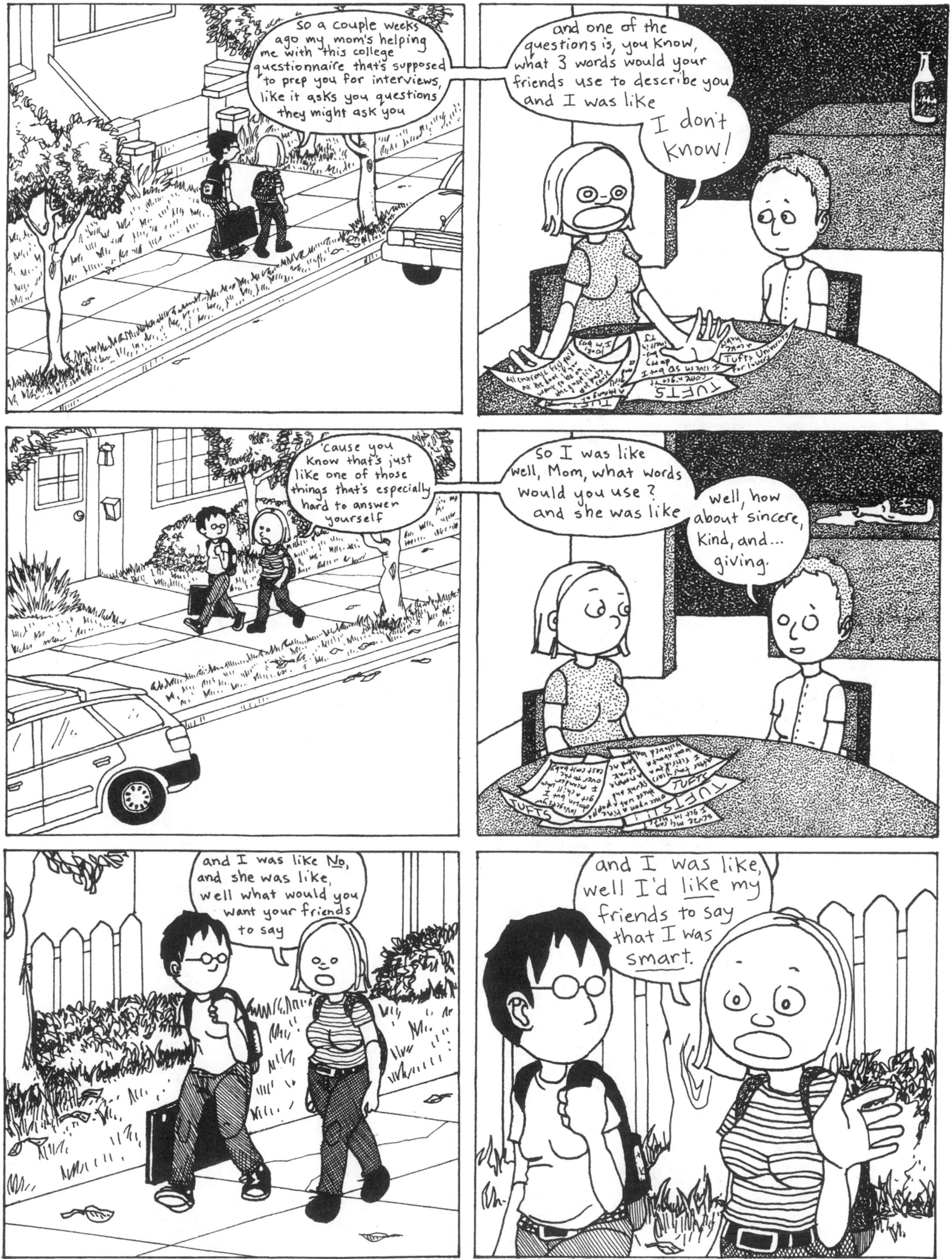
so a couple weeks ago my mom's helping me with this college questionnaire that's supposed to prep you for interviews, like it asks you questions they might ask you
and one of the questions is, you Know, what 3 words would your friends use to describe you and I was like
I don't Know!
'cause you Know that's just like one of those things that's especially hard to answer yourself
So I was like well, Mom, what words would you use? and she was like
Well, how about sincere, Kind, and... giving.
and I was like No, and she was like, well what would you want your friends to say
and I was like, well I'd like my friends to say that I was smart.

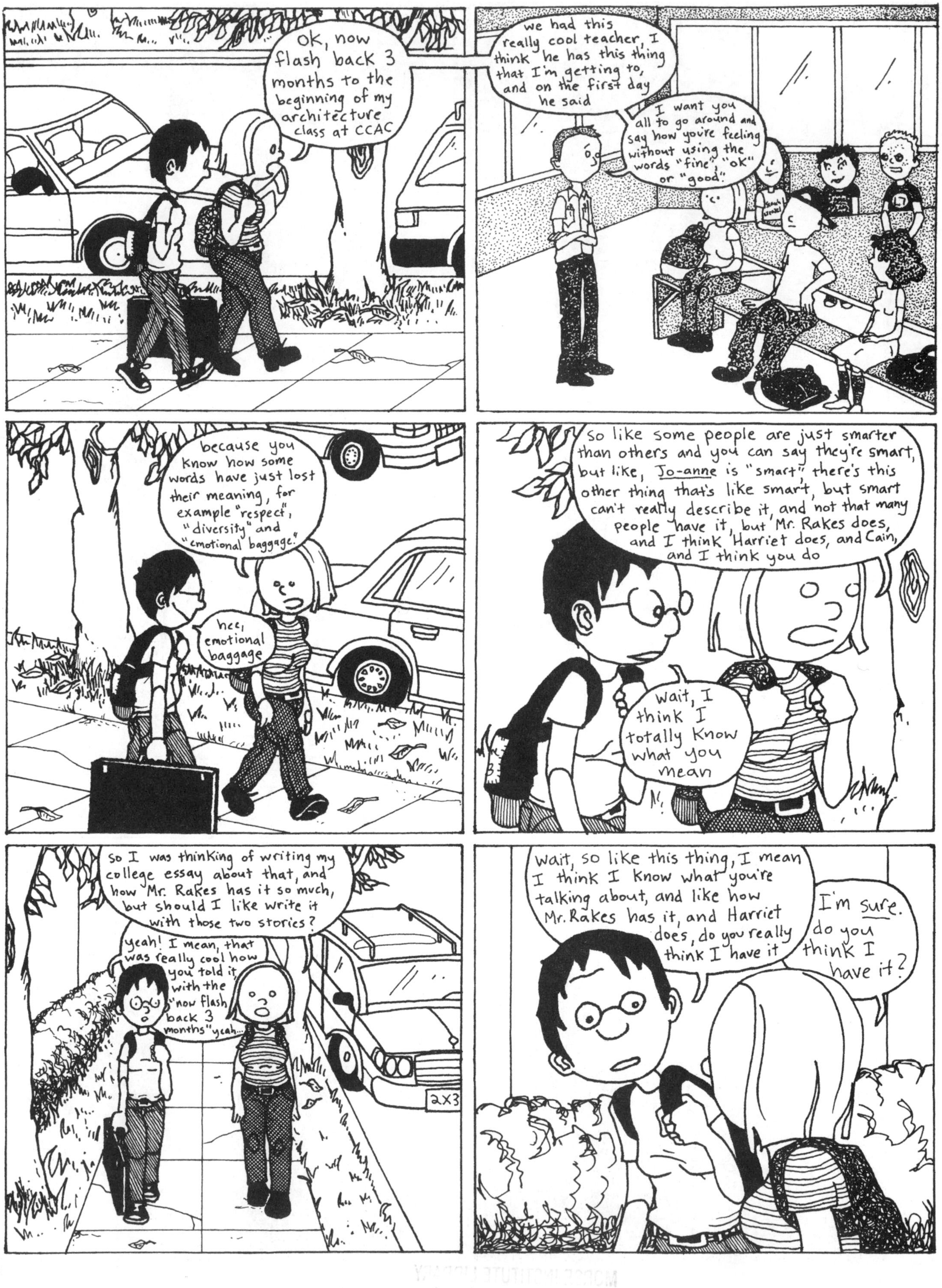
ok, now flash back 3 months to the beginning of my architecture class at CCAC
we had this really cool teacher, I think he has this thing that I'm getting to, and on the first day he said
I want you all to go around and say how you're feeling without using the words "fine", "ok" or "good"
because you know how some words have just lost their meaning, for example "respect", "diversity" and "emotional baggage."
hee, emotional baggage
so like some people are just smarter than others and you can say they're smart, but like, Jo-anne is "smart", there's this other thing that's like smart, but smart can't really describe it, and not that many people have it, but Mr. Rakes does, and I think Harriet does, and Cain, and I think you do
wait, I think I totally know what you mean
so I was thinking of writing my college essay about that, and how Mr. Rakes has it so much, but should I like write it with those two stories?
yeah! I mean, that was really cool how you told it with the "now flash back 3 months" yeah...
2X3
wait, so like this thing, I mean I think I know what you're talking about, and like how Mr. Rakes has it, and Harriet does, do you really think I have it
I'm sure. do you think I have it?

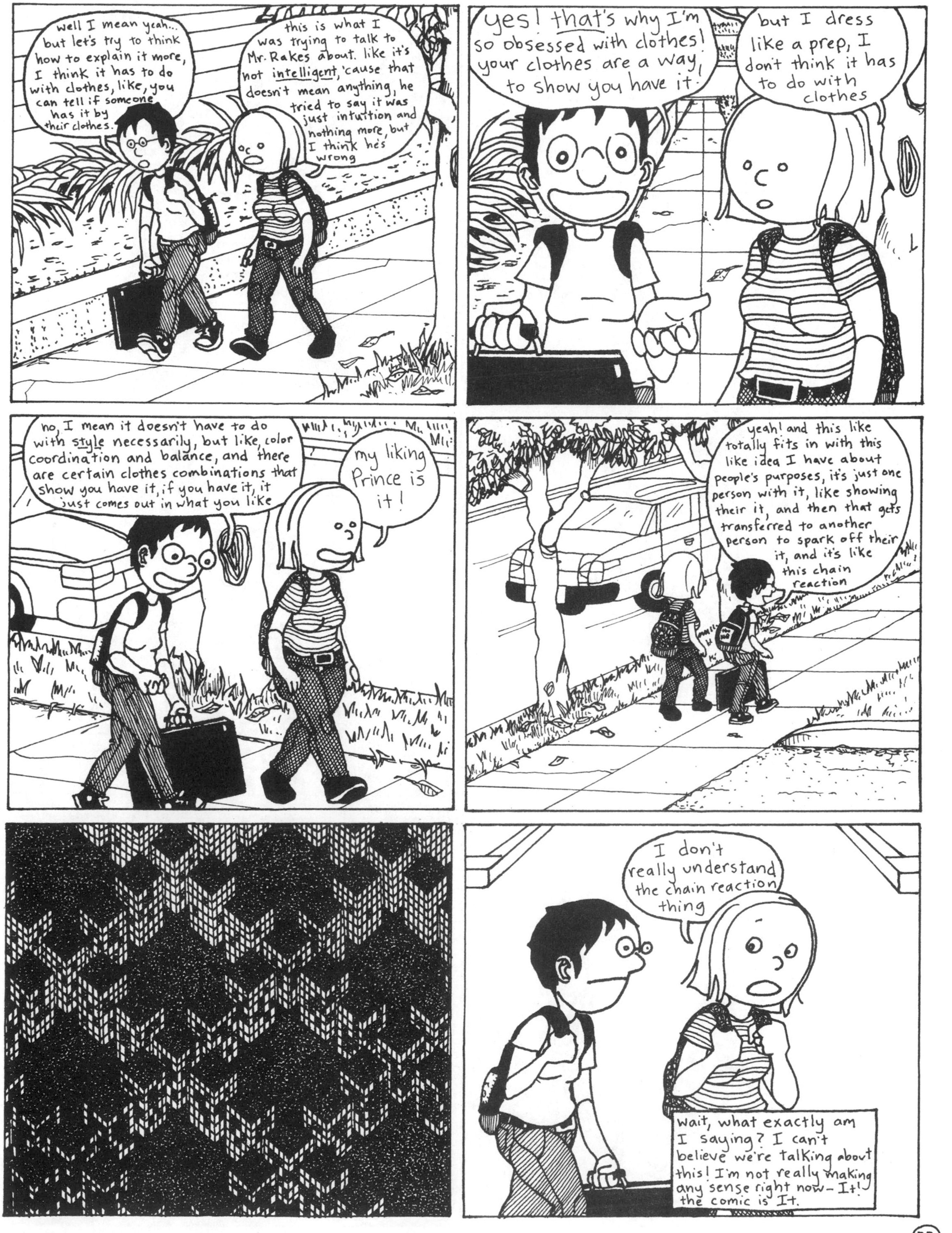
well I mean yeah... but let's try to think how to explain it more, I think it has to do with clothes, like, you can tell if someone has it by their clothes.
this is what I was trying to talk to Mr. Rakes about. like it's not intelligent, 'cause that doesn't mean anything, he tried to say it was just intuition and nothing more, but I think he's wrong
yes! that's why I'm so obsessed with clothes! your clothes are a way to show you have it.
but I dress like a prep, I don't think it has to do with clothes
no, I mean it doesn't have to do with style necessarily, but like, color coordination and balance, and there are certain clothes combinations that show you have it, if you have it, it just comes out in what you like
my liking Prince is it!
yeah! and this like totally fits in with this like idea I have about people's purposes, it's just one person with it, like showing their it, and then that gets transferred to another person to spark off their it, and it's like this chain reaction
I don't really understand the chain reaction thing
wait, what exactly am I saying? I can't believe we're talking about this! I'm not really making any sense right now– It! the comic is It.

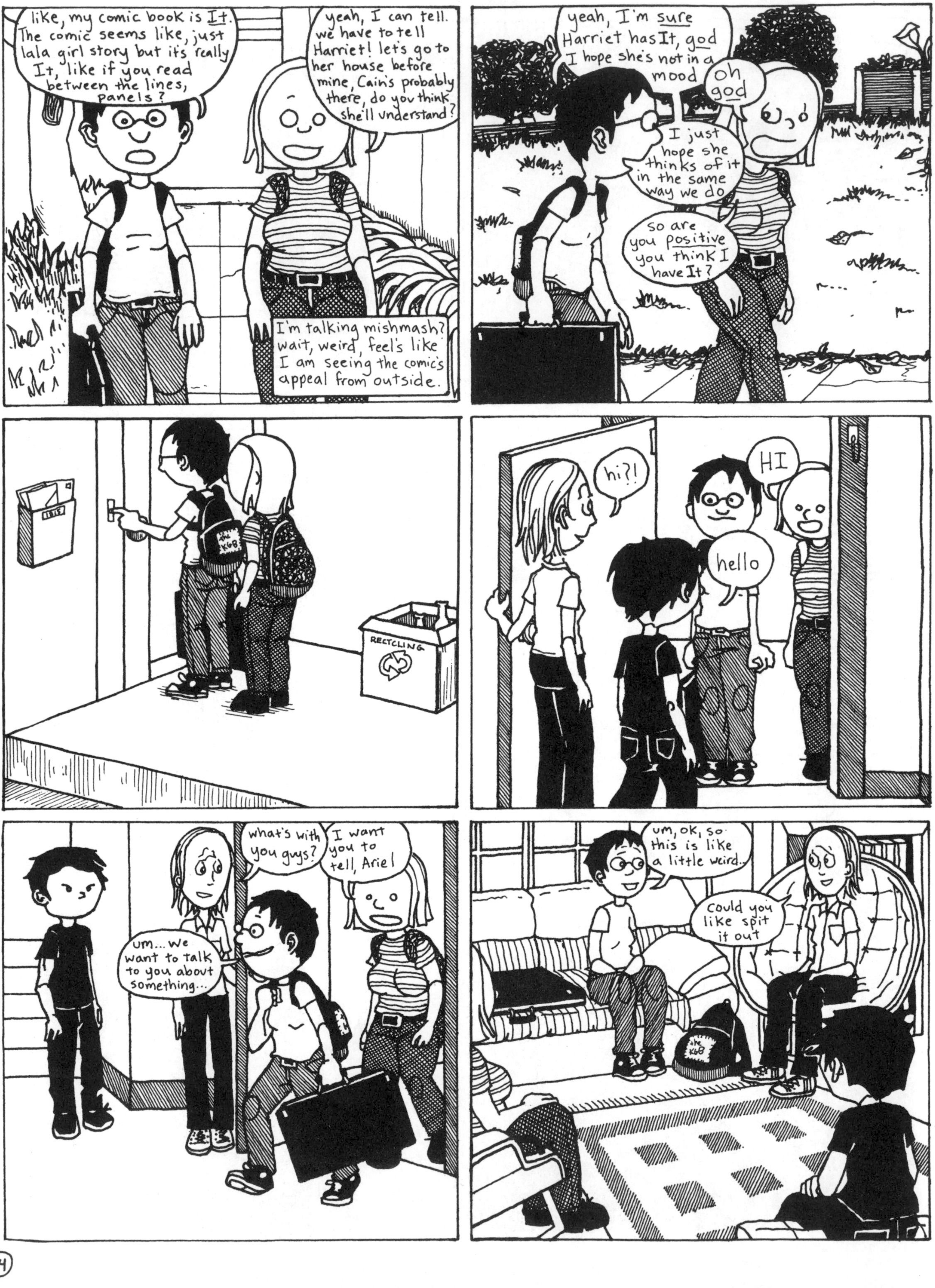
like, my comic book is It. The comic seems like, just lala girl story but it's really It, like if you read between the lines, panels?
yeah, I can tell. we have to tell Harriet! let's go to her house before mine, Cain's probably there, do you think she'll understand?
I'm talking mishmash? wait, weird, feel's like I am seeing the comic's appeal from outside.
yeah, I'm sure Harriet has It, god I hope she's not in a mood
oh god
I just hope she thinks of it in the same way we do
so are you positive you think I have It?
RECYCLING
hi?!
HI
hello
what's with you guys?
I want you to tell, Ariel
um... we want to talk to you about something...
um, ok, so this is like a little weird...
could you like spit it out

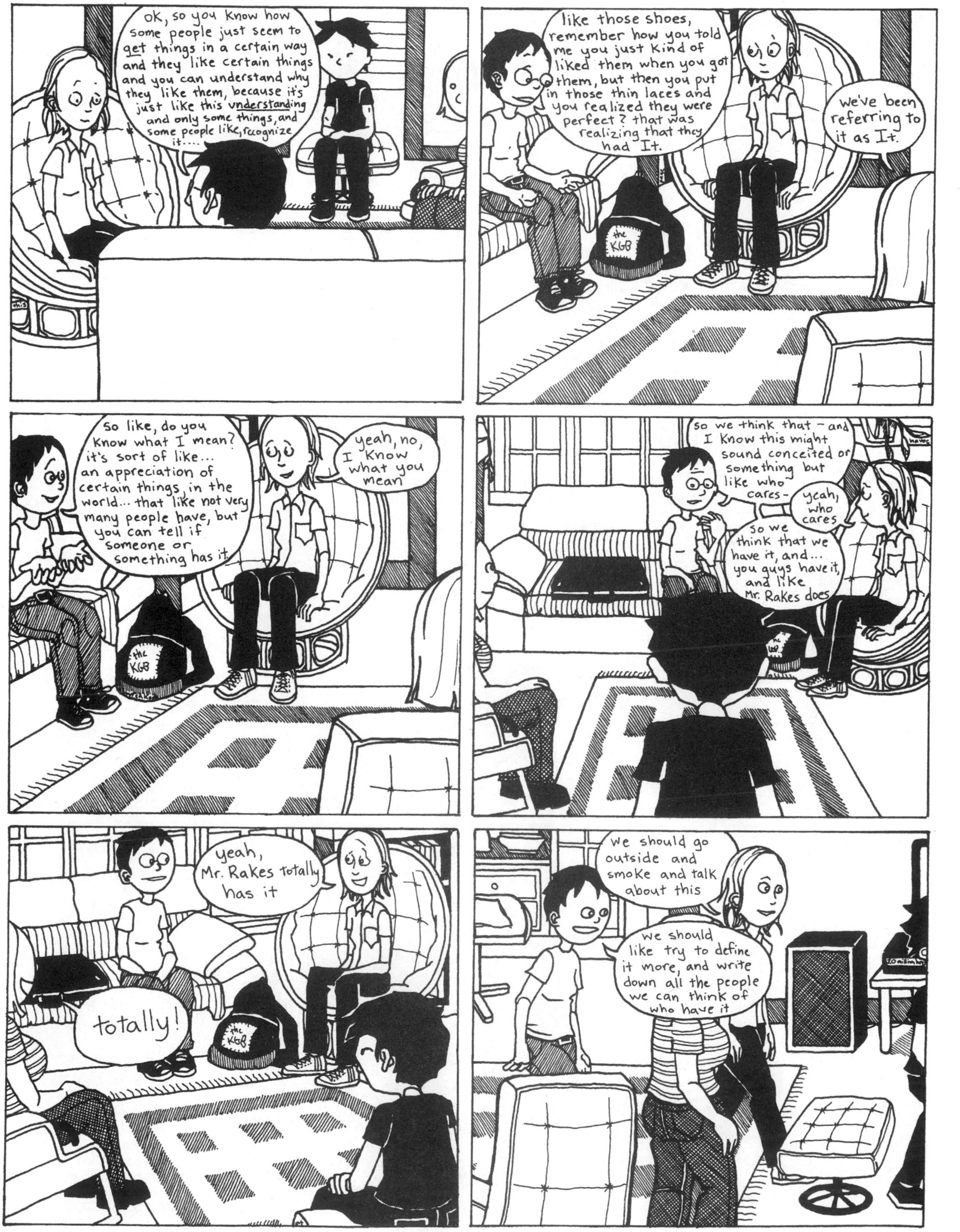
OK, so you know how some people just seem to get things in a certain way and they like certain things and you can understand why they like them, because it's just like this understanding and only some things, and some people like, recognize it....
like those shoes, remember how you told me you just kind of liked them when you got them, but then you put in those thin laces and you realized they were perfect? that was realizing that they had It.
We've been referring to it as It.
the KGB
So like, do you know what I mean? it's sort of like... an appreciation of certain things, in the world... that like not very many people have, but you can tell if someone or something has it.
yeah, no, I know what you mean
the KGB
So we think that - and I know this might sound conceited or something but like who cares-
yeah, who cares
So we think that we have it, and... you guys have it, and like Mr. Rakes does
yeah, Mr. Rakes totally has it
totally!
the KGB
We should go outside and smoke and talk about this
we should like try to define it more, and write down all the people we can think of who have it

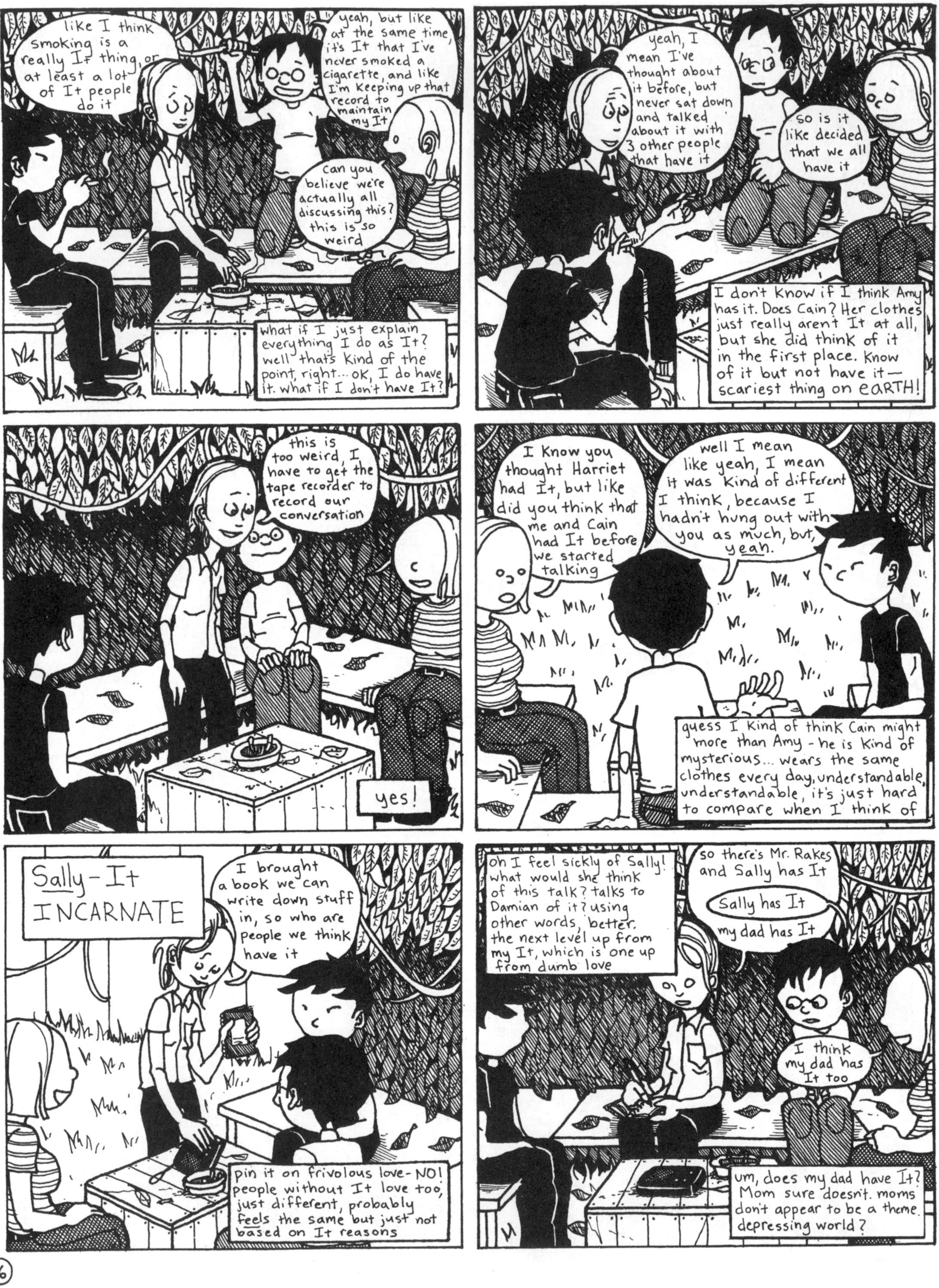
like I think smoking is a really It thing, or at least a lot of It people do it
yeah, but like at the same time, it's It that I've never smoked a cigarette, and like I'm keeping up that record to maintain my It
can you believe we're actually all discussing this? this is so weird
what if I just explain everything I do as It? well that's kind of the point, right... ok, I do have it. what if I don't have It?
yeah, I mean I've thought about it before, but never sat down and talked about it with 3 other people that have it
so is it like decided that we all have it
I don't know if I think Amy has it. Does Cain? Her clothes just really aren't It at all, but she did think of it in the first place. Know of it but not have it— scariest thing on EARTH!
this is too weird, I have to get the tape recorder to record our conversation
yes!
I know you thought Harriet had It, but like did you think that me and Cain had It before we started talking
well I mean like yeah, I mean it was kind of different I think, because I hadn't hung out with you as much, but, yeah.
guess I kind of think Cain might more than Amy - he is kind of mysterious... wears the same clothes every day, understandable, understandable, it's just hard to compare when I think of
Sally - It INCARNATE
I brought a book we can write down stuff in, so who are people we think have it
pin it on frivolous love - NO! people without It love too, just different, probably feels the same but just not based on It reasons
oh I feel sickly of Sally! what would she think of this talk? talks to Damian of it? using other words, better. the next level up from my It, which is one up from dumb love
so there's Mr. Rakes and Sally has It
Sally has It
my dad has It
I think my dad has It too
um, does my dad have It? Mom sure doesn't. moms don't appear to be a theme. depressing world?

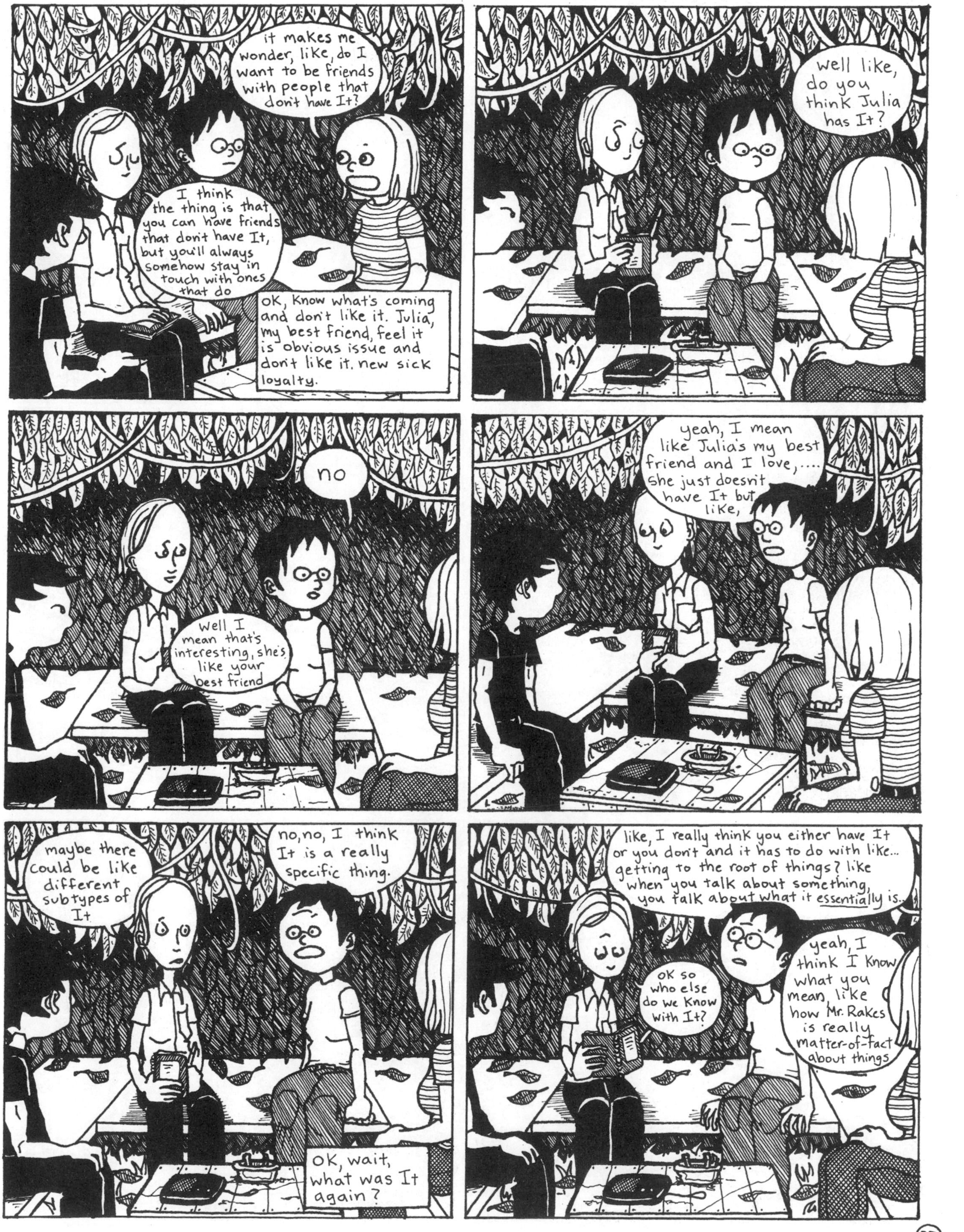
it makes me wonder, like, do I want to be friends with people that don't have It?
I think the thing is that you can have friends that don't have It, but you'll always somehow stay in touch with ones that do
OK, Know what's coming and don't like it. Julia, my best friend, feel it is obvious issue and don't like it. new sick loyalty.
well like, do you think Julia has It?
no
Well I mean that's interesting, she's like your best friend
yeah, I mean like Julia's my best friend and I love, ... She just doesn't have It but like,
maybe there could be like different subtypes of It
no, no, I think It is a really specific thing.
OK, wait, what was It again?
like, I really think you either have It or you don't and it has to do with like... getting to the root of things? like when you talk about something, you talk about what it essentially is...
OK so who else do we Know with It?
yeah, I think I Know what you mean, like how Mr. Rakes is really matter-of-fact about things

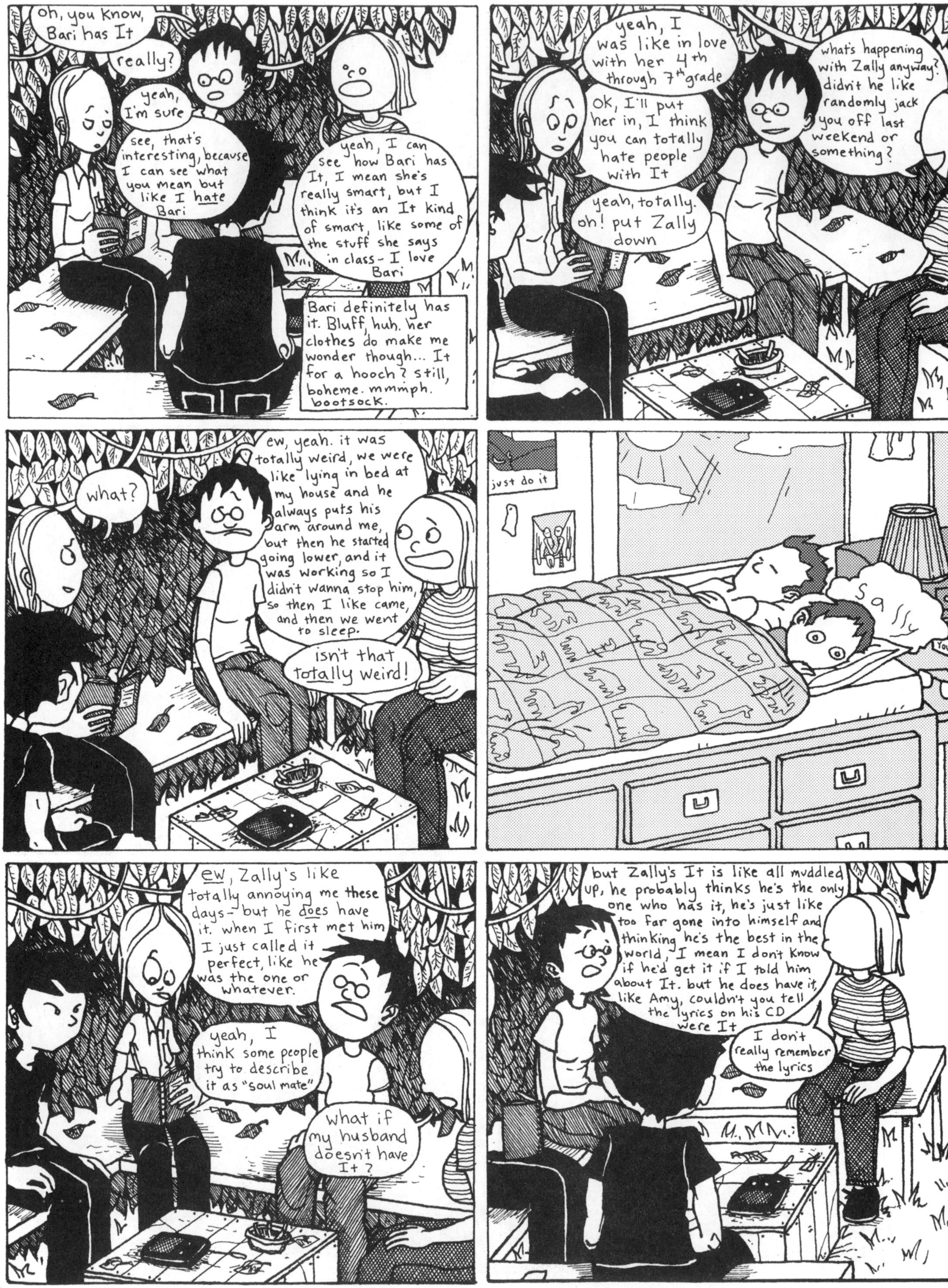
oh, you know, Bari has It
really?
yeah, I'm sure
see, that's interesting, because I can see what you mean but like I hate Bari
yeah, I can see how Bari has It, I mean she's really smart, but I think it's an It kind of smart, like some of the stuff she says in class- I love Bari
Bari definitely has it. Bluff, huh. her clothes do make me wonder though... It for a hooch? still, boheme. mmmph. bootsock.
yeah, I was like in love with her 4th through 7th grade
what's happening with Zally anyway? didn't he like randomly jack you off last weekend or something?
ok, I'll put her in, I think you can totally hate people with It
yeah, totally. oh! put Zally down
what?
ew, yeah. it was totally weird, we were like lying in bed at my house and he always puts his arm around me, but then he started going lower, and it was working so I didn't wanna stop him, so then I like came, and then we went to sleep.
isn't that totally weird!
just do it
Sally
YOUTH
ew, Zally's like totally annoying me these days- but he does have it. when I first met him I just called it perfect, like he was the one or whatever.
yeah, I think some people try to describe it as "soul mate"
what if my husband doesn't have It?
but Zally's It is like all muddled up, he probably thinks he's the only one who has it, he's just like too far gone into himself and thinking he's the best in the world, I mean I don't know if he'd get it if I told him about It. but he does have it, like Amy, couldn't you tell the lyrics on his CD were It
I don't really remember the lyrics

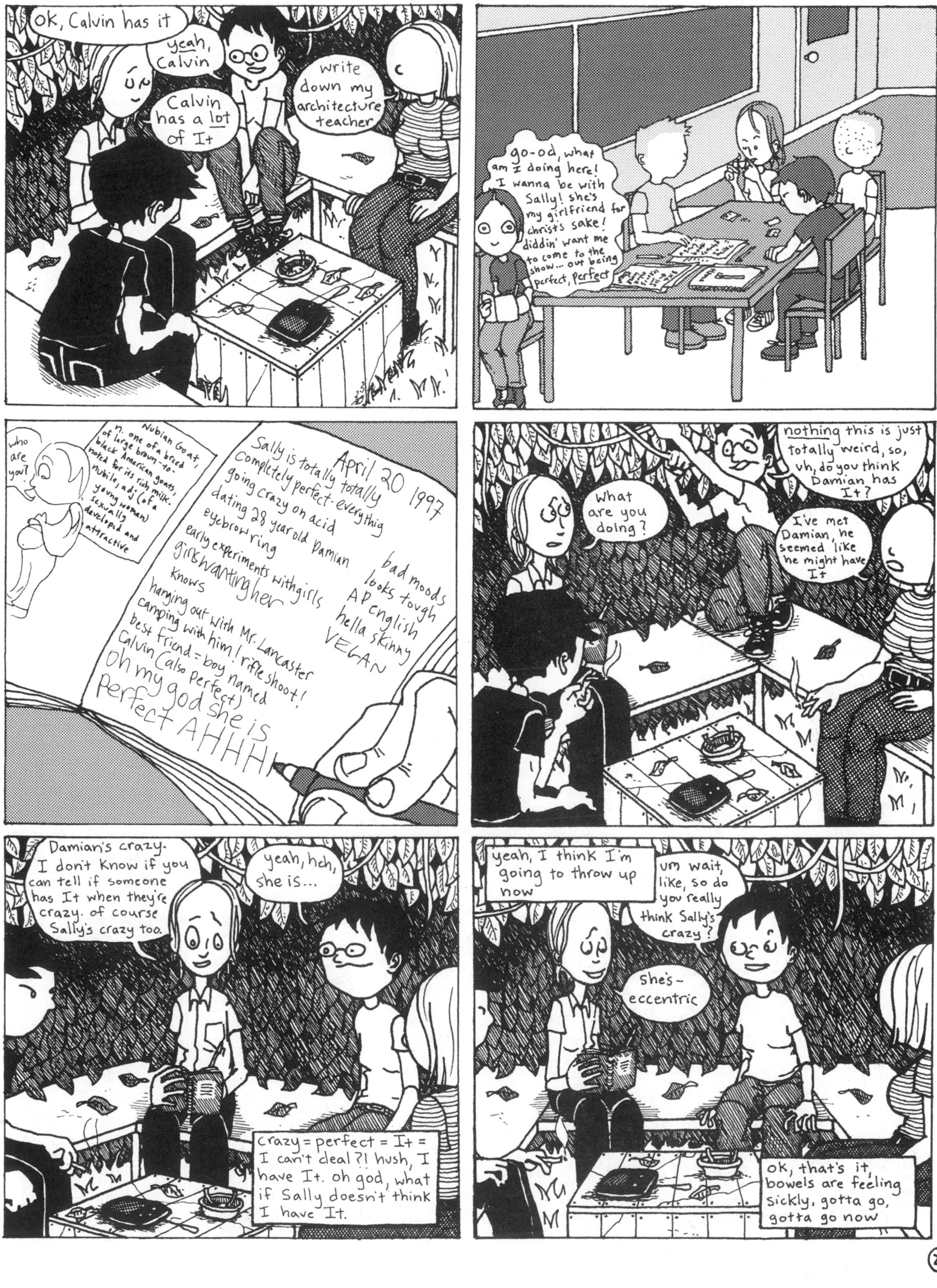

OK, Calvin has it
yeah, Calvin
Calvin has a lot of It
write down my architecture teacher
go-od, what am I doing here! I wanna be with Sally! she's my girlfriend for christ's sake! diddin' want me to come to the show... out being perfect, Perfect
who are you?
Nubian Goat, n. one of a breed of large brown-to-black American goats, noted for its rich milk.
nubile, adj (of a young woman) sexually developed and attractive
April 20 1997
Sally is totally totally completely perfect. everythig going crazy on acid
dating 28 year old Damian
eyebrow ring
early experiments with girls
girls wanting her
knows
hanging out with Mr. Lancaster
camping with him! rifle shoot!
best friend = boy named Calvin (also perfect)
bad moods
looks tough
AP english
hella skinny
VEGAN
oh my god she is perfect AHHH
What are you doing?
nothing this is just totally weird, so, uh, do you think Damian has It?
I've met Damian, he seemed like he might have It
Damian's crazy. I don't know if you can tell if someone has It when they're crazy. of course Sally's crazy too.
yeah, hch, she is...
crazy = perfect = It = I can't deal?! hush, I have It. oh god, what if Sally doesn't think I have It.
yeah, I think I'm going to throw up now
um wait, like, so do you really think Sally's crazy?
She's— eccentric
ok, that's it, bowels are feeling sickly, gotta go, gotta go now

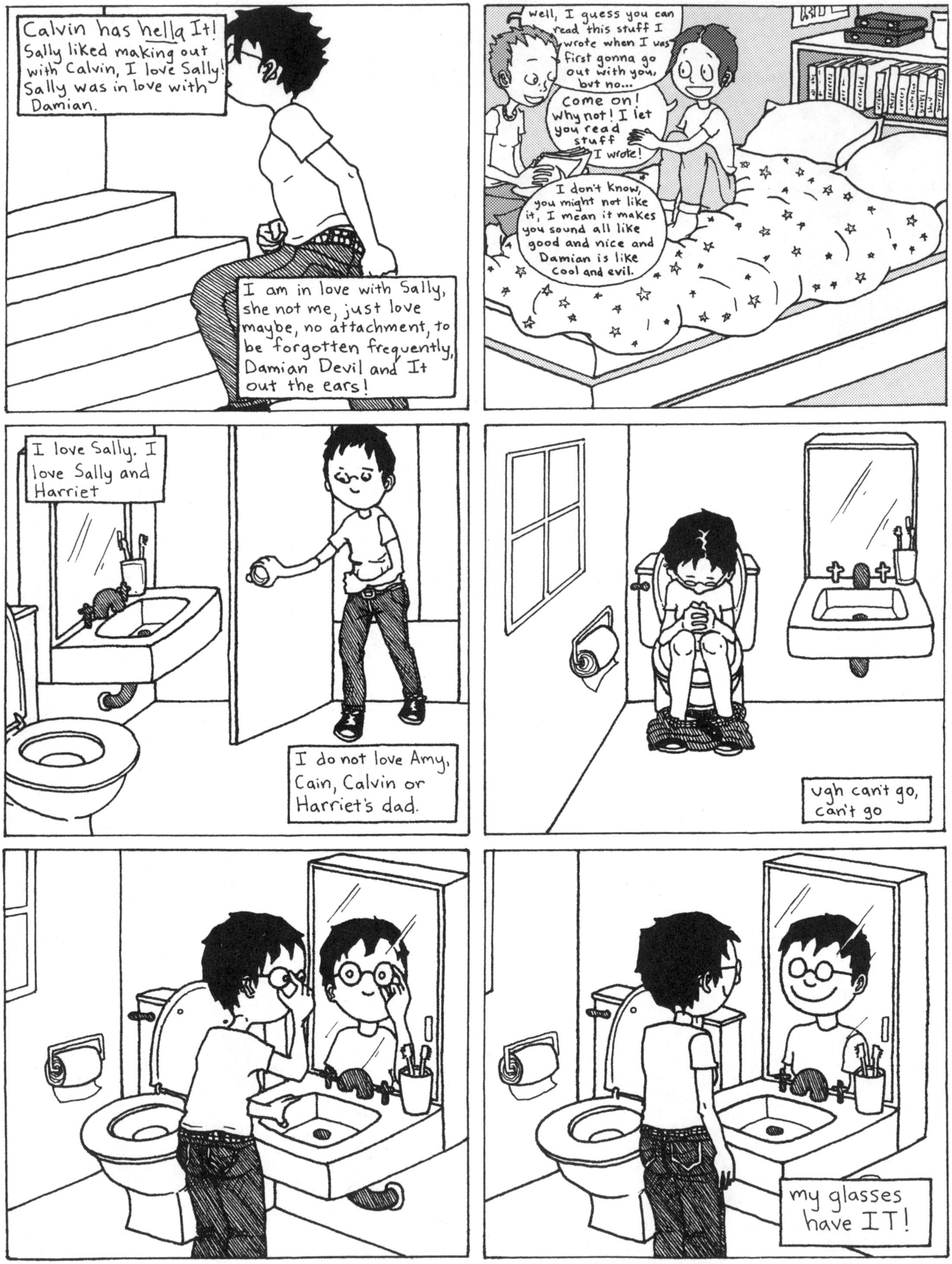
Calvin has hella It! Sally liked making out with Calvin, I love Sally! Sally was in love with Damian.
I am in love with Sally, she not me, just love maybe, no attachment, to be forgotten frequently, Damian Devil and It out the ears!
well, I guess you can read this stuff I wrote when I was first gonna go out with you, but no...
come on! why not! I let you read stuff I wrote!
I don't know, you might not like it, I mean it makes you sound all like good and nice and Damian is like cool and evil.
I love Sally. I love Sally and Harriet
I do not love Amy, Cain, Calvin or Harriet's dad.
ugh can't go, can't go
my glasses have IT!

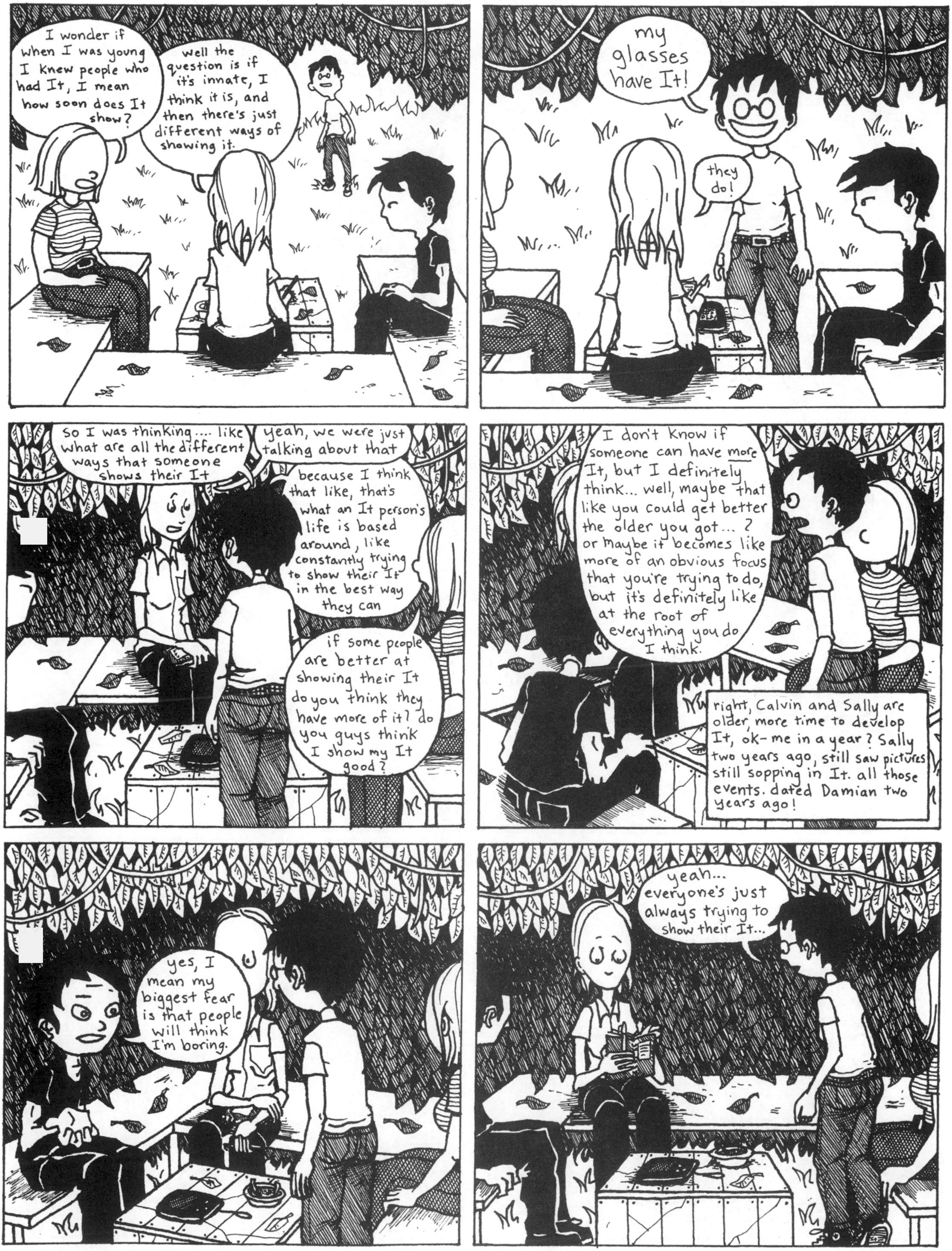

I wonder if when I was young I knew people who had It, I mean how soon does It show?
well the question is if it's innate, I think it is, and then there's just different ways of showing it.
my glasses have It!
they do!
So I was thinking.... like what are all the different ways that someone shows their It
yeah, we were just talking about that
because I think that like, that's what an It person's life is based around, like constantly trying to show their It in the best way they can
if some people are better at showing their It do you think they have more of it? do you guys think I show my It good?
I don't know if someone can have more It, but I definitely think... well, maybe that like you could get better the older you got... ? or maybe it becomes like more of an obvious focus that you're trying to do, but it's definitely like at the root of everything you do I think.
right, Calvin and Sally are older, more time to develop It, ok- me in a year? Sally two years ago, still saw pictures still sopping in It. all those events. dated Damian two years ago!
yes, I mean my biggest fear is that people will think I'm boring.
yeah... everyone's just always trying to show their It...

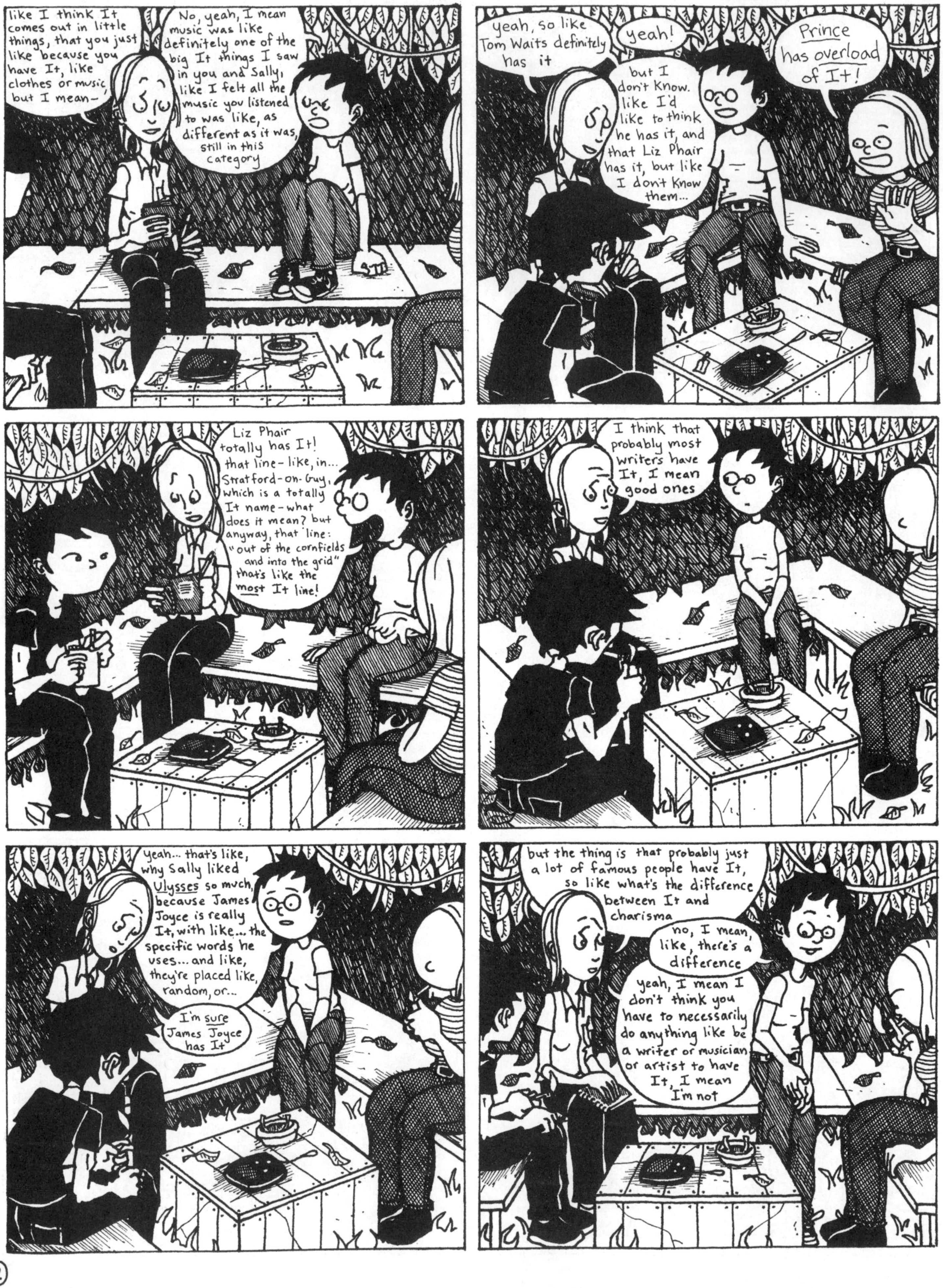

like I think It comes out in little things, that you just like because you have It, like clothes or music but I mean—
No, yeah, I mean music was like definitely one of the big It things I saw in you and Sally, like I felt all the music you listened to was like, as different as it was, still in this category
Yeah, so like Tom Waits definitely has it
yeah!
but I don't Know. like I'd like to think he has it, and that Liz Phair has it, but like I don't Know them...
Prince has overload of It!
Liz Phair totally has It! that line- like, in... Stratford-on-Guy, which is a totally It name- what does it mean? but anyway, that line: "out of the cornfields and into the grid" that's like the most It line!
I think that probably most writers have It, I mean good ones
yeah... that's like, why Sally liked Ulysses so much, because James Joyce is really It, with like... the specific words he uses... and like, they're placed like, random, or...
I'm sure James Joyce has It
but the thing is that probably just a lot of famous people have It, so like what's the difference between It and charisma
no, I mean, like, there's a difference
yeah, I mean I don't think you have to necessarily do anything like be a writer or musician or artist to have It, I mean I'm not

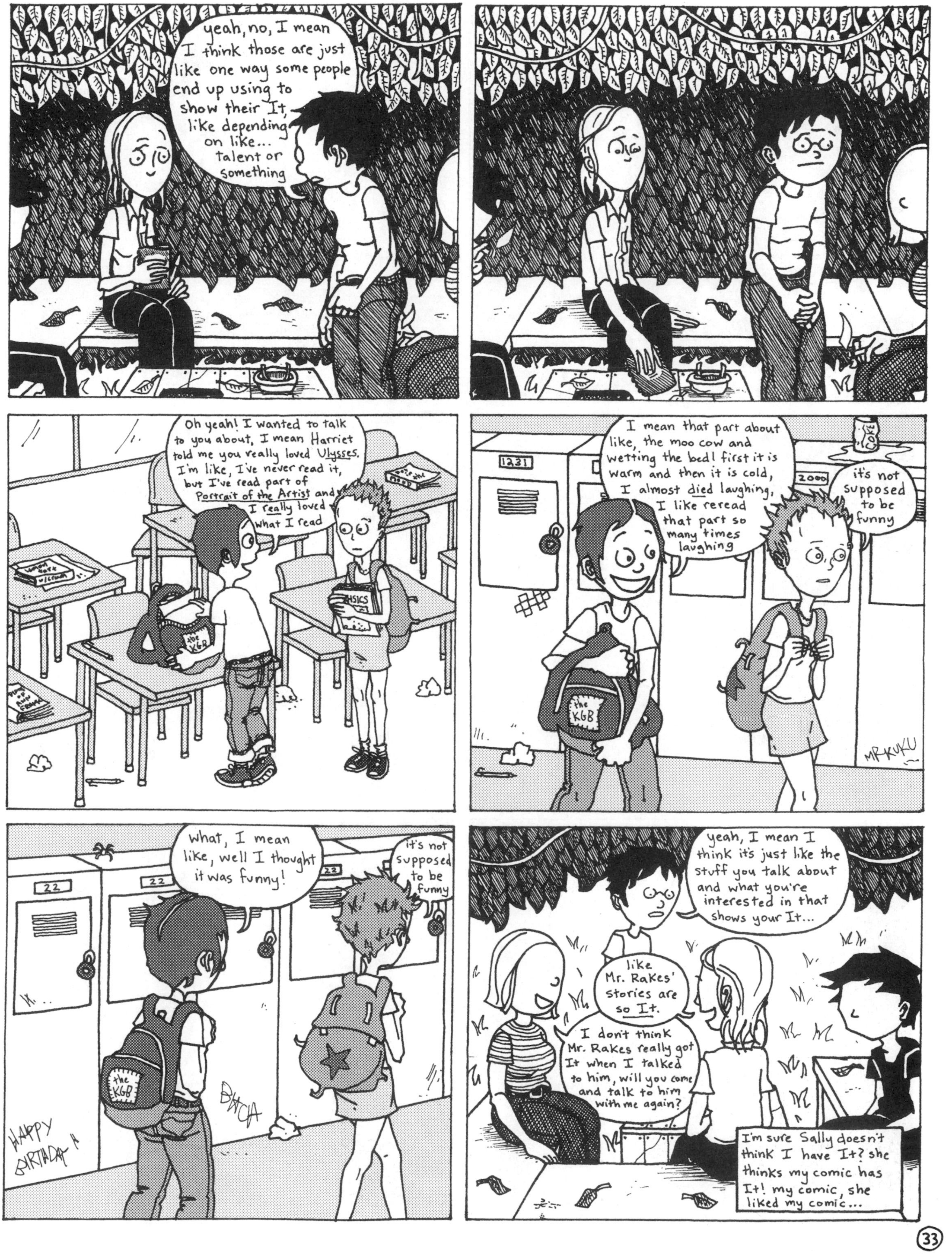
yeah, no, I mean I think those are just like one way some people end up using to show their It, like depending on like... talent or something
Oh yeah! I wanted to talk to you about, I mean Harriet told me you really loved Ulysses. I'm like, I've never read it, but I've read part of Portrait of the Artist and I really loved what I read
I mean that part about like, the moo cow and wetting the bed! first it is warm and then it is cold, I almost died laughing, I like reread that part so many times laughing
it's not supposed to be funny
MR KUKU
what, I mean like, well I thought it was funny!
it's not supposed to be funny
HAPPY BIRTHDAY
yeah, I mean I think it's just like the stuff you talk about and what you're interested in that shows your It...
like Mr. Rakes' stories are so It.
I don't think Mr. Rakes really got It when I talked to him, will you come and talk to him with me again?
I'm sure Sally doesn't think I have It? she thinks my comic has It! my comic, she liked my comic...

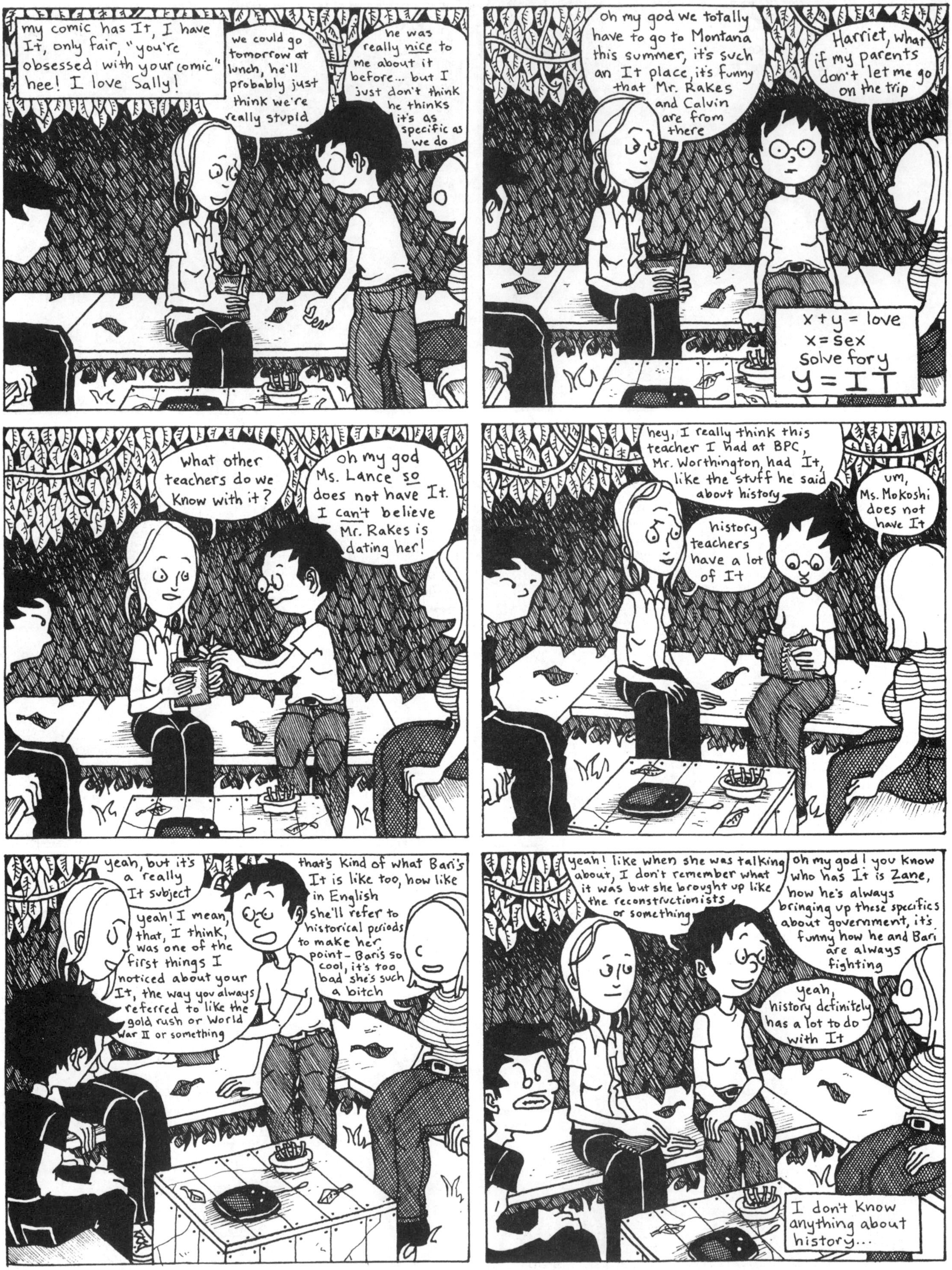

my comic has It, I have It, only fair, "you're obsessed with your comic" hee! I love Sally!
we could go tomorrow at lunch, he'll probably just think we're really stupid
he was really nice to me about it before... but I just don't think he thinks it's as specific as we do
oh my god we totally have to go to Montana this summer, it's such an It place, it's funny that Mr. Rakes and Calvin are from there
Harriet, what if my parents don't let me go on the trip
x + y = love
x = sex
solve for y
y = IT
What other teachers do we know with it?
oh my god Ms. Lance so does not have It. I can't believe Mr. Rakes is dating her!
hey, I really think this teacher I had at BPC, Mr. Worthington, had It, like the stuff he said about history
history teachers have a lot of It
um, Ms. Mokoshi does not have It
yeah, but it's a really It subject
yeah! I mean, that, I think, was one of the first things I noticed about your It, the way you always referred to like the gold rush or World War II or something
that's kind of what Bari's It is like too, how like in English she'll refer to historical periods to make her point - Bari's so cool, it's too bad she's such a bitch
yeah! like when she was talking about, I don't remember what it was but she brought up like the reconstructionists or something
oh my god! you know who has It is Zane, how he's always bringing up these specifics about government, it's funny how he and Bari are always fighting
yeah, history definitely has a lot to do with It
I don't know anything about history...

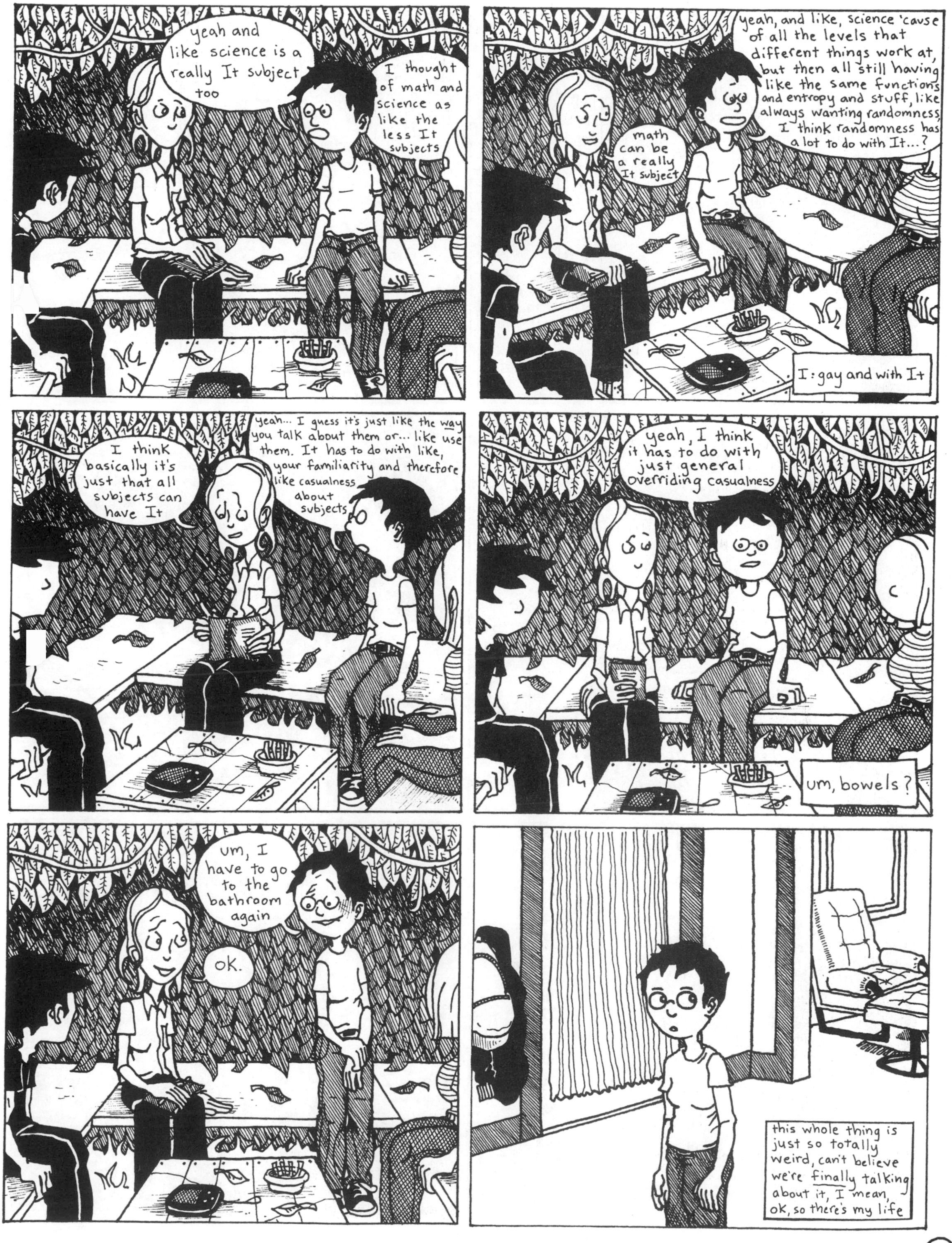
yeah and like science is a really It subject too
I thought of math and science as like the less It subjects
yeah, and like, science 'cause of all the levels that different things work at, but then all still having like the same functions and entropy and stuff, like always wanting randomness, I think randomness has a lot to do with It...?
math can be a really It subject
I: gay and with It
I think basically it's just that all subjects can have It
yeah... I guess it's just like the way you talk about them or... like use them. It has to do with like, your familiarity and therefore like casualness about subjects
yeah, I think it has to do with just general overriding casualness
um, bowels?
um, I have to go to the bathroom again
ok.
this whole thing is just so totally weird, can't believe we're finally talking about it, I mean, ok, so there's my life

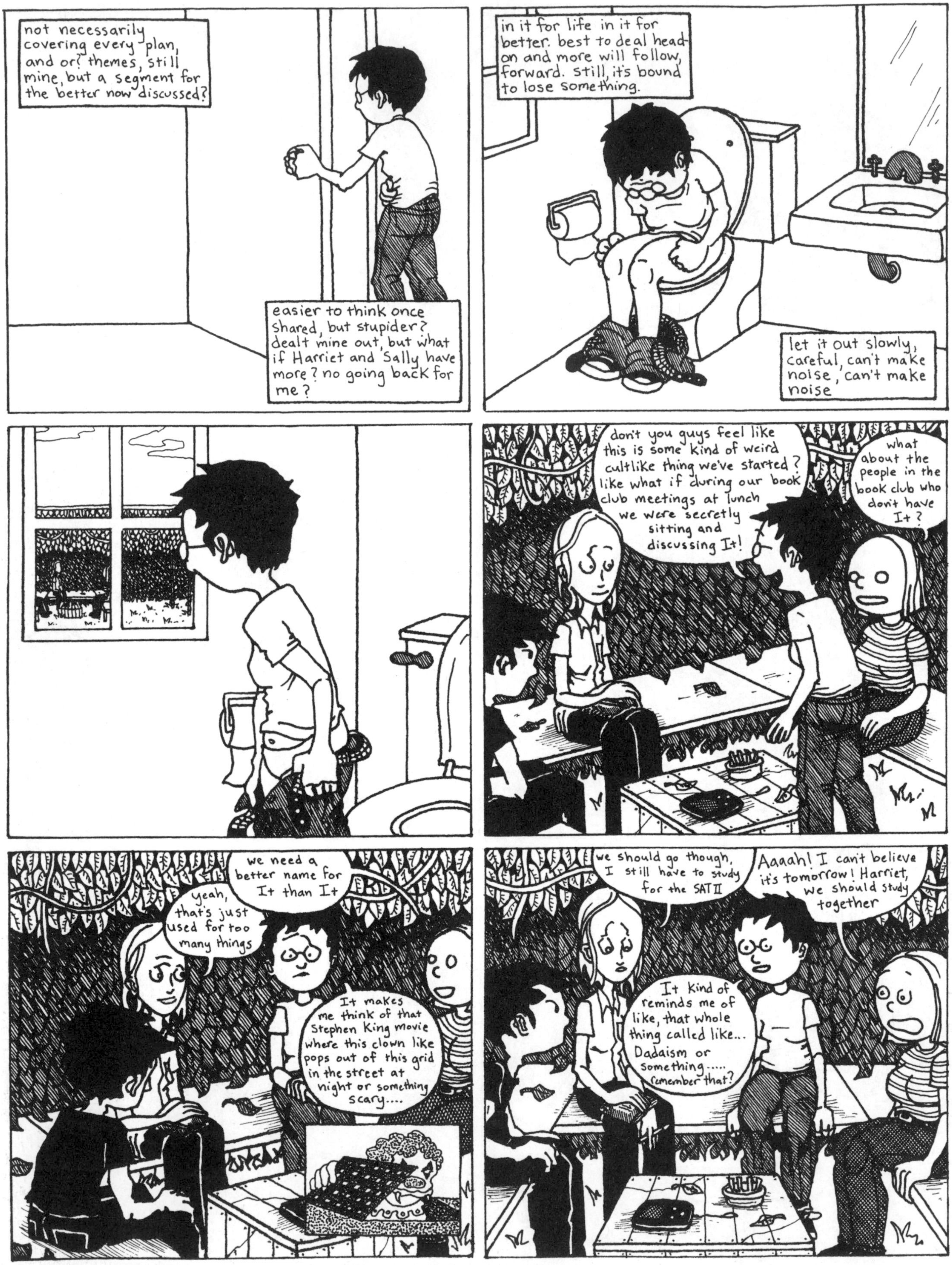
not necessarily covering every plan, and or? themes, still mine, but a segment for the better now discussed?
easier to think once shared, but stupider? dealt mine out, but what if Harriet and Sally have more? no going back for me?
in it for life in it for better. best to deal head on and more will follow, forward. still, it's bound to lose something.
let it out slowly, careful, can't make noise, can't make noise
don't you guys feel like this is some kind of weird cultlike thing we've started? like what if during our book club meetings at lunch we were secretly sitting and discussing It!
what about the people in the book club who don't have It?
we need a better name for It than It
yeah, that's just used for too many things
It makes me think of that Stephen King movie where this clown like pops out of this grid in the street at night or something scary....
we should go though, I still have to study for the SAT II
Aaaah! I can't believe it's tomorrow! Harriet, we should study together
It kind of reminds me of like, that whole thing called like... Dadaism or something..... remember that?

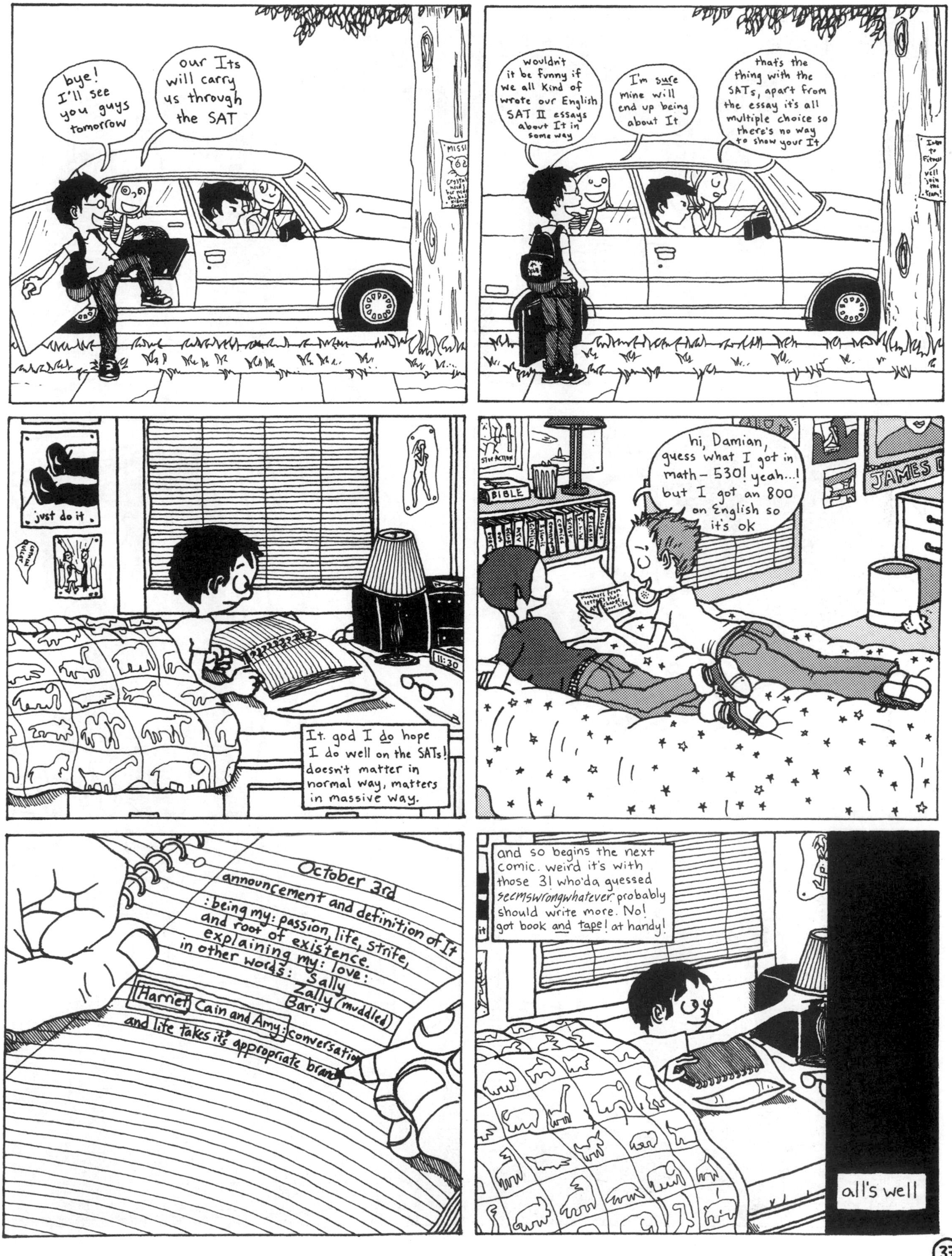
bye! I'll see you guys tomorrow
our Its will carry us through the SAT
wouldn't it be funny if we all kind of wrote our English SAT II essays about It in some way
I'm sure mine will end up being about It
that's the thing with the SATs, apart from the essay it's all multiple choice so there's no way to show your It
just do it
11:30
It. god I do hope I do well on the SATs! doesn't matter in normal way, matters in massive way.
BIBLE
JAMES D
hi, Damian, guess what I got in math – 530! yeah...! but I got an 800 on English so it's ok
October 3rd
announcement and definition of It
: being my: passion, life, strife, and root of existence.
explaining my: love:
in other words: Sally
Zally (muddled)
Bari
Harriet Cain and Amy: conversation
and life takes it's appropriate branch
and so begins the next comic. weird it's with those 3! who'da guessed seemswrongwhatever. probably should write more. No! got book and tape! at handy!
all's well

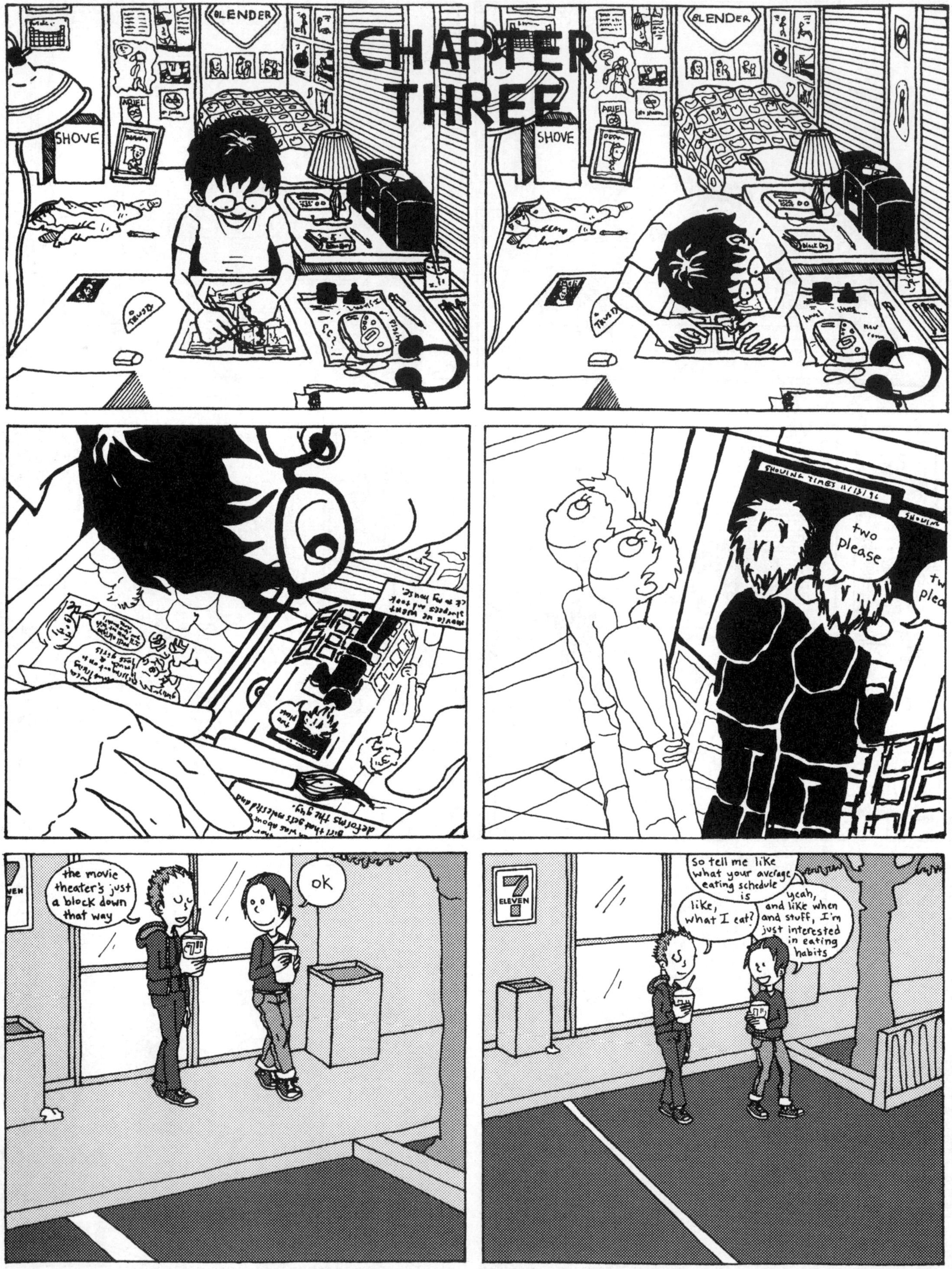
CHAPTER THREE
BLENDER
SHOVE
ARIEL
SHOWING TIMES 11/13/96
two please
the movie theater's just a block down that way
ok
ELEVEN
So tell me like what your average eating schedule is
like, what I eat?
yeah, and like when and stuff, I'm just interested in eating habits

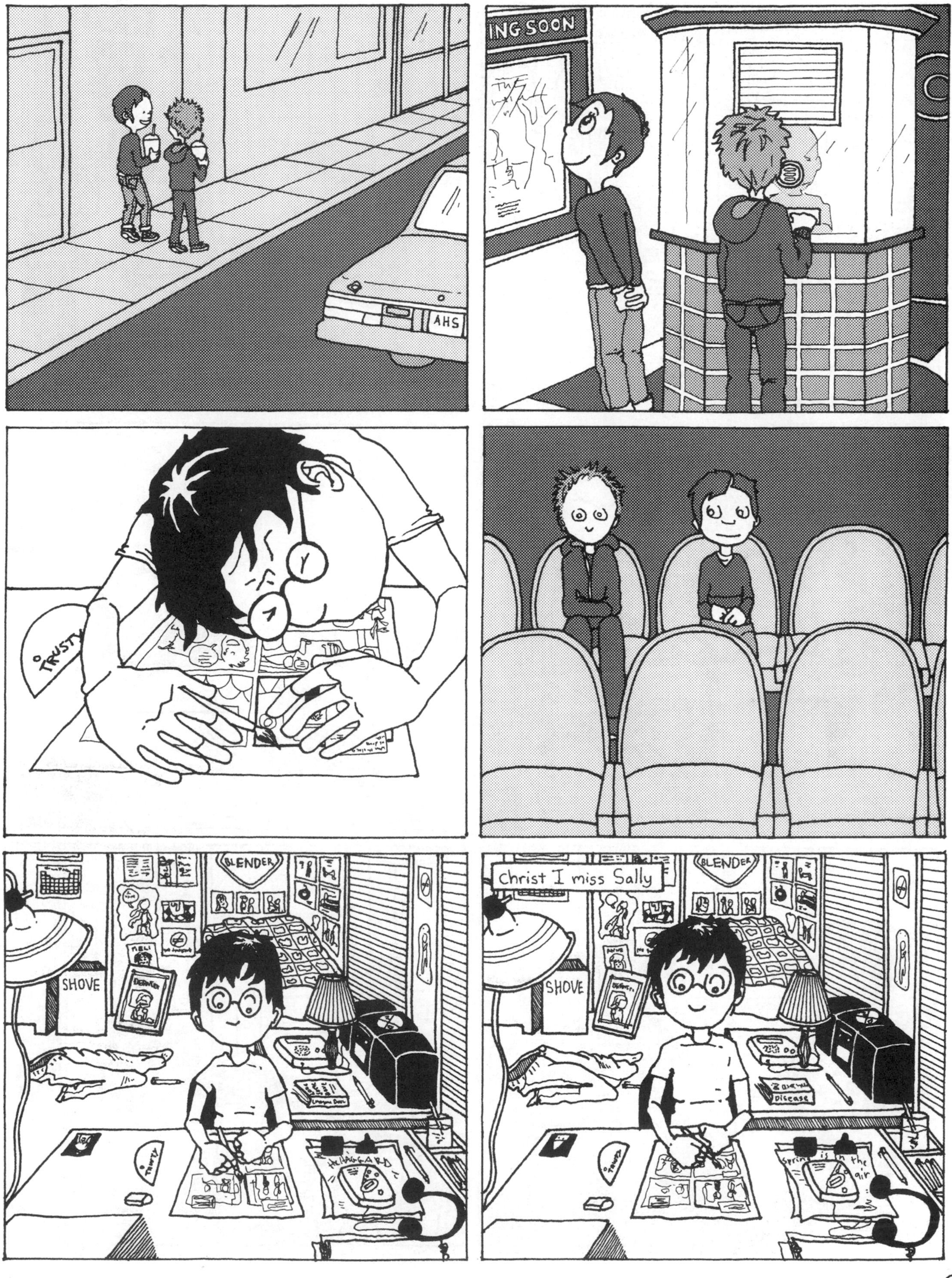
AHS
ING SOON
TRUSTY
BLENDER
SHOVE
HAGGARD
Christ I miss Sally
BLENDER
SHOVE
Disease

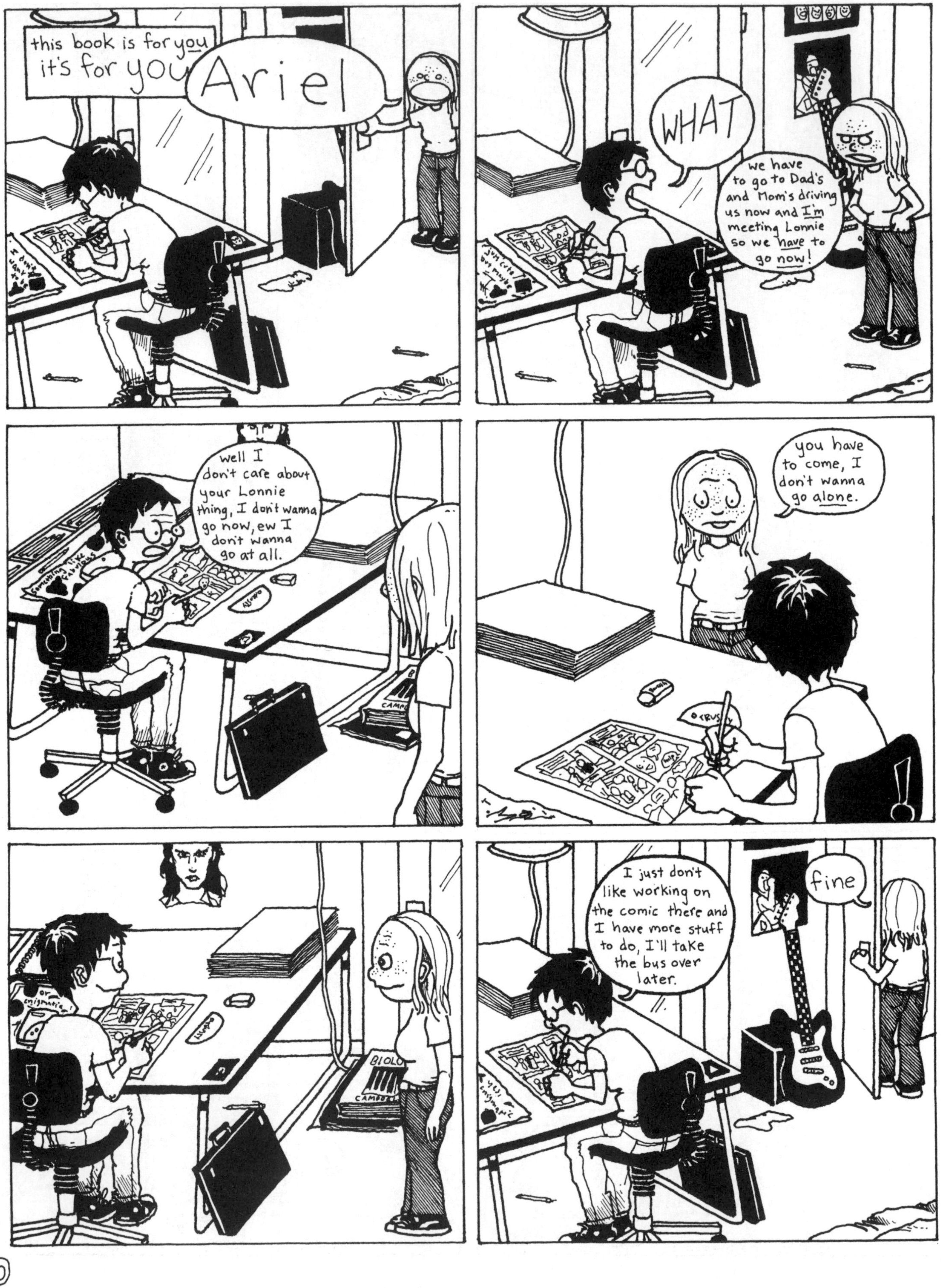

this book is for you
it's for you
Ariel
WHAT
we have to go to Dad's and Mom's driving us now and I'm meeting Lonnie so we have to go now!
well I don't care about your Lonnie thing, I don't wanna go now, ew I don't wanna go at all.
you have to come, I don't wanna go alone.
I just don't like working on the comic there and I have more stuff to do, I'll take the bus over later.
fine

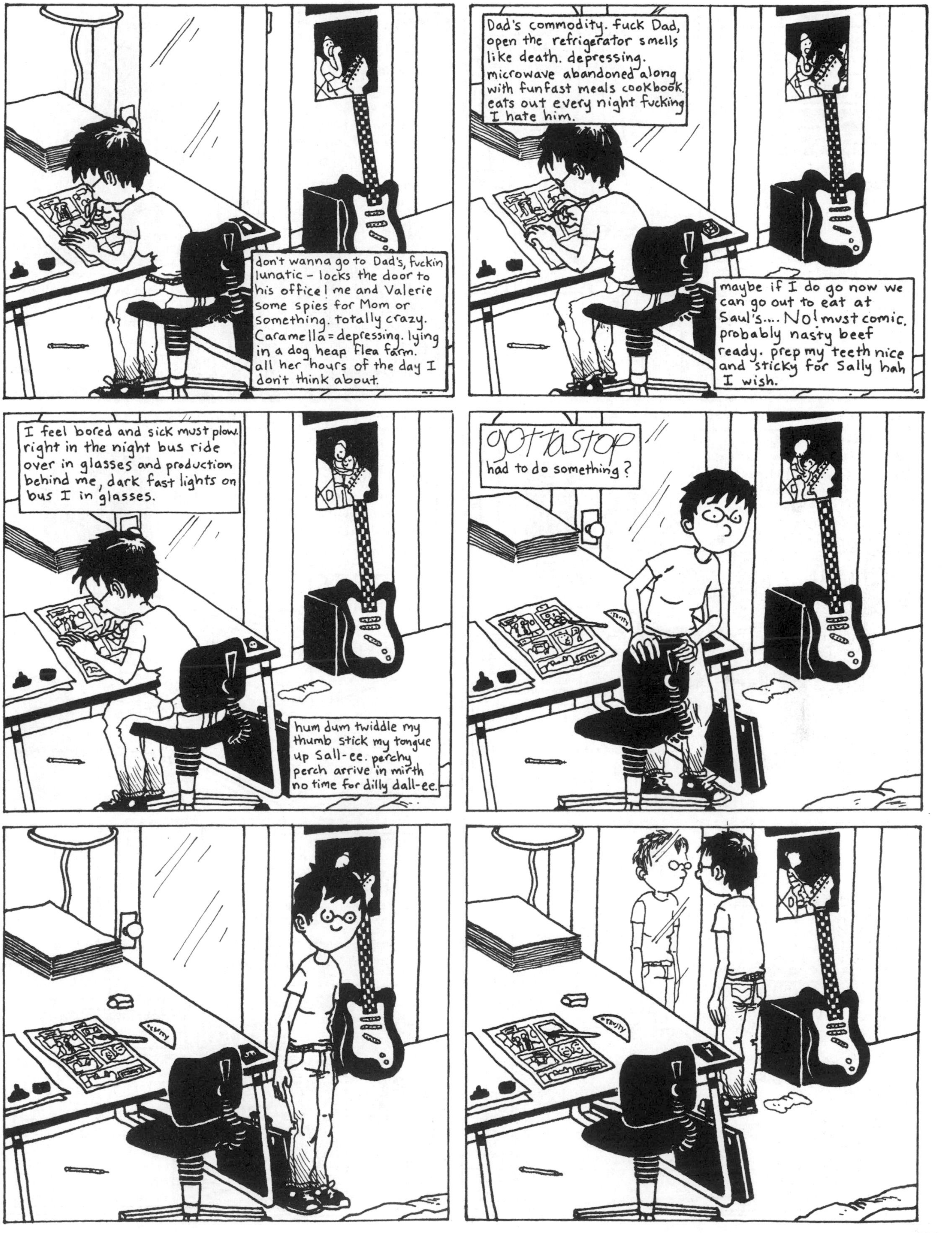
don't wanna go to Dad's, fuckin lunatic - locks the door to his office! me and Valerie some spies for Mom or something. totally crazy. Caramella = depressing. lying in a dog heap flea farm. all her hours of the day I don't think about.
Dad's commodity. fuck Dad, open the refrigerator smells like death. depressing. microwave abandoned along with funfast meals cookbook. eats out every night fucking I hate him.
maybe if I do go now we can go out to eat at Saul's.... No! must comic. probably nasty beef ready. prep my teeth nice and sticky for Sally hah I wish.
I feel bored and sick must plow. right in the night bus ride over in glasses and production behind me, dark fast lights on bus I in glasses.
hum dum twiddle my thumb stick my tongue up Sall-ee. perchy perch arrive in mirth no time for dilly dall-ee.
gottastop
had to do something?

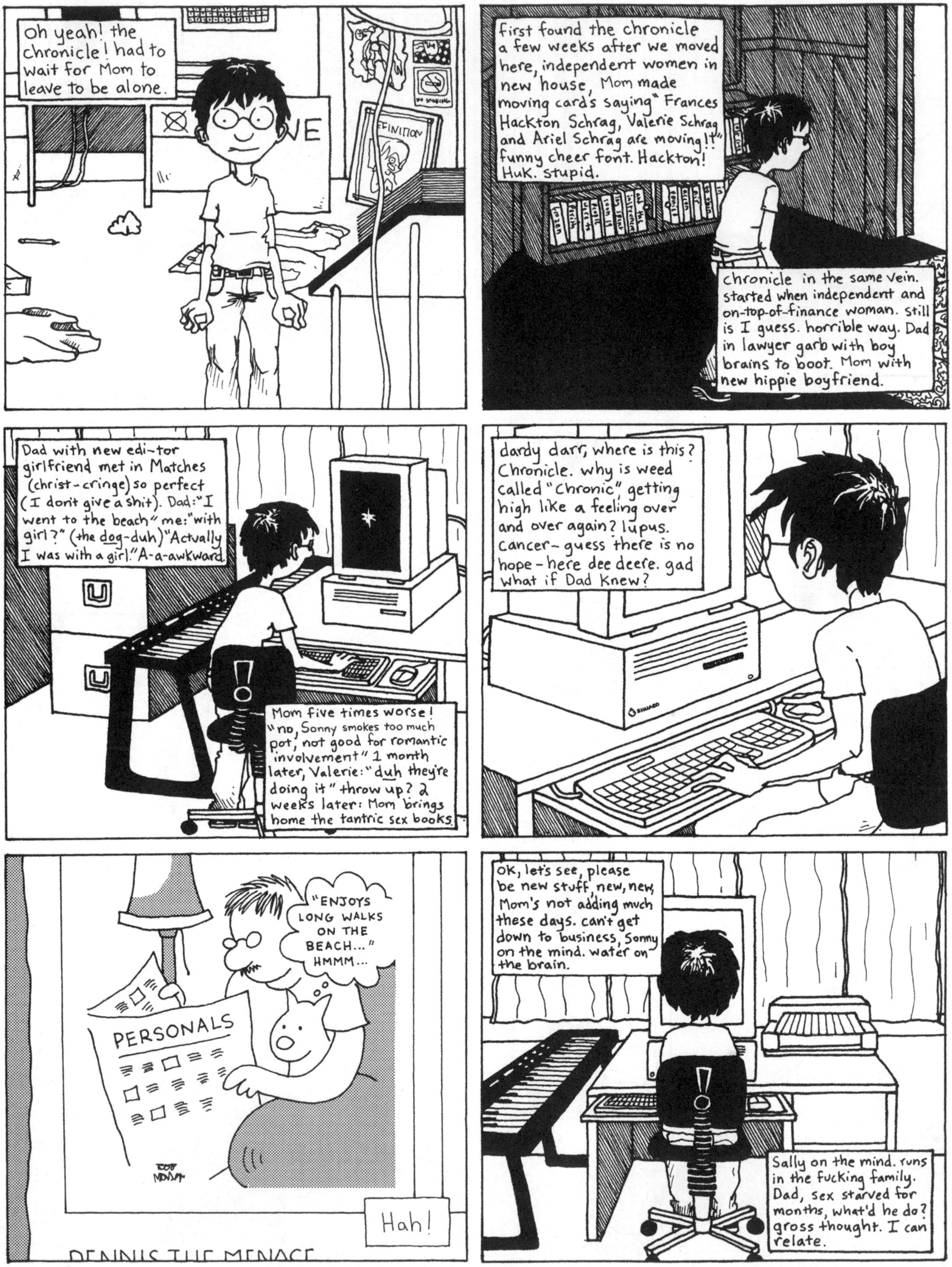
Oh yeah! the chronicle! had to wait for Mom to leave to be alone.
first found the chronicle a few weeks after we moved here, independent women in new house, Mom made moving cards saying "Frances Hackton Schrag, Valerie Schrag and Ariel Schrag are moving!" funny cheer font. Hackton! HuK. stupid.
chronicle in the same vein. started when independent and on-top-of-finance woman. still is I guess. horrible way. Dad in lawyer garb with boy brains to boot. Mom with new hippie boyfriend.
Dad with new edi-tor girlfriend met in Matches (christ-cringe) so perfect (I don't give a shit). Dad: "I went to the beach" me: "with girl?" (the dog-duh) "Actually I was with a girl." A-a-awkward.
Mom five times worse! "no, Sonny smokes too much pot, not good for romantic involvement" 1 month later, Valerie: "duh they're doing it" throw up? 2 weeks later: Mom brings home the tantric sex books.
dardy darr, where is this? Chronicle. why is weed called "Chronic", getting high like a feeling over and over again? lupus. cancer- guess there is no hope- here dee deere. gad What if Dad Knew?
"ENJOYS LONG WALKS ON THE BEACH..." HMMM...
PERSONALS
Hah!
DENNIS THE MENACE
OK, let's see, please be new stuff, new, new, Mom's not adding much these days. can't get down to business, Sonny on the mind. water on the brain.
Sally on the mind. runs in the fucking family. Dad, sex starved for months, what'd he do? gross thought. I can relate.

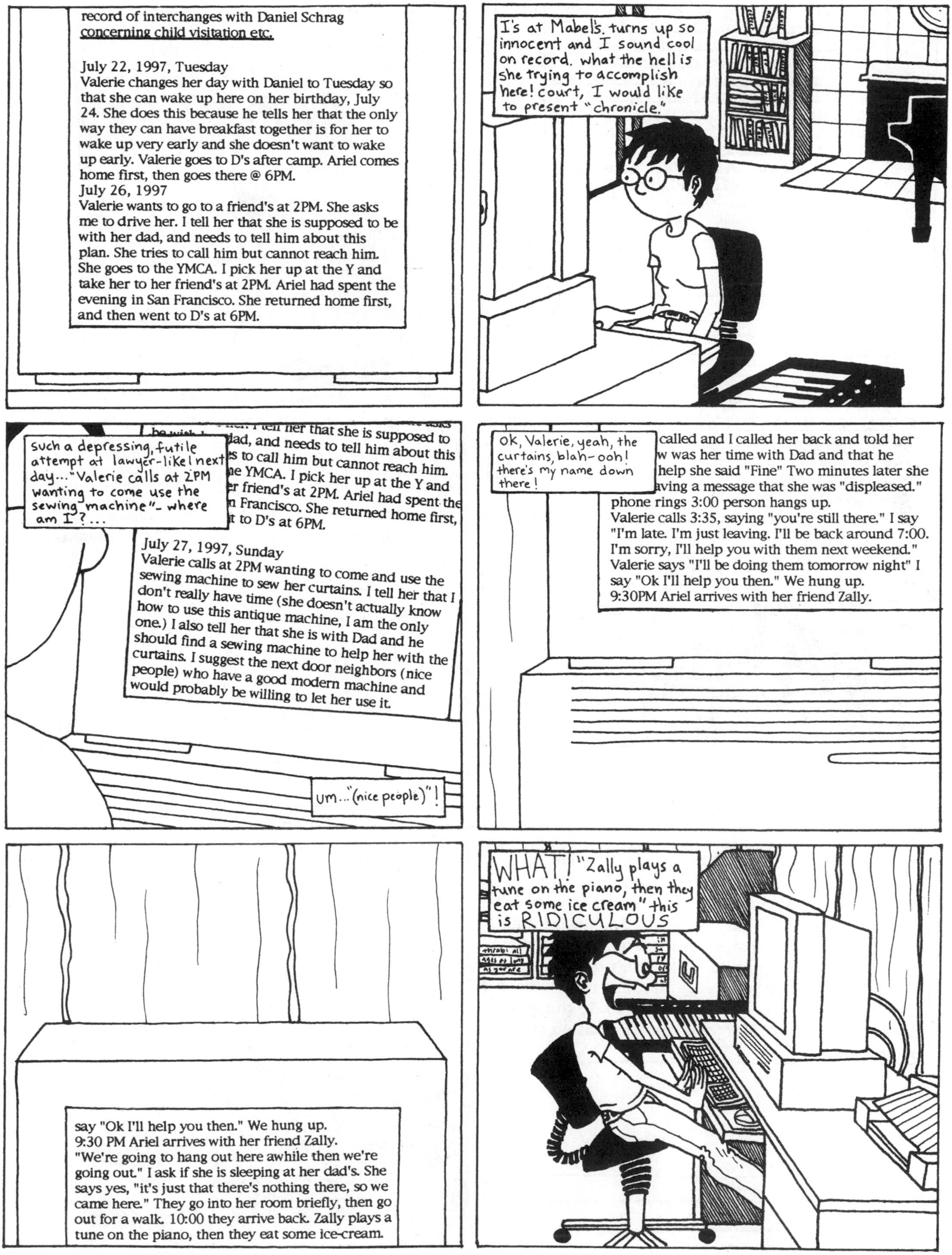
record of interchanges with Daniel Schrag
concerning child visitation etc.
July 22, 1997, Tuesday
Valerie changes her day with Daniel to Tuesday so that she can wake up here on her birthday, July 24. She does this because he tells her that the only way they can have breakfast together is for her to wake up very early and she doesn't want to wake up early. Valerie goes to D's after camp. Ariel comes home first, then goes there @ 6PM.
July 26, 1997
Valerie wants to go to a friend's at 2PM. She asks me to drive her. I tell her that she is supposed to be with her dad, and needs to tell him about this plan. She tries to call him but cannot reach him. She goes to the YMCA. I pick her up at the Y and take her to her friend's at 2PM. Ariel had spent the evening in San Francisco. She returned home first, and then went to D's at 6PM.
I's at Mabel's. turns up so innocent and I sound cool on record. what the hell is she trying to accomplish here! court, I would like to present "chronicle."
such a depressing, futile attempt at lawyer-like! next day..."Valerie calls at 2PM wanting to come use the sewing machine"- where am I?...
I tell her that she is supposed to
dad, and needs to tell him about this
s to call him but cannot reach him.
e YMCA. I pick her up at the Y and
r friend's at 2PM. Ariel had spent the
n Francisco. She returned home first,
t to D's at 6PM.
July 27, 1997, Sunday
Valerie calls at 2PM wanting to come and use the sewing machine to sew her curtains. I tell her that I don't really have time (she doesn't actually know how to use this antique machine, I am the only one.) I also tell her that she is with Dad and he should find a sewing machine to help her with the curtains. I suggest the next door neighbors (nice people) who have a good modern machine and would probably be willing to let her use it.
um..."(nice people)"!
ok, Valerie, yeah, the curtains, blah-ooh! there's my name down there!
called and I called her back and told her
w was her time with Dad and that he
help she said "Fine" Two minutes later she
aving a message that she was "displeased."
phone rings 3:00 person hangs up.
Valerie calls 3:35, saying "you're still there." I say "I'm late. I'm just leaving. I'll be back around 7:00. I'm sorry, I'll help you with them next weekend." Valerie says "I'll be doing them tomorrow night" I say "Ok I'll help you then." We hung up.
9:30PM Ariel arrives with her friend Zally.
say "Ok I'll help you then." We hung up.
9:30 PM Ariel arrives with her friend Zally.
"We're going to hang out here awhile then we're going out." I ask if she is sleeping at her dad's. She says yes, "it's just that there's nothing there, so we came here." They go into her room briefly, then go out for a walk. 10:00 they arrive back. Zally plays a tune on the piano, then they eat some ice-cream.
WHAT! "Zally plays a tune on the piano, then they eat some ice cream" this is RIDICULOUS

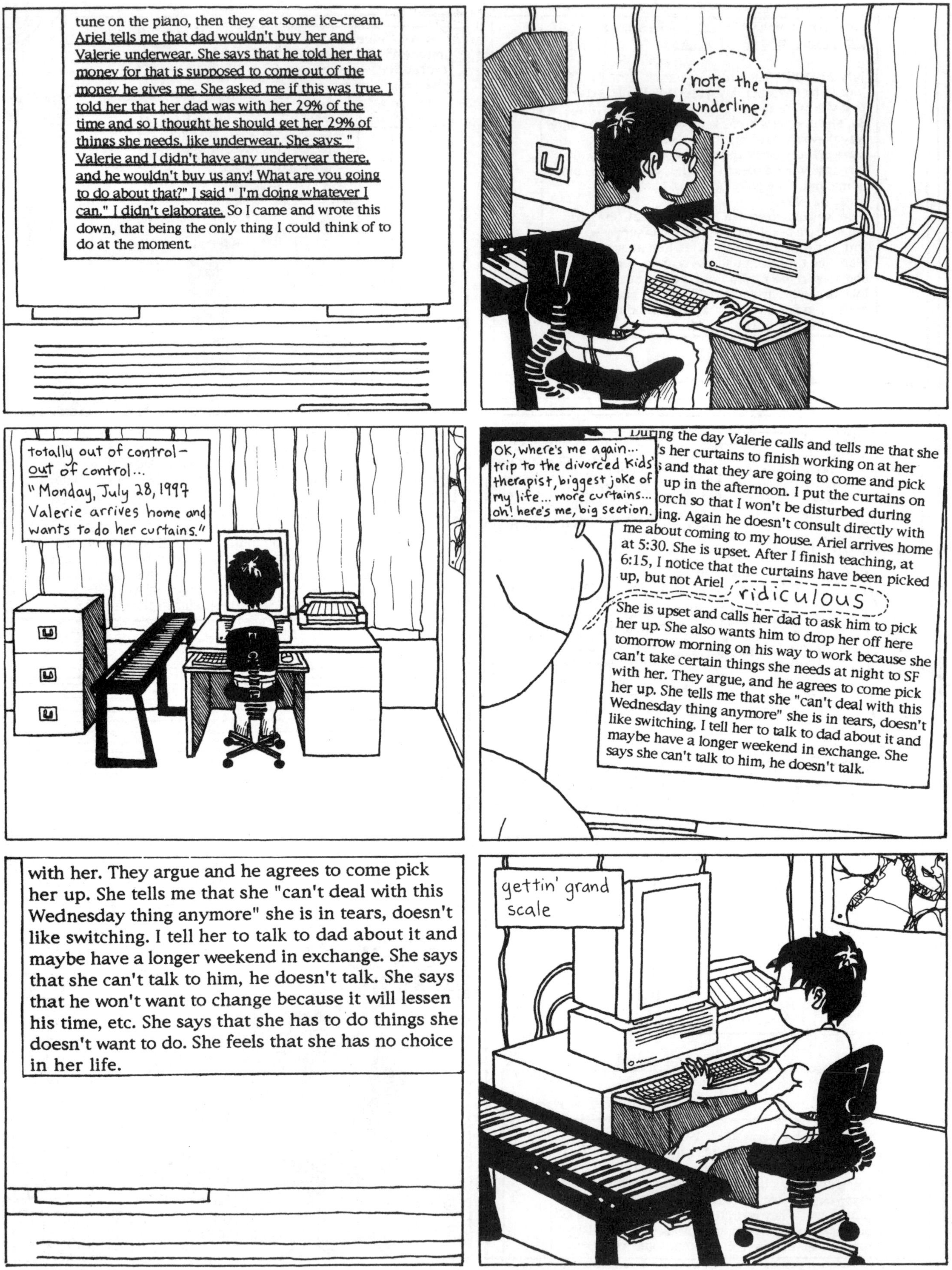

tune on the piano, then they eat some ice-cream. Ariel tells me that dad wouldn't buy her and Valerie underwear. She says that he told her that money for that is supposed to come out of the money he gives me. She asked me if this was true. I told her that her dad was with her 29% of the time and so I thought he should get her 29% of things she needs, like underwear. She says: " Valerie and I didn't have any underwear there, and he wouldn't buy us any! What are you going to do about that?" I said " I'm doing whatever I can." I didn't elaborate. So I came and wrote this down, that being the only thing I could think of to do at the moment.
note the underline
totally out of control - out of control... "Monday, July 28, 1997 Valerie arrives home and wants to do her curtains."
ok, where's me again... trip to the divorced kids' therapist, biggest joke of my life... more curtains... oh! here's me, big section.
ing the day Valerie calls and tells me that she
's her curtains to finish working on at her
and that they are going to come and pick
up in the afternoon. I put the curtains on
orch so that I won't be disturbed during
ing. Again he doesn't consult directly with me about coming to my house. Ariel arrives home at 5:30. She is upset. After I finish teaching, at 6:15, I notice that the curtains have been picked up, but not Ariel
ridiculous
She is upset and calls her dad to ask him to pick her up. She also wants him to drop her off here tomorrow morning on his way to work because she can't take certain things she needs at night to SF with her. They argue, and he agrees to come pick her up. She tells me that she "can't deal with this Wednesday thing anymore" she is in tears, doesn't like switching. I tell her to talk to dad about it and maybe have a longer weekend in exchange. She says she can't talk to him, he doesn't talk.
with her. They argue and he agrees to come pick her up. She tells me that she "can't deal with this Wednesday thing anymore" she is in tears, doesn't like switching. I tell her to talk to dad about it and maybe have a longer weekend in exchange. She says that she can't talk to him, he doesn't talk. She says that he won't want to change because it will lessen his time, etc. She says that she has to do things she doesn't want to do. She feels that she has no choice in her life.
gettin' grand scale

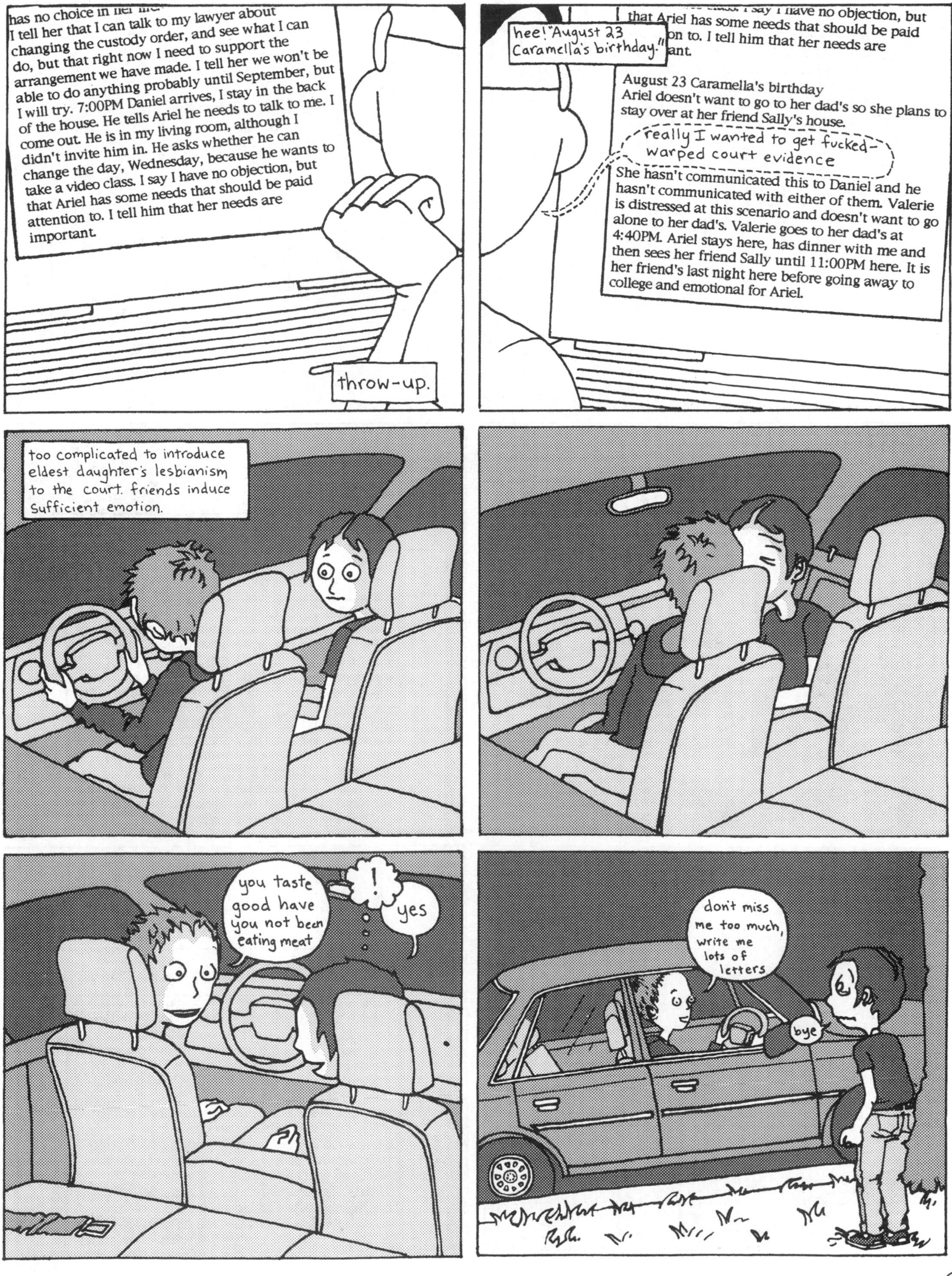

has no choice in her life
I tell her that I can talk to my lawyer about changing the custody order, and see what I can do, but that right now I need to support the arrangement we have made. I tell her we won't be able to do anything probably until September, but I will try. 7:00PM Daniel arrives, I stay in the back of the house. He tells Ariel he needs to talk to me. I come out. He is in my living room, although I didn't invite him in. He asks whether he can change the day, Wednesday, because he wants to take a video class. I say I have no objection, but that Ariel has some needs that should be paid attention to. I tell him that her needs are important.
throw-up.
hee! "August 23 Caramella's birthday."
that Ariel has some needs that should be paid attention to. I tell him that her needs are important.
August 23 Caramella's birthday
Ariel doesn't want to go to her dad's so she plans to stay over at her friend Sally's house.
really I wanted to get fucked-warped court evidence
She hasn't communicated this to Daniel and he hasn't communicated with either of them. Valerie is distressed at this scenario and doesn't want to go alone to her dad's. Valerie goes to her dad's at 4:40PM. Ariel stays here, has dinner with me and then sees her friend Sally until 11:00PM here. It is her friend's last night here before going away to college and emotional for Ariel.
too complicated to introduce eldest daughter's lesbianism to the court. friends induce sufficient emotion.
you taste good have you not been eating meat
!
yes
don't miss me too much, write me lots of letters
bye

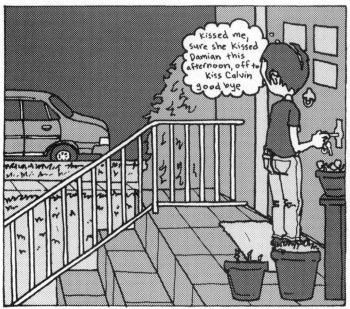

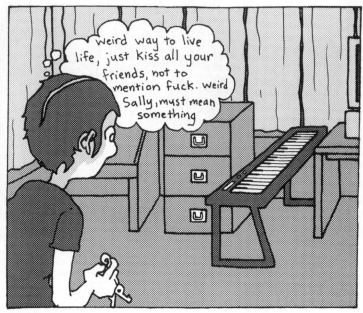

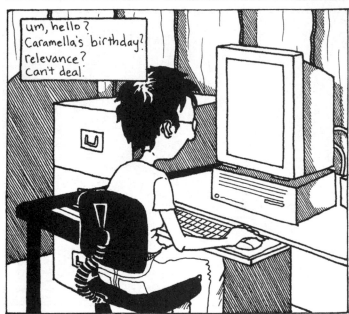

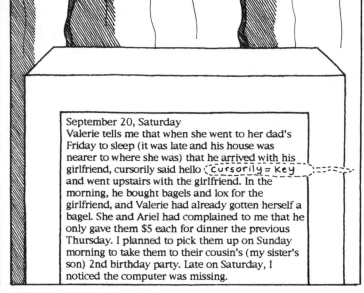

kissed me, sure she kissed Damian this afternoon, off to kiss Calvin good bye
weird way to live life, just kiss all your friends, not to mention fuck. Weird Sally, must mean something
um, hello? Caramella's birthday? relevance? can't deal.
September 20, Saturday
Valerie tells me that when she went to her dad's Friday to sleep (it was late and his house was nearer to where she was) that he arrived with his girlfriend, cursorily said hello and went upstairs with the girlfriend. In the morning, he bought bagels and lox for the girlfriend, and Valerie had already gotten herself a bagel. She and Ariel had complained to me that he only gave them $5 each for dinner the previous Thursday. I planned to pick them up on Sunday morning to take them to their cousin's (my sister's son) 2nd birthday party. Late on Saturday, I noticed the computer was missing.
cursorily = key
WHAT
can't deal, funny, late Saturday I noticed the computer missing, funny! can't deal....
September 21, Sunday
I arrive to take Ariel and Valerie to the birthday party at 10:00AM. I call the dog, wanting to visit with her. I am on the porch. Daniel refuses to let the dog out of his bedroom. Ariel is crying and screaming at him that it is her dog and she will take her if she wants. Somehow, the dog escapes, and I get to see her on the porch. Daniel comes down, and tells me that I need to ask his permission to see Caramella. I don't answer, I am busy with the dog. Ariel says that she is going to take the dog. She says "Take Caramella Mom!" Daniel hits Ariel and tells her that she is not taking anything out of this house anymore. Ariel says "You hit me!" I say goodbye to the dog and lead the girls to the car.
hee!
oh jesus christ

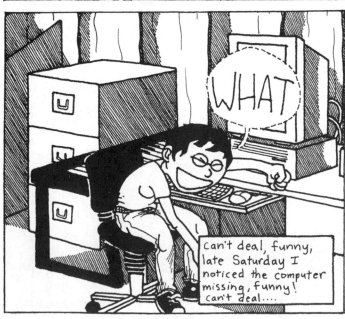

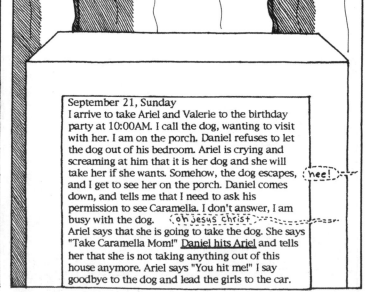

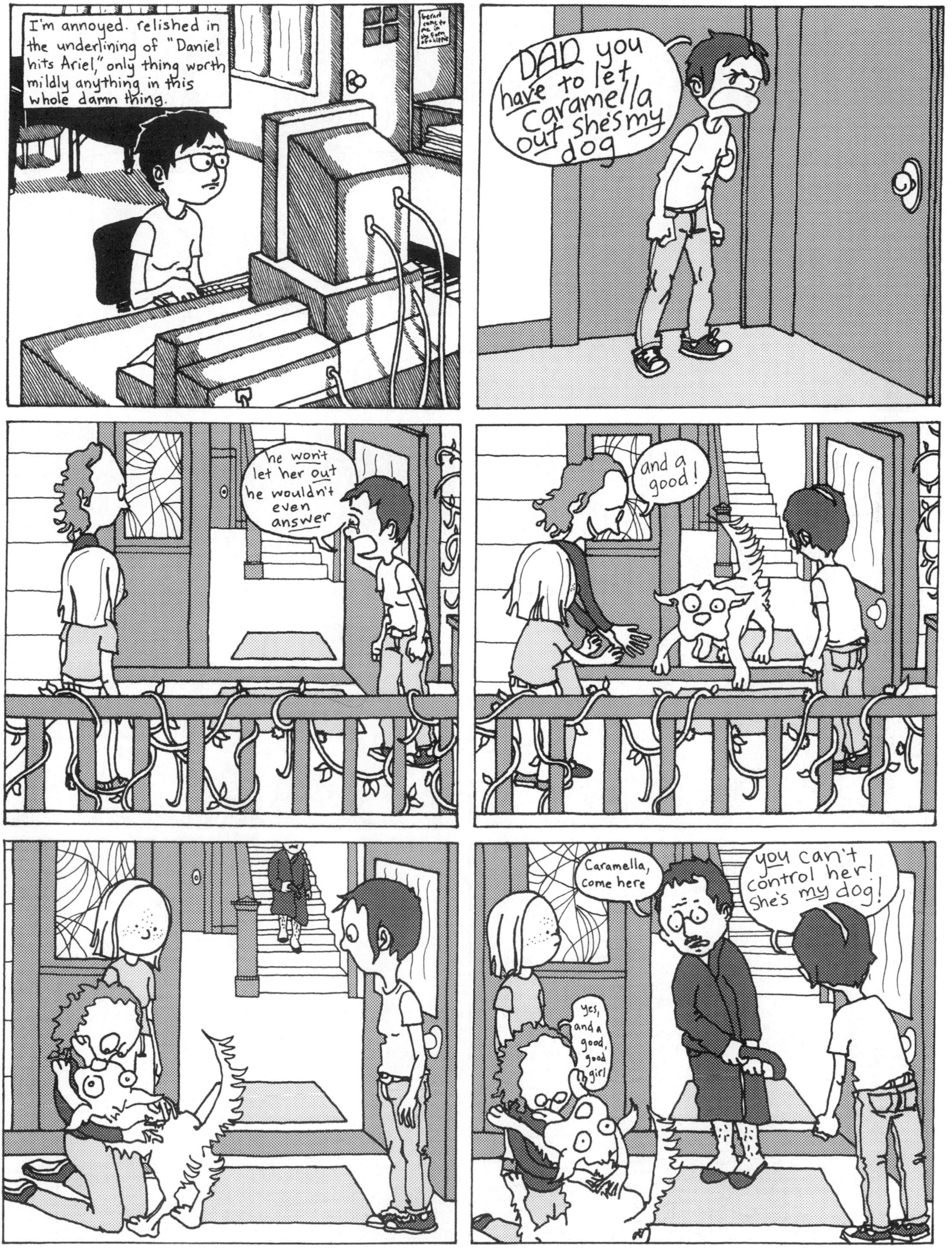
I'm annoyed. relished in the underlining of "Daniel hits Ariel," only thing worth mildly anything in this whole damn thing.
DAD you have to let Caramella out she's my dog
he won't let her out he wouldn't even answer
and a good!
Caramella, come here
you can't control her! She's my dog!
yes, and a good, good girl

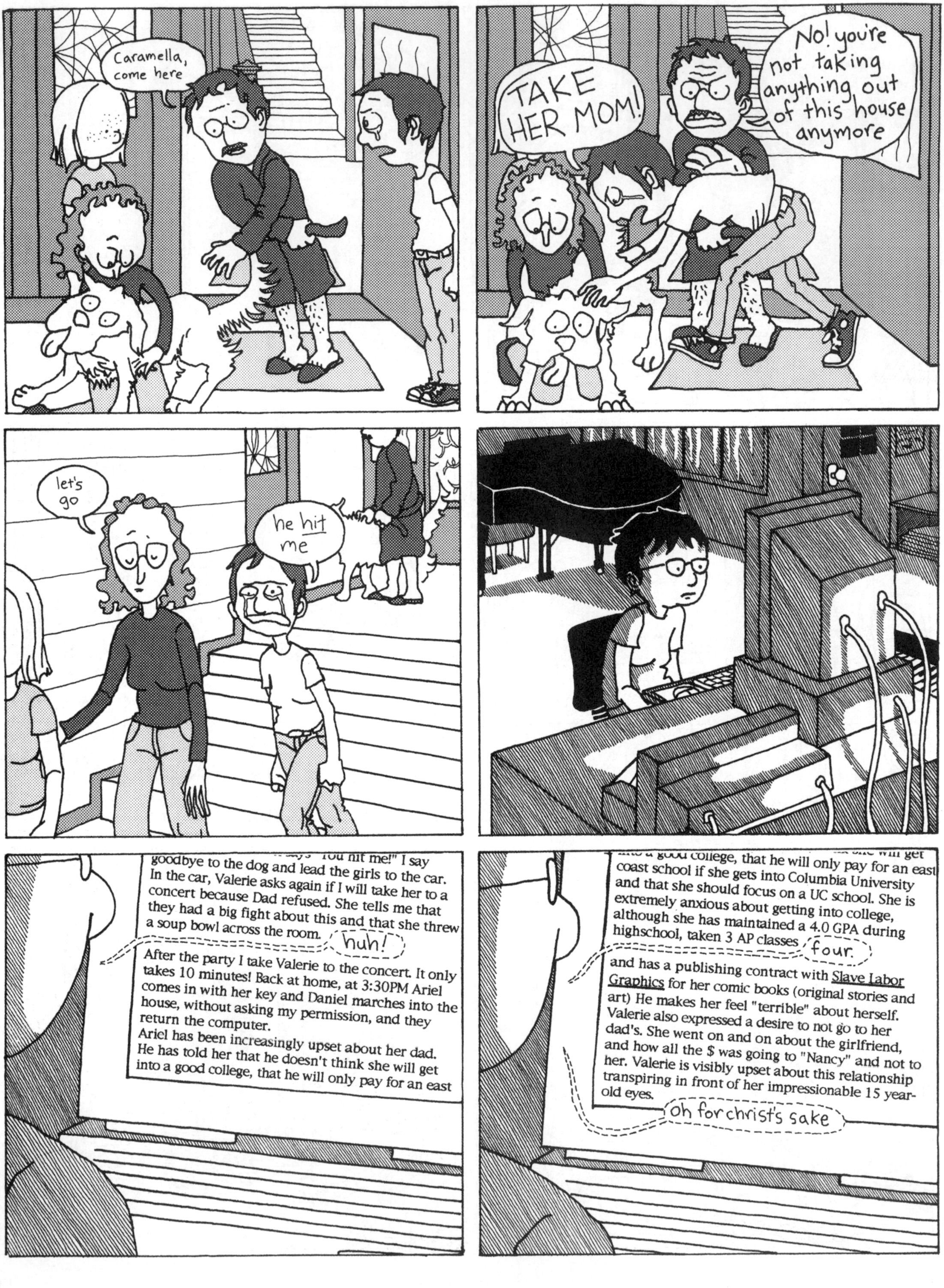

Caramella, come here
TAKE HER MOM!
No! you're not taking anything out of this house anymore
let's go
he hit me
goodbye to the dog and lead the girls to the car.
In the car, Valerie asks again if I will take her to a concert because Dad refused. She tells me that they had a big fight about this and that she threw a soup bowl across the room.
huh!
After the party I take Valerie to the concert. It only takes 10 minutes! Back at home, at 3:30PM Ariel comes in with her key and Daniel marches into the house, without asking my permission, and they return the computer.
Ariel has been increasingly upset about her dad. He has told her that he doesn't think she will get into a good college, that he will only pay for an east
coast school if she gets into Columbia University and that she should focus on a UC school. She is extremely anxious about getting into college, although she has maintained a 4.0 GPA during highschool, taken 3 AP classes
four.
and has a publishing contract with Slave Labor Graphics for her comic books (original stories and art) He makes her feel "terrible" about herself.
Valerie also expressed a desire to not go to her dad's. She went on and on about the girlfriend, and how all the $ was going to "Nancy" and not to her. Valerie is visibly upset about this relationship transpiring in front of her impressionable 15 year-old eyes.
oh for christ's sake

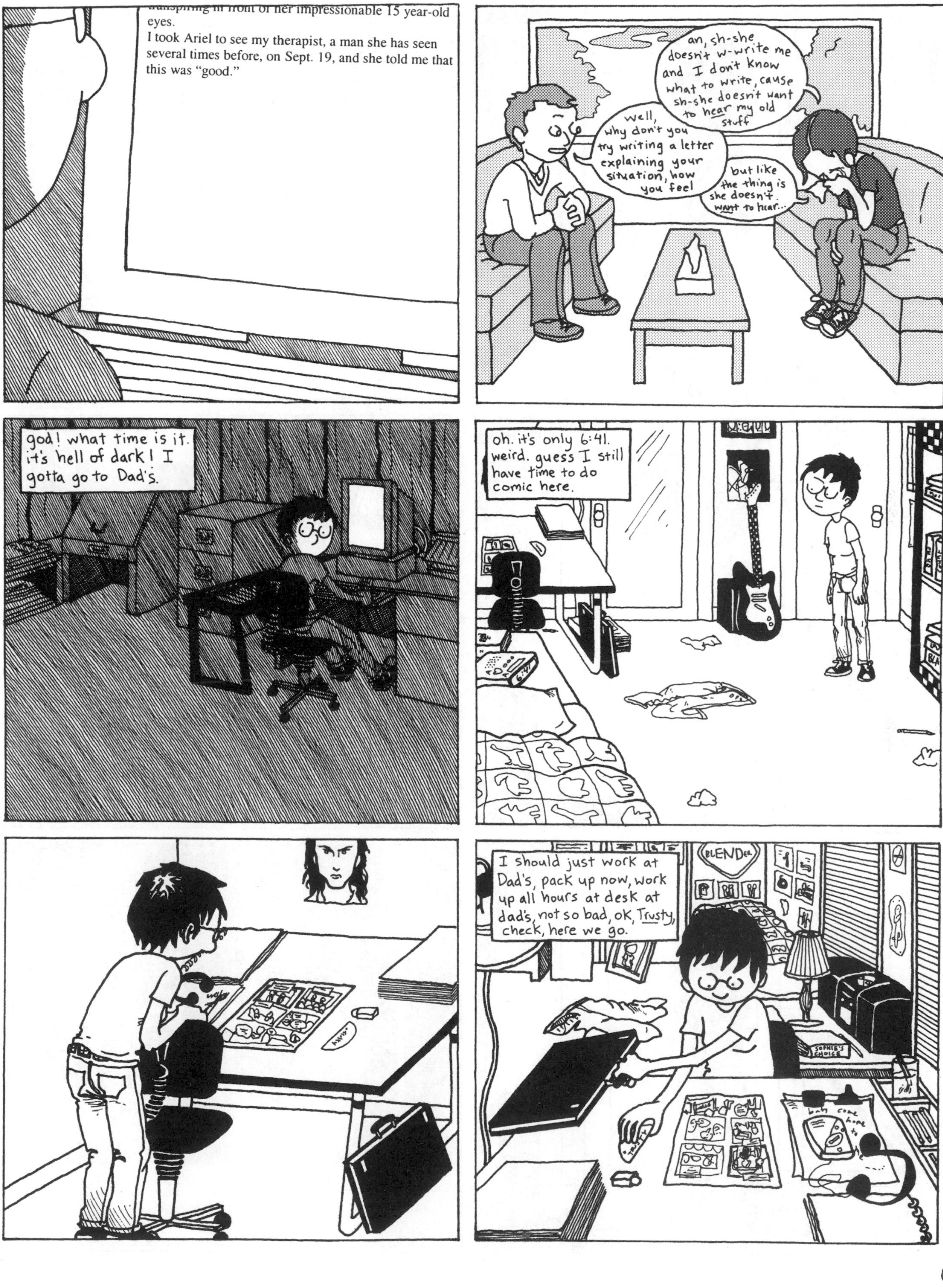
transpiring in front of her impressionable 15 year-old eyes.
I took Ariel to see my therapist, a man she has seen several times before, on Sept. 19, and she told me that this was "good."
an, sh-she doesn't w-write me and I don't know what to write, cause sh-she doesn't want to hear my old stuff
well, why don't you try writing a letter explaining your situation, how you feel
but like the thing is she doesn't want to hear...
god! what time is it. it's hell of dark! I gotta go to Dad's.
oh. it's only 6:41. weird. guess I still have time to do comic here.
I should just work at Dad's, pack up now, work up all hours at desk at dad's, not so bad, ok, Trusty, check, here we go.

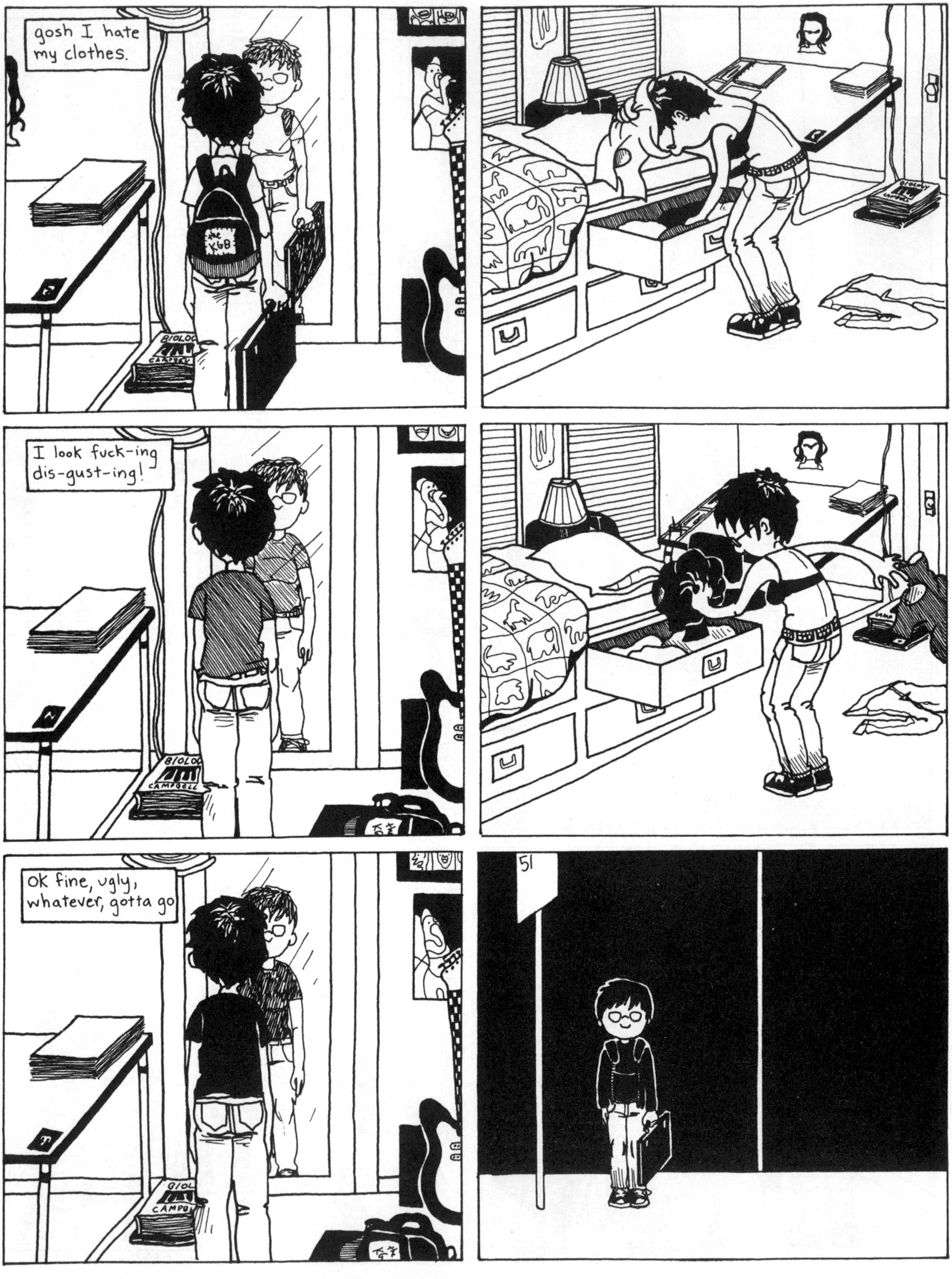
gosh I hate my clothes.
I look fuck-ing dis-gust-ing!
OK fine, ugly, whatever, gotta go
51

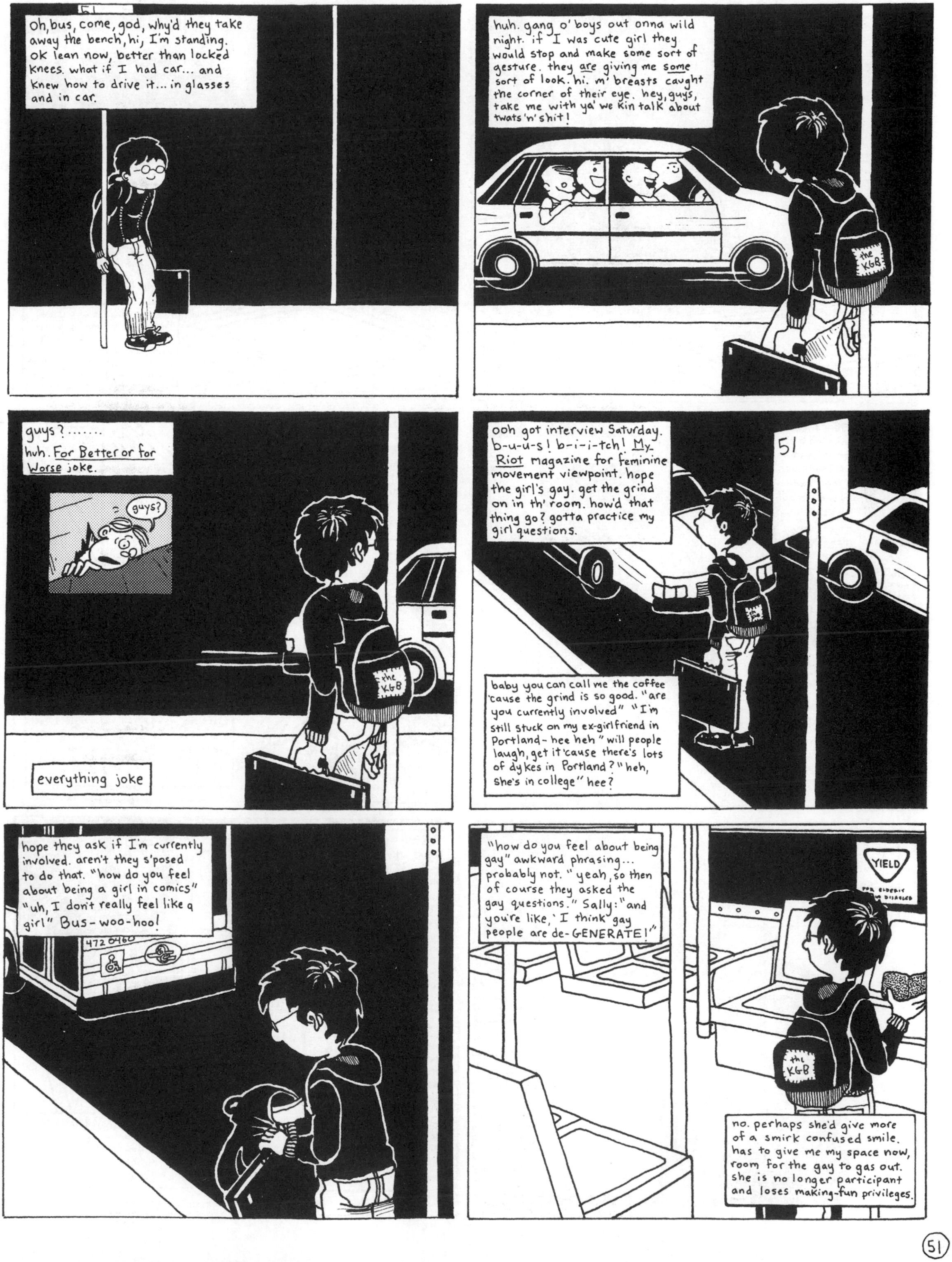
51
oh, bus, come, god, why'd they take away the bench, hi, I'm standing. ok lean now, better than locked knees. what if I had car... and knew how to drive it... in glasses and in car.
huh. gang o' boys out onna wild night. if I was cute girl they would stop and make some sort of gesture. they are giving me some sort of look. hi. m' breasts caught the corner of their eye. hey, guys, take me with ya' we kin talk about twats 'n' shit!
the KGB
guys?.......
huh. For Better or for Worse joke.
guys?
the KGB
everything joke
ooh got interview Saturday. b-u-u-s! b-i-i-tch! My Riot magazine for feminine movement viewpoint. hope the girl's gay. get the grind on in th' room. how'd that thing go? gotta practice my girl questions.
51
baby you can call me the coffee 'cause the grind is so good. "are you currently involved" "I'm still stuck on my ex-girlfriend in Portland - hee heh" will people laugh, get it 'cause there's lots of dykes in Portland?" heh, she's in college" hee?
hope they ask if I'm currently involved. aren't they s'posed to do that. "how do you feel about being a girl in comics" "uh, I don't really feel like a girl" Bus-woo-hoo!
472 0460
"how do you feel about being gay" awkward phrasing... probably not. "yeah, so then of course they asked the gay questions." Sally: "and you're like, 'I think gay people are de-GENERATE!'"
YIELD
the KGB
no. perhaps she'd give more of a smirk confused smile. has to give me my space now, room for the gay to gas out. she is no longer participant and loses making-fun privileges.

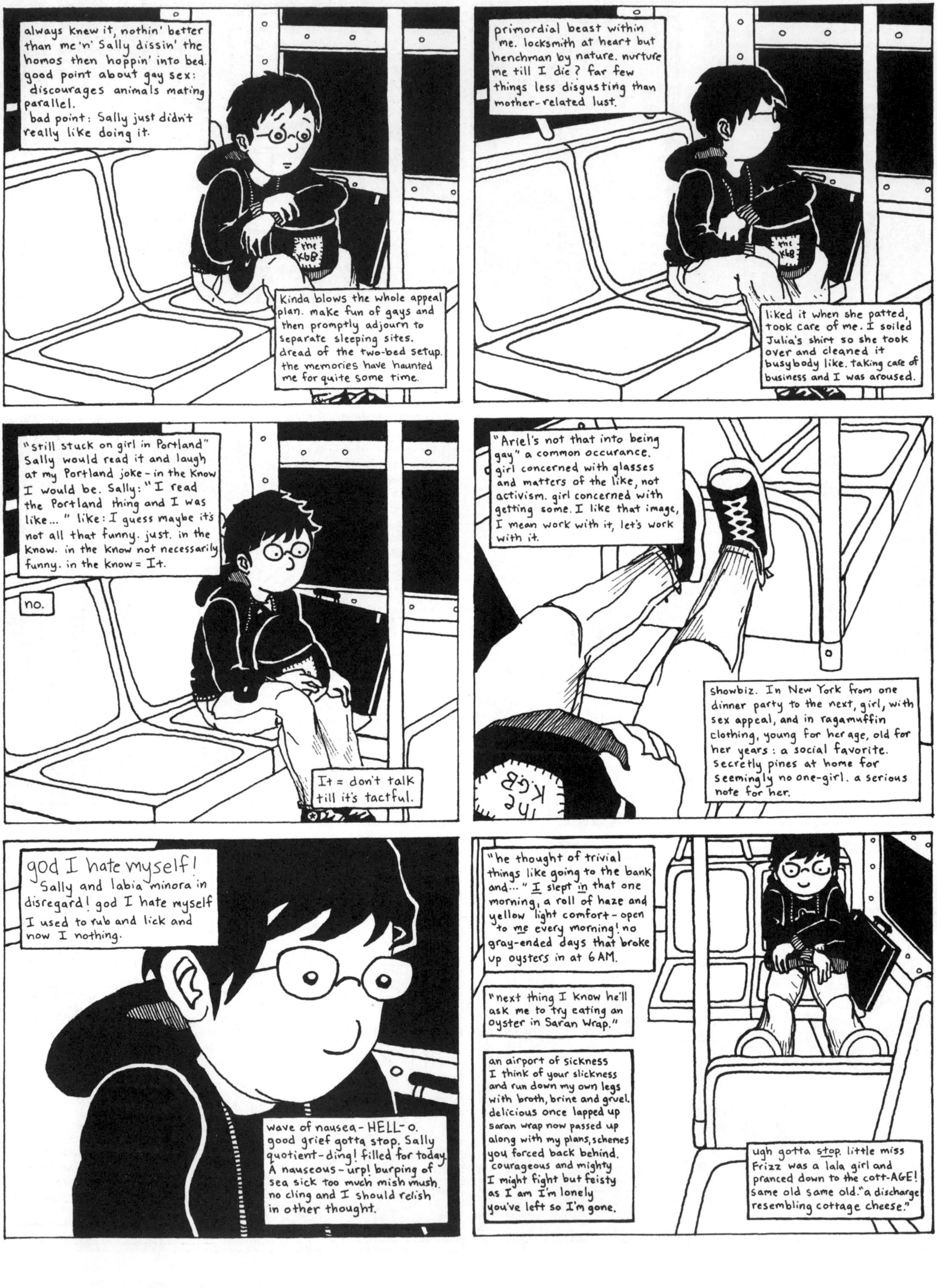
always knew it, nothin' better than me'n' Sally dissin' the homos then hoppin' into bed. good point about gay sex: discourages animals mating parallel. bad point: Sally just didn't really like doing it.
Kinda blows the whole appeal plan. make fun of gays and then promptly adjourn to separate sleeping sites. dread of the two-bed setup. the memories have haunted me for quite some time.
the KGB
primordial beast within me. locksmith at heart but henchman by nature. nurture me till I die? far few things less disgusting than mother-related lust.
liked it when she patted, took care of me. I soiled Julia's shirt so she took over and cleaned it busybody like. taking care of business and I was aroused.
"still stuck on girl in Portland" Sally would read it and laugh at my Portland joke - in the Know I would be. Sally: "I read the Portland thing and I was like..." like: I guess maybe it's not all that funny. just. in the Know. in the know not necessarily funny. in the know = It.
no.
It = don't talk till it's tactful.
"Ariel's not that into being gay" a common occurance. girl concerned with glasses and matters of the like, not activism. girl concerned with getting some. I like that image, I mean work with it, let's work with it.
showbiz. In New York from one dinner party to the next, girl, with sex appeal, and in ragamuffin clothing, young for her age, old for her years: a social favorite. secretly pines at home for seemingly no one-girl. a serious note for her.
god I hate myself! Sally and labia minora in disregard! god I hate myself I used to rub and lick and now I nothing.
wave of nausea - HELL-o. good grief gotta stop. Sally quotient-ding! filled for today. A nauseous-urp! burping of sea sick too much mish mush. no cling and I should relish in other thought.
"he thought of trivial things like going to the bank and..." I slept in that one morning, a roll of haze and yellow light comfort - open to me every morning! no gray-ended days that broke up oysters in at 6 AM.
"next thing I know he'll ask me to try eating an oyster in Saran Wrap."
an airport of sickness I think of your slickness and run down my own legs with broth, brine and gruel. delicious once lapped up saran wrap now passed up along with my plans, schemes you forced back behind. courageous and mighty I might fight but feisty as I am I'm lonely you've left so I'm gone.
ugh gotta stop. little miss Frizz was a lala girl and pranced down to the cott-AGE! same old same old. "a discharge resembling cottage cheese."

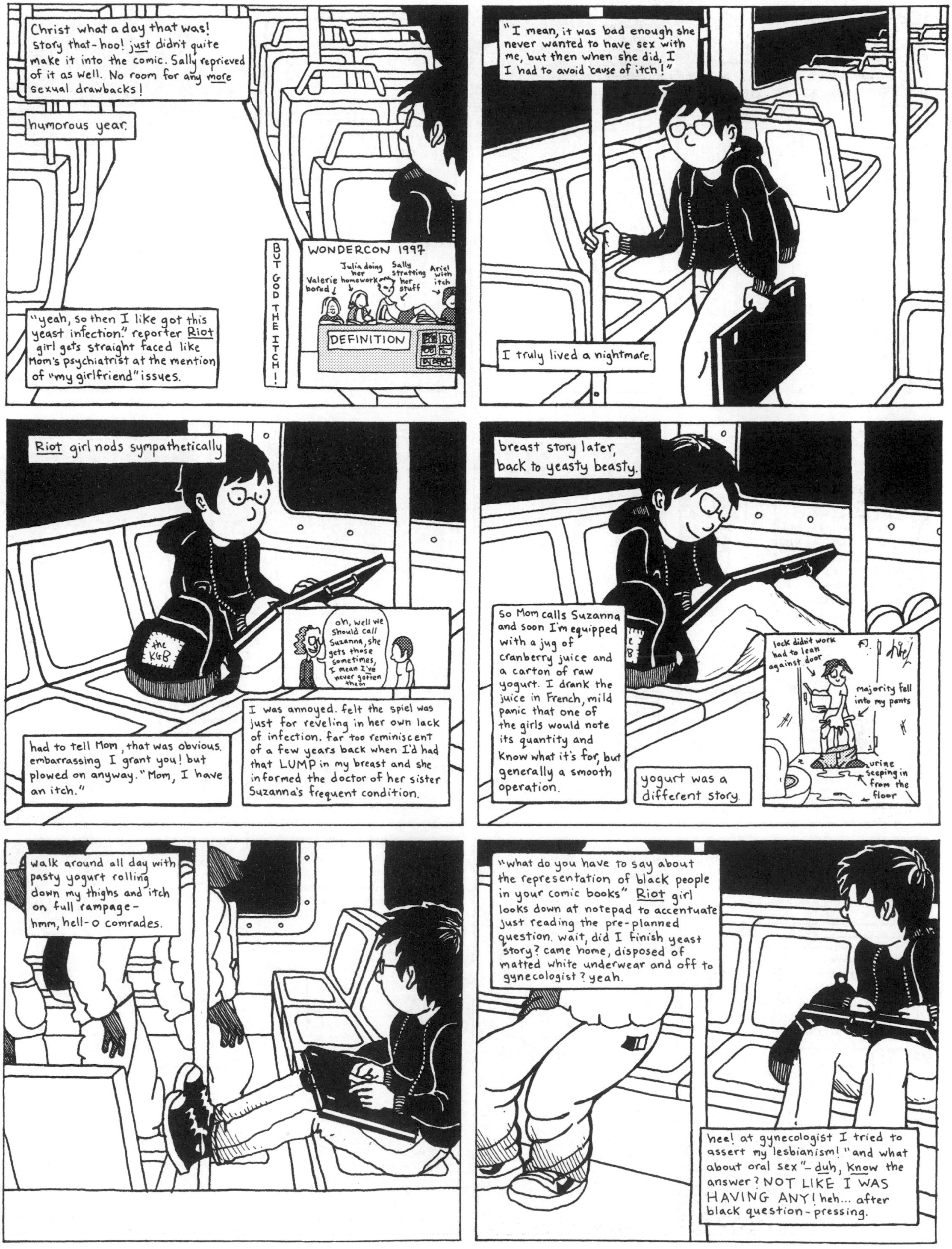

Christ what a day that was! story that-hoo! just didn't quite make it into the comic. Sally reprieved of it as well. No room for any more sexual drawbacks!
humorous year.
"yeah, so then I like got this yeast infection." reporter Riot girl gets straight faced like Mom's psychiatrist at the mention of "my girlfriend" issues.
BUT GOD THE ITCH!
WONDERCON 1997
Valerie bored
Julia doing her homework
Sally strutting her stuff
Ariel with itch
DEFINITION
"I mean, it was bad enough she never wanted to have sex with me, but then when she did, I had to avoid 'cause of itch!"
I truly lived a nightmare.
Riot girl nods sympathetically
the KGB
oh, well we should call Suzanna, she gets those sometimes, I mean I've never gotten them
had to tell Mom, that was obvious. embarrassing I grant you! but plowed on anyway. "Mom, I have an itch."
I was annoyed. felt the spiel was just for reveling in her own lack of infection. far too reminiscent of a few years back when I'd had that LUMP in my breast and she informed the doctor of her sister Suzanna's frequent condition.
breast story later, back to yeasty beasty.
So Mom calls Suzanna and soon I'm equipped with a jug of cranberry juice and a carton of raw yogurt. I drank the juice in French, mild panic that one of the girls would note its quantity and know what it's for, but generally a smooth operation.
yogurt was a different story.
lock didn't work had to lean against door
majority fell into my pants
urine seeping in from the floor
walk around all day with pasty yogurt rolling down my thighs and itch on full rampage- hmm, hell-o comrades.
"what do you have to say about the representation of black people in your comic books" Riot girl looks down at notepad to accentuate just reading the pre-planned question. wait, did I finish yeast story? came home, disposed of matted white underwear and off to gynecologist? yeah.
hee! at gynecologist I tried to assert my lesbianism! "and what about oral sex"- duh, know the answer? NOT LIKE I WAS HAVING ANY! heh... after black question-pressing.

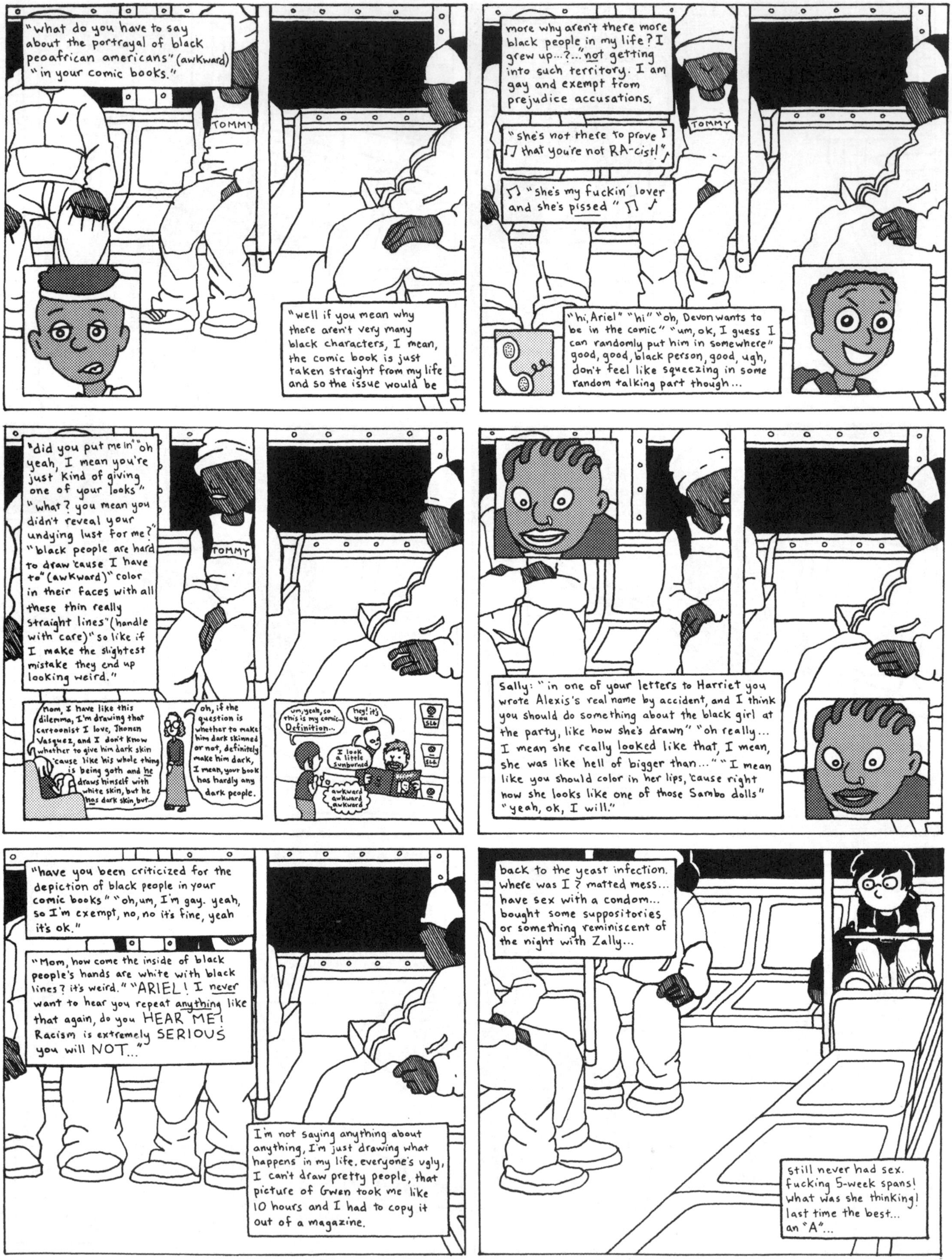
"what do you have to say about the portrayal of black peoafrican americans" (awkward) "in your comic books."
TOMMY
"well if you mean why there aren't very many black characters, I mean, the comic book is just taken straight from my life and so the issue would be
more why aren't there more black people in my life? I grew up...?..." not getting into such territory. I am gay and exempt from prejudice accusations.
TOMMY
"she's not there to prove that you're not RA-cist!"
"she's my fuckin' lover and she's pissed"
"hi, Ariel" "hi" "oh, Devon wants to be in the comic" "um, ok, I guess I can randomly put him in somewhere" good, good, black person, good, ugh, don't feel like squeezing in some random talking part though...
"did you put me in" "oh yeah, I mean you're just kind of giving one of your looks" "what? you mean you didn't reveal your undying lust for me?" "black people are hard to draw 'cause I have to" (awkward) "color in their faces with all these thin really straight lines" (handle with care) "so like if I make the slightest mistake they end up looking weird."
TOMMY
mom, I have like this dilemma, I'm drawing that cartoonist I love, Jhonen Vasquez, and I don't know whether to give him dark skin 'cause like his whole thing is being goth and he draws himself with white skin, but he has dark skin, but...
oh, if the question is whether to make him dark skinned or not, definitely make him dark, I mean, your book has hardly any dark people.
um, yeah, so this is my comic... Definition...
hey! it's you
I look a little sunburned
awkward awkward awkward
SLG
SLG
Sally: "in one of your letters to Harriet you wrote Alexis's real name by accident, and I think you should do something about the black girl at the party, like how she's drawn" "oh really... I mean she really looked like that, I mean, she was like hell of bigger than..." "I mean like you should color in her lips, 'cause right now she looks like one of those Sambo dolls" "yeah, ok, I will."
"have you been criticized for the depiction of black people in your comic books" "oh, um, I'm gay. yeah, so I'm exempt, no, no it's fine, yeah it's ok."
"Mom, how come the inside of black people's hands are white with black lines? it's weird." "ARIEL! I never want to hear you repeat anything like that again, do you HEAR ME! Racism is extremely SERIOUS you will NOT..."
I'm not saying anything about anything, I'm just drawing what happens in my life. everyone's ugly, I can't draw pretty people, that picture of Gwen took me like 10 hours and I had to copy it out of a magazine.
back to the yeast infection. where was I? matted mess... have sex with a condom... bought some suppositories or something reminiscent of the night with Zally...
still never had sex. fucking 5-week spans! what was she thinking! last time the best... an "A"...

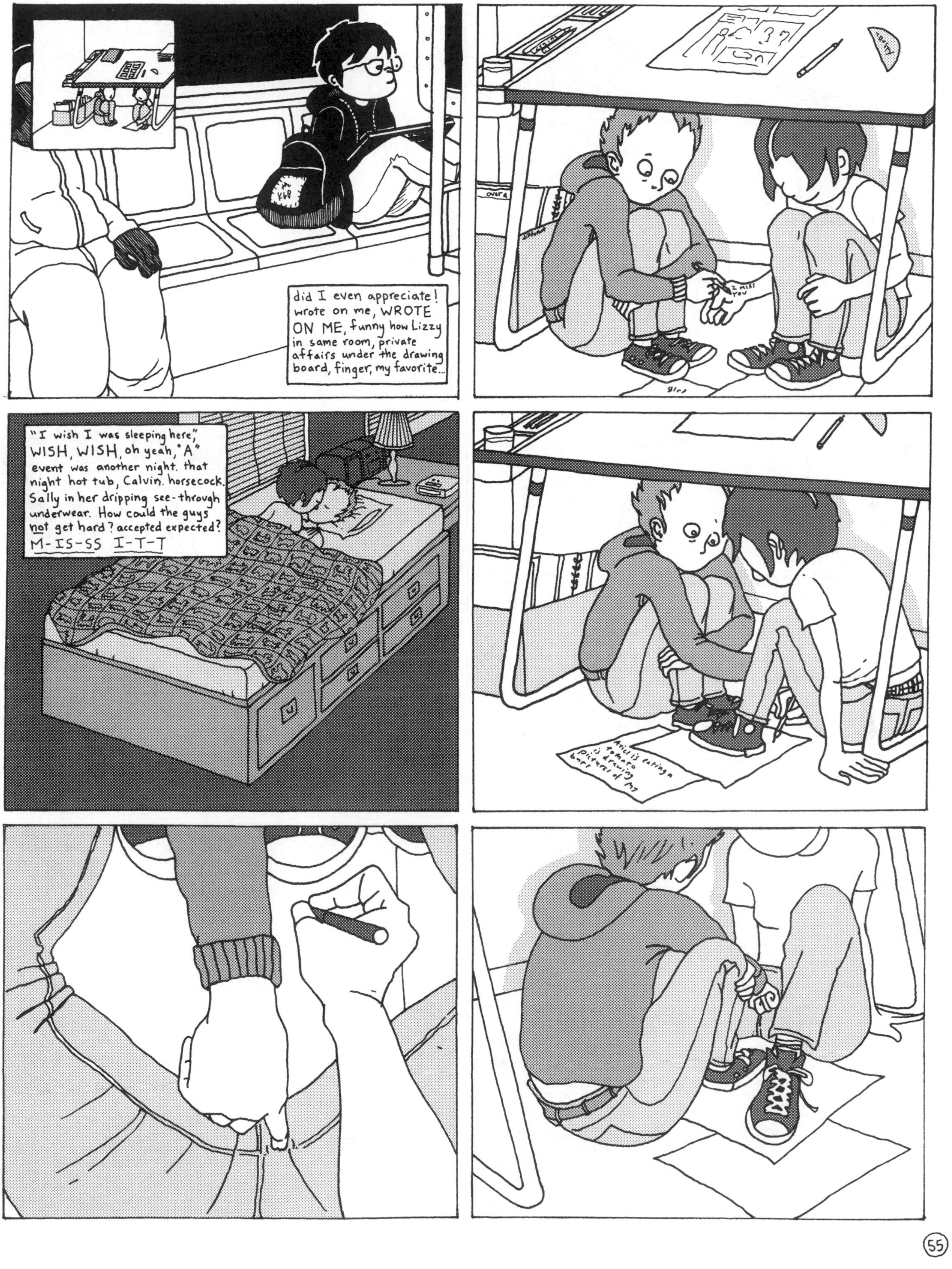

did I even appreciate! wrote on me, WROTE ON ME, funny how Lizzy in same room, private affairs under the drawing board, finger, my favorite...
I MISS YOU
"I wish I was sleeping here," WISH, WISH, oh yeah, "A" event was another night. that night hot tub, Calvin. horsecock. Sally in her dripping see-through underwear. How could the guys not get hard? accepted expected? M-IS-SS I-T-T
Ariel is eating a tomato is drawing pictures of my butt

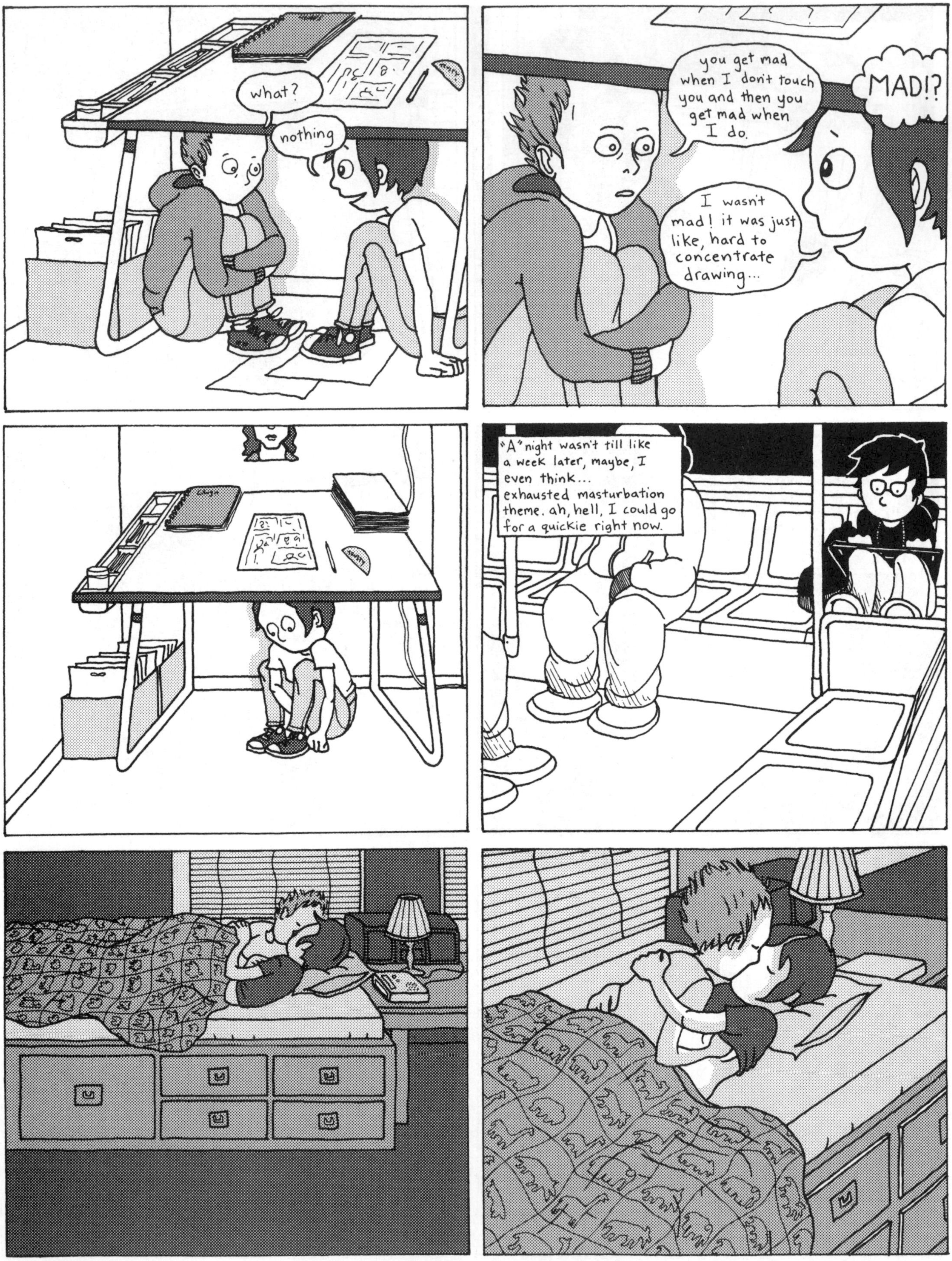
what?
nothing
you get mad when I don't touch you and then you get mad when I do.
MAD!?
I wasn't mad! it was just like, hard to concentrate drawing...
"A" night wasn't till like a week later, maybe, I even think... exhausted masturbation theme. ah, hell, I could go for a quickie right now.

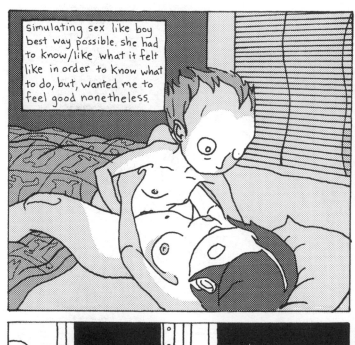

simulating sex like boy best way possible. she had to know/like what it felt like in order to know what to do, but, wanted me to feel good nonetheless.

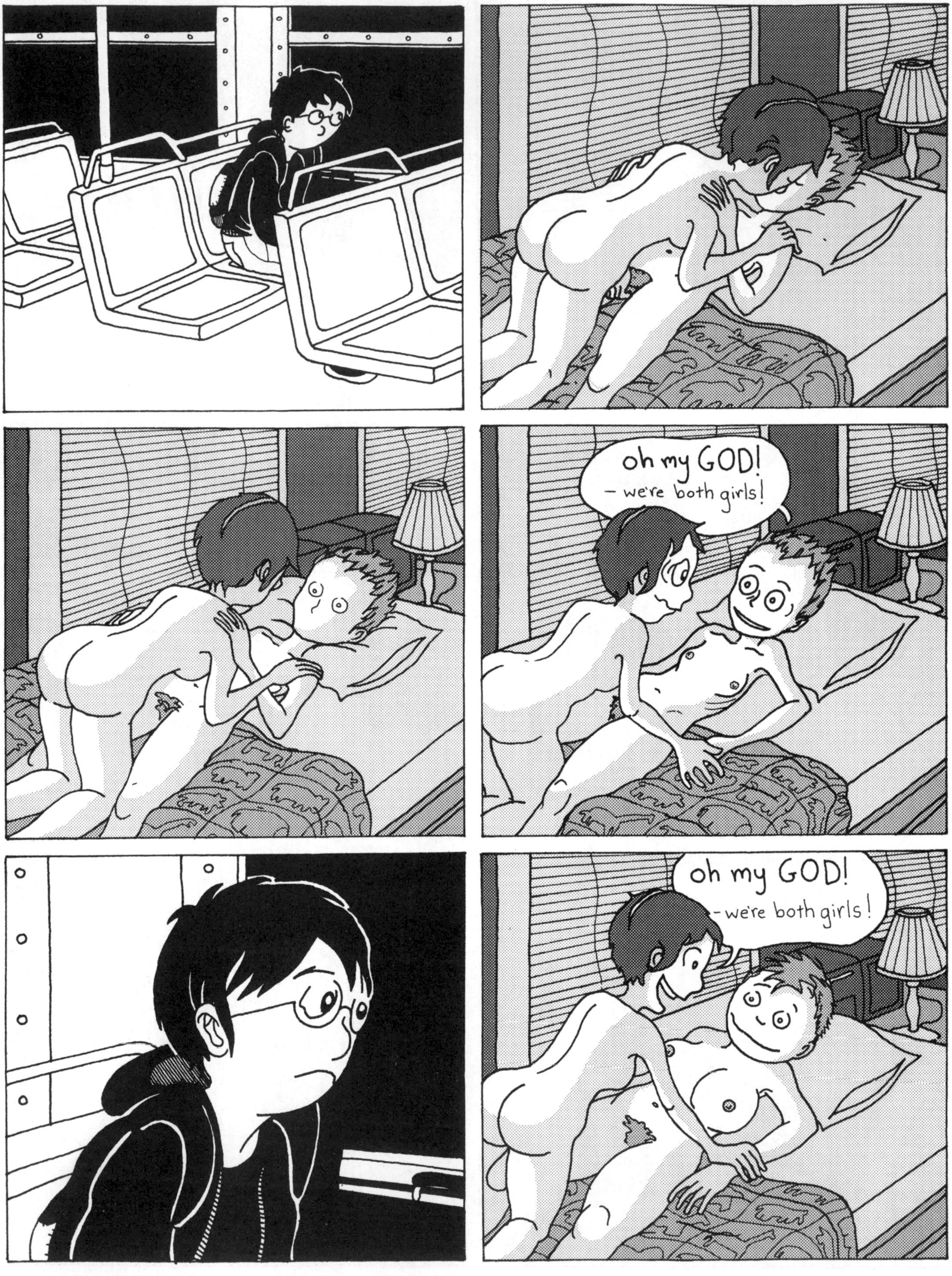
oh my GOD!
– we're both girls!
oh my GOD!
– we're both girls!

never want to speak to again, back to business with Sally:

oh my god oh my god

biggest, wettest gape I ever got in my life.

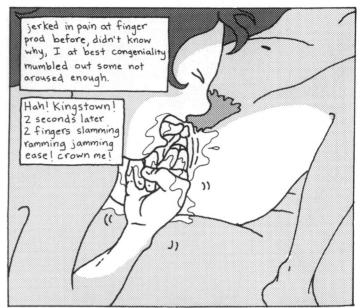

jerked in pain at finger prod before, didn't know why, I at best congeniality mumbled out some not aroused enough.

Hah! Kingstown! 2 seconds later 2 fingers slamming ramming jamming ease! crown me!

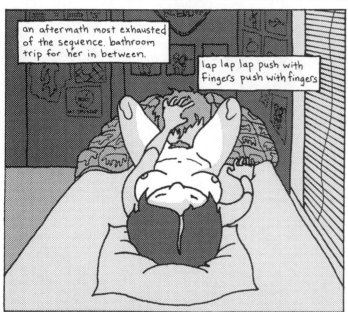

an aftermath most exhausted of the sequence. bathroom trip for her in between.

lap lap lap push with fingers push with fingers

hello! wait, forgot most important part!

that was an "A"

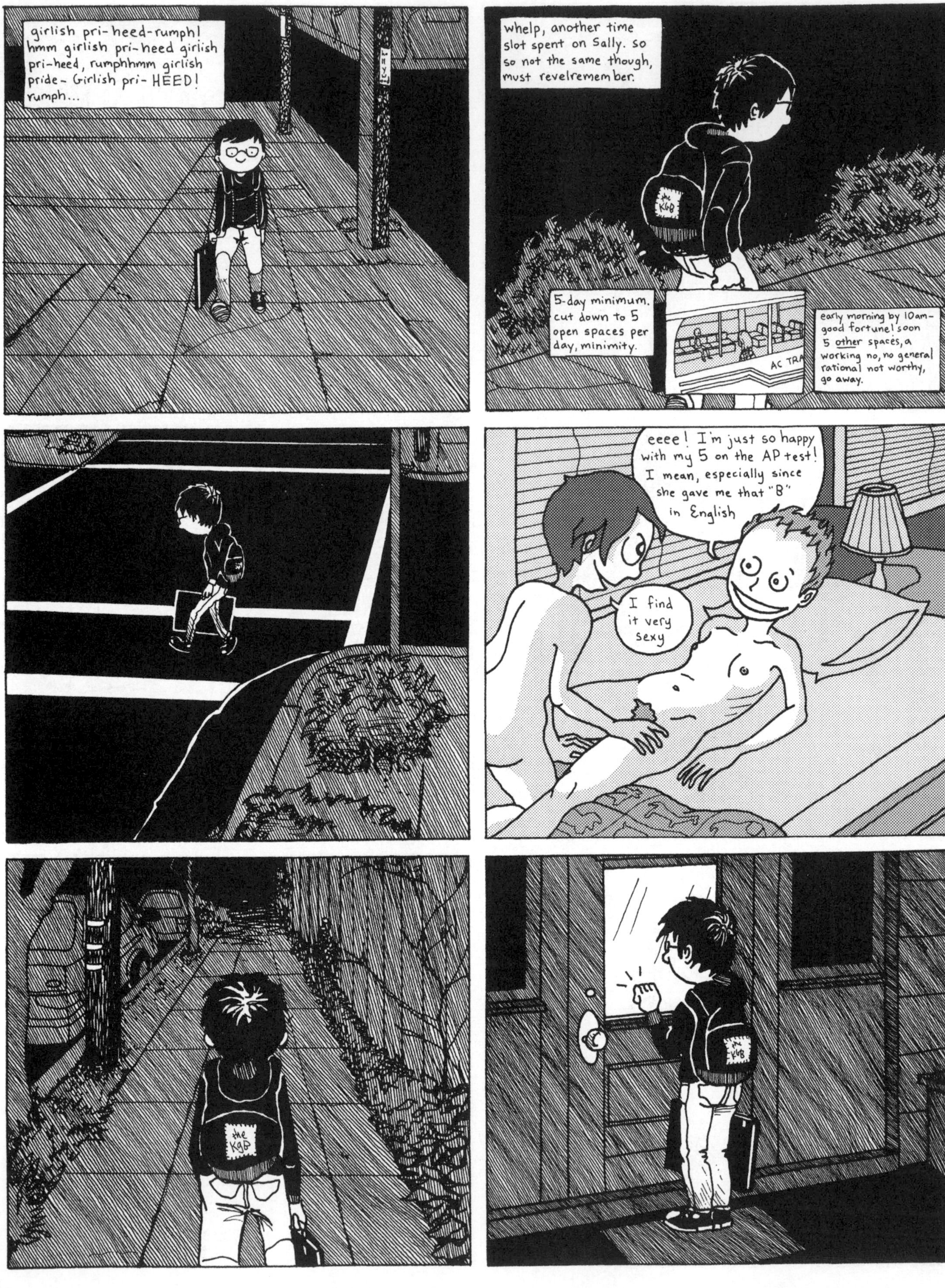
girlish pri-heed-rumph! hmm girlish pri-heed girlish pri-heed, rumphhmm girlish pride- Girlish pri-HEED! rumph...
whelp, another time slot spent on Sally. so so not the same though, must revelremember.
5-day minimum. cut down to 5 open spaces per day, minimity.
AC TRA
early morning by 10am- good fortune! soon 5 other spaces, a working no, no general rational not worthy, go away.
eeee! I'm just so happy with my 5 on the AP test! I mean, especially since she gave me that "B" in English
I find it very sexy

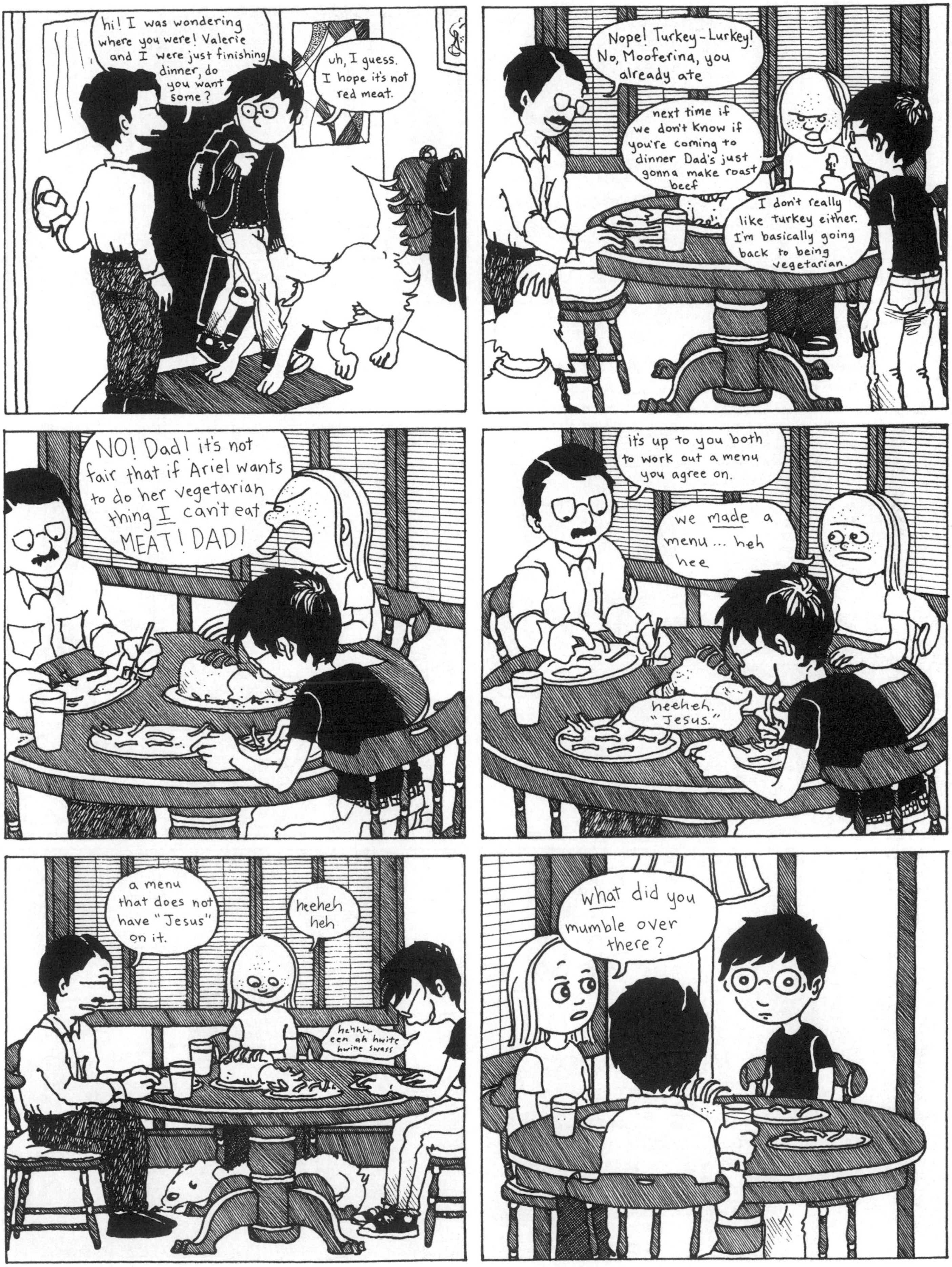
hi! I was wondering where you were! Valerie and I were just finishing dinner, do you want some?
uh, I guess. I hope it's not red meat.
Nope! Turkey-Lurkey! No, Mooferina, you already ate
next time if we don't know if you're coming to dinner Dad's just gonna make roast beef
I don't really like turkey either. I'm basically going back to being vegetarian.
NO! Dad! it's not fair that if Ariel wants to do her vegetarian thing I can't eat MEAT! DAD!
it's up to you both to work out a menu you agree on.
we made a menu... heh hee
heeheh. "Jesus."
a menu that does not have "Jesus" on it.
heeheh heh
hehhh een ah hwite hwine swass
what did you mumble over there?

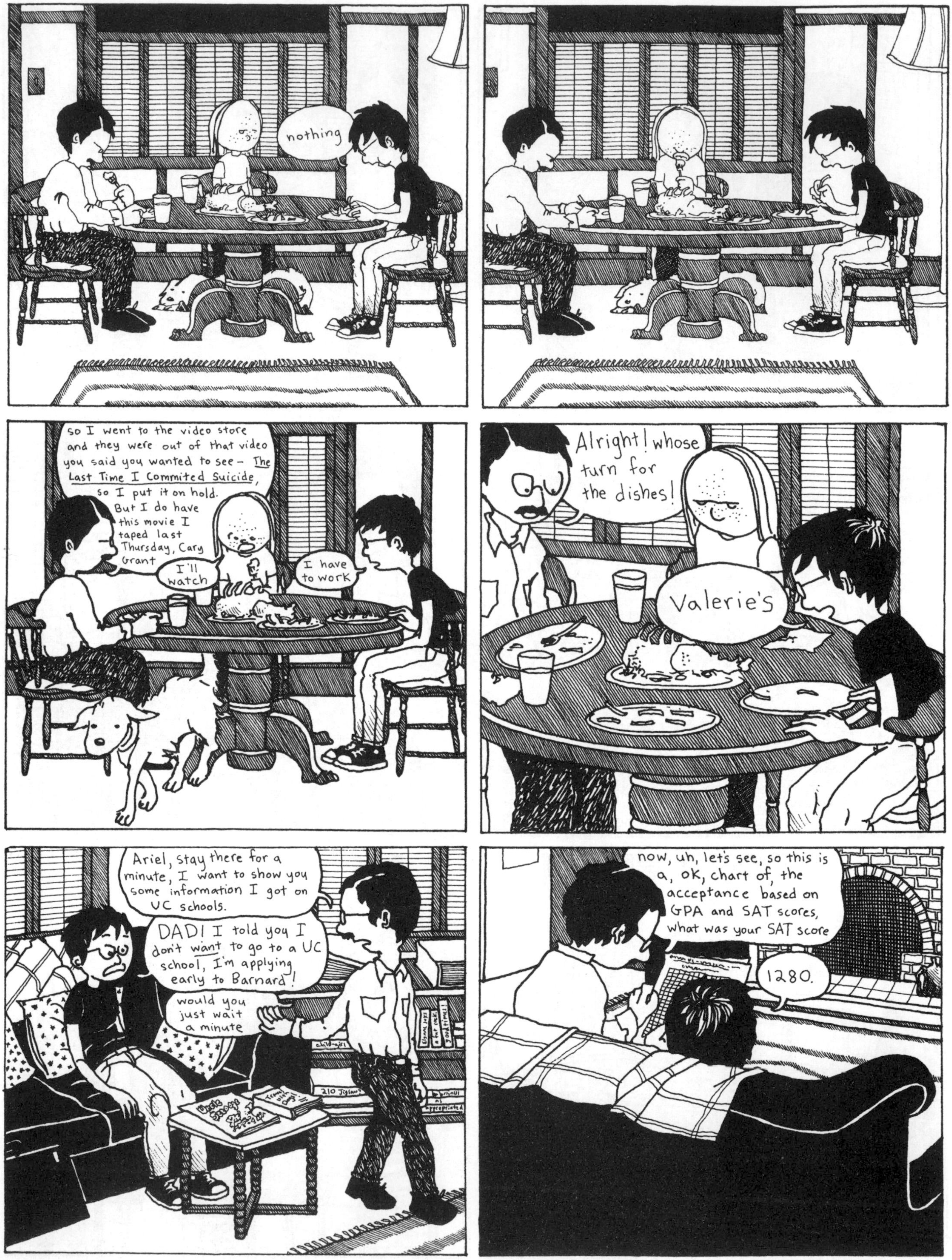
nothing
so I went to the video store and they were out of that video you said you wanted to see– The Last Time I Commited Suicide, so I put it on hold. But I do have this movie I taped last Thursday, Cary Grant
I'll watch
I have to work
Alright! whose turn for the dishes!
Valerie's
Ariel, stay there for a minute, I want to show you some information I got on UC schools.
DAD! I told you I don't want to go to a UC school, I'm applying early to Barnard!
would you just wait a minute
now, uh, let's see, so this is a, ok, chart of, the acceptance based on GPA and SAT scores, what was your SAT score
1280.

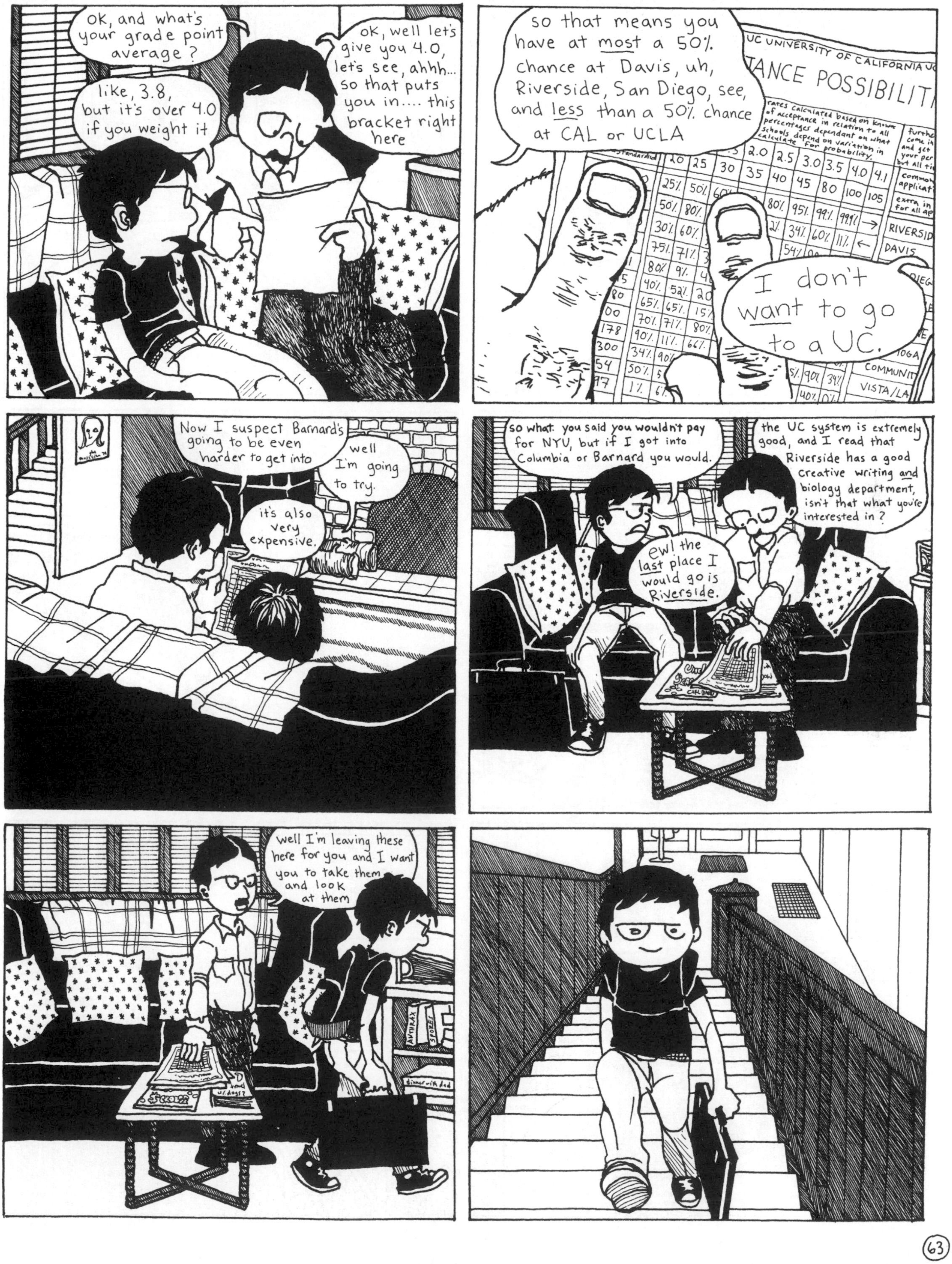

ok, and what's your grade point average?
like, 3.8, but it's over 4.0 if you weight it
ok, well let's give you 4.0, let's see, ahhh... so that puts you in.... this bracket right here
so that means you have at most a 50% chance at Davis, uh, Riverside, San Diego, see, and less than a 50% chance at CAL or UCLA
UC UNIVERSITY OF CALIFORNIA
I don't want to go to a UC.
Now I suspect Barnard's going to be even harder to get into
well I'm going to try.
it's also very expensive.
so what. you said you wouldn't pay for NYU, but if I got into Columbia or Barnard you would.
the UC system is extremely good, and I read that Riverside has a good creative writing and biology department, isn't that what you're interested in?
ew! the last place I would go is Riverside.
well I'm leaving these here for you and I want you to take them and look at them

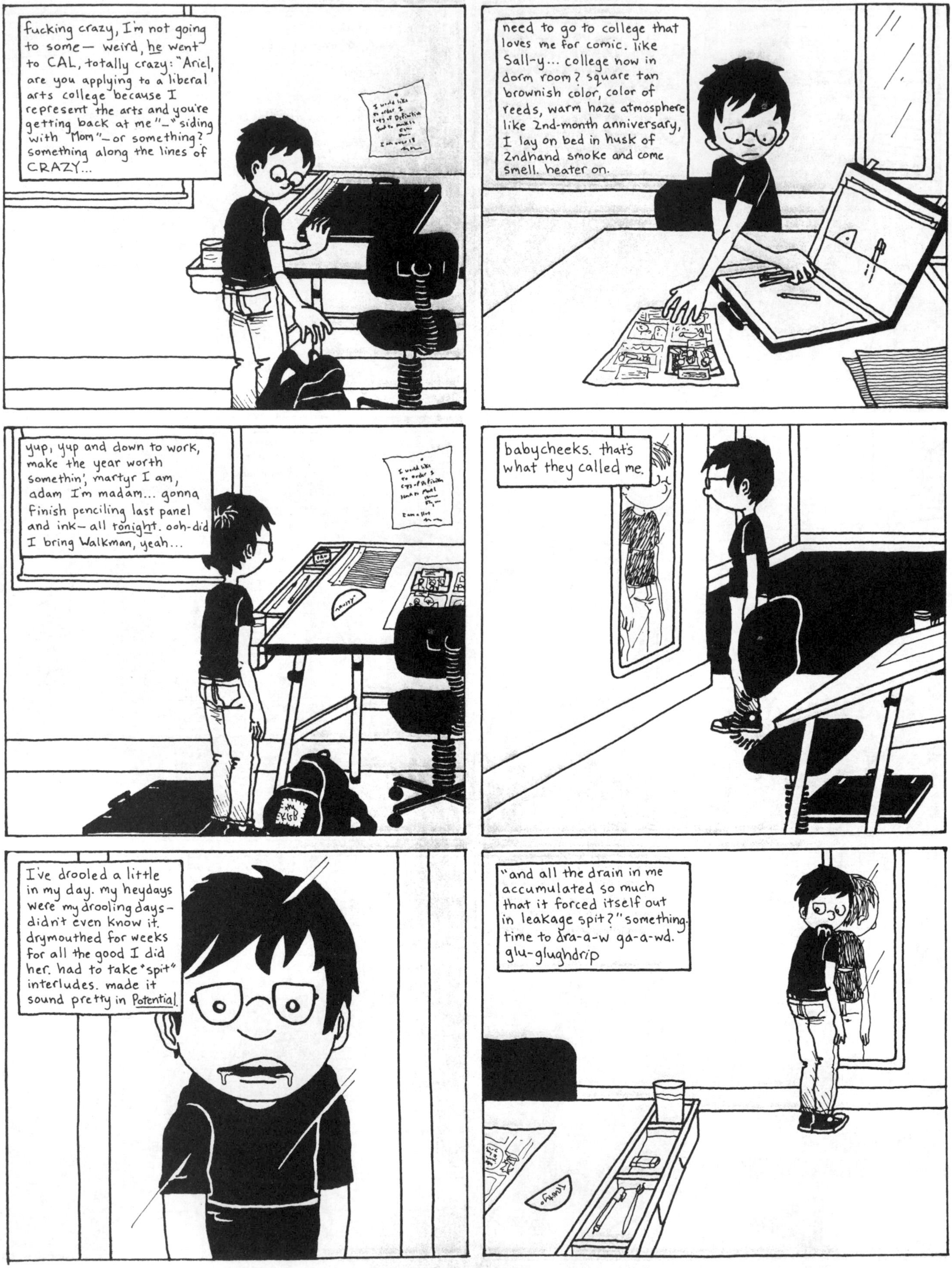
fucking crazy, I'm not going to some— weird, he went to CAL, totally crazy: "Ariel, are you applying to a liberal arts college because I represent the arts and you're getting back at me"—"siding with Mom"—or something? something along the lines of CRAZY...
need to go to college that loves me for comic. like Sall-y... college now in dorm room? square tan brownish color, color of reeds, warm haze atmosphere like 2nd-month anniversary, I lay on bed in husk of 2ndhand smoke and come smell. heater on.
yup, yup and down to work, make the year worth somethin', martyr I am, adam I'm madam... gonna finish penciling last panel and ink—all tonight. ooh-did I bring Walkman, yeah...
babycheeks. that's what they called me.
I've drooled a little in my day. my heydays were my drooling days-didn't even know it. drymouthed for weeks for all the good I did her. had to take "spit" interludes. made it sound pretty in Potential.
"and all the drain in me accumulated so much that it forced itself out in leakage spit?" something. time to dra-a-w ga-a-wd. glu-glughdrip

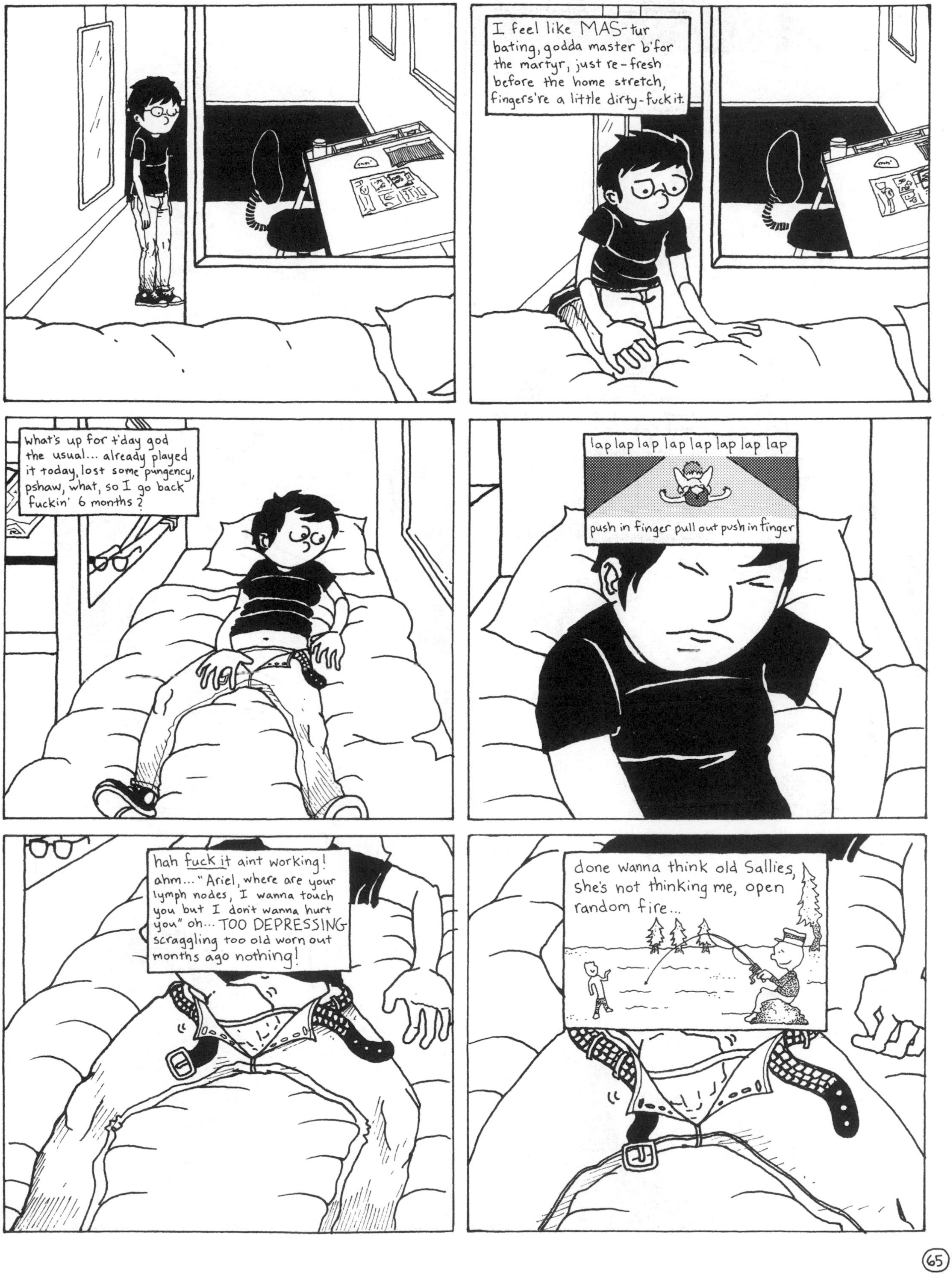
I feel like MAS-tur bating, godda master b'for the martyr, just re-fresh before the home stretch, fingers're a little dirty-fuck it.
what's up for t'day god the usual... already played it today, lost some pungency, pshaw, what, so I go back fuckin' 6 months?
lap lap lap lap lap lap lap lap
push in finger pull out push in finger
hah fuck it aint working! ahm... "Ariel, where are your lymph nodes, I wanna touch you but I don't wanna hurt you" oh... TOO DEPRESSING scraggling too old worn out months ago nothing!
done wanna think old Sallies, she's not thinking me, open random fire...

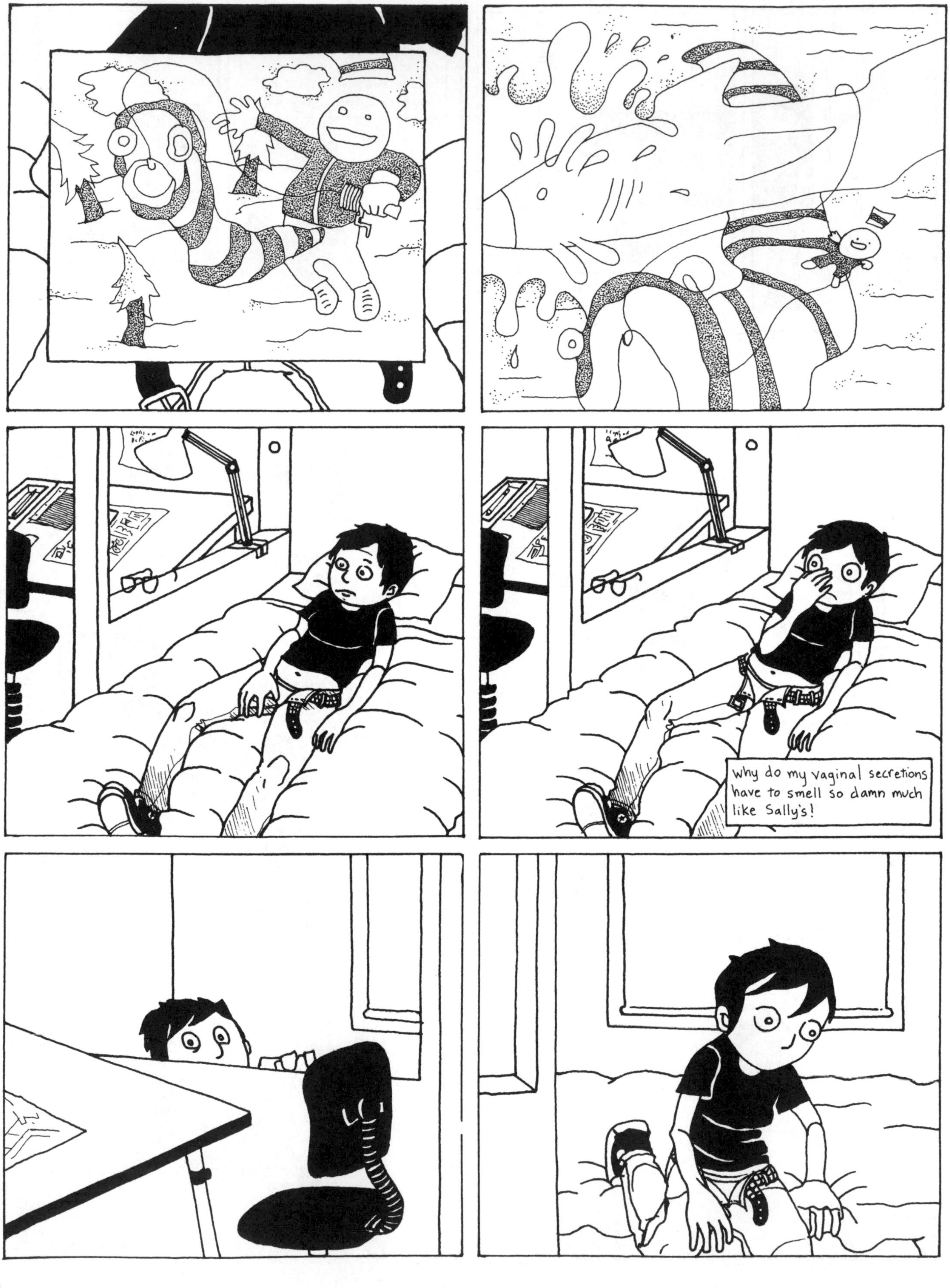
why do my vaginal secretions have to smell so damn much like Sally's!

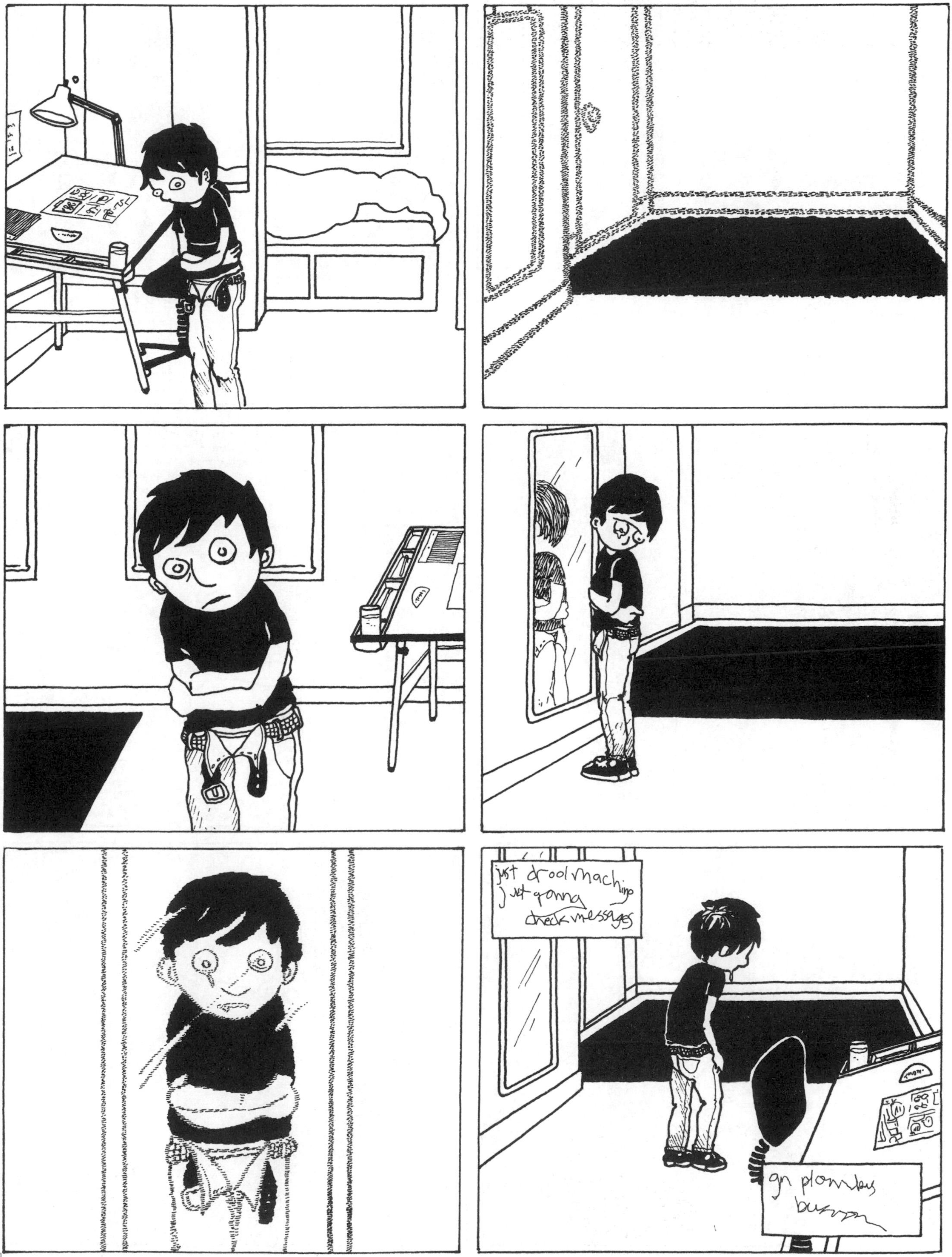
just drool machine
just gonna
check messages

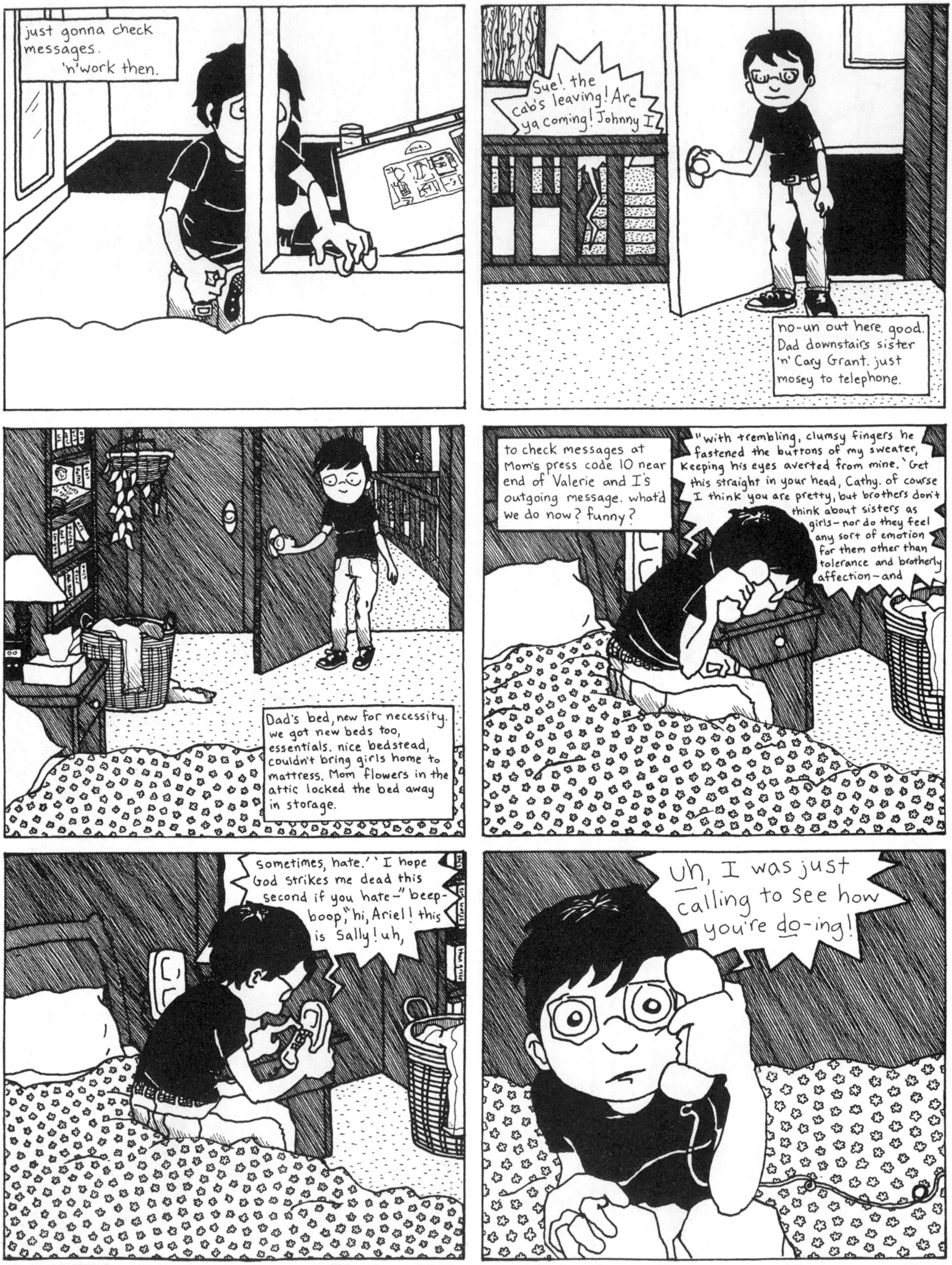
just gonna check messages. 'n'work then.
Sue! the cab's leaving! Are ya coming! Johnny I
no-un out here. good. Dad downstairs sister 'n' Cary Grant. just mosey to telephone.
Dad's bed, new for necessity. we got new beds too, essentials. nice bedstead, couldn't bring girls home to mattress. Mom flowers in the attic locked the bed away in storage.
to check messages at Mom's press code 10 near end of Valerie and I's outgoing message. what'd we do now? funny?
"with trembling, clumsy fingers he fastened the buttons of my sweater, keeping his eyes averted from mine. 'Get this straight in your head, Cathy. of course I think you are pretty, but brothers don't think about sisters as girls—nor do they feel any sort of emotion for them other than tolerance and brotherly affection—and
sometimes, hate.' 'I hope God strikes me dead this second if you hate—" beep-boop, "hi, Ariel! this is Sally! uh,
uh, I was just calling to see how you're do-ing!

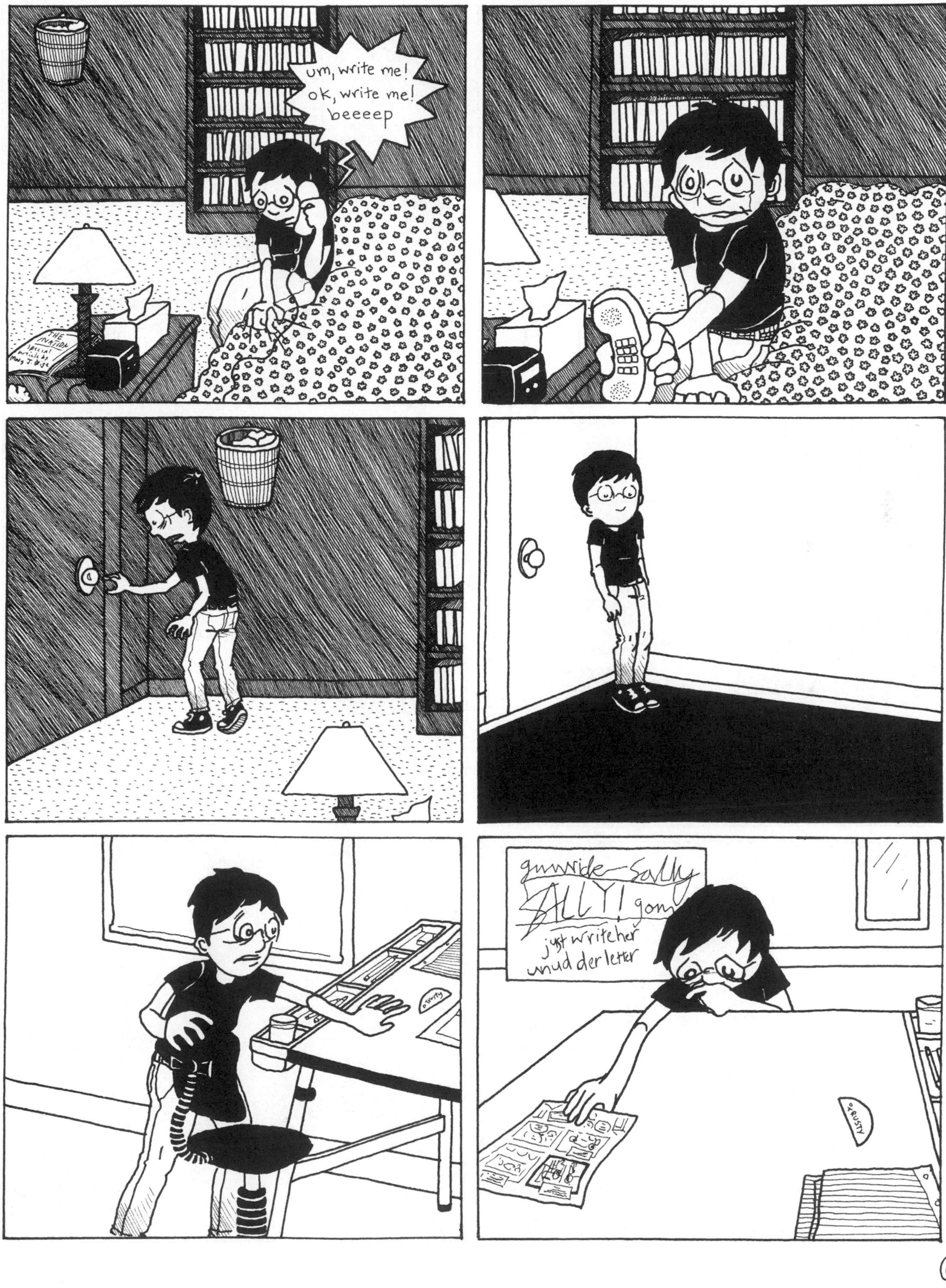
um, write me! ok, write me! beeeep
THE NATION
special article by
gunride Sally
SALLY! gom
just writeher
unud derletter

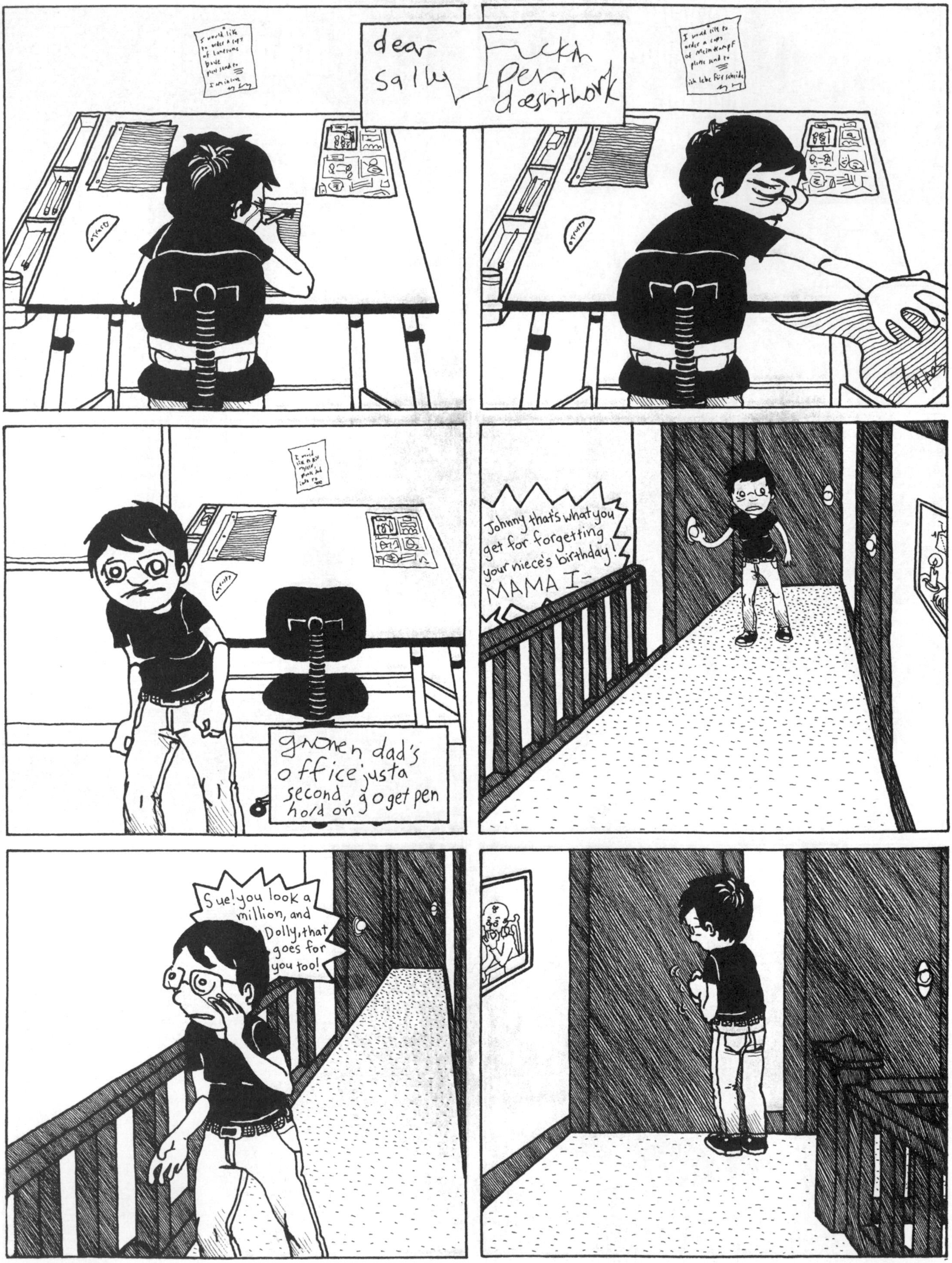
dear sally
Fuckin pen doesnt work
gnonen dad's office justa second, hold on go get pen
Johnny that's what you get for forgetting your niece's birthday! MAMA I-
Sue! you look a million, and Dolly, that goes for you too!

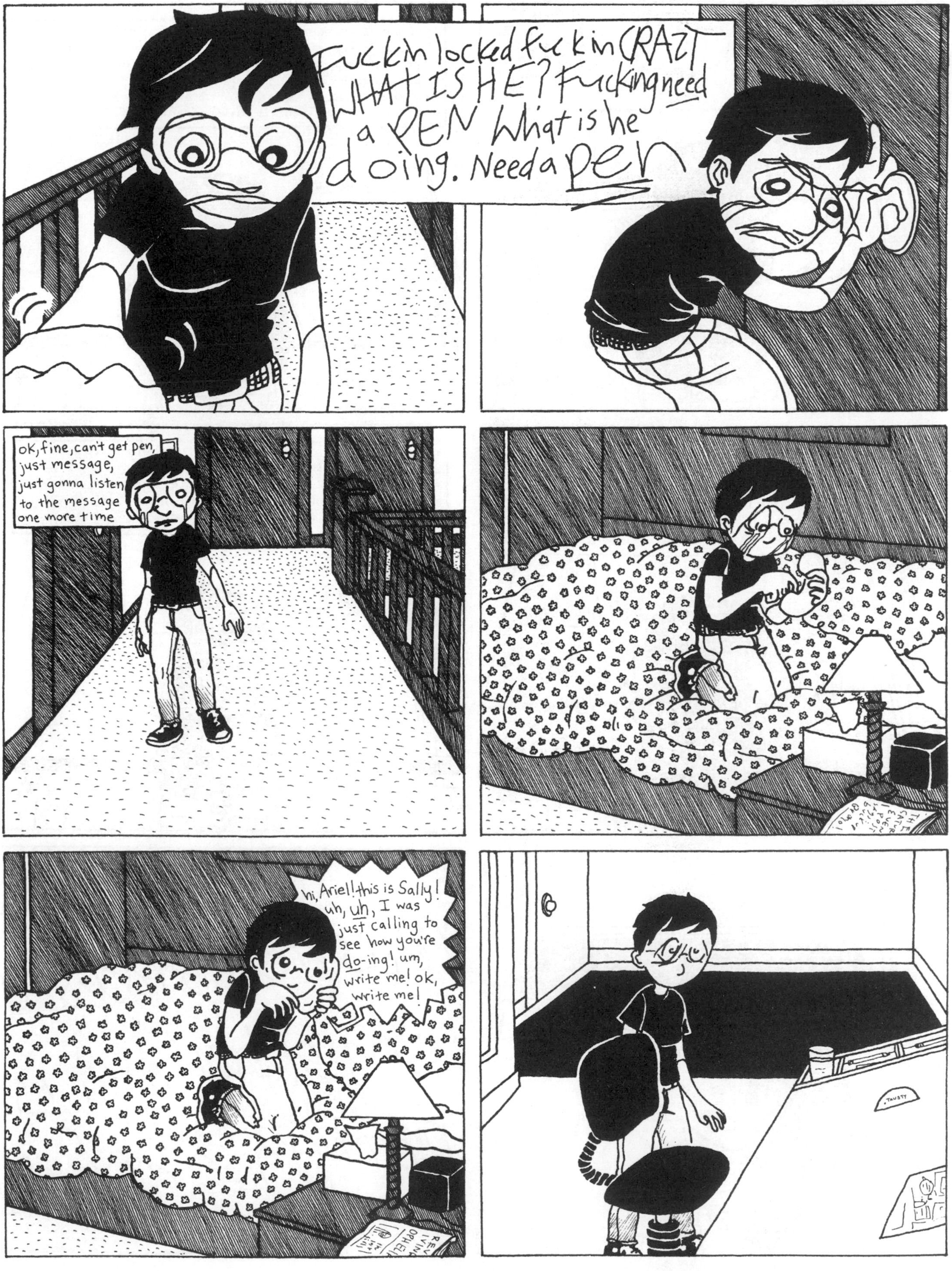

Fuckin locked fuckin CRAZY WHAT IS HE? Fucking need a PEN What is he doing. Need a pen
ok, fine, can't get pen, just message, just gonna listen to the message one more time
hi, Ariel! this is Sally! uh, uh, I was just calling to see how you're do-ing! um, write me! ok, write me!

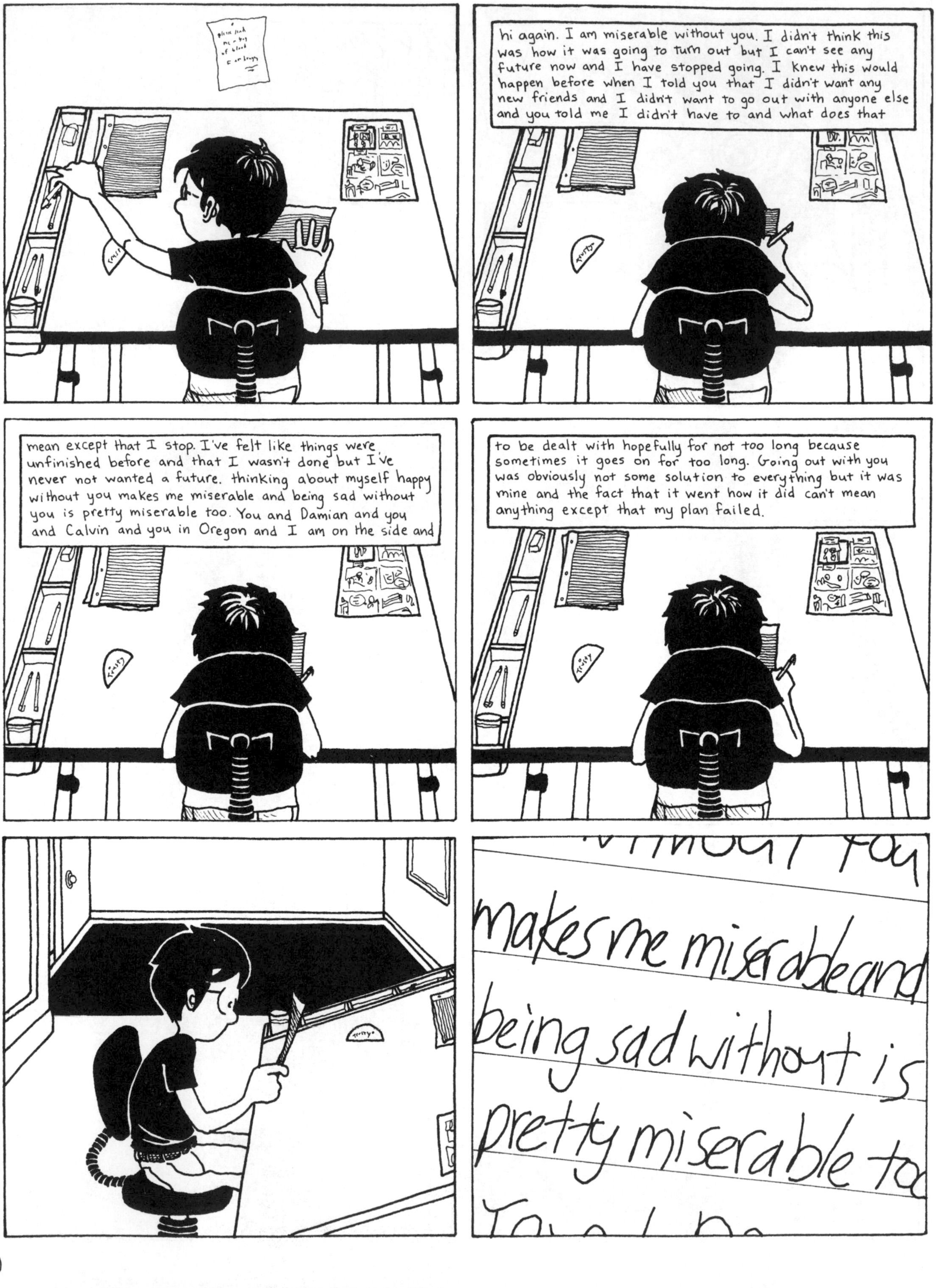
hi again. I am miserable without you. I didn't think this was how it was going to turn out but I can't see any future now and I have stopped going. I knew this would happen before when I told you that I didn't want any new friends and I didn't want to go out with anyone else and you told me I didn't have to and what does that
mean except that I stop. I've felt like things were unfinished before and that I wasn't done but I've never not wanted a future. thinking about myself happy without you makes me miserable and being sad without you is pretty miserable too. You and Damian and you and Calvin and you in Oregon and I am on the side and
to be dealt with hopefully for not too long because sometimes it goes on for too long. Going out with you was obviously not some solution to everything but it was mine and the fact that it went how it did can't mean anything except that my plan failed.
makes me miserable and
being sad without is
pretty miserable too

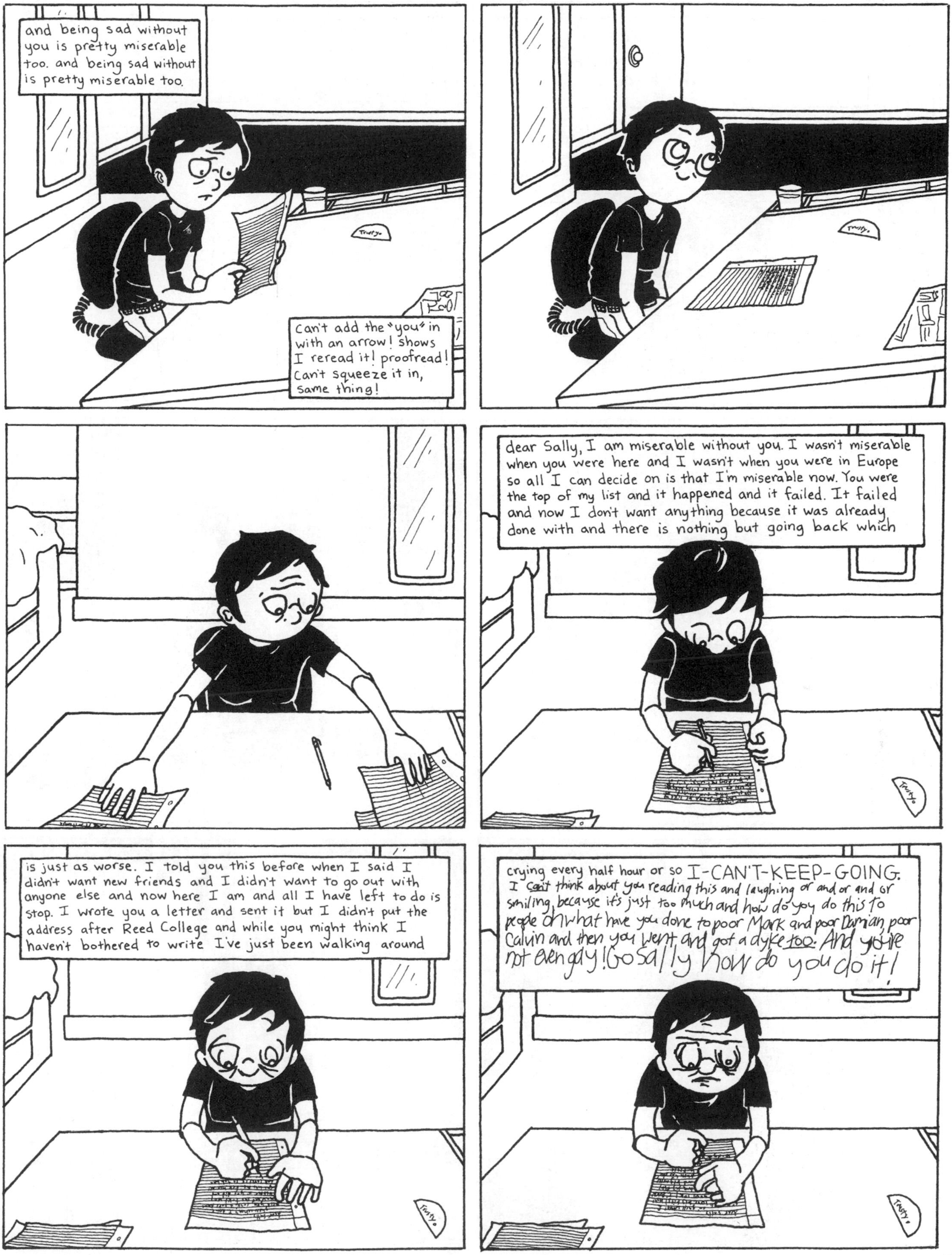

and being sad without you is pretty miserable too. and being sad without is pretty miserable too.
Can't add the "you" in with an arrow! shows I reread it! proofread! Can't squeeze it in, same thing!
dear Sally, I am miserable without you. I wasn't miserable when you were here and I wasn't when you were in Europe so all I can decide on is that I'm miserable now. You were the top of my list and it happened and it failed. It failed and now I don't want anything because it was already done with and there is nothing but going back which
is just as worse. I told you this before when I said I didn't want new friends and I didn't want to go out with anyone else and now here I am and all I have left to do is stop. I wrote you a letter and sent it but I didn't put the address after Reed College and while you might think I haven't bothered to write I've just been walking around
crying every half hour or so I-CAN'T-KEEP-GOING. I can't think about you reading this and laughing or and or and or smiling, because it's just too much and how do you do this to people oh what have you done to poor Mark and poor Damian, poor Calvin and then you went and got a dyke too. And you're not even gay! Go Sally how do you do it!

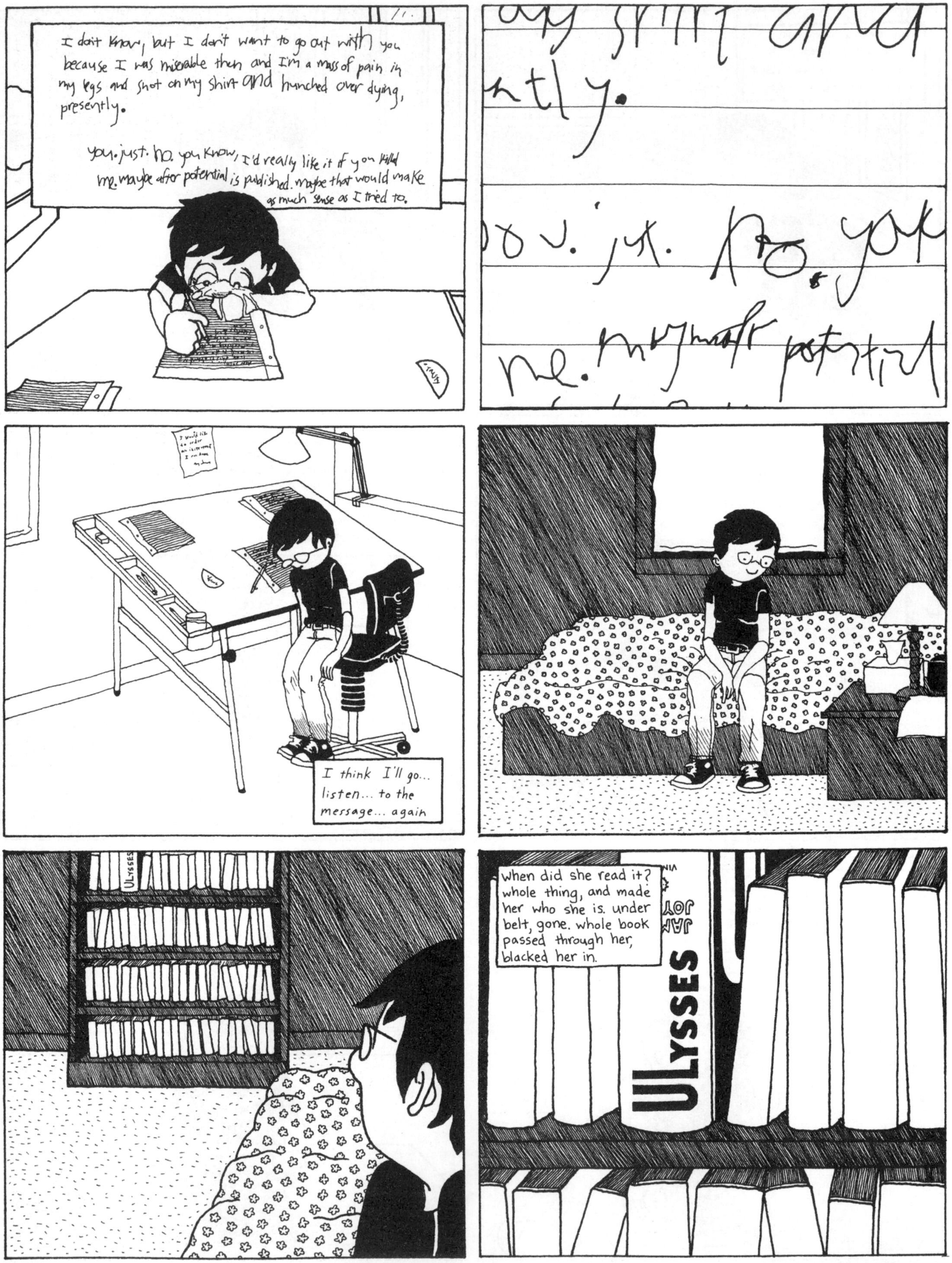
I don't know, but I don't want to go out with you because I was miserable then and I'm a mass of pain in my legs and snot on my shirt and hunched over dying, presently.
you. just. no. you know, I'd really like it if you killed me. maybe after potential is published. maybe that would make as much sense as I tried to.
I think I'll go... listen... to the message... again
ULYSSES
when did she read it? whole thing, and made her who she is. under belt, gone. whole book passed through her, blacked her in.
ULYSSES

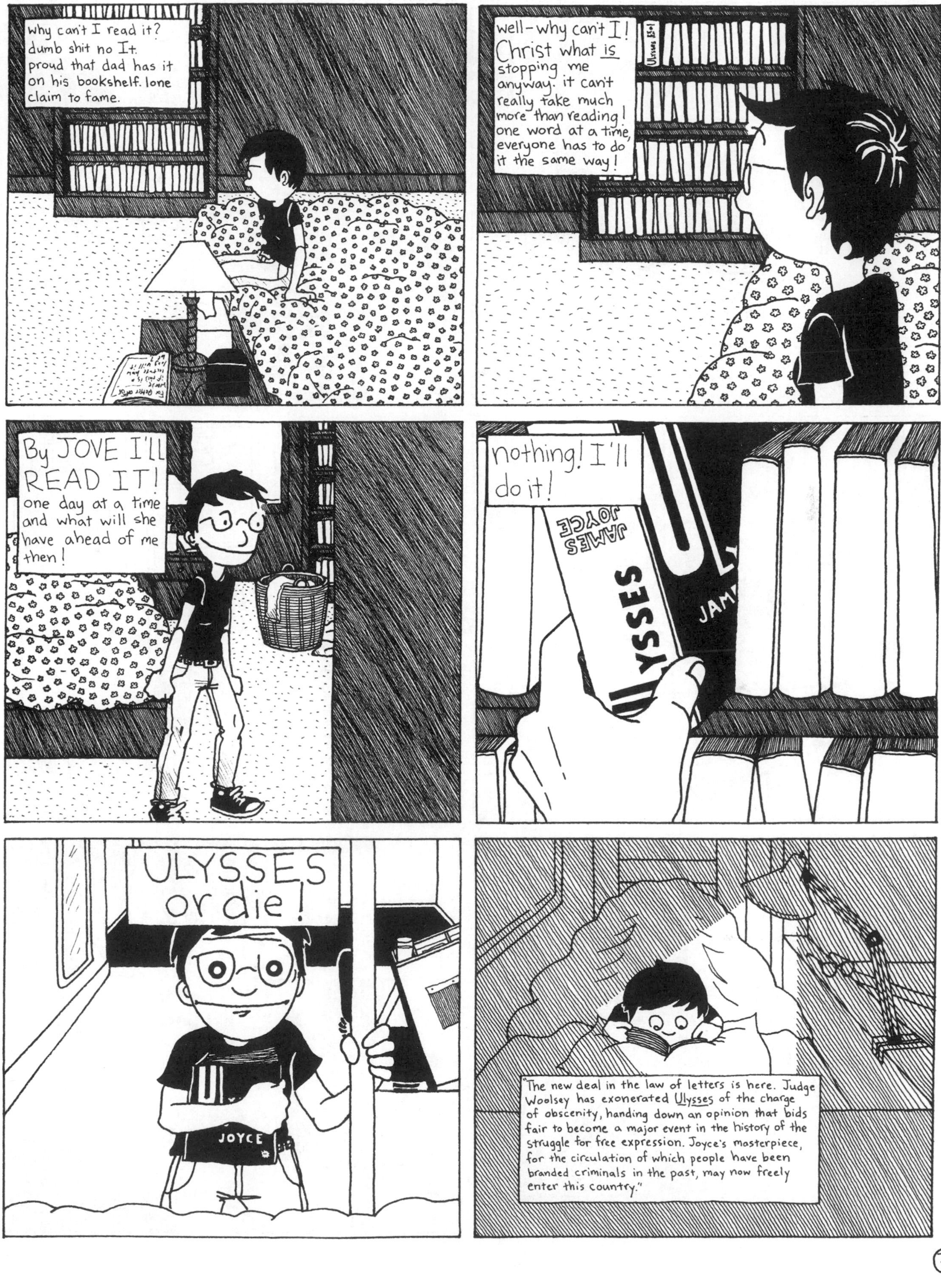
why can't I read it? dumb shit no It. proud that dad has it on his bookshelf. lone claim to fame.
well-why can't I! Christ what is stopping me anyway. it can't really take much more than reading! one word at a time, everyone has to do it the same way!
By JOVE I'LL READ IT! one day at a time and what will she have ahead of me then!
nothing! I'll do it!
JAMES JOYCE
ULYSSES
ULYSSES or die!
JOYCE
"The new deal in the law of letters is here. Judge Woolsey has exonerated Ulysses of the charge of obscenity, handing down an opinion that bids fair to become a major event in the history of the struggle for free expression. Joyce's masterpiece, for the circulation of which people have been branded criminals in the past, may now freely enter this country."

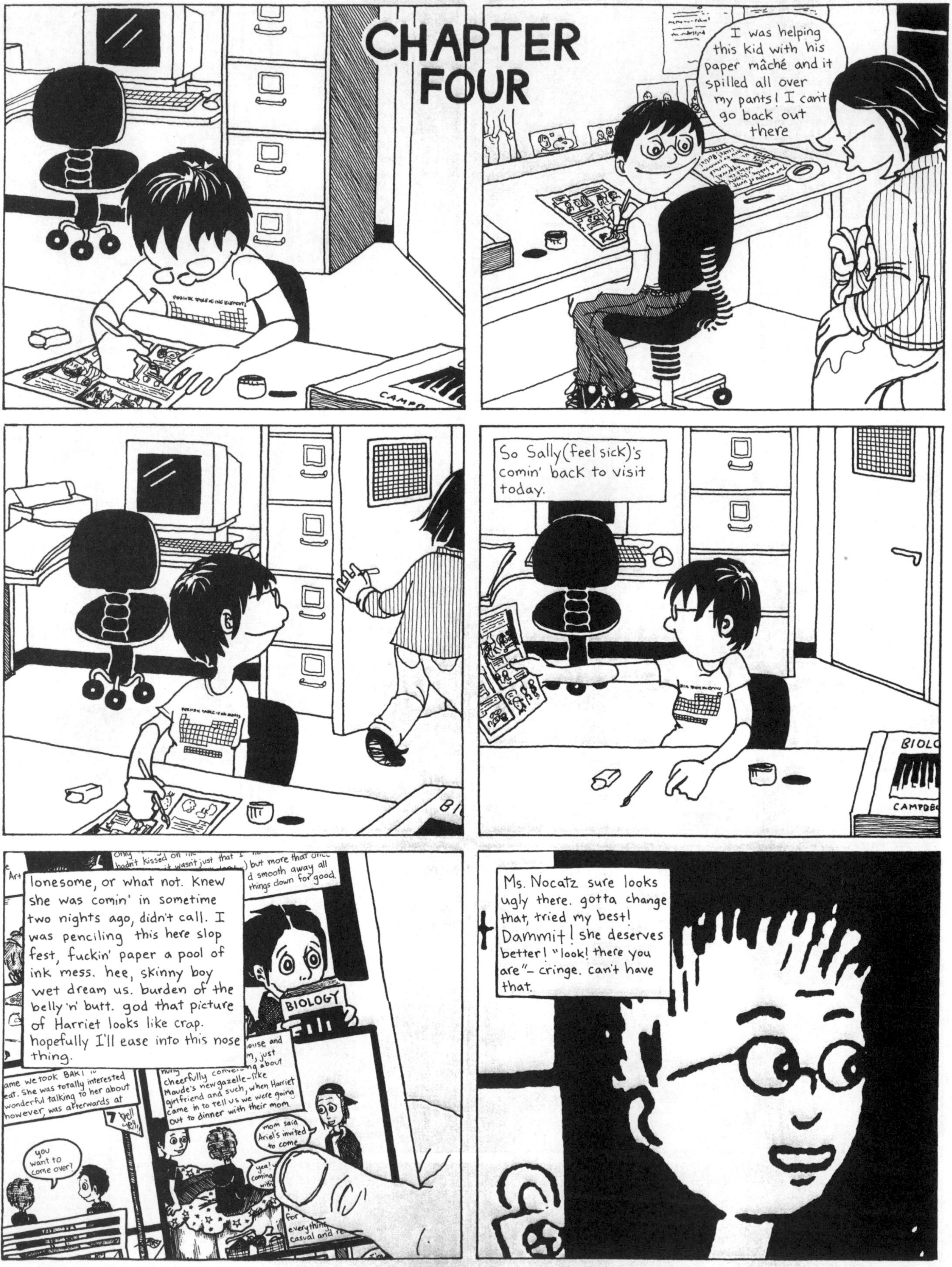
CHAPTER FOUR
I was helping this kid with his paper mâché and it spilled all over my pants! I can't go back out there
So Sally(feel sick)'s comin' back to visit today.
lonesome, or what not. Knew she was comin' in sometime two nights ago, didn't call. I was penciling this here slop fest, fuckin' paper a pool of ink mess. hee, skinny boy wet dream us. burden of the belly 'n' butt. god that picture of Harriet looks like crap. hopefully I'll ease into this nose thing.
BIOLOGY
cheerfully conve... Maude's new gazelle-like girlfriend and such, when Harriet came in to tell us we were going out to dinner with their mom.
you want to come over?
mom said Ariel's invited to come
Ms. Nocatz sure looks ugly there. gotta change that, tried my best! Dammit! she deserves better! "look! there you are"– cringe. can't have that.

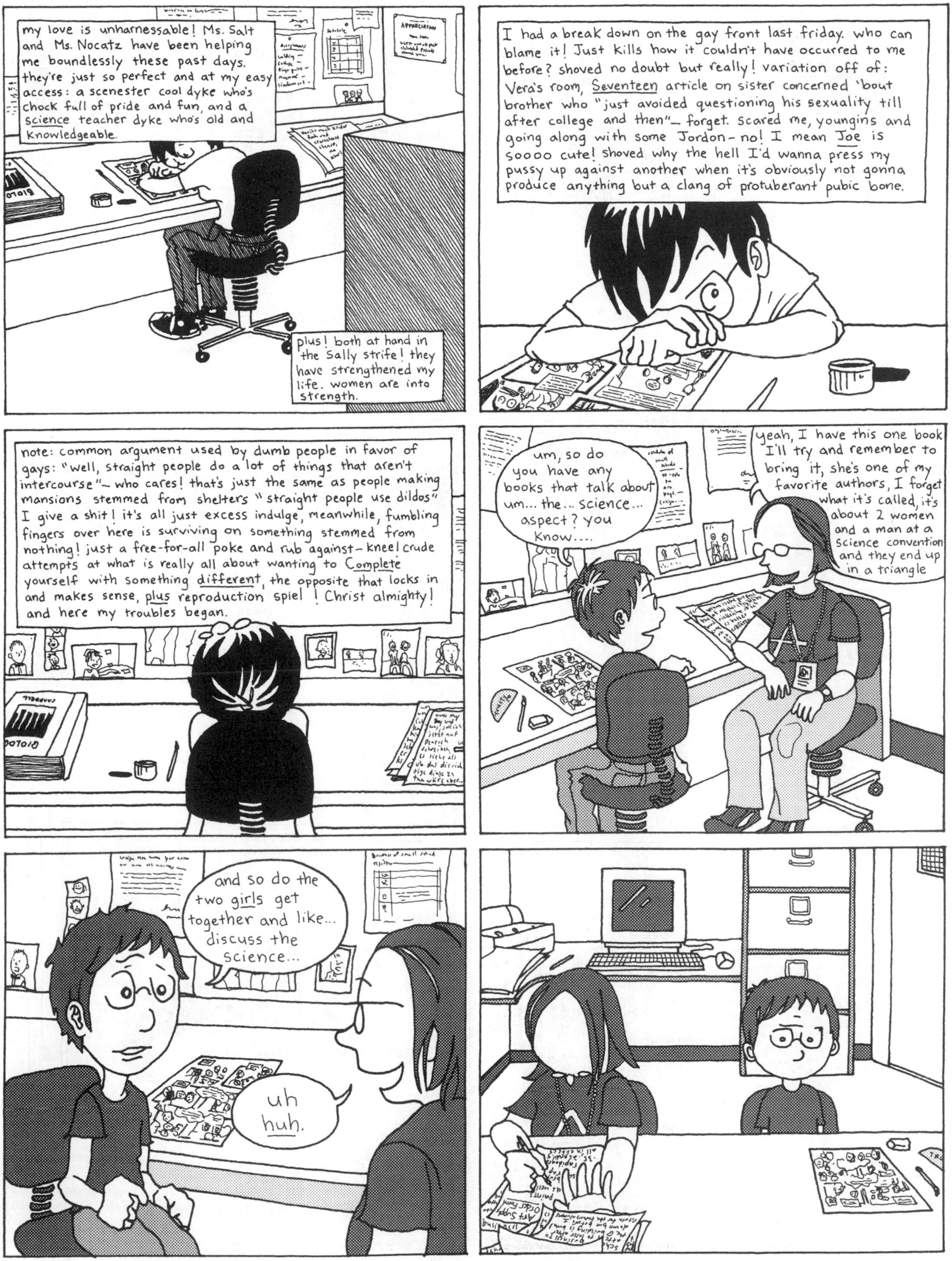

my love is unharnessable! Ms. Salt and Ms. Nocatz have been helping me boundlessly these past days. they're just so perfect and at my easy access: a scenester cool dyke who's chock full of pride and fun, and a science teacher dyke who's old and knowledgeable.
plus! both at hand in the Sally strife! they have strengthened my life. women are into strength.
I had a break down on the gay front last friday. who can blame it! Just kills how it couldn't have occurred to me before? shoved no doubt but really! variation off of: Vera's room, Seventeen article on sister concerned 'bout brother who "just avoided questioning his sexuality till after college and then"_ forget. Scared me, youngins and going along with some Jordon - no! I mean Joe is soooo cute! shoved why the hell I'd wanna press my pussy up against another when it's obviously not gonna produce anything but a clang of protuberant pubic bone.
note: common argument used by dumb people in favor of gays: "well, straight people do a lot of things that aren't intercourse"_ who cares! that's just the same as people making mansions stemmed from shelters "straight people use dildos" I give a shit! it's all just excess indulge, meanwhile, fumbling fingers over here is surviving on something stemmed from nothing! just a free-for-all poke and rub against-kneel crude attempts at what is really all about wanting to Complete yourself with something different, the opposite that locks in and makes sense, plus reproduction spiel! Christ almighty! and here my troubles began.
um, so do you have any books that talk about um... the... science... aspect? you know....
yeah, I have this one book I'll try and remember to bring it, she's one of my favorite authors, I forget what it's called, it's about 2 women and a man at a science convention and they end up in a triangle
and so do the two girls get together and like... discuss the science...
uh huh.

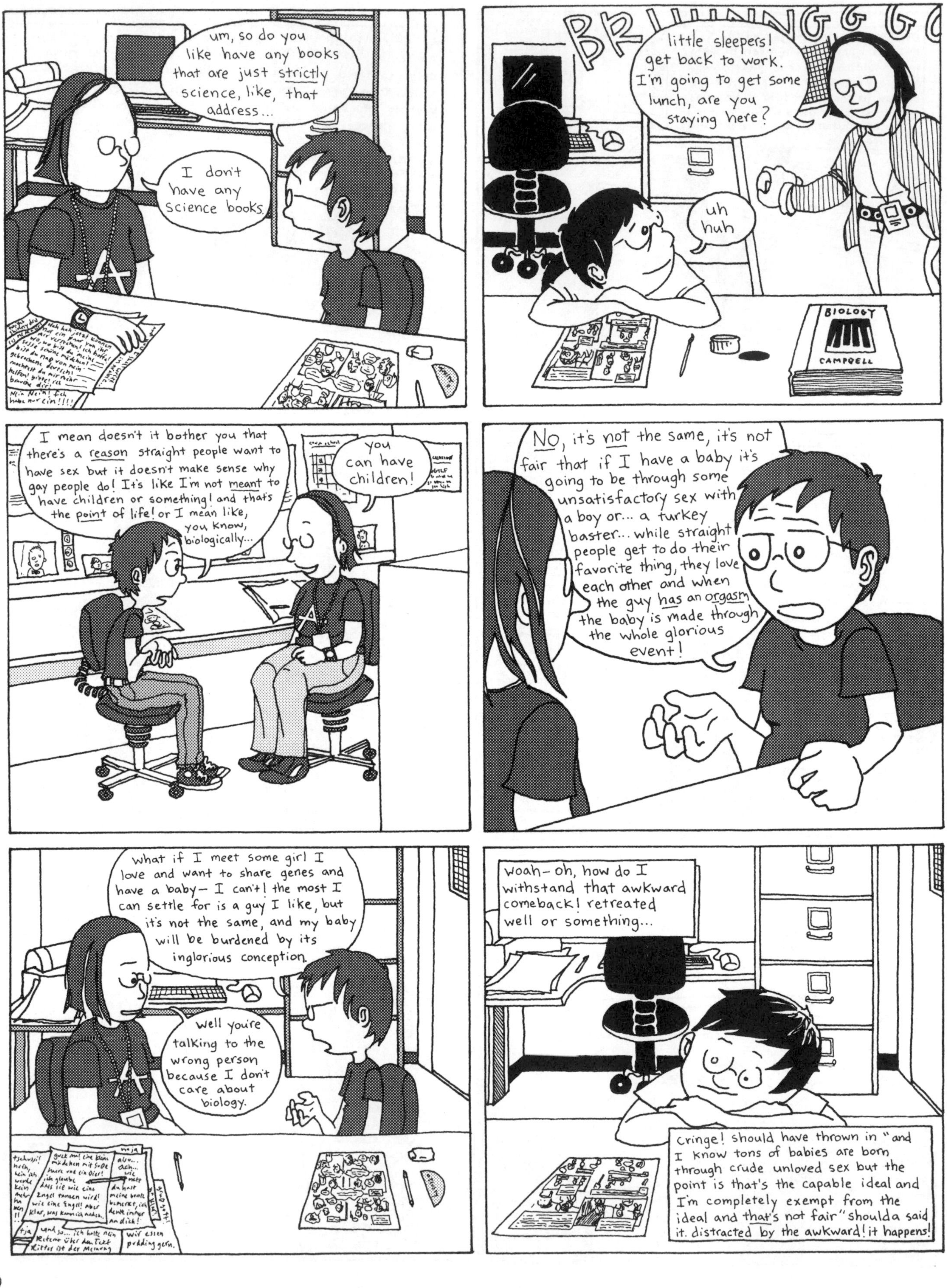
um, so do you like have any books that are just strictly science, like, that address...
I don't have any science books.
BRUUNNGGGG
little sleepers! get back to work. I'm going to get some lunch, are you staying here?
uh huh
BIOLOGY
CAMPBELL
I mean doesn't it bother you that there's a reason straight people want to have sex but it doesn't make sense why gay people do! It's like I'm not meant to have children or something! and that's the point of life! or I mean like, you know, biologically...
you can have children!
No, it's not the same, it's not fair that if I have a baby it's going to be through some unsatisfactory sex with a boy or... a turkey baster... while straight people get to do their favorite thing, they love each other and when the guy has an orgasm the baby is made through the whole glorious event!
what if I meet some girl I love and want to share genes and have a baby– I can't! the most I can settle for is a guy I like, but it's not the same, and my baby will be burdened by its inglorious conception.
well you're talking to the wrong person because I don't care about biology.
woah– oh, how do I withstand that awkward comeback! retreated well or something...
cringe! should have thrown in "and I know tons of babies are born through crude unloved sex but the point is that's the capable ideal and I'm completely exempt from the ideal and that's not fair" shoulda said it. distracted by the awkward! it happens!

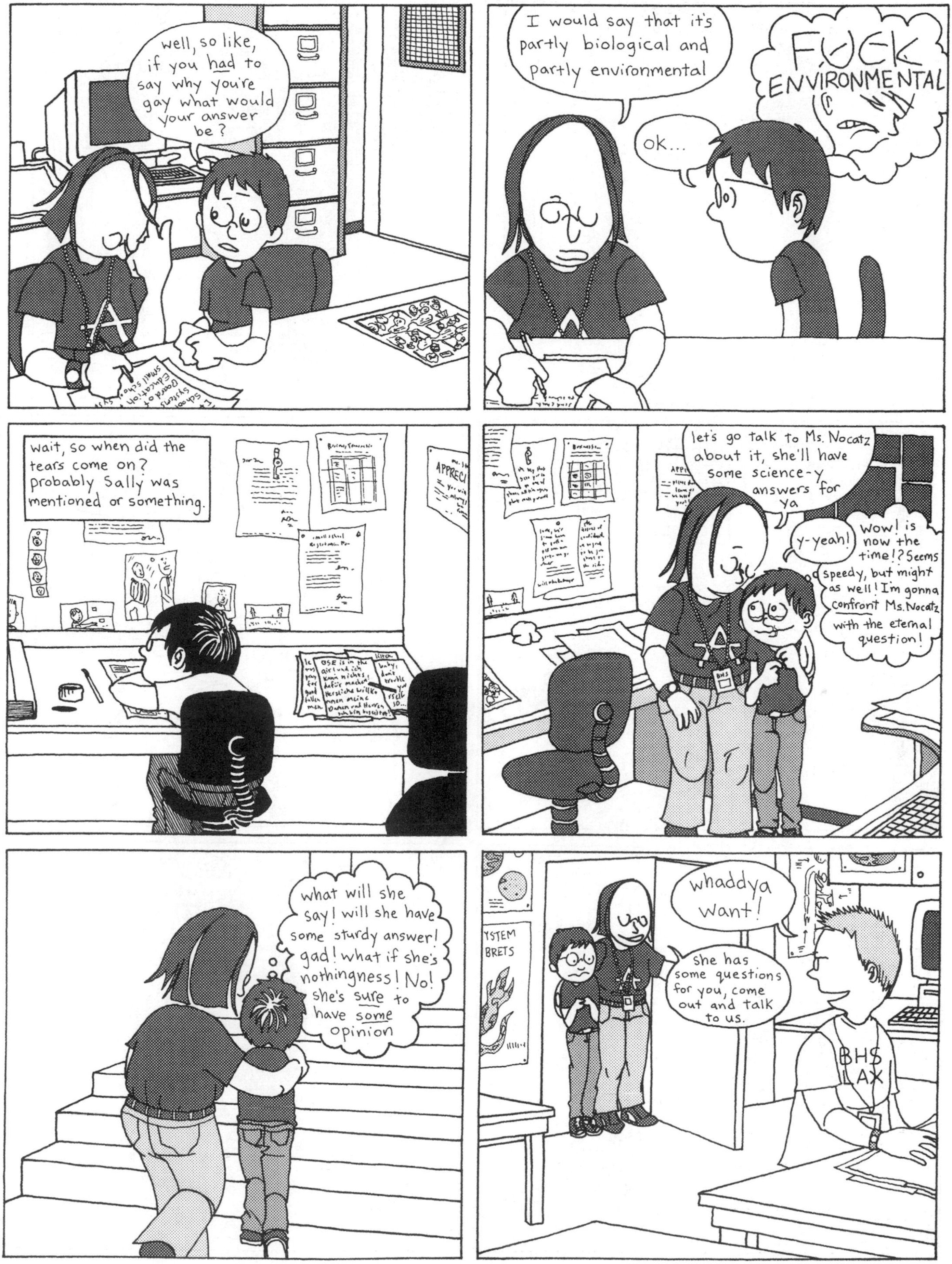

well, so like, if you had to say why you're gay what would your answer be?
I would say that it's partly biological and partly environmental
ok...
FUCK ENVIRONMENTAL
wait, so when did the tears come on? probably Sally was mentioned or something.
let's go talk to Ms. Nocatz about it, she'll have some science-y answers for ya
y-yeah!
wow! is now the time!? Seems speedy, but might as well! I'm gonna confront Ms. Nocatz with the eternal question!
what will she say! will she have some sturdy answer! gad! what if she's nothingness! No! she's sure to have some opinion
whaddya want!
she has some questions for you, come out and talk to us.
BHS LAX

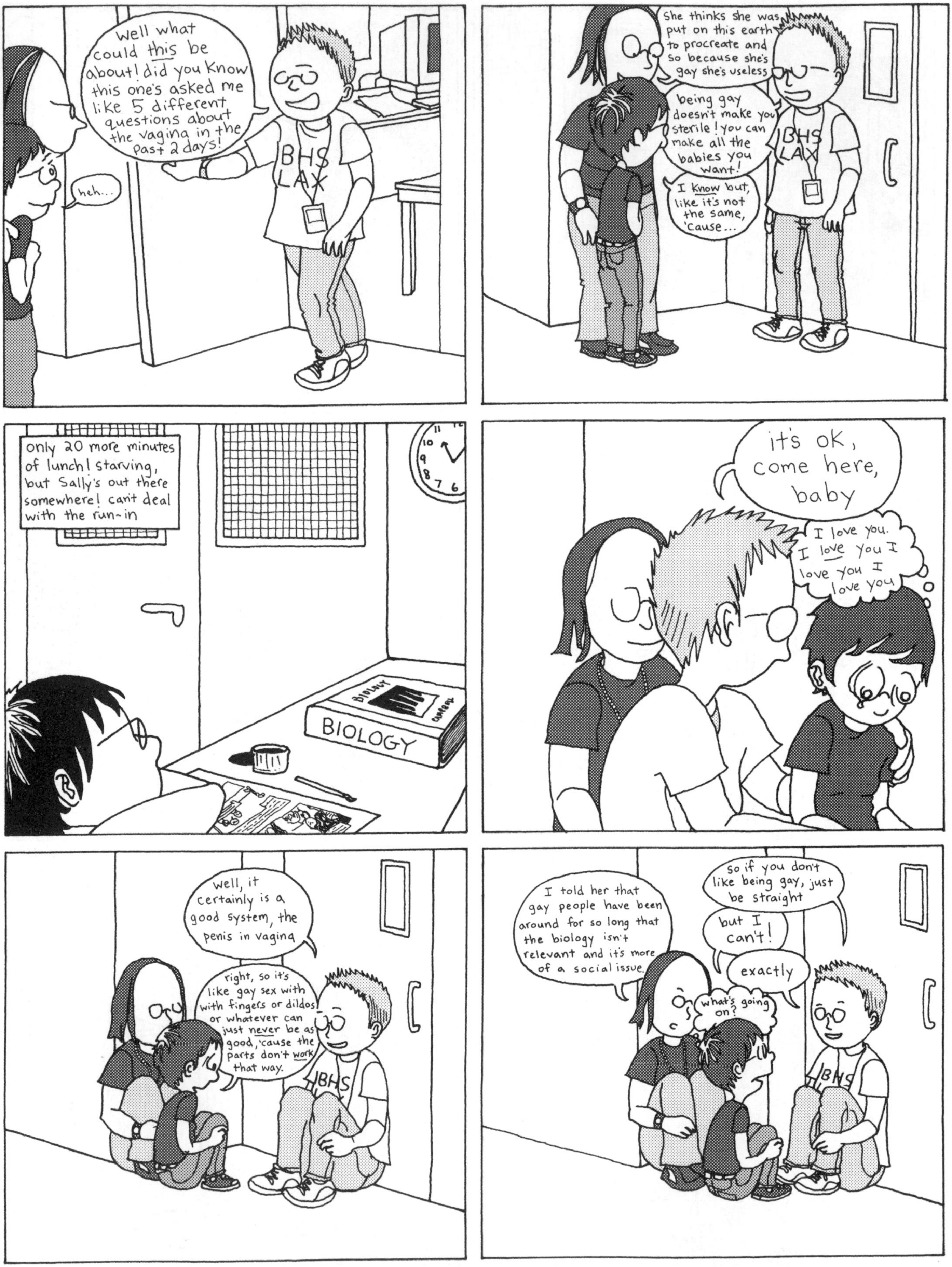
Well what could this be about! did you know this one's asked me like 5 different questions about the vagina in the past 2 days!
heh...
She thinks she was put on this earth to procreate and so because she's gay she's useless
being gay doesn't make you sterile! you can make all the babies you want!
I know but, like it's not the same, 'cause...
only 20 more minutes of lunch! starving, but Sally's out there somewhere! can't deal with the run-in
BIOLOGY
it's ok, come here, baby
I love you. I love you I love you I love you
well, it certainly is a good system, the penis in vagina
right, so it's like gay sex with with fingers or dildos or whatever can just never be as good, 'cause the parts don't work that way.
I told her that gay people have been around for so long that the biology isn't relevant and it's more of a social issue.
so if you don't like being gay, just be straight
but I can't!
exactly
what's going on?

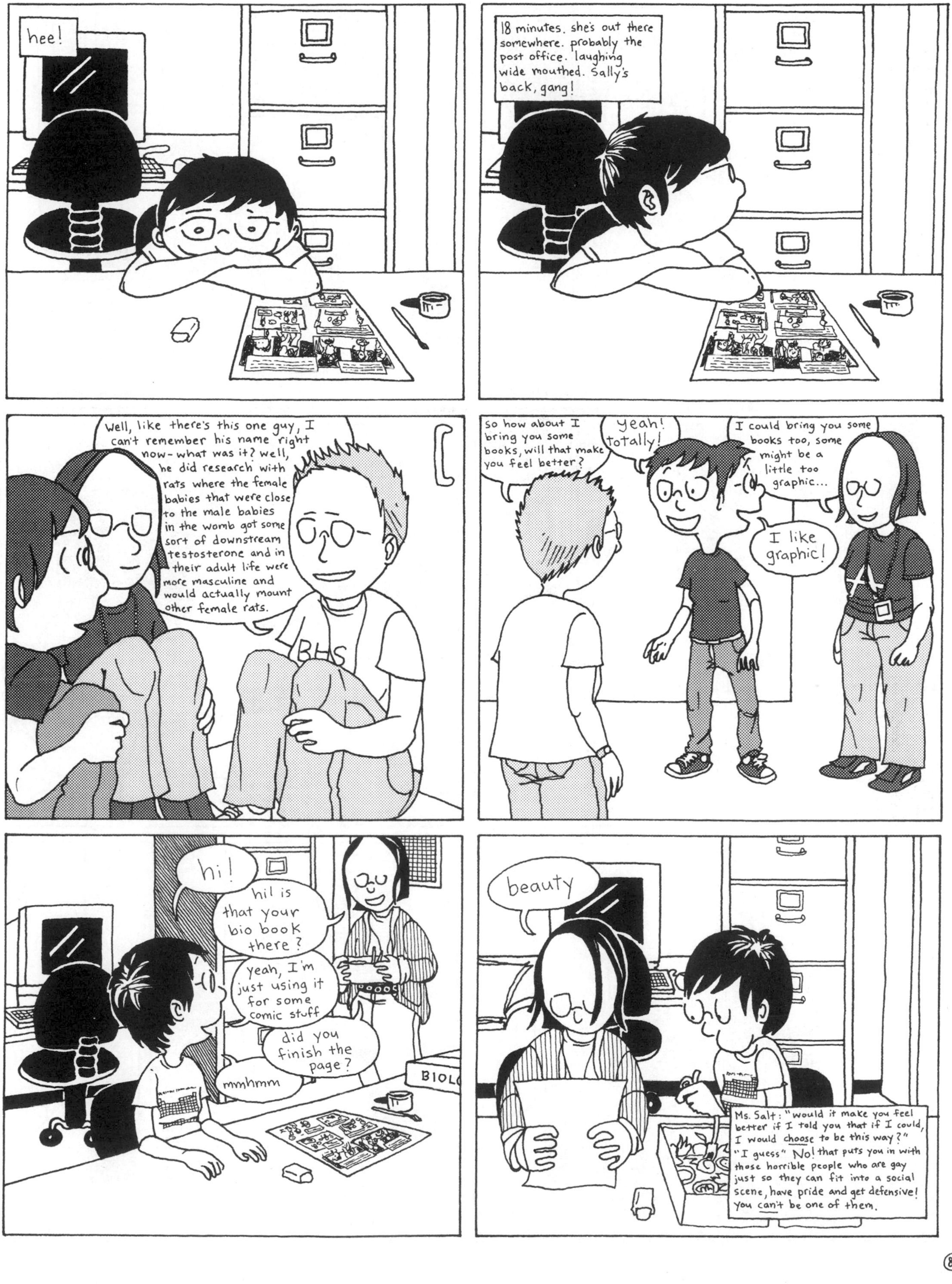

hee!
18 minutes. she's out there somewhere. probably the post office. laughing wide mouthed. Sally's back, gang!
Well, like there's this one guy, I can't remember his name right now- what was it? well, he did research with rats where the female babies that were close to the male babies in the womb got some sort of downstream testosterone and in their adult life were more masculine and would actually mount other female rats.
BHS
so how about I bring you some books, will that make you feel better?
yeah! totally!
I could bring you some books too, some might be a little too graphic...
I like graphic!
hi!
hi! is that your bio book there?
yeah, I'm just using it for some comic stuff
did you finish the page?
mmhmm
BIOL
beauty
Ms. Salt: "would it make you feel better if I told you that if I could, I would choose to be this way?" "I guess" No! that puts you in with those horrible people who are gay just so they can fit into a social scene, have pride and get defensive! You can't be one of them.

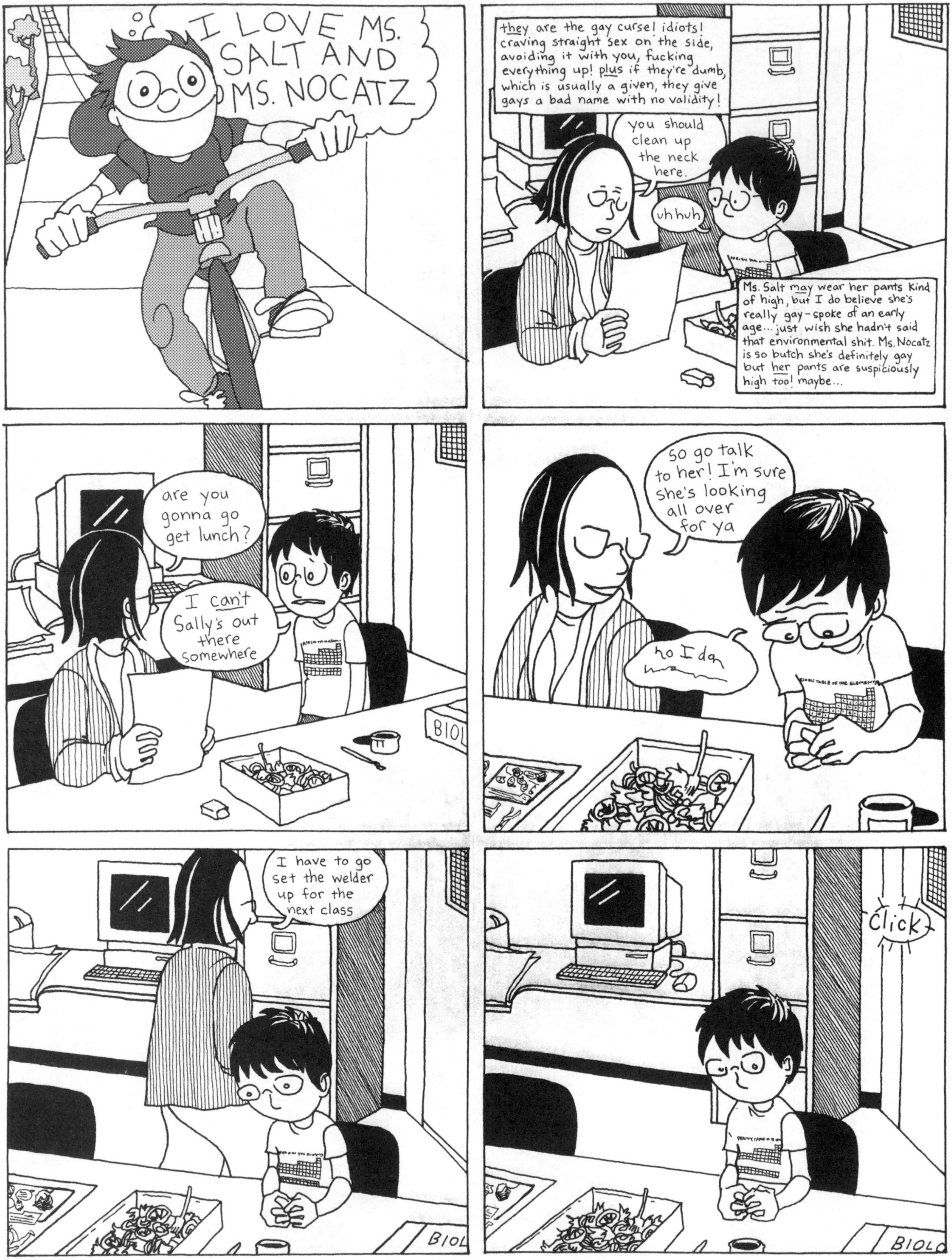
I LOVE MS. SALT AND MS. NOCATZ
they are the gay curse! idiots! craving straight sex on the side, avoiding it with you, fucking everything up! plus if they're dumb, which is usually a given, they give gays a bad name with no validity!
you should clean up the neck here.
uh huh
Ms. Salt may wear her pants kind of high, but I do believe she's really gay - spoke of an early age... just wish she hadn't said that environmental shit. Ms. Nocatz is so butch she's definitely gay but her pants are suspiciously high too! maybe...
are you gonna go get lunch?
I can't Sally's out there somewhere
BIOL
so go talk to her! I'm sure she's looking all over for ya
I have to go set the welder up for the next class
BIOL
Click
BIOLO

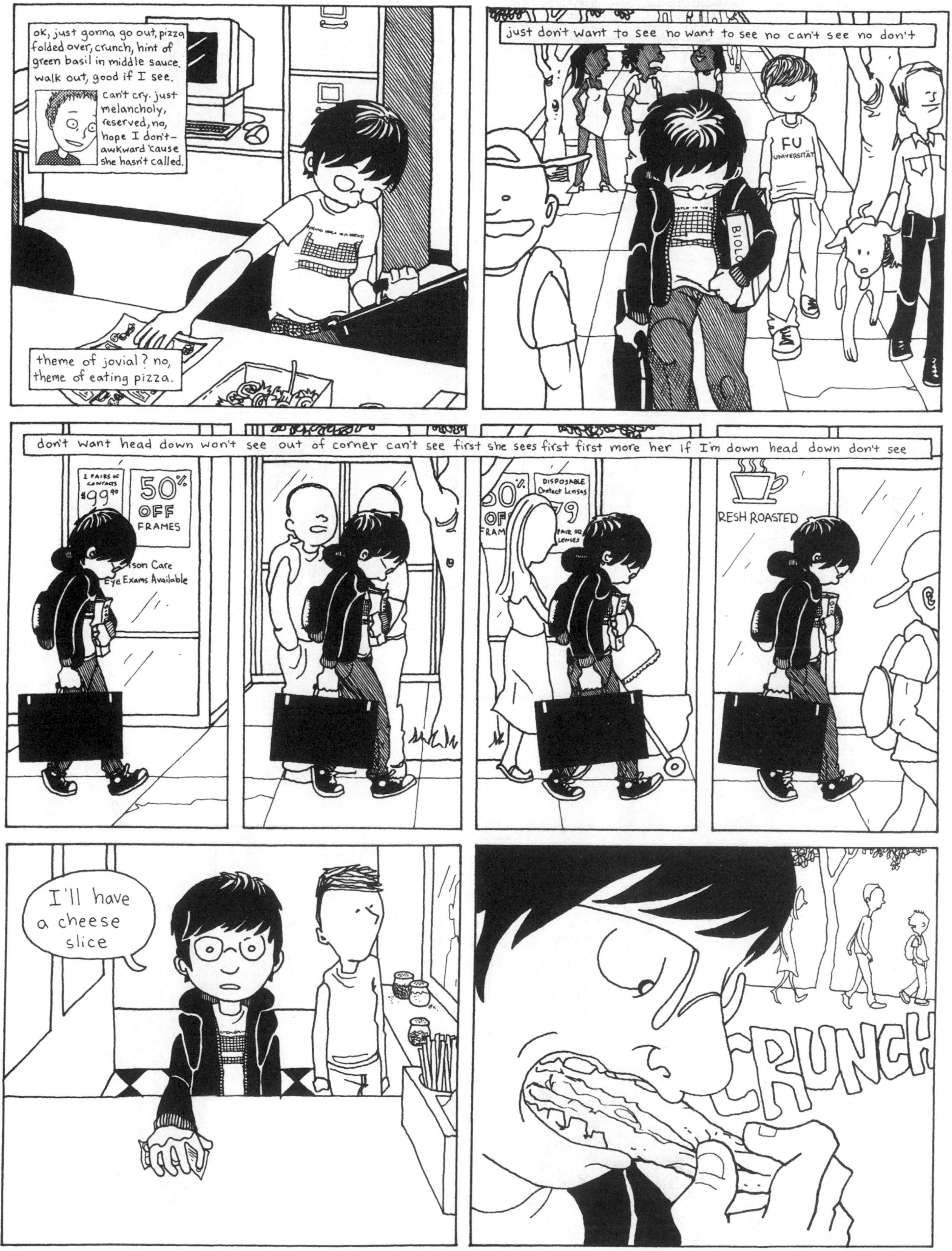
ok, just gonna go out, pizza folded over, crunch, hint of green basil in middle sauce. walk out, good if I see.
can't cry. just melancholy, reserved, no, hope I don't- awkward 'cause she hasn't called.
theme of jovial? no, theme of eating pizza.
just don't want to see no want to see no can't see no don't
FU UNIVERSITÄT
BIOLO
don't want head down won't see out of corner can't see first she sees first first more her if I'm down head down don't see
2 PAIRS OF CONTACTS $99.90
50% OFF FRAMES
Eye Exams Available
DISPOSABLE Contact Lenses
RESH ROASTED
I'll have a cheese slice
CRUNCH

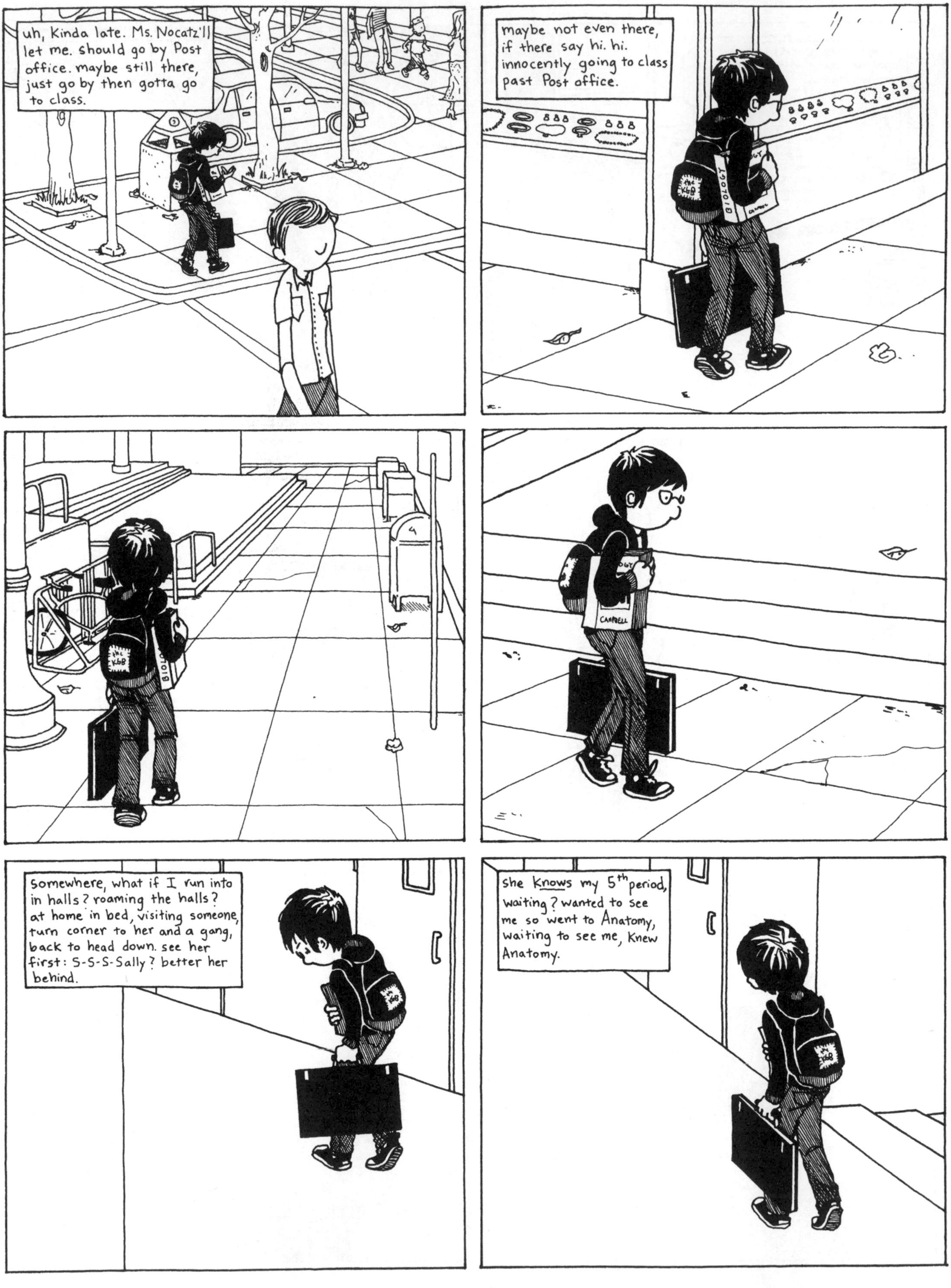

uh, Kinda late. Ms. Nocatz'll let me. should go by Post office. maybe still there, just go by then gotta go to class.
maybe not even there, if there say hi. hi. innocently going to class past Post office.
Somewhere, what if I run into in halls? roaming the halls? at home in bed, visiting someone, turn corner to her and a gang, back to head down. see her first: S-S-S-Sally? better her behind.
she Knows my 5th period, waiting? wanted to see me so went to Anatomy, waiting to see me, Knew Anatomy.

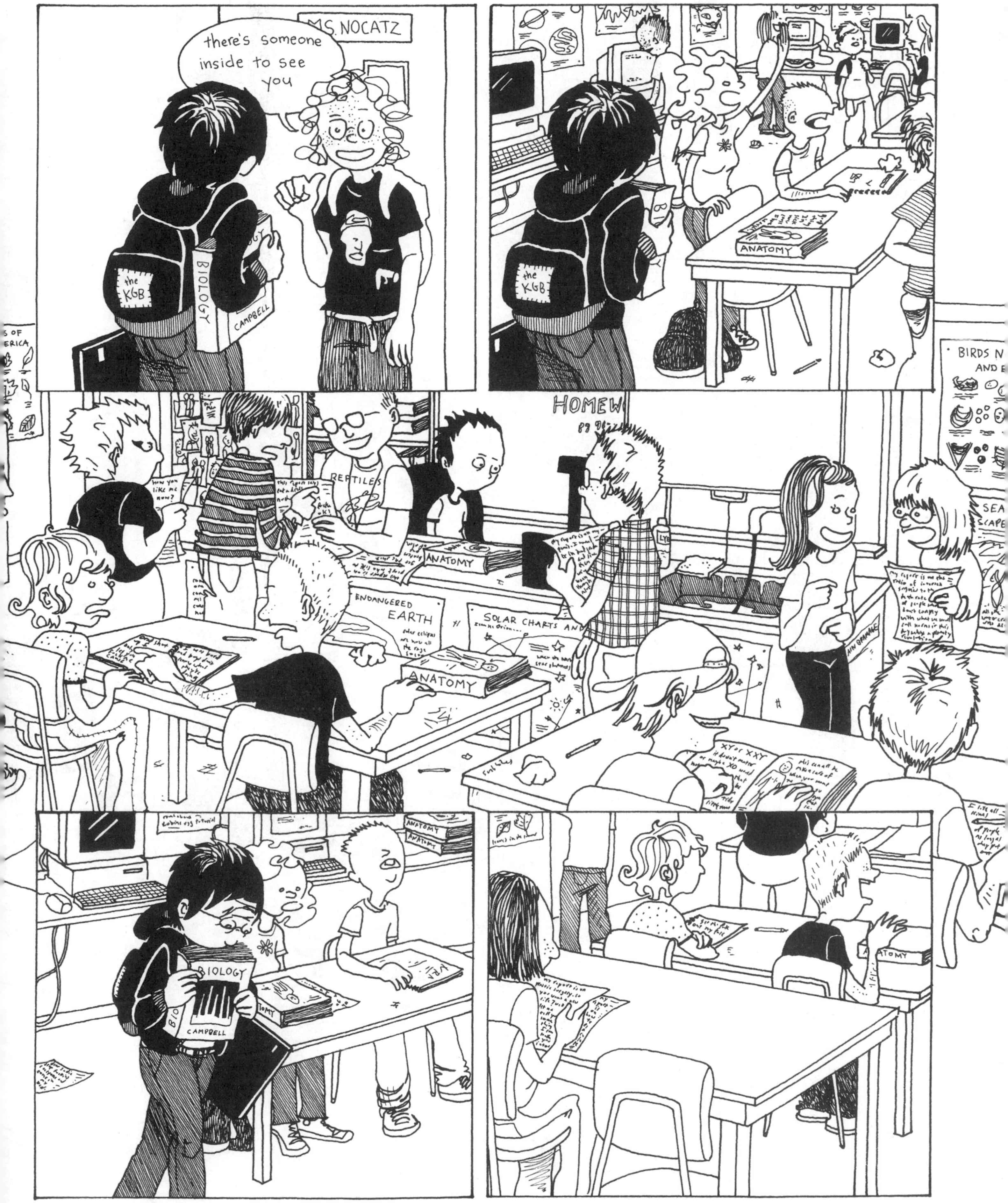
MS. NOCATZ
there's someone inside to see you
the KGB
BIOLOGY
CAMPBELL
ANATOMY
HOMEW
REPTILES
ENDANGERED EARTH
SOLAR CHARTS AN
BIRDS N AND E
XY or XXY
BIOLOGY
CAMPBELL

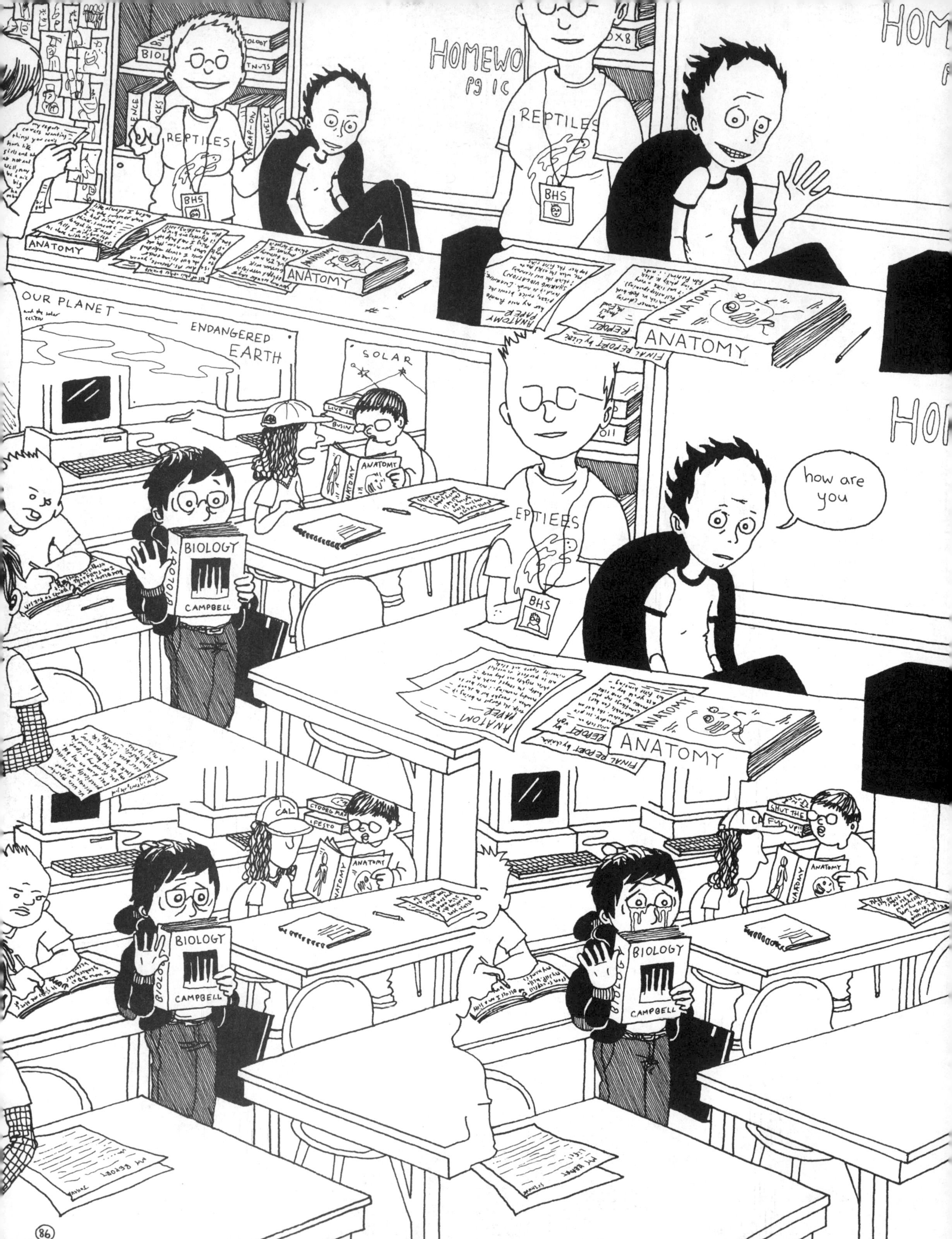

how are you
HOMEWO
pg 1C
REPTILES
BHS
ANATOMY
OUR PLANET
ENDANGERED EARTH
SOLAR
BIOLOGY
CAMPBELL
FINAL REPORT
ANATOMY PAPER
CAL
SHUT THE FUCK UP!

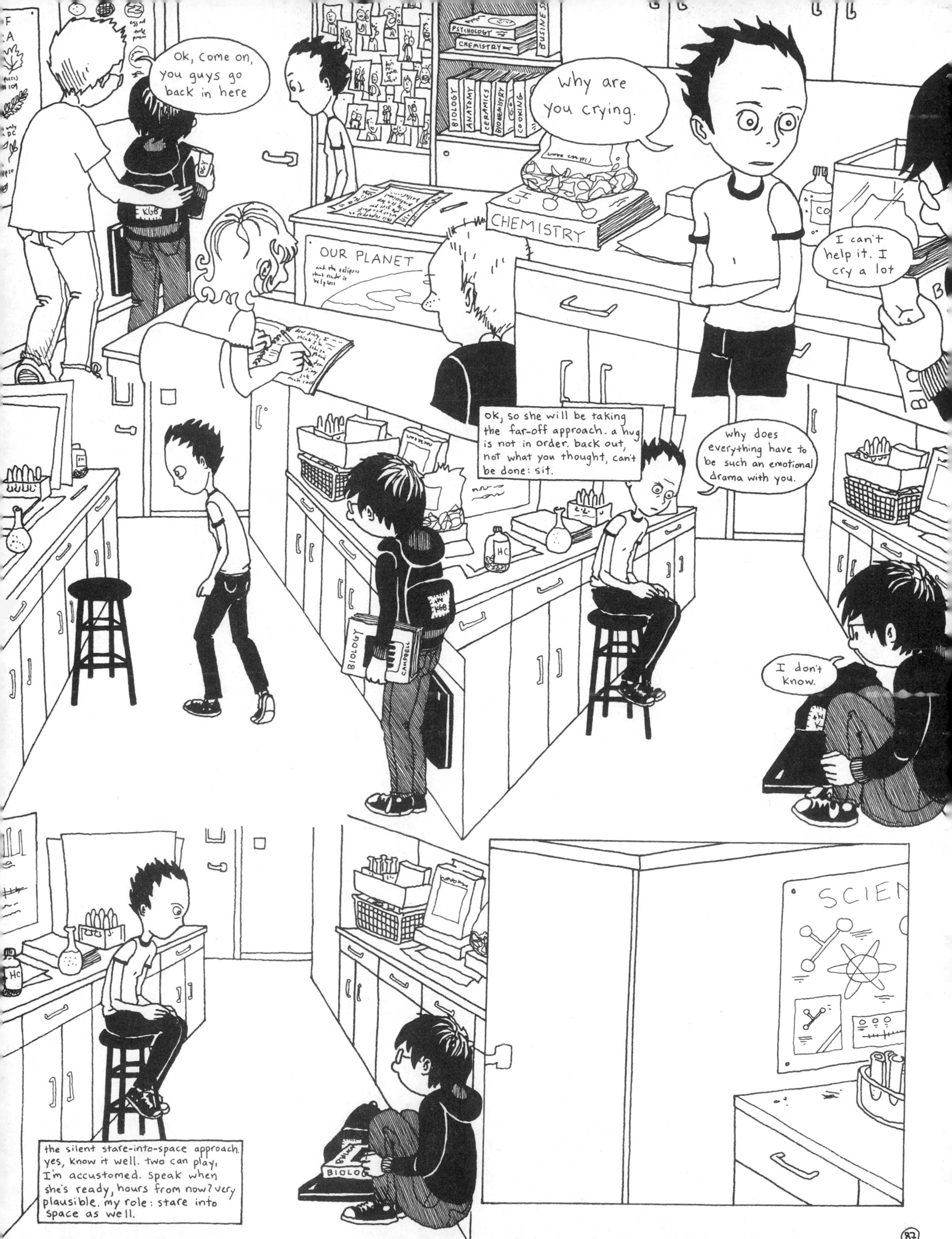

Ok, come on, you guys go back in here
Why are you crying.
I can't help it. I cry a lot
CHEMISTRY
OUR PLANET
ok, so she will be taking the far-off approach. a hug is not in order. back out, not what you thought, can't be done: sit.
why does everything have to be such an emotional drama with you.
I don't know.
BIOLOGY
CAMPBELL
SCIEN
the silent stare-into-space approach. yes, know it well. two can play, I'm accustomed. speak when she's ready, hours from now? very plausible. my role: stare into space as well.

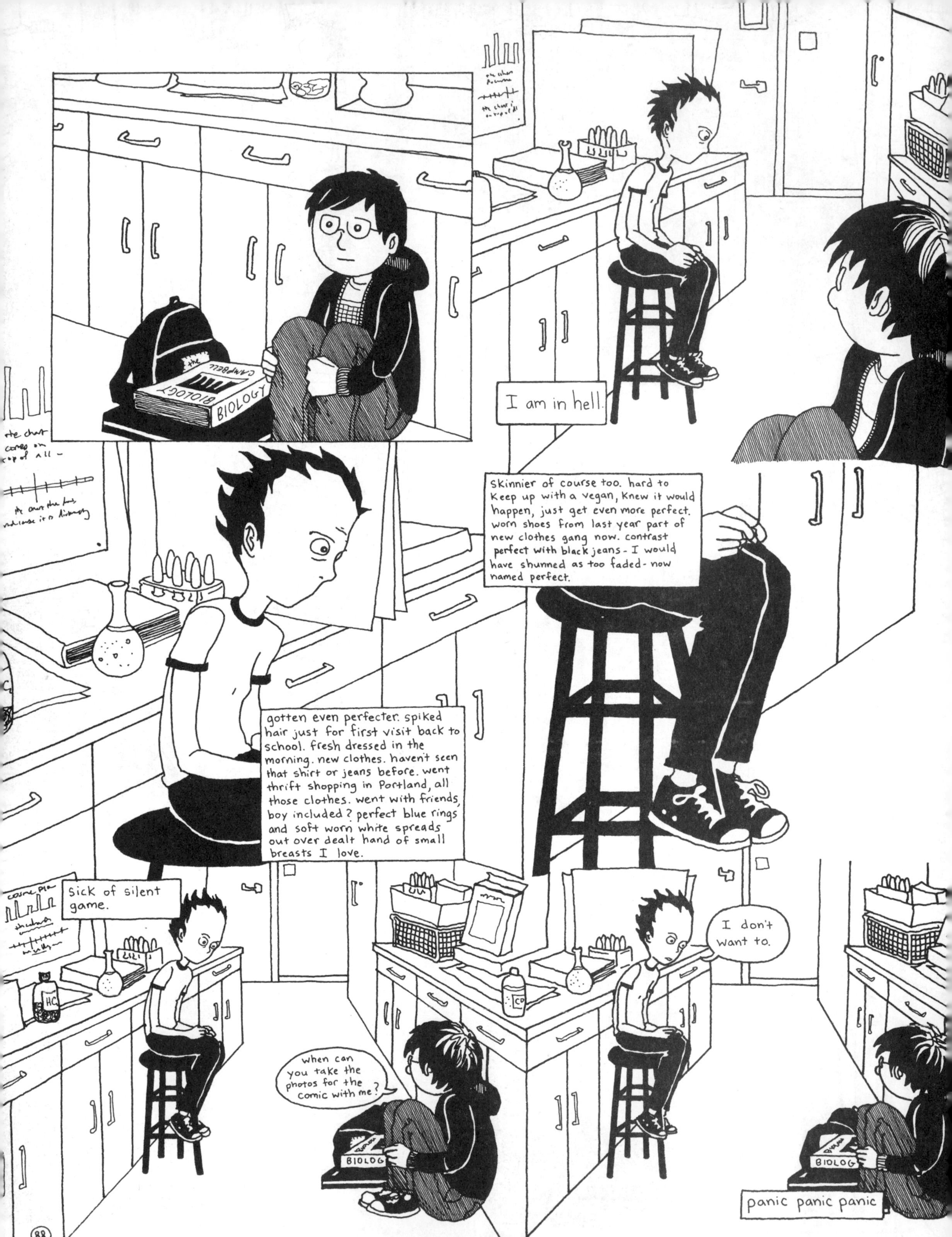
I am in hell.
gotten even perfecter. spiked hair just for first visit back to school. fresh dressed in the morning. new clothes. haven't seen that shirt or jeans before. went thrift shopping in Portland, all those clothes. went with friends, boy included? perfect blue rings and soft worn white spreads out over dealt hand of small breasts I love.
Skinnier of course too. hard to Keep up with a vegan, Knew it would happen, just get even more perfect. worn shoes from last year part of new clothes gang now. contrast perfect with black jeans - I would have shunned as too faded - now named perfect.
Sick of silent game.
when can you take the photos for the comic with me?
I don't want to.
panic panic panic

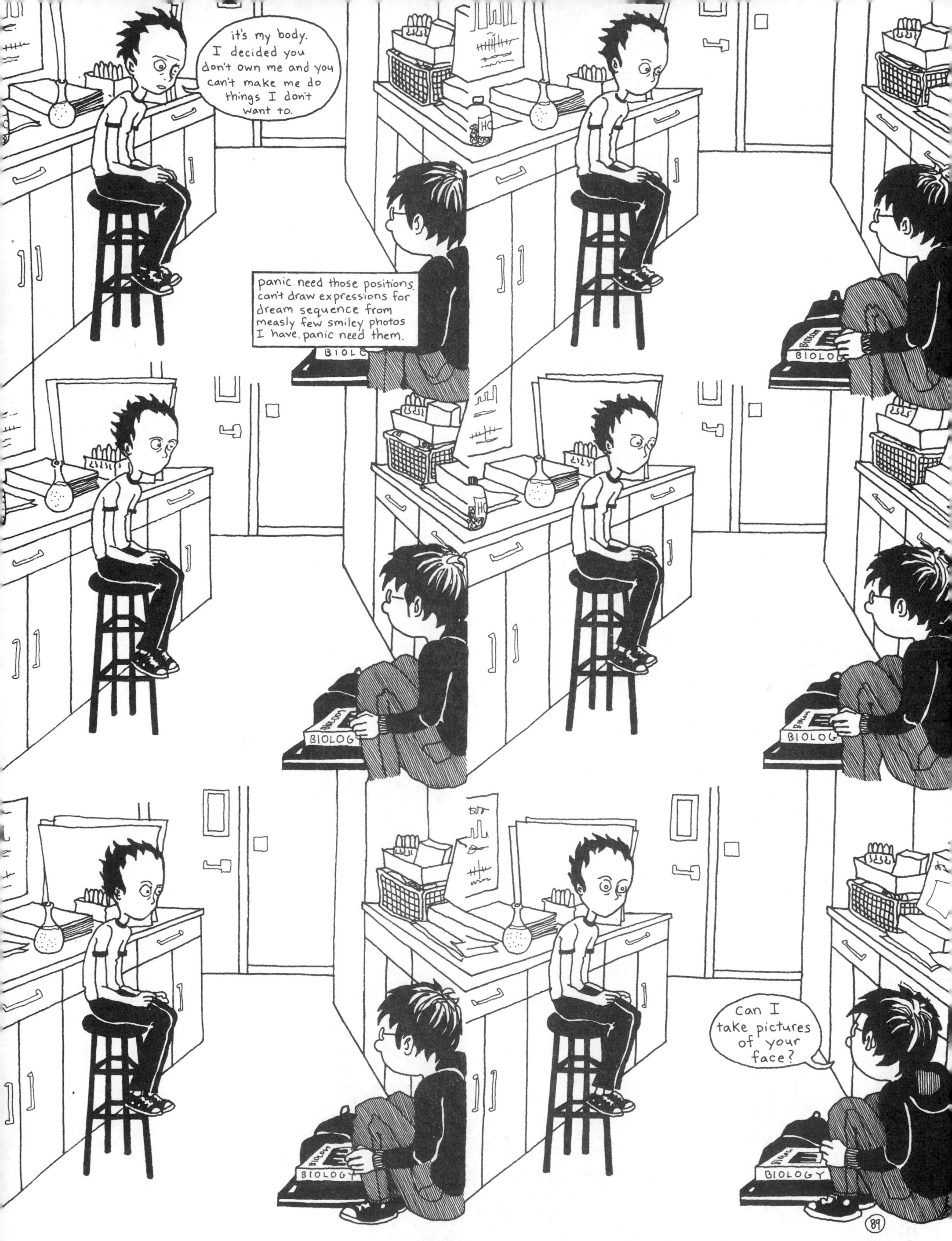
it's my body. I decided you don't own me and you can't make me do things I don't want to.
panic need those positions. can't draw expressions for dream sequence from measly few smiley photos I have. panic need them.
BIOLO
BIOLOG
BIOLOG
BIOLOG
BIOLOGY
Can I take pictures of your face?
BIOLOGY

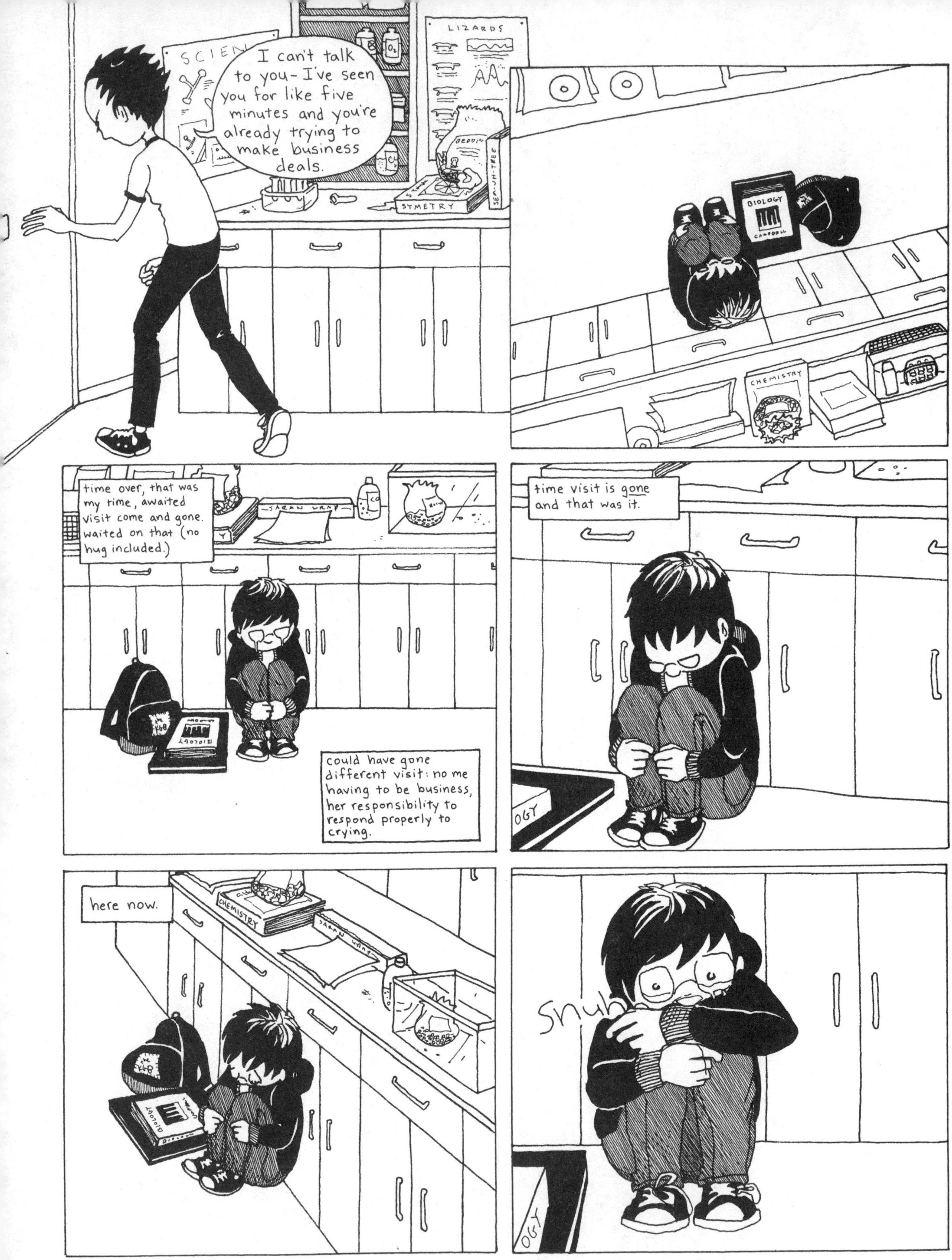
SCIEN
LIZARDS
I can't talk to you- I've seen you for like five minutes and you're already trying to make business deals.
SYMETRY
SEA-UH-TREE
BIOLOGY
CHEMISTRY
time over, that was my time, awaited visit come and gone. waited on that (no hug included.)
SARAN WRAP
could have gone different visit: no me having to be business, her responsibility to respond properly to crying.
time visit is gone and that was it.
here now.
CHEMISTRY
SARAN WRAP
BIOLOGY
Snub

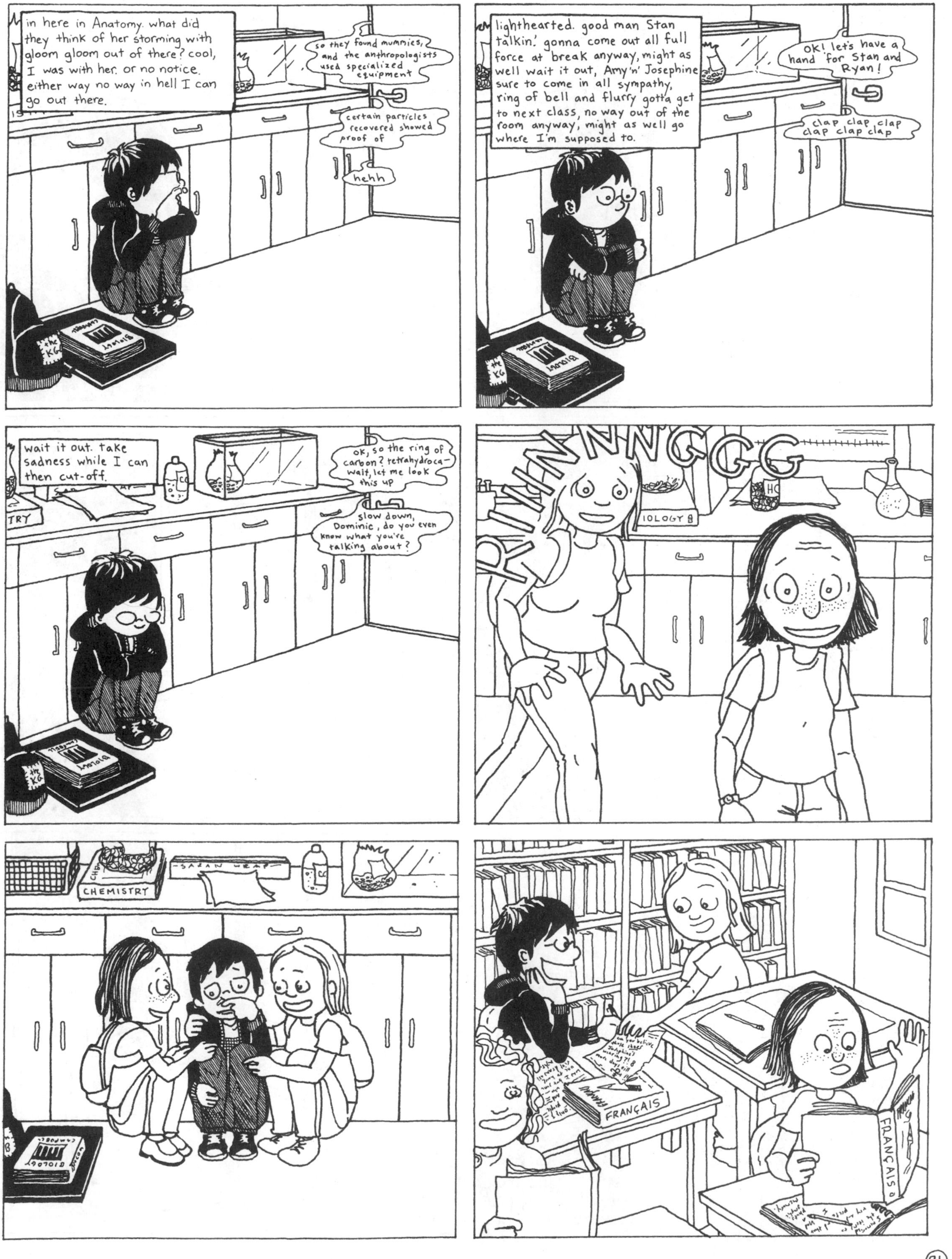

in here in Anatomy. what did they think of her storming with gloom gloom out of there? cool, I was with her. or no notice. either way no way in hell I can go out there.
so they found mummies, and the anthropologists used specialized equipment
certain particles recovered showed proof of
hehh
lighthearted. good man Stan talkin.' gonna come out all full force at break anyway, might as well wait it out, Amy 'n' Josephine sure to come in all sympathy, ring of bell and flurry gotta get to next class, no way out of the room anyway, might as well go where I'm supposed to.
OK! let's have a hand for Stan and Ryan!
clap clap clap clap clap clap
wait it out. take sadness while I can then cut-off.
ok, so the ring of carbon? tetrahydroca- wait, let me look this up
slow down, Dominic, do you even know what you're talking about?
RIIINNNNGGG
IOLOGY
CHEMISTRY
SARAN WRAP
FRANÇAIS
FRANÇAIS

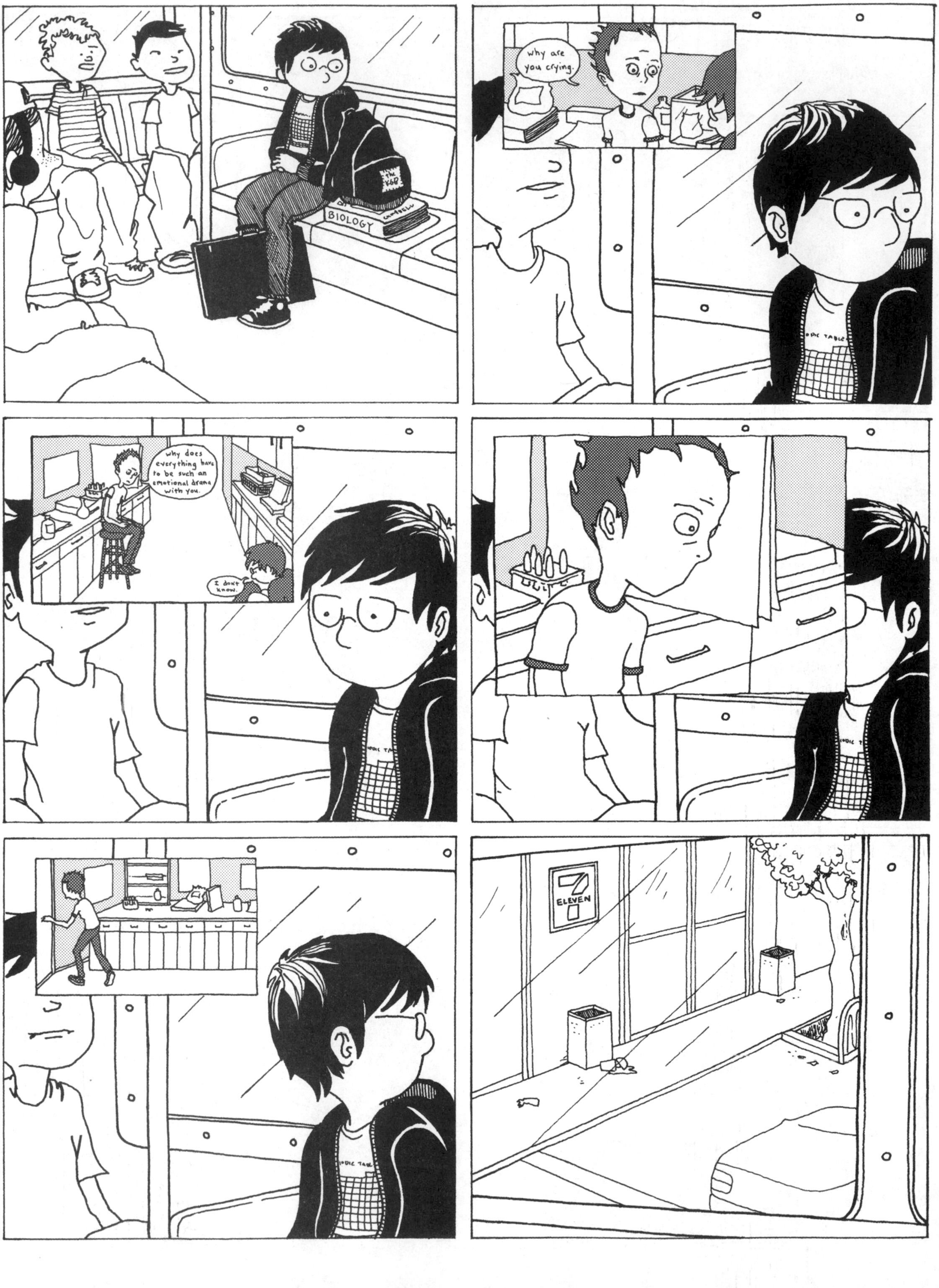

BIOLOGY
why are you crying.
why does everything have to be such an emotional drama with you.
I don't know.
7
ELEVEN

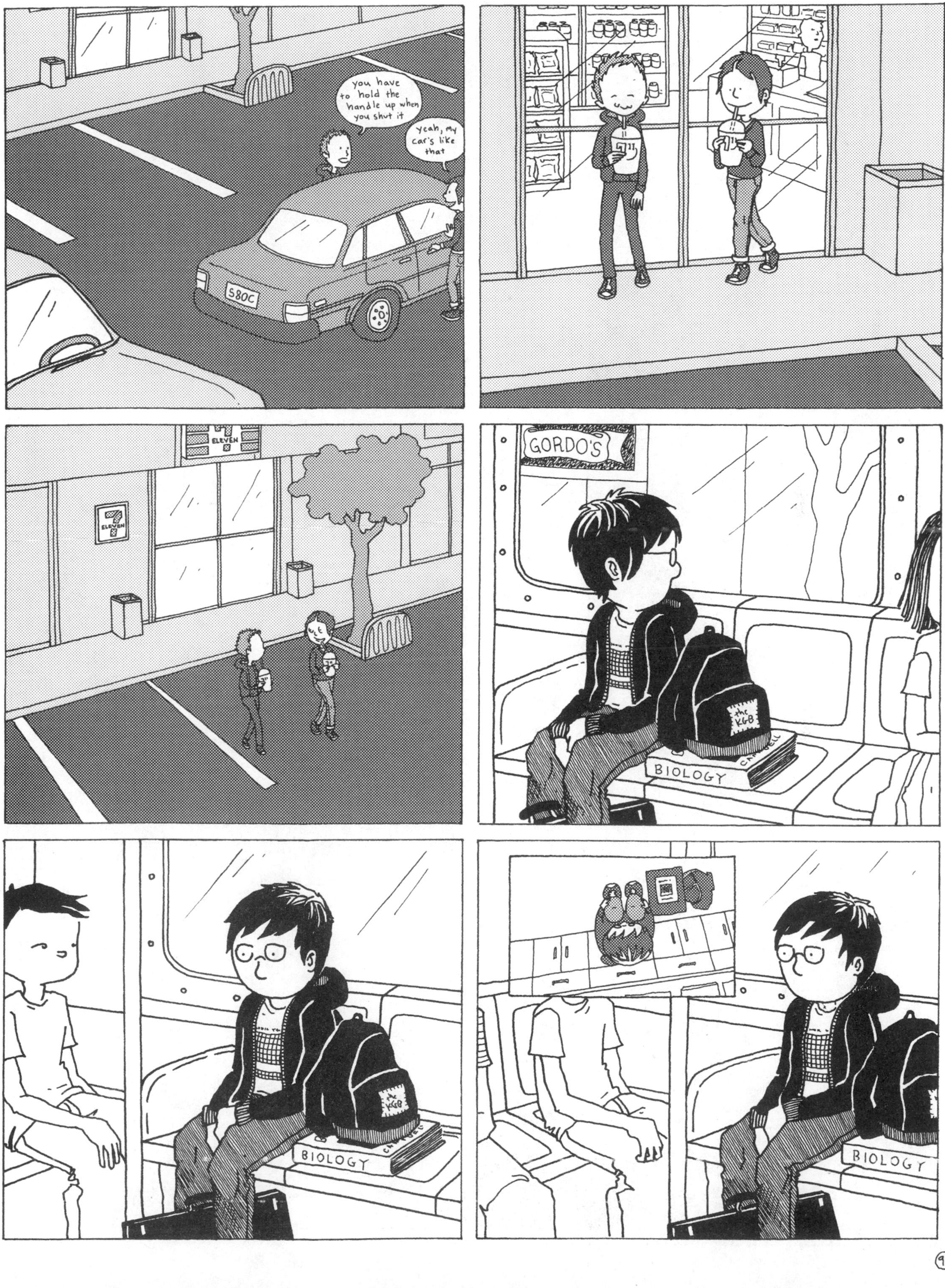
you have to hold the handle up when you shut it
Yeah, my car's like that
S80C
ELEVEN
GORDO'S
the KGB
BIOLOGY
CAMPBELL
BIOLOGY

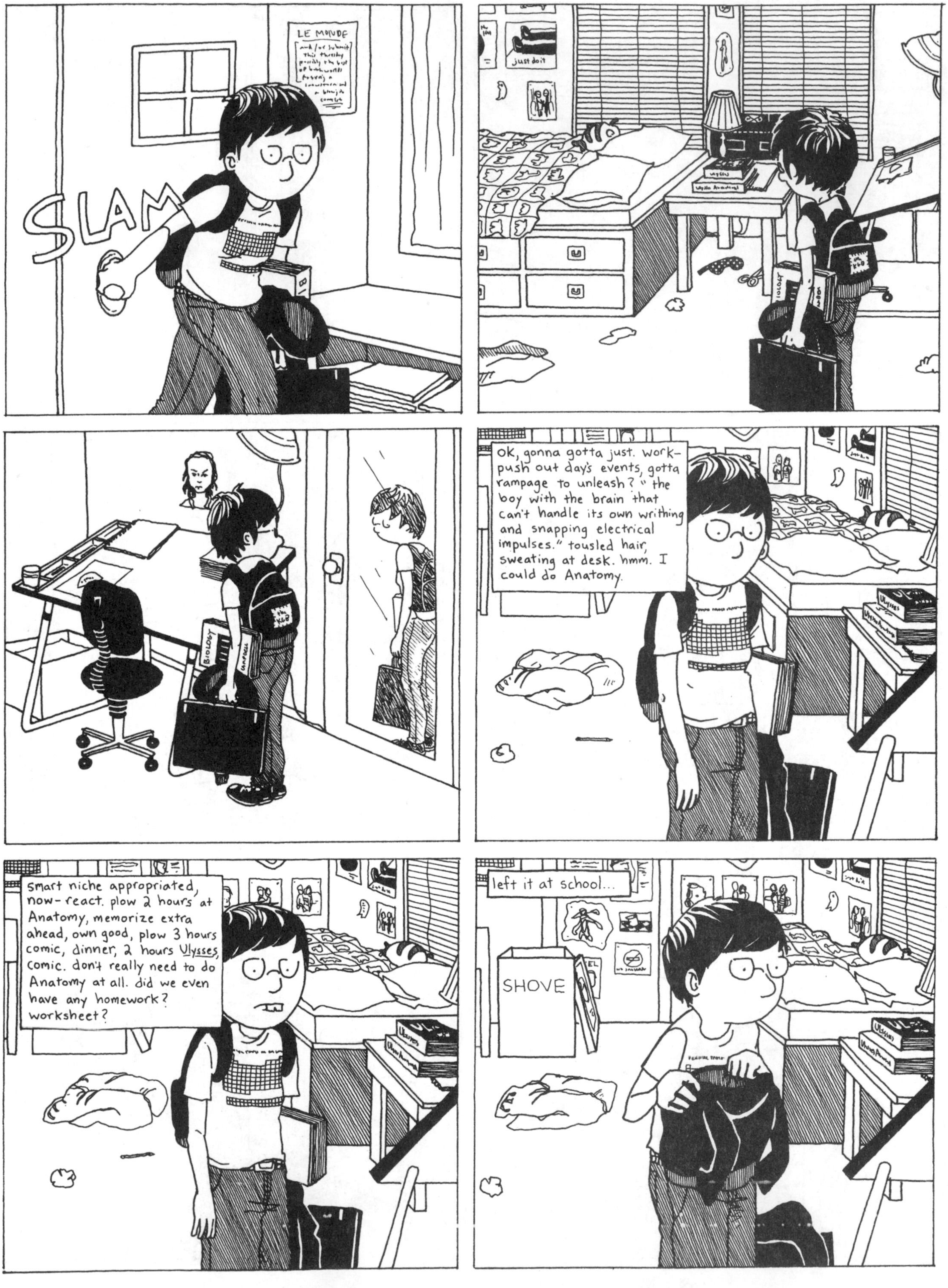
SLAM
ok, gonna gotta just. work-push out day's events, gotta rampage to unleash? "the boy with the brain that can't handle its own writhing and snapping electrical impulses." tousled hair, sweating at desk. hmm. I could do Anatomy.
smart niche appropriated, now-react. plow 2 hours at Anatomy, memorize extra ahead, own good, plow 3 hours comic, dinner, 2 hours Ulysses, comic. don't really need to do Anatomy at all. did we even have any homework? worksheet?
left it at school...
SHOVE

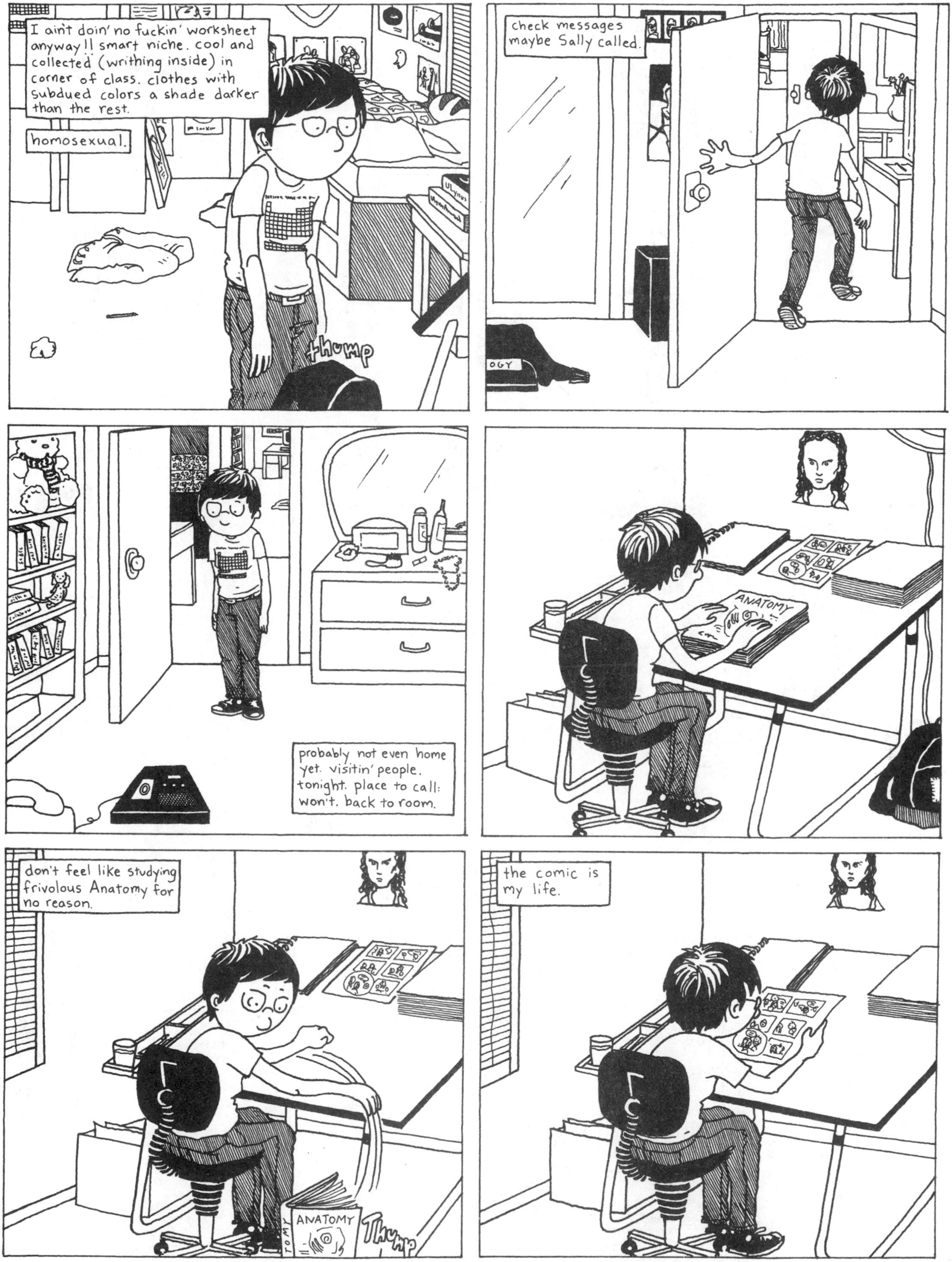
I ain't doin' no fuckin' worksheet anyway!! smart niche. cool and collected (writhing inside) in corner of class. clothes with subdued colors a shade darker than the rest.
homosexual.
thump
check messages maybe Sally called.
probably not even home yet. visitin' people. tonight. place to call: won't. back to room.
ANATOMY
don't feel like studying frivolous Anatomy for no reason.
ANATOMY
Thump
the comic is my life.

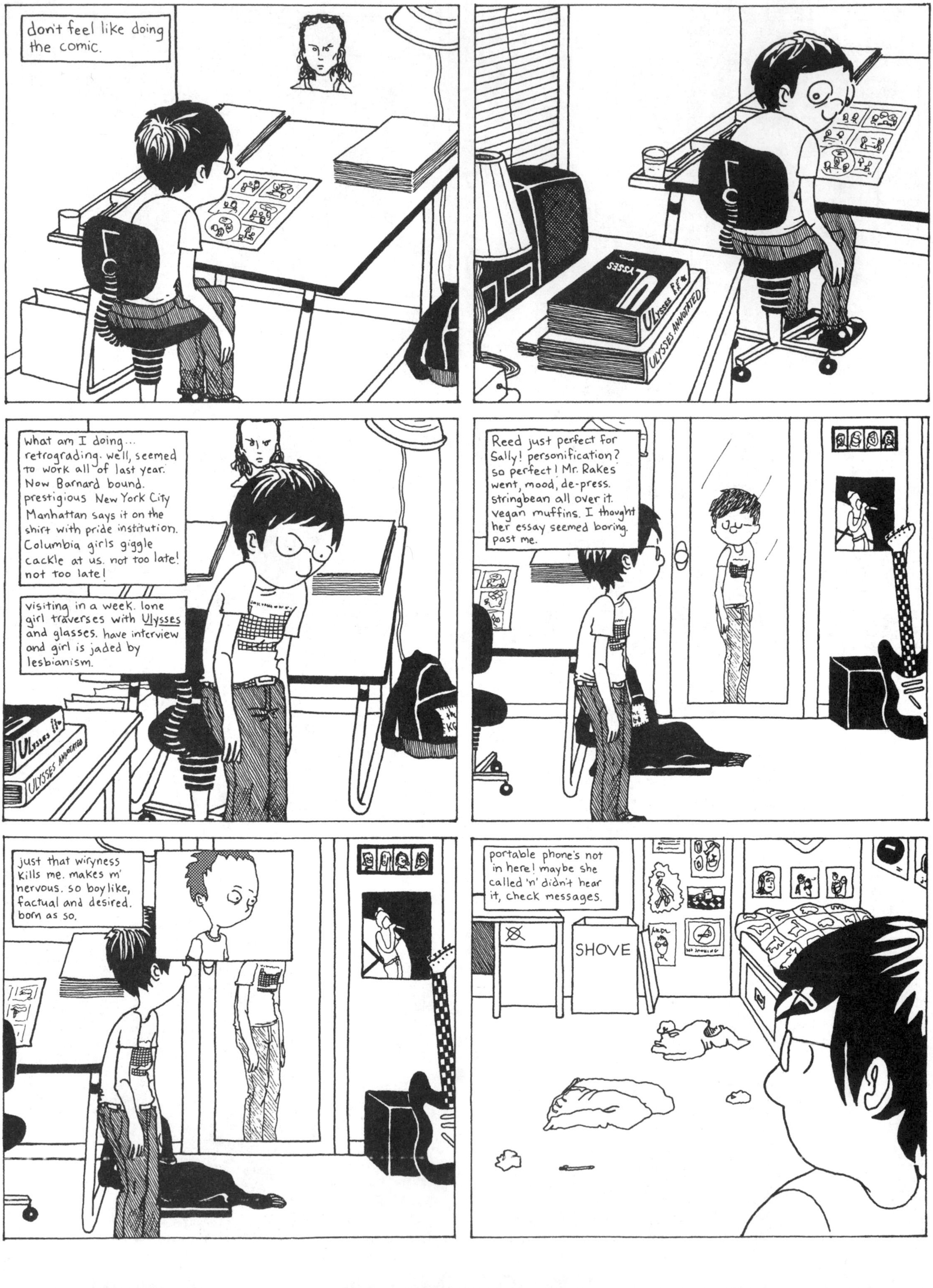
don't feel like doing the comic.
ULYSSES
ULYSSES ANNOTATED
what am I doing... retrograding. well, seemed to work all of last year. Now Barnard bound. prestigious New York City Manhattan says it on the shirt with pride institution. Columbia girls giggle cackle at us. not too late! not too late!
visiting in a week. lone girl traverses with Ulysses and glasses. have interview and girl is jaded by lesbianism.
ULYSSES ANNOTATED
Reed just perfect for Sally! personification? so perfect! Mr. Rakes went, mood, de-press. stringbean all over it. vegan muffins. I thought her essay seemed boring. past me.
just that wiryness kills me. makes m' nervous. so boy like, factual and desired. born as so.
portable phone's not in here! maybe she called 'n' didn't hear it, check messages.
SHOVE

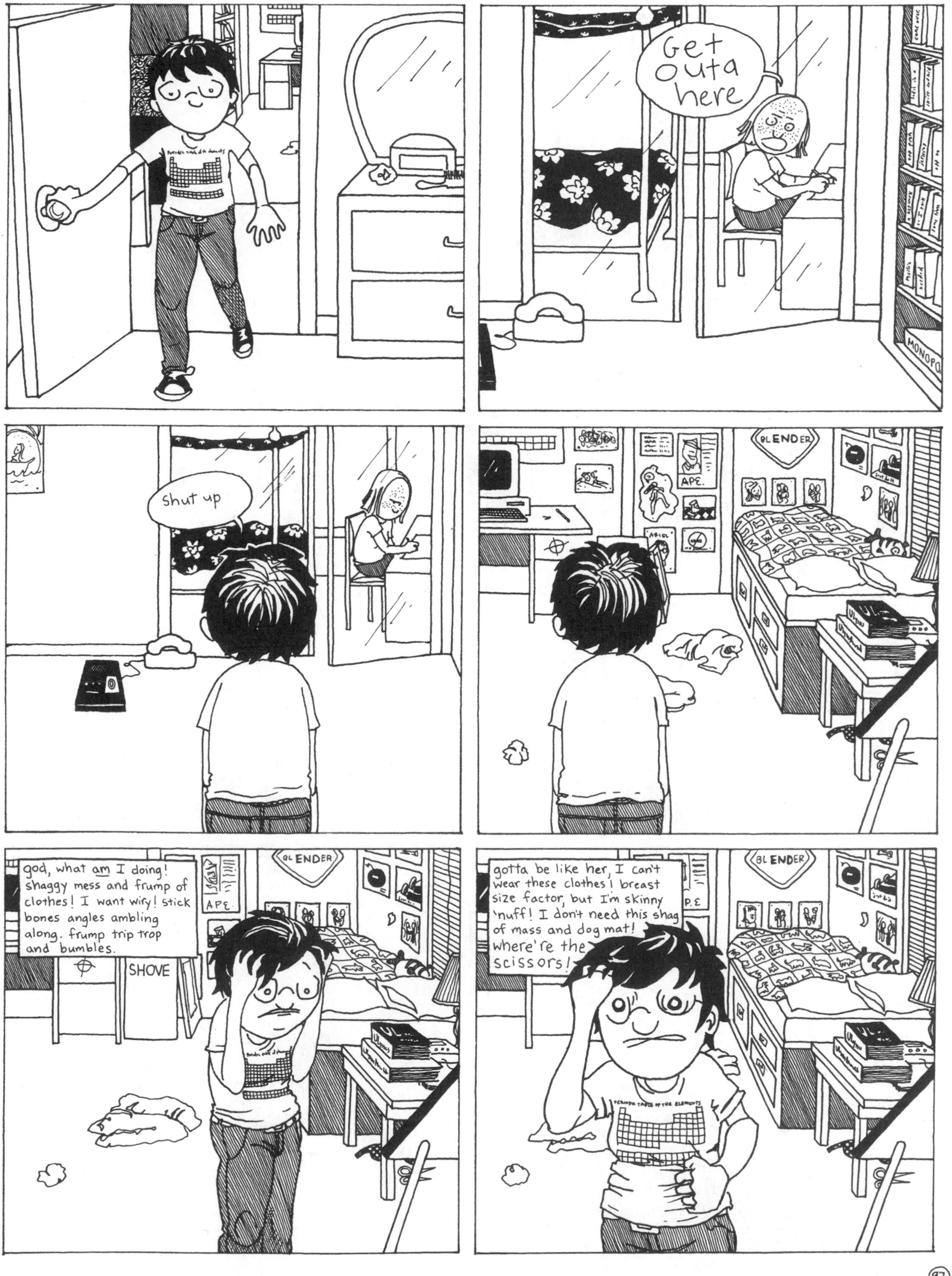
Get outa here
shut up
god, what am I doing! shaggy mess and frump of clothes! I want wiry! stick bones angles ambling along. frump trip trop and bumbles.
SHOVE
gotta be like her, I can't wear these clothes! breast size factor, but I'm skinny 'nuff! I don't need this shag of mass and dog mat! where're the scissors!

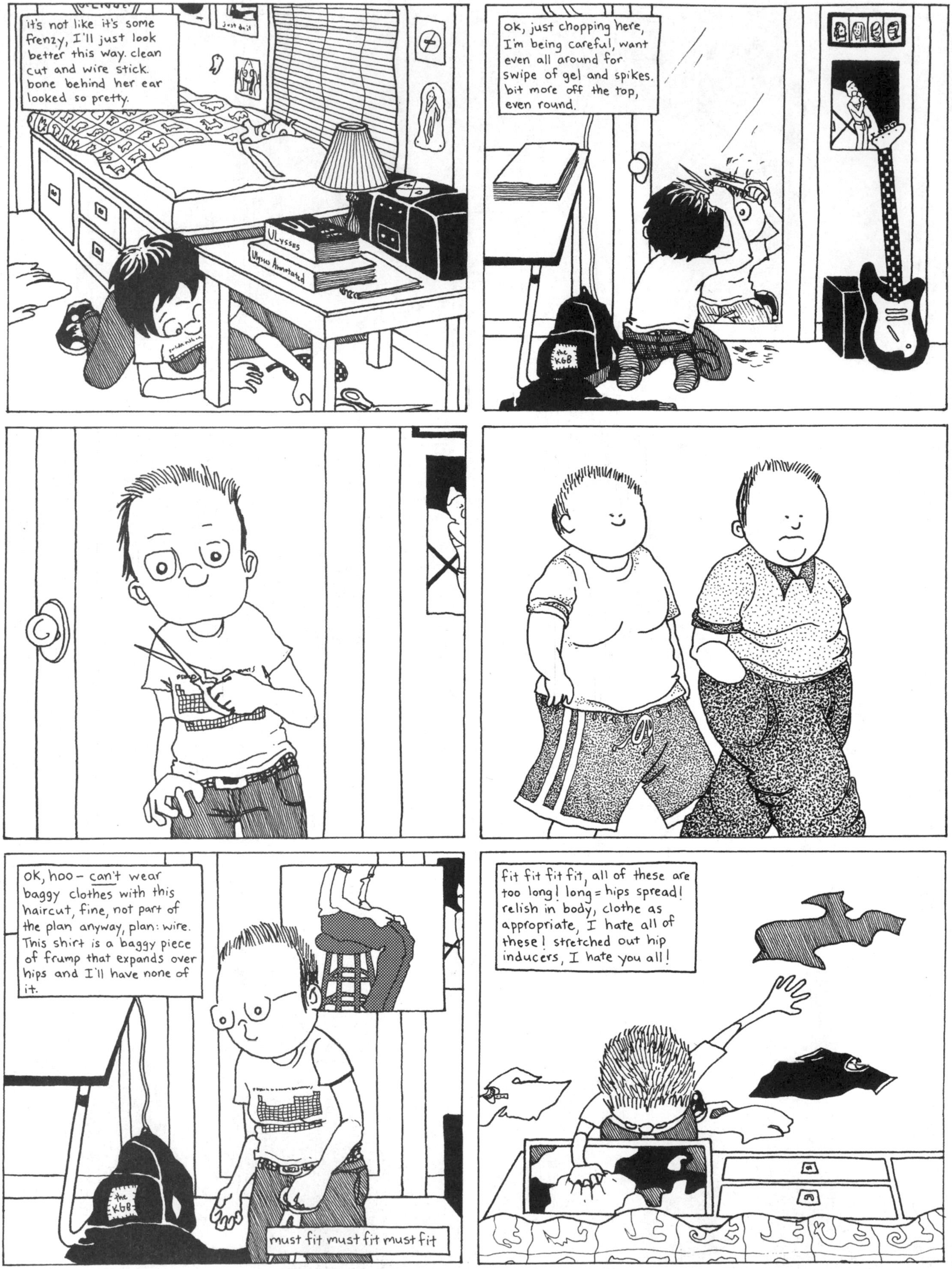
it's not like it's some frenzy, I'll just look better this way. clean cut and wire stick. bone behind her ear looked so pretty.
just do it
ULysses
Ulysses Annotated
Ok, just chopping here, I'm being careful, want even all around for swipe of gel and spikes. bit more off the top, even round.
the KGB
OK, hoo- can't wear baggy clothes with this haircut, fine, not part of the plan anyway, plan: wire. This shirt is a baggy piece of frump that expands over hips and I'll have none of it.
the KGB
must fit must fit must fit
fit fit fit fit, all of these are too long! long = hips spread! relish in body, clothe as appropriate, I hate all of these! stretched out hip inducers, I hate you all!

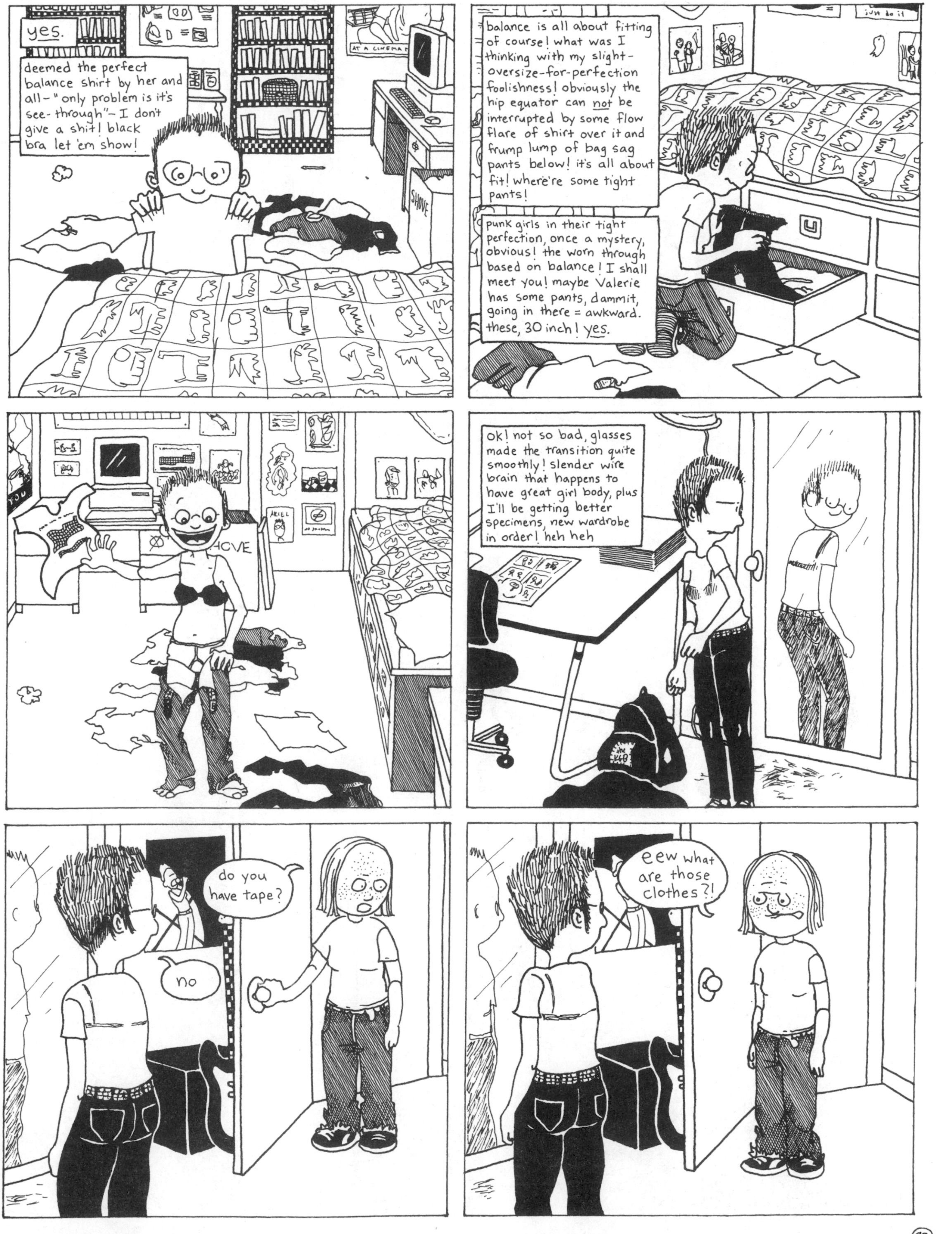
yes.
deemed the perfect balance shirt by her and all- "only problem is it's see-through"- I don't give a shit! black bra let 'em show!
SHOVE
balance is all about fitting of course! what was I thinking with my slight-oversize-for-perfection foolishness! obviously the hip equator can not be interrupted by some flow flare of shirt over it and frump lump of bag sag pants below! it's all about fit! where're some tight pants!
punk girls in their tight perfection, once a mystery, obvious! the worn through based on balance! I shall meet you! maybe Valerie has some pants, dammit, going in there = awkward. these, 30 inch! yes.
SHOVE
ok! not so bad, glasses made the transition quite smoothly! slender wire brain that happens to have great girl body, plus I'll be getting better specimens, new wardrobe in order! heh heh
do you have tape?
no
eew what are those clothes?!

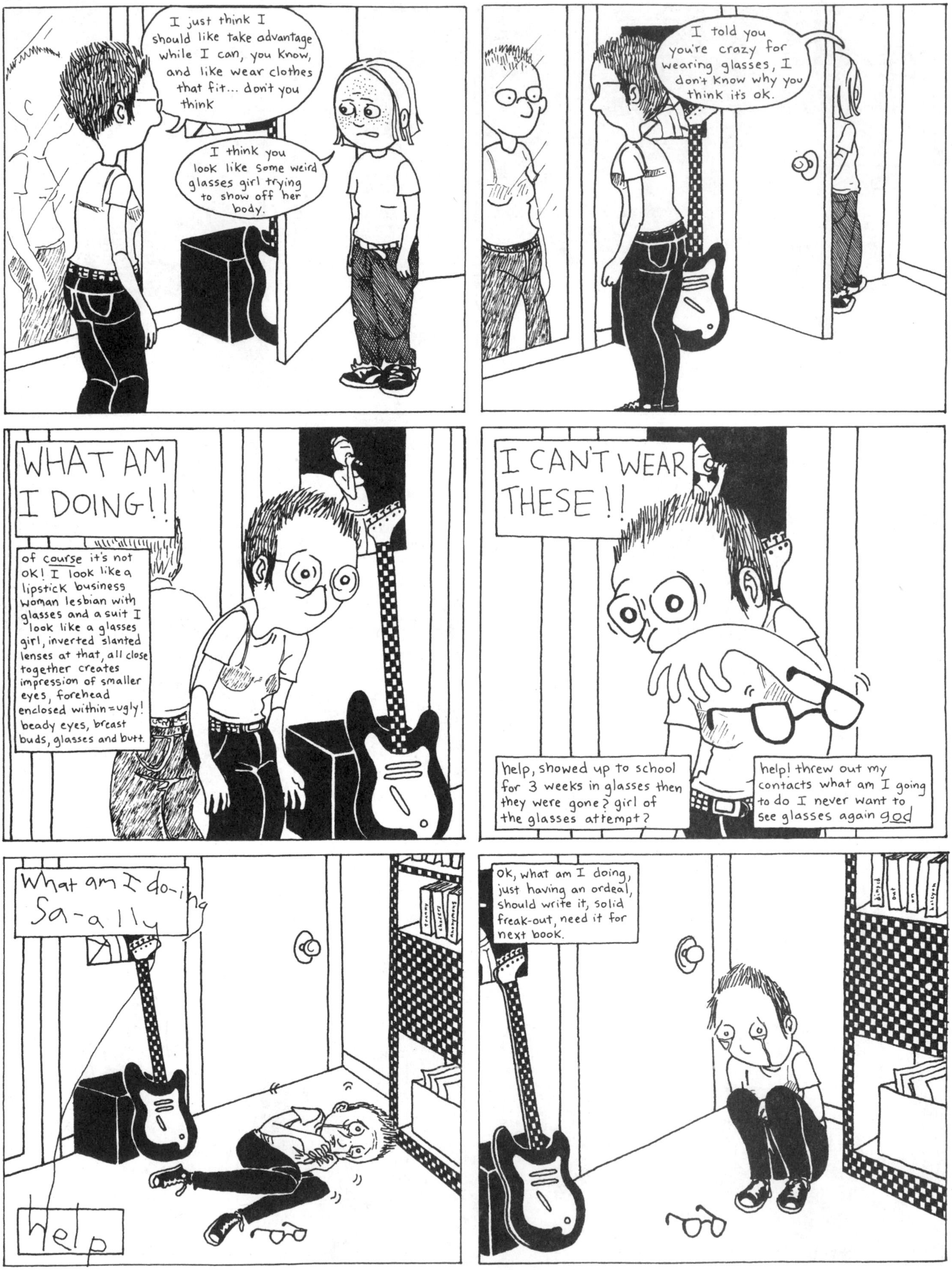
I just think I should like take advantage while I can, you know, and like wear clothes that fit... don't you think
I think you look like some weird glasses girl trying to show off her body.
I told you you're crazy for wearing glasses, I don't know why you think it's ok.
WHAT AM I DOING!!
of course it's not OK! I look like a lipstick business woman lesbian with glasses and a suit I look like a glasses girl, inverted slanted lenses at that, all close together creates impression of smaller eyes, forehead enclosed within=ugly! beady eyes, breast buds, glasses and butt.
I CAN'T WEAR THESE!!
help, showed up to school for 3 weeks in glasses then they were gone? girl of the glasses attempt?
help! threw out my contacts what am I going to do I never want to see glasses again god
What am I do-ing Sa-ally
Help
Ok, what am I doing, just having an ordeal, should write it, solid freak-out, need it for next book.

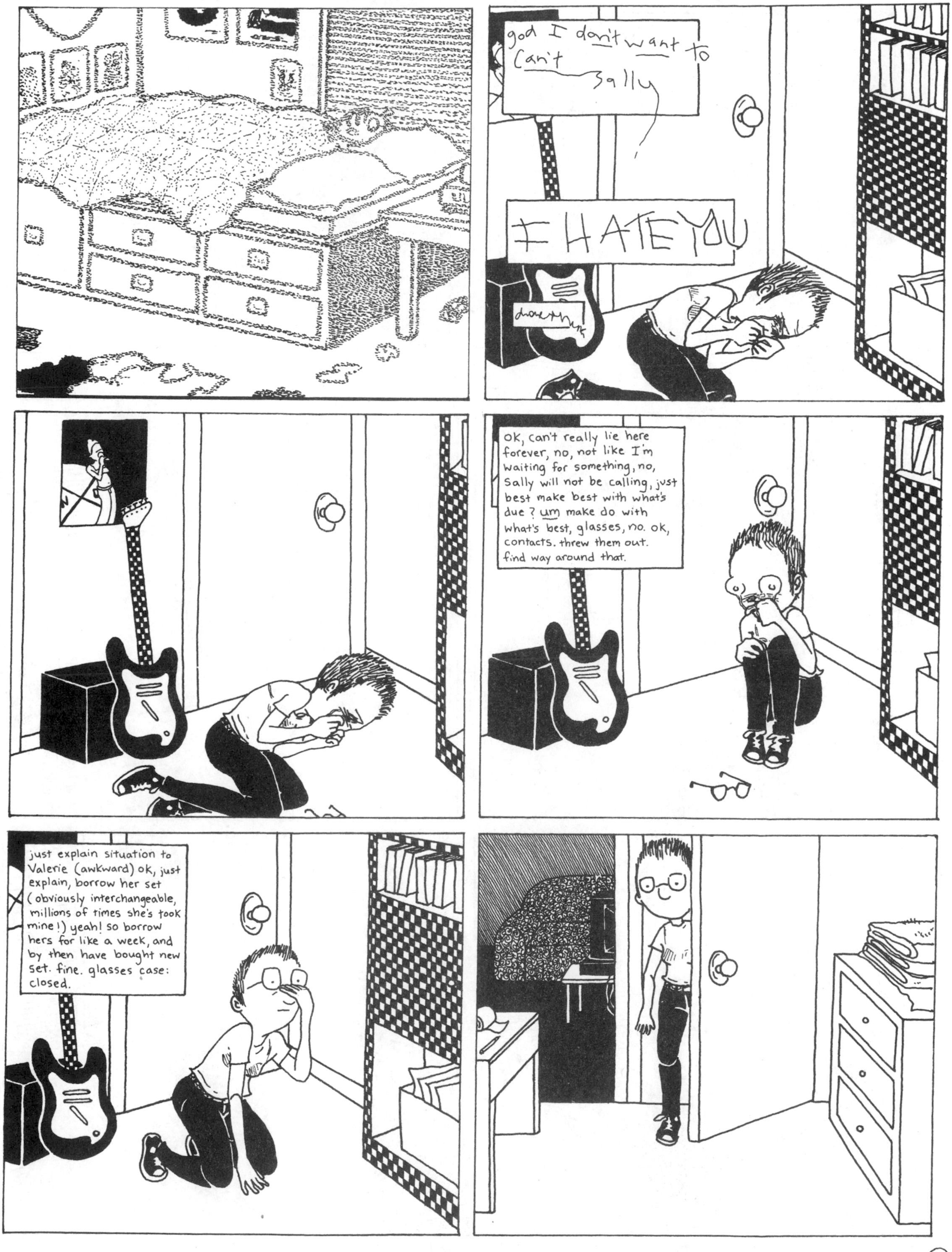
god I don't want to
Can't
Sally
I HATE YOU
ok, can't really lie here forever, no, not like I'm waiting for something, no, Sally will not be calling, just best make best with what's due? um make do with what's best, glasses, no. ok, contacts. threw them out. find way around that.
just explain situation to Valerie (awkward) ok, just explain, borrow her set (obviously interchangeable, millions of times she's took mine!) yeah! so borrow hers for like a week, and by then have bought new set. fine. glasses case: closed.

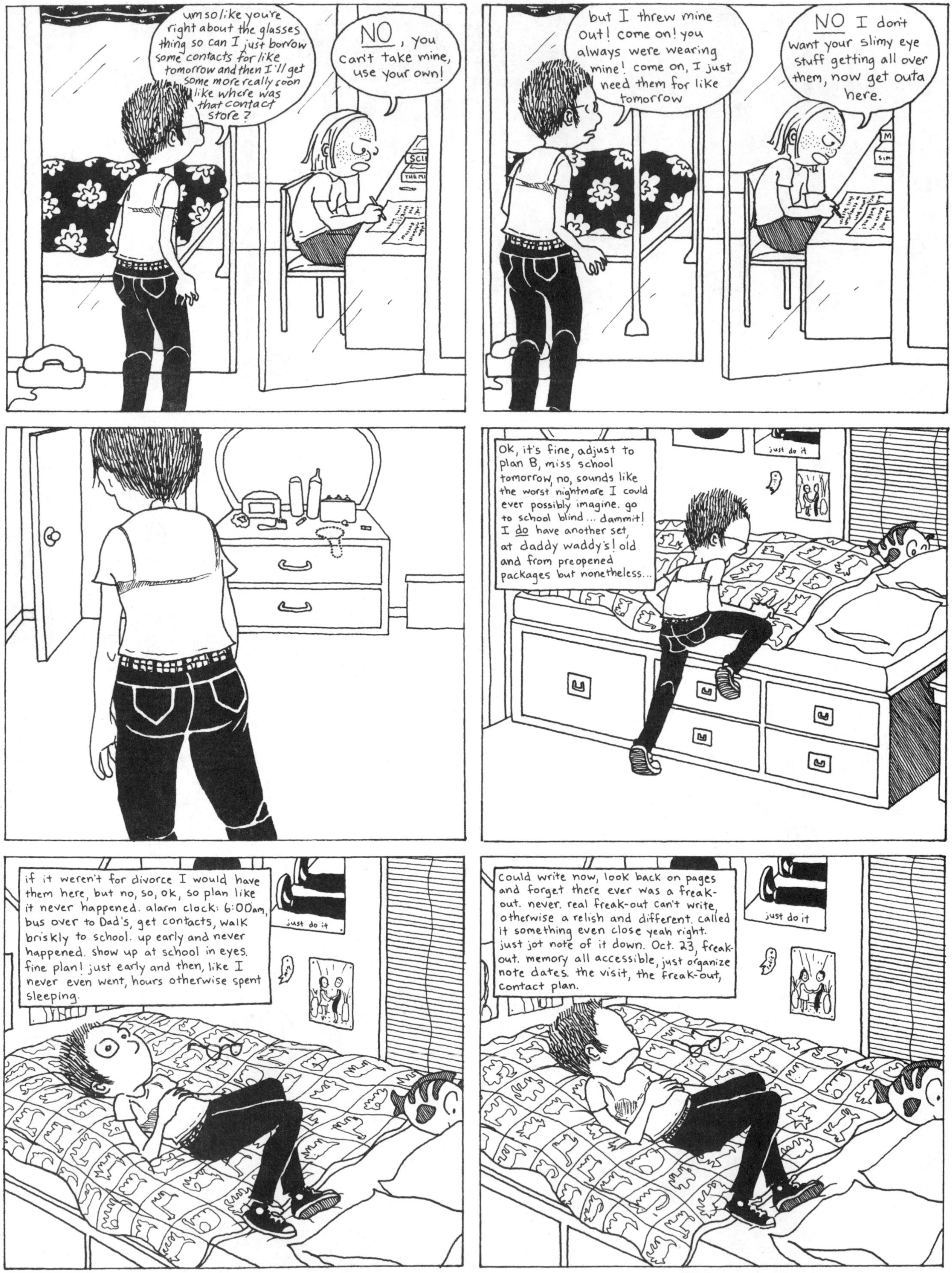

um so like you're right about the glasses thing so can I just borrow some contacts for like tomorrow and then I'll get some more really soon like where was that contact store?
NO, you can't take mine, use your own!
but I threw mine out! come on! you always were wearing mine! come on, I just need them for like tomorrow
NO I don't want your slimy eye stuff getting all over them, now get outa here.
just do it
Ok, it's fine, adjust to plan B, miss school tomorrow, no, sounds like the worst nightmare I could ever possibly imagine. go to school blind... dammit! I do have another set, at daddy waddy's! old and from preopened packages but nonetheless...
if it weren't for divorce I would have them here, but no, so, ok, so plan like it never happened. alarm clock: 6:00am, bus over to Dad's, get contacts, walk briskly to school. up early and never happened. show up at school in eyes. fine plan! just early and then, like I never even went, hours otherwise spent sleeping.
just do it
could write now, look back on pages and forget there ever was a freak-out. never. real freak-out can't write, otherwise a relish and different. called it something even close yeah right. just jot note of it down. Oct. 23, freak-out. memory all accessible, just organize note dates. the visit, the freak-out, contact plan.
just do it

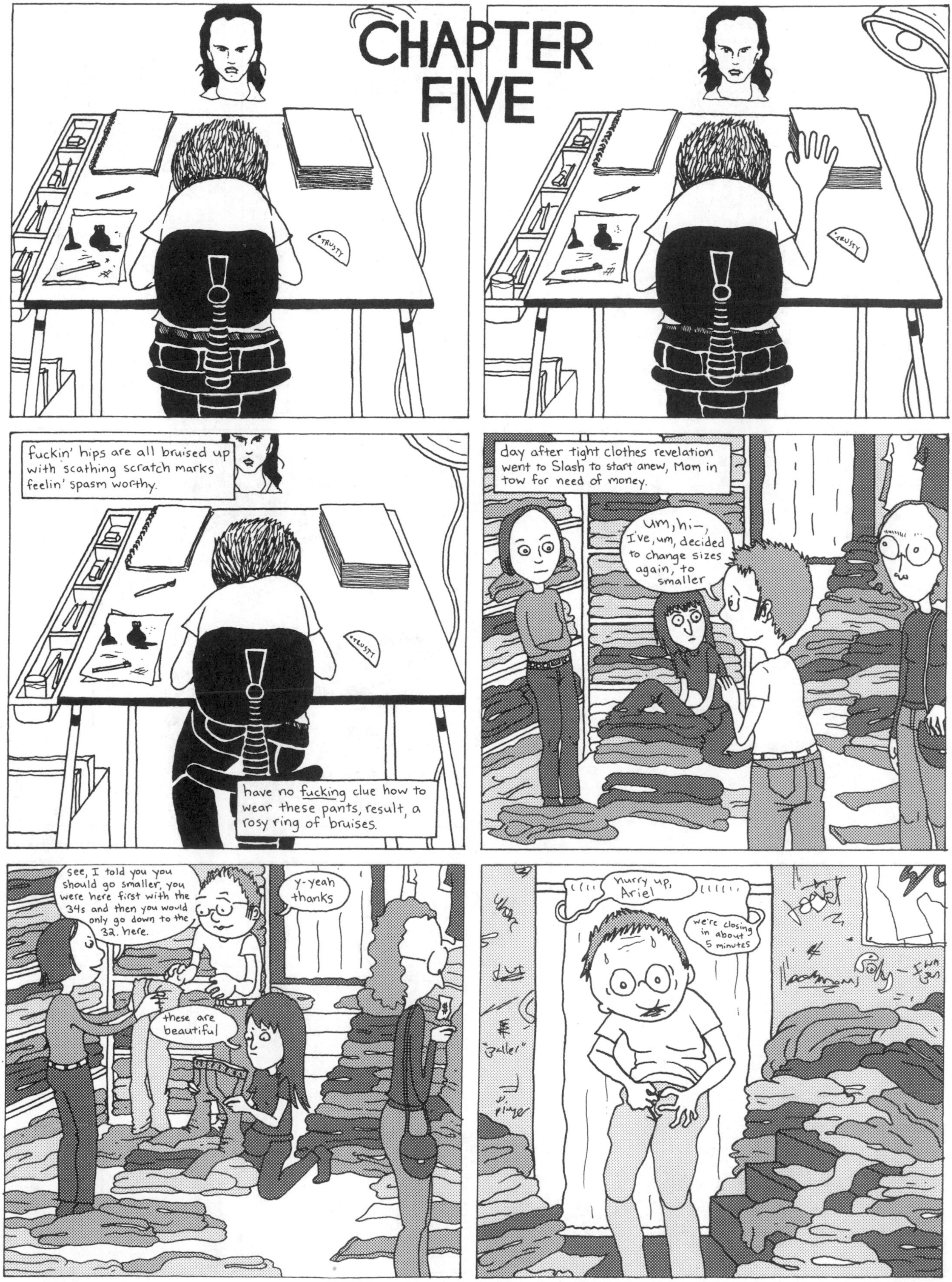
CHAPTER FIVE
TRUSTY
TRUSTY
fuckin' hips are all bruised up with scathing scratch marks feelin' spasm worthy.
TRUSTY
have no fucking clue how to wear these pants, result, a rosy ring of bruises.
day after tight clothes revelation went to Slash to start anew, Mom in tow for need of money.
um, hi—, I've, um, decided to change sizes again, to smaller
see, I told you you should go smaller, you were here first with the 34s and then you would only go down to the 32. here.
y-yeah thanks
these are beautiful
hurry up, Ariel
we're closing in about 5 minutes

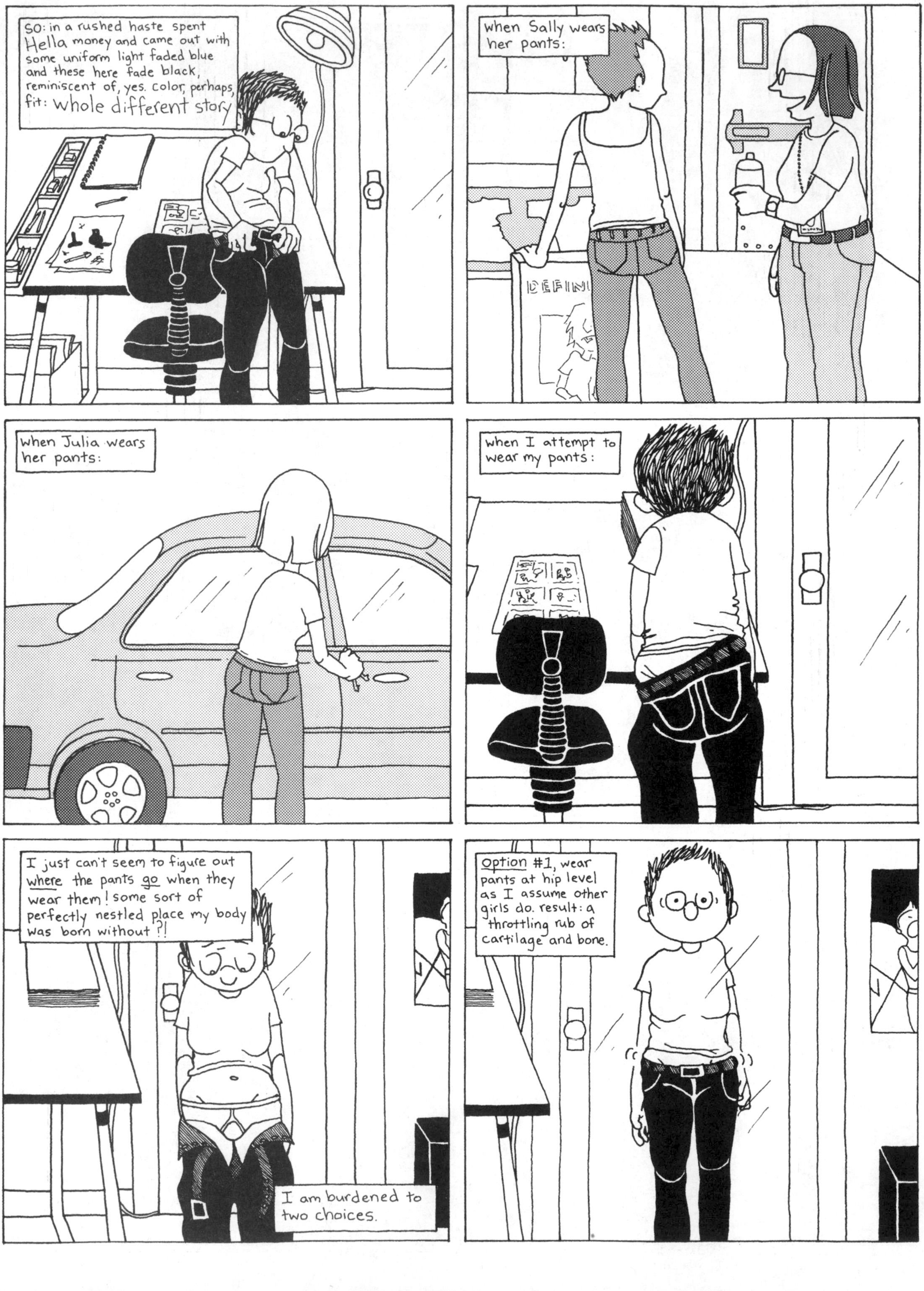
SO: in a rushed haste spent Hella money and came out with some uniform light faded blue and these here fade black, reminiscent of, yes. color, perhaps, fit: whole different story
when Sally wears her pants:
when Julia wears her pants:
when I attempt to wear my pants:
I just can't seem to figure out where the pants go when they wear them! some sort of perfectly nestled place my body was born without?!
I am burdened to two choices.
Option #1, wear pants at hip level as I assume other girls do. result: a throttling rub of cartilage and bone.

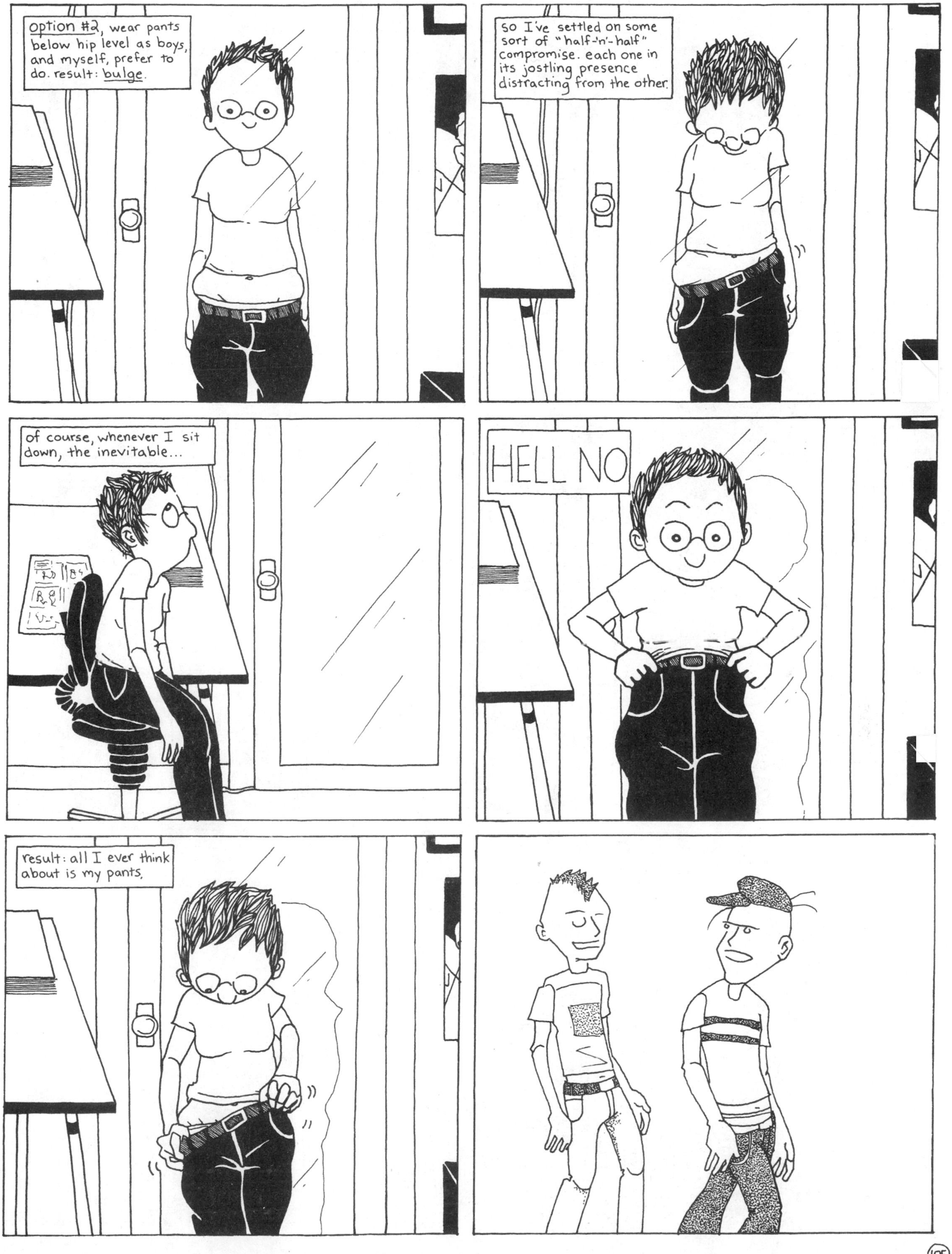
option #2, wear pants below hip level as boys, and myself, prefer to do. result: bulge.
so I've settled on some sort of "half-'n'-half" compromise. each one in its jostling presence distracting from the other.
of course, whenever I sit down, the inevitable...
HELL NO
result: all I ever think about is my pants.

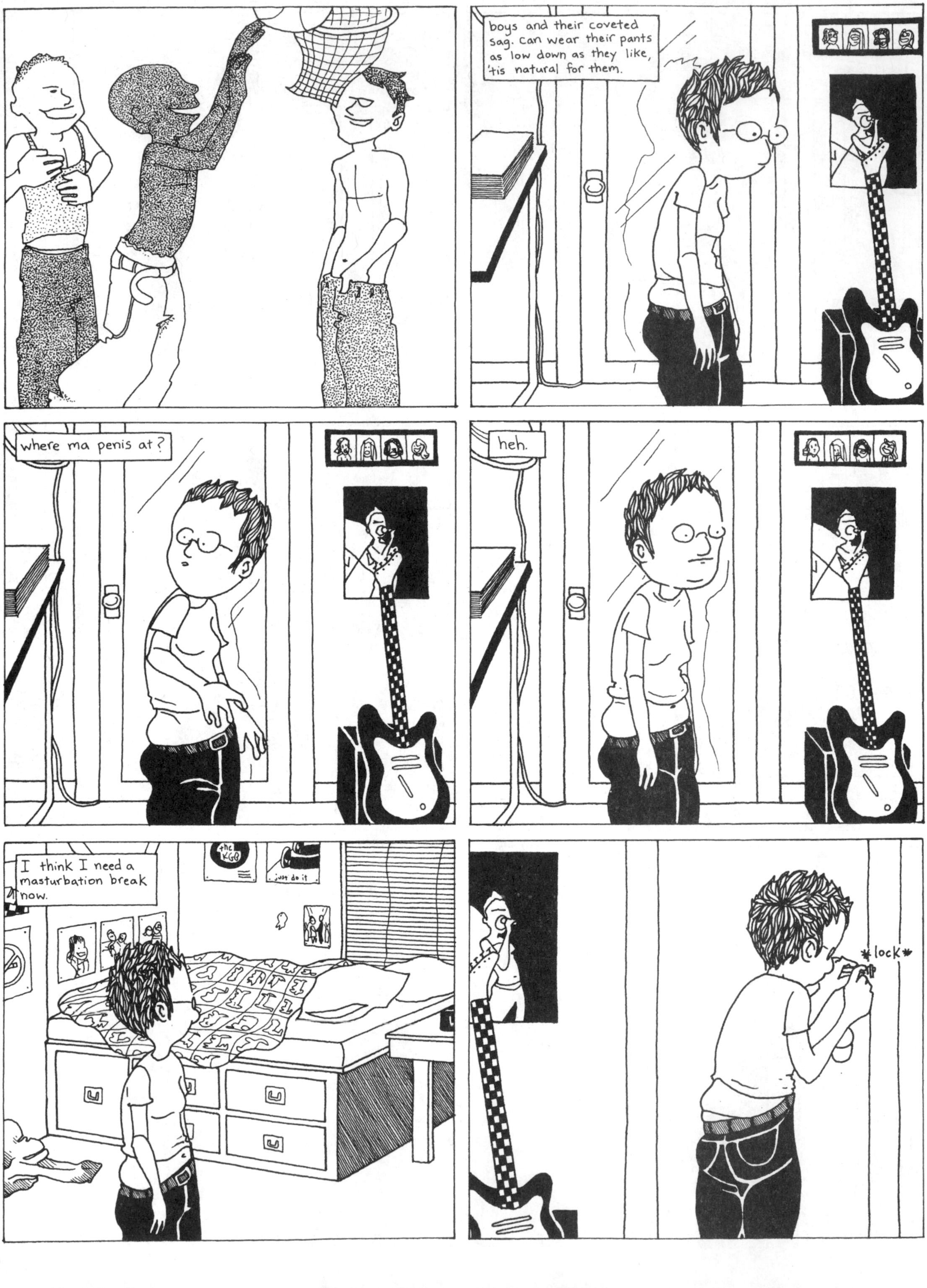
boys and their coveted sag. can wear their pants as low down as they like, 'tis natural for them.
where ma penis at?
heh.
I think I need a masturbation break now.
just do it
lock

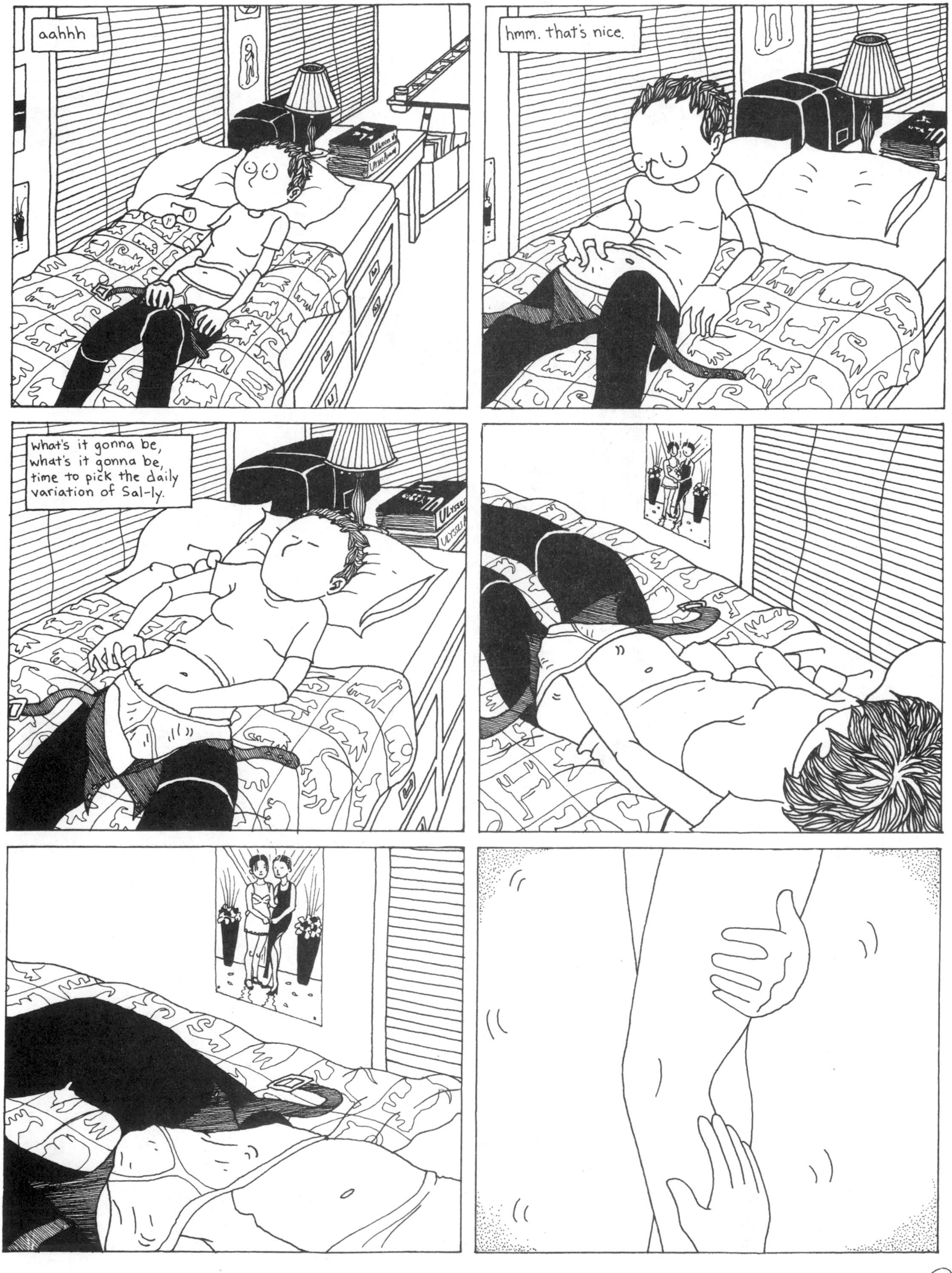
aahhh
hmm. that's nice.
what's it gonna be, what's it gonna be, time to pick the daily variation of Sal-ly.

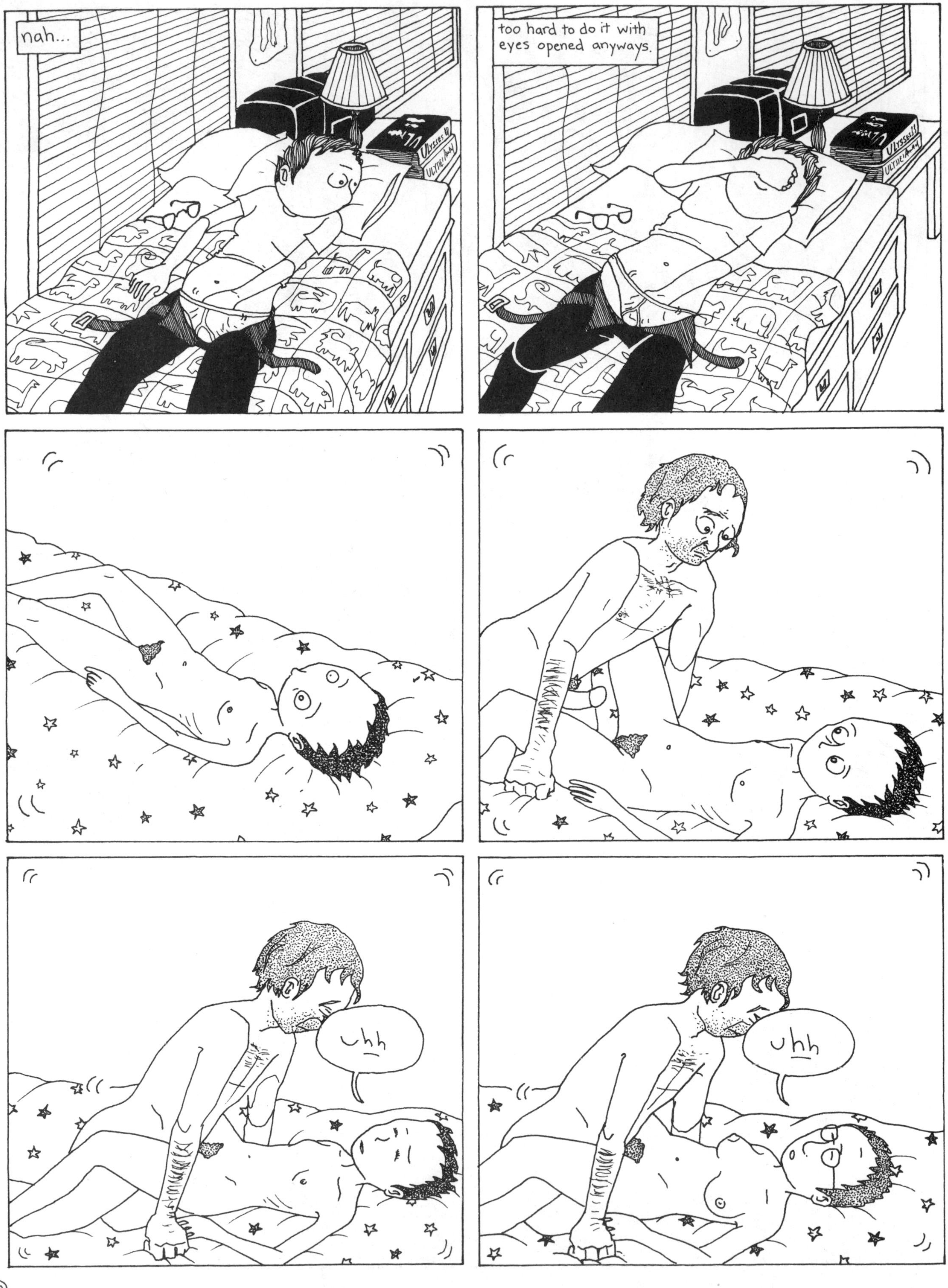
nah...
too hard to do it with
eyes opened anyways.
uhh
uhh

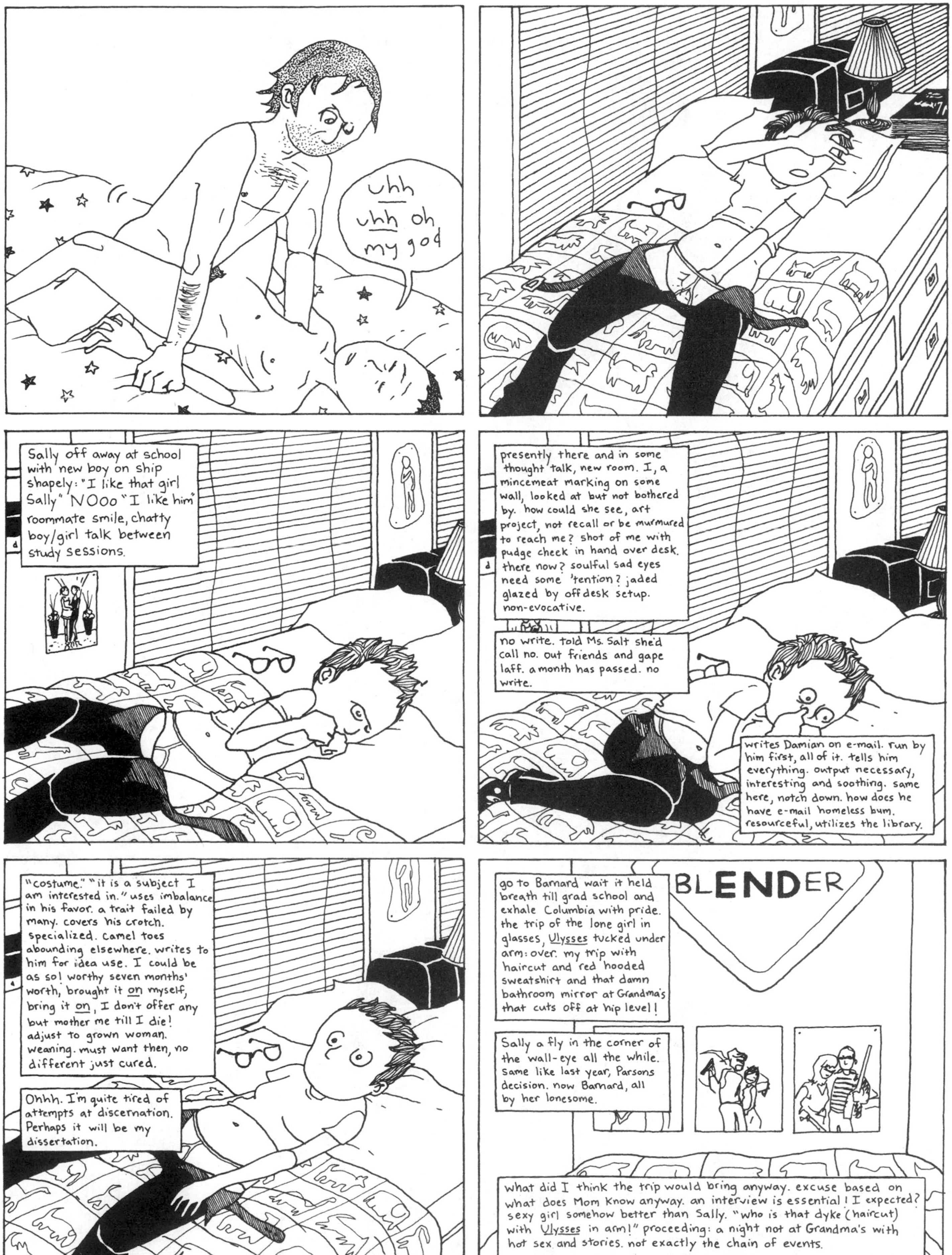

uhh uhh oh my god
Sally off away at school with new boy on ship shapely: "I like that girl Sally" NOoo "I like him" roommate smile, chatty boy/girl talk between study sessions.
presently there and in some thought talk, new room. I, a mincemeat marking on some wall, looked at but not bothered by. how could she see, art project, not recall or be murmured to reach me? shot of me with pudge cheek in hand over desk. there now? soulful sad eyes need some 'tention? jaded glazed by off desk setup. non-evocative.
no write. told Ms. Salt she'd call no. out friends and gape laff. a month has passed. no write.
writes Damian on e-mail. run by him first, all of it. tells him everything. output necessary, interesting and soothing. same here, notch down. how does he have e-mail homeless bum. resourceful, utilizes the library.
"costume." "it is a subject I am interested in." uses imbalance in his favor. a trait failed by many. covers his crotch. specialized. camel toes abounding elsewhere. writes to him for idea use. I could be as so! worthy seven months' worth, brought it on myself, bring it on, I don't offer any but mother me till I die! adjust to grown woman. weaning. must want then, no different just cured.
Ohhh. I'm quite tired of attempts at discernation. Perhaps it will be my dissertation.
BLENDER
go to Barnard wait it held breath till grad school and exhale Columbia with pride. the trip of the lone girl in glasses, Ulysses tucked under arm: over. my trip with haircut and red hooded sweatshirt and that damn bathroom mirror at Grandma's that cuts off at hip level!
Sally a fly in the corner of the wall-eye all the while. same like last year, Parsons decision. now Barnard, all by her lonesome.
what did I think the trip would bring anyway. excuse based on what does Mom know anyway. an interview is essential! I expected? sexy girl somehow better than Sally. "who is that dyke (haircut) with Ulysses in arm!" proceeding: a night not at Grandma's with hot sex and stories. not exactly the chain of events.

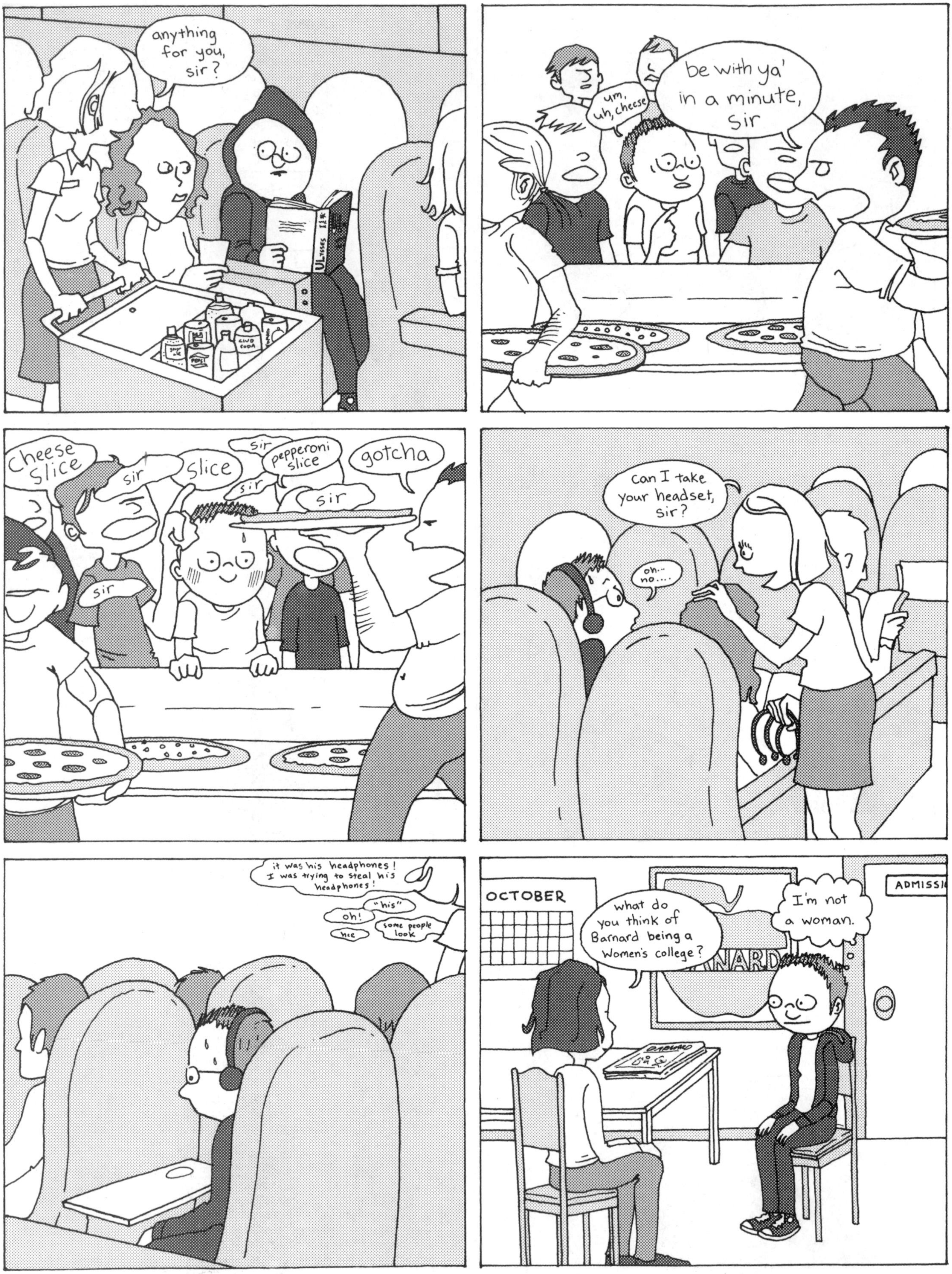
anything for you, sir?
um, uh, cheese
be with ya' in a minute, sir
Cheese slice
sir
slice
sir
sir
pepperoni slice
sir
gotcha
sir
can I take your headset, sir?
oh... no....
it was his headphones! I was trying to steal his headphones!
"his"
oh!
hee
some people look
OCTOBER
what do you think of Barnard being a Women's college?
I'm not a woman.

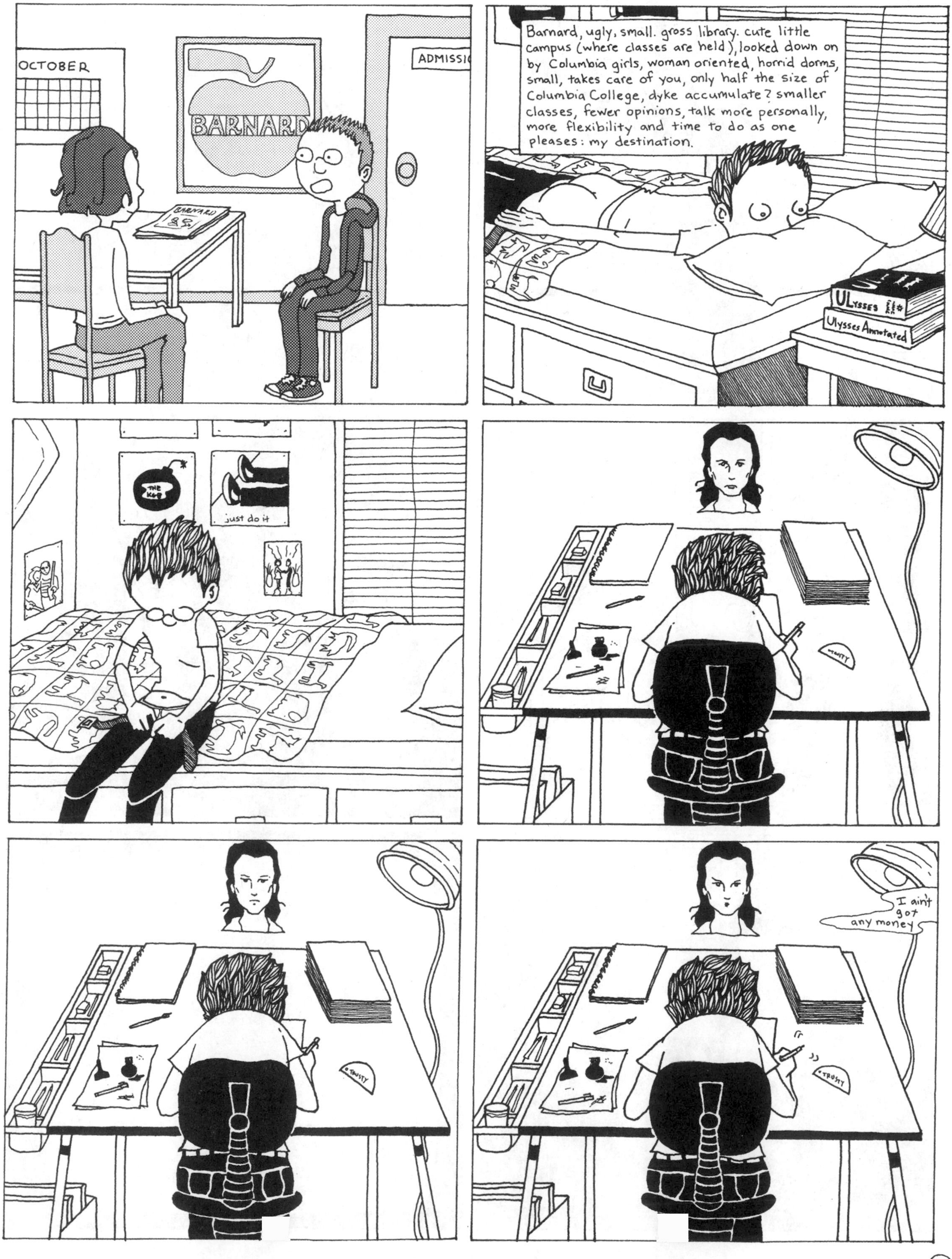
OCTOBER
ADMISSI
BARNARD
Barnard, ugly, small. gross library. cute little campus (where classes are held), looked down on by Columbia girls, woman oriented, horrid dorms, small, takes care of you, only half the size of Columbia College, dyke accumulate? smaller classes, fewer opinions, talk more personally, more flexibility and time to do as one pleases: my destination.
ULysses
Ulysses Annotated
just do it
I ain't got any money

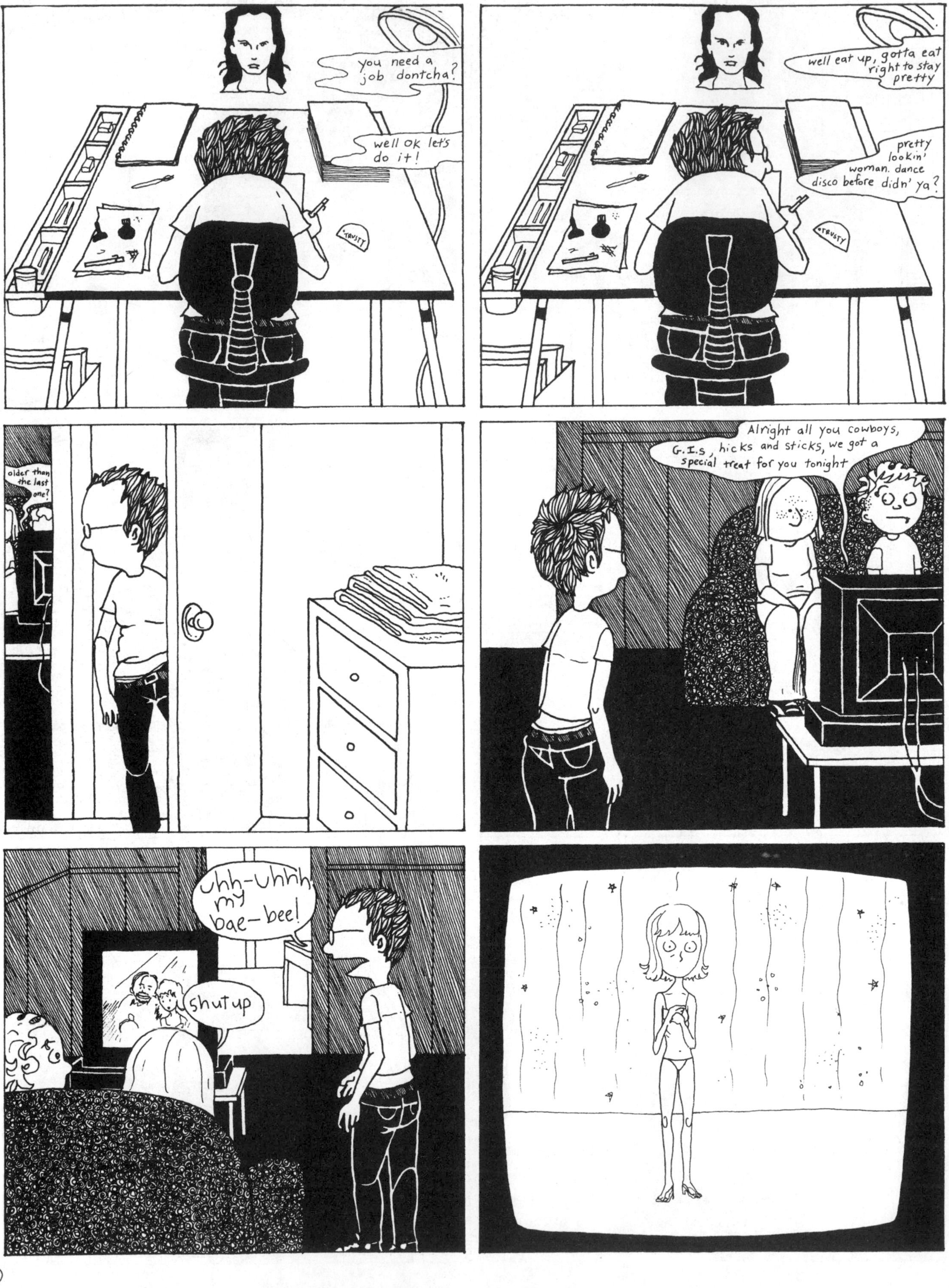
you need a job dontcha?
well OK let's do it!
TRUSTY
well eat up, gotta eat right to stay pretty
pretty lookin' woman. dance disco before didn' ya?
TRUSTY
older than the last one?
Alright all you cowboys, G.I.s, hicks and sticks, we got a special treat for you tonight
uhh-uhhh my bae-bee!
shutup

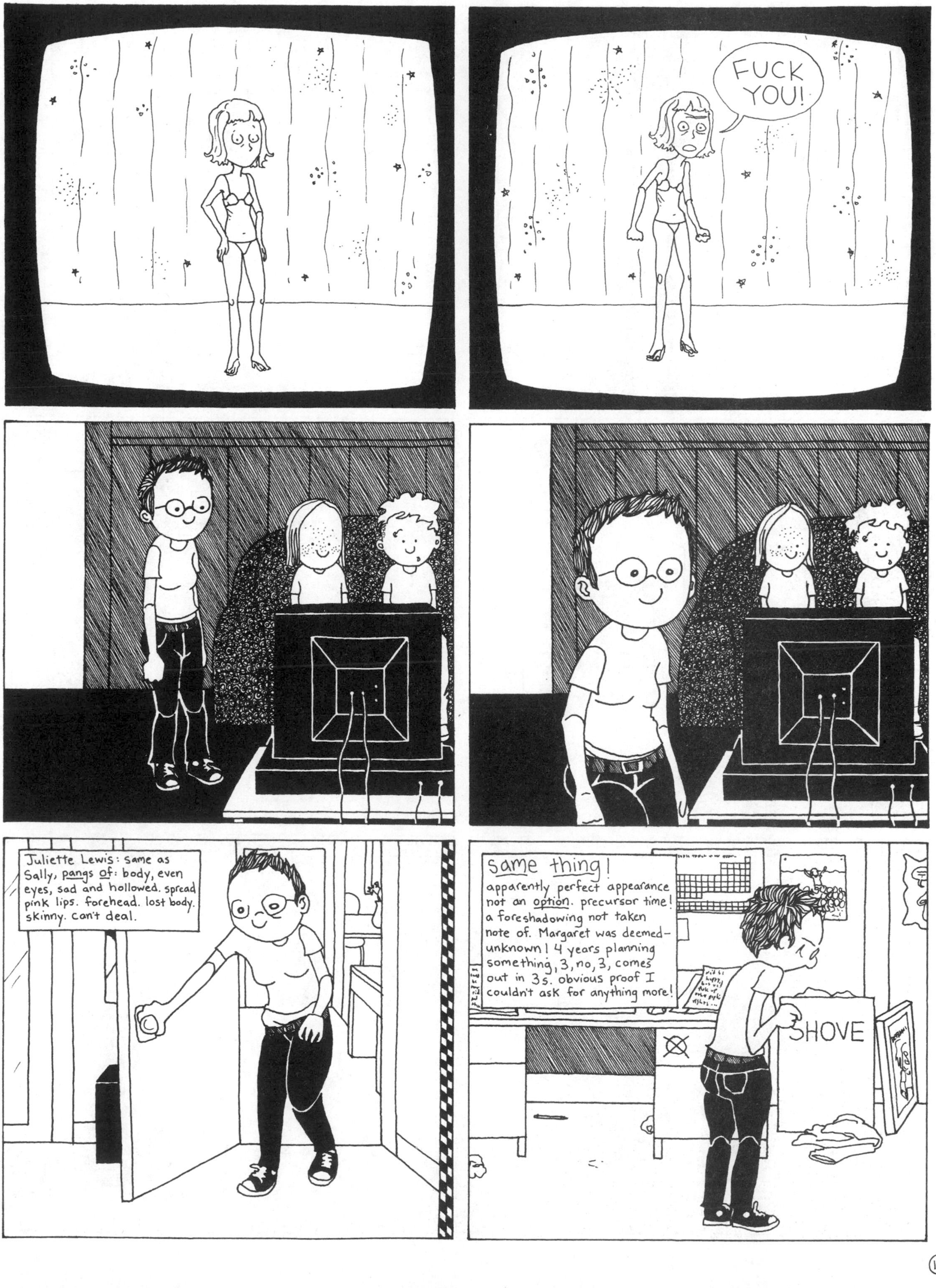
FUCK YOU!
Juliette Lewis: same as Sally, pangs of: body, even eyes, sad and hollowed. spread pink lips. forehead. lost body. skinny. can't deal.
same thing!
apparently perfect appearance not an option. precursor time! a foreshadowing not taken note of. Margaret was deemed-unknown! 4 years planning something, 3, no, 3, comes out in 3s. obvious proof I couldn't ask for anything more!
SHOVE

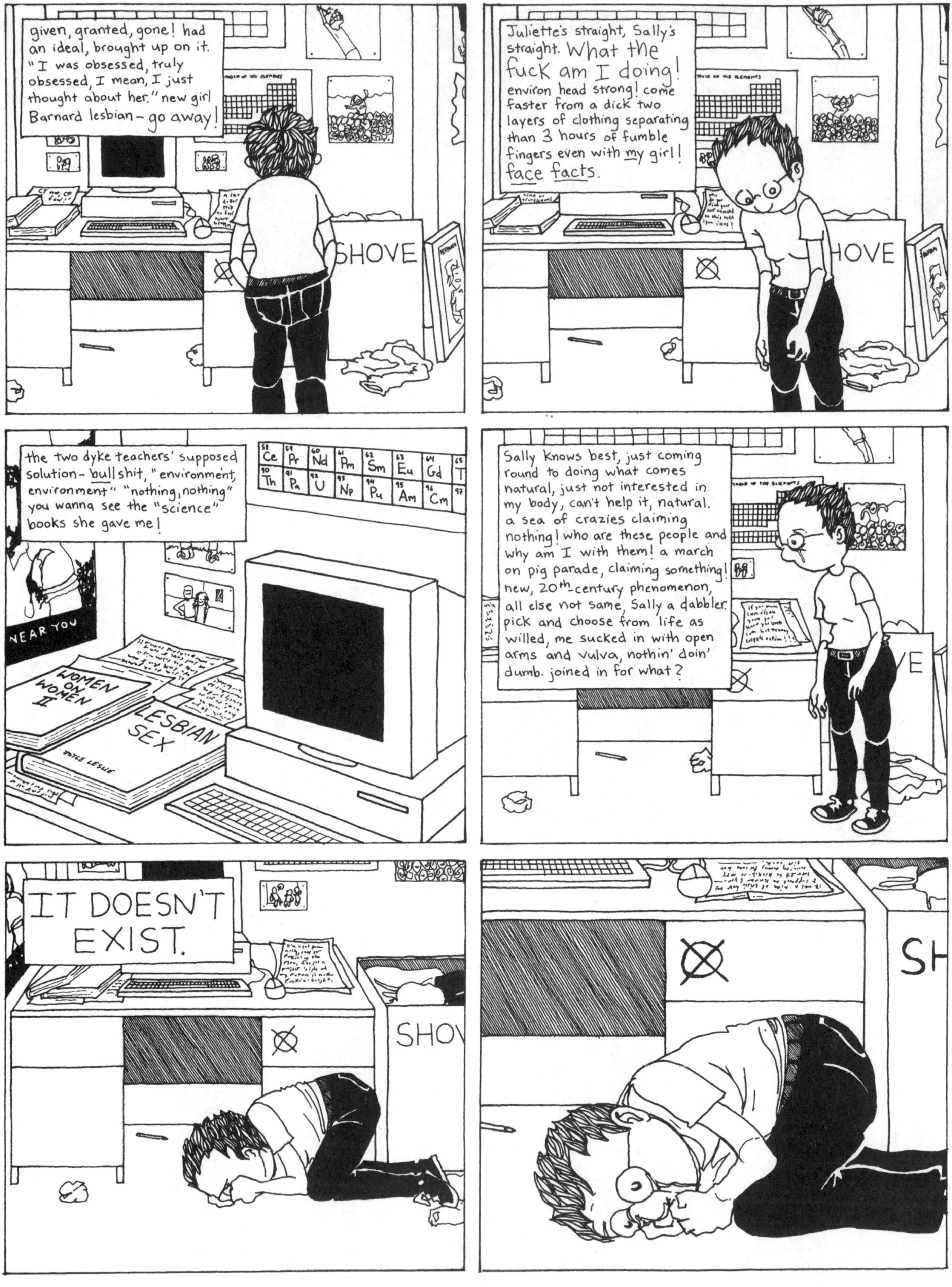
given, granted, gone! had an ideal, brought up on it. "I was obsessed, truly obsessed, I mean, I just thought about her." new girl Barnard lesbian – go away!
SHOVE
Juliette's straight, Sally's straight. What the fuck am I doing! environ head strong! come faster from a dick two layers of clothing separating than 3 hours of fumble fingers even with my girl! face facts.
HOVE
the two dyke teachers' supposed solution – bullshit, "environment, environment" "nothing, nothing" you wanna see the "science" books she gave me!
58 Ce
59 Pr
60 Nd
61 Pm
62 Sm
63 Eu
64 Gd
90 Th
91 Pa
92 U
93 Np
94 Pu
95 Am
96 Cm
NEAR YOU
WOMEN ON WOMEN II
LESBIAN SEX
JOYCE LESLIE
Sally knows best, just coming round to doing what comes natural, just not interested in my body, can't help it, natural. a sea of crazies claiming nothing! who are these people and why am I with them! a march on pig parade, claiming something! new, 20th-century phenomenon, all else not same, Sally a dabbler. pick and choose from life as willed, me sucked in with open arms and vulva, nothin' doin' dumb. joined in for what?
IT DOESN'T EXIST.
SHOV
SH

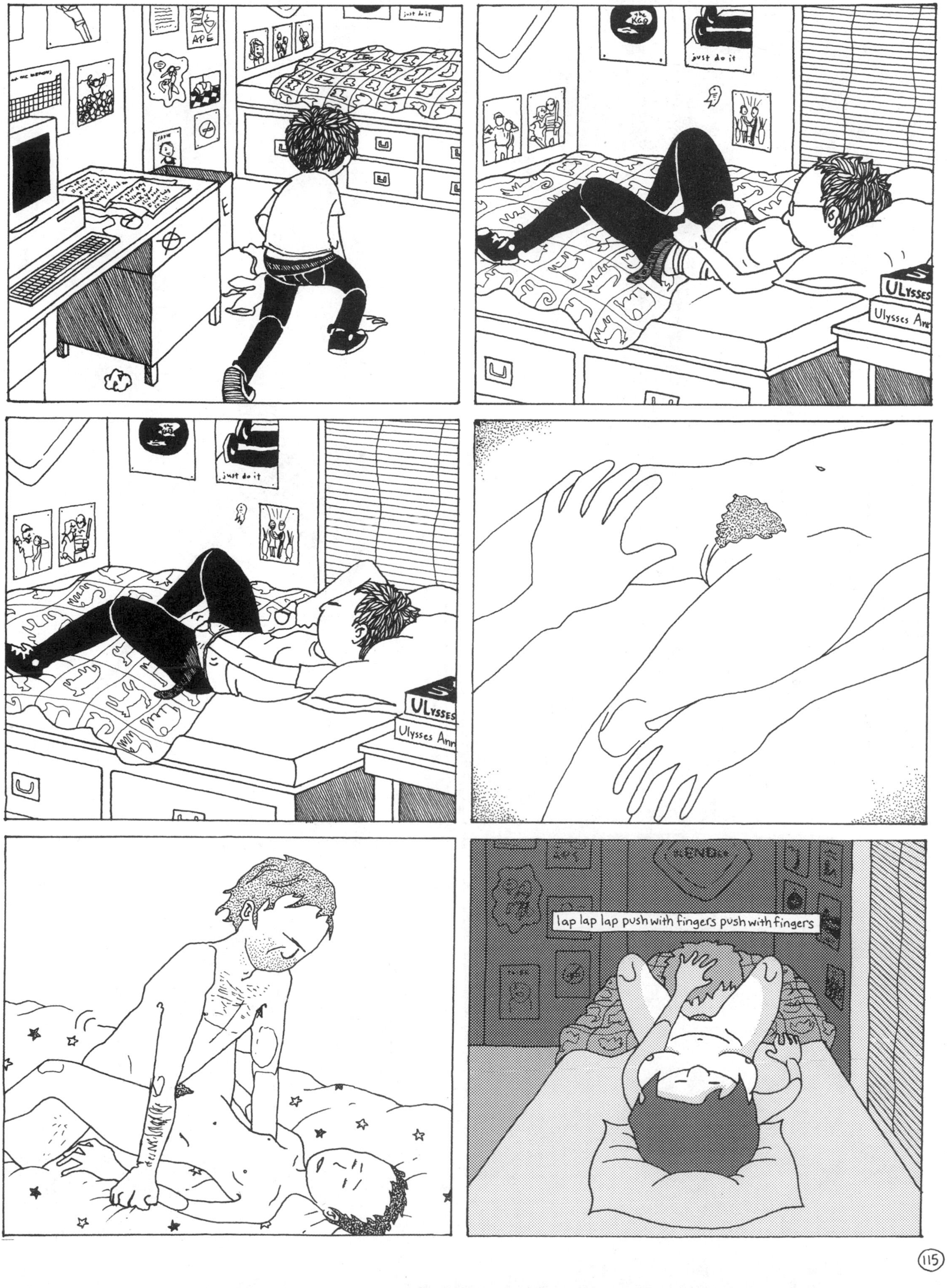
just do it
APE
ULYSSES
lap lap lap push with fingers push with fingers

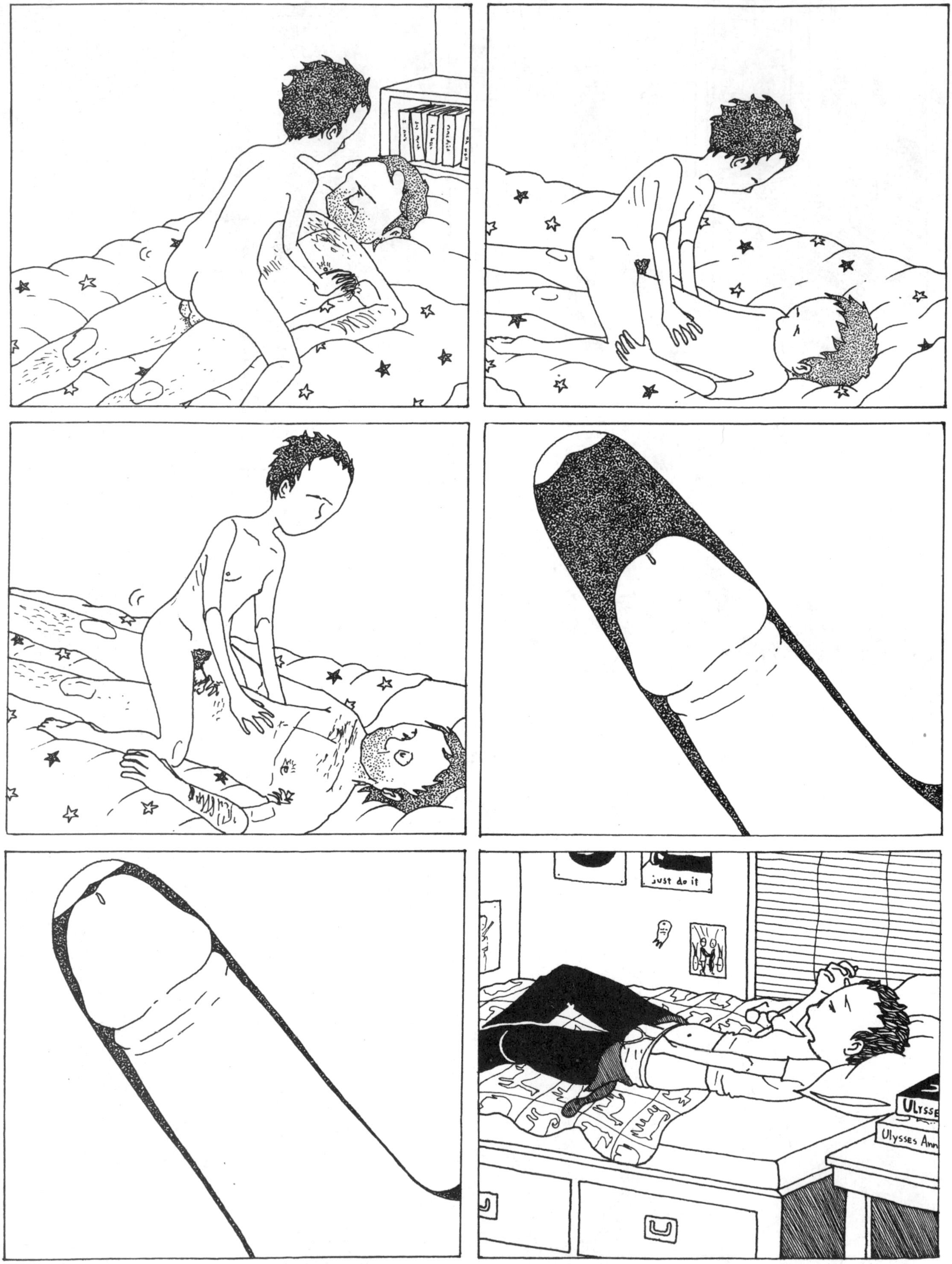
just do it
ULYSSE
Ulysses Ann

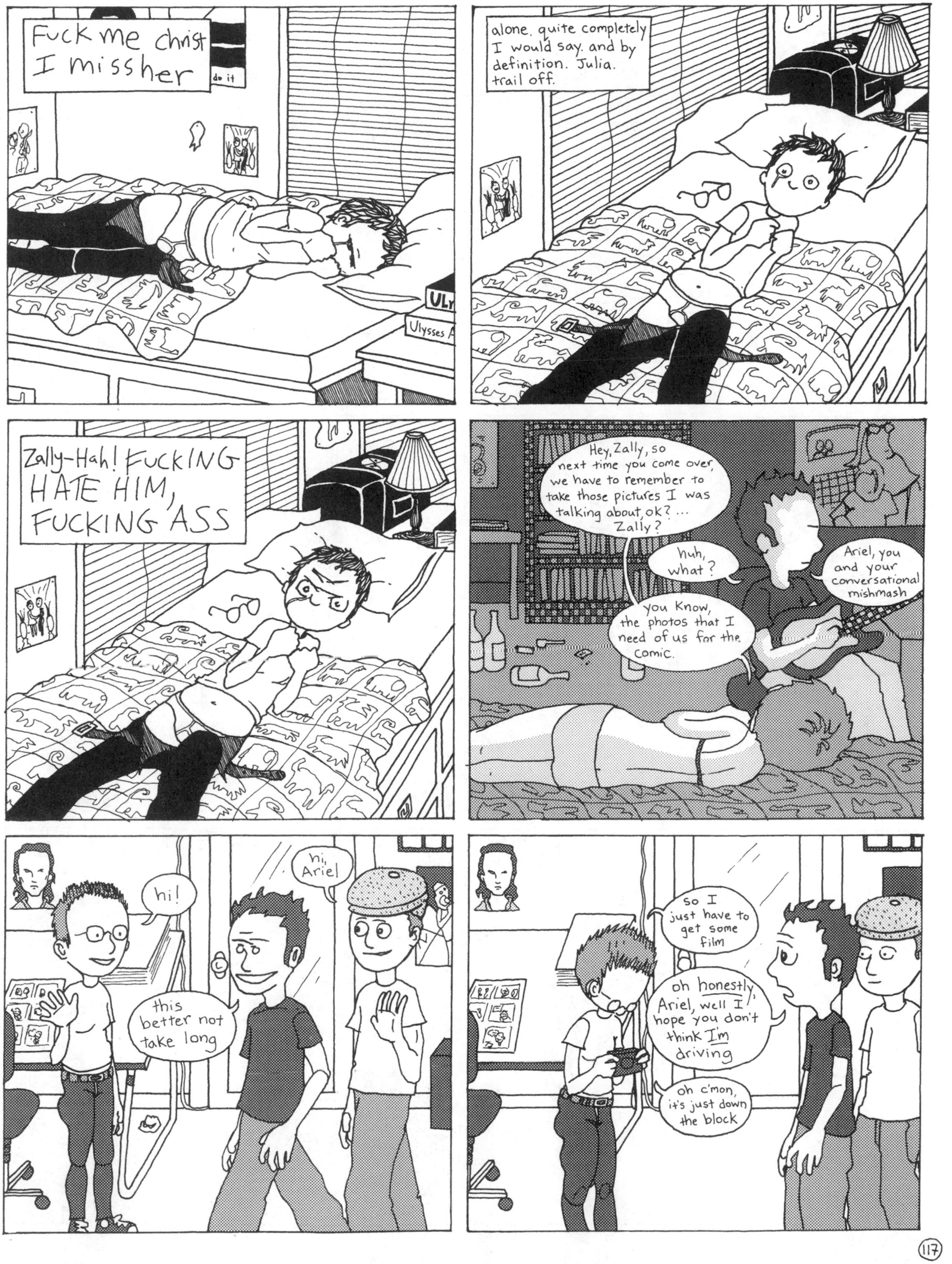
Fuck me christ I miss her
do it
Ulysses
alone. quite completely I would say. and by definition. Julia. trail off.
Zally-Hah! FUCKING HATE HIM, FUCKING ASS
Hey, Zally, so next time you come over, we have to remember to take those pictures I was talking about, ok? ... Zally?
huh, what?
Ariel, you and your conversational mishmash
you Know, the photos that I need of us for the comic.
hi!
hi, Ariel
this better not take long
so I just have to get some film
oh honestly, Ariel, well I hope you don't think I'm driving
oh c'mon, it's just down the block

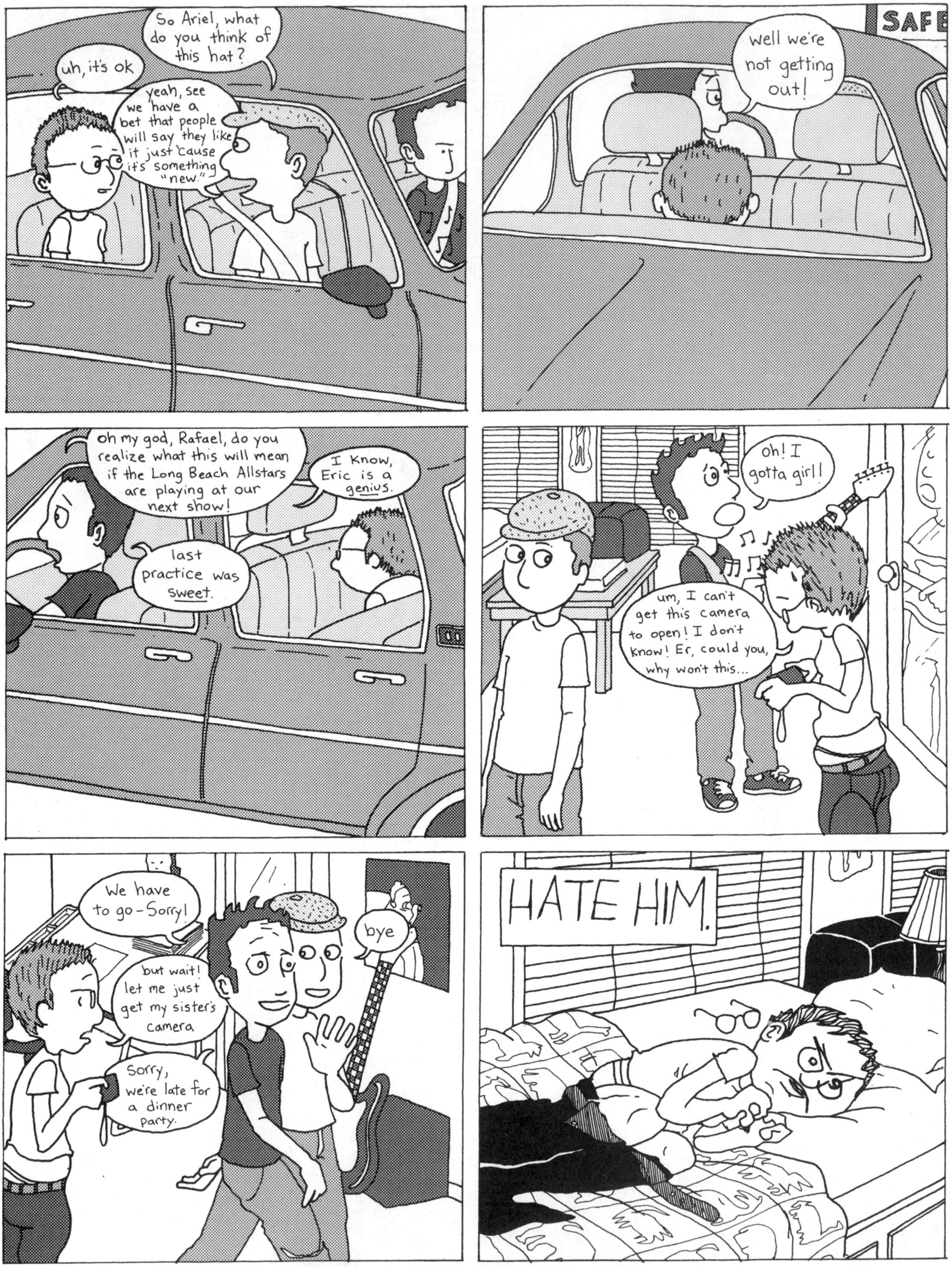

So Ariel, what do you think of this hat?
uh, it's ok
yeah, see we have a bet that people will say they like it just 'cause it's something "new."
well we're not getting out!
SAFE
oh my god, Rafael, do you realize what this will mean if the Long Beach Allstars are playing at our next show!
I know, Eric is a genius.
last practice was sweet.
oh! I gotta girl!
um, I can't get this camera to open! I don't know! Er, could you, why won't this...
We have to go - Sorry!
but wait! let me just get my sister's camera
Sorry, we're late for a dinner party.
bye
HATE HIM.

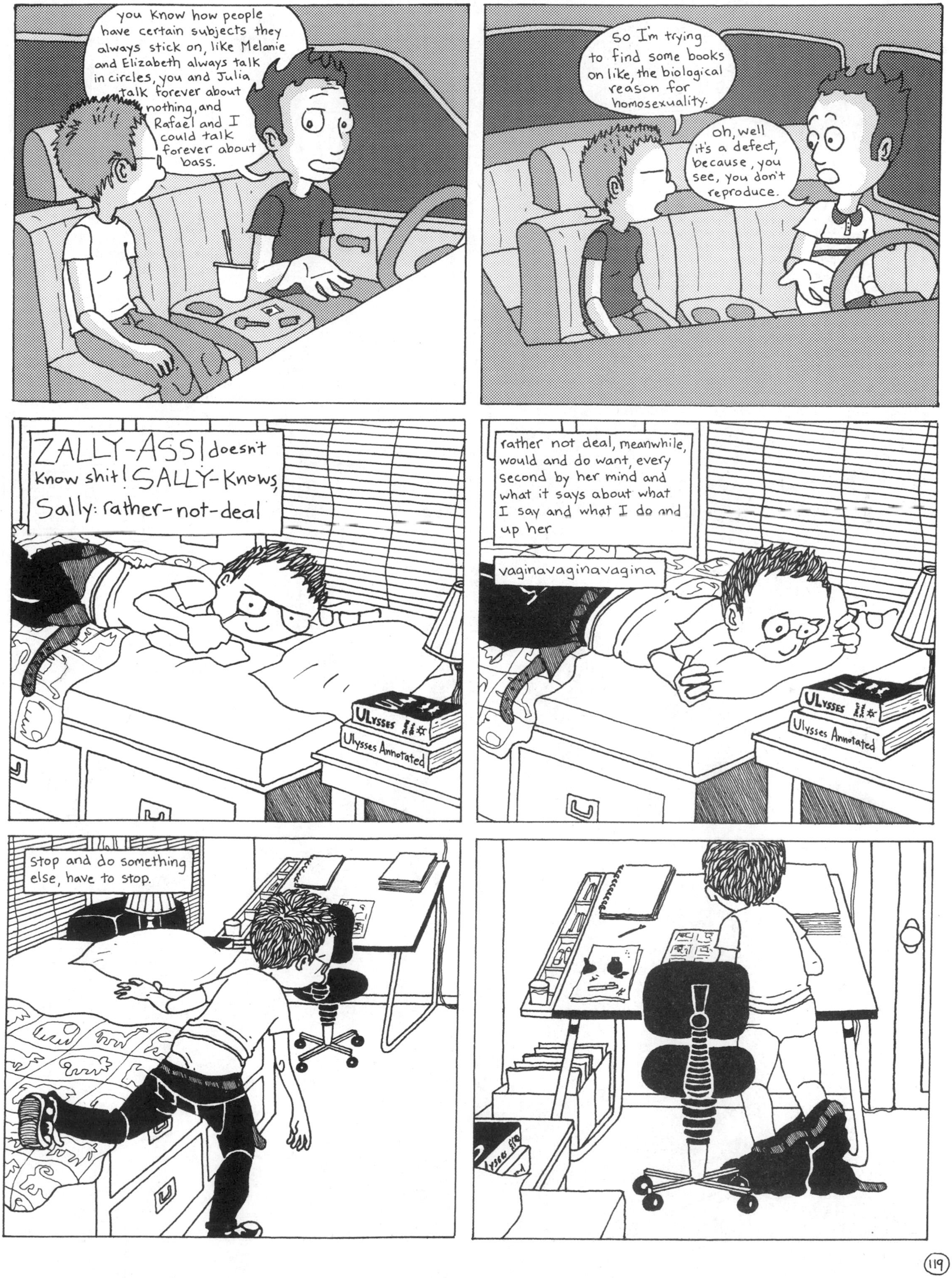
you know how people have certain subjects they always stick on, like Melanie and Elizabeth always talk in circles, you and Julia talk forever about nothing, and Rafael and I could talk forever about bass.
So I'm trying to find some books on like, the biological reason for homosexuality.
oh, well it's a defect, because, you see, you don't reproduce.
ZALLY-ASS I doesn't know shit! SALLY-Knows, Sally: rather-not-deal
Ulysses
Ulysses Annotated
rather not deal, meanwhile, would and do want, every second by her mind and what it says about what I say and what I do and up her
vaginavaginavagina
Ulysses
Ulysses Annotated
stop and do something else, have to stop.

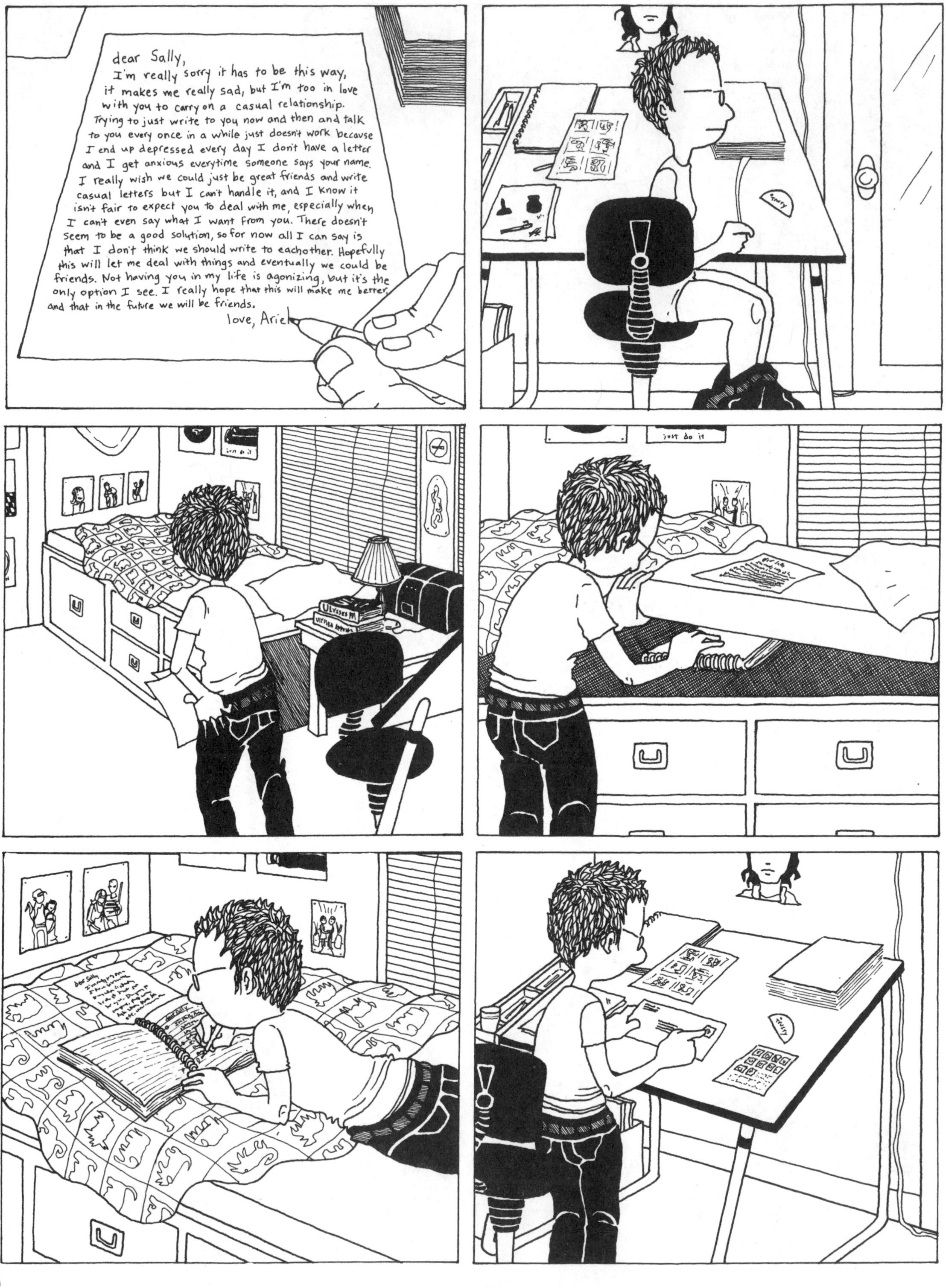
dear Sally,
I'm really sorry it has to be this way,
it makes me really sad, but I'm too in love
with you to carry on a casual relationship.
Trying to just write to you now and then and talk
to you every once in a while just doesn't work because
I end up depressed every day I don't have a letter
and I get anxious everytime someone says your name.
I really wish we could just be great friends and write
casual letters but I can't handle it, and I know it
isn't fair to expect you to deal with me, especially when
I can't even say what I want from you. There doesn't
seem to be a good solution, so for now all I can say is
that I don't think we should write to eachother. Hopefully
this will let me deal with things and eventually we could be
friends. Not having you in my life is agonizing, but it's the
only option I see. I really hope that this will make me better,
and that in the future we will be friends.
love, Ariel
just do it

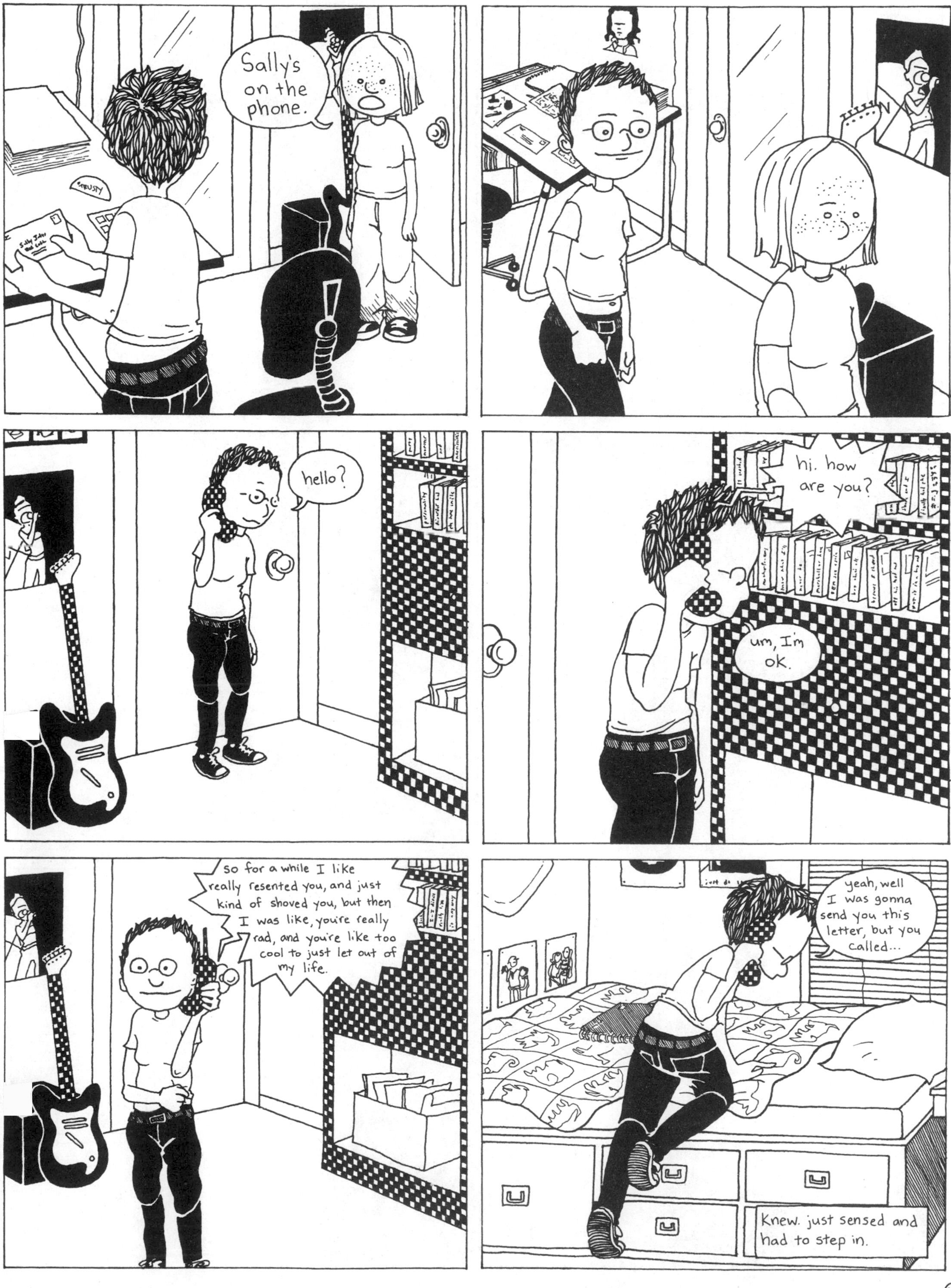

Sally's on the phone.
hello?
hi. how are you?
um, I'm ok.
so for a while I like really resented you, and just kind of shoved you, but then I was like, you're really rad, and you're like too cool to just let out of my life.
yeah, well I was gonna send you this letter, but you called...
Knew. just sensed and had to step in.

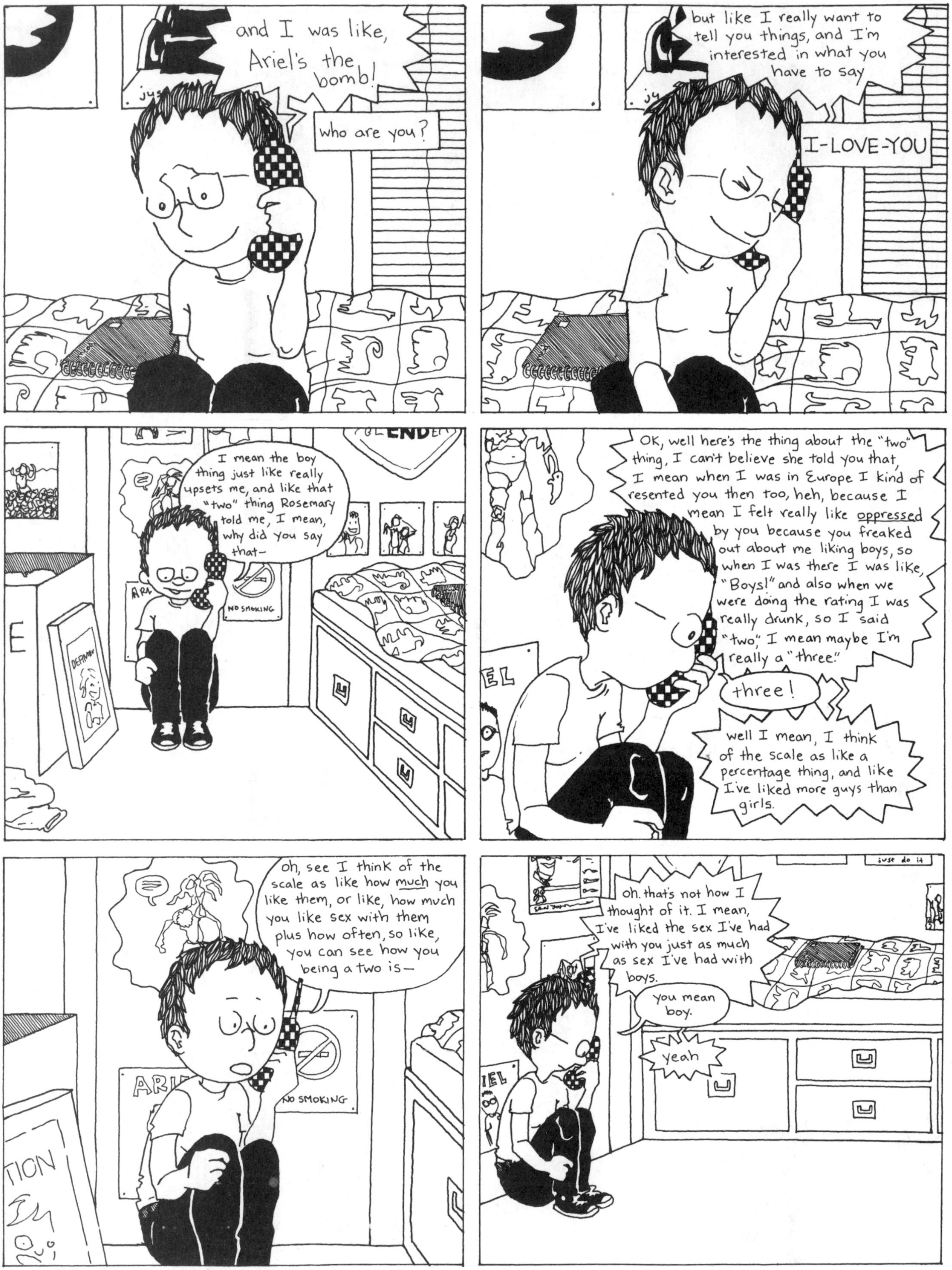
and I was like, Ariel's the bomb!
who are you?
but like I really want to tell you things, and I'm interested in what you have to say
I-LOVE-YOU
I mean the boy thing just like really upsets me, and like that "two" thing Rosemary told me, I mean, why did you say that—
NO SMOKING
OK, well here's the thing about the "two" thing, I can't believe she told you that, I mean when I was in Europe I kind of resented you then too, heh, because I mean I felt really like oppressed by you because you freaked out about me liking boys, so when I was there I was like, "Boys!" and also when we were doing the rating I was really drunk, so I said "two," I mean maybe I'm really a "three."
three!
well I mean, I think of the scale as like a percentage thing, and like I've liked more guys than girls.
oh, see I think of the scale as like how much you like them, or like, how much you like sex with them plus how often, so like, you can see how you being a two is—
NO SMOKING
just do it
oh. that's not how I thought of it. I mean, I've liked the sex I've had with you just as much as sex I've had with boys.
you mean boy.
yeah

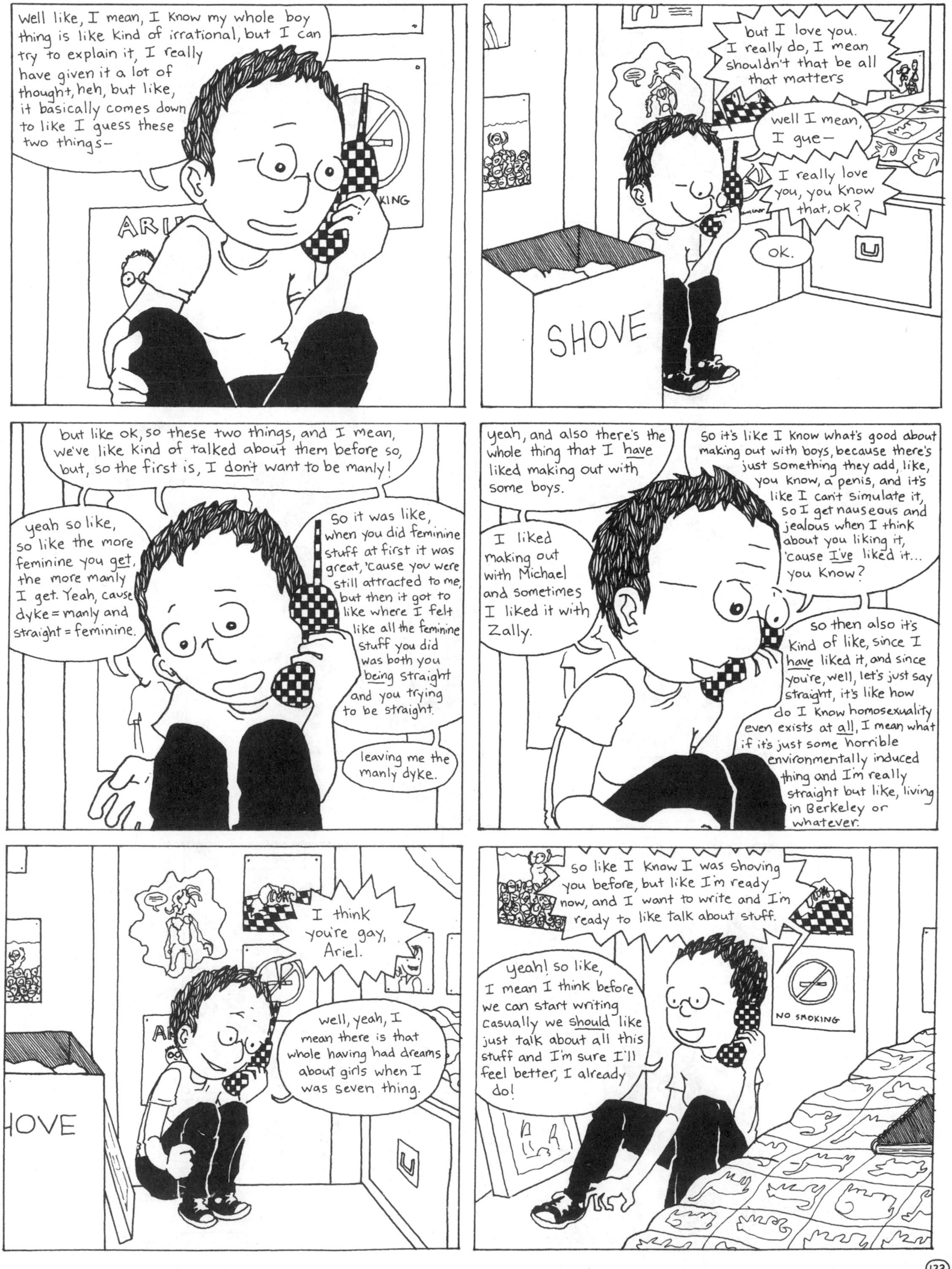

Well like, I mean, I know my whole boy thing is like kind of irrational, but I can try to explain it, I really have given it a lot of thought, heh, but like, it basically comes down to like I guess these two things—
but I love you. I really do, I mean shouldn't that be all that matters
well I mean, I gue—
I really love you, you know that, ok?
ok.
SHOVE
but like ok, so these two things, and I mean, we've like kind of talked about them before so, but, so the first is, I don't want to be manly!
yeah so like, so like the more feminine you get, the more manly I get. Yeah, cause dyke = manly and straight = feminine.
So it was like, when you did feminine stuff at first it was great, 'cause you were still attracted to me, but then it got to like where I felt like all the feminine stuff you did was both you being straight and you trying to be straight.
leaving me the manly dyke.
yeah, and also there's the whole thing that I have liked making out with some boys.
I liked making out with Michael and sometimes I liked it with Zally.
So it's like I know what's good about making out with boys, because there's just something they add, like, you know, a penis, and it's like I can't simulate it, so I get nauseous and jealous when I think about you liking it, 'cause I've liked it... you know?
so then also it's kind of like, since I have liked it, and since you're, well, let's just say straight, it's like how do I know homosexuality even exists at all, I mean what if it's just some horrible environmentally induced thing and I'm really straight but like, living in Berkeley or whatever.
I think you're gay, Ariel.
well, yeah, I mean there is that whole having had dreams about girls when I was seven thing.
HOVE
so like I know I was shoving you before, but like I'm ready now, and I want to write and I'm ready to like talk about stuff.
yeah! so like, I mean I think before we can start writing casually we should like just talk about all this stuff and I'm sure I'll feel better, I already do!
NO SMOKING

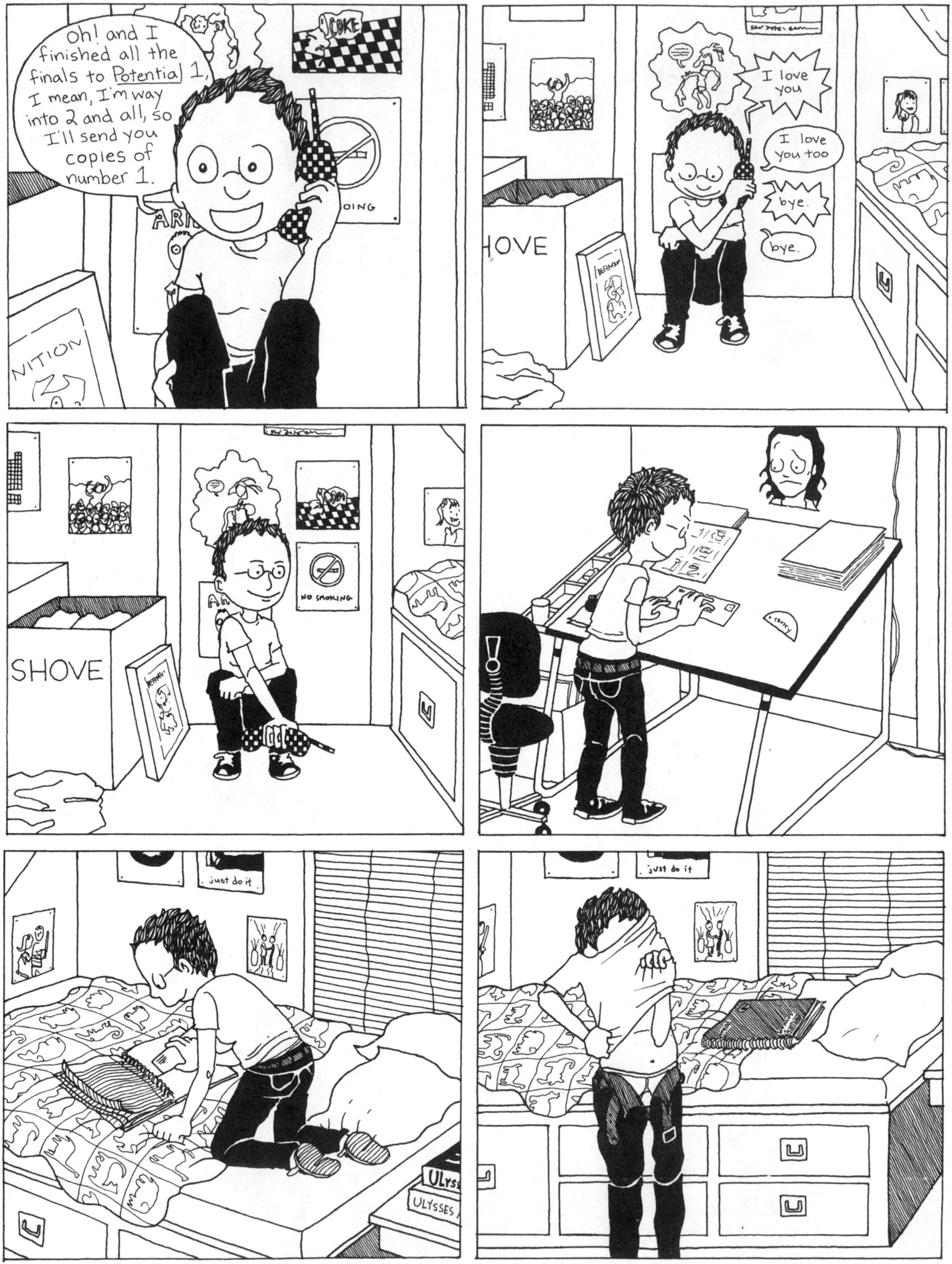
Oh! and I finished all the finals to Potential 1, I mean, I'm way into 2 and all, so I'll send you copies of number 1.
I love you
I love you too
bye.
bye.
SHOVE
NO SMOKING
just do it
ULYSSES

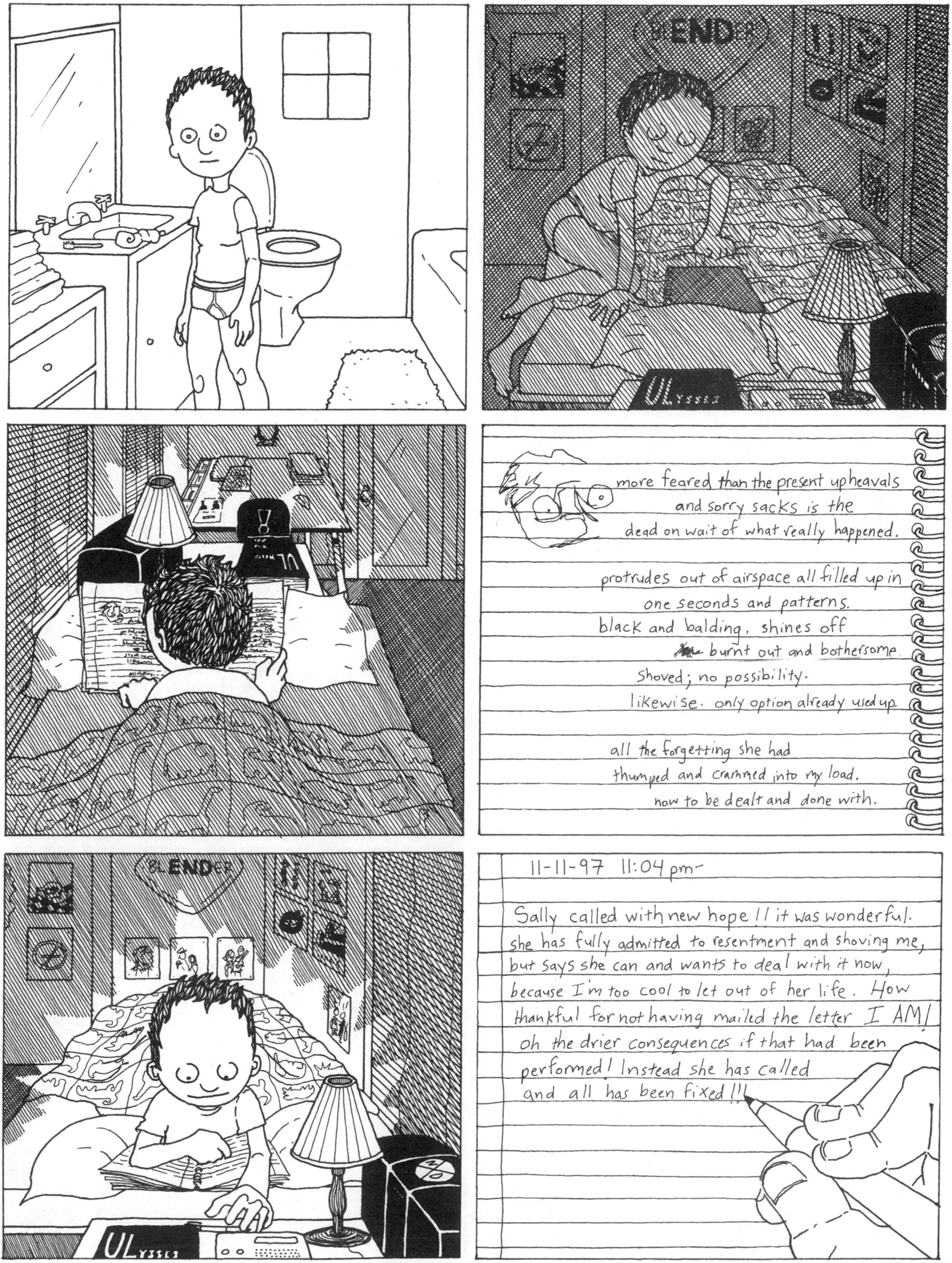
BLENDER
ULYSSES
more feared than the present upheavals
and sorry sacks is the
dead on wait of what really happened.
protrudes out of airspace all filled up in
one seconds and patterns.
black and balding, shines off
burnt out and bothersome
shoved; no possibility.
likewise. only option already used up.
all the forgetting she had
thumped and crammed into my load.
now to be dealt and done with.
BLENDER
ULYSSES
11-11-97 11:04 pm-
Sally called with new hope!! it was wonderful.
she has fully admitted to resentment and shoving me,
but says she can and wants to deal with it now,
because I'm too cool to let out of her life. How
thankful for not having mailed the letter I AM!
oh the drier consequences if that had been
performed! Instead she has called
and all has been fixed!!!

I AM SO OPTIMISTIC!
JOY PERVADES!!
she said she missed me and loved me so many times! "I love you" "I love you too". we talked of lesbianism!

we talked of lesbianism!
Oh hope for such a future!
I brought up the 2 issue and explained the homosexual fear, she understands - she knows I'll meet others and wants to be friends! we acknowledged how our relationship got bad in the beginning, but how there was always something there. true, I liked her more towards the end, but we her open so joyous! we will write!
I AM FREE!!
so happy!!

a solace no greater than my out weight crater of cavernous joy comes floods in splashes round. for as I am penning my futures relenting has ceased, halted, stopped now I'm free for all cries. Alone, still, still eager, with no outlets

of lesbianist
Oh hope for s
I brought up t
explained the h
fear, she understar
others and wants t
acknowledged how
got bad in the b
vas always somethi
true, I liked her
the end, but we
so joyous! h
I AM F
so h

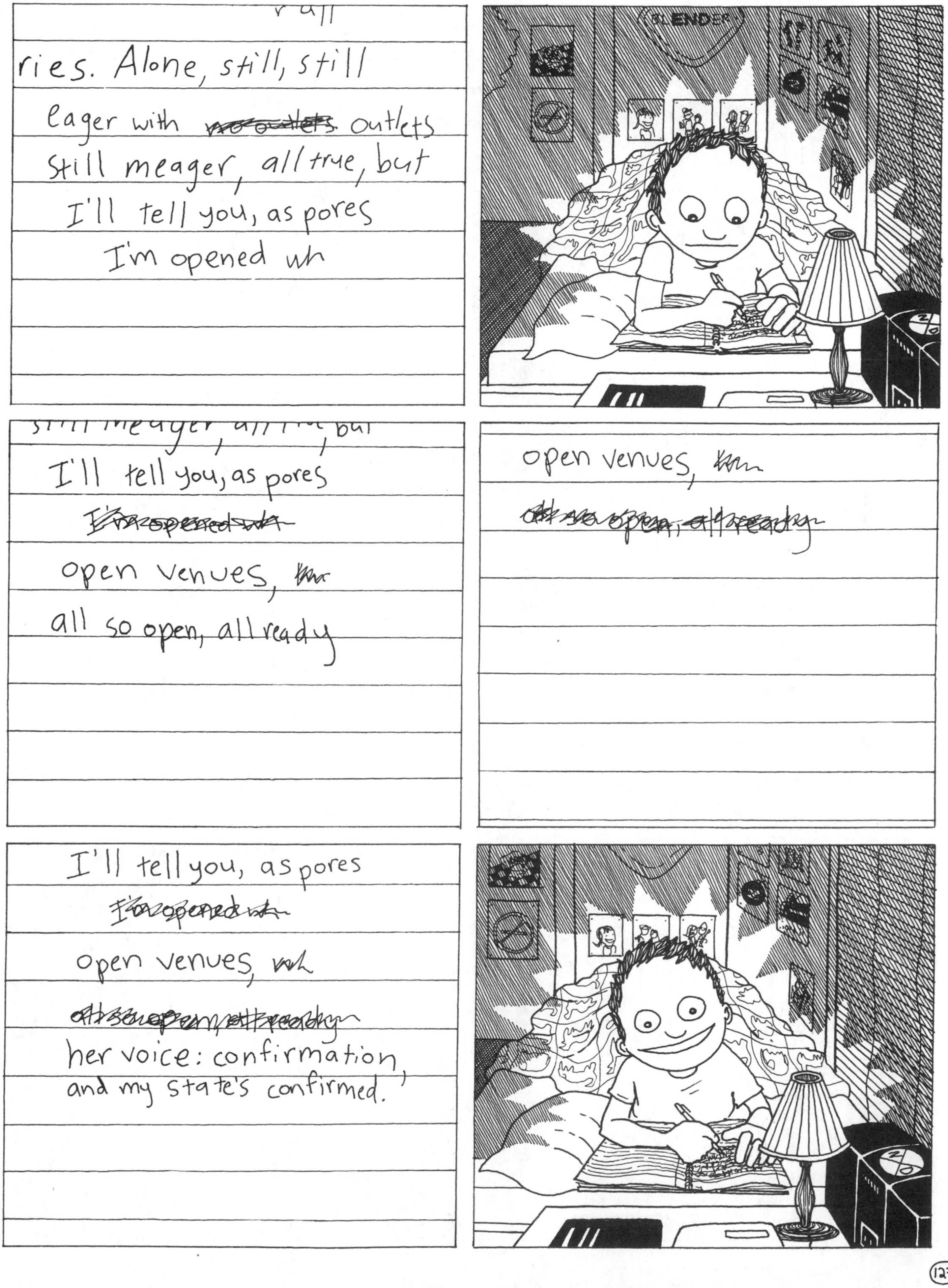

ri.es. Alone, still, still
eager with ~~no outlets.~~ outlets.
Still meager, all true, but
I'll tell you, as pores
I'm opened uh

~~still meager, all true, but~~
I'll tell you, as pores
~~I'm opened uh~~
open venues, ~~km~~
all so open, allready

open venues, ~~km~~
~~all so open, allready~~

I'll tell you, as pores
~~I'm opened uh~~
open venues, uh
~~all so open, allready~~
her voice: confirmation,
and my state's confirmed.

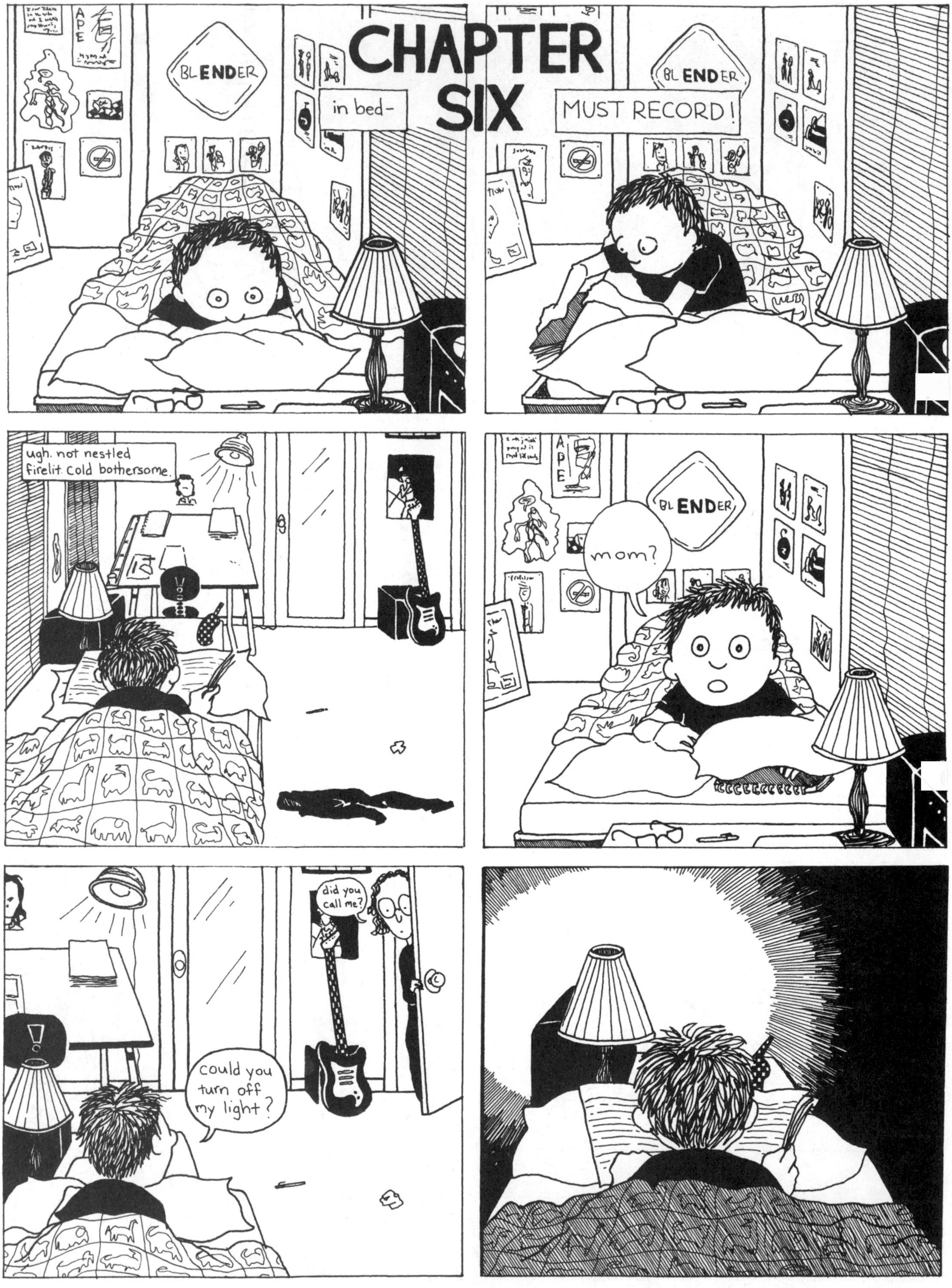
CHAPTER SIX
in bed-
MUST RECORD!
ugh. not nestled firelit. Cold bothersome.
mom?
did you call me?
could you turn off my light?

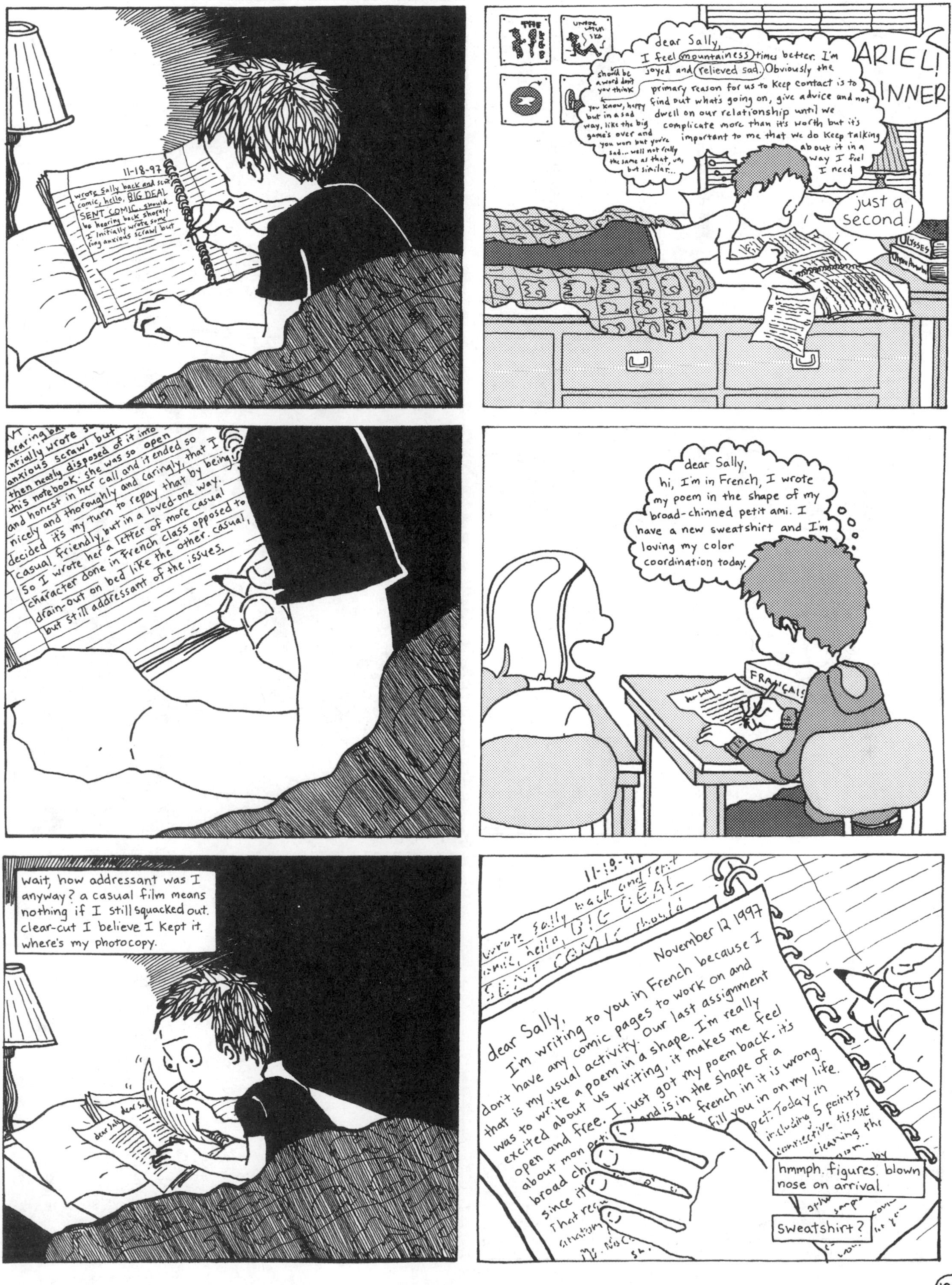
11-18-97
wrote Sally back and sent comic, hello, BIG DEAL SENT COMIC. should be hearing back shortly. I initially wrote some long anxious scrawl but
dear Sally,
I feel mountainess times better. I'm joyed and relieved sad. Obviously the primary reason for us to keep contact is to find out what's going on, give advice and not dwell on our relationship until we complicate more than it's worth but it's important to me that we do keep talking about it in a way I feel I need
should be a word don't you think
you know, happy but in a sad way, like the big game's over and you won but you're sad... well not really the same as that, um, but similar...
ARIEL! DINNER
just a second!
ULYSSES
initially wrote some anxious scrawl but then neatly disposed of it into this notebook. she was so open and honest in her call and it ended so nicely and thoroughly and caringly, that I decided it's my turn to repay that by being casual friendly, but in a loved-one way. So I wrote her a letter of more casual character done in French class opposed to drain-out on bed like the other. casual, but still addressant of the issues.
dear Sally,
hi, I'm in French, I wrote my poem in the shape of my broad-chinned petit ami. I have a new sweatshirt and I'm loving my color coordination today.
FRANÇAIS
wait, how addressant was I anyway? a casual film means nothing if I still squacked out. clear-cut I believe I kept it. where's my photocopy.
November 12 1997
dear Sally,
I'm writing to you in French because I don't have any comic pages to work on and that is my usual activity. Our last assignment was to write a poem in a shape. I'm really excited about us writing, it makes me feel open and free. I just got my poem back. it's
hmmph. figures. blown nose on arrival.
sweatshirt?

11-18-97
#2
tell me more about your college friends. what are Alexis and Leo like? I got a message from Berlyn. It depressed me, but in a way made me happy. Because if I used to get all excited and thrilled about a friendship with someone like her then I must have made considerable progress. unless one is swayed by the ignorance-is-bliss factor. but no, I am happy.
I can't believe I have to go through another semester of this. I can't believe how depressing my next comic is going to be.
cheap shot for humor. doesn't have to mean anything. Sally pardoned.
#3
that said I'll move on to the issue of seeing you- seeing you is difficult because (yes, this is going to be very boyish) I can't not think about wanting to have sex with you. Here in my numb state I get along alright, but seeing you is like cracking the ice off a frostbitten finger but not giving the blood a chance to flow back. very painful.
total squacking!
I'm cool.
I got my grades and they were A's and a C in French. I attribute this to my. lack of a girlfriend - more time to study, but no one to parler la langue de l'amour avec.
Well worded that one was.
I'm going with Amy to look for her prom dress. I'm only going to the prom if I have a girlfriend that really wants to go.
#4
#2
#3
hee. Christ, gotta get back to business.
11-18-97
this whole thing has made me abominably selfish. The publisher thing only bolstered and I am annoying. I've got to change. It's weird that last year I was all freaked and earnest about studying and SATs and being skinn
NOT-THAT-DIFFICULT STAY-ON-TRACK
4.0 SKINNY

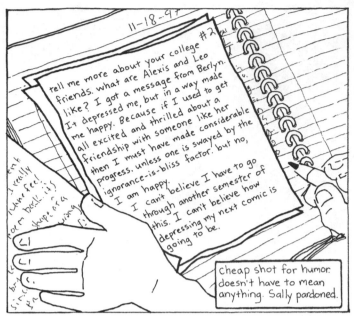

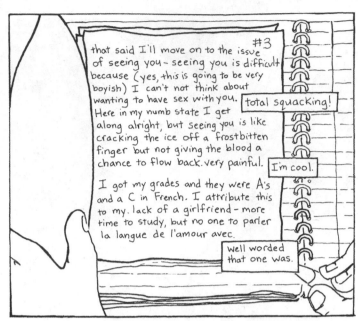

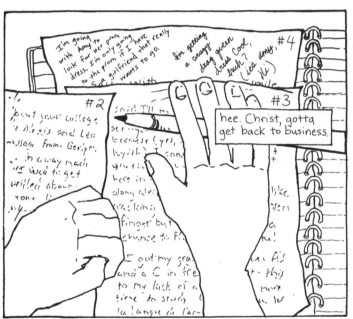

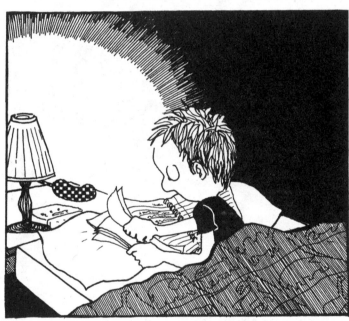

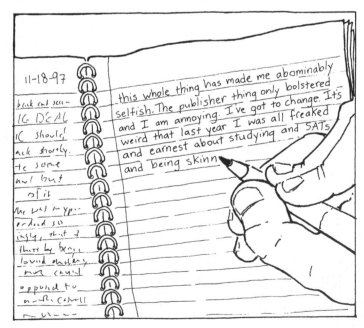

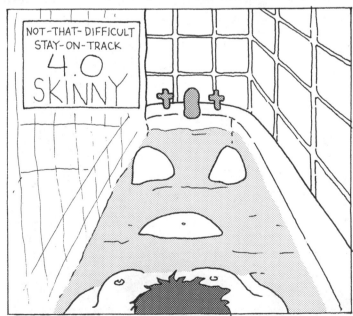

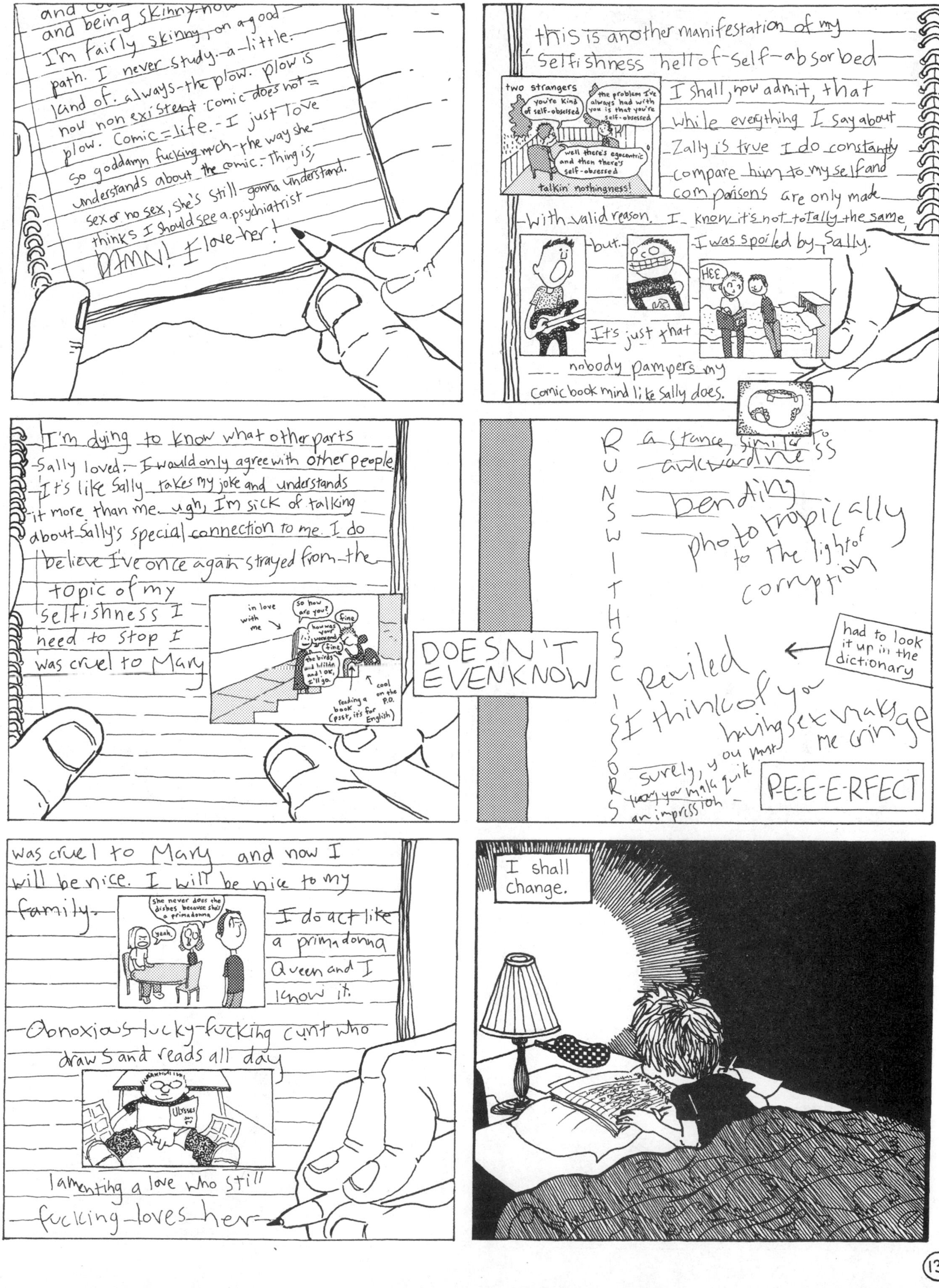

and being skinny now I'm fairly skinny, on a good path. I never study a little. kind of. always-the plow. plow is now non existent comic does not = plow. Comic = life. - I just love so goddamn fucking much the way she understands about the comic. thing is, sex or no sex, she's still gonna understand. thinks I should see a psychiatrist
DAMN! I love her!
this is another manifestation of my selfishness hell of self-absorbed
two strangers
you're kind of self-obsessed
the problem I've always had with you is that you're self-obsessed
well there's egocentric and then there's self-obsessed
talkin nothingness!
I shall, now admit, that while everything I say about Zally is true I do constantly compare him to myself and comparisons are only made with valid reason. I know it's not totally the same, but. I was spoiled by Sally.
HEE.
It's just that nobody pampers my comic book mind like Sally does.
I'm dying to know what other parts Sally loved. I would only agree with other people. It's like Sally takes my joke and understands it more than me. ugh, I'm sick of talking about Sally's special connection to me. I do believe I've once again strayed from the topic of my selfishness I need to stop I was cruel to Mary
in love with me
so how are you?
fine
how was your weekend
fine
the birds and I ok, I'll go.
cool on the P.O.
reading a book (psst, it's for English)
DOESN'T EVEN KNOW
RUN WITH SCISSORS
a stance, similar to awkwardness
bending phototropically to the light of corruption
had to look it up in the dictionary
Reviled
I think of you having sex makes me cringe
surely, you must make quite an impression
P-E-E-E-RFECT
was cruel to Mary and now I will be nice. I will be nice to my family.
she never does the dishes because she's a primadonna
yeah.
I do act like a prima donna Queen and I know it.
Obnoxious lucky fucking cunt who draws and reads all day
Ulysses
lamenting a love who still fucking loves her
I shall change.

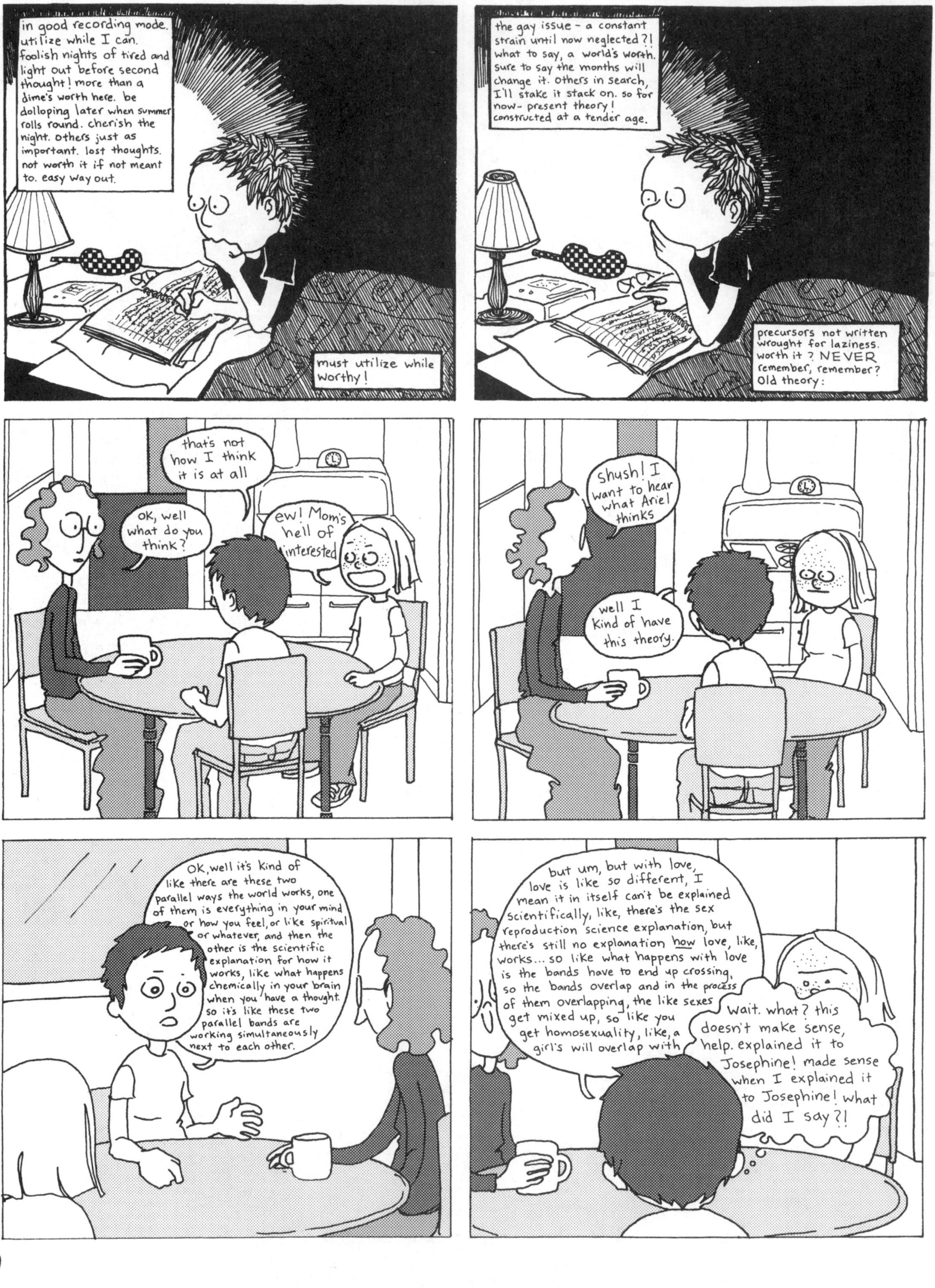

in good recording mode. utilize while I can. foolish nights of tired and light out before second thought! more than a dime's worth here. be dolloping later when summer rolls round. cherish the night. others just as important. lost thoughts. not worth it if not meant to. easy way out.
must utilize while worthy!
the gay issue - a constant strain until now neglected?! what to say, a world's worth. sure to say the months will change it. others in search, I'll stake it stack on. so for now- present theory! constructed at a tender age.
precursors not written wrought for laziness. worth it? NEVER remember, remember? Old theory:
that's not how I think it is at all
OK, well what do you think?
ew! Mom's hell of interested
shush! I want to hear what Ariel thinks
well I kind of have this theory.
OK, well it's kind of like there are these two parallel ways the world works, one of them is everything in your mind or how you feel, or like spiritual or whatever, and then the other is the scientific explanation for how it works, like what happens chemically in your brain when you have a thought. so it's like these two parallel bands are working simultaneously next to each other.
but um, but with love, love is like so different, I mean it in itself can't be explained scientifically, like, there's the sex reproduction science explanation, but there's still no explanation how love, like, works... so like what happens with love is the bands have to end up crossing, so the bands overlap and in the process of them overlapping, the like sexes get mixed up, so like you get homosexuality, like, a girl's will overlap with
Wait. what? this doesn't make sense, help. explained it to Josephine! made sense when I explained it to Josephine! what did I say?!

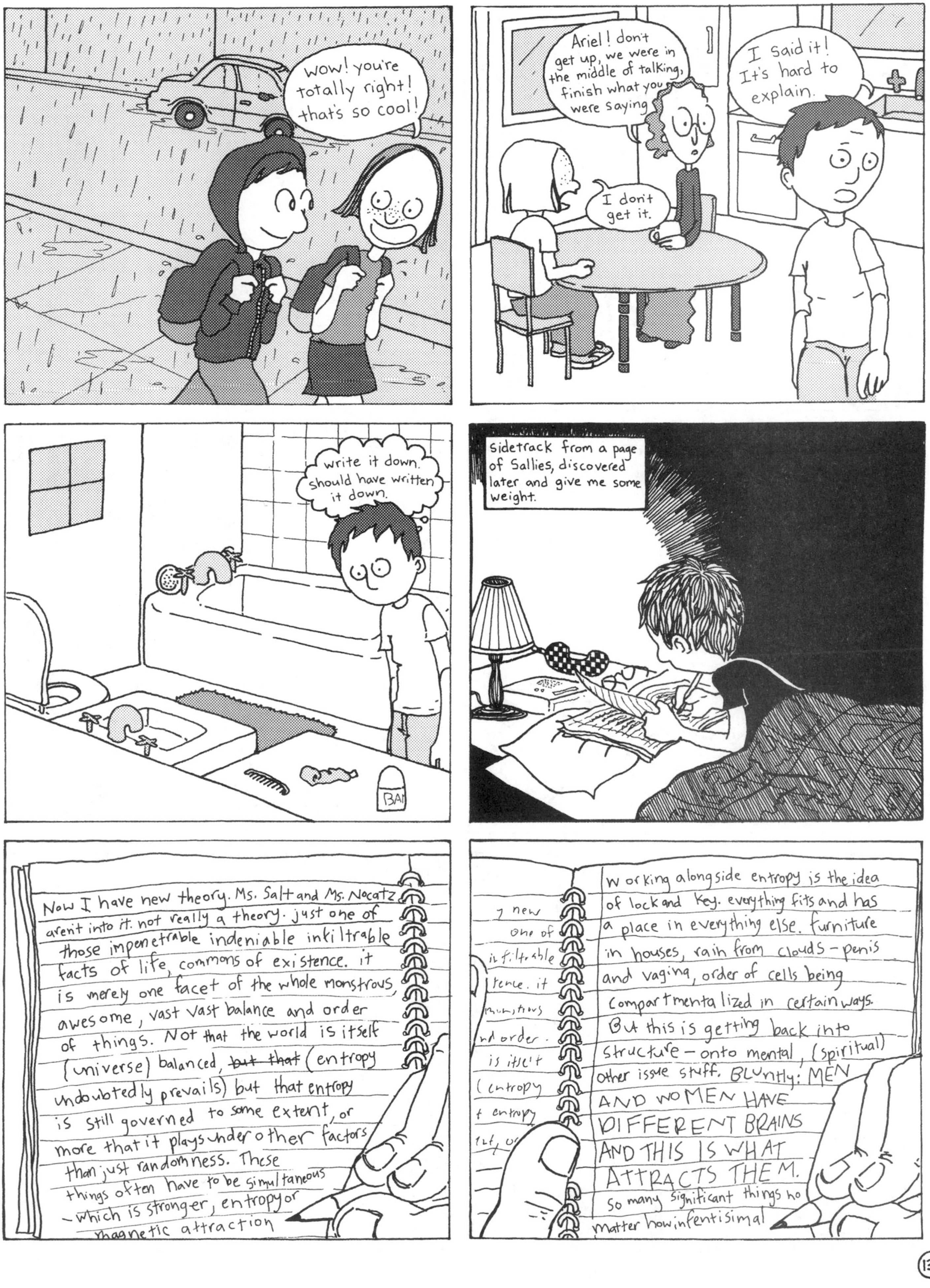
wow! you're totally right! that's so cool!
Ariel! don't get up, we were in the middle of talking, finish what you were saying
I don't get it.
I said it! It's hard to explain.
write it down. should have written it down.
BA
Sidetrack from a page of Sallies, discovered later and give me some weight.
Now I have new theory. Ms. Salt and Ms. Nocatz aren't into it. not really a theory. just one of those impenetrable indeniable infiltrable facts of life, commons of existence. it is merely one facet of the whole monstrous, awesome, vast vast balance and order of things. Not that the world is itself (universe) balanced, ~~but that~~ (entropy undoubtedly prevails) but that entropy is still governed to some extent, or more that it plays under other factors than just randomness. These things often have to be simultaneous - which is stronger, entropy or magnetic attraction
working alongside entropy is the idea of lock and key. everything fits and has a place in everything else. furniture in houses, rain from clouds - penis and vagina, order of cells being compartmentalized in certain ways. But this is getting back into structure - onto mental, (spiritual) other issue stuff. BLUntly: MEN AND WOMEN HAVE DIFFERENT BRAINS AND THIS IS WHAT ATTRACTS THEM. So many significant things no matter how infentisimal

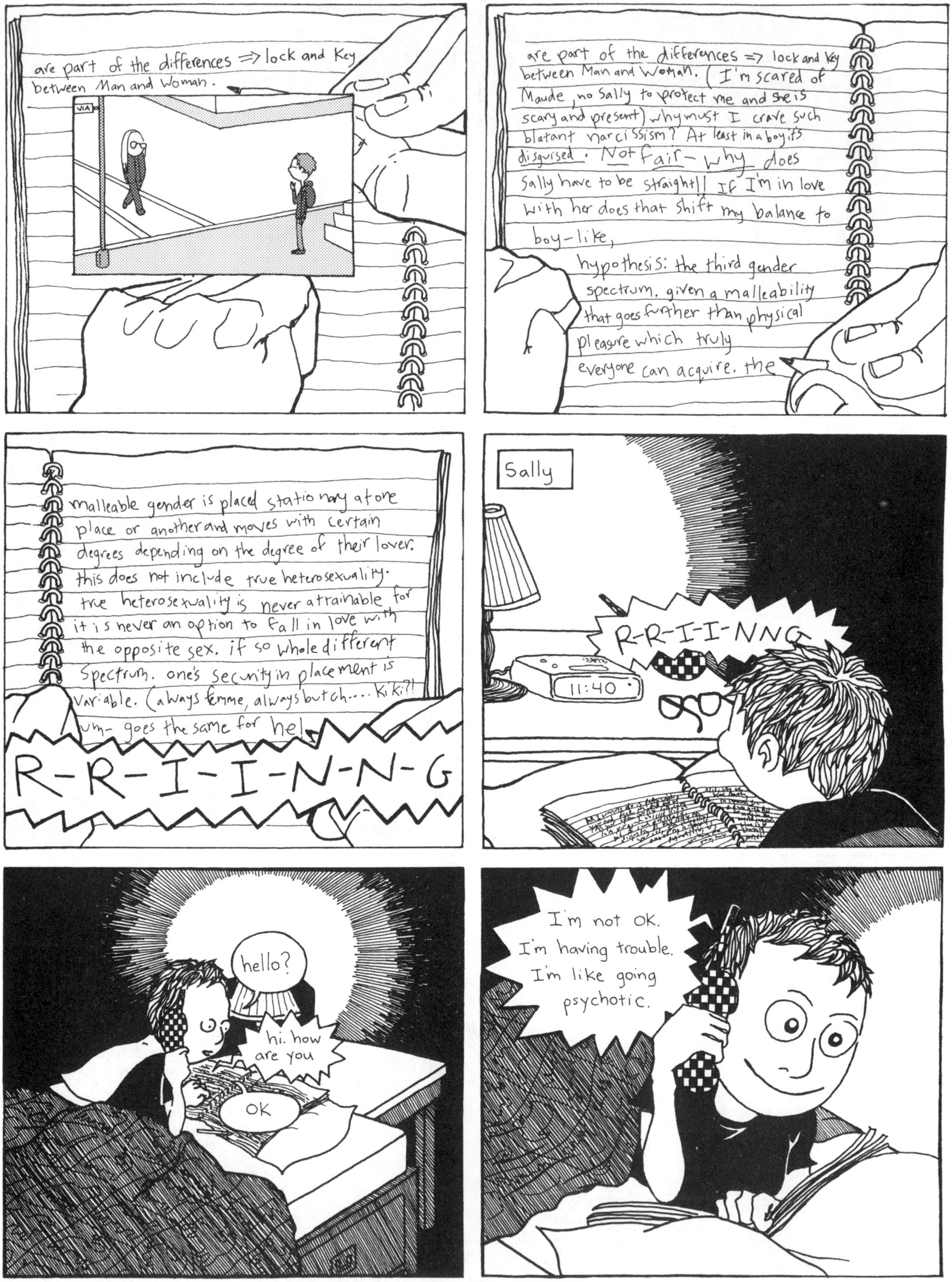
are part of the differences => lock and Key
between Man and Woman.
VIA
are part of the differences => lock and Key
between Man and Woman. (I'm scared of
Maude, no Sally to protect me and she is
scary and present) why must I crave such
blatant narcissism? At least in a boy it's
disguised. Not fair - why does
Sally have to be straight!! If I'm in love
with her does that shift my balance to
boy-like,
hypothesis: the third gender
spectrum. given a malleability
that goes further than physical
pleasure which truly
everyone can acquire. the
malleable gender is placed stationary at one
place or another and moves with certain
degrees depending on the degree of their lover.
this does not include true heterosexuality.
true heterosexuality is never attrainable for
it is never an option to fall in love with
the opposite sex. if so whole different
Spectrum. one's security in placement is
variable. (always femme, always butch.... kiki?!
um- goes the same for he!
R-R-I-I-N-N-G
Sally
R-R-I-I-NNG
11:40
hello?
hi. how are you
OK
I'm not OK.
I'm having trouble.
I'm like going
psychotic.

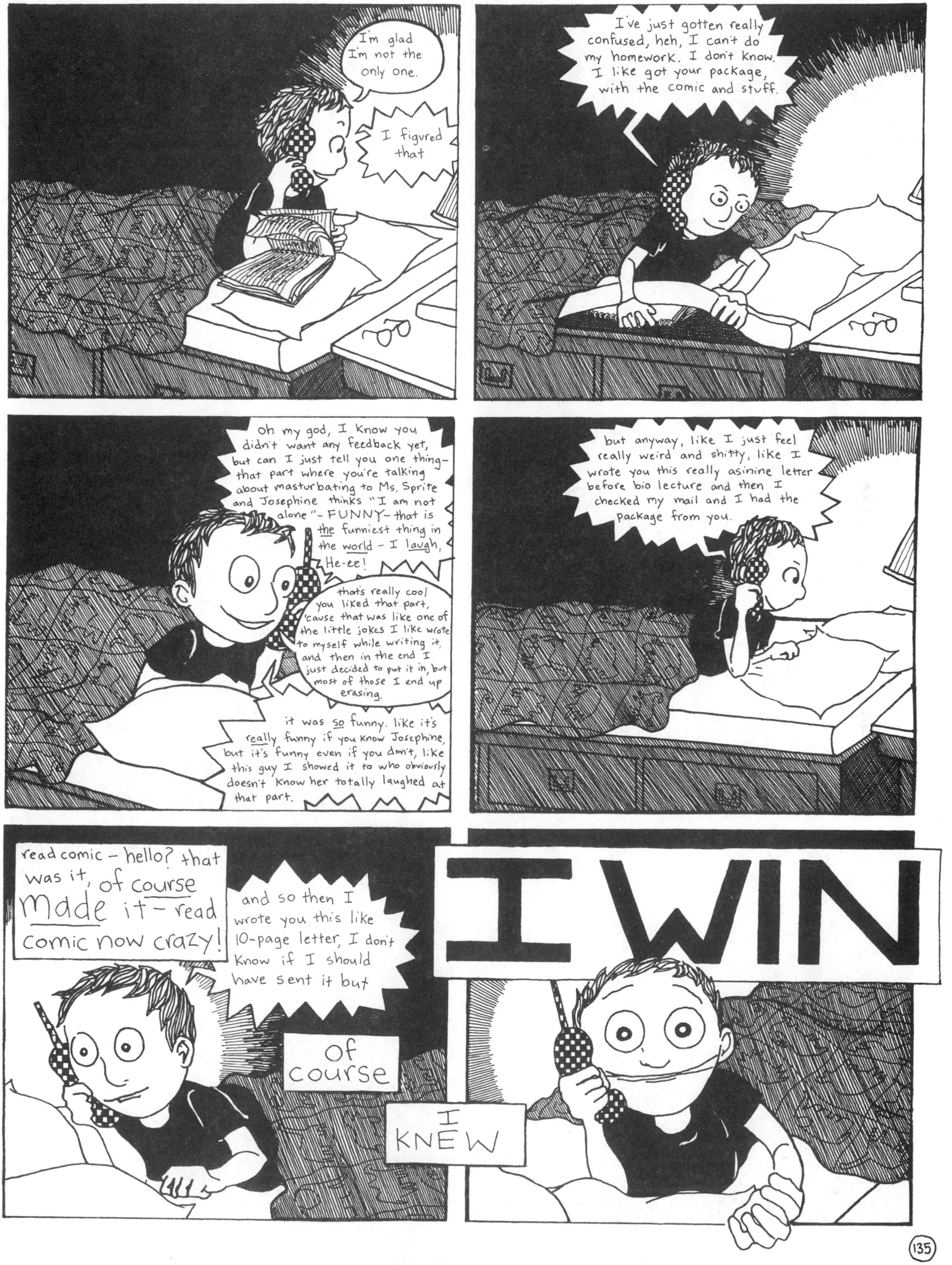
I'm glad I'm not the only one.
I figured that
I've just gotten really confused, heh, I can't do my homework. I don't know. I like got your package, with the comic and stuff.
oh my god, I know you didn't want any feedback yet, but can I just tell you one thing- that part where you're talking about masturbating to Ms. Sprite and Josephine thinks "I am not alone" - FUNNY - that is the funniest thing in the world - I laugh, He-ee!
that's really cool you liked that part, 'cause that was like one of the little jokes I like wrote to myself while writing it, and then in the end I just decided to put it in, but most of those I end up erasing.
it was so funny. like it's really funny if you know Josephine, but it's funny even if you don't, like this guy I showed it to who obviously doesn't know her totally laughed at that part.
but anyway, like I just feel really weird and shitty, like I wrote you this really asinine letter before bio lecture and then I checked my mail and I had the package from you.
read comic - hello? that was it, of course made it - read comic now crazy!
and so then I wrote you this like 10-page letter, I don't know if I should have sent it but
of course
I KNEW
I WIN

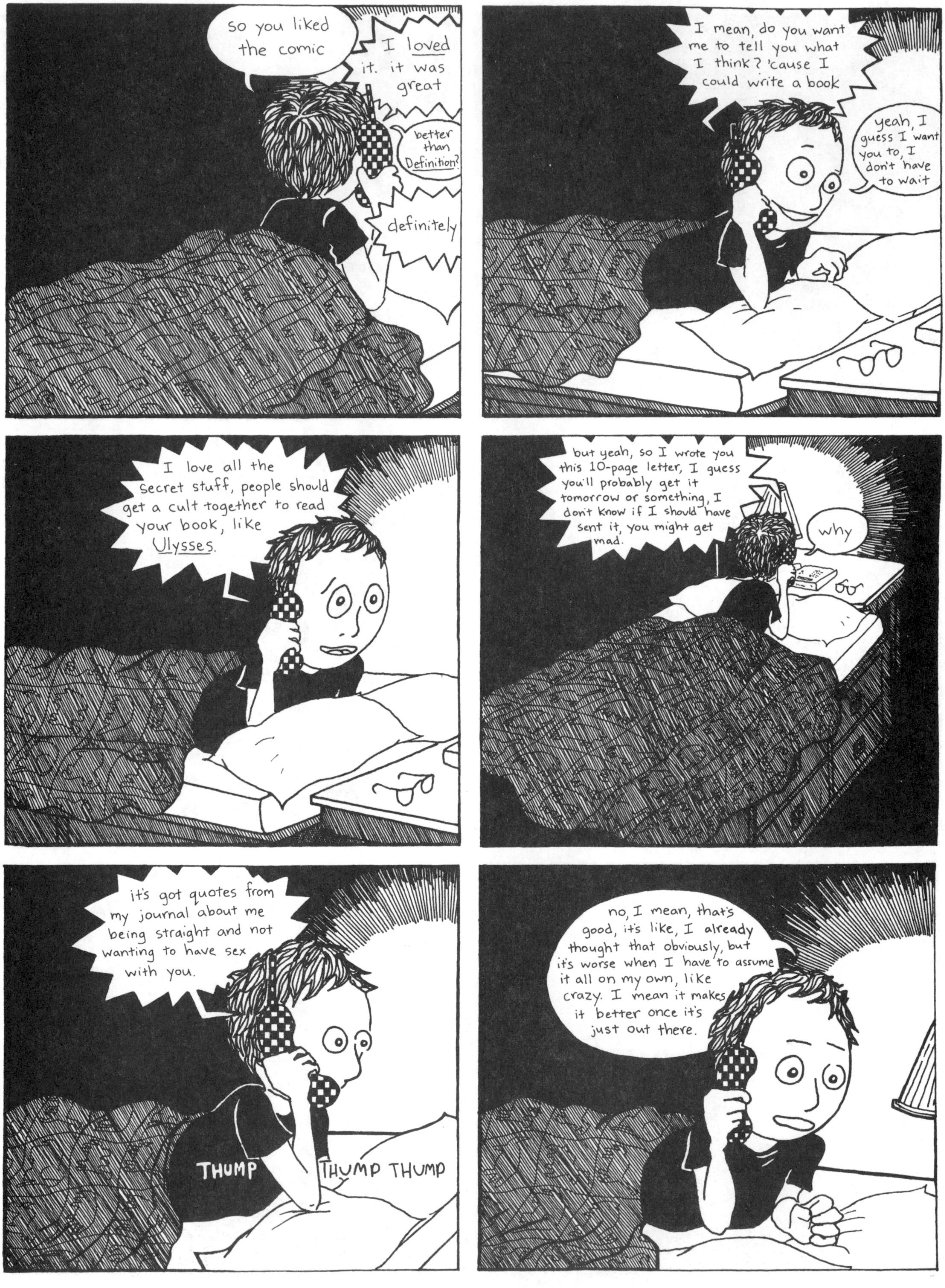
so you liked the comic
I loved it. it was great
better than Definition?
definitely
I mean, do you want me to tell you what I think? 'cause I could write a book
yeah, I guess I want you to, I don't have to wait
I love all the secret stuff, people should get a cult together to read your book, like Ulysses.
but yeah, so I wrote you this 10-page letter, I guess you'll probably get it tomorrow or something, I don't know if I should have sent it, you might get mad.
why
it's got quotes from my journal about me being straight and not wanting to have sex with you.
THUMP THUMP THUMP
no, I mean, that's good, it's like, I already thought that obviously, but it's worse when I have to assume it all on my own, like crazy. I mean it makes it better once it's just out there.

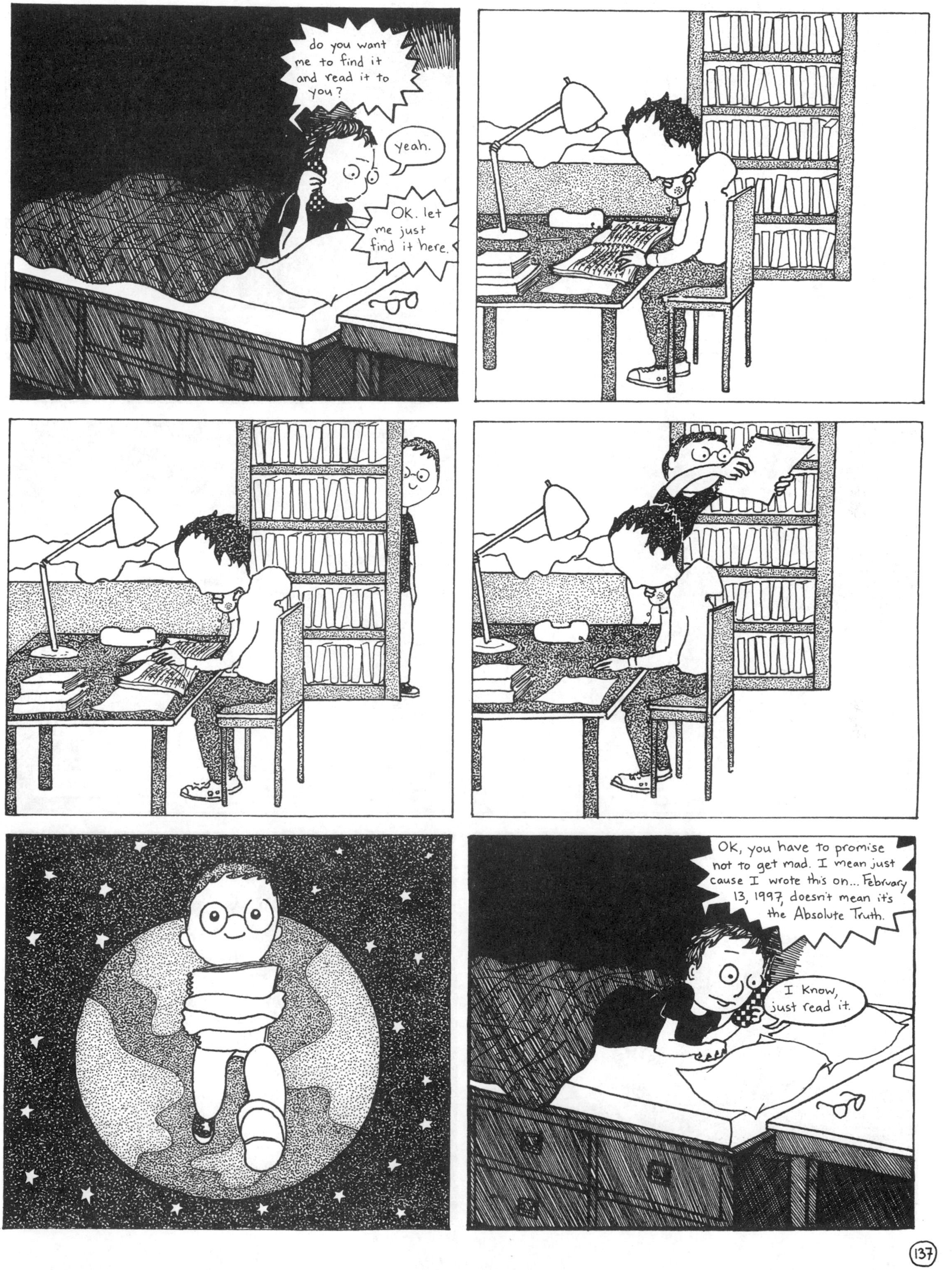

do you want me to find it and read it to you?
yeah.
OK. let me just find it here.
OK, you have to promise not to get mad. I mean just cause I wrote this on... February 13, 1997, doesn't mean it's the Absolute Truth.
I know, just read it.

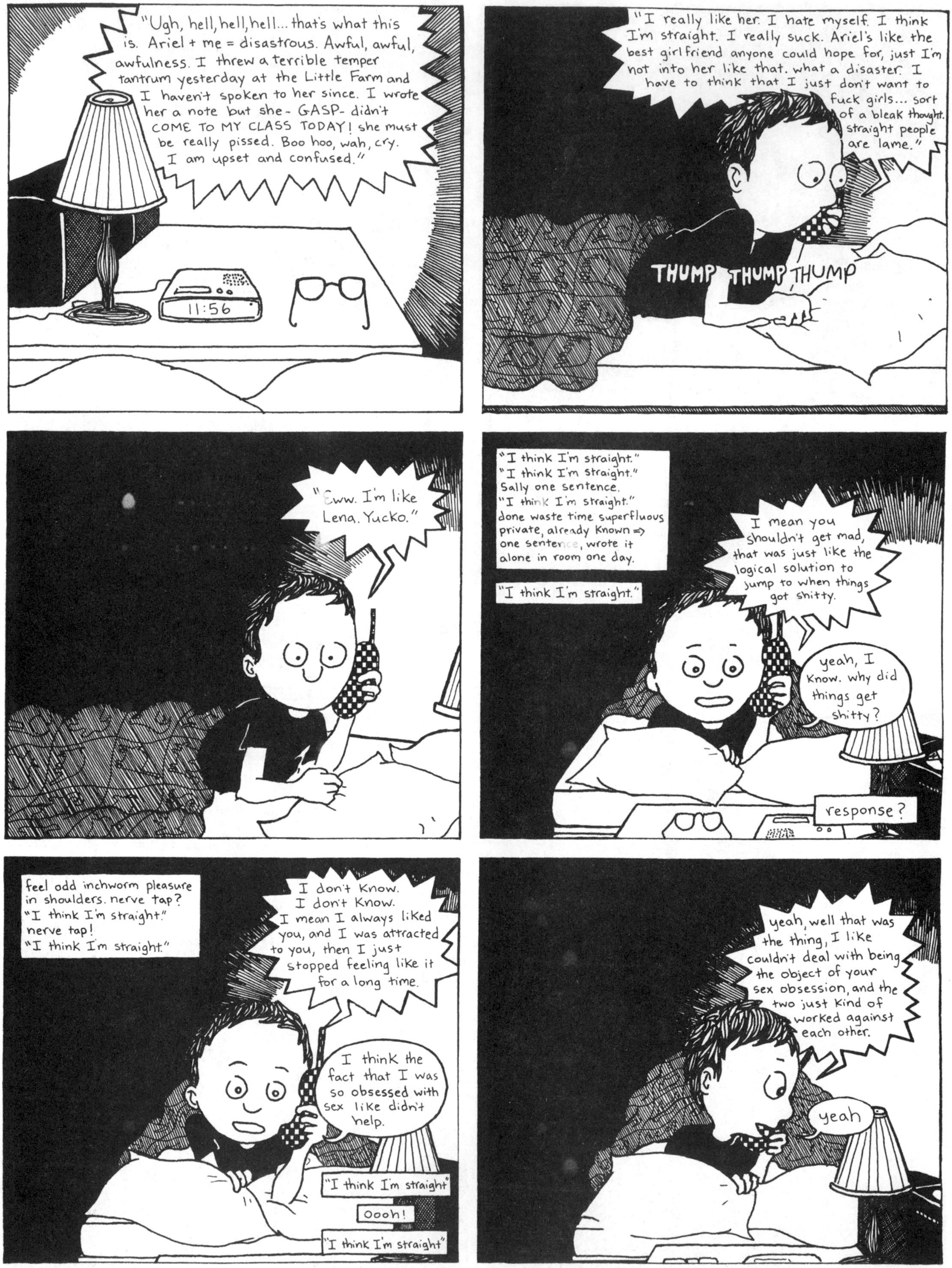

"Ugh, hell, hell, hell... that's what this is. Ariel + me = disastrous. Awful, awful, awfulness. I threw a terrible temper tantrum yesterday at the Little Farm and I haven't spoken to her since. I wrote her a note but she - GASP - didn't COME TO MY CLASS TODAY! she must be really pissed. Boo hoo, wah, cry. I am upset and confused."
11:56
"I really like her. I hate myself. I think I'm straight. I really suck. Ariel's like the best girlfriend anyone could hope for, just I'm not into her like that. what a disaster. I have to think that I just don't want to fuck girls... sort of a bleak thought. straight people are lame."
THUMP THUMP THUMP
"Eww. I'm like Lena. Yucko."
"I think I'm straight." "I think I'm straight." Sally one sentence. "I think I'm straight." done waste time superfluous private, already Known ⇒ one sentence, wrote it alone in room one day.
"I think I'm straight."
I mean you shouldn't get mad, that was just like the logical solution to jump to when things got shitty.
yeah, I Know. why did things get shitty?
response?
feel odd inchworm pleasure in shoulders. nerve tap? "I think I'm straight." nerve tap! "I think I'm straight."
I don't Know. I don't Know. I mean I always liked you, and I was attracted to you, then I just stopped feeling like it for a long time.
I think the fact that I was so obsessed with sex like didn't help.
"I think I'm straight"
Oooh!
"I think I'm straight"
yeah, well that was the thing, I like couldn't deal with being the object of your sex obsession, and the two just Kind of worked against each other.
yeah

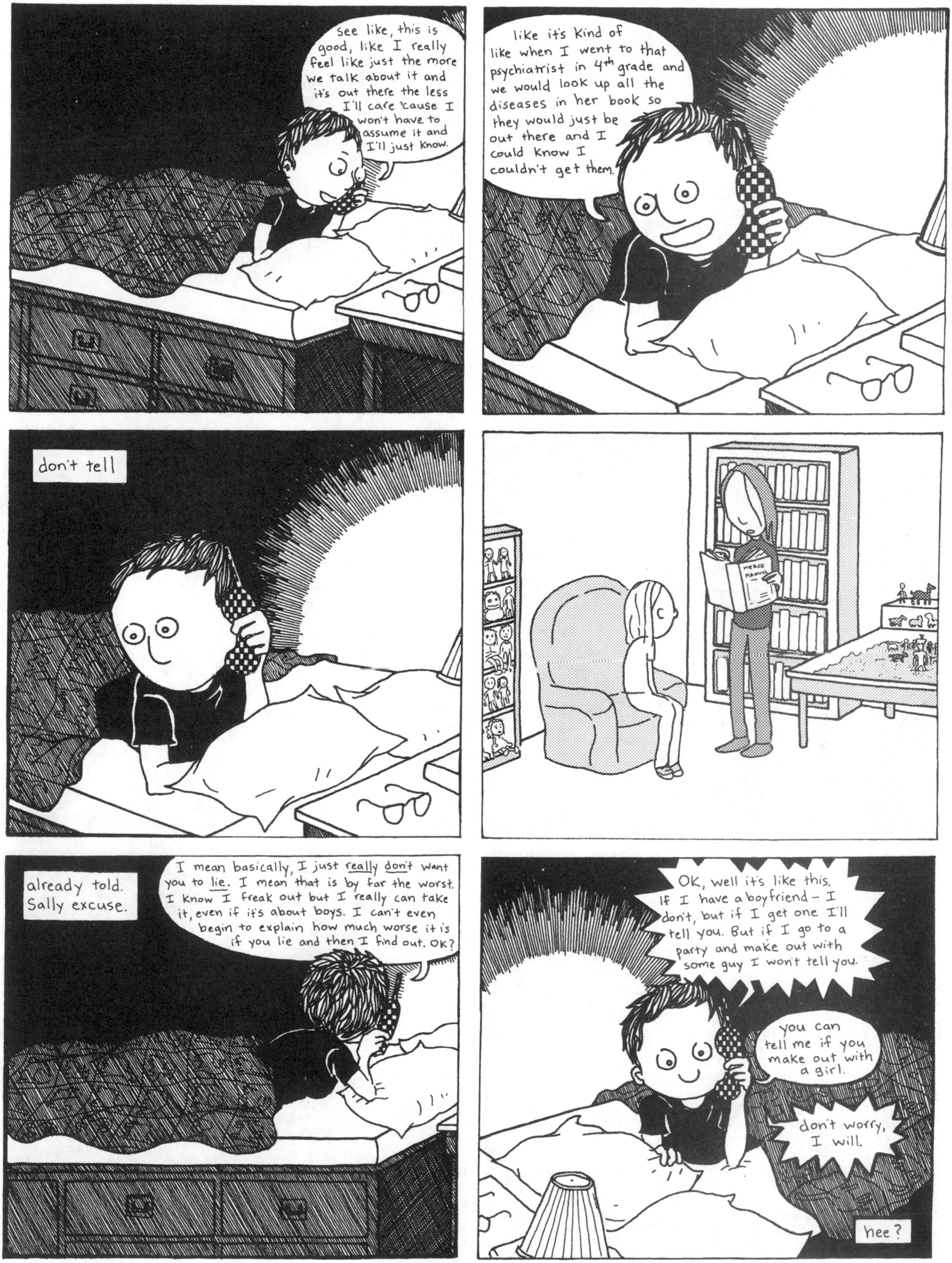

See like, this is good, like I really feel like just the more we talk about it and it's out there the less I'll care 'cause I won't have to assume it and I'll just know.
like it's kind of like when I went to that psychiatrist in 4th grade and we would look up all the diseases in her book so they would just be out there and I could know I couldn't get them.
don't tell
MERCK MANUAL
already told. Sally excuse.
I mean basically, I just really don't want you to lie. I mean that is by far the worst. I know I freak out but I really can take it, even if it's about boys. I can't even begin to explain how much worse it is if you lie and then I find out. OK?
OK, well it's like this. If I have a boyfriend – I don't, but if I get one I'll tell you. But if I go to a party and make out with some guy I won't tell you.
you can tell me if you make out with a girl.
don't worry, I will.
hee?

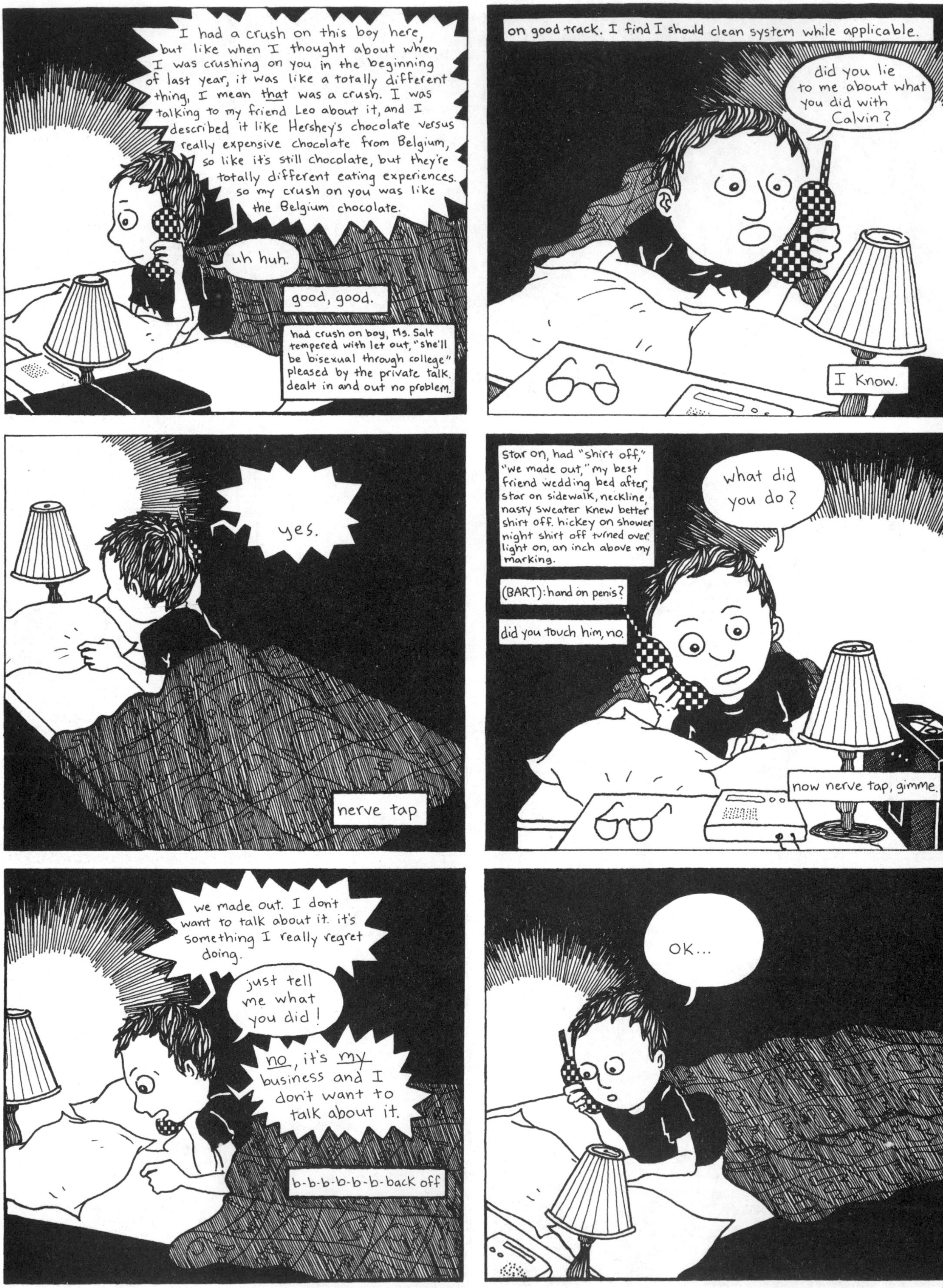
I had a crush on this boy here, but like when I thought about when I was crushing on you in the beginning of last year, it was like a totally different thing, I mean that was a crush. I was talking to my friend Leo about it, and I described it like Hershey's chocolate versus really expensive chocolate from Belgium, so like it's still chocolate, but they're totally different eating experiences. so my crush on you was like the Belgium chocolate.
uh huh.
good, good.
had crush on boy, Ms. Salt tempered with let out, "she'll be bisexual through college" pleased by the private talk. dealt in and out no problem.
on good track. I find I should clean system while applicable.
did you lie to me about what you did with Calvin?
I Know.
yes.
nerve tap
Star on, had "shirt off," "we made out," my best friend wedding bed after, star on sidewalk, neckline, nasty sweater knew better shirt off. hickey on shower night shirt off turned over. light on, an inch above my marking.
(BART): hand on penis?
did you touch him, no.
what did you do?
now nerve tap, gimme.
we made out. I don't want to talk about it. it's something I really regret doing.
just tell me what you did!
no, it's my business and I don't want to talk about it.
b-b-b-b-b-b-back off
OK...

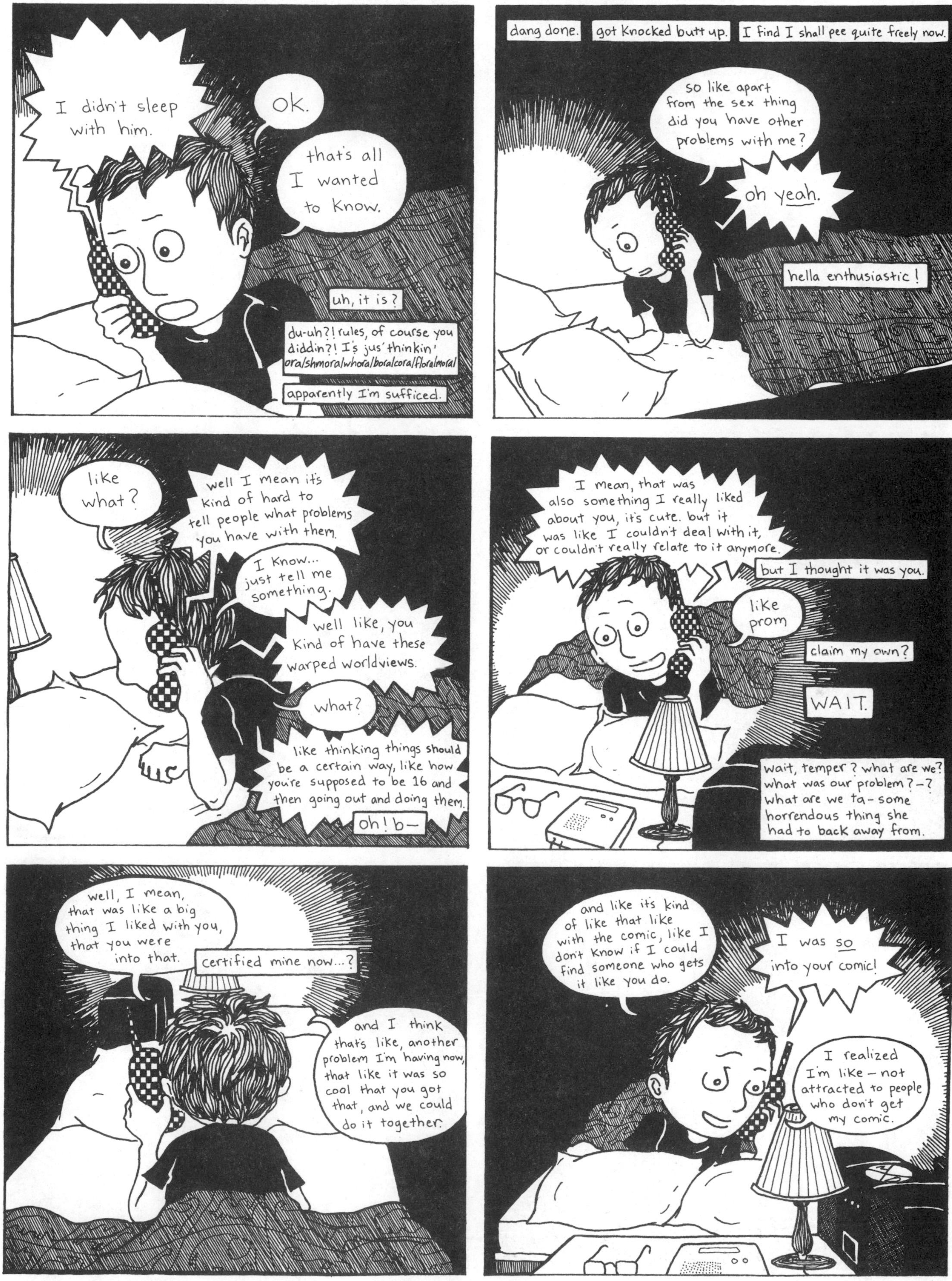
I didn't sleep with him.
ok.
that's all I wanted to know.
uh, it is?
du-uh?! rules, of course you diddin?! I's jus' thinkin' oral/shmoral/whoral/boral/coral/floral/moral
apparently I'm sufficed.
dang done.
got knocked butt up.
I find I shall pee quite freely now.
so like apart from the sex thing did you have other problems with me?
oh yeah.
hella enthusiastic!
like what?
well I mean it's kind of hard to tell people what problems you have with them.
I know... just tell me something.
well like, you kind of have these warped worldviews.
what?
like thinking things should be a certain way, like how you're supposed to be 16 and then going out and doing them.
oh! b–
I mean, that was also something I really liked about you, it's cute. but it was like I couldn't deal with it, or couldn't really relate to it anymore.
but I thought it was you.
like prom
claim my own?
WAIT.
wait, temper? what are we? what was our problem?–? what are we ta– some horrendous thing she had to back away from.
well, I mean, that was like a big thing I liked with you, that you were into that.
certified mine now...?
and I think that's like, another problem I'm having now, that like it was so cool that you got that, and we could do it together.
and like it's kind of like that like with the comic, like I don't know if I could find someone who gets it like you do.
I was so into your comic!
I realized I'm like – not attracted to people who don't get my comic.

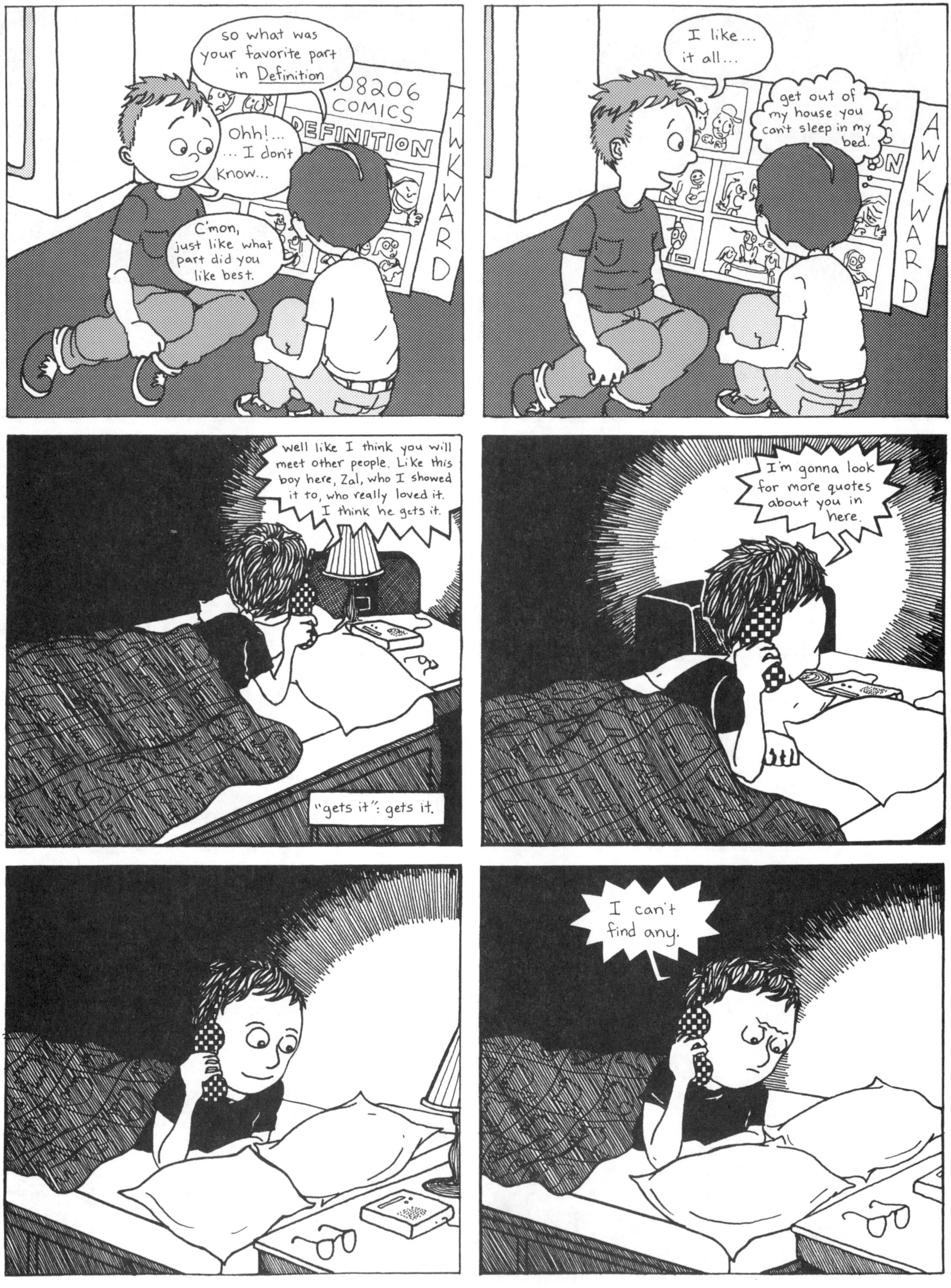
so what was your favorite part in Definition
.08206 COMICS
DEFINITION
AWKWARD
Ohh!... ... I don't know...
C'mon, just like what part did you like best.
I like... it all...
get out of my house you can't sleep in my bed.
AWKWARD
well like I think you will meet other people. Like this boy here, Zal, who I showed it to, who really loved it. I think he gets it.
"gets it": gets it.
I'm gonna look for more quotes about you in here.
I can't find any.

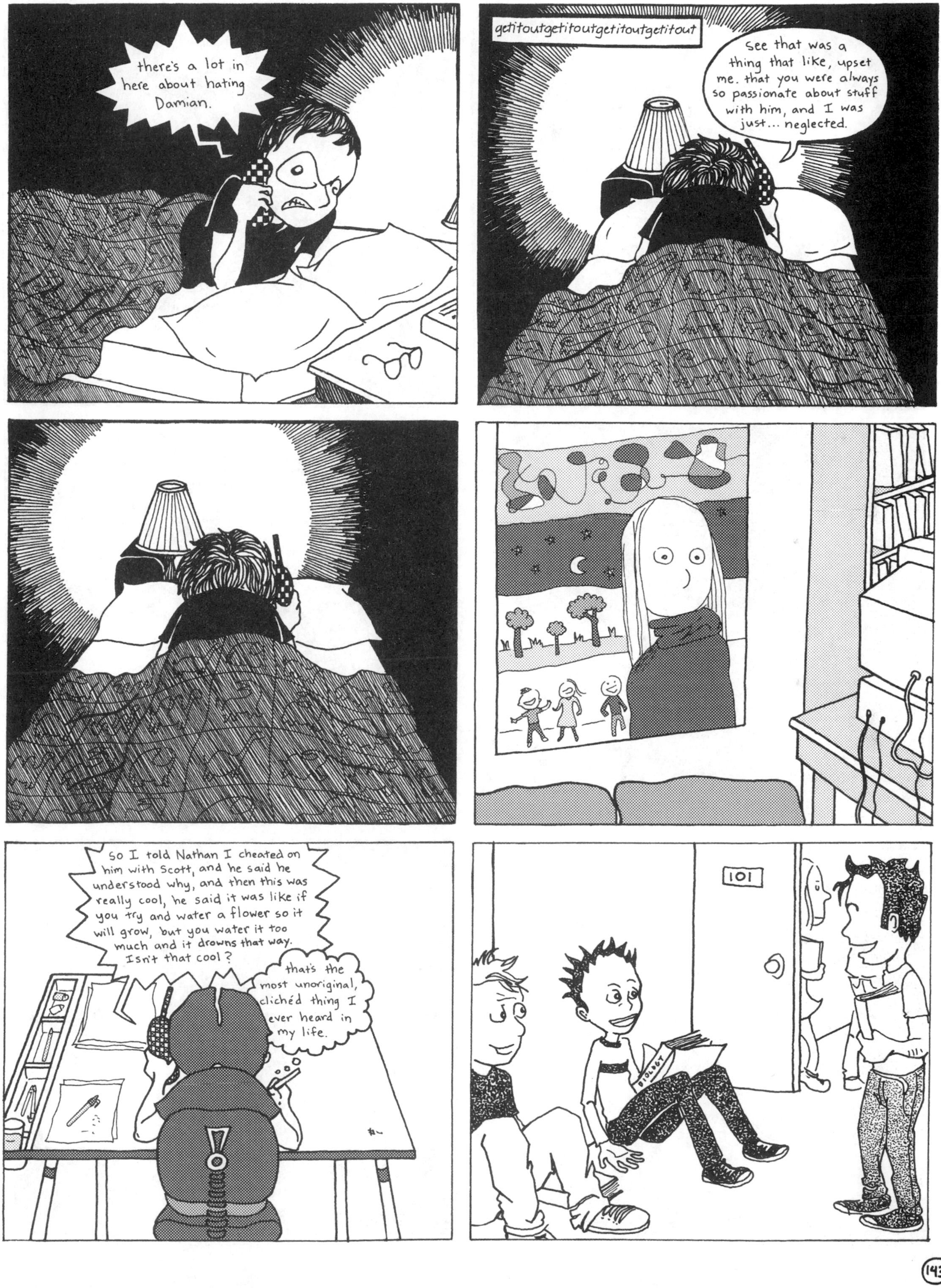

there's a lot in here about hating Damian.
getitoutgetitoutgetitoutgetitout
See that was a thing that like, upset me. that you were always so passionate about stuff with him, and I was just... neglected.
So I told Nathan I cheated on him with Scott, and he said he understood why, and then this was really cool, he said it was like if you try and water a flower so it will grow, but you water it too much and it drowns that way. Isn't that cool?
that's the most unoriginal, clichéd thing I ever heard in my life.
101
BIOLOGY

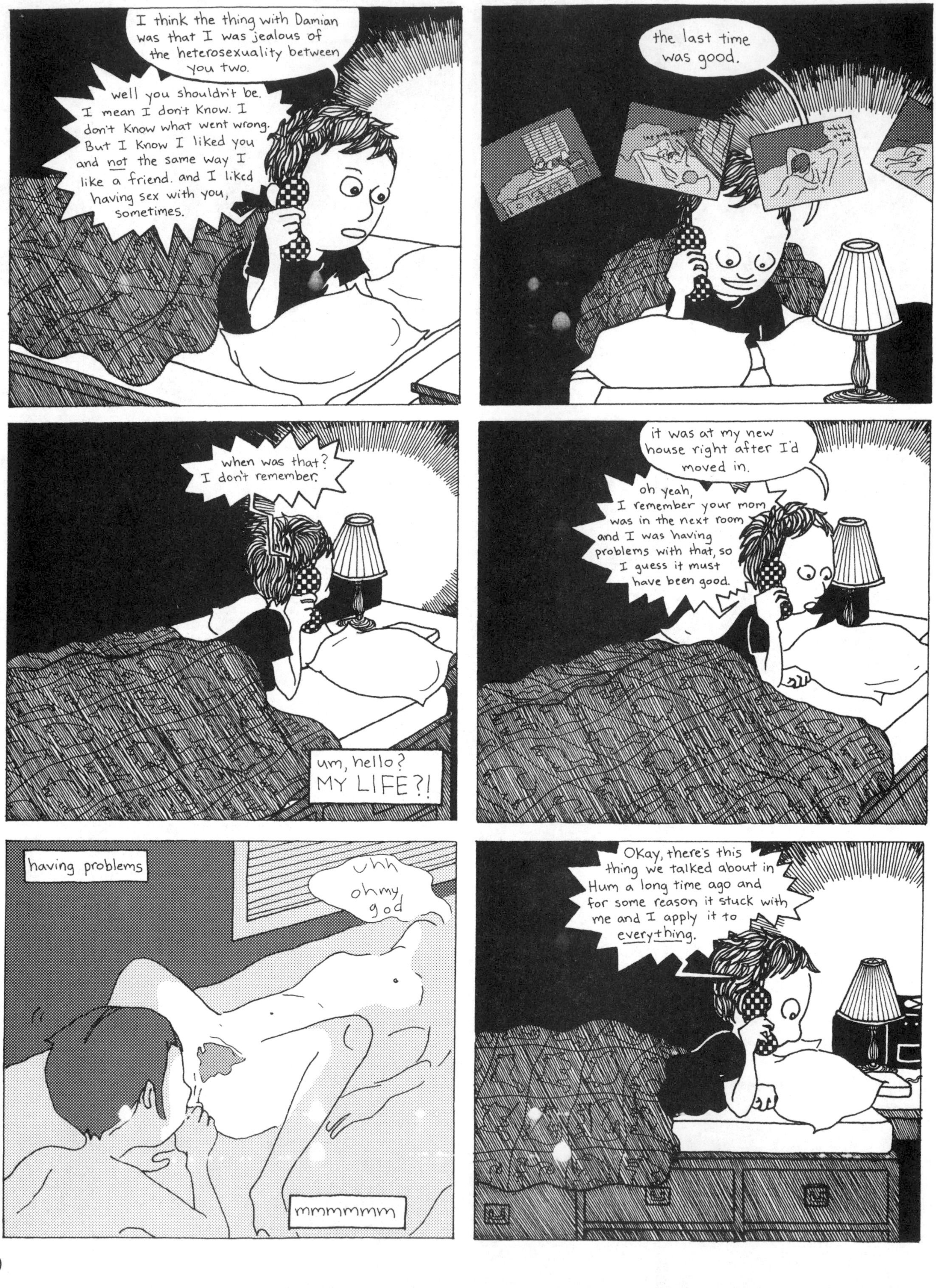

I think the thing with Damian was that I was jealous of the heterosexuality between you two.
well you shouldn't be. I mean I don't Know. I don't Know what went wrong. But I Know I liked you and not the same way I like a friend. and I liked having sex with you, sometimes.
the last time was good.
when was that? I don't remember.
um, hello? MY LIFE?!
it was at my new house right after I'd moved in.
oh yeah, I remember your mom was in the next room and I was having problems with that, so I guess it must have been good.
having problems
uhh ohmy god
mmmmmm
OKay, there's this thing we talked about in Hum a long time ago and for some reason it stuck with me and I apply it to everything.

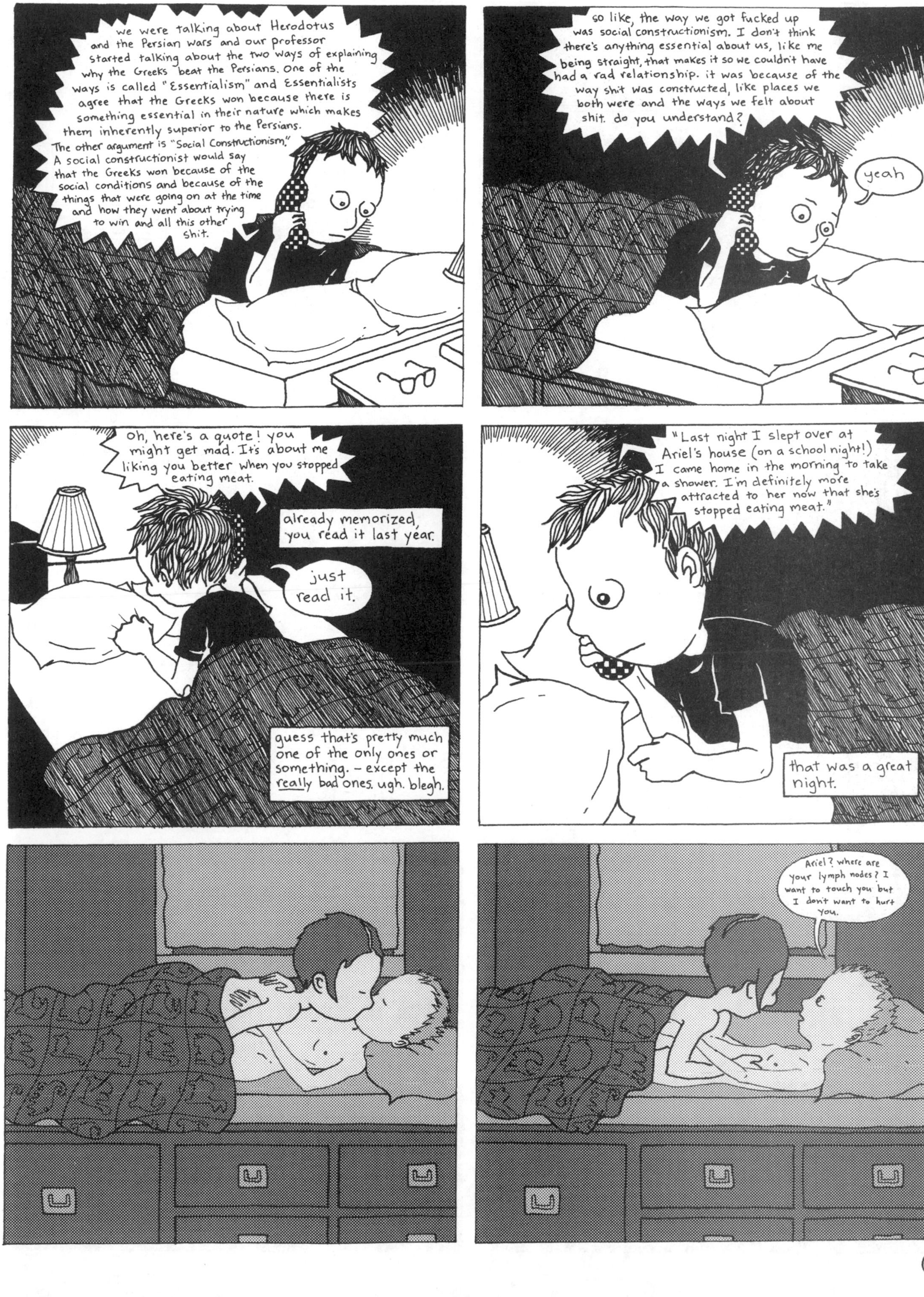
we were talking about Herodotus and the Persian wars and our professor started talking about the two ways of explaining why the Greeks beat the Persians. One of the ways is called "Essentialism" and Essentialists agree that the Greeks won because there is something essential in their nature which makes them inherently superior to the Persians. The other argument is "Social Constructionism." A social constructionist would say that the Greeks won because of the social conditions and because of the things that were going on at the time and how they went about trying to win and all this other shit.
so like, the way we got fucked up was social constructionism. I don't think there's anything essential about us, like me being straight, that makes it so we couldn't have had a rad relationship. it was because of the way shit was constructed, like places we both were and the ways we felt about shit. do you understand?
yeah
Oh, here's a quote! you might get mad. It's about me liking you better when you stopped eating meat.
already memorized, you read it last year.
just read it.
guess that's pretty much one of the only ones or something. - except the really bad ones. ugh. blegh.
"Last night I slept over at Ariel's house (on a school night!) I came home in the morning to take a shower. I'm definitely more attracted to her now that she's stopped eating meat."
that was a great night.
Ariel? where are your lymph nodes? I want to touch you but I don't want to hurt you.

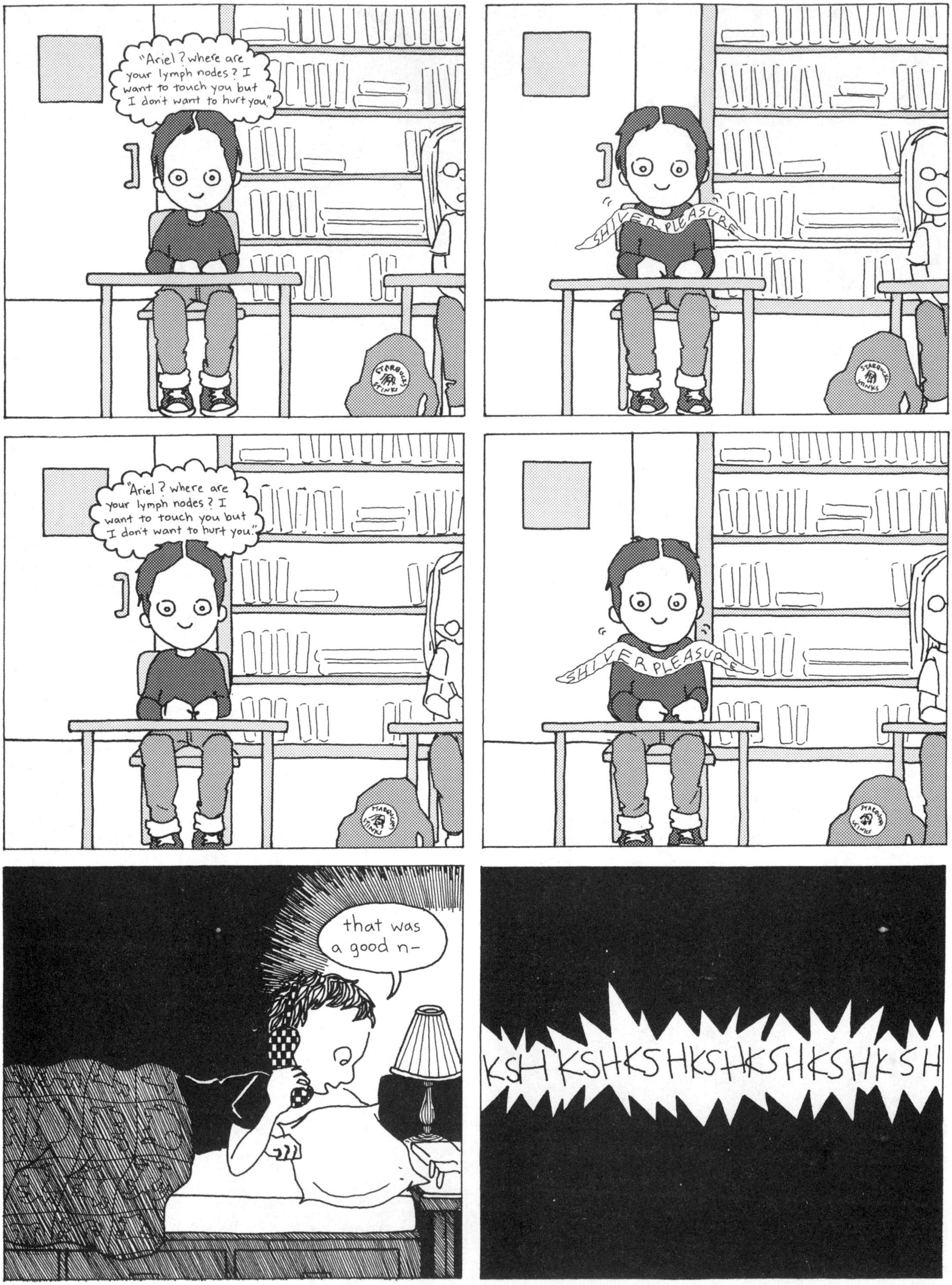
"Ariel? where are your lymph nodes? I want to touch you but I don't want to hurt you."
STARBUCKS STINKS
SHIVER PLEASURE
STARBUCKS STINKS
"Ariel? where are your lymph nodes? I want to touch you but I don't want to hurt you."
STARBUCKS STINKS
SHIVER PLEASURE
STARBUCKS STINKS
that was a good n-
KSHKSHKSHKSHKSHKSHKSHKSH

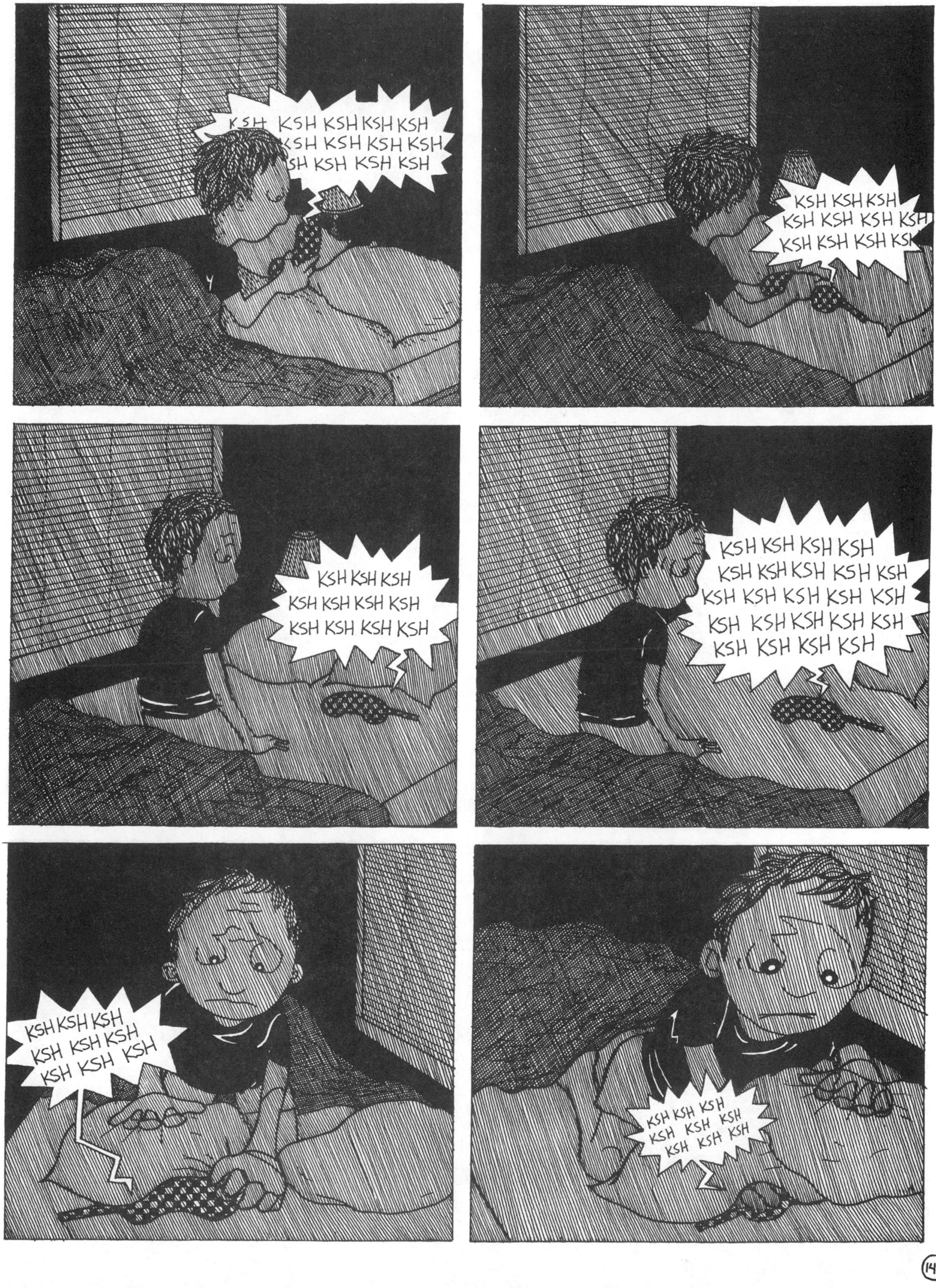
KSH KSH KSH KSH KSH
KSH KSH KSH KSH
SH KSH KSH KSH
KSH KSH KSH
KSH KSH KSH KSH
KSH KSH KSH KSH
KSH KSH KSH
KSH KSH KSH KSH
KSH KSH KSH KSH
KSH KSH KSH KSH
KSH KSH KSH KSH KSH
KSH KSH KSH KSH KSH
KSH KSH KSH KSH KSH
KSH KSH KSH KSH
KSH KSH KSH
KSH KSH KSH
KSH KSH KSH
KSH KSH KSH
KSH KSH KSH
KSH KSH KSH

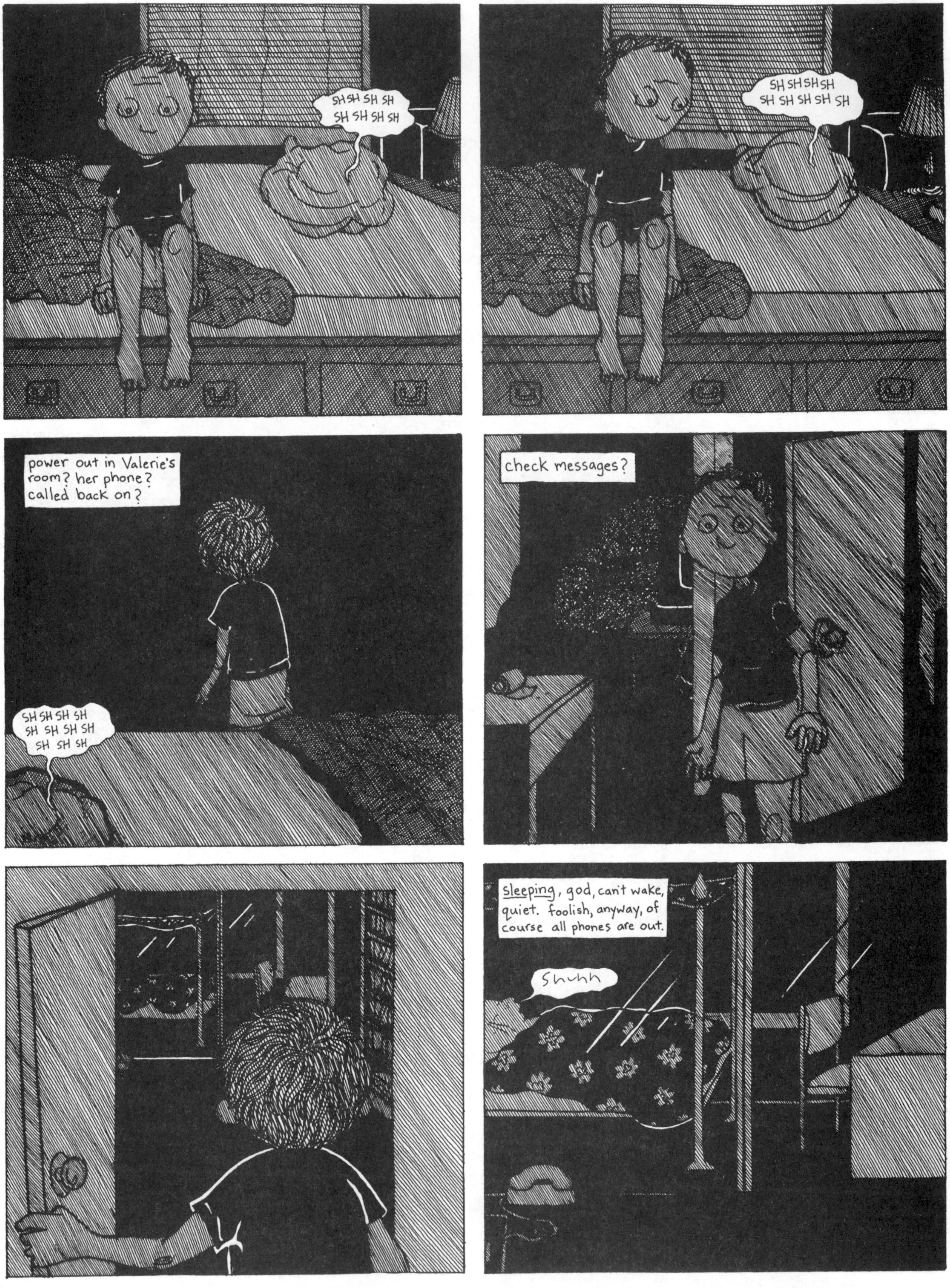
SH SH SH SH
SH SH SH SH
SH SH SH SH
SH SH SH SH SH
power out in Valerie's room? her phone? called back on?
SH SH SH SH
SH SH SH SH
SH SH SH
check messages?
sleeping, god, can't wake, quiet. foolish, anyway, of course all phones are out.
Shuhh

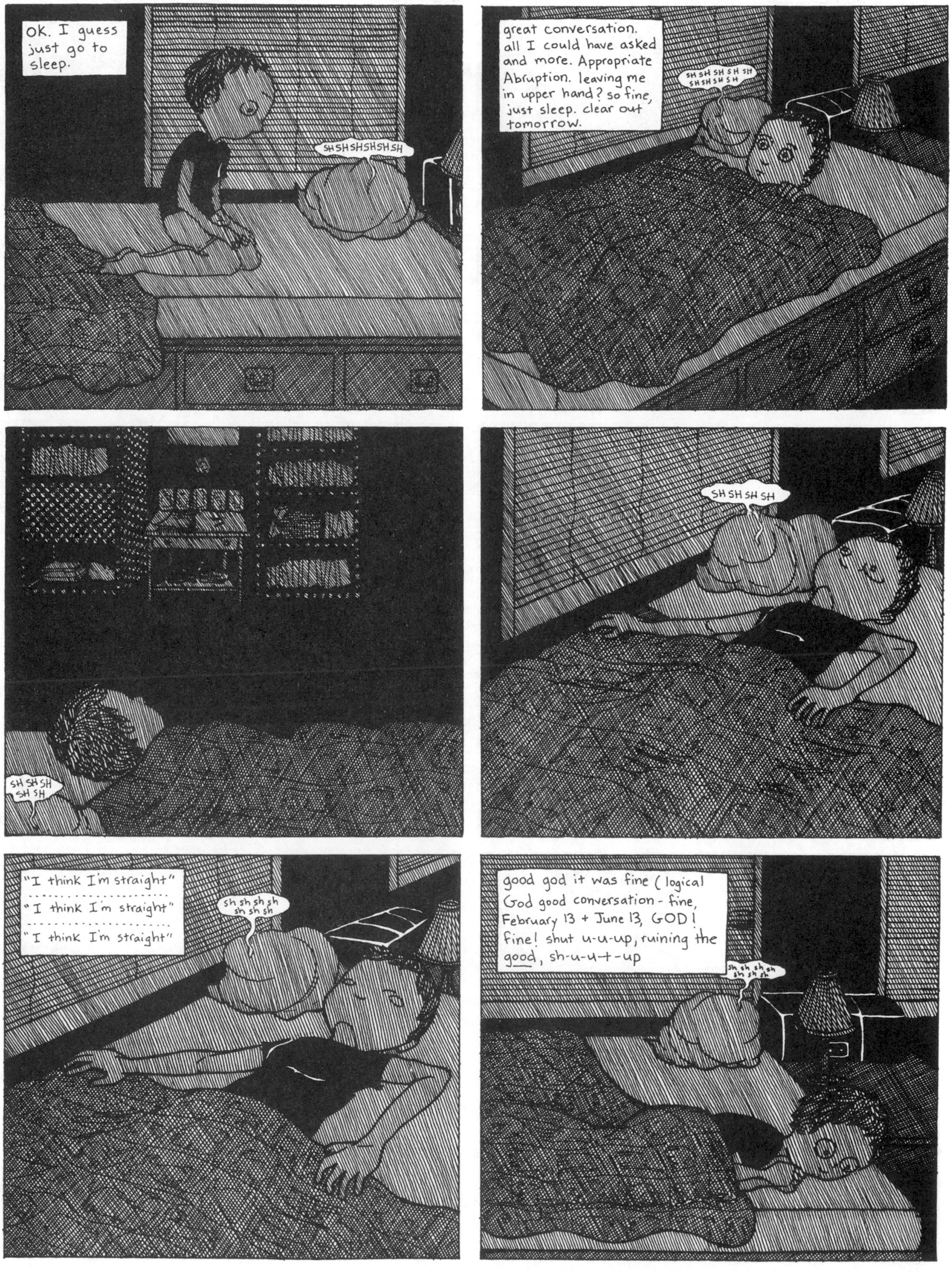
OK. I guess just go to sleep.
SH SH SH SH SH SH SH
great conversation. all I could have asked and more. Appropriate Abruption. leaving me in upper hand? so fine, just sleep. clear out tomorrow.
SH SH SH SH SH SH SH SH SH
SH SH SH SH SH
SH SH SH SH
"I think I'm straight"
"I think I'm straight"
"I think I'm straight"
sh sh sh sh sh sh sh
good god it was fine (logical God good conversation - fine, February 13 + June 13, GOD! fine! shut u-u-up, ruining the good, sh-u-u-t-up
sh sh sh sh sh sh sh

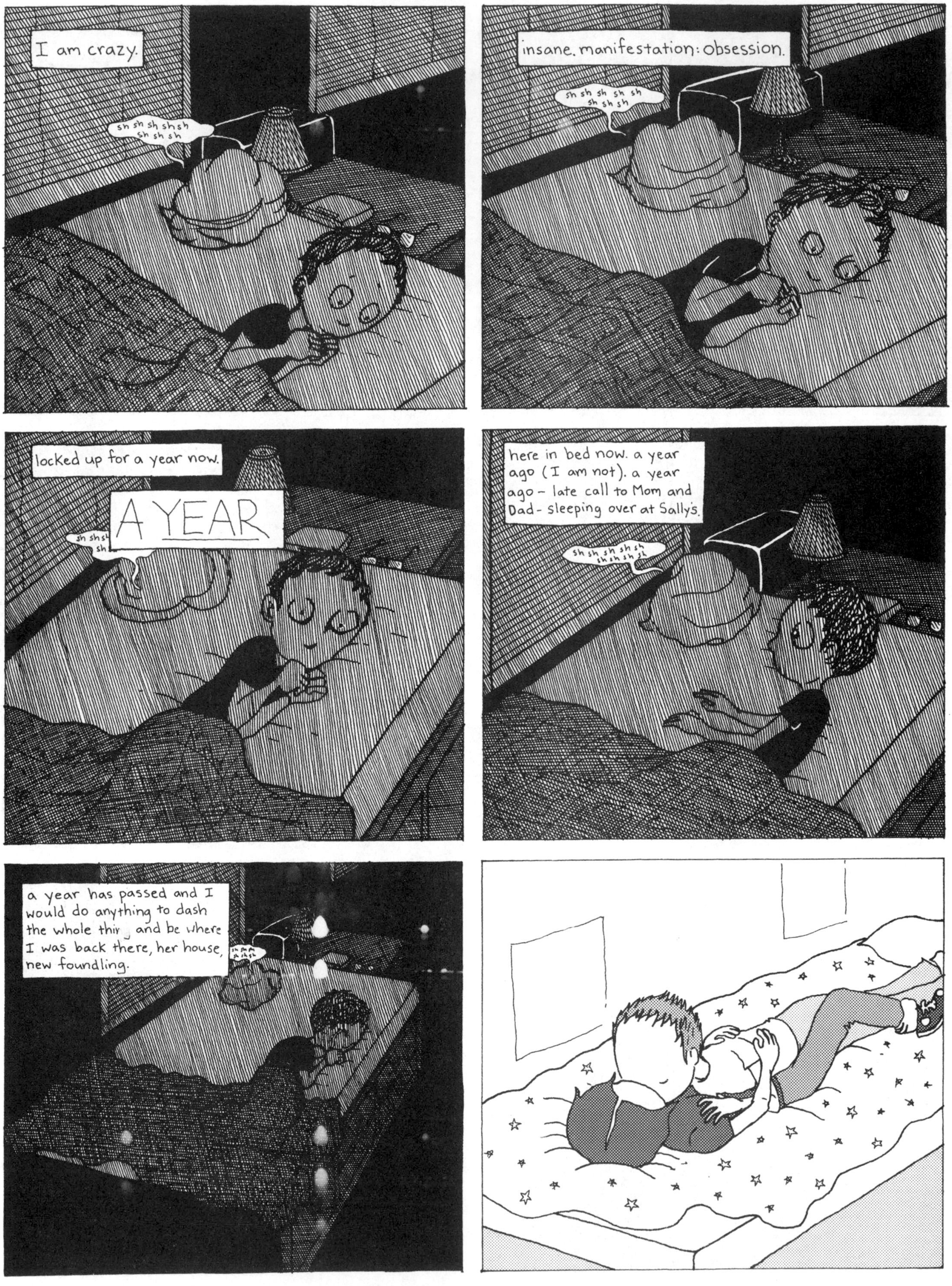
I am crazy.
sh sh sh shsh sh sh sh
insane. manifestation: obsession.
sh sh sh sh sh sh sh sh
locked up for a year now.
A YEAR
here in bed now. a year ago (I am not). a year ago – late call to Mom and Dad – sleeping over at Sally's.
sh sh sh sh sh sh sh sh sh sh
a year has passed and I would do anything to dash the whole thing and be where I was back there, her house, new foundling.

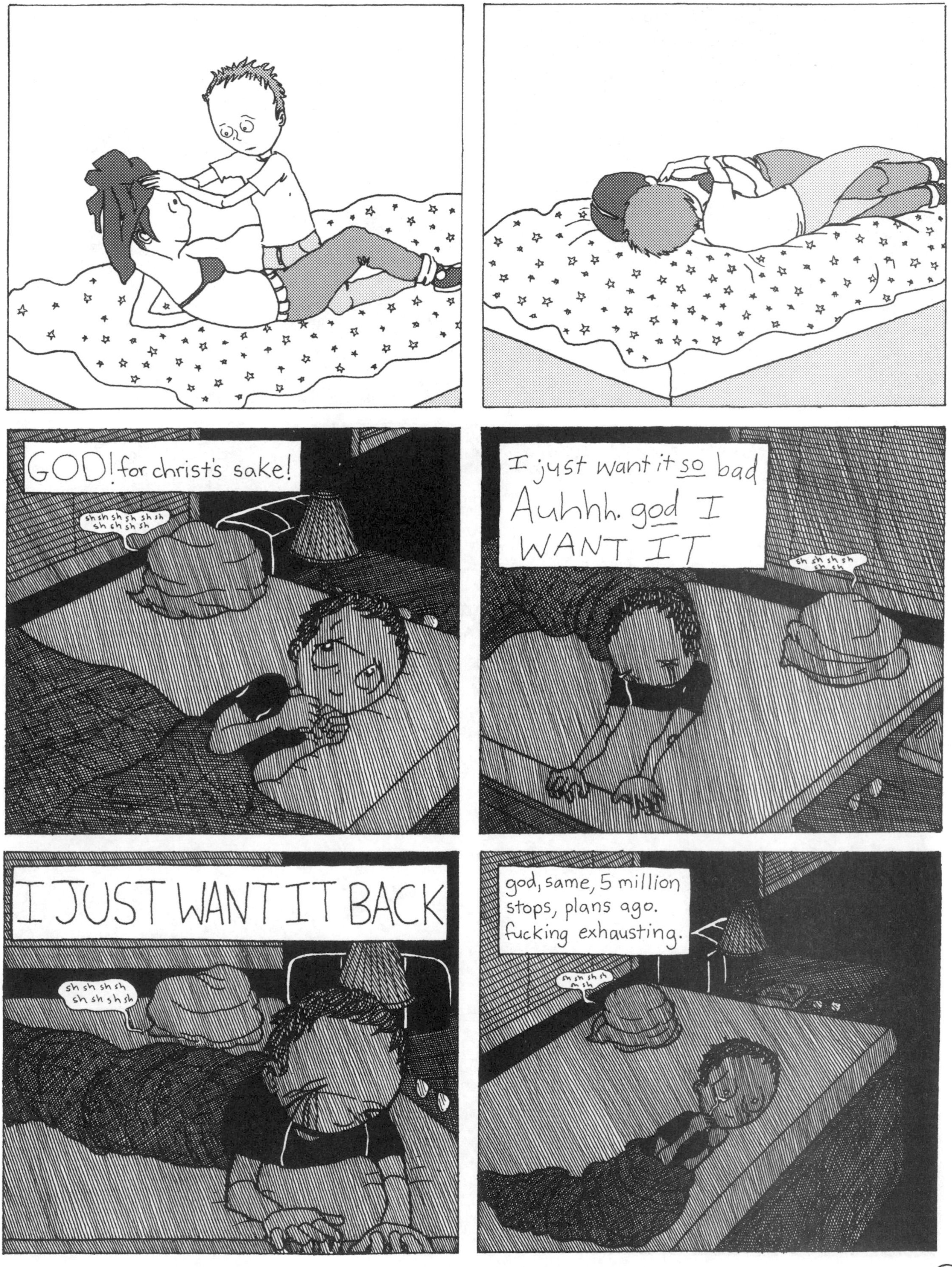
GOD! for christ's sake!
I just want it so bad
Auhhh. god I WANT IT
I JUST WANT IT BACK
god, same, 5 million stops, plans ago. fucking exhausting.

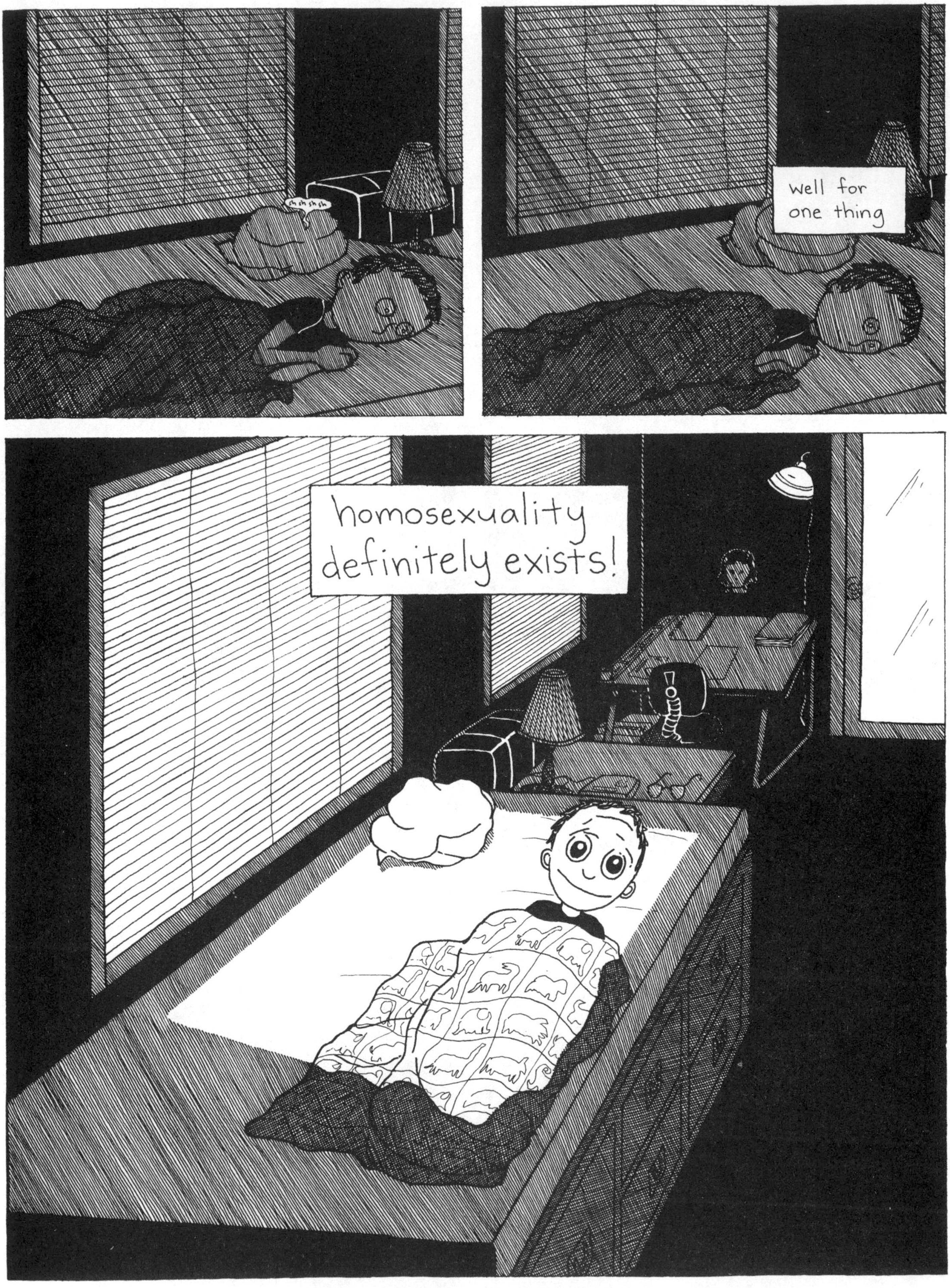
sh sh sh sh
well for one thing
homosexuality definitely exists!

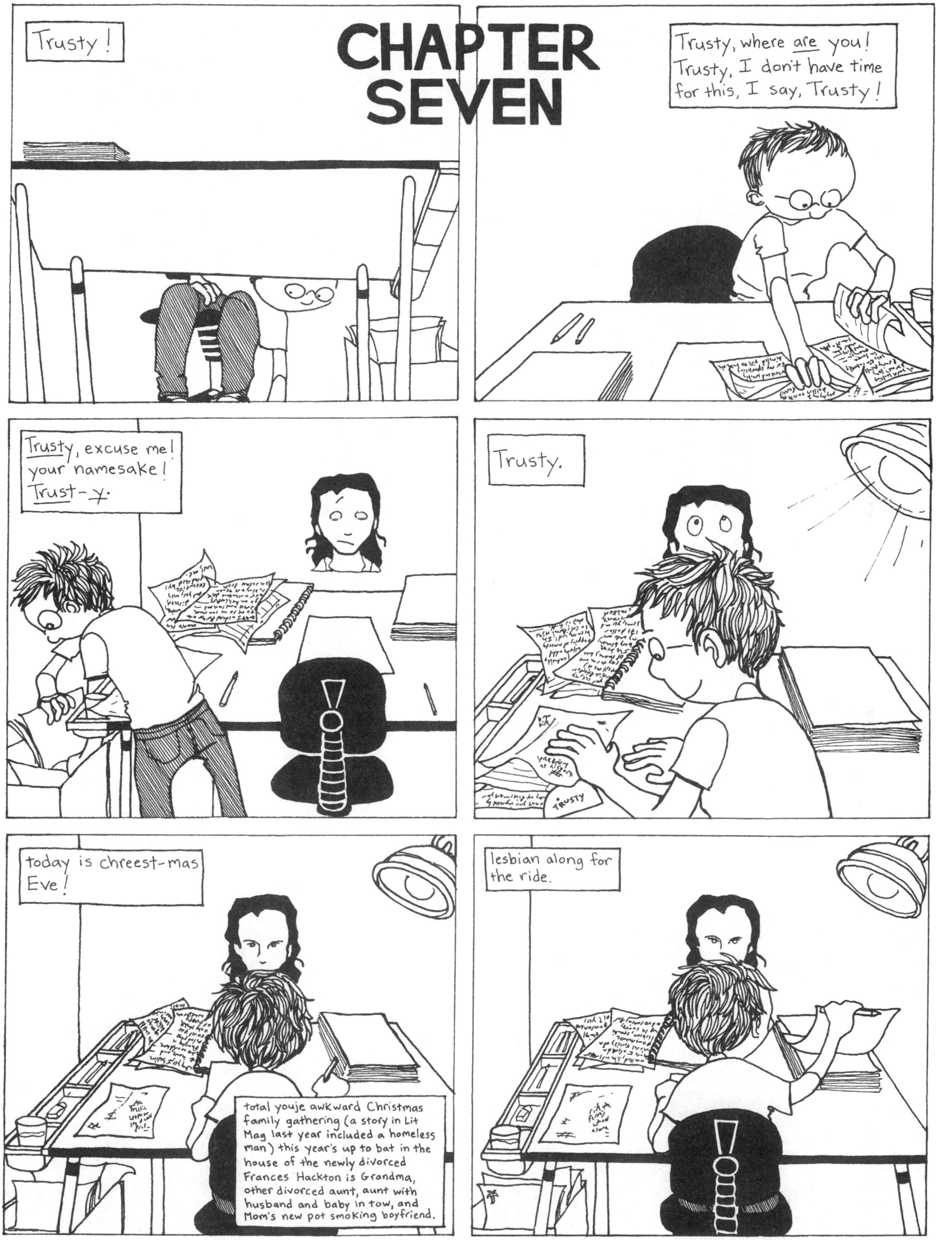

CHAPTER SEVEN
Trusty!
Trusty, where are you! Trusty, I don't have time for this, I say, Trusty!
Trusty, excuse me! your namesake! Trust-y.
Trusty.
TRUSTY
today is chreest-mas Eve!
total youje awkward Christmas family gathering (a story in Lit Mag last year included a homeless man) this year's up to bat in the house of the newly divorced Frances Hackton is Grandma, other divorced aunt, aunt with husband and baby in tow, and Mom's new pot smoking boyfriend.
lesbian along for the ride.

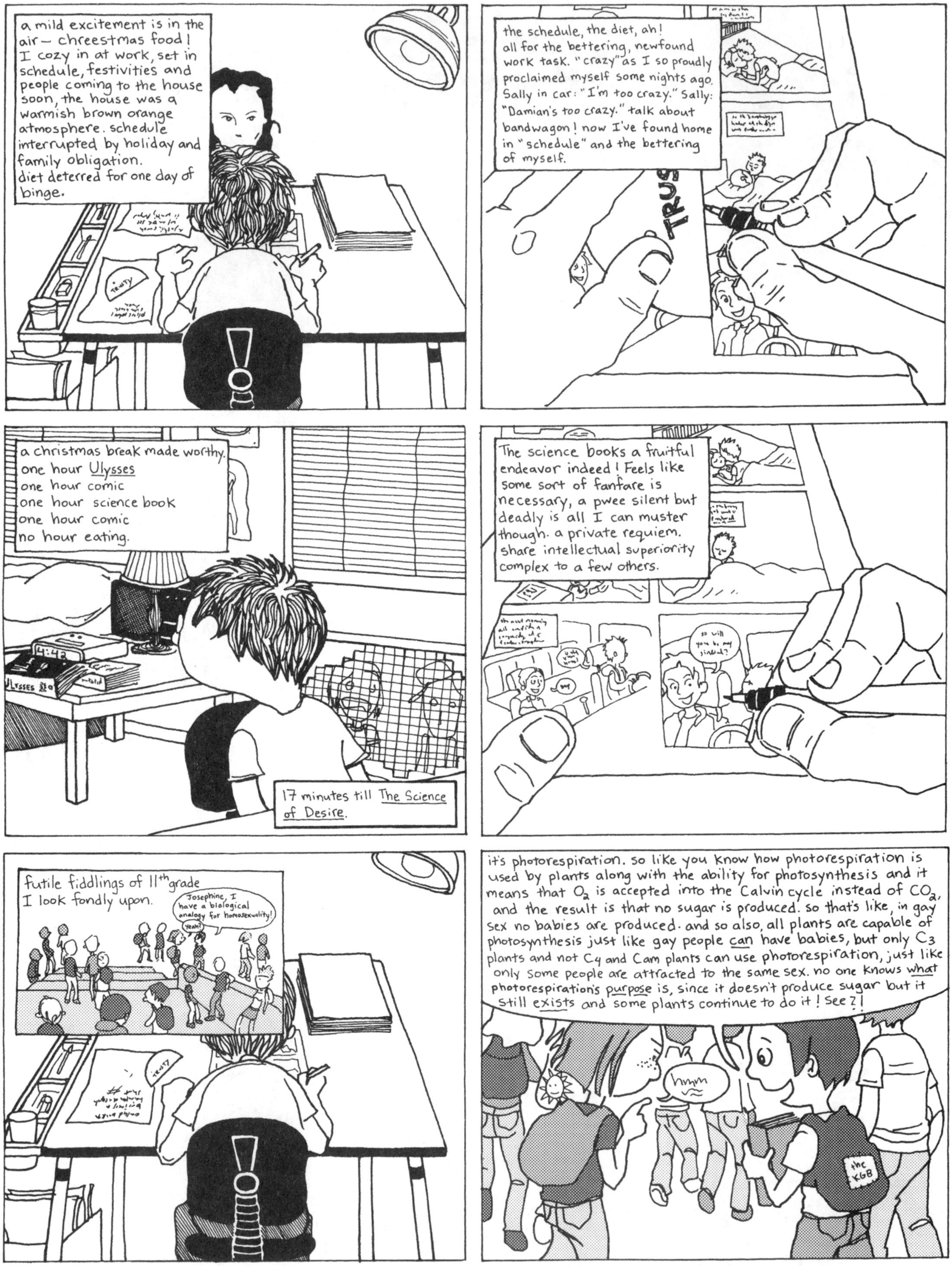
a mild excitement is in the air— chreestmas food! I cozy in at work, set in schedule, festivities and people coming to the house soon, the house was a warmish brown orange atmosphere. schedule interrupted by holiday and family obligation. diet deterred for one day of binge.
the schedule, the diet, ah! all for the bettering, newfound work task. "crazy" as I so proudly proclaimed myself some nights ago. Sally in car: "I'm too crazy." Sally: "Damian's too crazy." talk about bandwagon! now I've found home in "schedule" and the bettering of myself.
TRUS
a christmas break made worthy. one hour Ulysses one hour comic one hour science book one hour comic no hour eating.
17 minutes till The Science of Desire.
The science books a fruitful endeavor indeed! Feels like some sort of fanfare is necessary, a pwee silent but deadly is all I can muster though. a private requiem. share intellectual superiority complex to a few others.
futile fiddlings of 11th grade I look fondly upon.
Josephine, I have a biological analogy for homosexuality!
Yeah?
it's photorespiration. so like you know how photorespiration is used by plants along with the ability for photosynthesis and it means that O2 is accepted into the Calvin cycle instead of CO2, and the result is that no sugar is produced. so that's like, in gay sex no babies are produced. and so also, all plants are capable of photosynthesis just like gay people can have babies, but only C3 plants and not C4 and Cam plants can use photorespiration, just like only some people are attracted to the same sex. no one knows what photorespiration's purpose is, since it doesn't produce sugar but it still exists and some plants continue to do it! See?!
hmm
the KGB

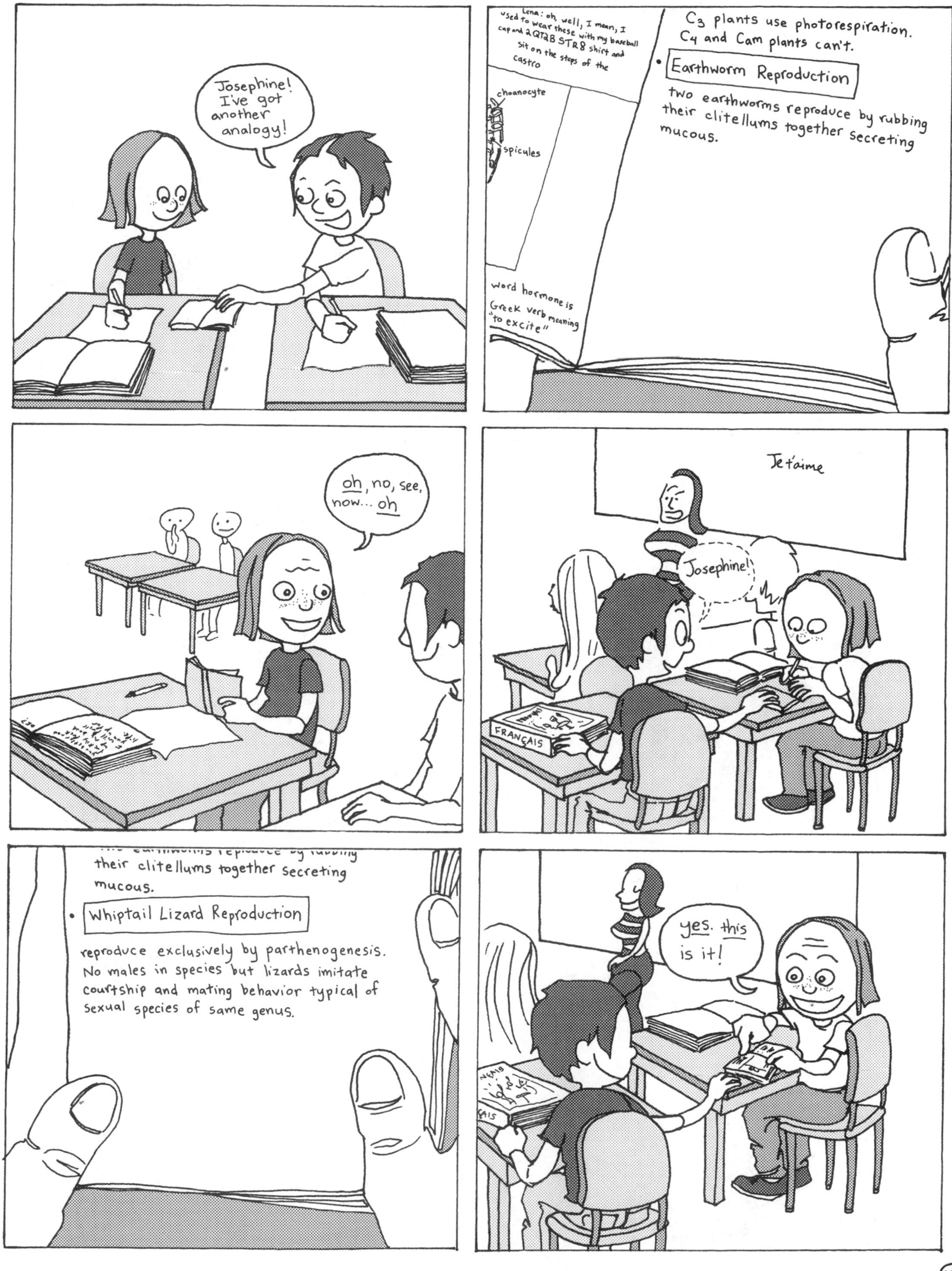
Josephine! I've got another analogy!
Lena: oh, well, I mean, I used to wear these with my baseball cap and a QT2B STR8 shirt and sit on the steps of the castro
choanocyte
spicules
word hormone is Greek verb meaning "to excite"
C_3 plants use photorespiration. C_4 and Cam plants can't.
• Earthworm Reproduction
two earthworms reproduce by rubbing their clitellums together secreting mucous.
oh, no, see, now... oh
Je t'aime
Josephine!
FRANÇAIS
their clitellums together secreting mucous.
• Whiptail Lizard Reproduction
reproduce exclusively by parthenogenesis. No males in species but lizards imitate courtship and mating behavior typical of sexual species of same genus.
yes. this is it!

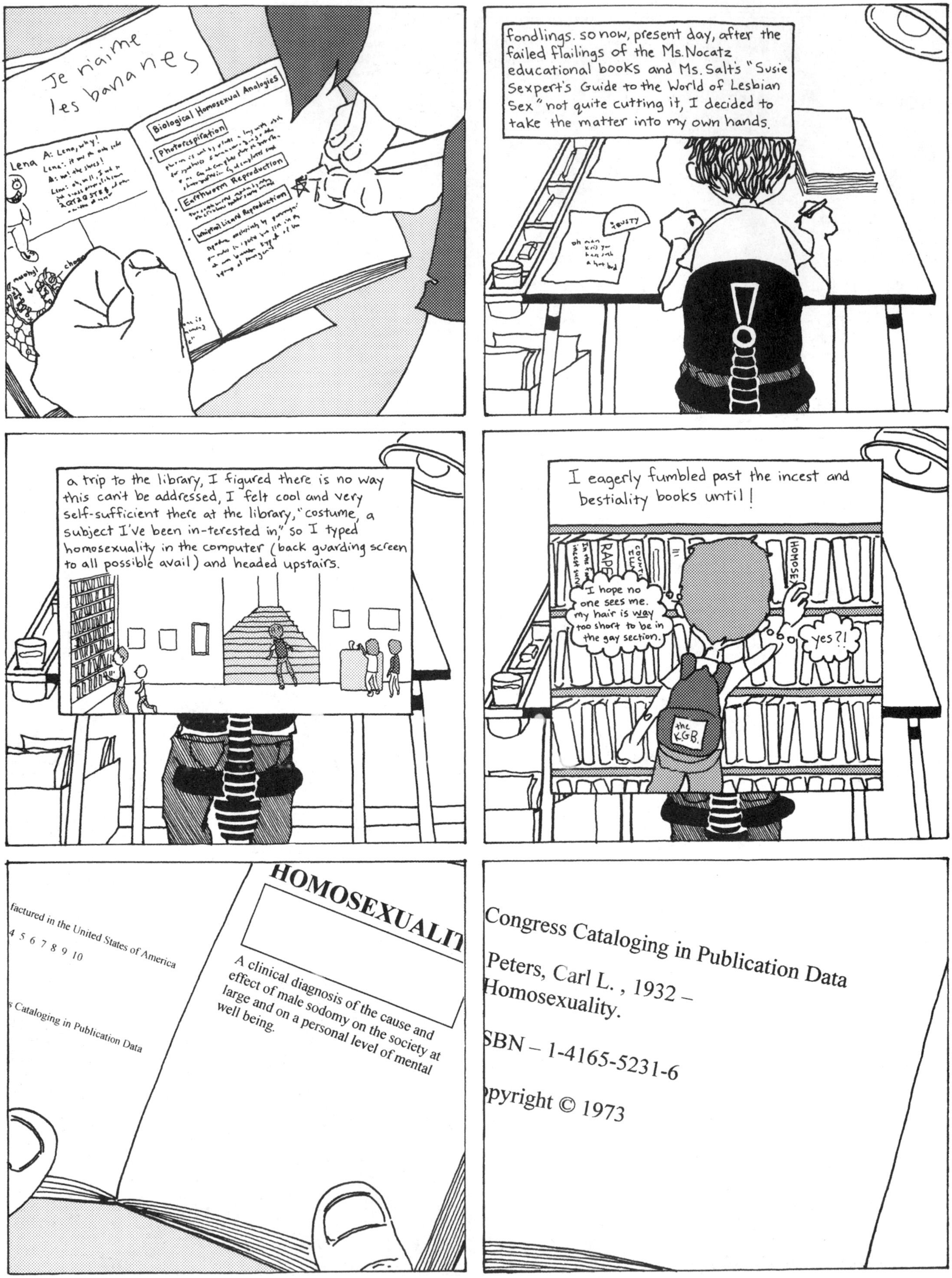
Je n'aime les bananes
Biological Homosexual Analogies
Photorespiration
Earthworm Reproduction
Whiptail Lizard Reproduction
Lena
fondlings. so now, present day, after the failed flailings of the Ms. Nocatz educational books and Ms. Salt's "Susie Sexpert's Guide to the World of Lesbian Sex" not quite cutting it, I decided to take the matter into my own hands.
a trip to the library, I figured there is no way this can't be addressed, I felt cool and very self-sufficient there at the library, "costume, a subject I've been in-terested in," so I typed homosexuality in the computer (back guarding screen to all possible avail) and headed upstairs.
I eagerly fumbled past the incest and bestiality books until!
RAPE
HOMOSEX
I hope no one sees me. my hair is way too short to be in the gay section.
yes?!
the KGB.
HOMOSEXUALIT
A clinical diagnosis of the cause and effect of male sodomy on the society at large and on a personal level of mental well being.
factured in the United States of America
4 5 6 7 8 9 10
s Cataloging in Publication Data
Congress Cataloging in Publication Data
Peters, Carl L. , 1932 –
Homosexuality.
SBN – 1-4165-5231-6
pyright © 1973

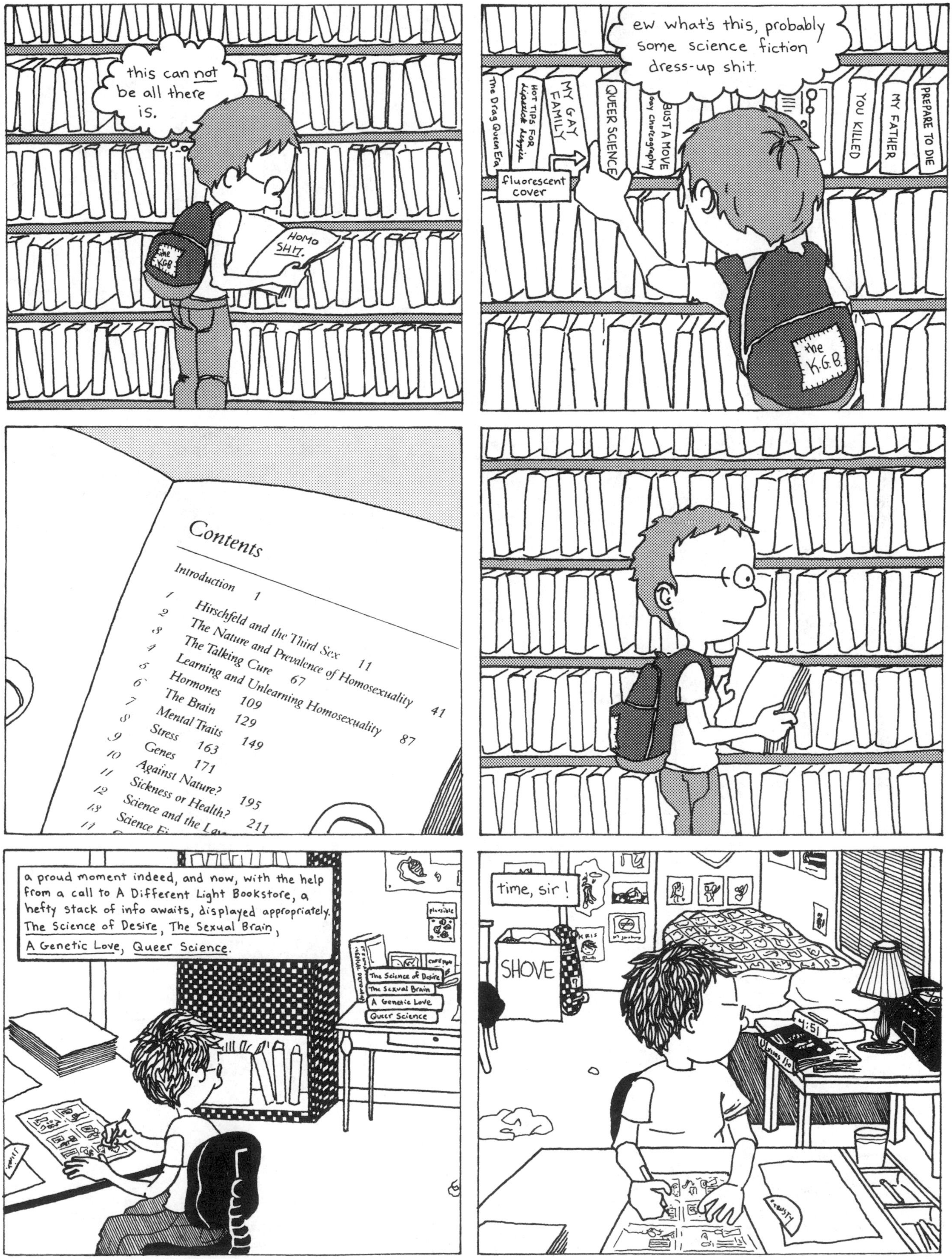

this can not be all there is.
HOMO SHIT.
ew what's this, probably some science fiction dress-up shit.
The Drag Queen Era
MY GAY FAMILY
QUEER SCIENCE
BUST A MOVE
gay choreography
YOU KILLED
MY FATHER
PREPARE TO DIE
fluorescent cover
the K.G.B.
Contents
Introduction 1
1 Hirschfeld and the Third Sex 11
2 The Nature and Prevalence of Homosexuality 41
3 The Talking Cure 67
4 Learning and Unlearning Homosexuality 87
5 Hormones 109
6 The Brain 129
7 Mental Traits 149
8 Stress 163
9 Genes 171
10 Against Nature?
11 Sickness or Health? 195
12 Science and the La 211
13 Science Fi
a proud moment indeed, and now, with the help from a call to A Different Light Bookstore, a hefty stack of info awaits, displayed appropriately. The Science of Desire, The Sexual Brain, A Genetic Love, Queer Science.
The Science of Desire
The Sexual Brain
A Genetic Love
Queer Science
time, sir!
SHOVE
4:51

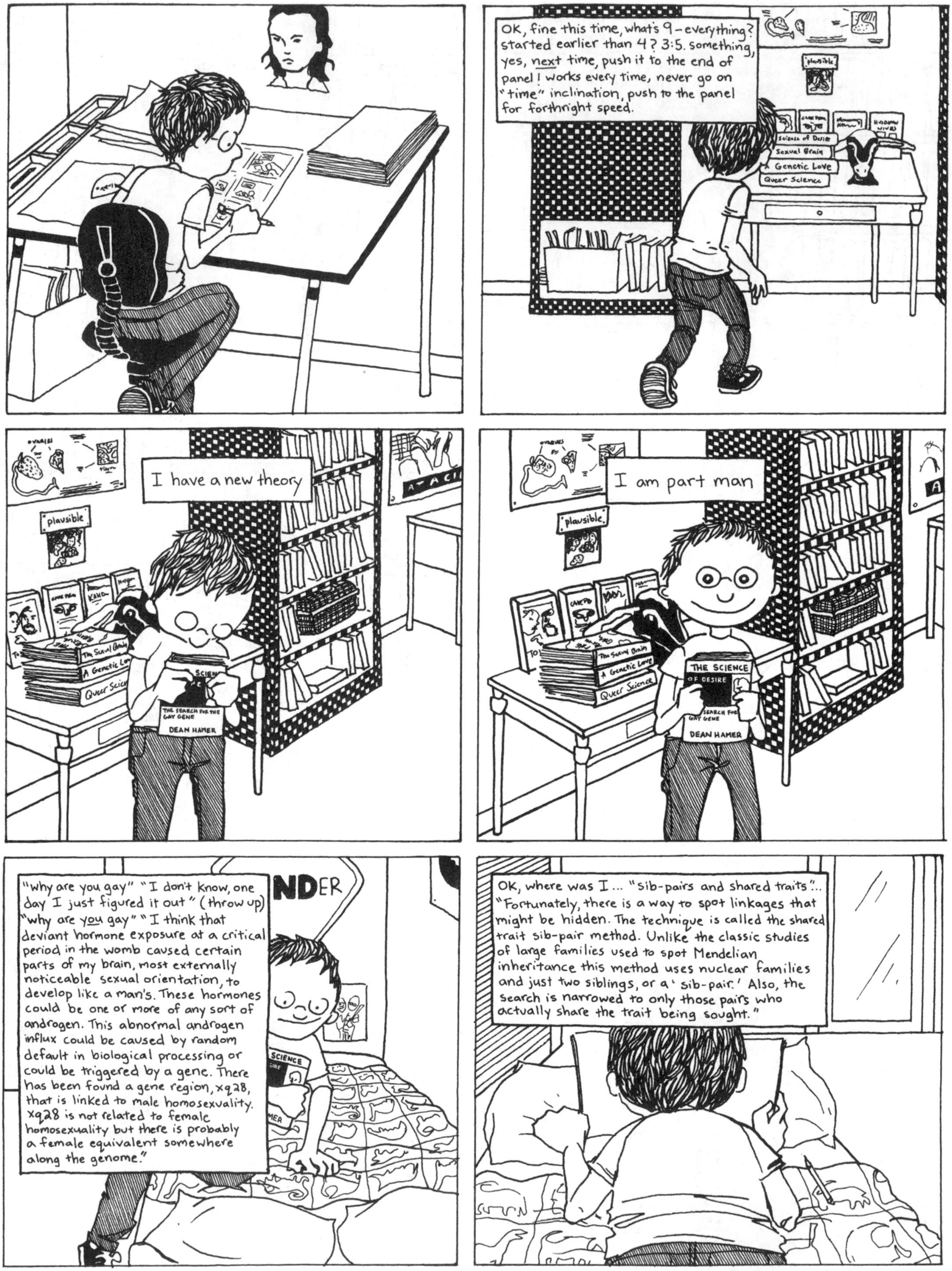
OK, fine this time, what's 9 – everything? started earlier than 4? 3:5. something, yes, next time, push it to the end of panel! works every time, never go on "time" inclination, push to the panel for forthright speed.
plausible
Science of Desire
Sexual Brain
Genetic Love
Queer Science
I have a new theory
plausible
The Sexual Brain
A Genetic Love
THE SEARCH FOR THE GAY GENE
DEAN HAMER
I am part man
plausible
The Sexual Brain
A Genetic Love
Queer Science
THE SCIENCE OF DESIRE
DEAN HAMER
"why are you gay" "I don't know, one day I just figured it out" (throw up) "why are you gay" "I think that deviant hormone exposure at a critical period in the womb caused certain parts of my brain, most externally noticeable sexual orientation, to develop like a man's. These hormones could be one or more of any sort of androgen. This abnormal androgen influx could be caused by random default in biological processing or could be triggered by a gene. There has been found a gene region, xq28, that is linked to male homosexuality. xq28 is not related to female homosexuality but there is probably a female equivalent somewhere along the genome."
NDER
OK, where was I... "sib-pairs and shared traits"... "Fortunately, there is a way to spot linkages that might be hidden. The technique is called the shared trait sib-pair method. Unlike the classic studies of large families used to spot Mendelian inheritance this method uses nuclear families and just two siblings, or a 'sib-pair.' Also, the search is narrowed to only those pairs who actually share the trait being sought."

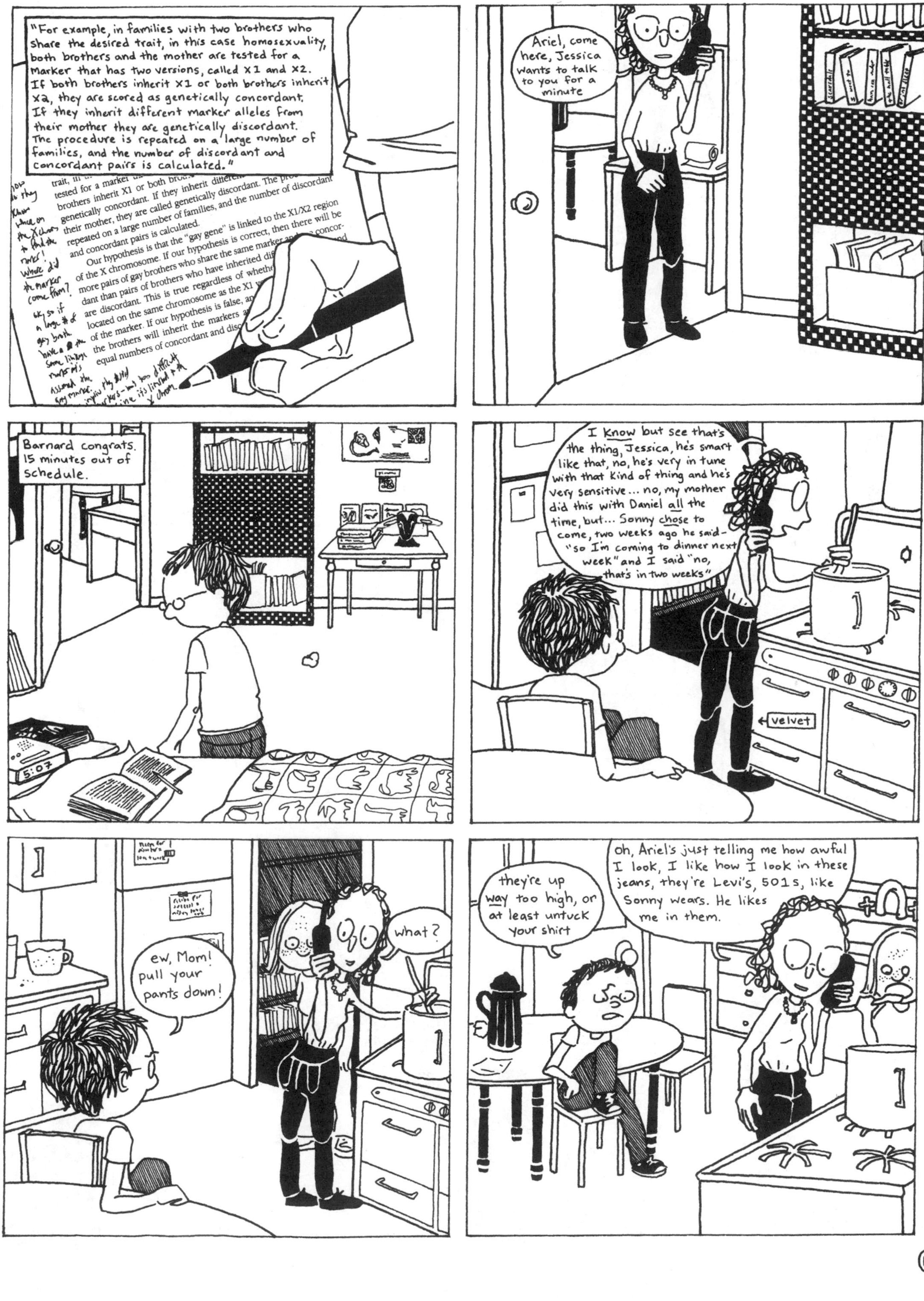
"For example, in families with two brothers who share the desired trait, in this case homosexuality, both brothers and the mother are tested for a marker that has two versions, called X1 and X2. If both brothers inherit X1 or both brothers inherit X2, they are scored as genetically concordant. If they inherit different marker alleles from their mother they are genetically discordant. The procedure is repeated on a large number of families, and the number of discordant and concordant pairs is calculated."
Ariel, come here, Jessica wants to talk to you for a minute
Barnard congrats. 15 minutes out of schedule.
I know but see that's the thing, Jessica, he's smart like that, no, he's very in tune with that kind of thing and he's very sensitive... no, my mother did this with Daniel all the time, but... Sonny chose to come, two weeks ago he said- "so I'm coming to dinner next week" and I said "no, that's in two weeks"
velvet
ew, Mom! pull your pants down!
what?
they're up way too high, or at least untuck your shirt
Oh, Ariel's just telling me how awful I look, I like how I look in these jeans, they're Levi's, 501s, like Sonny wears. He likes me in them.

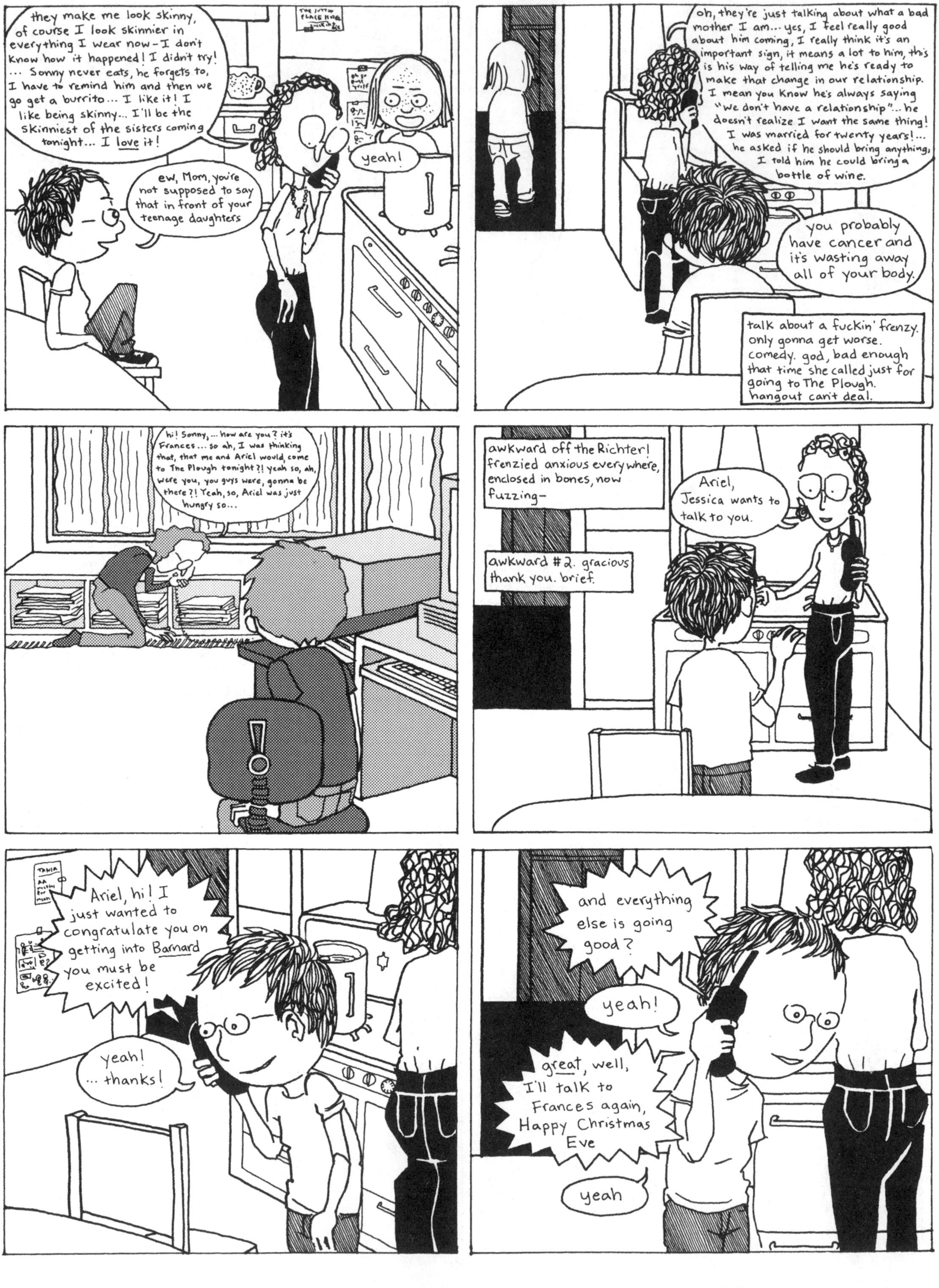
they make me look skinny, of course I look skinnier in everything I wear now - I don't know how it happened! I didn't try! ... Sonny never eats, he forgets to, I have to remind him and then we go get a burrito... I like it! I like being skinny... I'll be the skinniest of the sisters coming tonight... I love it!
yeah!
ew, Mom, you're not supposed to say that in front of your teenage daughters
oh, they're just talking about what a bad mother I am... yes, I feel really good about him coming, I really think it's an important sign, it means a lot to him, this is his way of telling me he's ready to make that change in our relationship. I mean you know he's always saying "we don't have a relationship"... he doesn't realize I want the same thing! I was married for twenty years!... he asked if he should bring anything, I told him he could bring a bottle of wine.
you probably have cancer and it's wasting away all of your body.
talk about a fuckin' frenzy. only gonna get worse. comedy. god, bad enough that time she called just for going to The Plough. hangout can't deal.
hi! Sonny, ... how are you? it's Frances... so ah, I was thinking that, that me and Ariel would, come to The Plough tonight?! yeah so, ah, were you, you guys were, gonna be there?! Yeah, so, Ariel was just hungry so...
awkward off the Richter! frenzied anxious everywhere, enclosed in bones, now fuzzing-
Ariel, Jessica wants to talk to you.
awkward #2. gracious thank you. brief.
Ariel, hi! I just wanted to congratulate you on getting into Barnard you must be excited!
yeah! ... thanks!
and everything else is going good?
yeah!
great, well, I'll talk to Frances again, Happy Christmas Eve
yeah

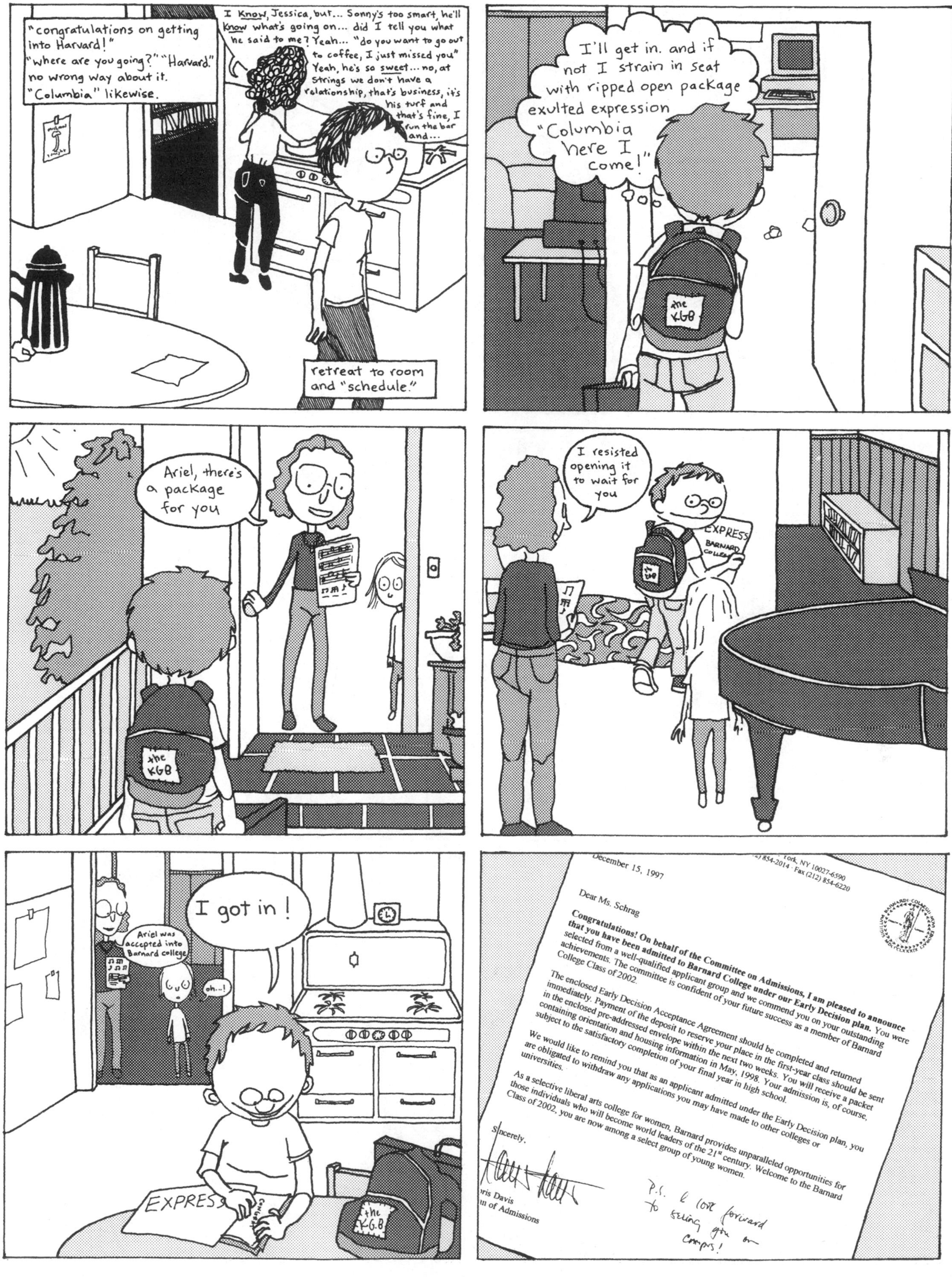

"congratulations on getting into Harvard!" "where are you going?" "Harvard." no wrong way about it. "Columbia" likewise.
I Know, Jessica, but... Sonny's too smart, he'll Know what's going on... did I tell you what he said to me? Yeah... "do you want to go out to coffee, I just missed you" Yeah, he's so sweet... no, at strings we don't have a relationship, that's business, it's his turf and that's fine, I run the bar and...
retreat to room and "schedule."
I'll get in. and if not I strain in seat with ripped open package exulted expression "Columbia here I come!"
the KGB
Ariel, there's a package for you
the KGB
I resisted opening it to wait for you
EXPRESS
BARNARD COLLEGE
I got in!
Ariel was accepted into Barnard college
oh...!
EXPRESS
the K.G.B
December 15, 1997
York, NY 10027-6590
854-2014 · Fax (212) 854-6220
Dear Ms. Schrag
Congratulations! On behalf of the Committee on Admissions, I am pleased to announce that you have been admitted to Barnard College under our Early Decision plan. You were selected from a well-qualified applicant group and we commend you on your outstanding achievements. The committee is confident of your future success as a member of Barnard College Class of 2002.
The enclosed Early Decision Acceptance Agreement should be completed and returned immediately. Payment of the deposit to reserve your place in the first-year class should be sent in the enclosed pre-addressed envelope within the next two weeks. You will receive a packet containing orientation and housing information in May, 1998. Your admission is, of course, subject to the satisfactory completion of your final year in high school.
We would like to remind you that as an applicant admitted under the Early Decision plan, you are obligated to withdraw any applications you may have made to other colleges or universities.
As a selective liberal arts college for women, Barnard provides unparalleled opportunities for those individuals who will become world leaders of the 21st century. Welcome to the Barnard Class of 2002, you are now among a select group of young women.
Sincerely,
oris Davis
n of Admissions
P.S. I look forward to seeing you on campus!

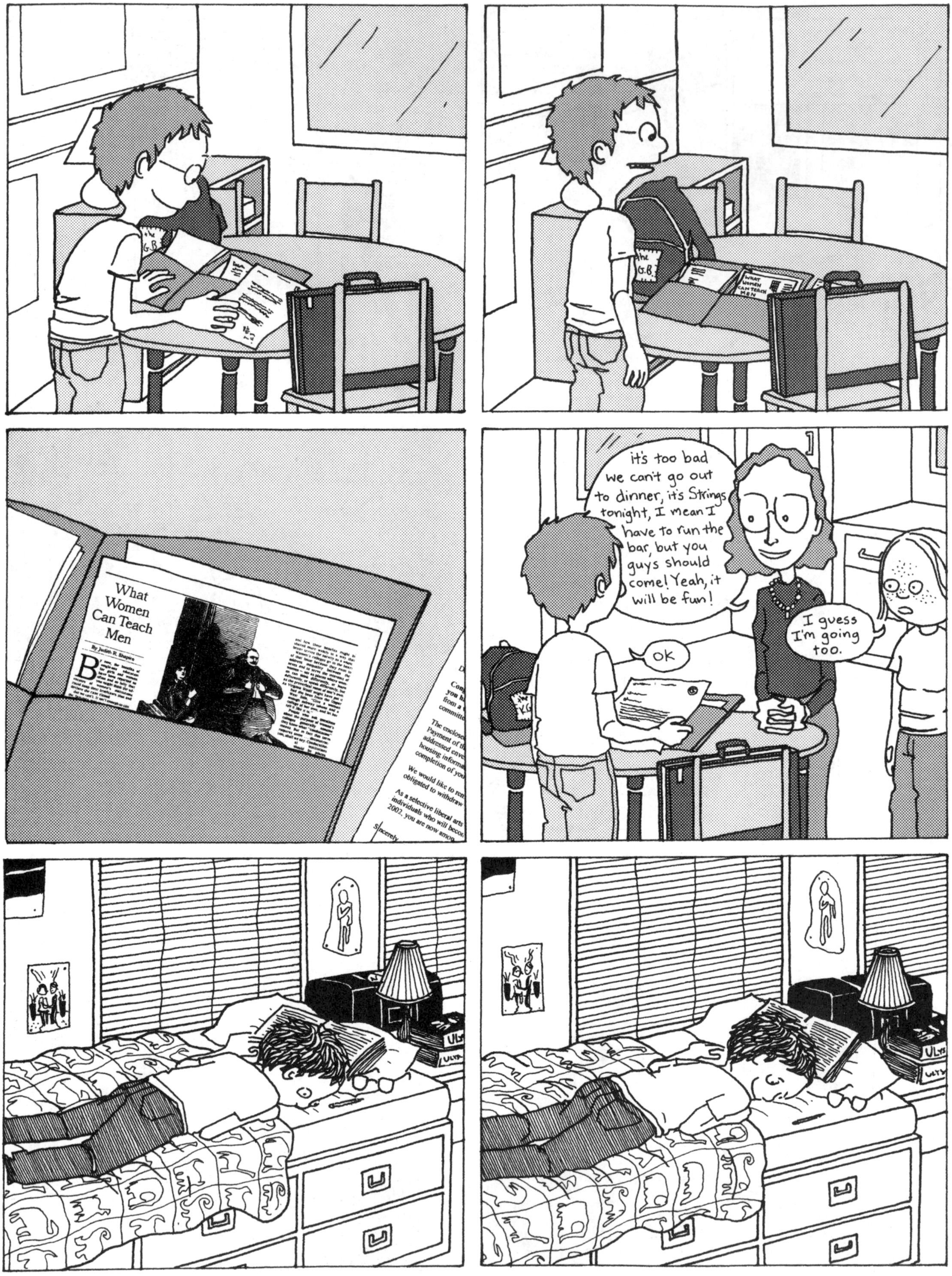

WHAT WOMEN CAN TEACH MEN
What Women Can Teach Men
it's too bad we can't go out to dinner, it's Strings tonight, I mean I have to run the bar, but you guys should come! Yeah, it will be fun!
I guess I'm going too.
OK

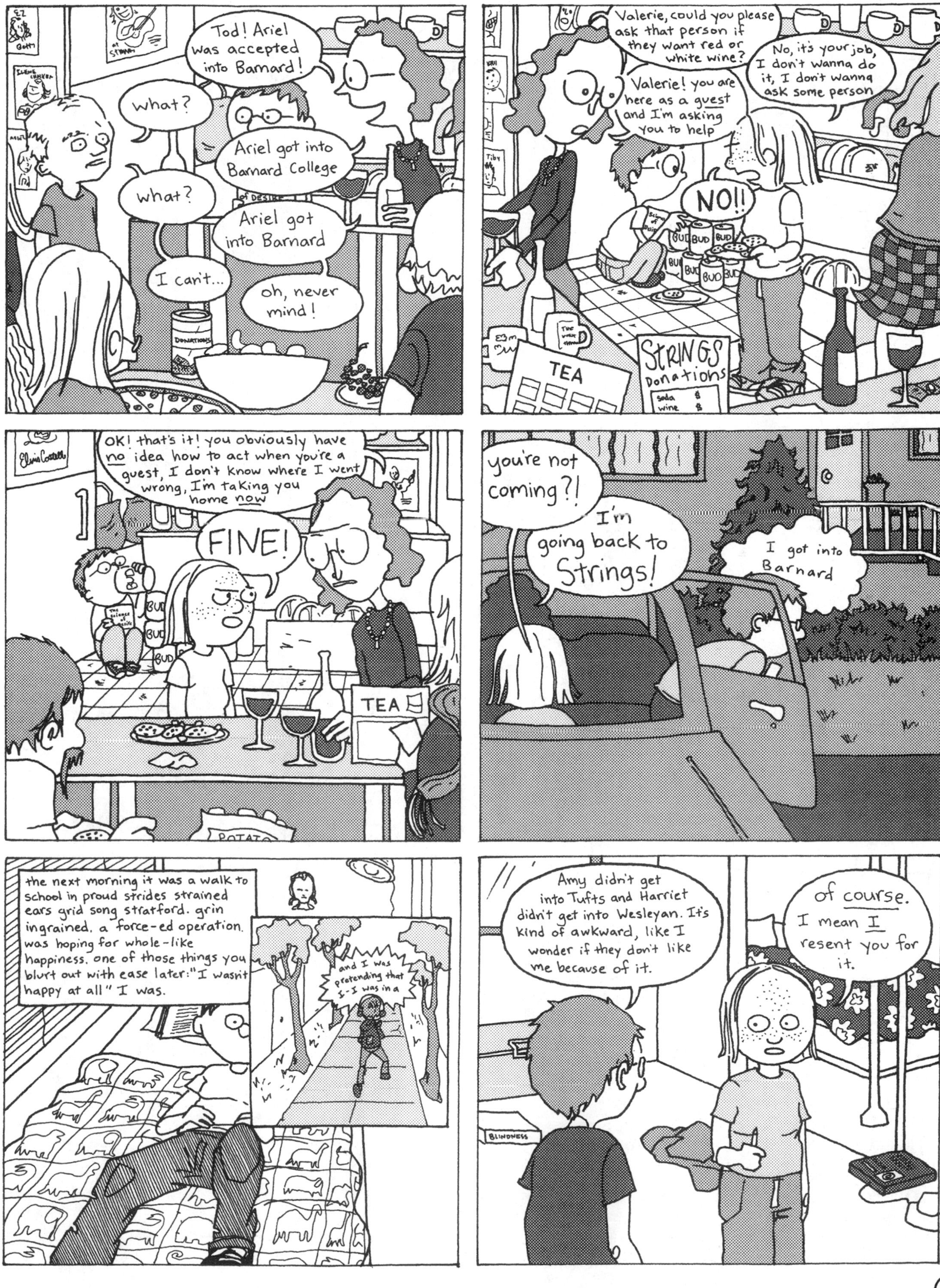
Tod! Ariel was accepted into Barnard!
what?
Ariel got into Barnard College
what?
Ariel got into Barnard
I can't...
oh, never mind!
DONATIONS
Valerie, could you please ask that person if they want red or white wine?
No, it's your job, I don't wanna do it, I don't wanna ask some person
Valerie! you are here as a guest and I'm asking you to help
NO!!
BUD
TEA
STRINGS Donations
soda $
wine $
OK! that's it! you obviously have no idea how to act when you're a guest, I don't know where I went wrong, I'm taking you home now
FINE!
TEA
you're not coming?!
I'm going back to Strings!
I got into Barnard
the next morning it was a walk to school in proud strides strained ears grid song stratford. grin ingrained. a force-ed operation. was hoping for whole-like happiness. one of those things you blurt out with ease later: "I wasn't happy at all" I was.
and I was pretending that I- I was in a
Amy didn't get into Tufts and Harriet didn't get into Wesleyan. It's kind of awkward, like I wonder if they don't like me because of it.
of course. I mean I resent you for it.
BLINDNESS

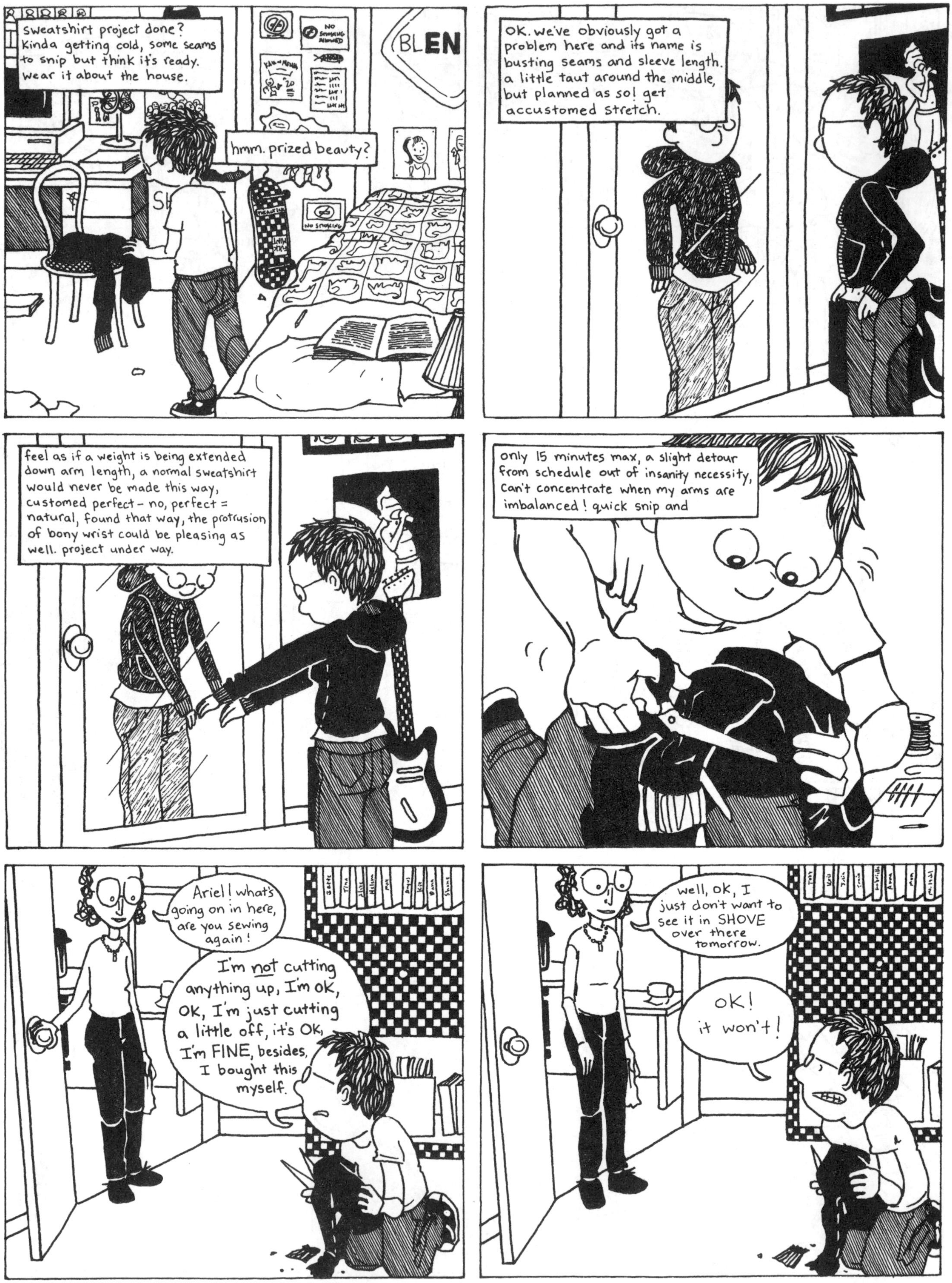

sweatshirt project done? Kinda getting cold, some seams to snip but think it's ready. wear it about the house.
hmm. prized beauty?
OK. we've obviously got a problem here and its name is busting seams and sleeve length. a little taut around the middle, but planned as so! get accustomed stretch.
feel as if a weight is being extended down arm length, a normal sweatshirt would never be made this way, customed perfect - no, perfect = natural, found that way, the protrusion of bony wrist could be pleasing as well. project under way.
only 15 minutes max, a slight detour from schedule out of insanity necessity, can't concentrate when my arms are imbalanced! quick snip and
Ariel! what's going on in here, are you sewing again!
I'm not cutting anything up, I'm OK, OK, I'm just cutting a little off, it's OK, I'm FINE, besides, I bought this myself.
well, OK, I just don't want to see it in SHOVE over there tomorrow.
OK! it won't!

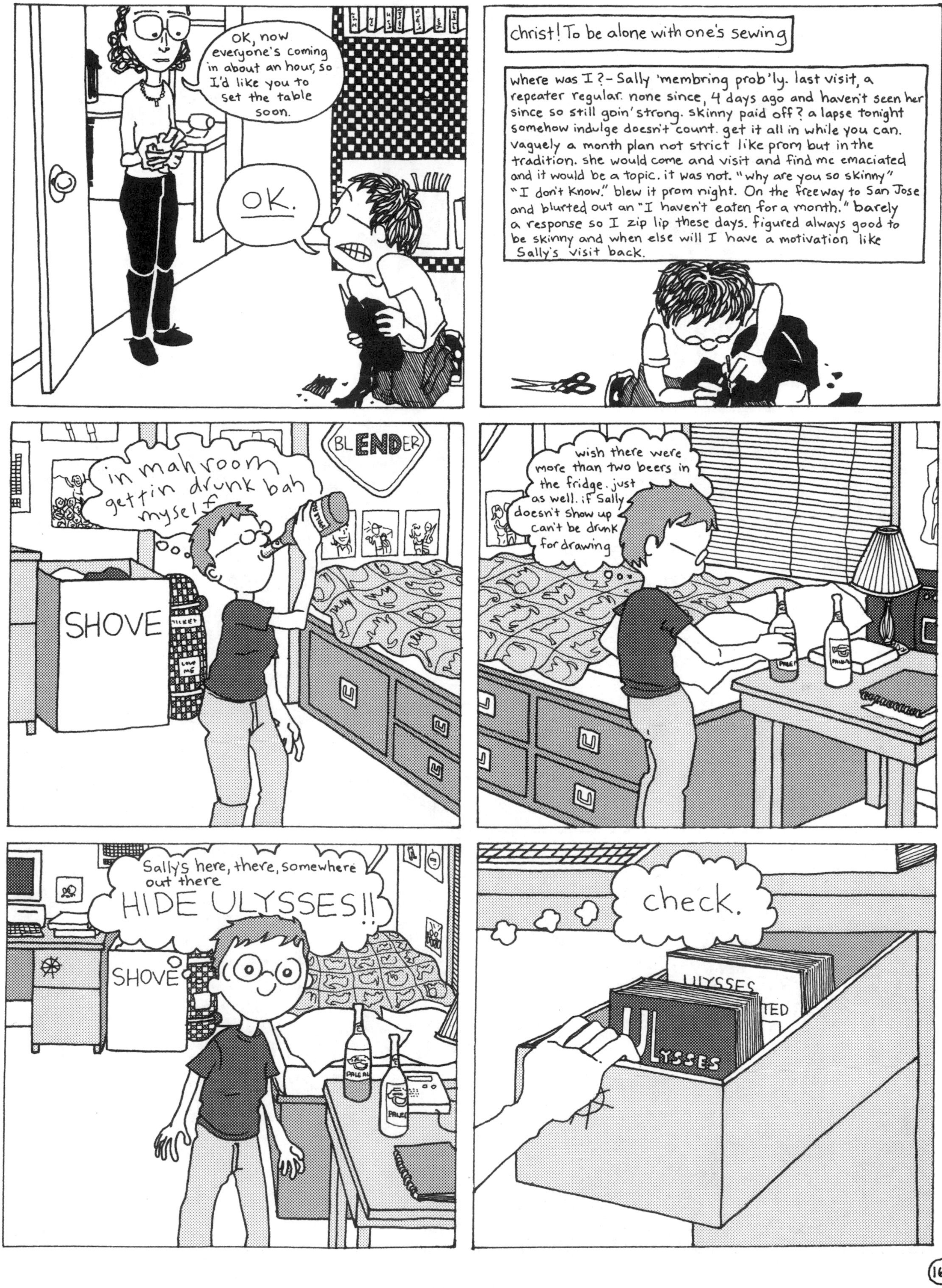
OK, now everyone's coming in about an hour, so I'd like you to set the table soon.
OK.
christ! To be alone with one's sewing
where was I?- Sally 'membring prob'ly. last visit, a repeater regular. none since, 4 days ago and haven't seen her since so still goin' strong. skinny paid off? a lapse tonight somehow indulge doesn't count. get it all in while you can. vaguely a month plan not strict like prom but in the tradition. she would come and visit and find me emaciated and it would be a topic. it was not. "why are you so skinny" "I don't know." blew it prom night. On the freeway to San Jose and blurted out an "I haven't eaten for a month." barely a response so I zip lip these days. figured always good to be skinny and when else will I have a motivation like Sally's visit back.
BLENDER
in mah room gettin drunk bah myself
SHOVE
wish there were more than two beers in the fridge. just as well. if Sally doesn't show up can't be drunk for drawing
Sally's here, there, somewhere out there
HIDE ULYSSES!!
SHOVE
check.

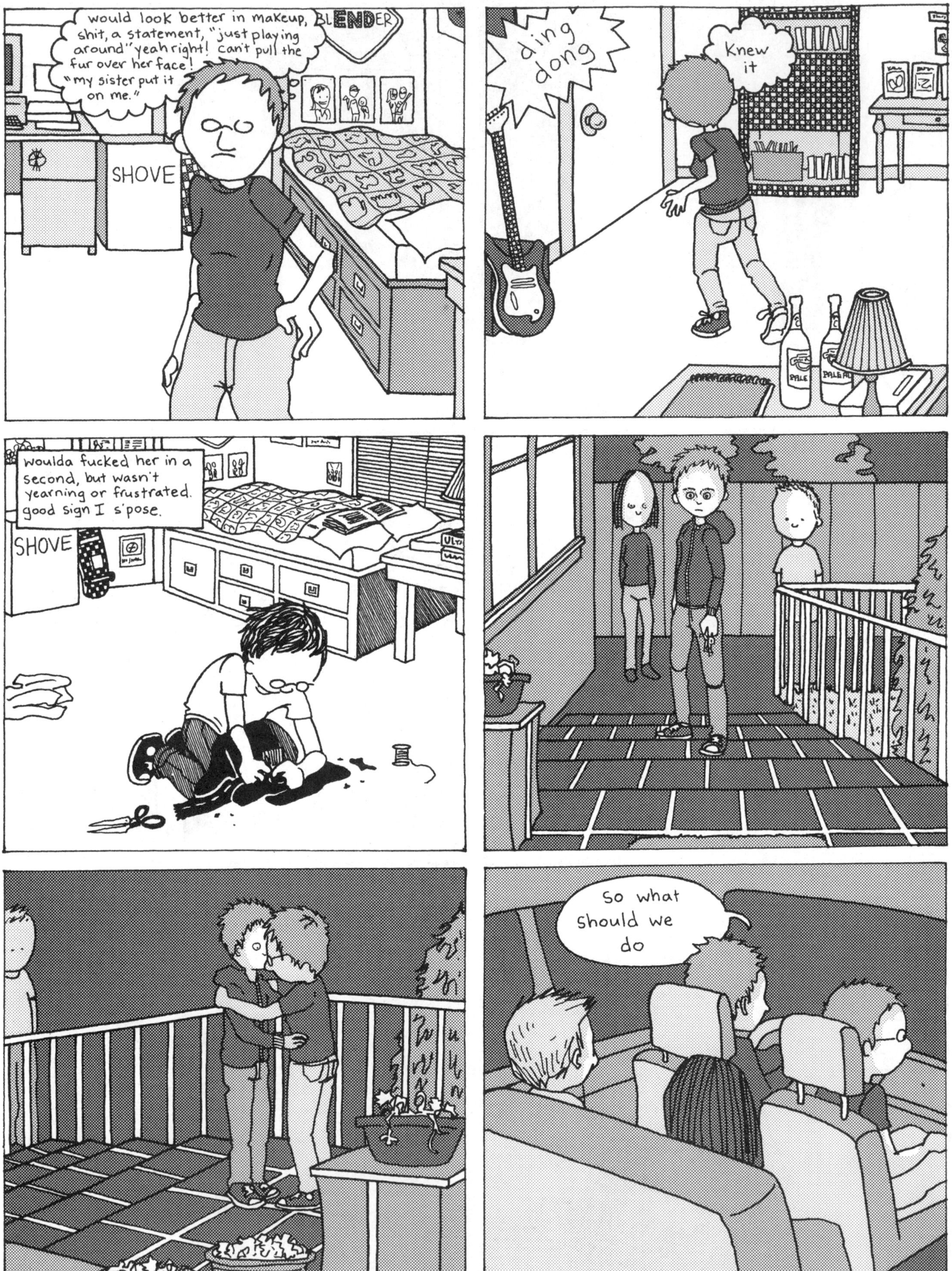
would look better in makeup, shit, a statement, "just playing around" yeah right! can't pull the fur over her face! "my sister put it on me."
BLENDER
SHOVE
ding dong
Knew it
PALE
PALE
woulda fucked her in a second, but wasn't yearning or frustrated. good sign I s'pose.
SHOVE
So what should we do

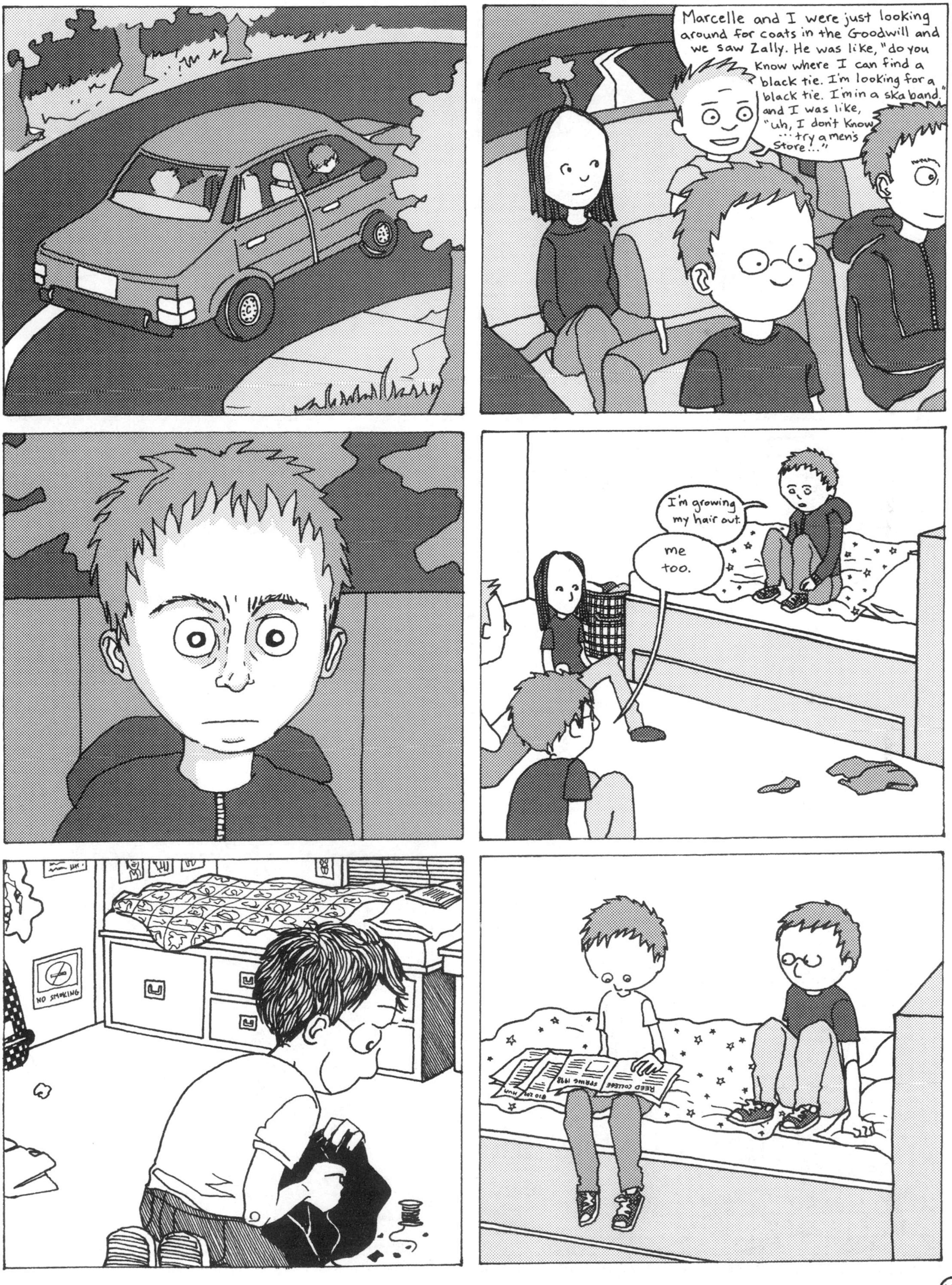
Marcelle and I were just looking around for coats in the Goodwill and we saw Zally. He was like, "do you know where I can find a black tie. I'm looking for a black tie. I'm in a ska band." and I was like, "uh, I don't know ...try a men's store..."
I'm growing my hair out.
me too.
NO SMOKING
REED COLLEGE
SPRING 1998

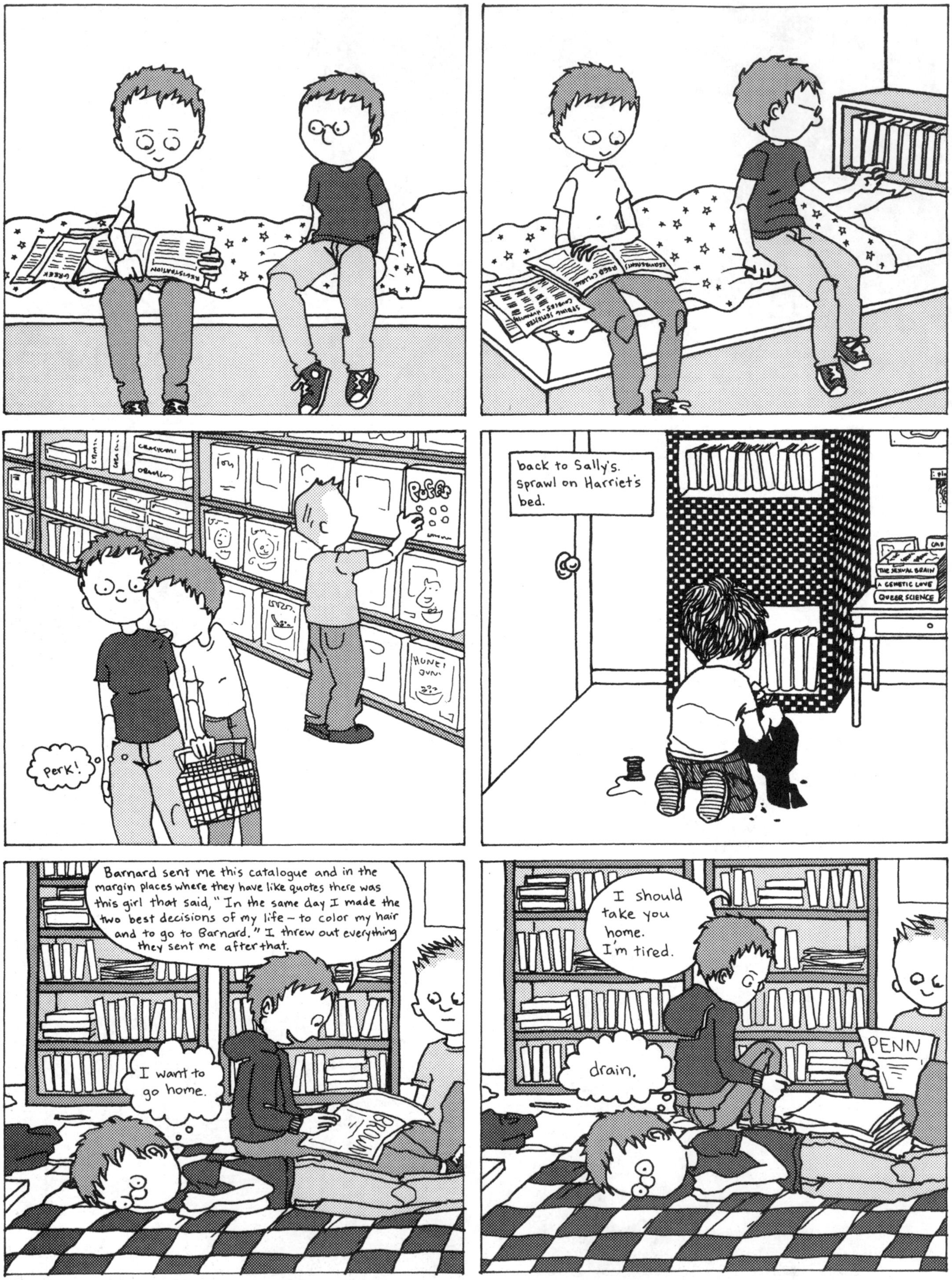
back to Sally's.
sprawl on Harriet's
bed.
THE SEXUAL BRAIN
A GENETIC LOVE
QUEER SCIENCE
Perk!
Barnard sent me this catalogue and in the margin places where they have like quotes there was this girl that said, "In the same day I made the two best decisions of my life – to color my hair and to go to Barnard." I threw out everything they sent me after that.
I want to go home.
BROWN
I should take you home. I'm tired.
drain.
PENN

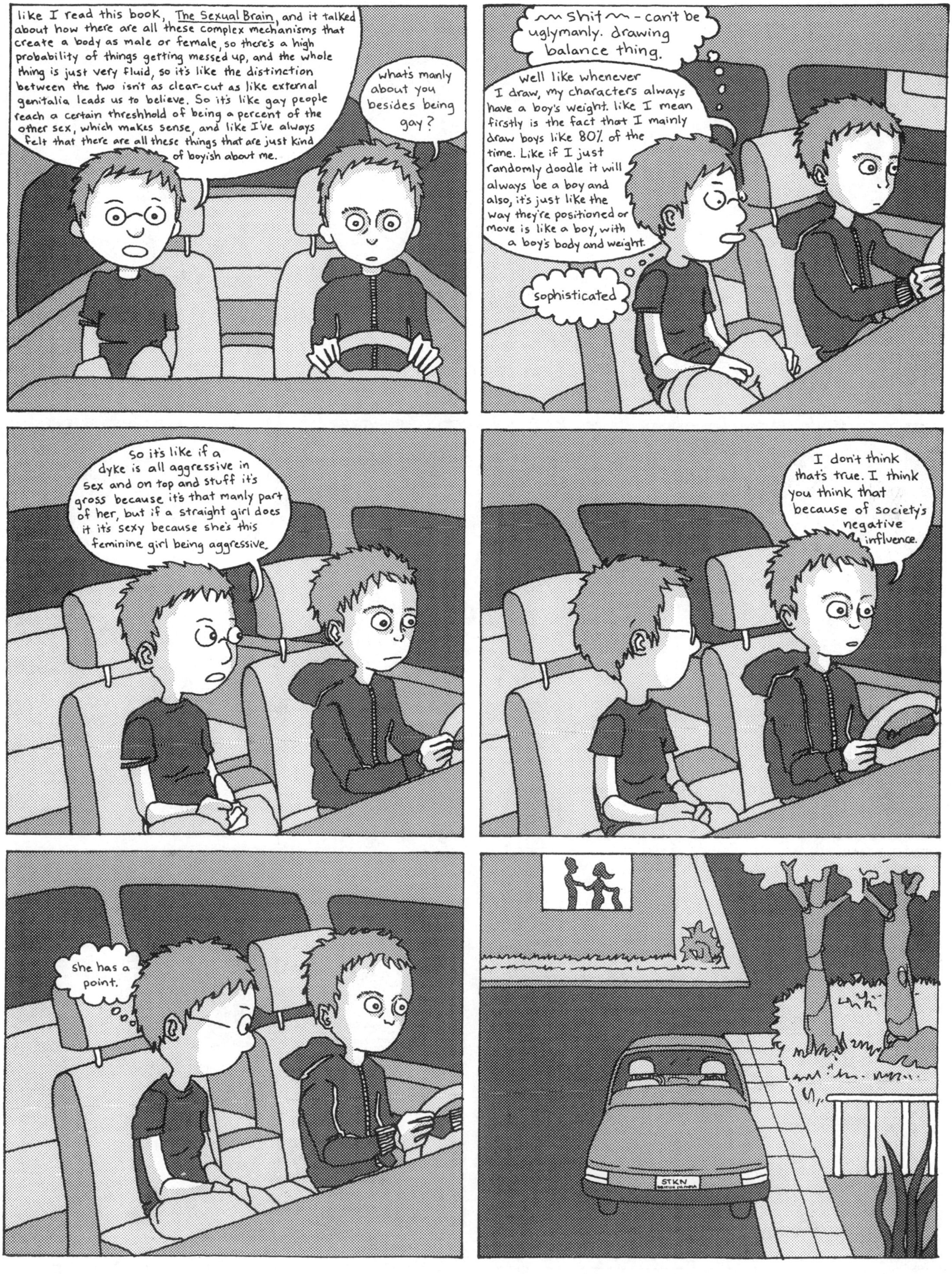
like I read this book, The Sexual Brain, and it talked about how there are all these complex mechanisms that create a body as male or female, so there's a high probability of things getting messed up, and the whole thing is just very fluid, so it's like the distinction between the two isn't as clear-cut as like external genitalia leads us to believe. So it's like gay people reach a certain threshhold of being a percent of the other sex, which makes sense, and like I've always felt that there are all these things that are just kind of boyish about me.
what's manly about you besides being gay?
shit - can't be uglymanly. drawing balance thing.
Well like whenever I draw, my characters always have a boy's weight. like I mean firstly is the fact that I mainly draw boys like 80% of the time. Like if I just randomly doodle it will always be a boy and also, it's just like the way they're positioned or move is like a boy, with a boy's body and weight.
sophisticated
So it's like if a dyke is all aggressive in sex and on top and stuff it's gross because it's that manly part of her, but if a straight girl does it it's sexy because she's this feminine girl being aggressive.
I don't think that's true. I think you think that because of society's negative influence.
she has a point.
STKN

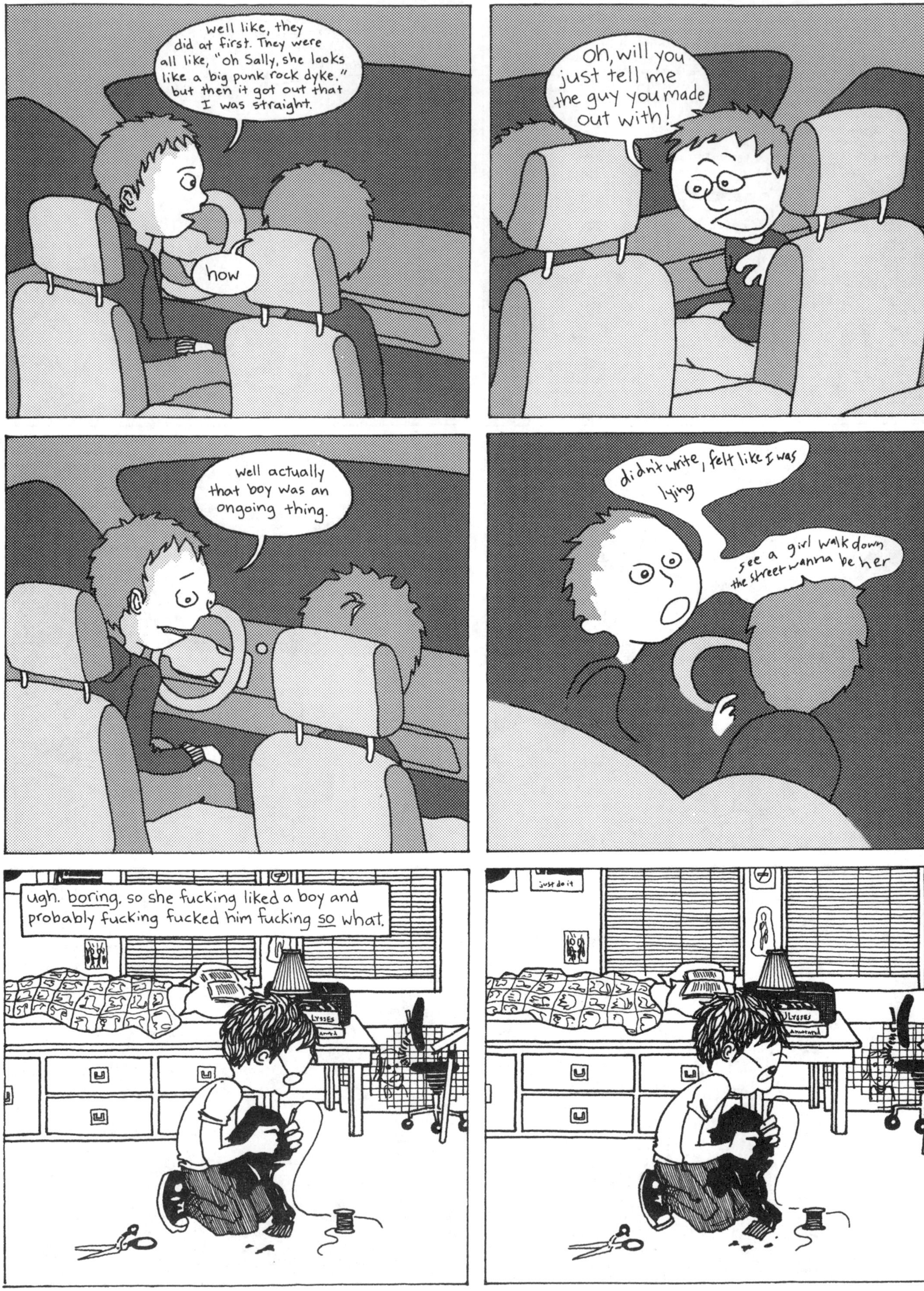
well like, they did at first. They were all like, "oh Sally, she looks like a big punk rock dyke." but then it got out that I was straight.
how
Oh, will you just tell me the guy you made out with!
well actually that boy was an ongoing thing.
didn't write, felt like I was lying
see a girl walk down the street wanna be her
ugh. boring. so she fucking liked a boy and probably fucking fucked him fucking so what.
just do it

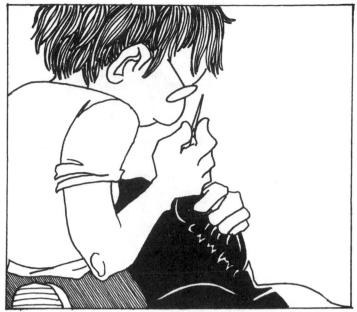

"Since then the only contact we've had is some awkward conversation about the plan of the buying of the dildo for my 18th birthday."

youje!

I can only stay for a second, I have like a million essays to write and 20 thousand college applications. my mom like wouldn't let me leave, I had to tell her I had to return these tapes to you. she didn't believe me. youje.

youje. I've been sewing this sweatshirt for an hour.

it looks cool!

I sewed this thermal on the inside so I can have like these hidden pockets for putting stuff in.

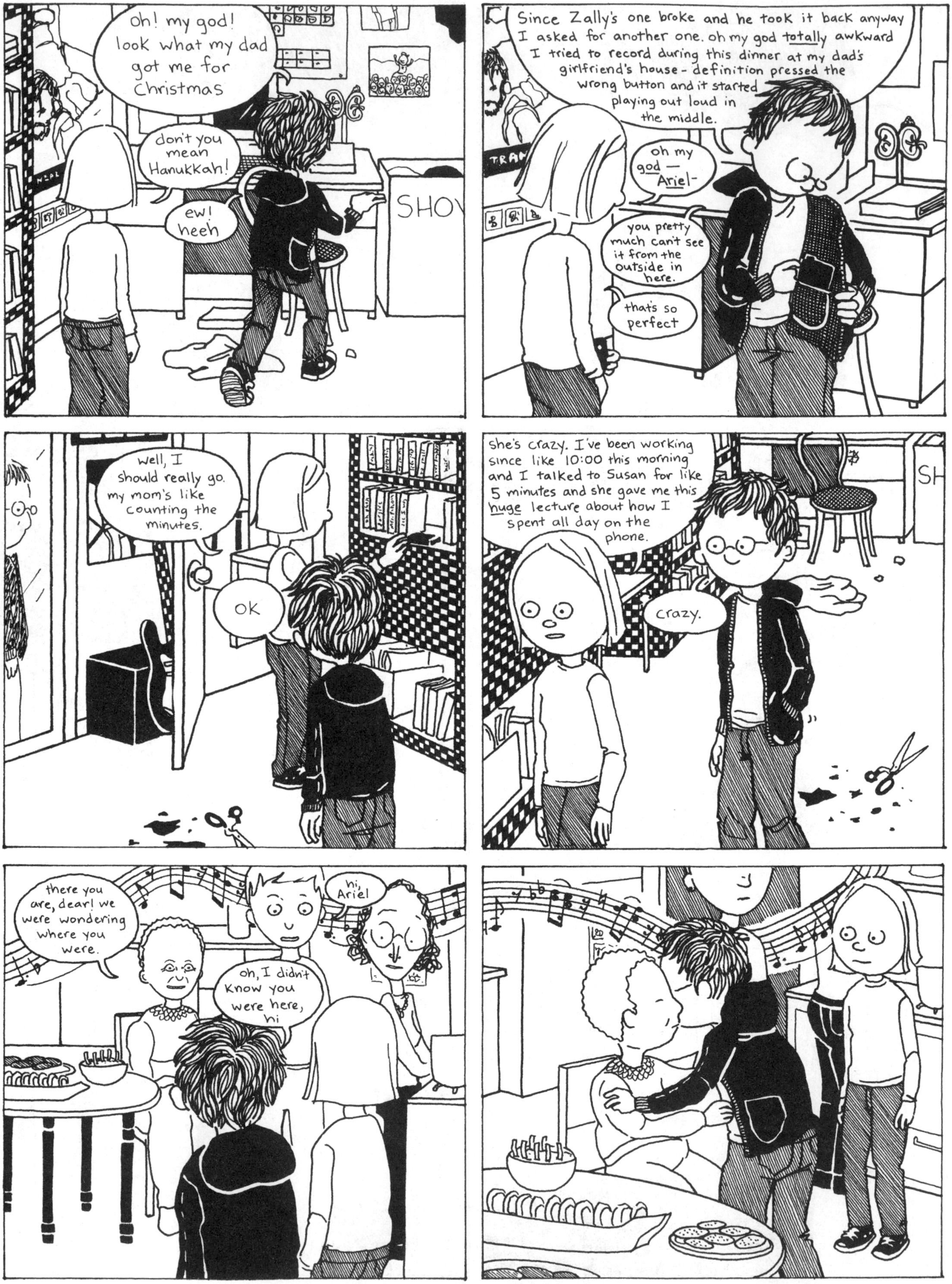
oh! my god! look what my dad got me for Christmas
don't you mean Hanukkah!
ew! heeh
Since Zally's one broke and he took it back anyway I asked for another one. oh my god totally awkward I tried to record during this dinner at my dad's girlfriend's house - definition pressed the wrong button and it started playing out loud in the middle.
oh my god — Ariel-
you pretty much can't see it from the outside in here.
that's so perfect
well, I should really go. my mom's like counting the minutes.
OK
she's crazy. I've been working since like 10:00 this morning and I talked to Susan for like 5 minutes and she gave me this huge lecture about how I spent all day on the phone.
crazy.
there you are, dear! we were wondering where you were.
hi, Ariel
oh, I didn't know you were here, hi

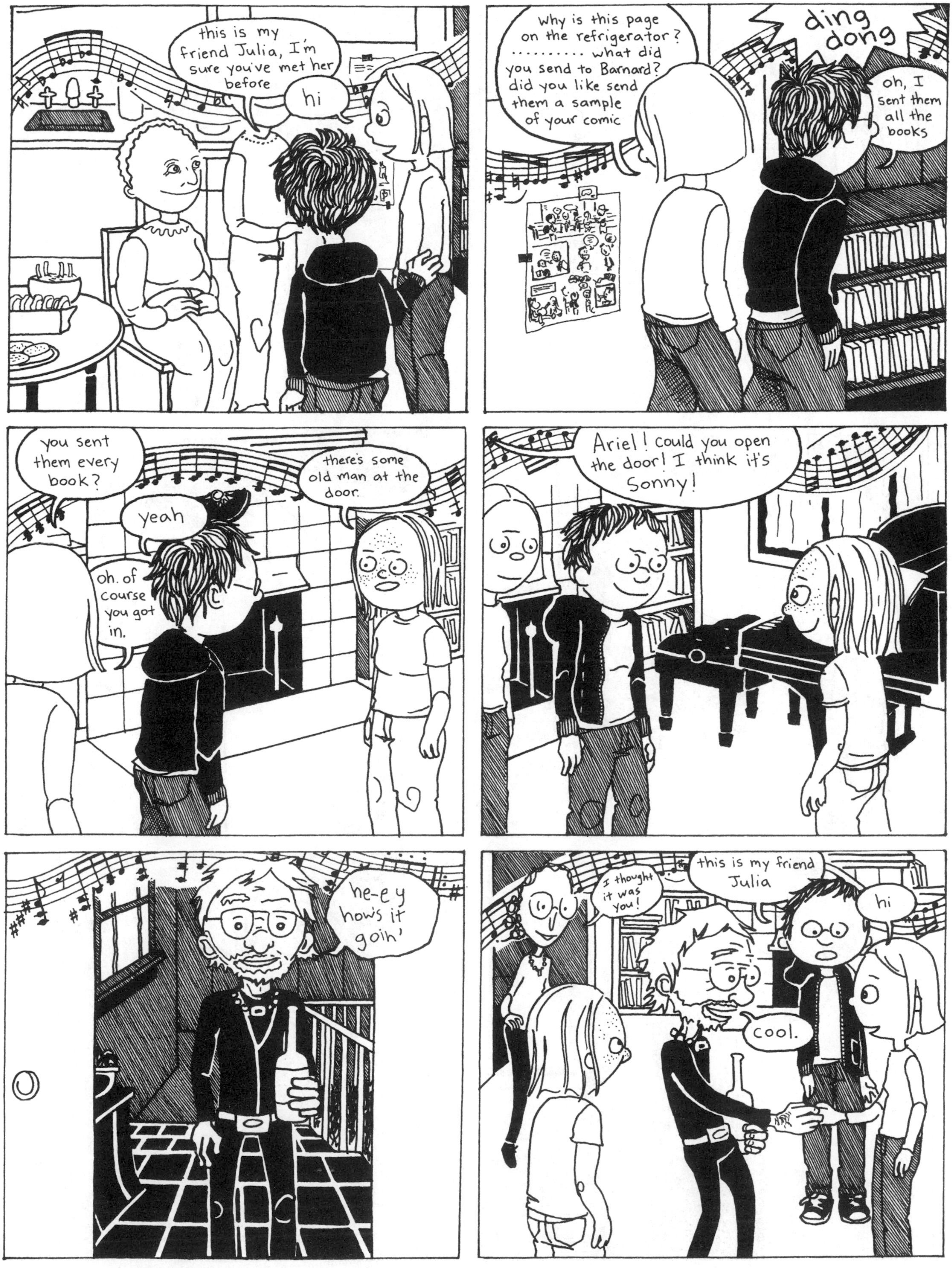
this is my friend Julia, I'm sure you've met her before
hi
why is this page on the refrigerator? .... what did you send to Barnard? did you like send them a sample of your comic
ding dong
oh, I sent them all the books
you sent them every book?
yeah
oh. of course you got in.
there's some old man at the door.
Ariel! could you open the door! I think it's Sonny!
he-ey hows it goin'
I thought it was you!
this is my friend Julia
hi
cool.

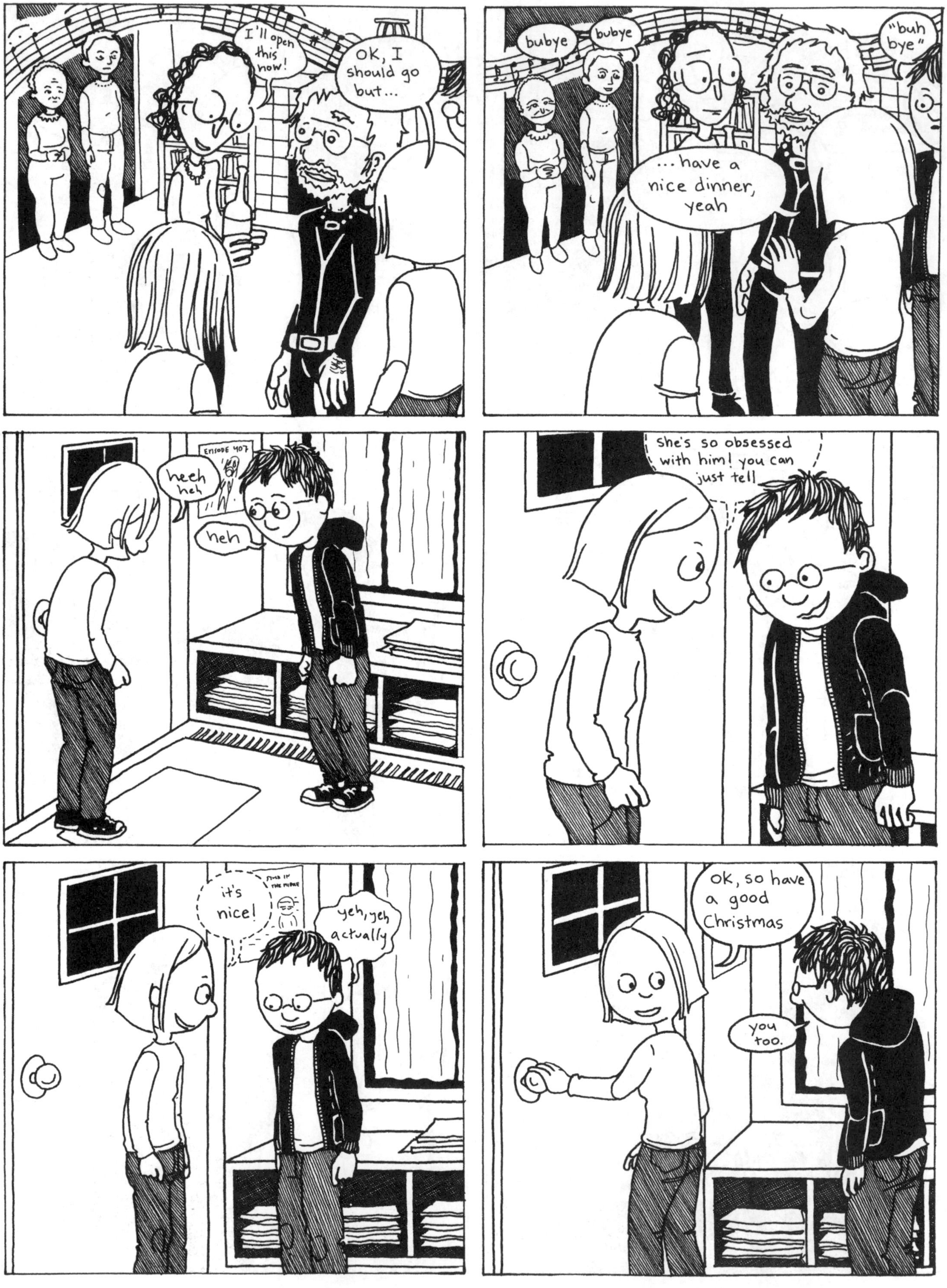

I'll open this now!
OK, I should go but...
bubye
bubye
"buh bye"
...have a nice dinner, yeah
EPISODE 407
heeh heh
heh
She's so obsessed with him! you can just tell
it's nice!
yeh, yeh actually
OK, so have a good Christmas
you too.

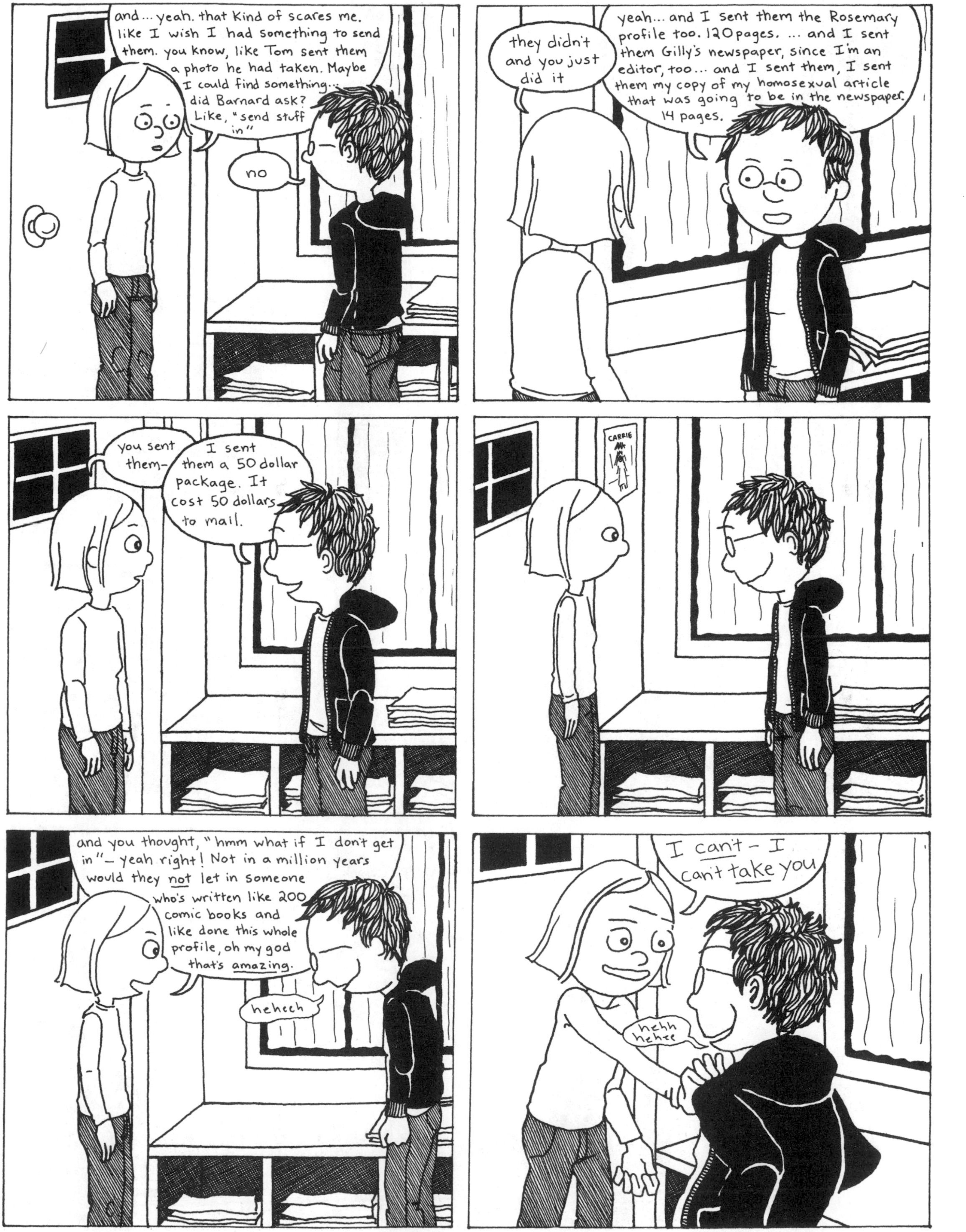
and... yeah. that kind of scares me. like I wish I had something to send them. you know, like Tom sent them a photo he had taken. Maybe I could find something... did Barnard ask? Like, "send stuff in"
no
they didn't and you just did it
yeah... and I sent them the Rosemary profile too. 120 pages. ... and I sent them Gilly's newspaper, since I'm an editor, too... and I sent them, I sent them my copy of my homosexual article that was going to be in the newspaper. 14 pages.
you sent them-
I sent them a 50 dollar package. It cost 50 dollars to mail.
CARRIE
and you thought, "hmm what if I don't get in" - yeah right! Not in a million years would they not let in someone who's written like 200 comic books and like done this whole profile, oh my god that's amazing.
heheeh
I can't - I can't take you
hehh hehee

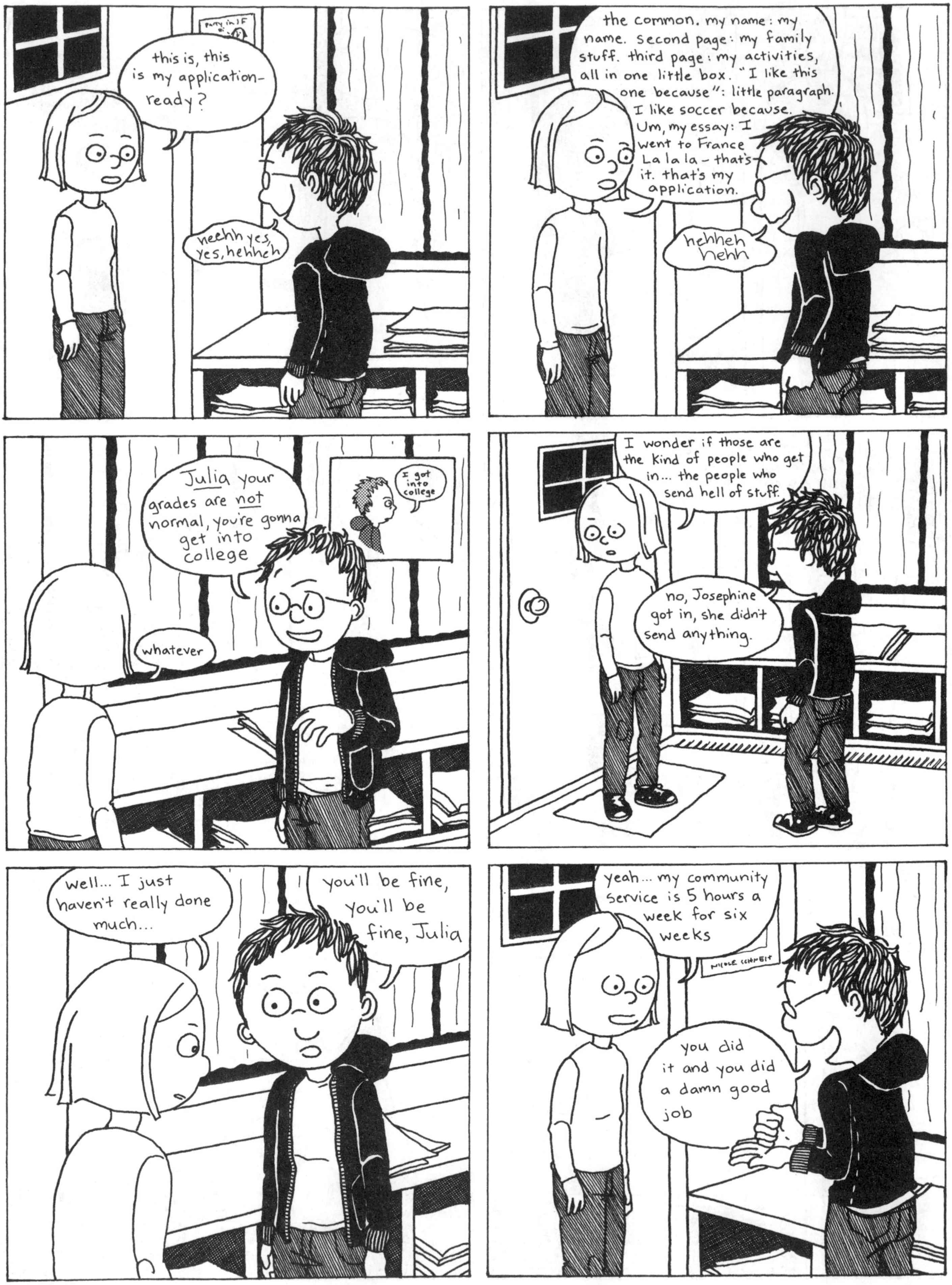

this is, this is my application- ready?
neehh yes, yes, hehheh
the common. my name: my name. second page: my family stuff. third page: my activities, all in one little box. "I like this one because": little paragraph. I like soccer because. Um, my essay: I went to France La la la - that's it. that's my application.
hehheh hehh
Julia your grades are not normal, you're gonna get into college
I got into college
whatever
I wonder if those are the kind of people who get in... the people who send hell of stuff.
no, Josephine got in, she didn't send anything.
well... I just haven't really done much...
you'll be fine, you'll be fine, Julia
yeah... my community service is 5 hours a week for six weeks
you did it and you did a damn good job

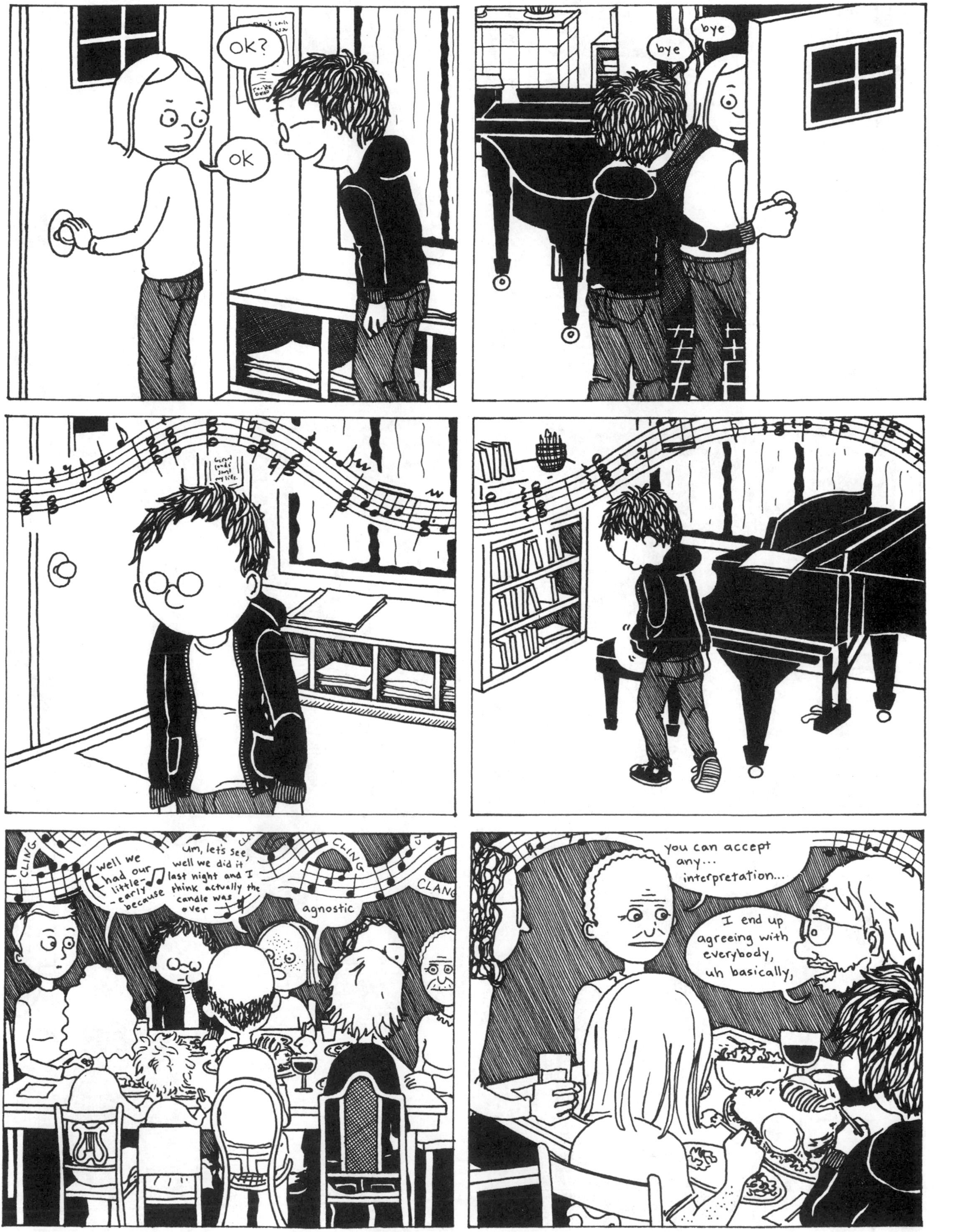
ok?
ok
bye
bye
CLING
well we had our little— early because
um, let's see, well we did it last night and I think actually the candle was over
CLING
agnostic
CLANG
you can accept any... interpretation...
I end up agreeing with everybody, uh basically,

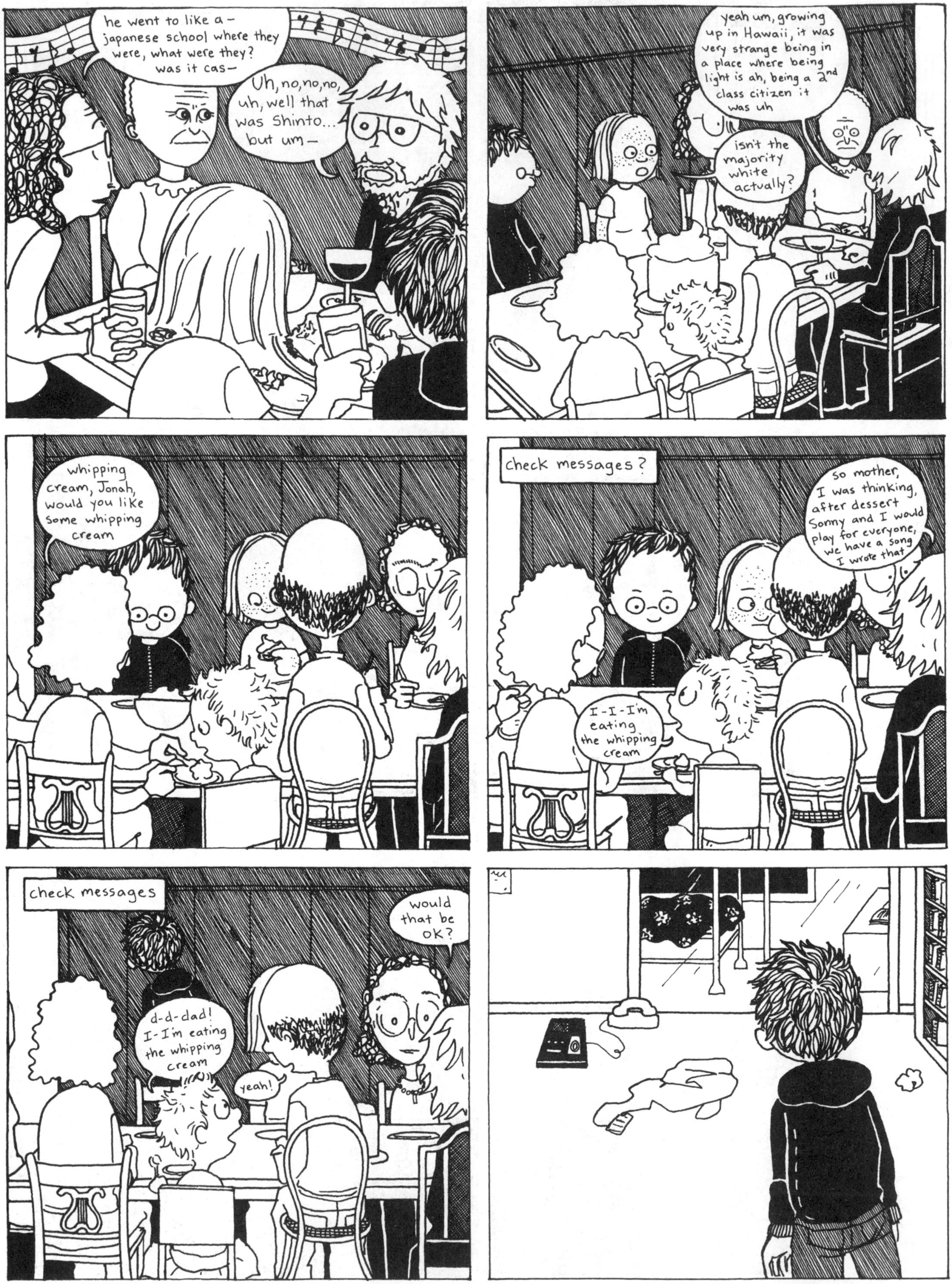
he went to like a- japanese school where they were, what were they? was it cas-
Uh, no, no, no, uh, well that was Shinto... but um-
yeah um, growing up in Hawaii, it was very strange being in a place where being light is ah, being a 2nd class citizen it was uh
isn't the majority white actually?
whipping cream, Jonah, would you like some whipping cream
check messages?
so mother, I was thinking, after dessert Sonny and I would play for everyone, we have a song I wrote that
I-I-I'm eating the whipping cream
check messages
would that be OK?
d-d-dad! I-I'm eating the whipping cream
yeah!

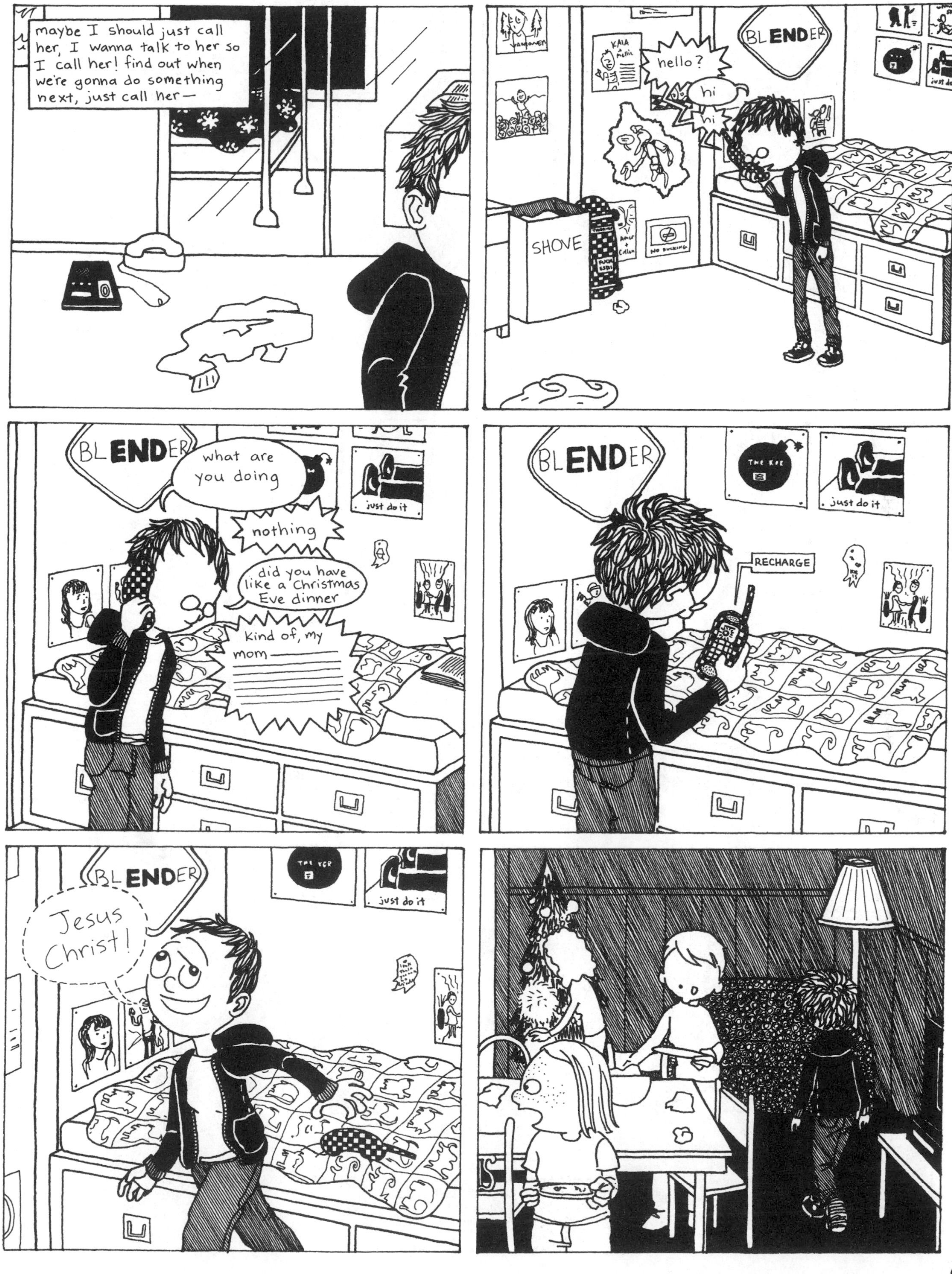
maybe I should just call her, I wanna talk to her so I call her! find out when we're gonna do something next, just call her—
BLENDER
hello?
hi
hi
SHOVE
NO DUCKING
what are you doing
nothing
did you have like a Christmas Eve dinner
kind of, my mom—
RECHARGE
just do it
Jesus Christ!

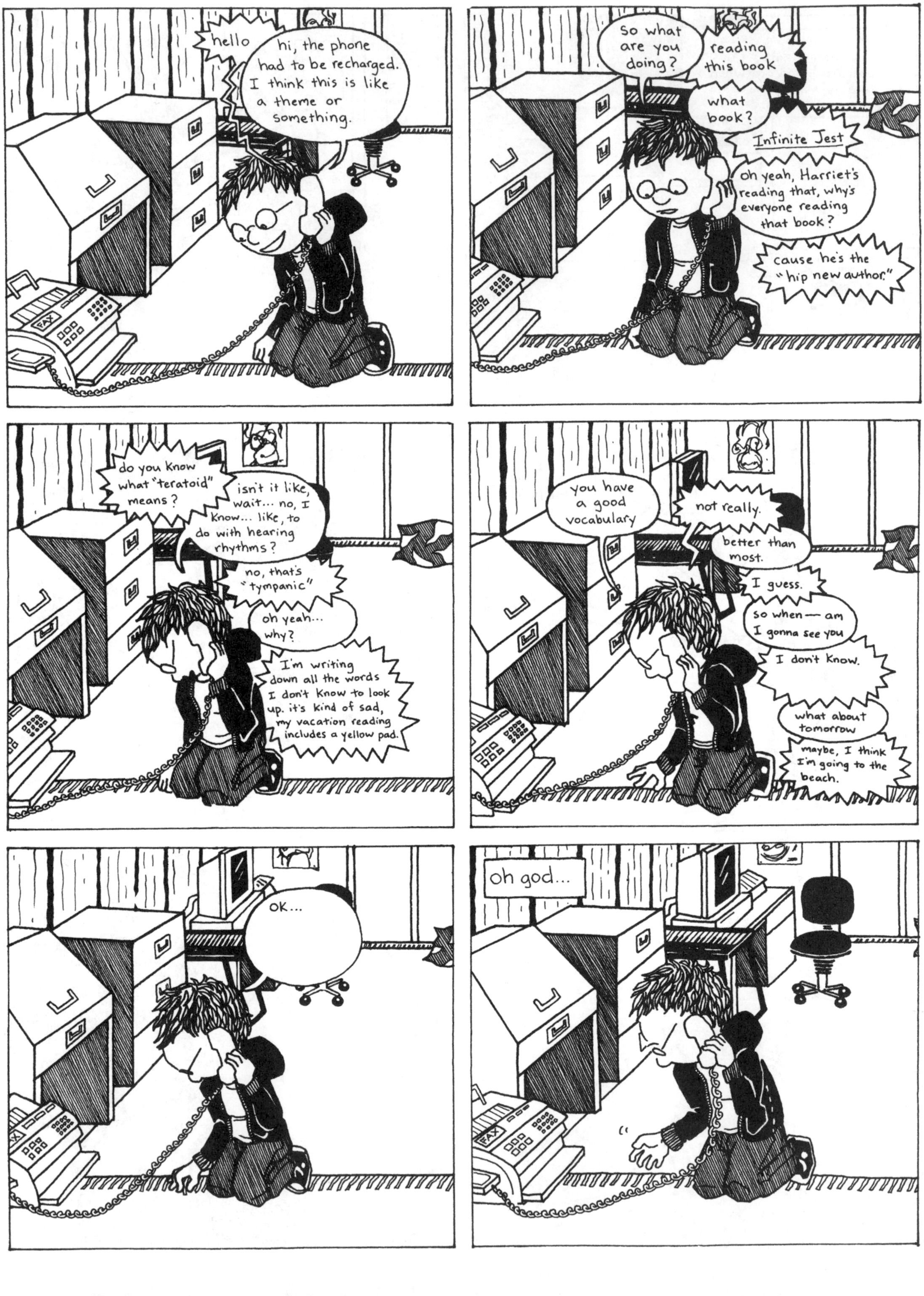

hello
hi, the phone had to be recharged. I think this is like a theme or something.
So what are you doing?
reading this book
what book?
Infinite Jest
oh yeah, Harriet's reading that, why's everyone reading that book?
cause he's the "hip new author."
do you Know what "teratoid" means?
isn't it like, wait... no, I Know... like, to do with hearing rhythms?
no, that's "tympanic"
oh yeah... why?
I'm writing down all the words I don't Know to look up. it's kind of sad, my vacation reading includes a yellow pad.
you have a good vocabulary
not really.
better than most.
I guess.
so when — am I gonna see you
I don't Know.
what about tomorrow
maybe, I think I'm going to the beach.
ok...
oh god...

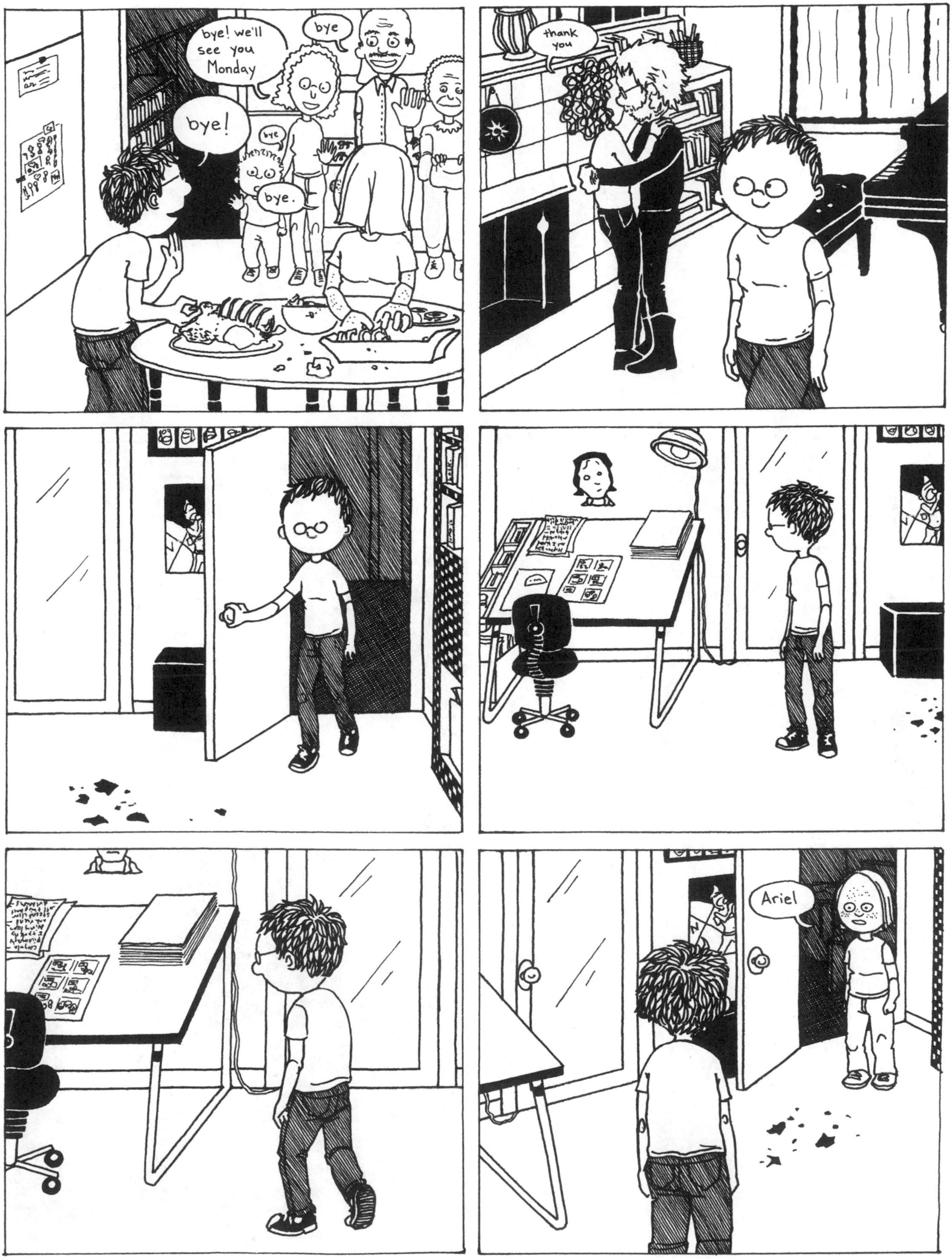
bye! we'll see you Monday
bye
bye!
bye
bye.
thank you
Ariel

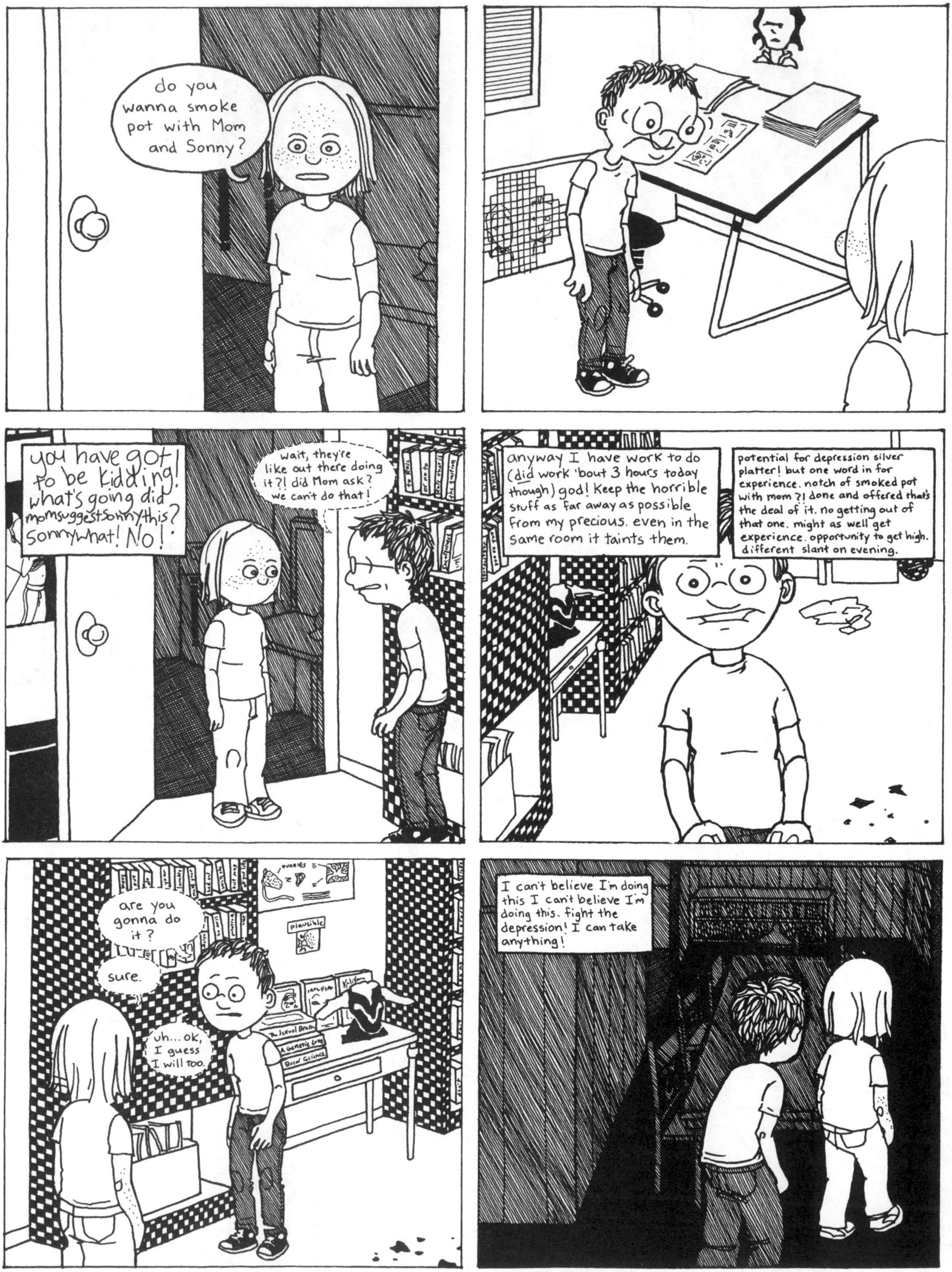
do you wanna smoke pot with Mom and Sonny?
you have got to be kidding! what's going did momsuggestSonnythis? Sonnywhat! No!
wait, they're like out there doing it?! did Mom ask? we can't do that!
anyway I have work to do (did work 'bout 3 hours today though) god! Keep the horrible stuff as far away as possible from my precious. even in the same room it taints them.
potential for depression silver platter! but one word in for experience. notch of smoked pot with mom?! done and offered that's the deal of it. no getting out of that one. might as well get experience. opportunity to get high. different slant on evening.
are you gonna do it?
sure.
uh... ok, I guess I will too.
I can't believe I'm doing this I can't believe I'm doing this. fight the depression! I can take anything!

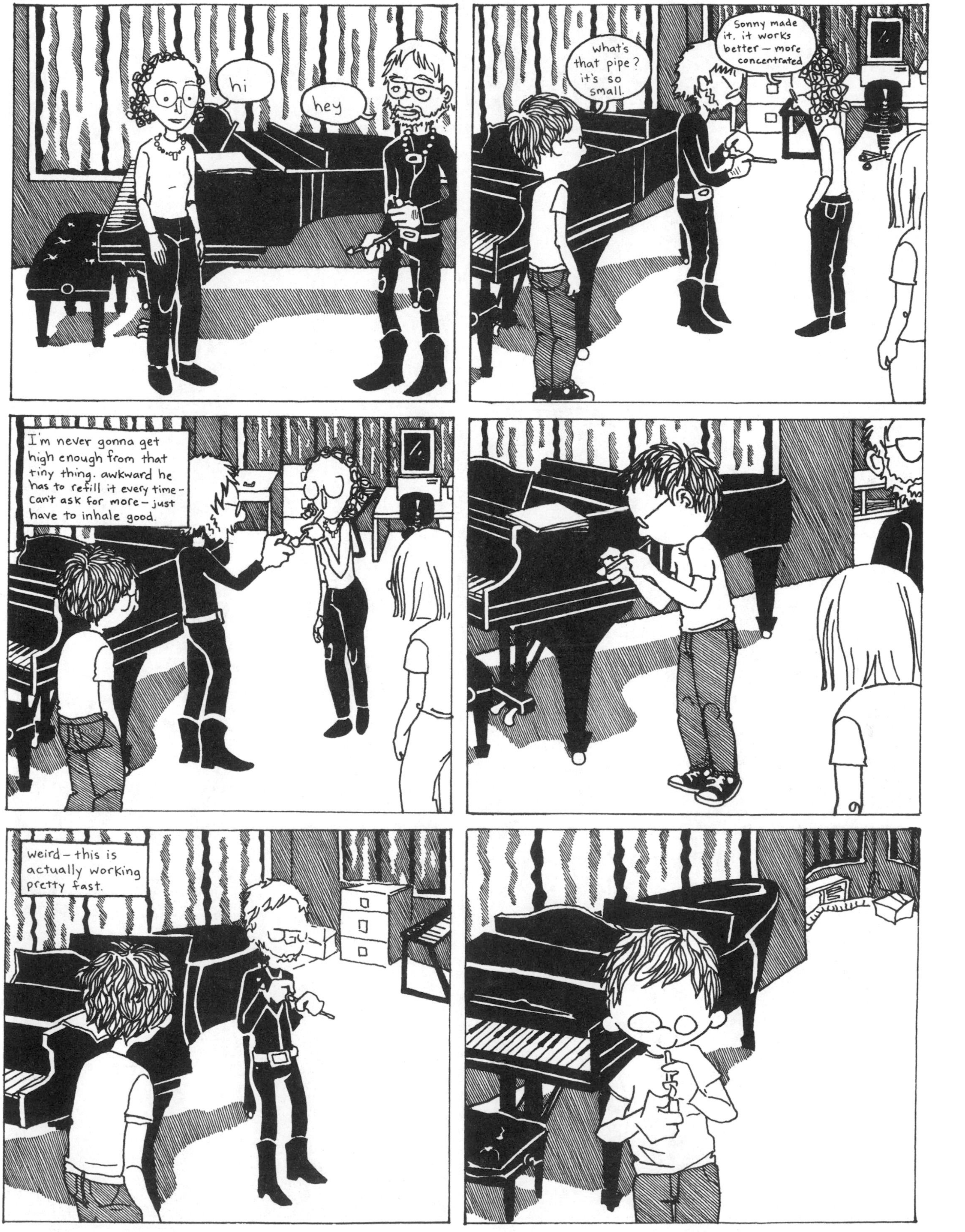
hi
hey
what's that pipe? it's so small.
Sonny made it. it works better — more concentrated
I'm never gonna get high enough from that tiny thing. awkward he has to refill it every time - can't ask for more - just have to inhale good.
weird - this is actually working pretty fast.

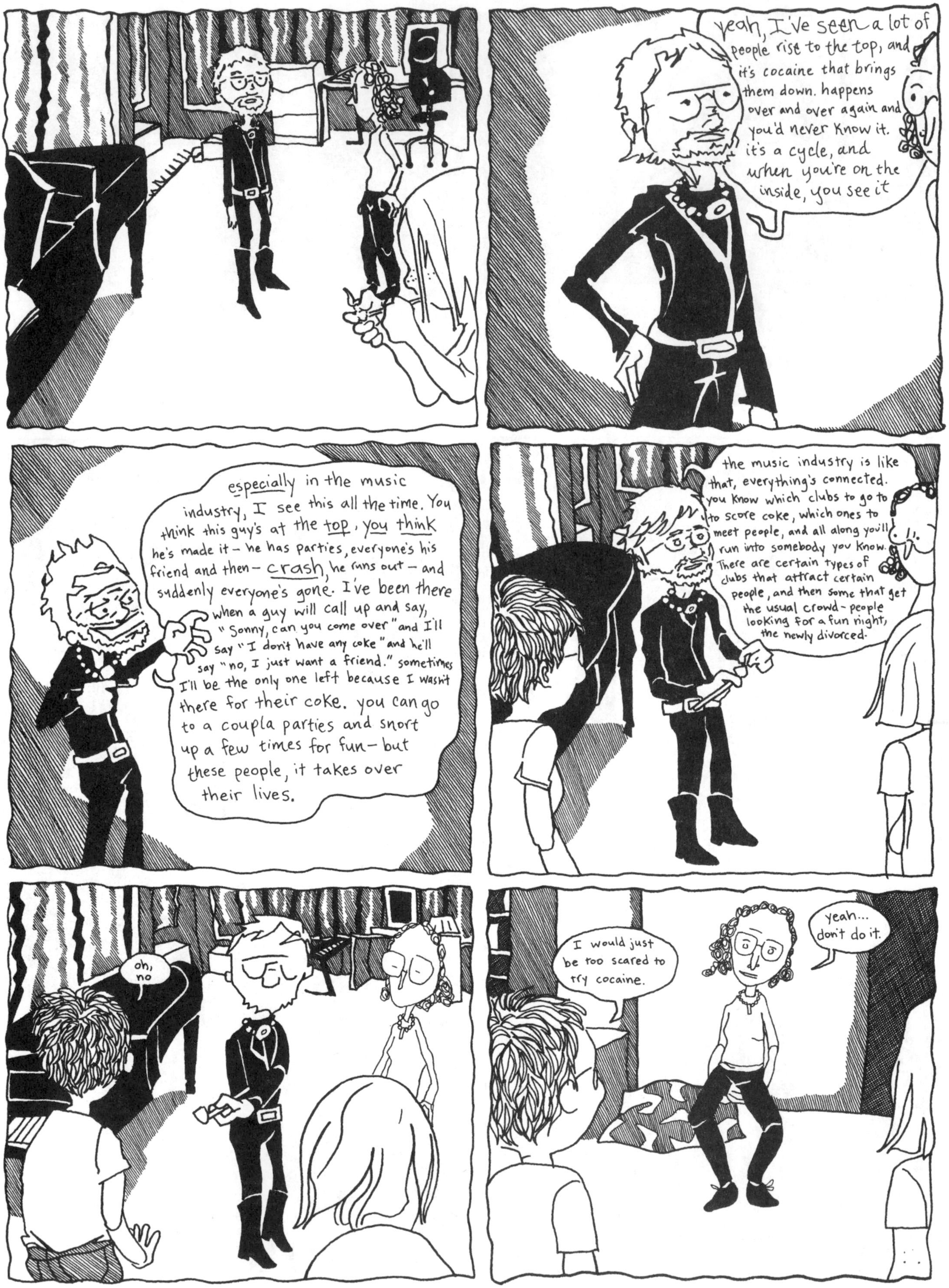
yeah, I've seen a lot of people rise to the top, and it's cocaine that brings them down. happens over and over again and you'd never know it. it's a cycle, and when you're on the inside, you see it
especially in the music industry, I see this all the time. You think this guy's at the top, you think he's made it – he has parties, everyone's his friend and then – crash, he runs out – and suddenly everyone's gone. I've been there when a guy will call up and say, "Sonny, can you come over" and I'll say "I don't have any coke" and he'll say "no, I just want a friend." sometimes I'll be the only one left because I wasn't there for their coke. you can go to a coupla parties and snort up a few times for fun – but these people, it takes over their lives.
the music industry is like that, everything's connected. you know which clubs to go to to score coke, which ones to meet people, and all along you'll run into somebody you know. There are certain types of clubs that attract certain people, and then some that get the usual crowd – people looking for a fun night, the newly divorced.
oh, no
I would just be too scared to try cocaine.
yeah... don't do it.

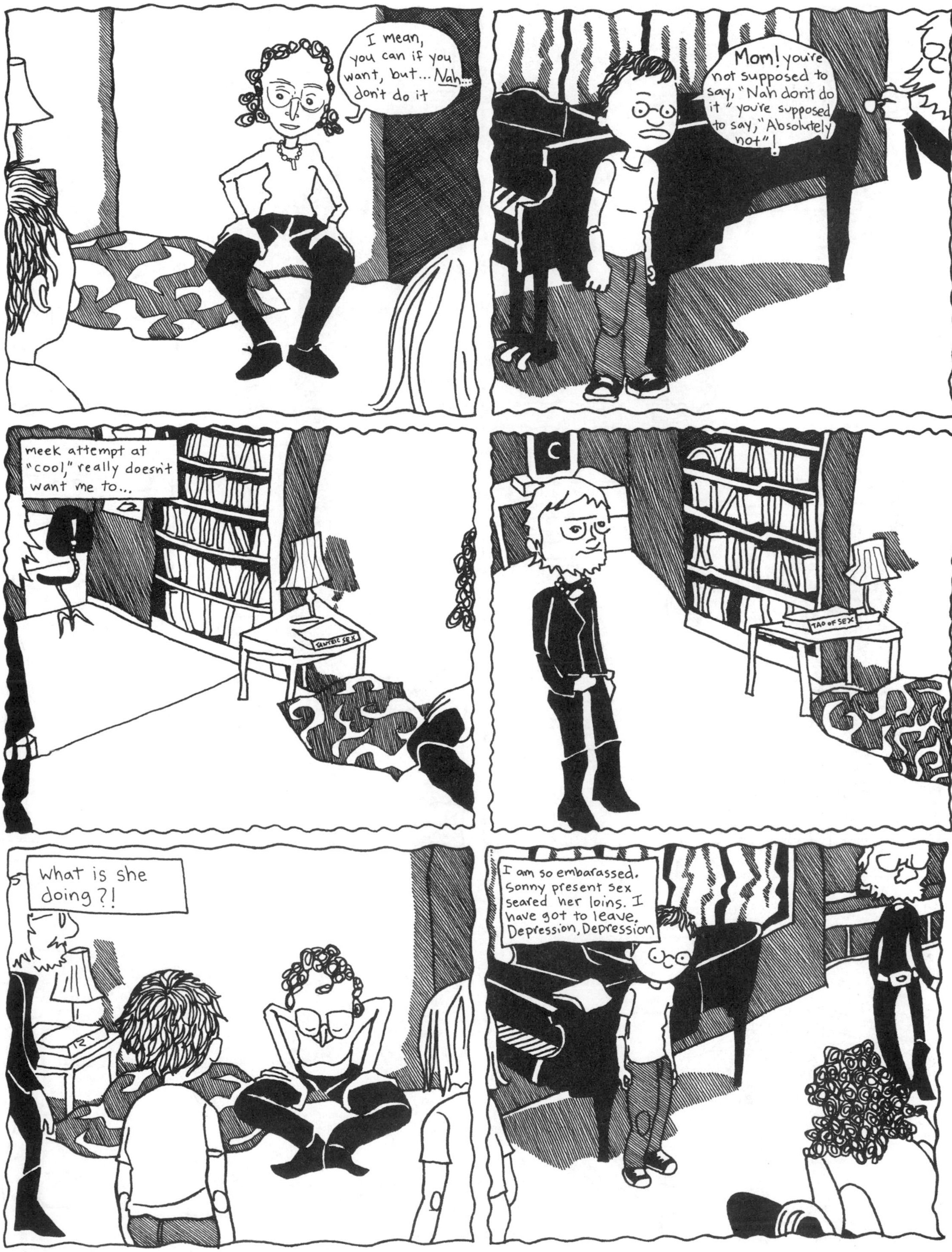
I mean, you can if you want, but... Nah... don't do it
Mom! you're not supposed to say, "Nah don't do it" you're supposed to say, "Absolutely not"!
meek attempt at "cool," really doesn't want me to...
TAO OF SEX
What is she doing?!
I am so embarassed. Sonny present sex seared her loins. I have got to leave. Depression, Depression

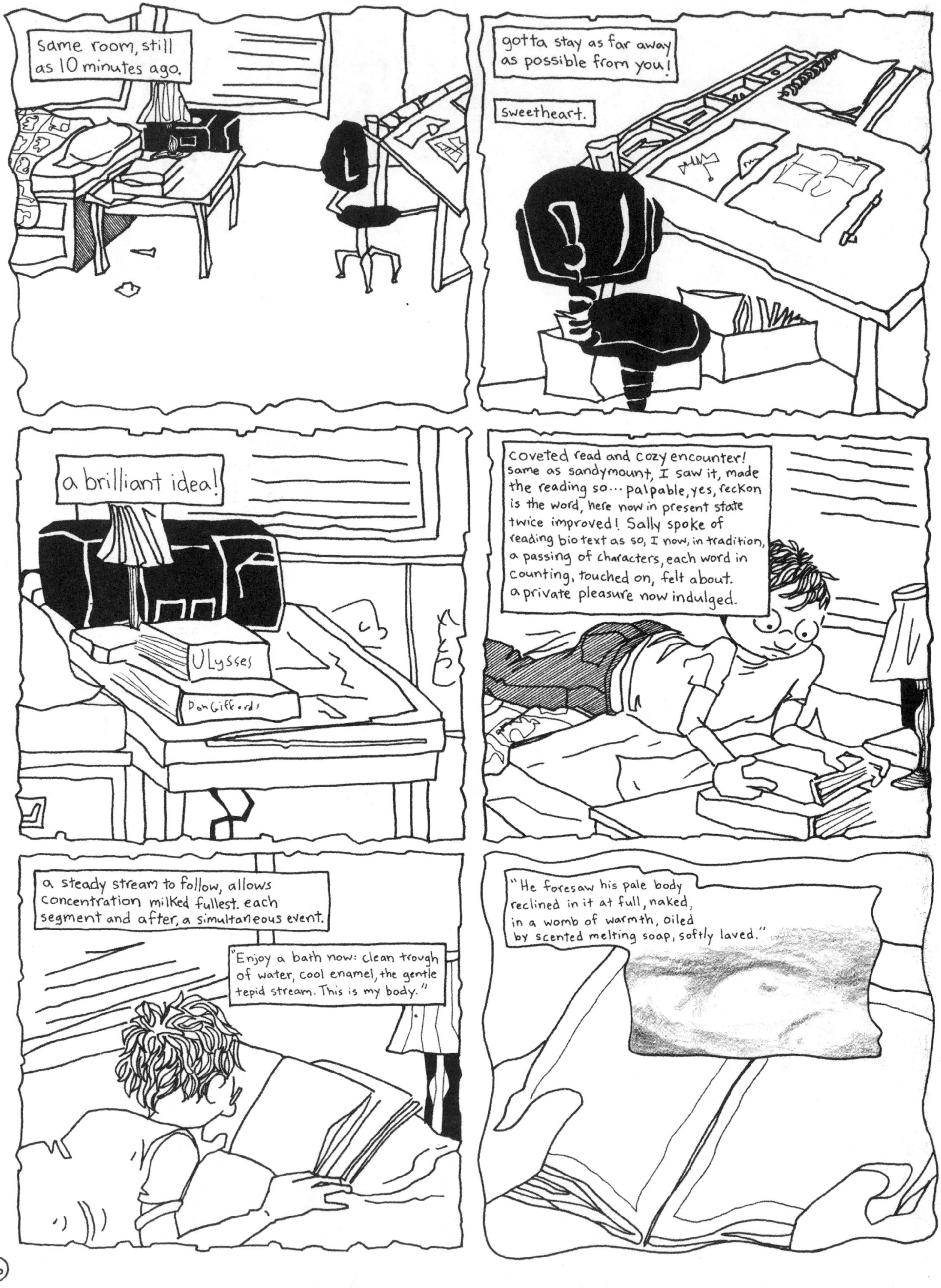

same room, still as 10 minutes ago.
gotta stay as far away as possible from you!
sweetheart.
a brilliant idea!
ULysses
Don Giffords
coveted read and cozy encounter! same as sandymount, I saw it, made the reading so... palpable, yes, reckon is the word, here now in present state twice improved! Sally spoke of reading bio text as so, I now, in tradition, a passing of characters, each word in counting, touched on, felt about. a private pleasure now indulged.
a steady stream to follow, allows concentration milked fullest. each segment and after, a simultaneous event.
"Enjoy a bath now: clean trough of water, cool enamel, the gentle tepid stream. This is my body."
"He foresaw his pale body reclined in it at full, naked, in a womb of warmth, oiled by scented melting soap, softly laved."

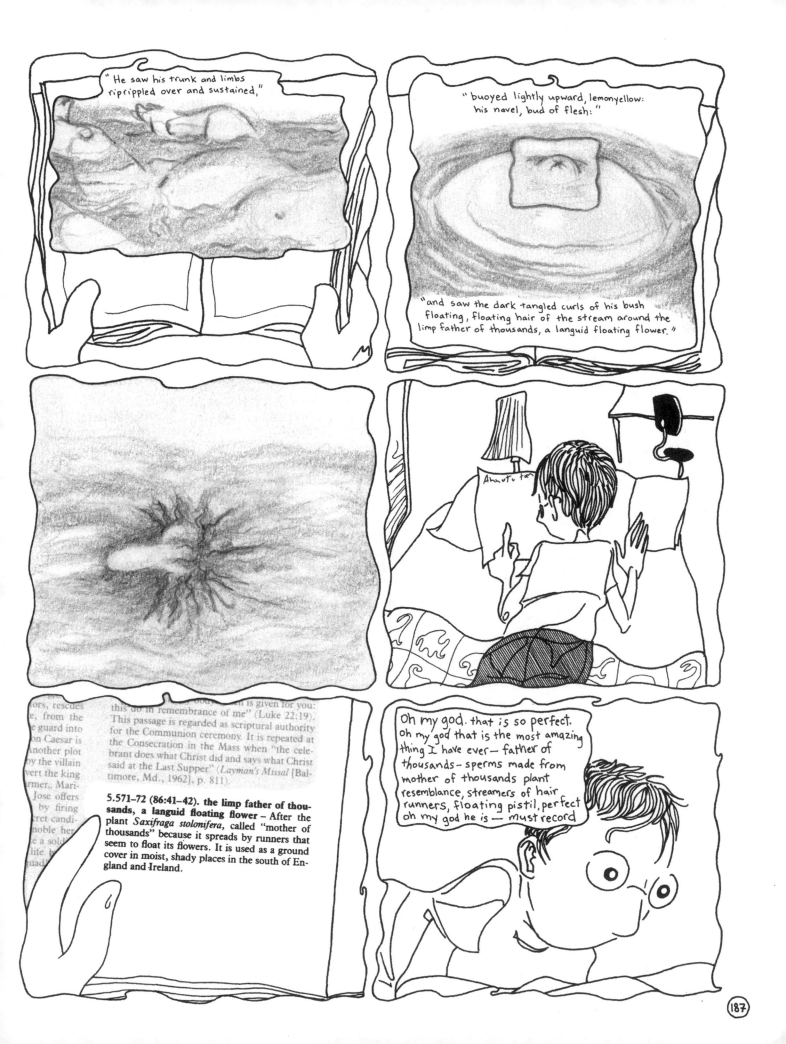

"He saw his trunk and limbs ripprippled over and sustained,"

"buoyed lightly upward, lemonyellow: his navel, bud of flesh: "

"and saw the dark tangled curls of his bush floating, floating hair of the stream around the limp father of thousands, a languid floating flower."

this do in remembrance of me" (Luke 22:19). This passage is regarded as scriptural authority for the Communion ceremony. It is repeated at the Consecration in the Mass when "the celebrant does what Christ did and says what Christ said at the Last Supper" (*Layman's Missal* [Baltimore, Md., 1962], p. 811).

5.571–72 (86:41–42). the limp father of thousands, a languid floating flower – After the plant *Saxifraga stolonifera*, called "mother of thousands" because it spreads by runners that seem to float its flowers. It is used as a ground cover in moist, shady places in the south of England and Ireland.

Oh my god. that *is* so perfect. oh my god that is the most amazing thing I have ever— father of thousands— sperms made from mother of thousands plant resemblance, streamers of hair runners, floating pistil, perfect oh my god he is — must record

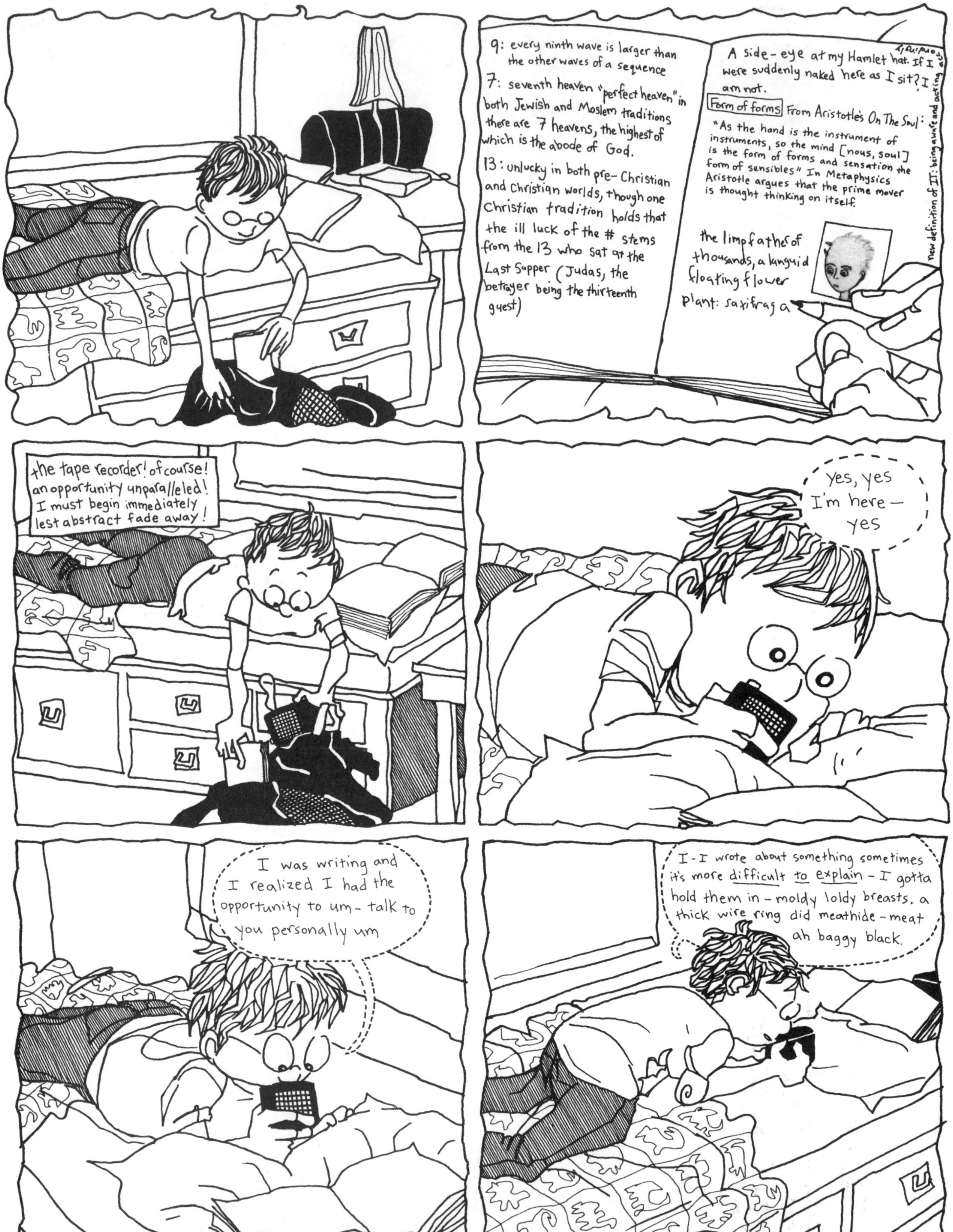
9: every ninth wave is larger than the other waves of a sequence
7: seventh heaven "perfect heaven" in both Jewish and Moslem traditions there are 7 heavens, the highest of which is the abode of God.
13: unlucky in both pre-Christian and Christian worlds, though one Christian tradition holds that the ill luck of the # stems from the 13 who sat at the Last Supper (Judas, the betrayer being the thirteenth guest)
A side-eye at my Hamlet hat. If I were suddenly naked here as I sit? I am not.
Form of forms From Aristotle's On The Soul:
"As the hand is the instrument of instruments, so the mind [nous, soul] is the form of forms and sensation the form of sensibles" In Metaphysics Aristotle argues that the prime mover is thought thinking on itself.
new definition of IT: being aware and acting accordingly
the limp father of thousands, a languid floating flower
plant: saxifraga
the tape recorder! of course! an opportunity unparalleled! I must begin immediately lest abstract fade away!
yes, yes I'm here—yes
I was writing and I realized I had the opportunity to um- talk to you personally um
I-I wrote about something sometimes it's more difficult to explain - I gotta hold them in - moldy loldy breasts. a thick wire ring did meathide - meat ah baggy black.

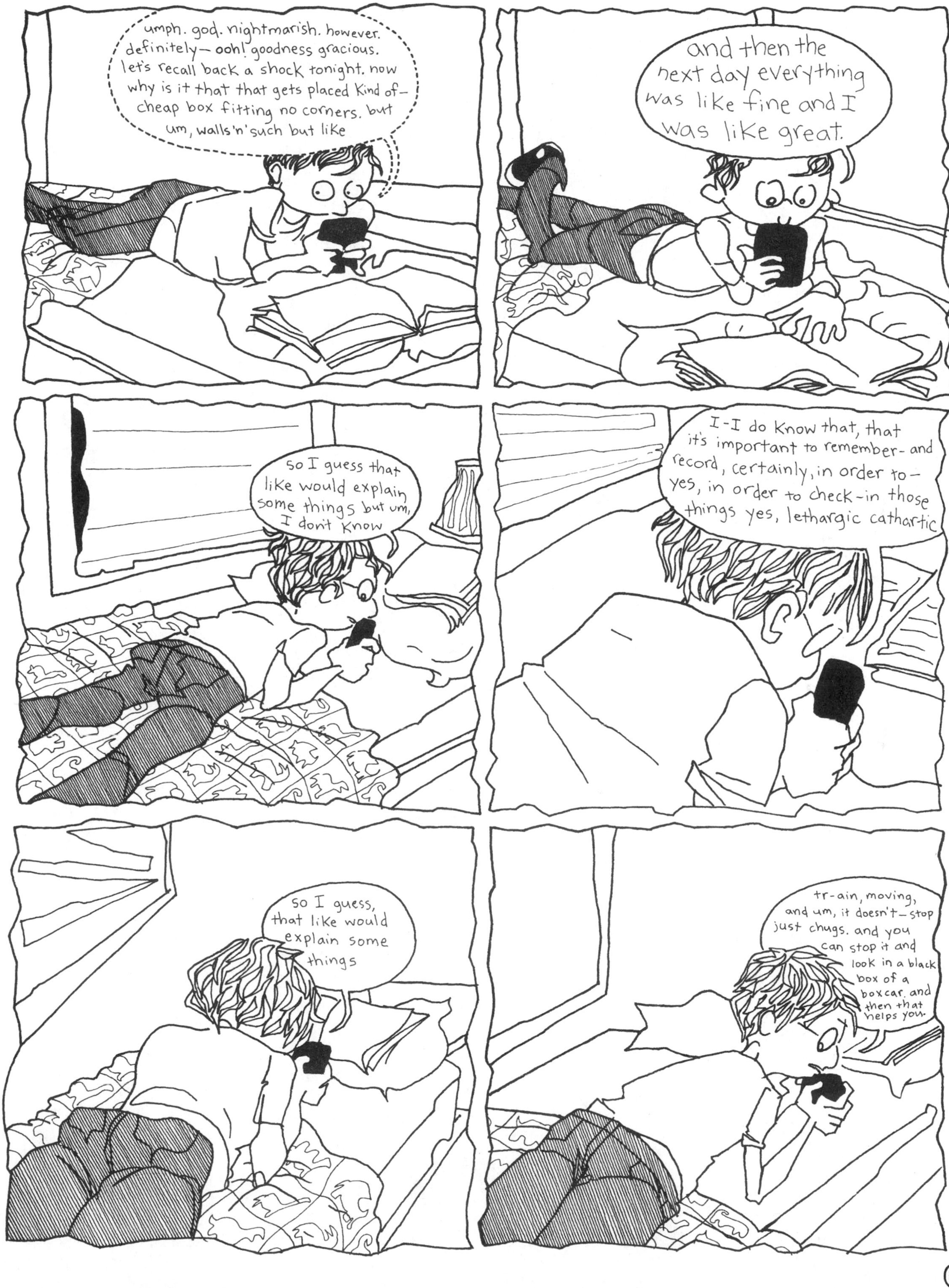
umph. god. nightmarish. however. definitely— ooh! goodness gracious. let's recall back a shock tonight. now why is it that that gets placed kind of— cheap box fitting no corners. but um, walls'n'such but like
and then the next day everything was like fine and I was like great.
so I guess that like would explain some things but um, I don't know
I-I do know that, that it's important to remember- and record, certainly, in order to— yes, in order to check-in those things yes, lethargic cathartic
so I guess, that like would explain some things
tr-ain, moving, and um, it doesn't— stop just chugs. and you can stop it and look in a black box of a boxcar. and then that helps you.

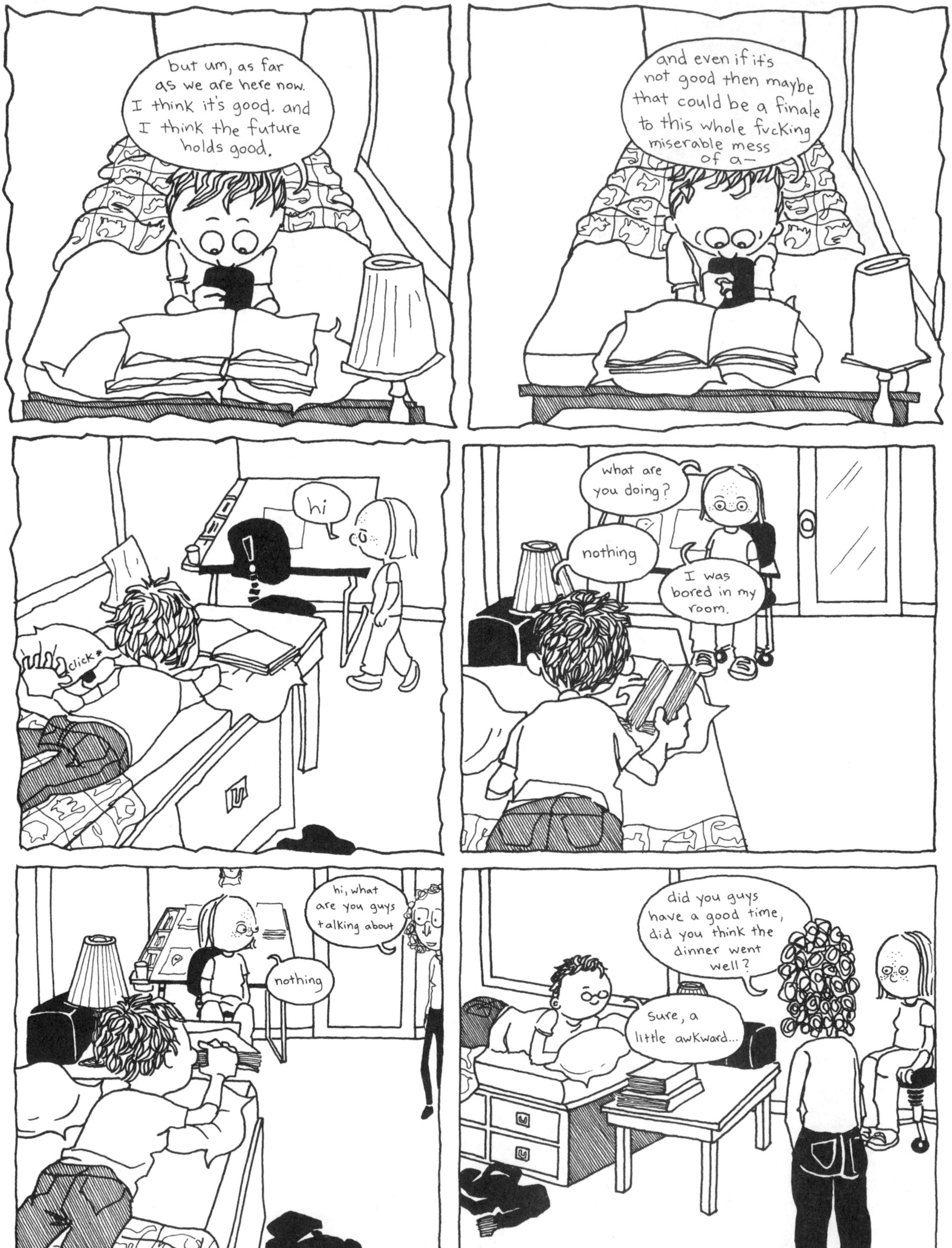
but um, as far as we are here now. I think it's good. and I think the future holds good.
and even if it's not good then maybe that could be a finale to this whole fucking miserable mess of a—
hi
click*
what are you doing?
nothing
I was bored in my room.
hi, what are you guys talking about
nothing
did you guys have a good time, did you think the dinner went well?
Sure, a little awkward...

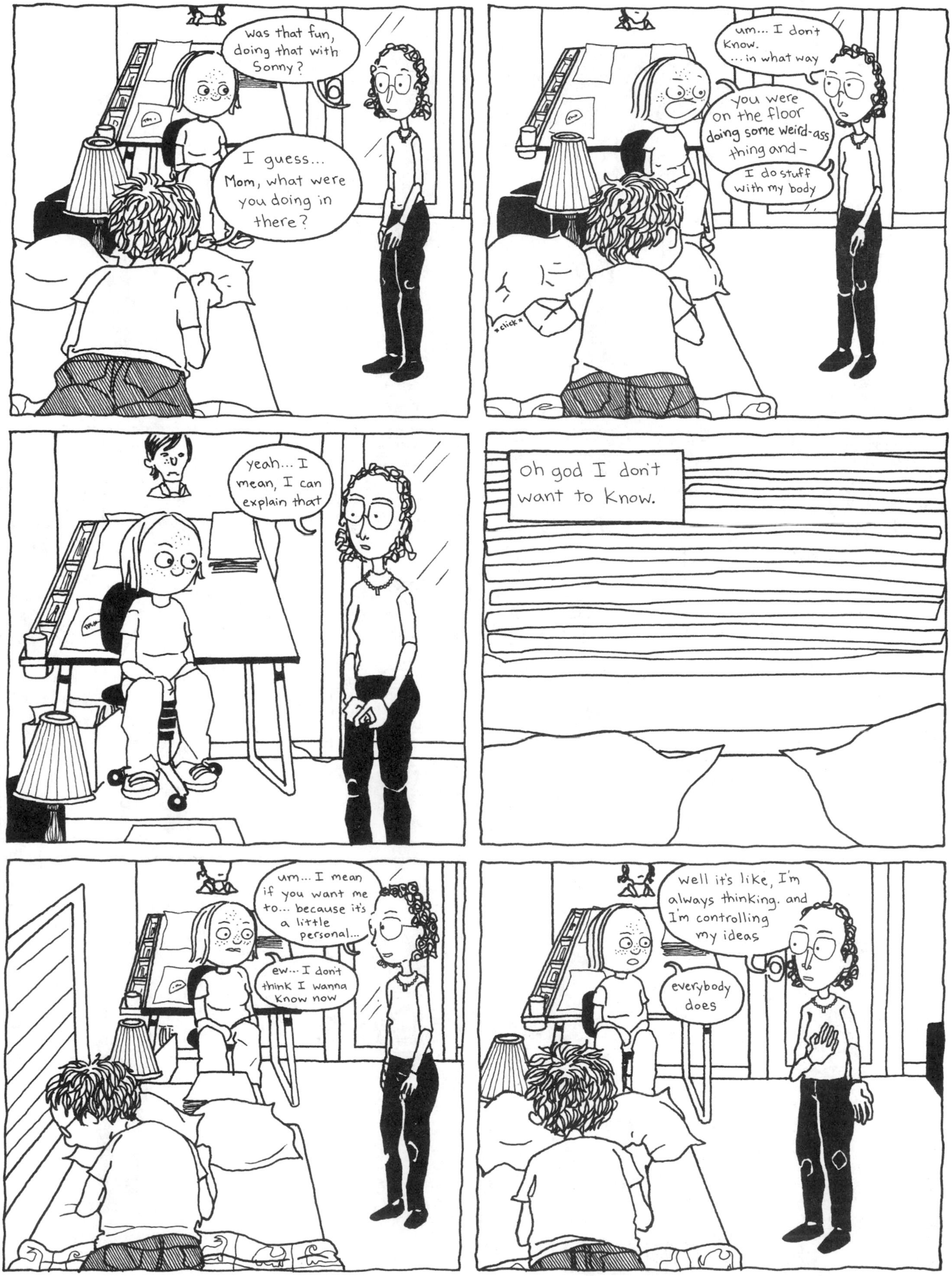
was that fun, doing that with Sonny?
I guess... Mom, what were you doing in there?
um... I don't know. ...in what way
you were on the floor doing some weird-ass thing and—
I do stuff with my body
click
yeah... I mean, I can explain that
oh god I don't want to know.
um... I mean if you want me to... because it's a little personal...
ew... I don't think I wanna know now
well it's like, I'm always thinking. and I'm controlling my ideas
everybody does

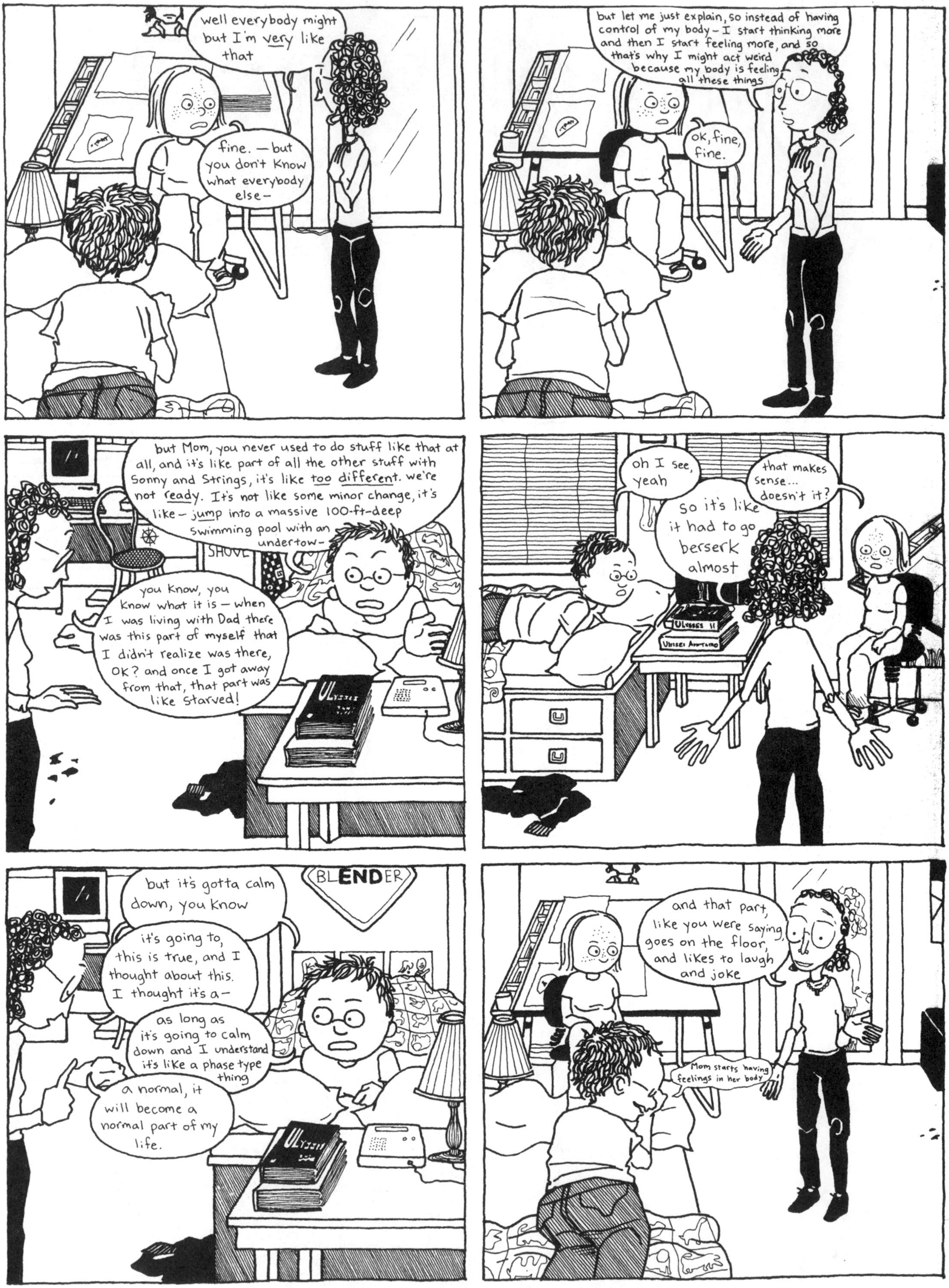

well everybody might but I'm very like that
fine. —but you don't know what everybody else—
but let me just explain, so instead of having control of my body—I start thinking more and then I start feeling more, and so that's why I might act weird because my body is feeling all these things
ok, fine, fine.
but Mom, you never used to do stuff like that at all, and it's like part of all the other stuff with Sonny and Strings, it's like too different. we're not ready. It's not like some minor change, it's like—jump into a massive 100-ft-deep swimming pool with an undertow—
you know, you know what it is—when I was living with Dad there was this part of myself that I didn't realize was there, OK? and once I got away from that, that part was like starved!
oh I see, yeah
that makes sense... doesn't it?
so it's like it had to go berserk almost
but it's gotta calm down, you know
it's going to, this is true, and I thought about this. I thought it's a—
as long as it's going to calm down and I understand it's like a phase type thing
a normal, it will become a normal part of my life.
and that part, like you were saying, goes on the floor, and likes to laugh and joke
Mom starts having feelings in her body

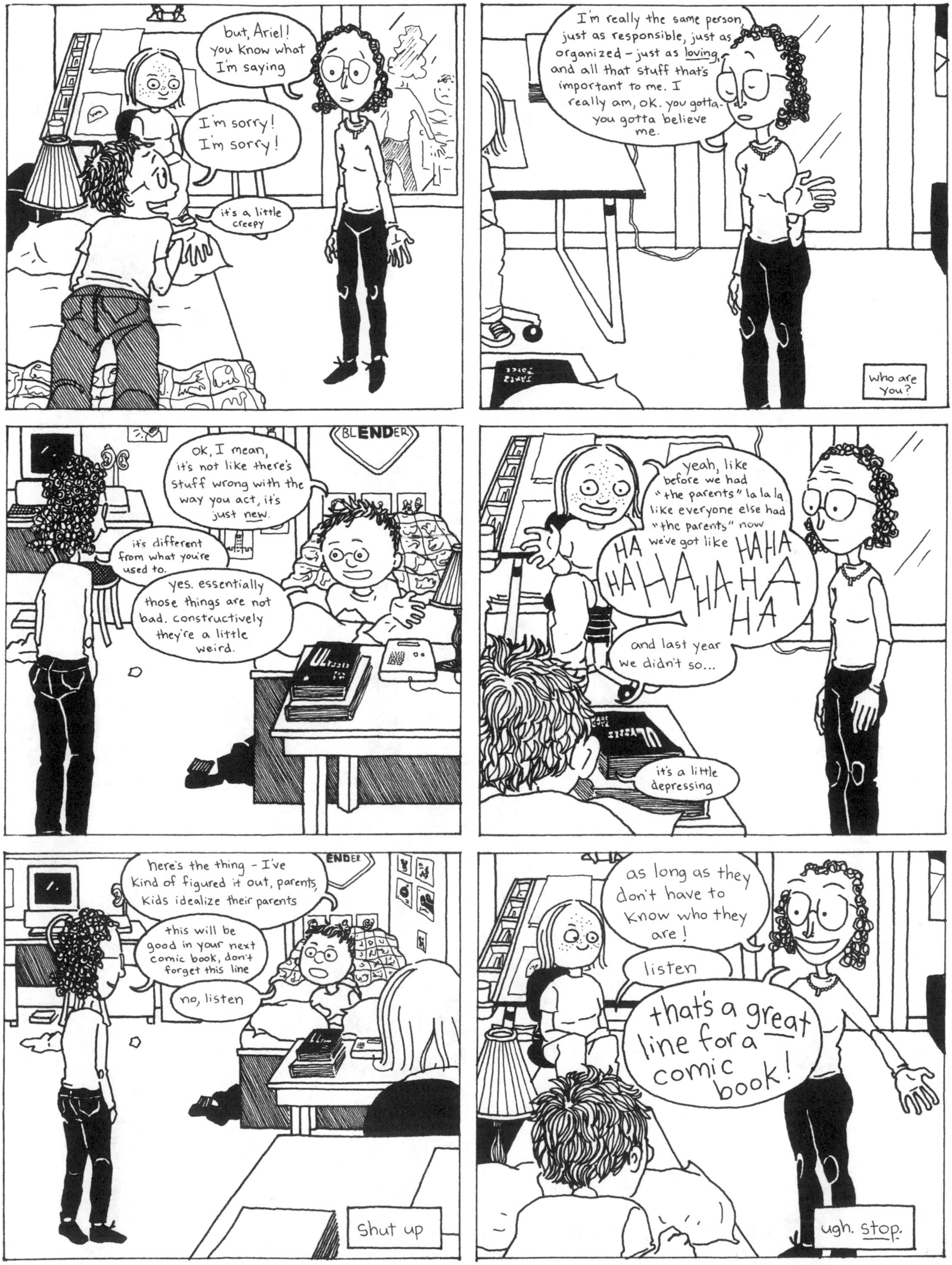
but, Ariel! you know what I'm saying
I'm sorry! I'm sorry!
it's a little creepy
I'm really the same person, just as responsible, just as organized - just as loving, and all that stuff that's important to me. I really am, OK. you gotta- you gotta believe me.
who are you?
OK, I mean, it's not like there's stuff wrong with the way you act, it's just new.
it's different from what you're used to.
yes. essentially those things are not bad. constructively they're a little weird.
BLENDER
yeah, like before we had "the parents" la la la like everyone else had "the parents" now we've got like
HA HAHA HAHA HAHA HA
and last year we didn't so...
it's a little depressing
here's the thing - I've kind of figured it out, parents, kids idealize their parents
this will be good in your next comic book, don't forget this line
no, listen
Shut up
as long as they don't have to know who they are!
listen
that's a great line for a comic book!
ugh. stop.

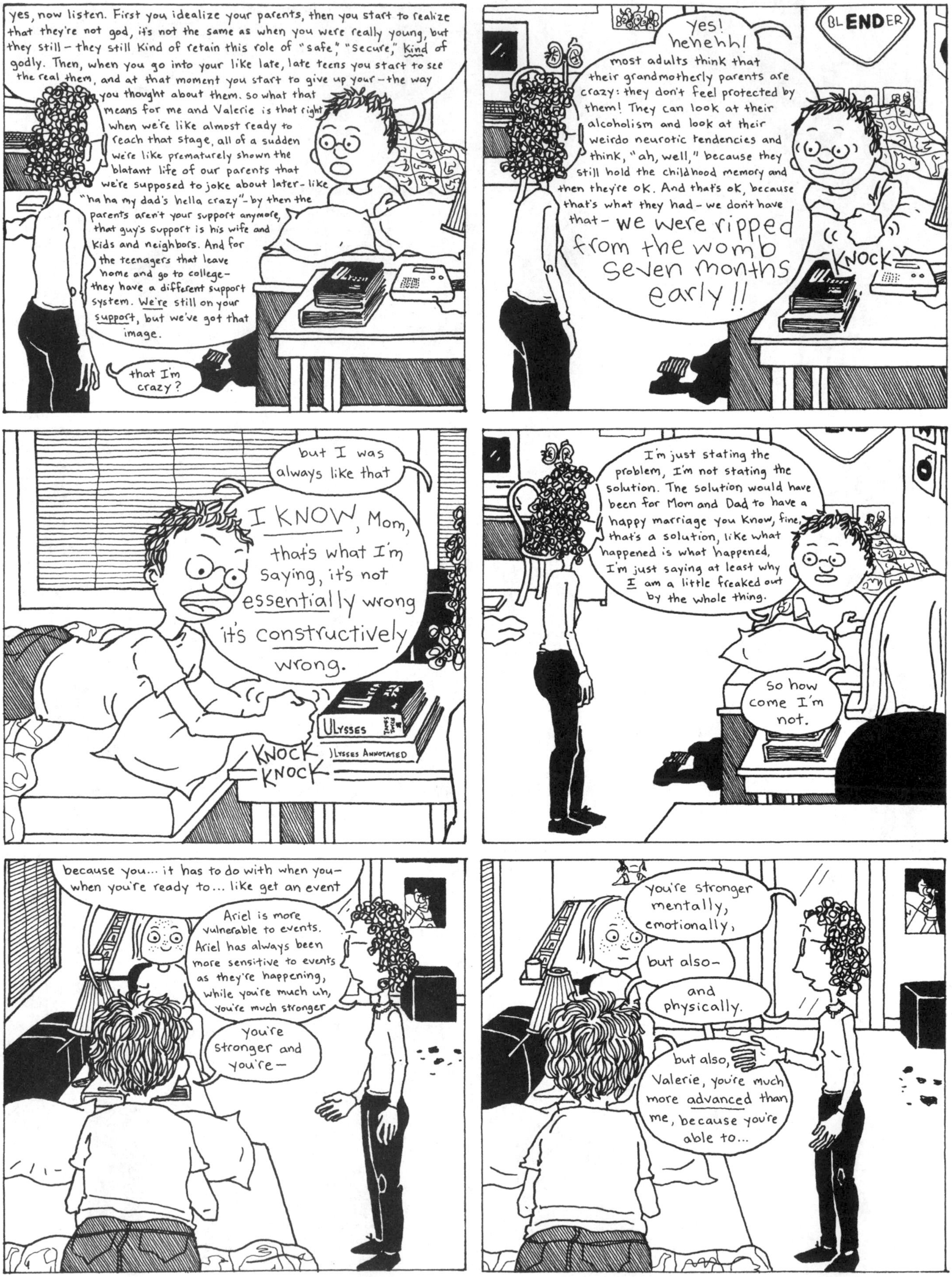
yes, now listen. First you idealize your parents, then you start to realize that they're not god, it's not the same as when you were really young, but they still – they still kind of retain this role of "safe," "secure," kind of godly. Then, when you go into your like late, late teens you start to see the real them, and at that moment you start to give up your – the way you thought about them. so what that means for me and Valerie is that right when we're like almost ready to reach that stage, all of a sudden we're like prematurely shown the blatant life of our parents that we're supposed to joke about later – like "ha ha my dad's hella crazy" – by then the parents aren't your support anymore, that guy's support is his wife and kids and neighbors. And for the teenagers that leave home and go to college – they have a different support system. We're still on your support, but we've got that image.
that I'm crazy?
BLENDER
yes! hehehh! most adults think that their grandmotherly parents are crazy: they don't feel protected by them! They can look at their alcoholism and look at their weirdo neurotic tendencies and think, "ah, well," because they still hold the childhood memory and then they're OK. And that's ok, because that's what they had – we don't have that – we were ripped from the womb seven months early!!
KNOCK
but I was always like that
I KNOW, Mom, that's what I'm saying, it's not essentially wrong it's constructively wrong.
KNOCK KNOCK
ULYSSES
ULYSSES ANNOTATED
I'm just stating the problem, I'm not stating the solution. The solution would have been for Mom and Dad to have a happy marriage you know, fine, that's a solution, like what happened is what happened, I'm just saying at least why I am a little freaked out by the whole thing.
So how come I'm not.
because you… it has to do with when you – when you're ready to… like get an event
Ariel is more vulnerable to events. Ariel has always been more sensitive to events as they're happening, while you're much uh, you're much stronger
you're stronger and you're –
you're stronger mentally, emotionally,
but also –
and physically.
but also, Valerie, you're much more advanced than me, because you're able to…

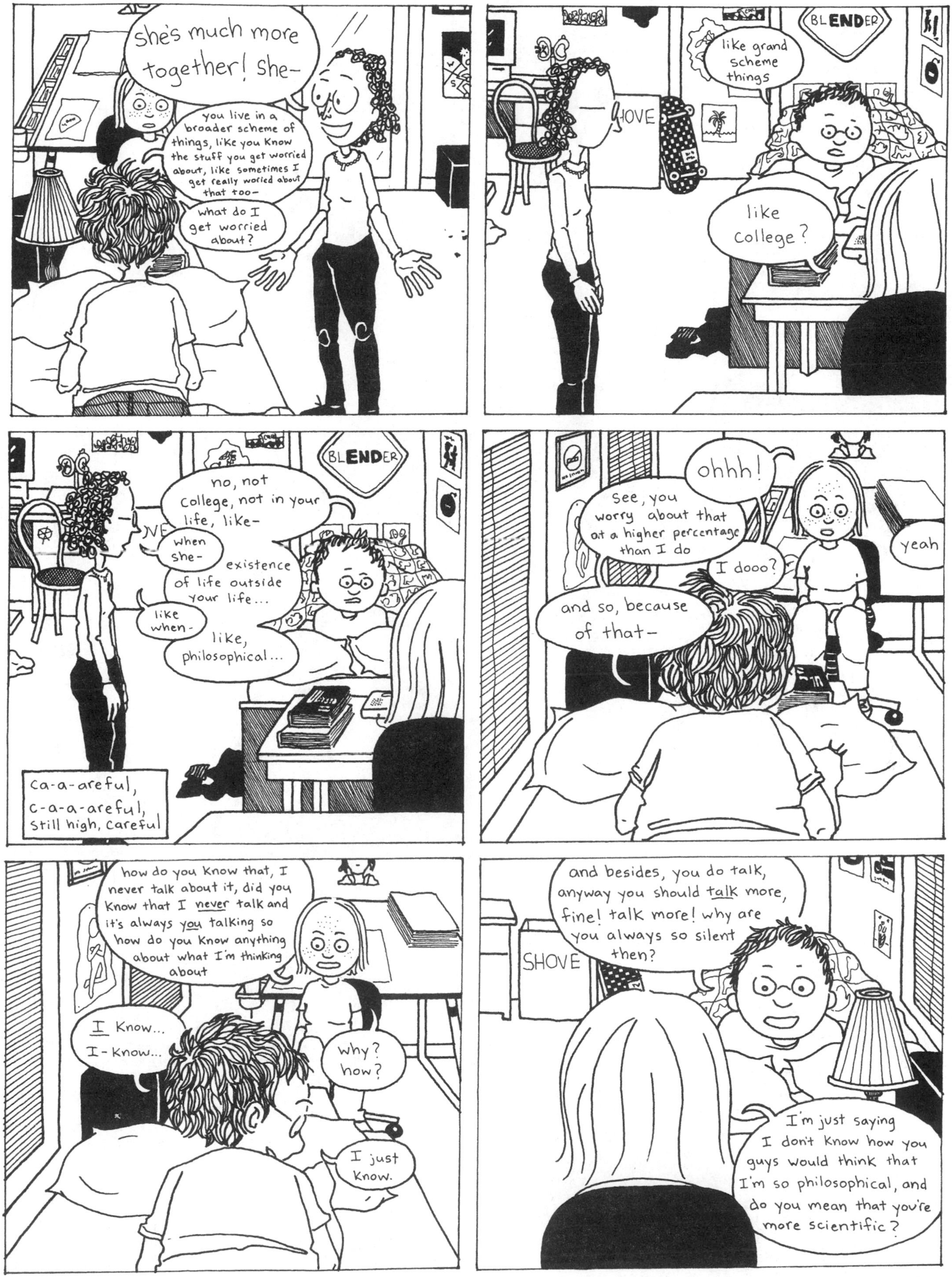

she's much more together! she-
you live in a broader scheme of things, like you know the stuff you get worried about, like sometimes I get really woried about that too-
what do I get worried about?
like grand scheme things
like college?
no, not college, not in your life, like-
when she-
existence of life outside your life...
like when-
like, philosophical...
ca-a-areful, c-a-a-areful, still high, careful
ohhh!
see, you worry about that at a higher percentage than I do
yeah
I dooo?
and so, because of that-
how do you know that, I never talk about it, did you know that I never talk and it's always you talking so how do you know anything about what I'm thinking about
I know... I-know...
why? how?
I just know.
and besides, you do talk, anyway you should talk more, fine! talk more! why are you always so silent then?
I'm just saying I don't know how you guys would think that I'm so philosophical, and do you mean that you're more scientific?

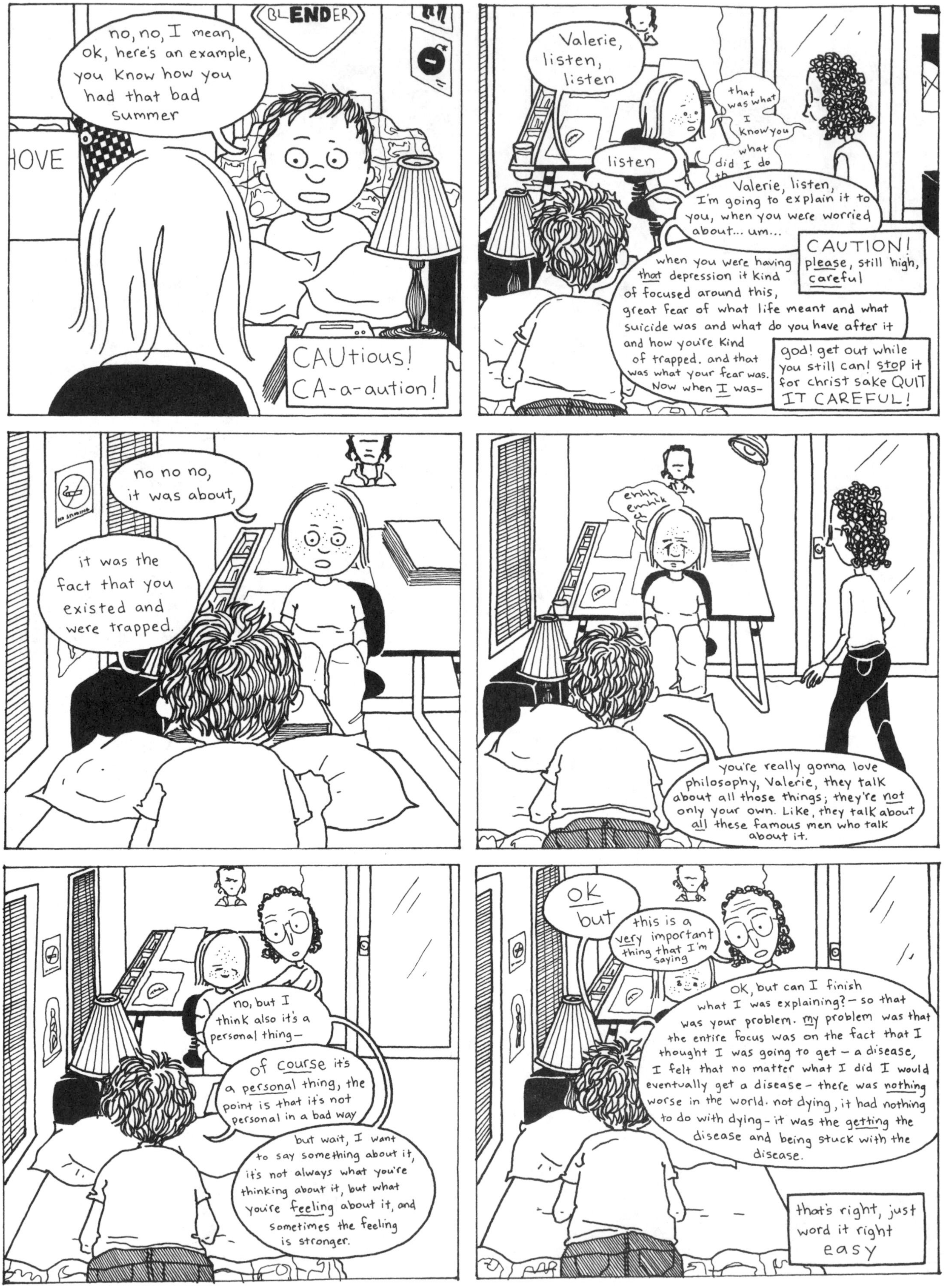
BLENDER
no, no, I mean, ok, here's an example, you know how you had that bad summer
HOVE
CAUtious! CA-a-aution!
Valerie, listen, listen
that was what
I know you
what did I do
listen
Valerie, listen, I'm going to explain it to you, when you were worried about... um...
CAUTION! please, still high, careful
when you were having that depression it kind of focused around this, great fear of what life meant and what suicide was and what do you have after it and how you're kind of trapped. and that was what your fear was. Now when I was-
god! get out while you still can! stop it for christ sake QUIT IT CAREFUL!
no no no, it was about,
it was the fact that you existed and were trapped.
ehhh ehhhk
you're really gonna love philosophy, Valerie, they talk about all those things; they're not only your own. Like, they talk about all these famous men who talk about it.
no, but I think also it's a personal thing—
of course it's a personal thing, the point is that it's not personal in a bad way
but wait, I want to say something about it, it's not always what you're thinking about it, but what you're feeling about it, and sometimes the feeling is stronger.
ok but
this is a very important thing that I'm saying
OK, but can I finish what I was explaining?—so that was your problem. my problem was that the entire focus was on the fact that I thought I was going to get—a disease, I felt that no matter what I did I would eventually get a disease—there was nothing worse in the world. not dying, it had nothing to do with dying—it was the getting the disease and being stuck with the disease.
that's right, just word it right easy

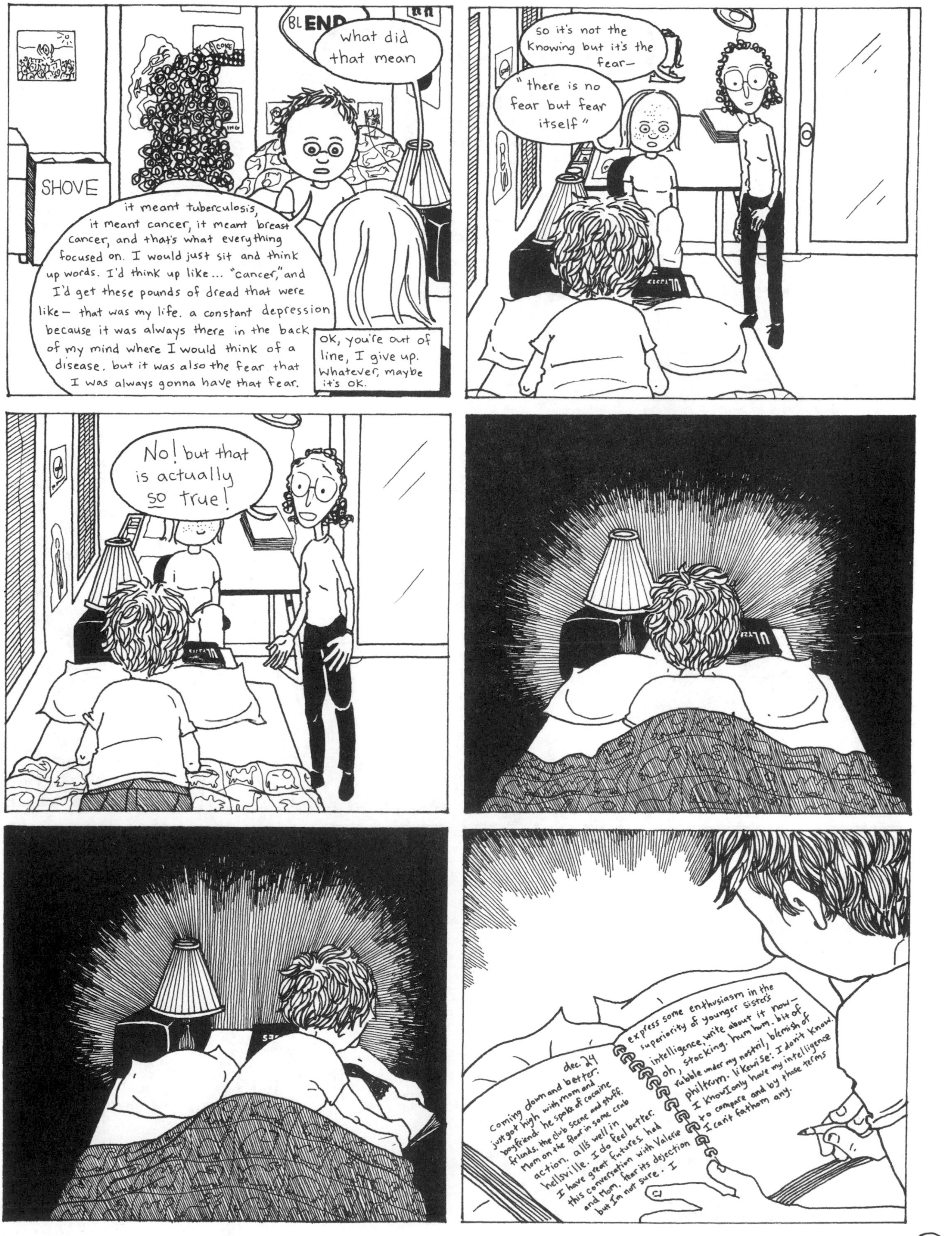
BLEND
SHOVE
what did that mean
it meant tuberculosis, it meant cancer, it meant breast cancer, and that's what everything focused on. I would just sit and think up words. I'd think up like... "cancer," and I'd get these pounds of dread that were like— that was my life. a constant depression because it was always there in the back of my mind where I would think of a disease. but it was also the fear that I was always gonna have that fear.
OK, you're out of line, I give up. Whatever, maybe it's OK.
so it's not the Knowing but it's the fear—
"there is no fear but fear itself"
No! but that is actually so true!
dec. 24
Coming down and better. just got high with mom and boyfriend. he spoke of cocaine friends. the club scene and stuff. Mom on the floor in some crab action. all's well in hellsville. I do feel better. I have great futures. had this conversation with Valerie and Mom. fear its dejection but I'm not sure. I
express some enthusiasm in the superiority of younger sister's intelligence, write about it now— oh, stocking. hum hum. bit of rubble under my nostril, blemish of philtrum. likewise: I don't know. I know I only have my intelligence to compare and by those terms I can't fathom any.

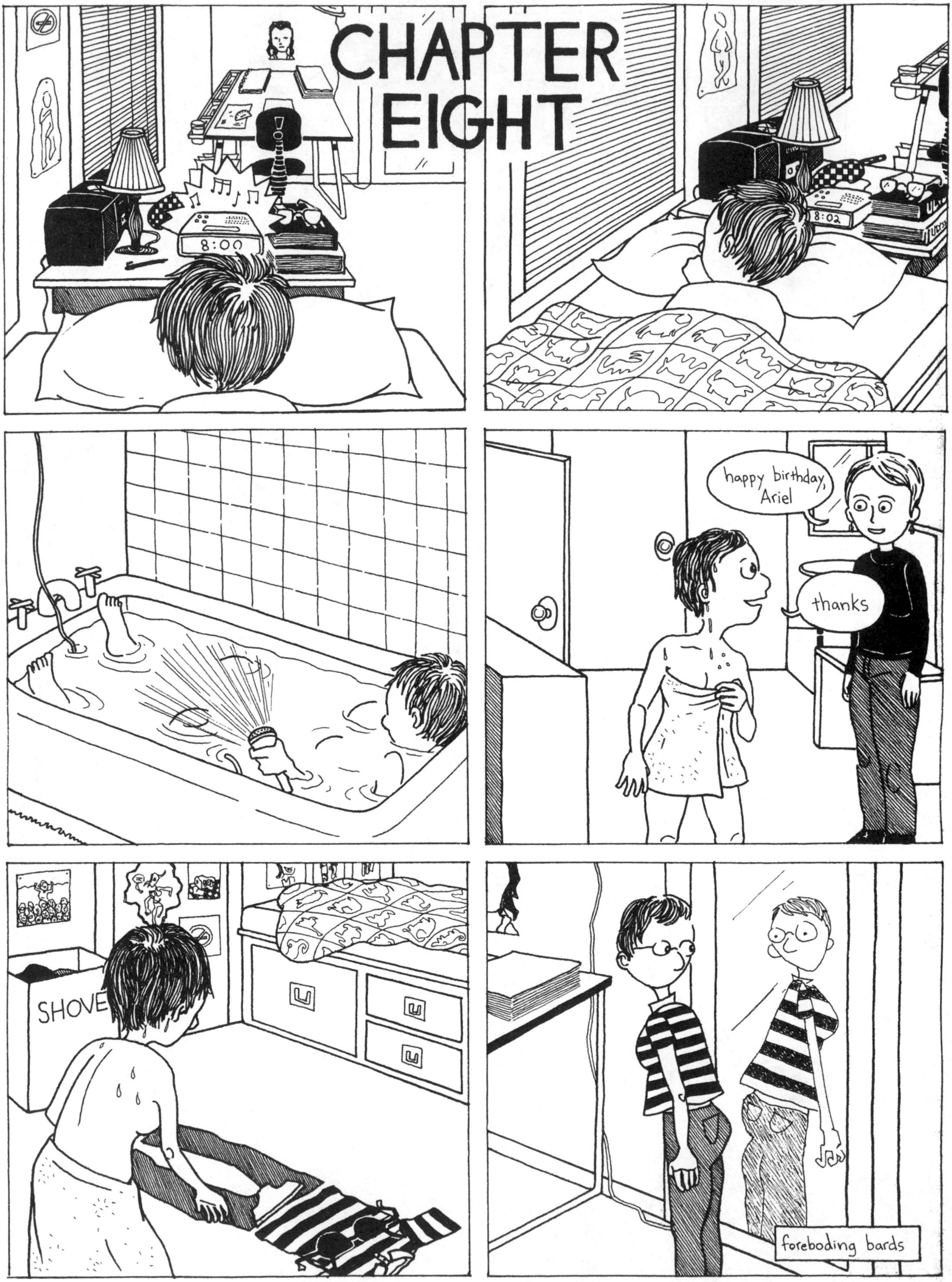
CHAPTER EIGHT
8:00
8:02
happy birthday, Ariel
thanks
SHOVE
foreboding bards

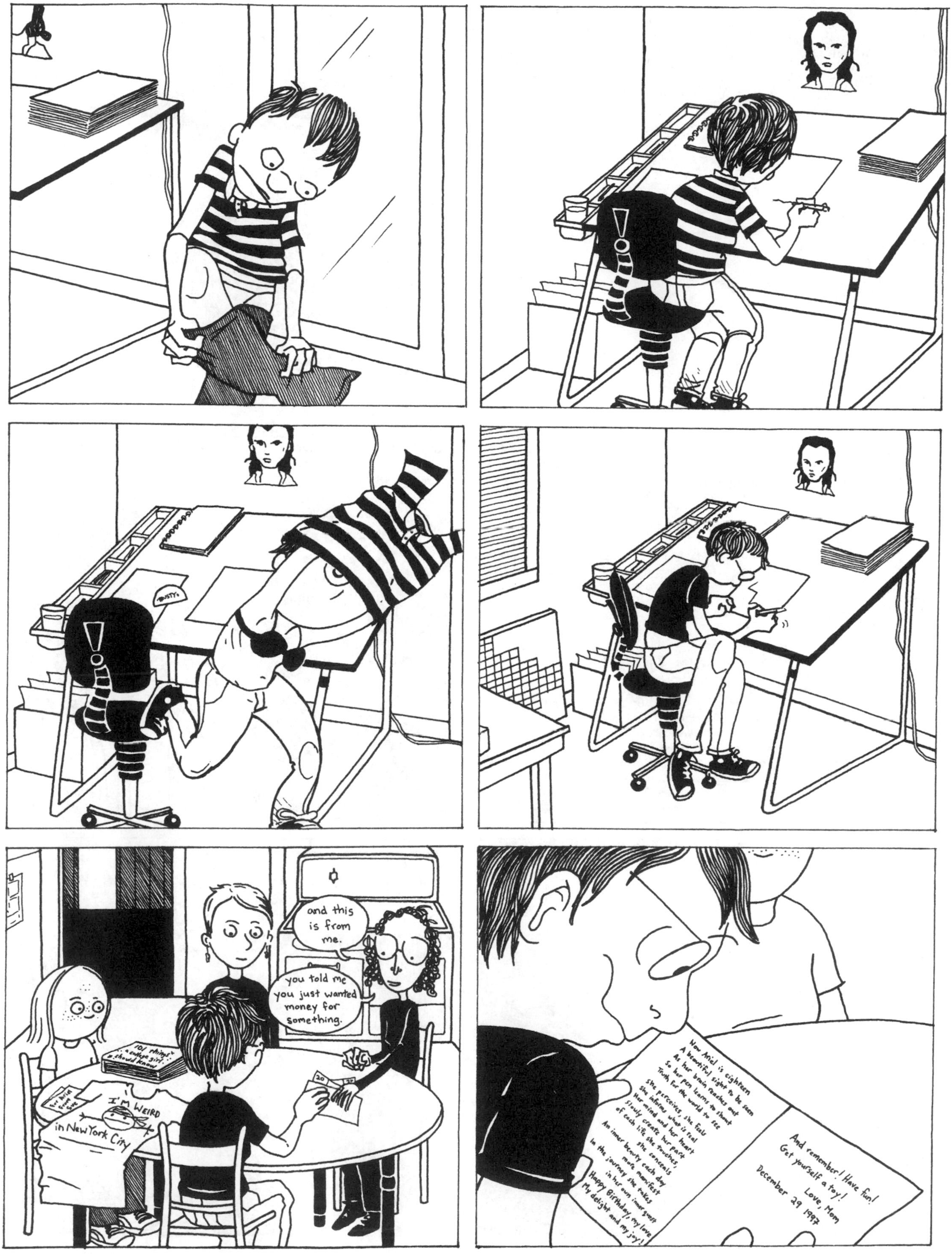
BUSTY's
101 things a college girl should know
For Ariel From Sue
I'M WEIRD
in New York City
you told me you just wanted money for something.
and this is from me.
Now Ariel is eighteen
A beautiful sight to be seen
As her brain reaches out
So her pen learns to shout
Truth for the world to see
She perceives, she feels
She informs what is real
Her mind and her heart
Slowly create her part
of each life she touches,
she conceals
An inner beauty each day
more manifest
In the journey she takes
in her own inner quest
Happy Birthday, my love
My delight and my joy!
And remember! Have fun!
Get yourself a toy!
Love, Mom
December 29 1997

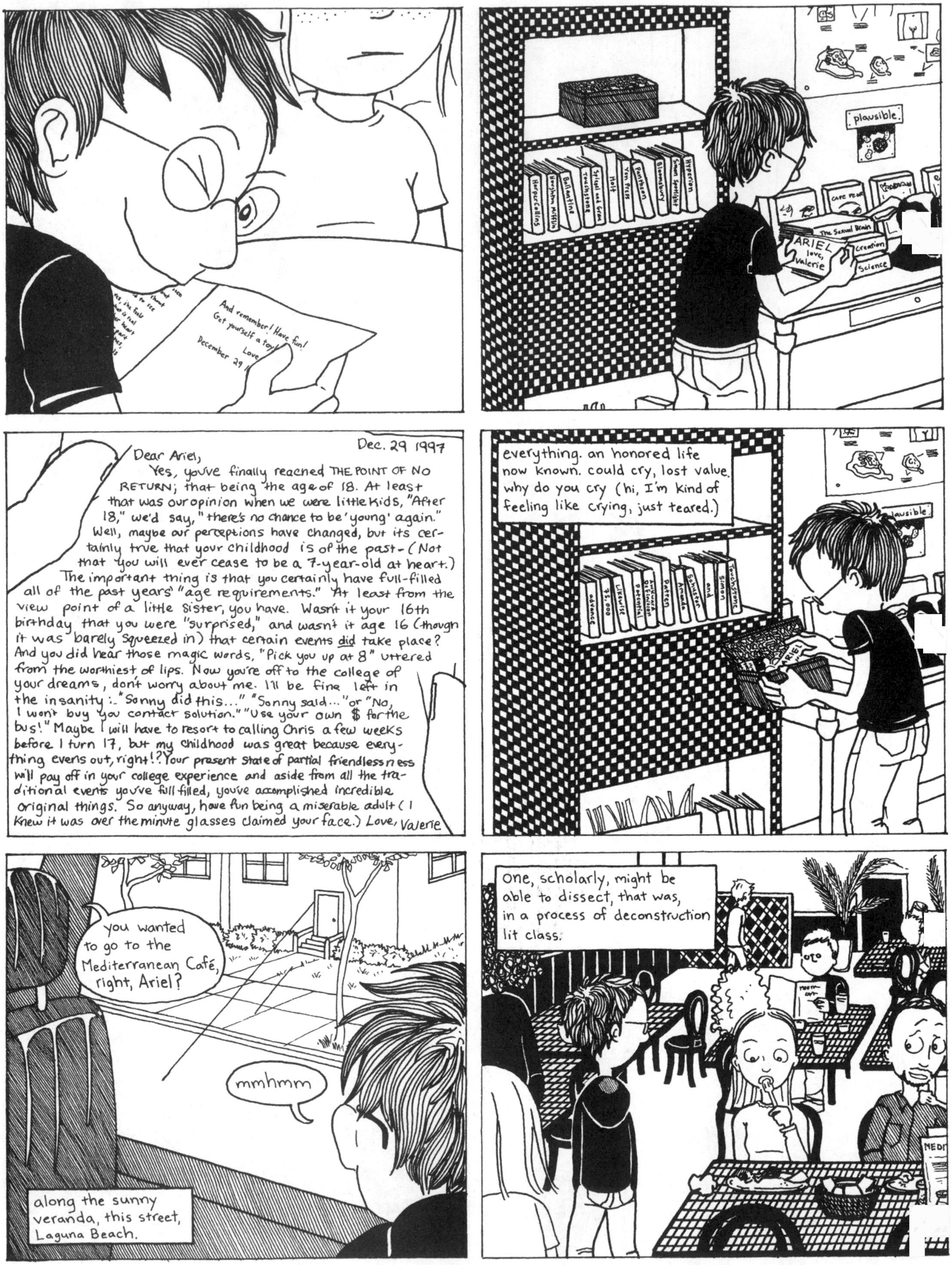
And remember! Have fun!
Get yourself a toy!
Love,
December 29
plausible.
ARIEL
love,
Valerie
The Sexual Brain
Creation
Science
Dec. 29 1997
Dear Ariel,
Yes, you've finally reached THE POINT OF NO RETURN; that being the age of 18. At least that was our opinion when we were little kids, "After 18," we'd say, "there's no chance to be 'young' again." Well, maybe our perceptions have changed, but its certainly true that your childhood is of the past- (Not that you will ever cease to be a 7-year-old at heart.)
The important thing is that you certainly have full-filled all of the past years' "age requirements." At least from the view point of a little sister, you have. Wasn't it your 16th birthday that you were "surprised," and wasn't it age 16 (though it was barely squeezed in) that certain events did take place? And you did hear those magic words, "Pick you up at 8" uttered from the worthiest of lips. Now you're off to the college of your dreams, don't worry about me. I'll be fine left in the insanity :- "Sonny did this..." "Sonny said..." or "No, I won't buy you contact solution." "Use your own $ for the bus!" Maybe I will have to resort to calling Chris a few weeks before I turn 17, but my childhood was great because everything evens out, right!? Your present state of partial friendlessness will pay off in your college experience and aside from all the traditional events you've full filled, you've accomplished incredible original things. So anyway, have fun being a miserable adult (I knew it was over the minute glasses claimed your face.) Love, Valerie
everything. an honored life now known. could cry, lost value. why do you cry (hi, I'm kind of feeling like crying, just teared.)
you wanted to go to the Mediterranean Café, right, Ariel?
mmhmm
along the sunny veranda, this street, Laguna Beach.
One, scholarly, might be able to dissect, that was, in a process of deconstruction lit class.

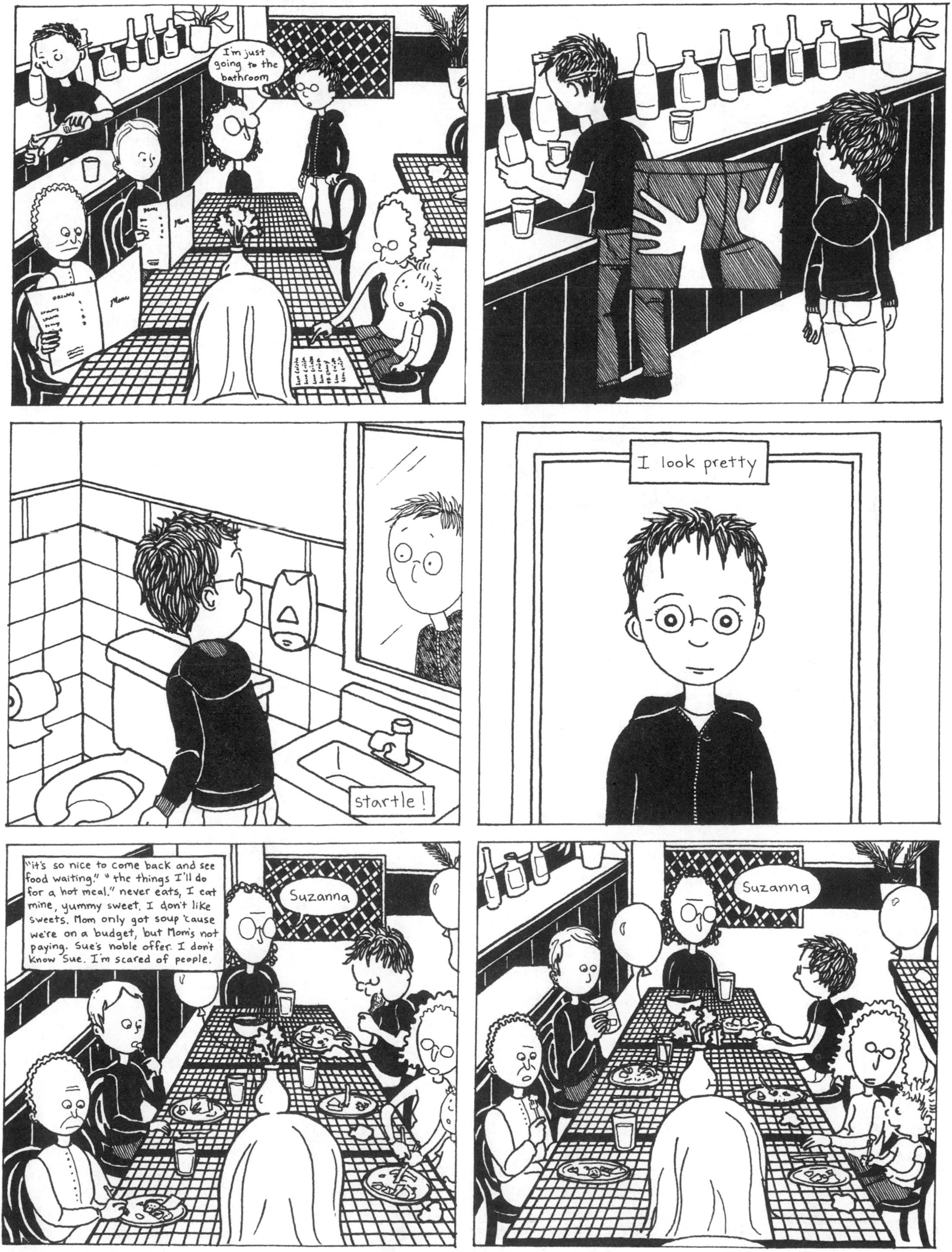
I'm just going to the bathroom
startle!
I look pretty
"it's so nice to come back and see food waiting." "the things I'll do for a hot meal." never eats, I eat mine, yummy sweet. I don't like sweets. Mom only got soup 'cause we're on a budget, but Mom's not paying. Sue's noble offer. I don't know Sue. I'm scared of people.
Suzanna
Suzanna

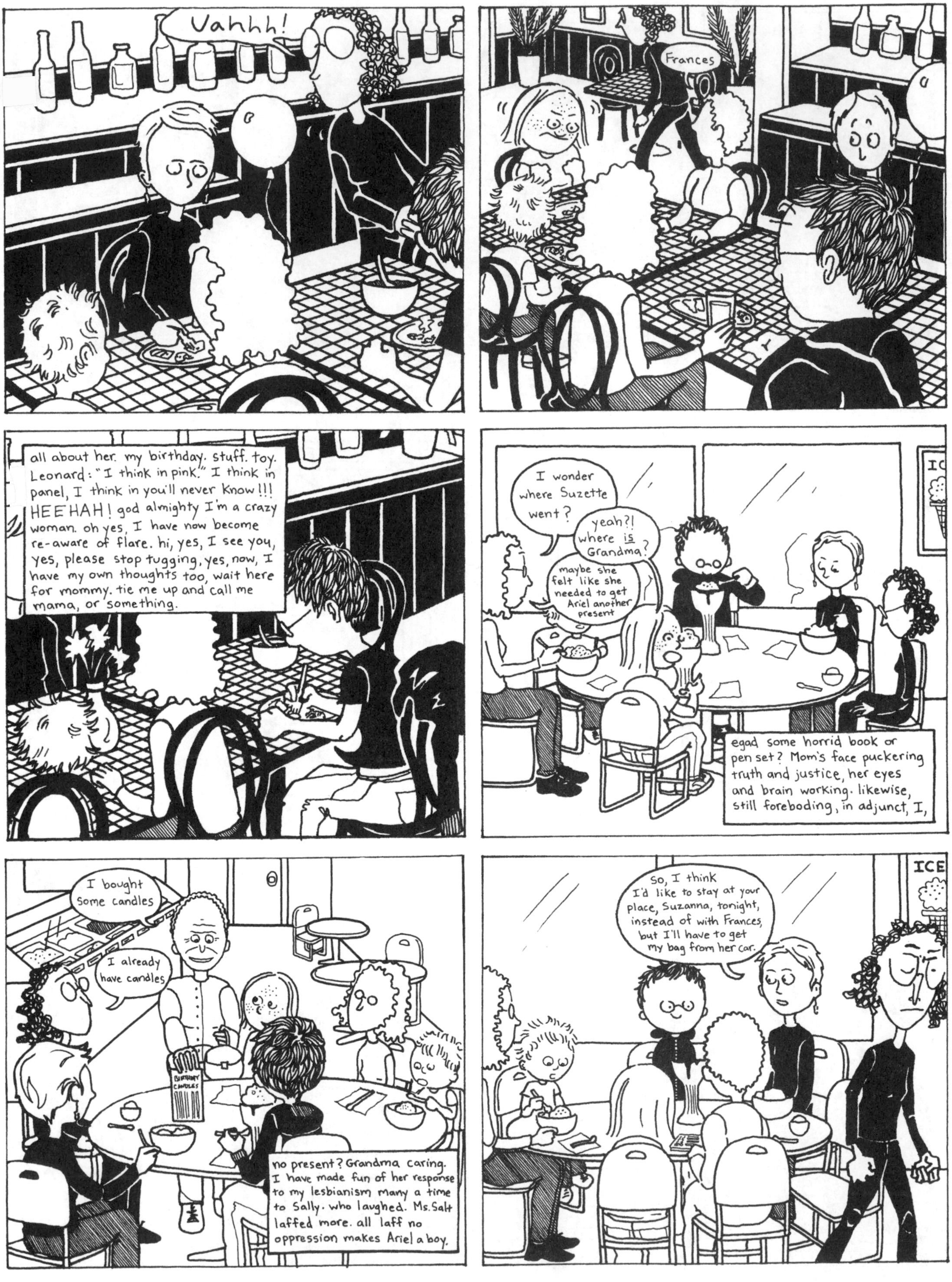

Vahhh!
Frances
all about her. my birthday. stuff. toy. Leonard: "I think in pink." I think in panel, I think in you'll never know!!! HEEHAH! god almighty I'm a crazy woman. oh yes, I have now become re-aware of flare. hi, yes, I see you, yes, please stop tugging, yes, now, I have my own thoughts too, wait here for mommy. tie me up and call me mama, or something.
I wonder where Suzette went?
yeah?! where is Grandma?
maybe she felt like she needed to get Ariel another present
ICE
egad some horrid book or pen set? Mom's face puckering truth and justice, her eyes and brain working. likewise, still foreboding, in adjunct, I,
I bought some candles
I already have candles
BIRTHDAY CANDLES
no present? Grandma caring. I have made fun of her response to my lesbianism many a time to Sally. who laughed. Ms. Salt laffed more. all laff no oppression makes Ariel a boy.
ICE
So, I think I'd like to stay at your place, Suzanna, tonight, instead of with Frances, but I'll have to get my bag from her car.

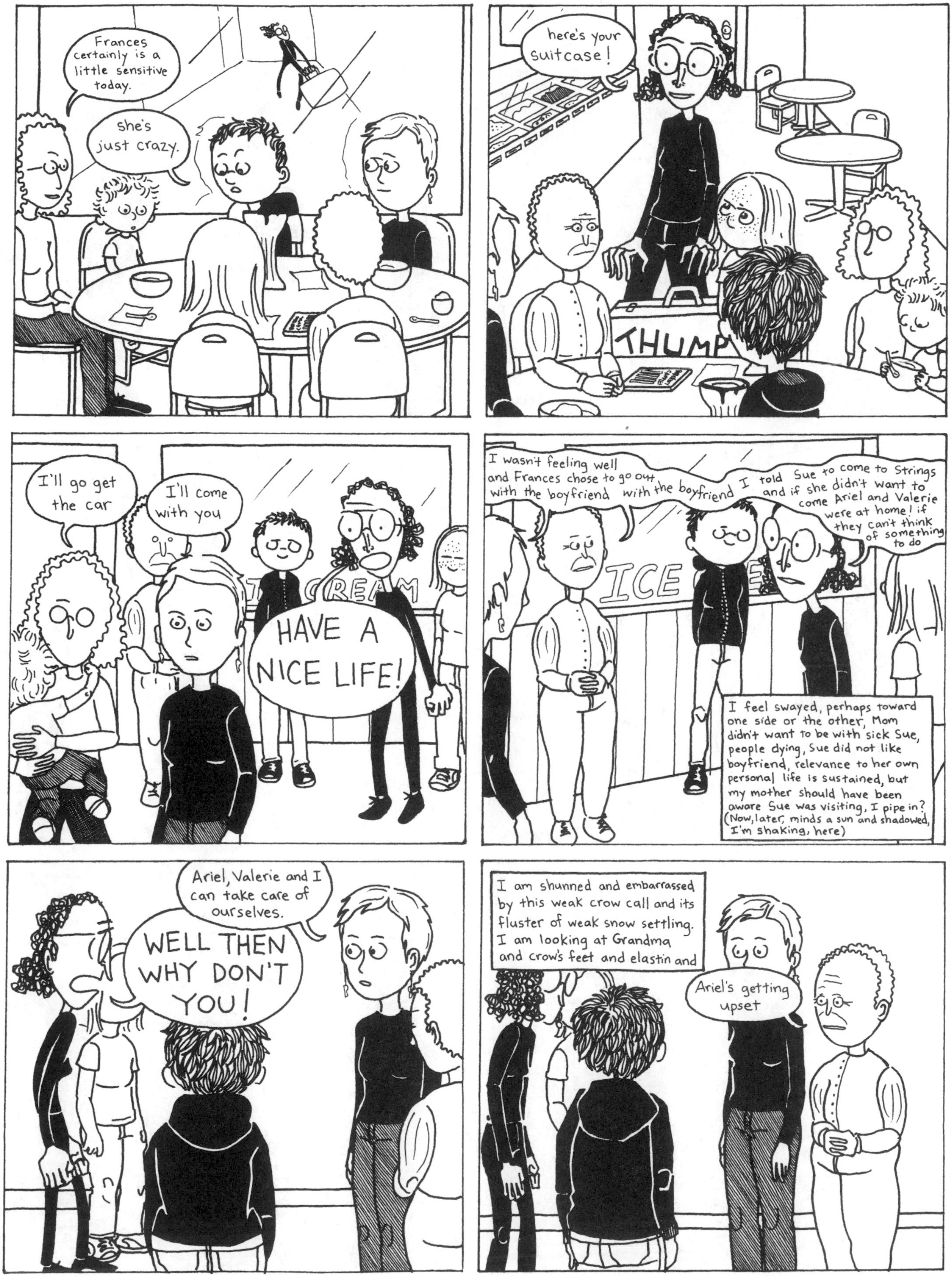
Frances certainly is a little sensitive today.
she's just crazy.
here's your suitcase!
THUMP
I'll go get the car
I'll come with you
HAVE A NICE LIFE!
I wasn't feeling well and Frances chose to go out with the boyfriend with the boyfriend
I told Sue to come to Strings and if she didn't want to come Ariel and Valerie were at home! if they can't think of something to do
ICE
I feel swayed, perhaps toward one side or the other, Mom didn't want to be with sick Sue, people dying, Sue did not like boyfriend, relevance to her own personal life is sustained, but my mother should have been aware Sue was visiting, I pipe in? (Now, later, minds a sun and shadowed, I'm shaking, here)
Ariel, Valerie and I can take care of ourselves.
WELL THEN WHY DON'T YOU!
I am shunned and embarrassed by this weak crow call and its fluster of weak snow settling. I am looking at Grandma and crow's feet and elastin and
Ariel's getting upset

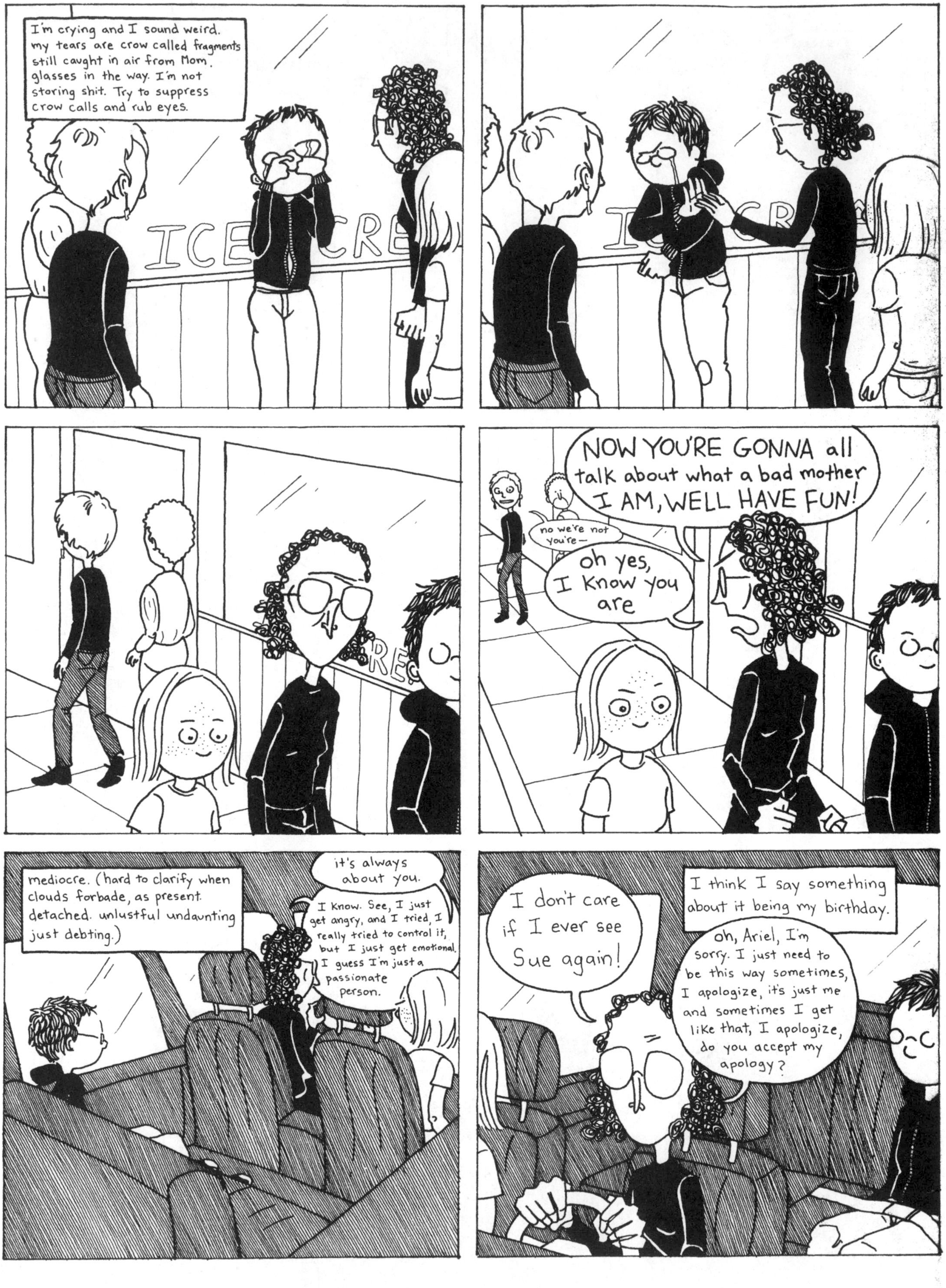
I'm crying and I sound weird. my tears are crow called fragments still caught in air from Mom. glasses in the way. I'm not storing shit. Try to suppress crow calls and rub eyes.
ICE CRE
ICE CR
RE
NOW YOU'RE GONNA all talk about what a bad mother I AM, WELL HAVE FUN!
no we're not you're—
oh yes, I know you are
mediocre. (hard to clarify when clouds forbade, as present. detached. unlustful undaunting just debting.)
it's always about you.
I know. See, I just get angry, and I tried, I really tried to control it, but I just get emotional. I guess I'm just a passionate person.
I don't care if I ever see Sue again!
I think I say something about it being my birthday.
oh, Ariel, I'm sorry. I just need to be this way sometimes, I apologize, it's just me and sometimes I get like that, I apologize, do you accept my apology?

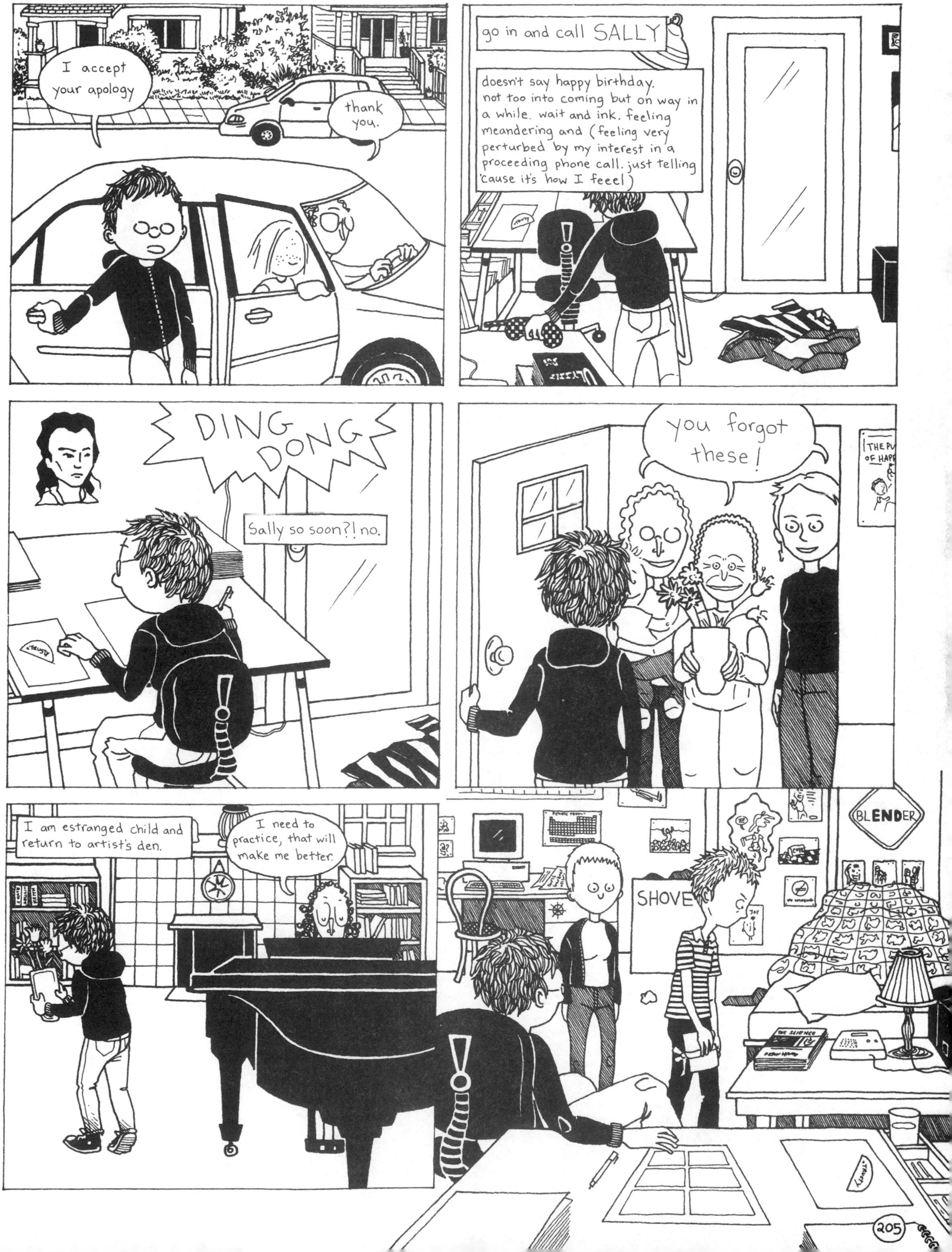

I accept your apology
thank you.
go in and call SALLY
doesn't say happy birthday. not too into coming but on way in a while. wait and ink. feeling meandering and (feeling very perturbed by my interest in a proceeding phone call. just telling 'cause it's how I feeel)
DING DONG
Sally so soon?! no.
you forgot these!
I am estranged child and return to artist's den.
I need to practice, that will make me better.
SHOVE
BLENDER

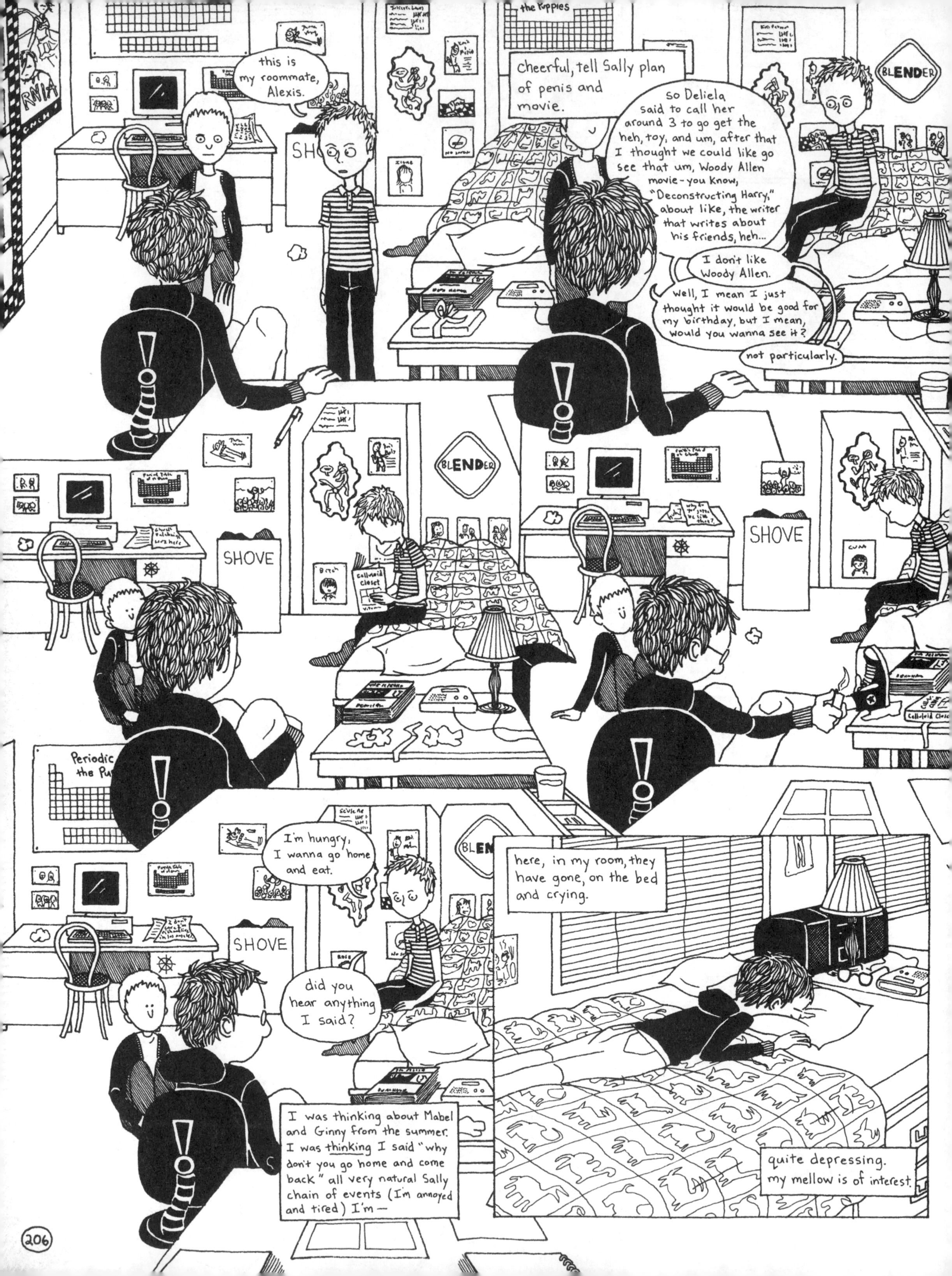
this is my roommate, Alexis.
SHOVE
cheerful, tell Sally plan of penis and movie.
BLENDER
so Deliela said to call her around 3 to go get the heh, toy, and um, after that I thought we could like go see that um, Woody Allen movie - you know, "Deconstructing Harry," about like, the writer that writes about his friends, heh...
I don't like Woody Allen.
well, I mean I just thought it would be good for my birthday, but I mean, would you wanna see it?
not particularly.
BLENDER
SHOVE
Celluloid Closet
SHOVE
Periodic the Pu
I'm hungry, I wanna go home and eat.
SHOVE
did you hear anything I said?
I was thinking about Mabel and Ginny from the summer. I was thinking I said "why don't you go home and come back" all very natural Sally chain of events (I'm annoyed and tired) I'm—
here, in my room, they have gone, on the bed and crying.
quite depressing. my mellow is of interest.

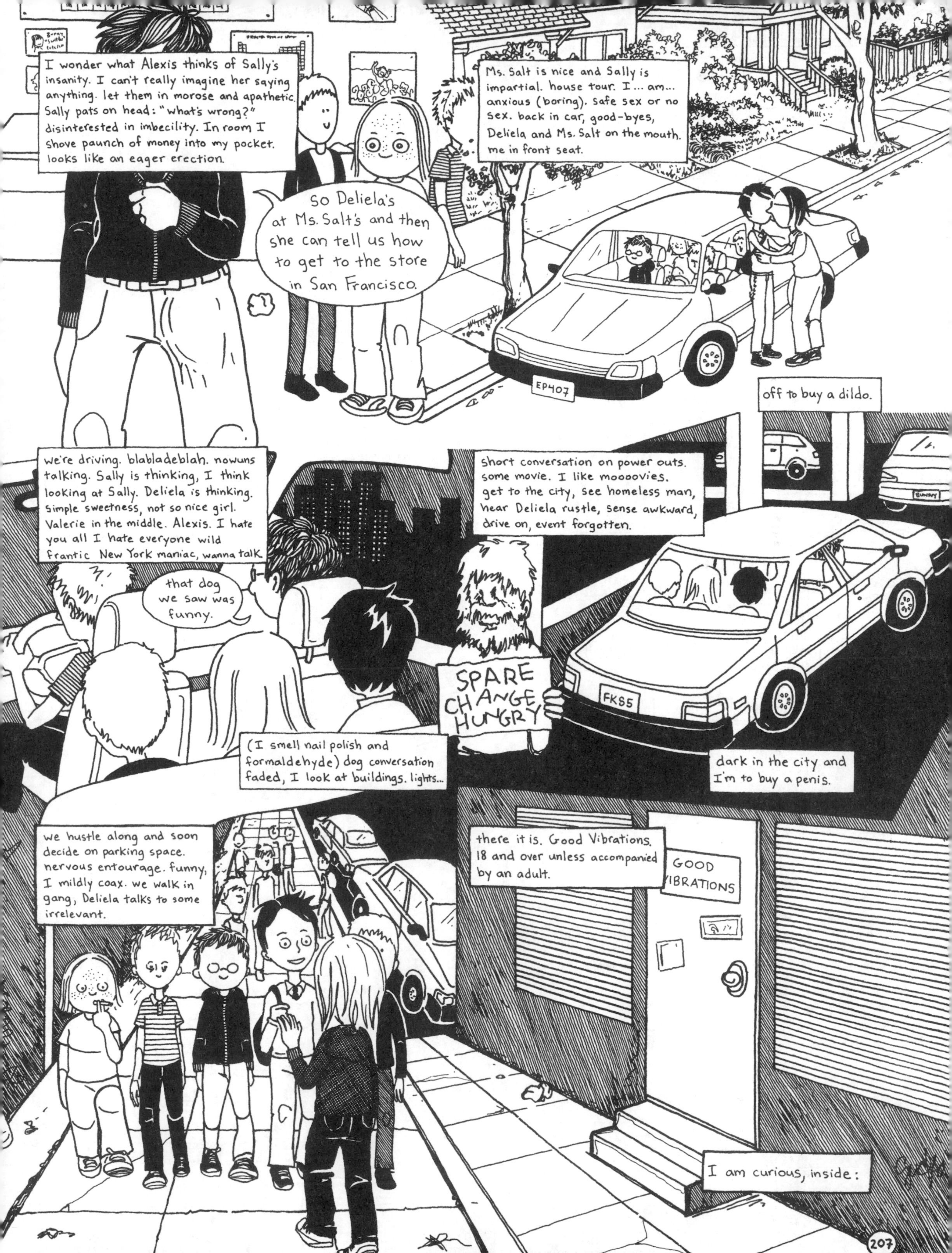

I wonder what Alexis thinks of Sally's insanity. I can't really imagine her saying anything. let them in morose and apathetic. Sally pats on head: "what's wrong?" disinterested in imbecility. In room I shove paunch of money into my pocket. looks like an eager erection.
So Deliela's at Ms. Salt's and then she can tell us how to get to the store in San Francisco.
Ms. Salt is nice and Sally is impartial. house tour. I... am... anxious (boring). safe sex or no sex. back in car, good-byes, Deliela and Ms. Salt on the mouth. me in front seat.
EP407
off to buy a dildo.
we're driving. blabladeblah. nowuns talking. Sally is thinking, I think looking at Sally. Deliela is thinking. simple sweetness, not so nice girl. Valerie in the middle. Alexis. I hate you all I hate everyone wild frantic New York maniac, wanna talk.
that dog we saw was funny.
short conversation on power outs. some movie. I like moooovies. get to the city, see homeless man, hear Deliela rustle, sense awkward, drive on, event forgotten.
SPARE CHANGE HUNGRY
FKS5
(I smell nail polish and formaldehyde) dog conversation faded, I look at buildings. lights...
dark in the city and I'm to buy a penis.
we hustle along and soon decide on parking space. nervous entourage. funny, I mildly coax. we walk in gang, Deliela talks to some irrelevant.
there it is. Good Vibrations. 18 and over unless accompanied by an adult.
GOOD VIBRATIONS
I am curious, inside:

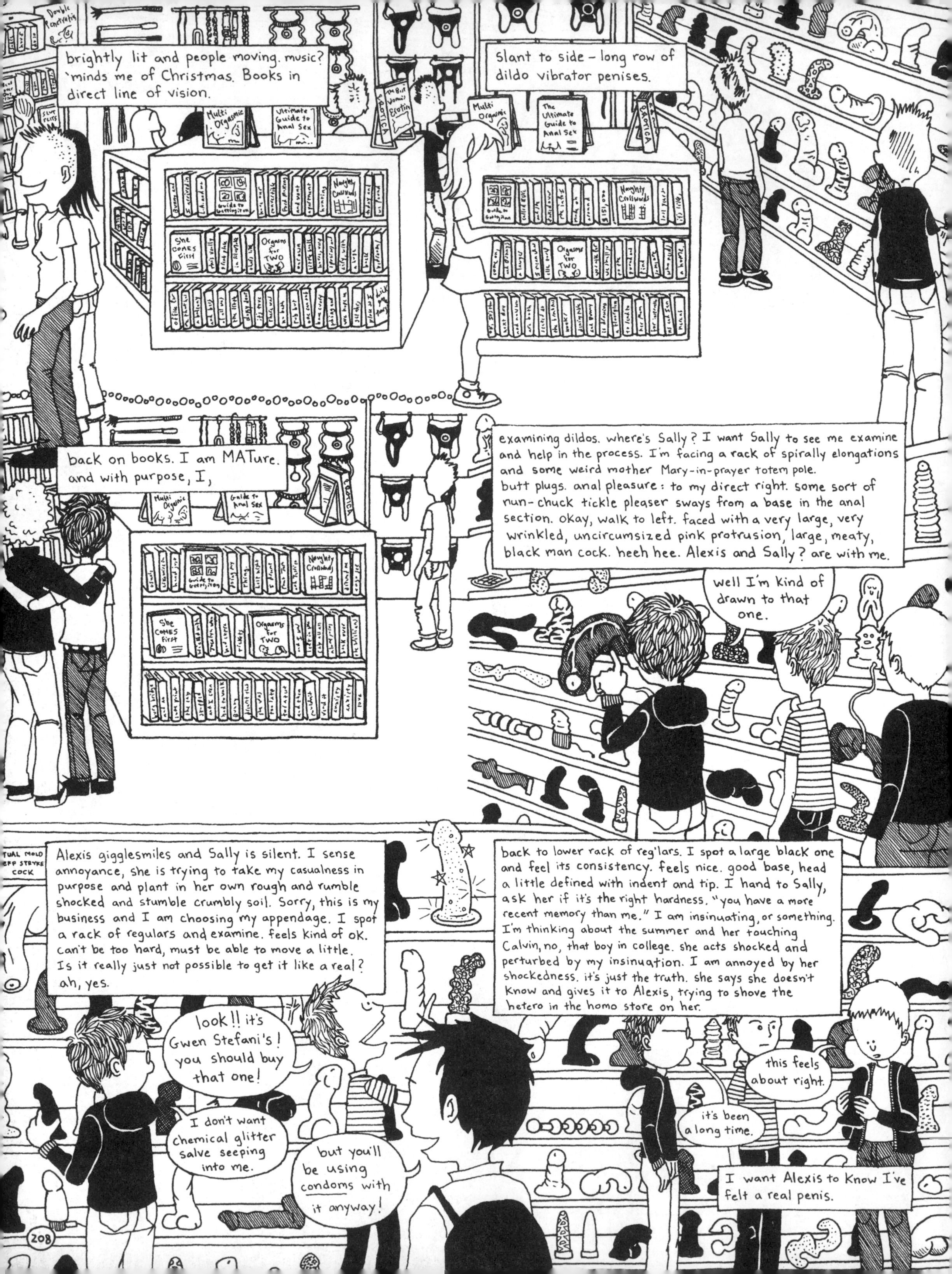

brightly lit and people moving. music? `minds me of Christmas. Books in direct line of vision.
Slant to side - long row of dildo vibrator penises.
Multi Orgasmic
Ultimate Guide to Anal Sex
EROTICA
Naughty Crosswords
She COMES First
Orgasms for TWO
back on books. I am MATure. and with purpose, I,
examining dildos. where's Sally? I want Sally to see me examine and help in the process. I'm facing a rack of spirally elongations and some weird mother Mary-in-prayer totem pole. butt plugs. anal pleasure: to my direct right. some sort of nun-chuck tickle pleaser sways from a base in the anal section. okay, walk to left. faced with a very large, very wrinkled, uncircumsized pink protrusion, large, meaty, black man cock. heeh hee. Alexis and Sally? are with me.
well I'm kind of drawn to that one.
Alexis gigglesmiles and Sally is silent. I sense annoyance, she is trying to take my casualness in purpose and plant in her own rough and rumble shocked and stumble crumbly soil. Sorry, this is my business and I am choosing my appendage. I spot a rack of regulars and examine. feels kind of OK. can't be too hard, must be able to move a little. Is it really just not possible to get it like a real? ah, yes.
back to lower rack of reg'lars. I spot a large black one and feel its consistency. feels nice. good base, head a little defined with indent and tip. I hand to Sally, ask her if it's the right hardness. "you have a more recent memory than me." I am insinuating, or something. I'm thinking about the summer and her touching Calvin, no, that boy in college. she acts shocked and perturbed by my insinuation. I am annoyed by her shockedness. it's just the truth. she says she doesn't know and gives it to Alexis, trying to shove the hetero in the homo store on her.
look!! it's Gwen Stefani's! you should buy that one!
I don't want chemical glitter salve seeping into me.
but you'll be using condoms with it anyway!
this feels about right.
it's been a long time.
I want Alexis to know I've felt a real penis.

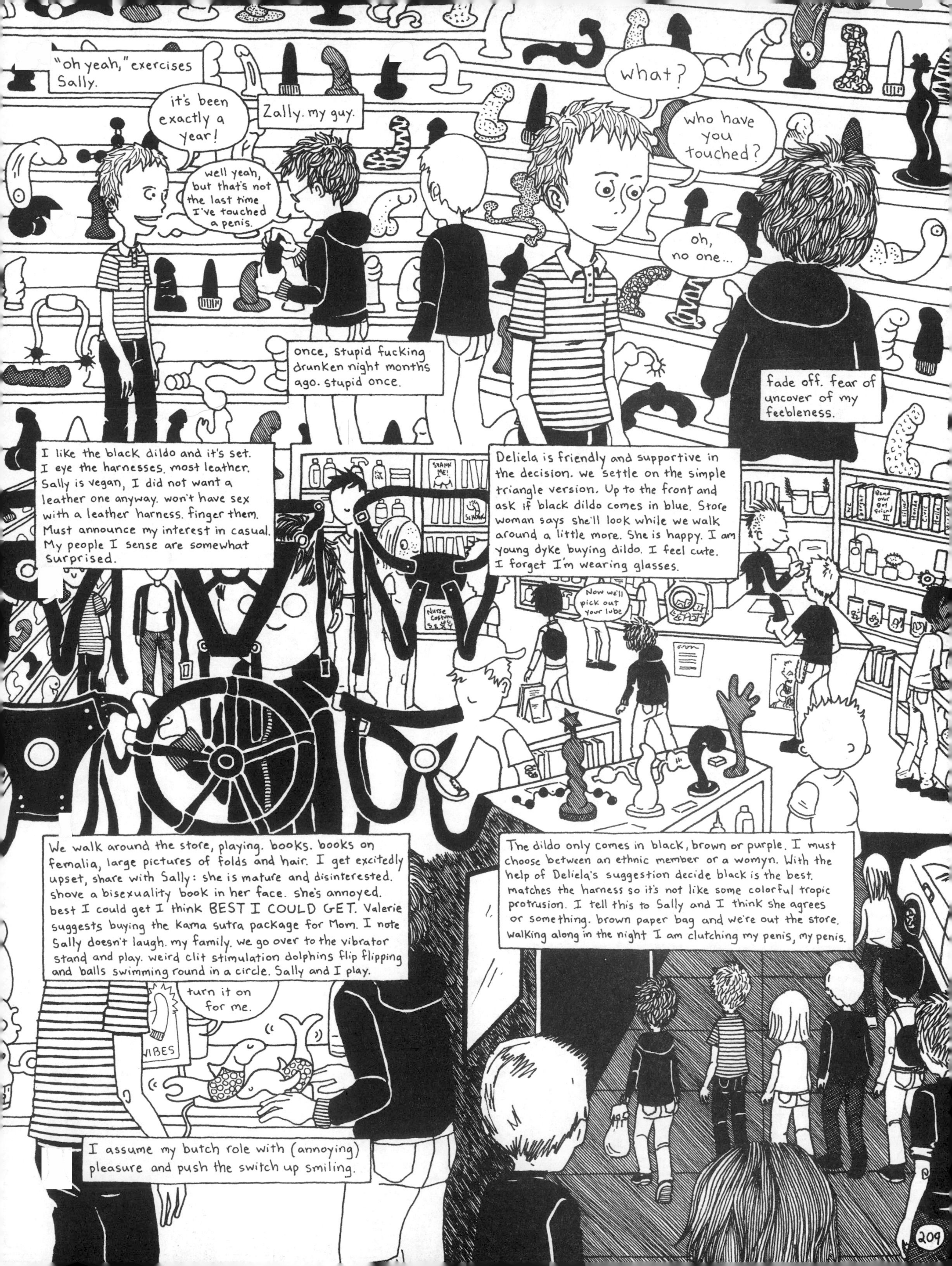
"oh yeah," exercises Sally.
it's been exactly a year!
Zally. my guy.
well yeah, but that's not the last time I've touched a penis.
what?
who have you touched?
oh, no one...
once, stupid fucking drunken night months ago. stupid once.
fade off. fear of uncover of my feebleness.
I like the black dildo and it's set. I eye the harnesses. most leather. Sally is vegan, I did not want a leather one anyway. won't have sex with a leather harness. finger them. Must announce my interest in casual. My people I sense are somewhat surprised.
Deliela is friendly and supportive in the decision. we settle on the simple triangle version. Up to the front and ask if black dildo comes in blue. Store woman says she'll look while we walk around a little more. She is happy. I am young dyke buying dildo. I feel cute. I forget I'm wearing glasses.
Now we'll pick out your lube
We walk around the store, playing. books. books on femalia, large pictures of folds and hair. I get excitedly upset, share with Sally: she is mature and disinterested. shove a bisexuality book in her face. she's annoyed. best I could get I think BEST I COULD GET. Valerie suggests buying the kama sutra package for Mom. I note Sally doesn't laugh. my family. we go over to the vibrator stand and play. weird clit stimulation dolphins flip flipping and balls swimming round in a circle. Sally and I play.
turn it on for me.
VIBES
I assume my butch role with (annoying) pleasure and push the switch up smiling.
The dildo only comes in black, brown or purple. I must choose between an ethnic member or a womyn. With the help of Deliela's suggestion decide black is the best. matches the harness so it's not like some colorful tropic protrusion. I tell this to Sally and I think she agrees or something. brown paper bag and we're out the store. walking along in the night I am clutching my penis, my penis.

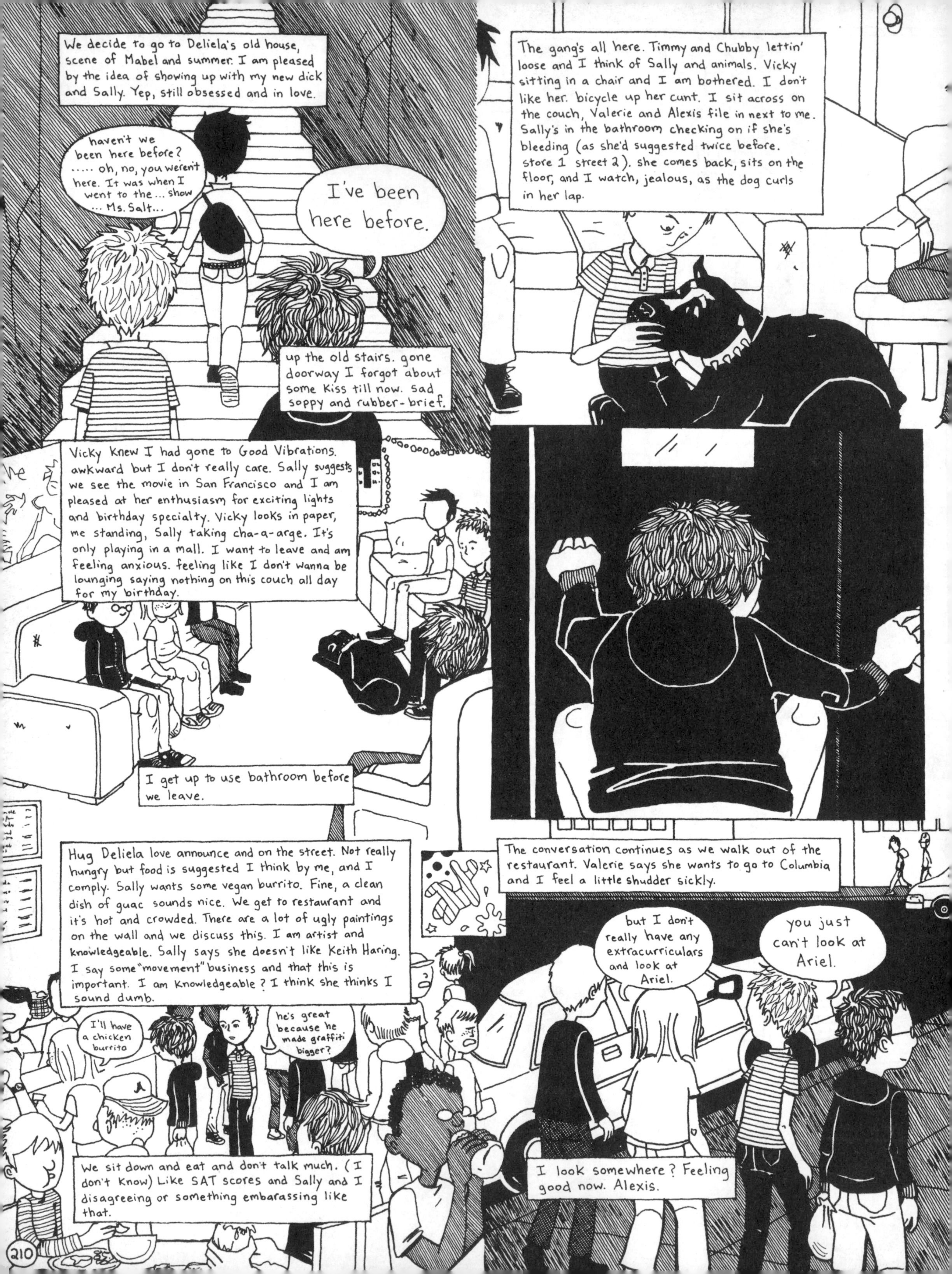

We decide to go to Deliela's old house, scene of Mabel and summer. I am pleased by the idea of showing up with my new dick and Sally. Yep, still obsessed and in love.
haven't we been here before? ..... oh, no, you weren't here. It was when I went to the ... show ... Ms. Salt...
I've been here before.
up the old stairs. gone doorway I forgot about some kiss till now. sad soppy and rubber-brief.
The gang's all here. Timmy and Chubby lettin' loose and I think of Sally and animals. Vicky sitting in a chair and I am bothered. I don't like her. bicycle up her cunt. I sit across on the couch, Valerie and Alexis file in next to me. Sally's in the bathroom checking on if she's bleeding (as she'd suggested twice before. store 1 street 2). she comes back, sits on the floor, and I watch, jealous, as the dog curls in her lap.
Vicky knew I had gone to Good Vibrations. awkward but I don't really care. Sally suggests we see the movie in San Francisco and I am pleased at her enthusiasm for exciting lights and birthday specialty. Vicky looks in paper, me standing, Sally taking cha-a-arge. It's only playing in a mall. I want to leave and am feeling anxious. feeling like I don't wanna be lounging saying nothing on this couch all day for my birthday.
I get up to use bathroom before we leave.
Hug Deliela love announce and on the street. Not really hungry but food is suggested I think by me, and I comply. Sally wants some vegan burrito. Fine, a clean dish of guac sounds nice. We get to restaurant and it's hot and crowded. There are a lot of ugly paintings on the wall and we discuss this. I am artist and knowledgeable. Sally says she doesn't like Keith Haring. I say some "movement" business and that this is important. I am knowledgeable? I think she thinks I sound dumb.
I'll have a chicken burrito
he's great because he made graffiti bigger?
We sit down and eat and don't talk much. (I don't know) Like SAT scores and Sally and I disagreeing or something embarassing like that.
The conversation continues as we walk out of the restaurant. Valerie says she wants to go to Columbia and I feel a little shudder sickly.
but I don't really have any extracurriculars and look at Ariel.
you just can't look at Ariel.
I look somewhere? Feeling good now. Alexis.

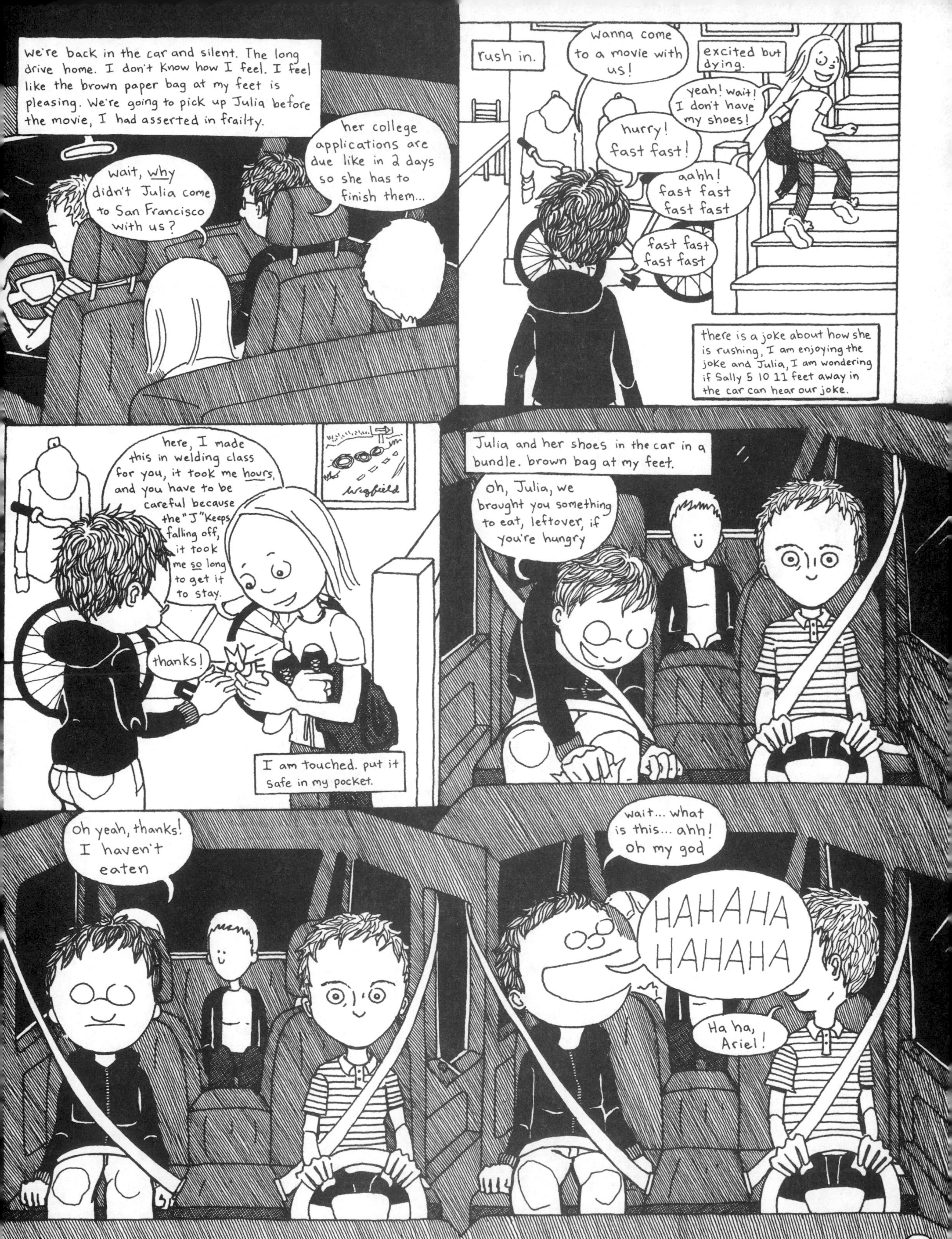
we're back in the car and silent. The long drive home. I don't know how I feel. I feel like the brown paper bag at my feet is pleasing. We're going to pick up Julia before the movie, I had asserted in frailty.
wait, why didn't Julia come to San Francisco with us?
her college applications are due like in 2 days so she has to finish them...
rush in.
wanna come to a movie with us!
excited but dying.
yeah! wait! I don't have my shoes!
hurry! fast fast!
aahh! fast fast fast fast
fast fast fast fast
there is a joke about how she is rushing, I am enjoying the joke and Julia, I am wondering if Sally 5 10 11 feet away in the car can hear our joke.
here, I made this in welding class for you, it took me hours, and you have to be careful because the "J" keeps falling off, it took me so long to get it to stay.
thanks!
I am touched. put it safe in my pocket.
Julia and her shoes in the car in a bundle. brown bag at my feet.
oh, Julia, we brought you something to eat, leftover, if you're hungry
oh yeah, thanks! I haven't eaten
wait... what is this... ahh! oh my god
HAHAHA HAHAHA
Ha ha, Ariel!

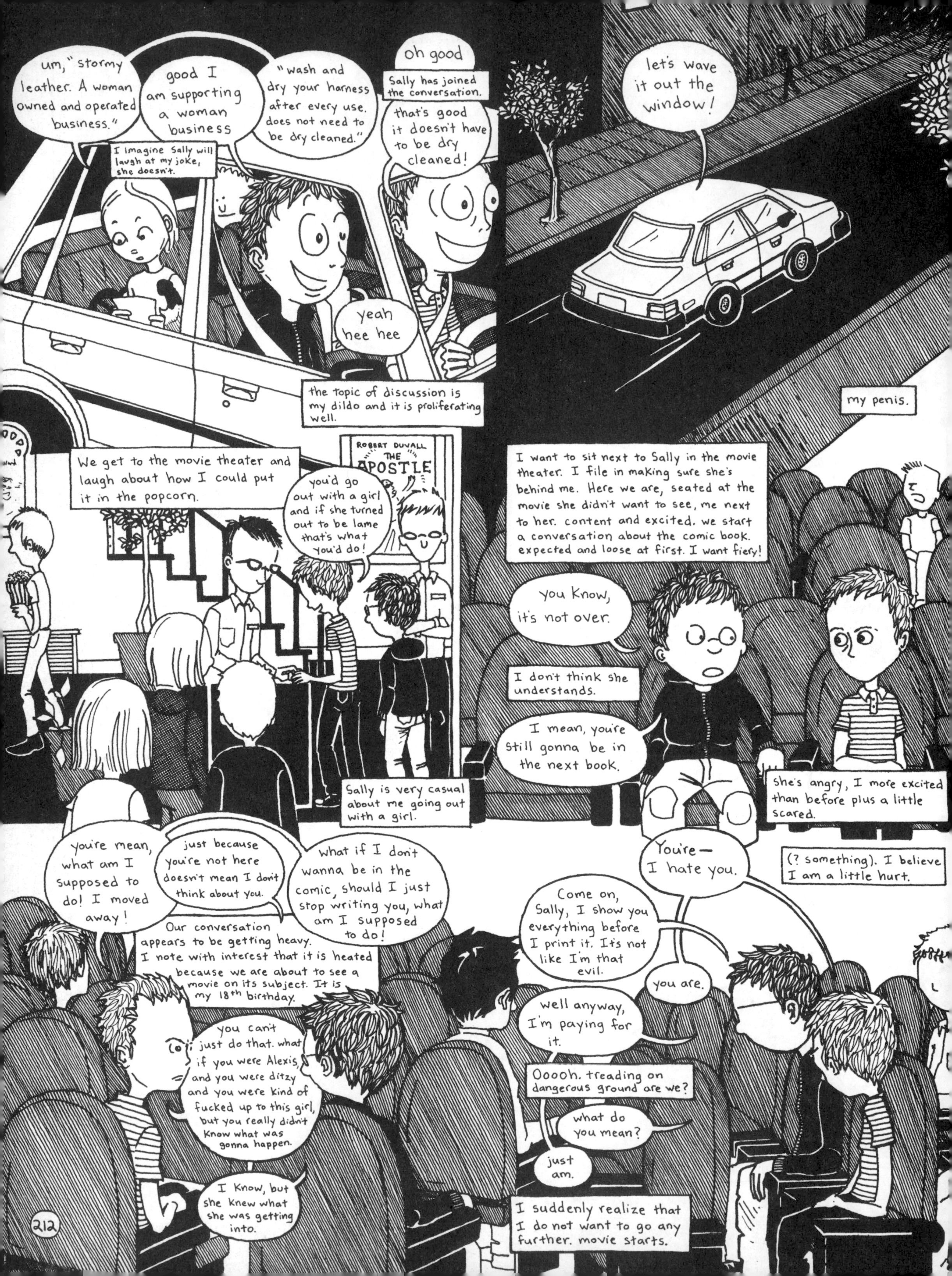
um," stormy leather. A woman owned and operated business."
good I am supporting a woman business
"wash and dry your harness after every use. does not need to be dry cleaned."
I imagine Sally will laugh at my joke, she doesn't.
oh good
Sally has joined the conversation.
that's good it doesn't have to be dry cleaned!
yeah hee hee
the topic of discussion is my dildo and it is proliferating well.
let's wave it out the window!
my penis.
We get to the movie theater and laugh about how I could put it in the popcorn.
ROBERT DUVALL THE APOSTLE
you'd go out with a girl and if she turned out to be lame that's what you'd do!
Sally is very casual about me going out with a girl.
I want to sit next to Sally in the movie theater. I file in making sure she's behind me. Here we are, seated at the movie she didn't want to see, me next to her. content and excited. we start a conversation about the comic book. expected and loose at first. I want fiery!
you know, it's not over.
I don't think she understands.
I mean, you're still gonna be in the next book.
she's angry, I more excited than before plus a little scared.
you're mean, what am I supposed to do! I moved away!
just because you're not here doesn't mean I don't think about you.
what if I don't wanna be in the comic, should I just stop writing you, what am I supposed to do!
Our conversation appears to be getting heavy. I note with interest that it is heated because we are about to see a movie on its subject. It is my 18th birthday.
you can't just do that. what if you were Alexis, and you were ditzy and you were kind of fucked up to this girl, but you really didn't know what was gonna happen.
I know, but she knew what she was getting into.
You're— I hate you.
(? something). I believe I am a little hurt.
Come on, Sally, I show you everything before I print it. It's not like I'm that evil.
you are.
well anyway, I'm paying for it.
Oooh. treading on dangerous ground are we?
what do you mean?
just am.
I suddenly realize that I do not want to go any further. movie starts.

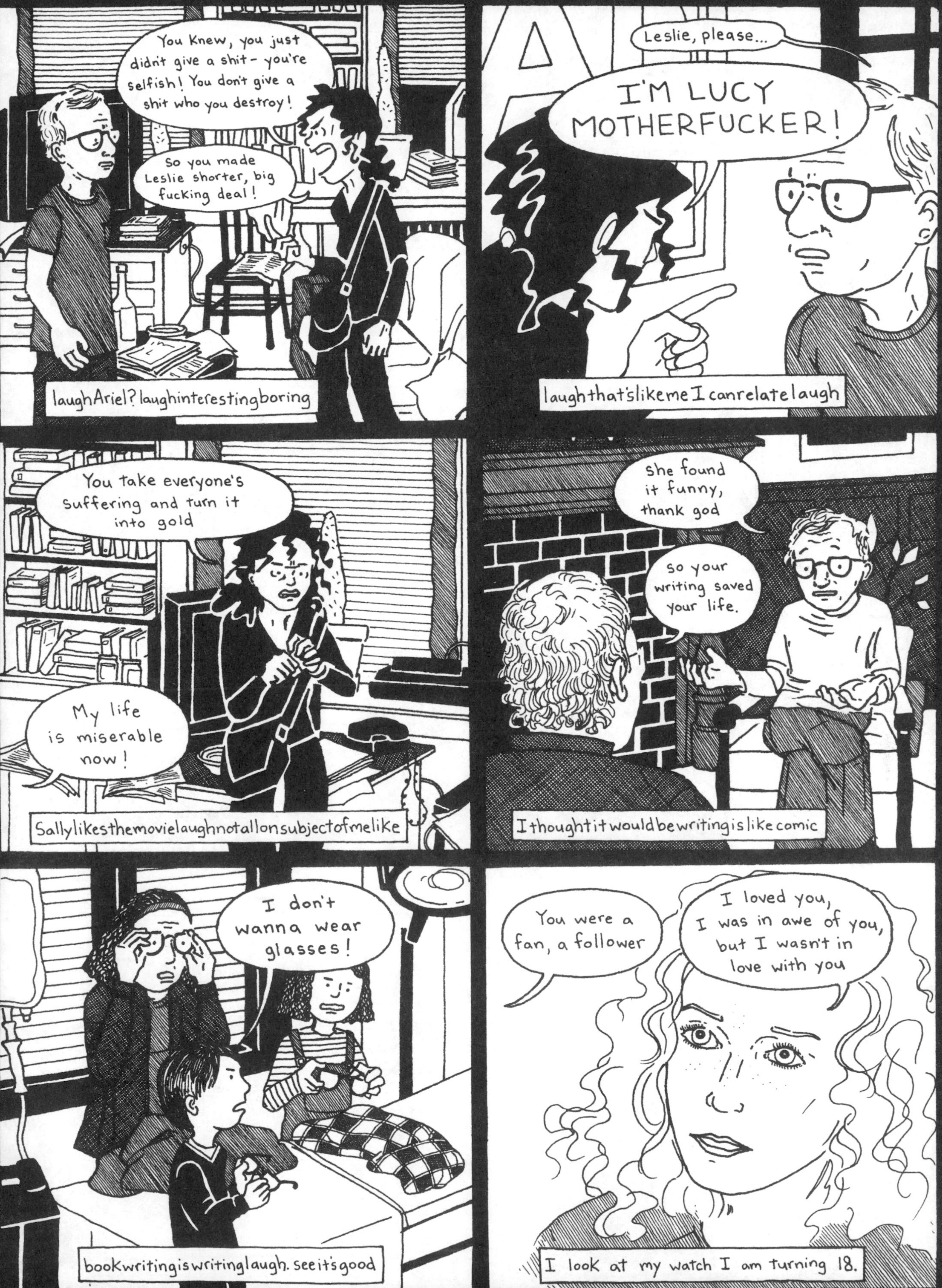

You Knew, you just didn't give a shit - you're selfish! You don't give a shit who you destroy!
So you made Leslie shorter, big fucking deal!
laughAriel? laughinterestingboring
Leslie, please...
I'M LUCY MOTHERFUCKER!
laughthat'slikeme I canrelatelaugh
You take everyone's suffering and turn it into gold
My life is miserable now!
Sallylikesthemovielaughnotallonsubjectofmelike
She found it funny, thank god
so your writing saved your life.
Ithoughtitwouldbewritingislike comic
I don't wanna wear glasses!
bookwritingiswritinglaugh. seeit'sgood
You were a fan, a follower
I loved you, I was in awe of you, but I wasn't in love with you
I look at my watch I am turning 18.

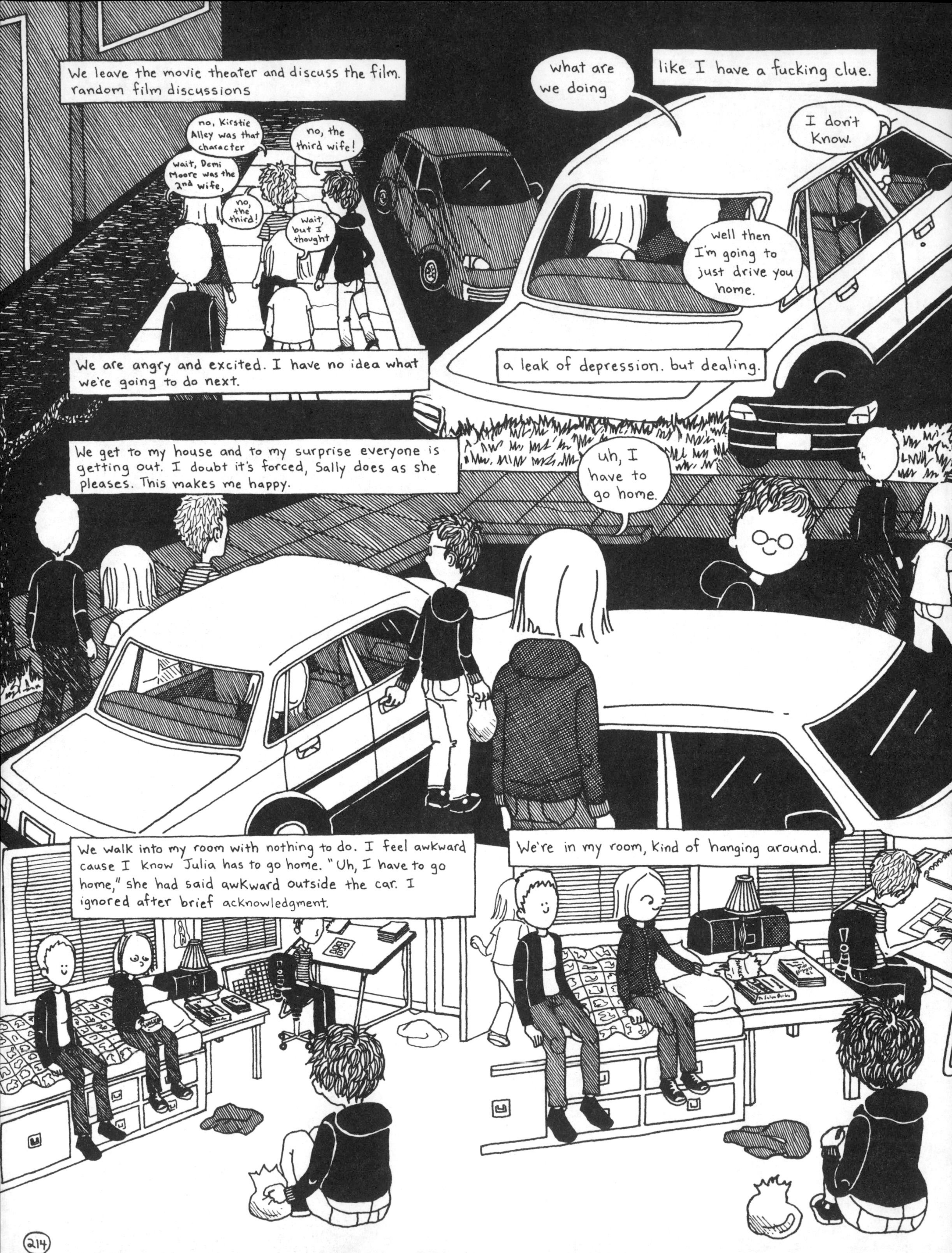

We leave the movie theater and discuss the film. random film discussions
no, Kirstie Alley was that character
no, the third wife!
wait, Demi Moore was the 2nd wife,
no, the third!
wait, but I thought
what are we doing
like I have a fucking clue.
I don't Know.
well then I'm going to just drive you home.
We are angry and excited. I have no idea what we're going to do next.
a leak of depression. but dealing.
We get to my house and to my surprise everyone is getting out. I doubt it's forced, Sally does as she pleases. This makes me happy.
uh, I have to go home.
We walk into my room with nothing to do. I feel awkward cause I know Julia has to go home. "Uh, I have to go home," she had said awkward outside the car. I ignored after brief acknowledgment.
We're in my room, kind of hanging around.

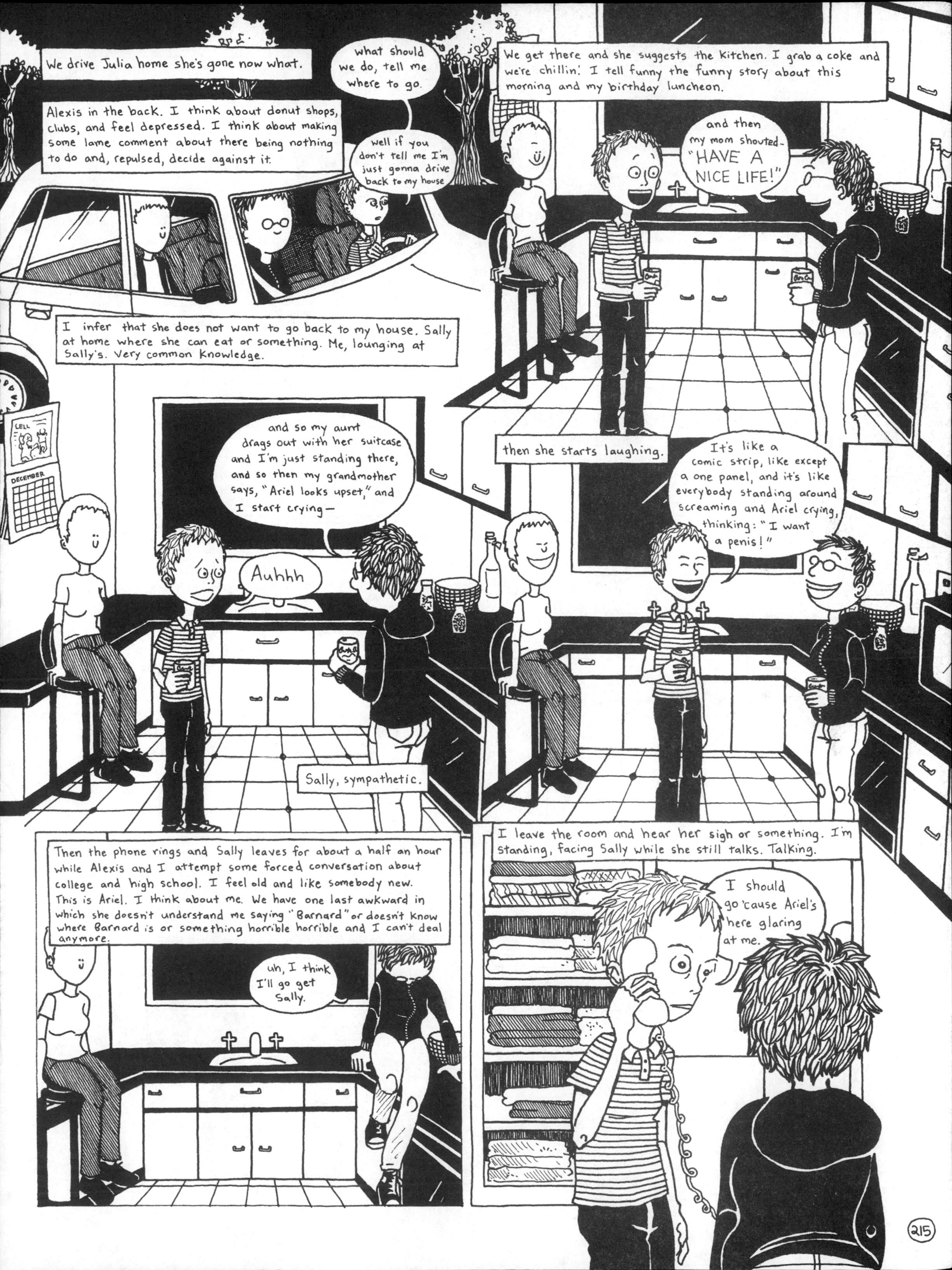
We drive Julia home she's gone now what.
what should we do, tell me where to go.
Alexis in the back. I think about donut shops, clubs, and feel depressed. I think about making some lame comment about there being nothing to do and, repulsed, decide against it.
well if you don't tell me I'm just gonna drive back to my house
I infer that she does not want to go back to my house. Sally at home where she can eat or something. Me, lounging at Sally's. Very common knowledge.
We get there and she suggests the kitchen. I grab a coke and we're chillin'. I tell funny the funny story about this morning and my birthday luncheon.
and then my mom shouted- "HAVE A NICE LIFE!"
and so my aunt drags out with her suitcase and I'm just standing there, and so then my grandmother says, "Ariel looks upset," and I start crying-
Auhhh
Sally, sympathetic.
then she starts laughing.
It's like a comic strip, like except a one panel, and it's like everybody standing around screaming and Ariel crying, thinking: "I want a penis!"
Then the phone rings and Sally leaves for about a half an hour while Alexis and I attempt some forced conversation about college and high school. I feel old and like somebody new. This is Ariel. I think about me. We have one last awkward in which she doesn't understand me saying "Barnard" or doesn't know where Barnard is or something horrible horrible and I can't deal anymore.
uh, I think I'll go get Sally.
I leave the room and hear her sigh or something. I'm standing, facing Sally while she still talks. Talking.
I should go 'cause Ariel's here glaring at me.

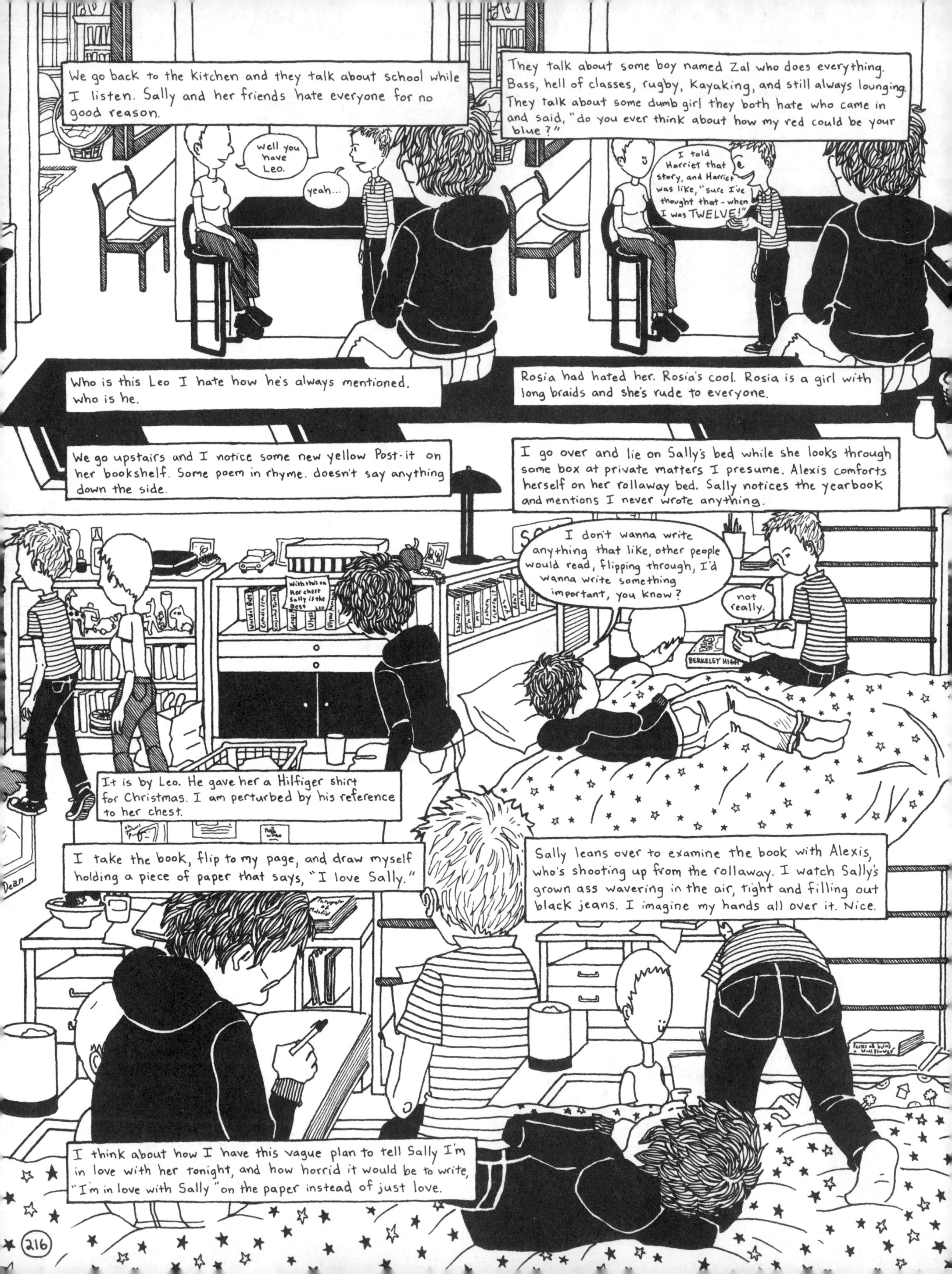

We go back to the kitchen and they talk about school while I listen. Sally and her friends hate everyone for no good reason.
well you have Leo.
yeah...
They talk about some boy named Zal who does everything. Bass, hell of classes, rugby, kayaking, and still always lounging. They talk about some dumb girl they both hate who came in and said, "do you ever think about how my red could be your blue?"
I told Harriet that story, and Harriet was like, "sure I've thought that - when I was TWELVE!"
Who is this Leo I hate how he's always mentioned. who is he.
Rosia had hated her. Rosia's cool. Rosia is a girl with long braids and she's rude to everyone.
We go upstairs and I notice some new yellow Post-it on her bookshelf. Some poem in rhyme. doesn't say anything down the side.
With this on her chest Sally is the Best Leo
I go over and lie on Sally's bed while she looks through some box at private matters I presume. Alexis comforts herself on her rollaway bed. Sally notices the yearbook and mentions I never wrote anything.
I don't wanna write anything that like, other people would read, flipping through, I'd wanna write something important, you know?
not really.
BERKELEY HIGH
It is by Leo. He gave her a Hilfiger shirt for Christmas. I am perturbed by his reference to her chest.
I take the book, flip to my page, and draw myself holding a piece of paper that says, "I love Sally."
Sally leans over to examine the book with Alexis, who's shooting up from the rollaway. I watch Sally's grown ass wavering in the air, tight and filling out black jeans. I imagine my hands all over it. Nice.
I think about how I have this vague plan to tell Sally I'm in love with her tonight, and how horrid it would be to write, "I'm in love with Sally" on the paper instead of just love.

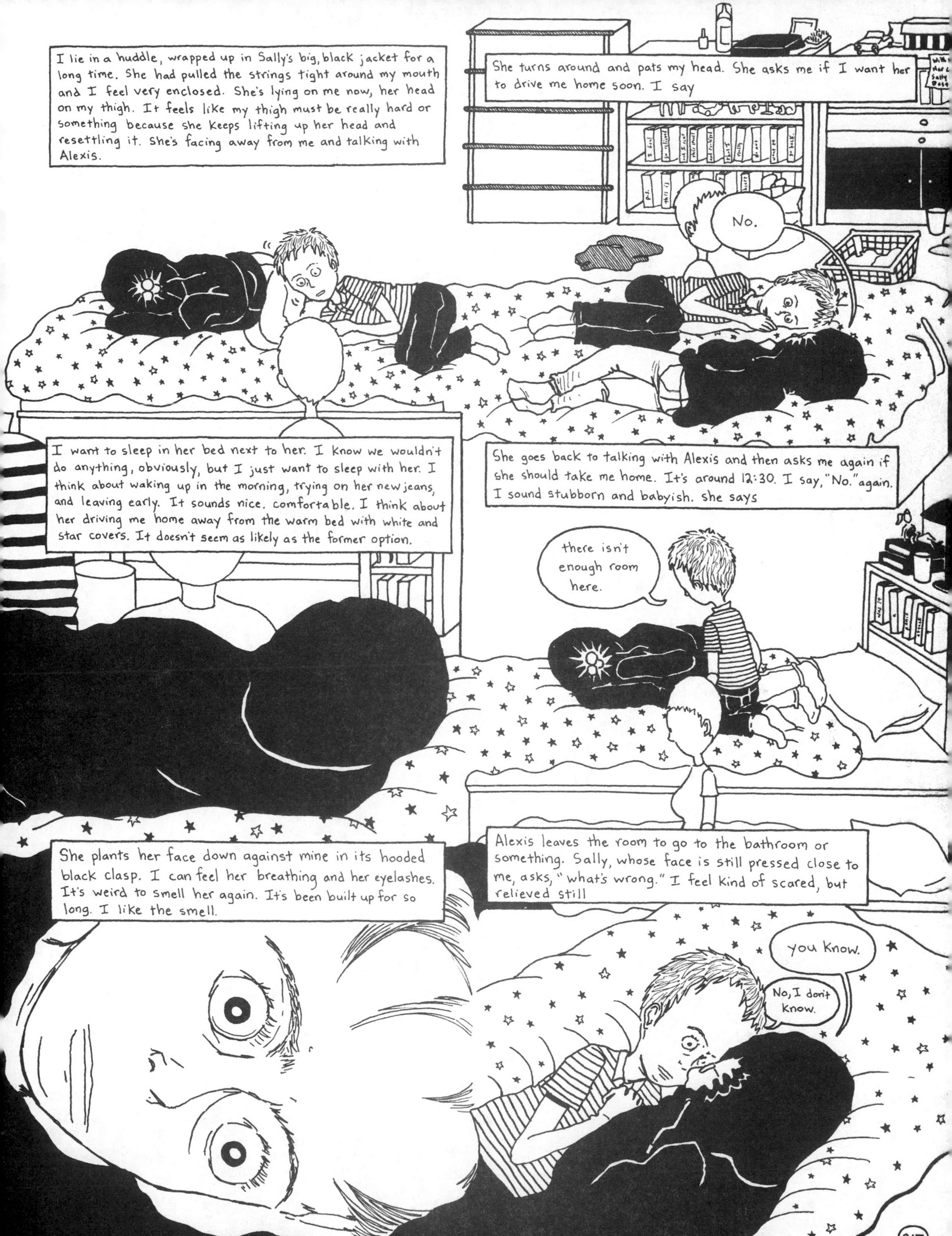

I lie in a huddle, wrapped up in Sally's big, black jacket for a long time. She had pulled the strings tight around my mouth and I feel very enclosed. She's lying on me now, her head on my thigh. It feels like my thigh must be really hard or something because she keeps lifting up her head and resettling it. She's facing away from me and talking with Alexis.
She turns around and pats my head. She asks me if I want her to drive me home soon. I say
No.
I want to sleep in her bed next to her. I know we wouldn't do anything, obviously, but I just want to sleep with her. I think about waking up in the morning, trying on her new jeans, and leaving early. It sounds nice. comfortable. I think about her driving me home away from the warm bed with white and star covers. It doesn't seem as likely as the former option.
She goes back to talking with Alexis and then asks me again if she should take me home. It's around 12:30. I say, "No." again. I sound stubborn and babyish. she says
there isn't enough room here.
She plants her face down against mine in its hooded black clasp. I can feel her breathing and her eyelashes. It's weird to smell her again. It's been built up for so long. I like the smell.
Alexis leaves the room to go to the bathroom or something. Sally, whose face is still pressed close to me, asks, "what's wrong." I feel kind of scared, but relieved still
you know.
No, I don't know.

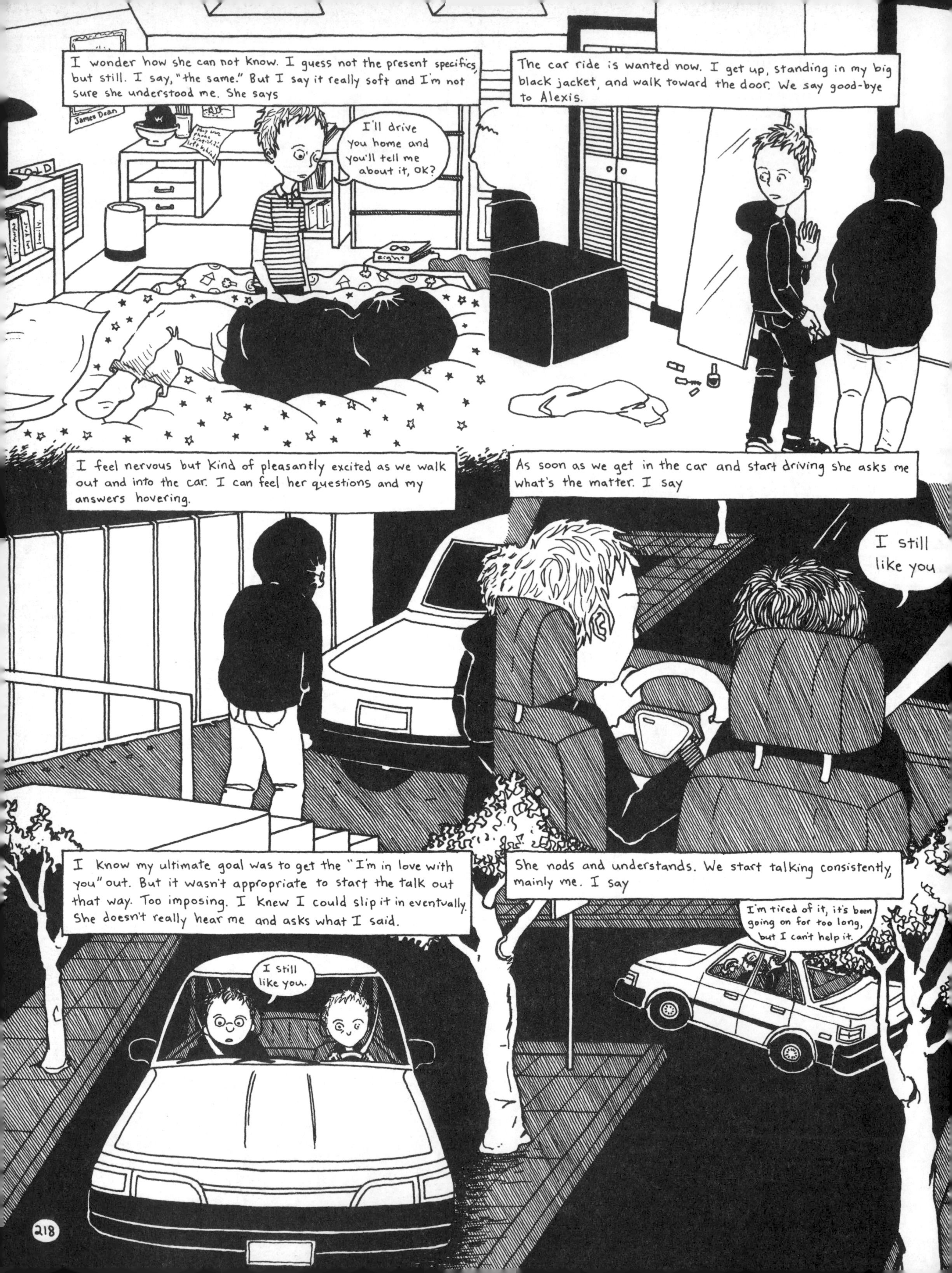
I wonder how she can not know. I guess not the present specifics, but still. I say, "the same." But I say it really soft and I'm not sure she understood me. She says
I'll drive you home and you'll tell me about it, OK?
The car ride is wanted now. I get up, standing in my big black jacket, and walk toward the door. We say good-bye to Alexis.
I feel nervous but kind of pleasantly excited as we walk out and into the car. I can feel her questions and my answers hovering.
As soon as we get in the car and start driving she asks me what's the matter. I say
I still like you
I know my ultimate goal was to get the "I'm in love with you" out. But it wasn't appropriate to start the talk out that way. Too imposing. I knew I could slip it in eventually. She doesn't really hear me and asks what I said.
I still like you.
She nods and understands. We start talking consistently, mainly me. I say
I'm tired of it, it's been going on for too long, but I can't help it.

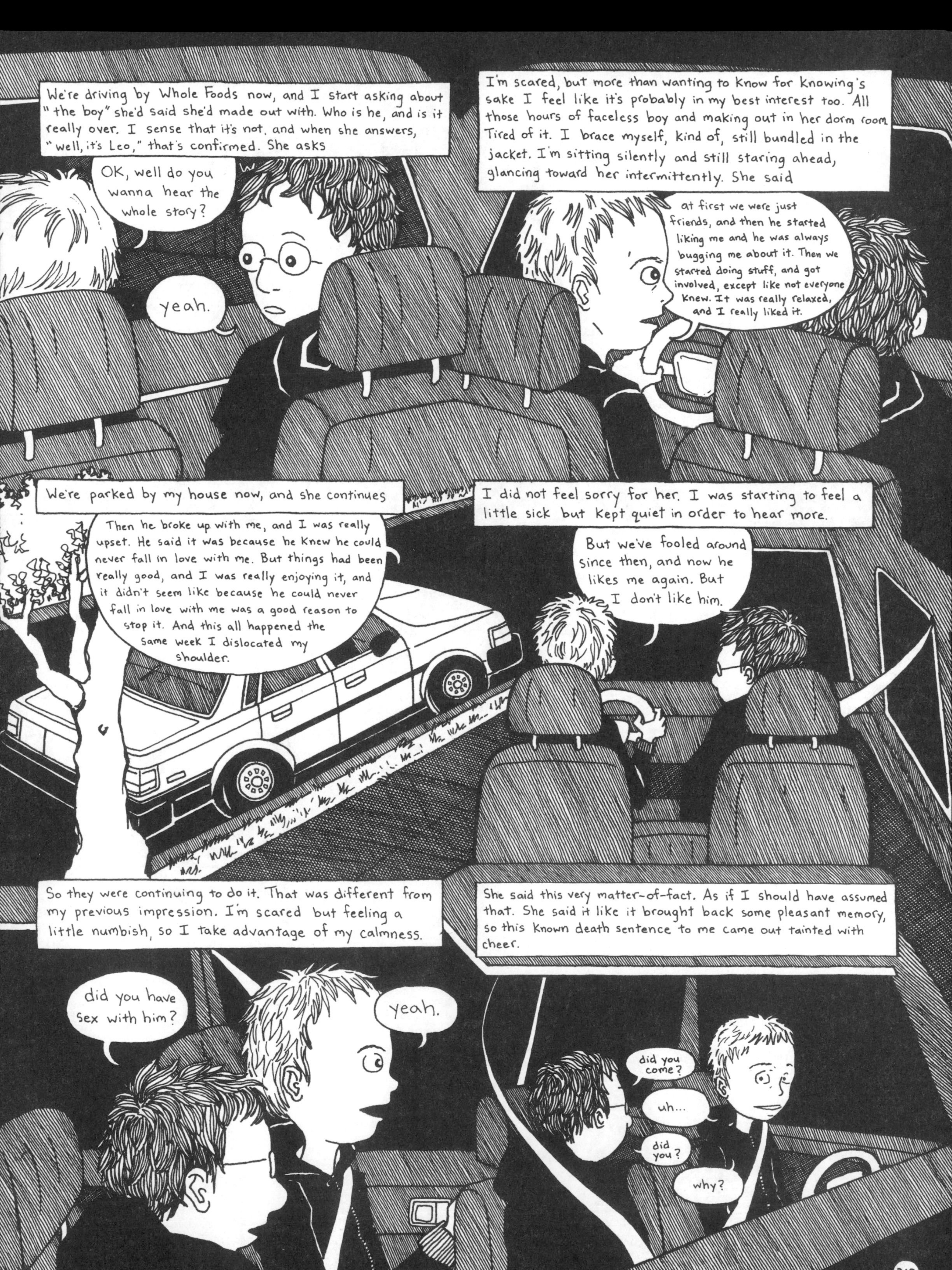
We're driving by Whole Foods now, and I start asking about "the boy" she'd said she'd made out with. Who is he, and is it really over. I sense that it's not, and when she answers, "well, it's Leo," that's confirmed. She asks
OK, well do you wanna hear the whole story?
yeah.
I'm scared, but more than wanting to know for knowing's sake I feel like it's probably in my best interest too. All those hours of faceless boy and making out in her dorm room. Tired of it. I brace myself, kind of, still bundled in the jacket. I'm sitting silently and still staring ahead, glancing toward her intermittently. She said
at first we were just friends, and then he started liking me and he was always bugging me about it. Then we started doing stuff, and got involved, except like not everyone knew. It was really relaxed, and I really liked it.
We're parked by my house now, and she continues
Then he broke up with me, and I was really upset. He said it was because he knew he could never fall in love with me. But things had been really good, and I was really enjoying it, and it didn't seem like because he could never fall in love with me was a good reason to stop it. And this all happened the same week I dislocated my shoulder.
I did not feel sorry for her. I was starting to feel a little sick but kept quiet in order to hear more.
But we've fooled around since then, and now he likes me again. But I don't like him.
So they were continuing to do it. That was different from my previous impression. I'm scared but feeling a little numbish, so I take advantage of my calmness.
did you have sex with him?
yeah.
She said this very matter-of-fact. As if I should have assumed that. She said it like it brought back some pleasant memory, so this known death sentence to me came out tainted with cheer.
did you come?
uh...
did you?
why?

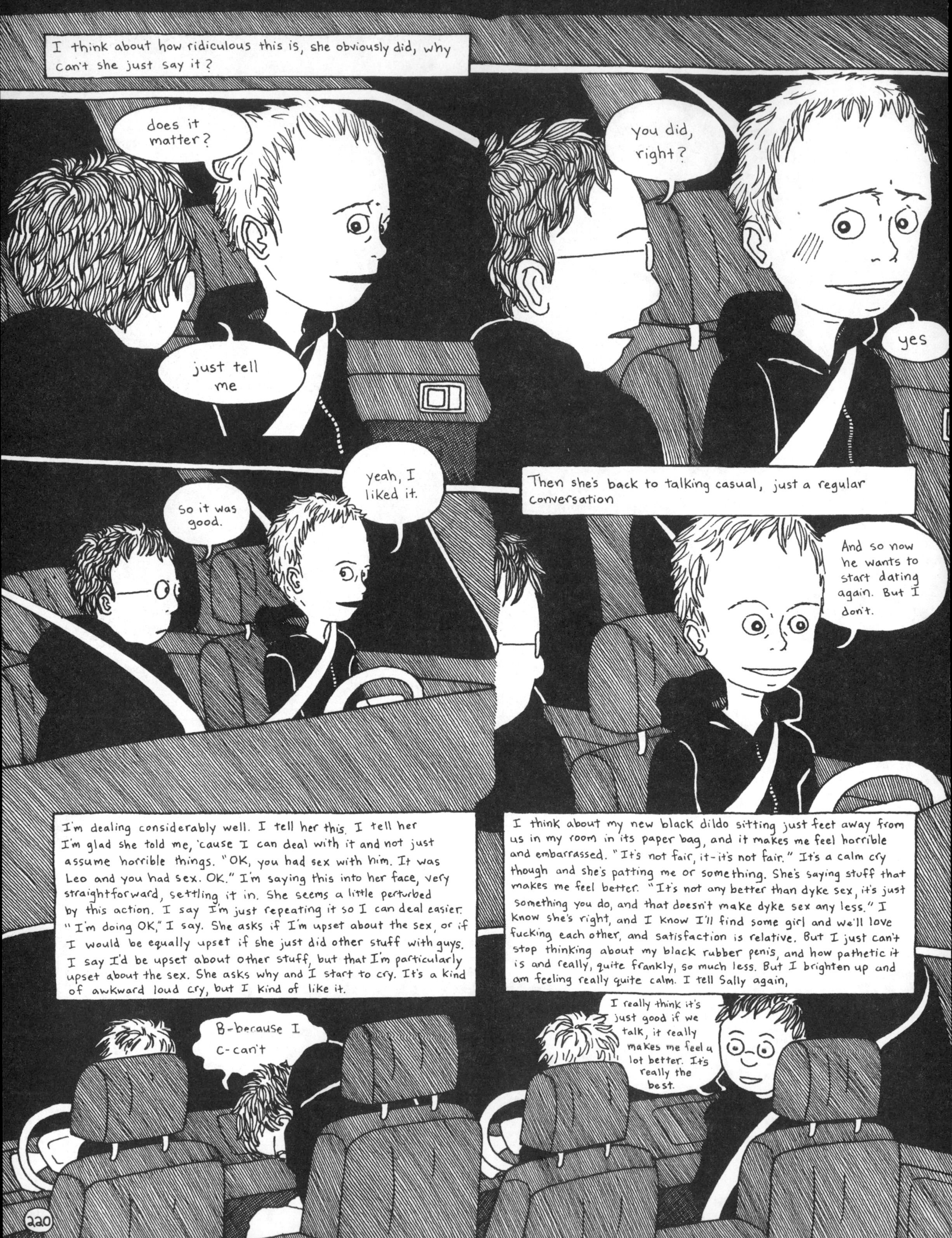

I think about how ridiculous this is, she obviously did, why can't she just say it?
does it matter?
just tell me
you did, right?
yes
So it was good.
yeah, I liked it.
Then she's back to talking casual, just a regular conversation
And so now he wants to start dating again. But I don't.
I'm dealing considerably well. I tell her this. I tell her I'm glad she told me, 'cause I can deal with it and not just assume horrible things. "OK, you had sex with him. It was Leo and you had sex. OK." I'm saying this into her face, very straightforward, settling it in. She seems a little perturbed by this action. I say I'm just repeating it so I can deal easier. "I'm doing OK," I say. She asks if I'm upset about the sex, or if I would be equally upset if she just did other stuff with guys. I say I'd be upset about other stuff, but that I'm particularly upset about the sex. She asks why and I start to cry. It's a kind of awkward loud cry, but I kind of like it.
I think about my new black dildo sitting just feet away from us in my room in its paper bag, and it makes me feel horrible and embarrassed. "It's not fair, it-it's not fair." It's a calm cry though and she's patting me or something. She's saying stuff that makes me feel better. "It's not any better than dyke sex, it's just something you do, and that doesn't make dyke sex any less." I know she's right, and I know I'll find some girl and we'll love fucking each other, and satisfaction is relative. But I just can't stop thinking about my black rubber penis, and how pathetic it is and really, quite frankly, so much less. But I brighten up and am feeling really quite calm. I tell Sally again,
B-because I c-can't
I really think it's just good if we talk, it really makes me feel a lot better. It's really the best.

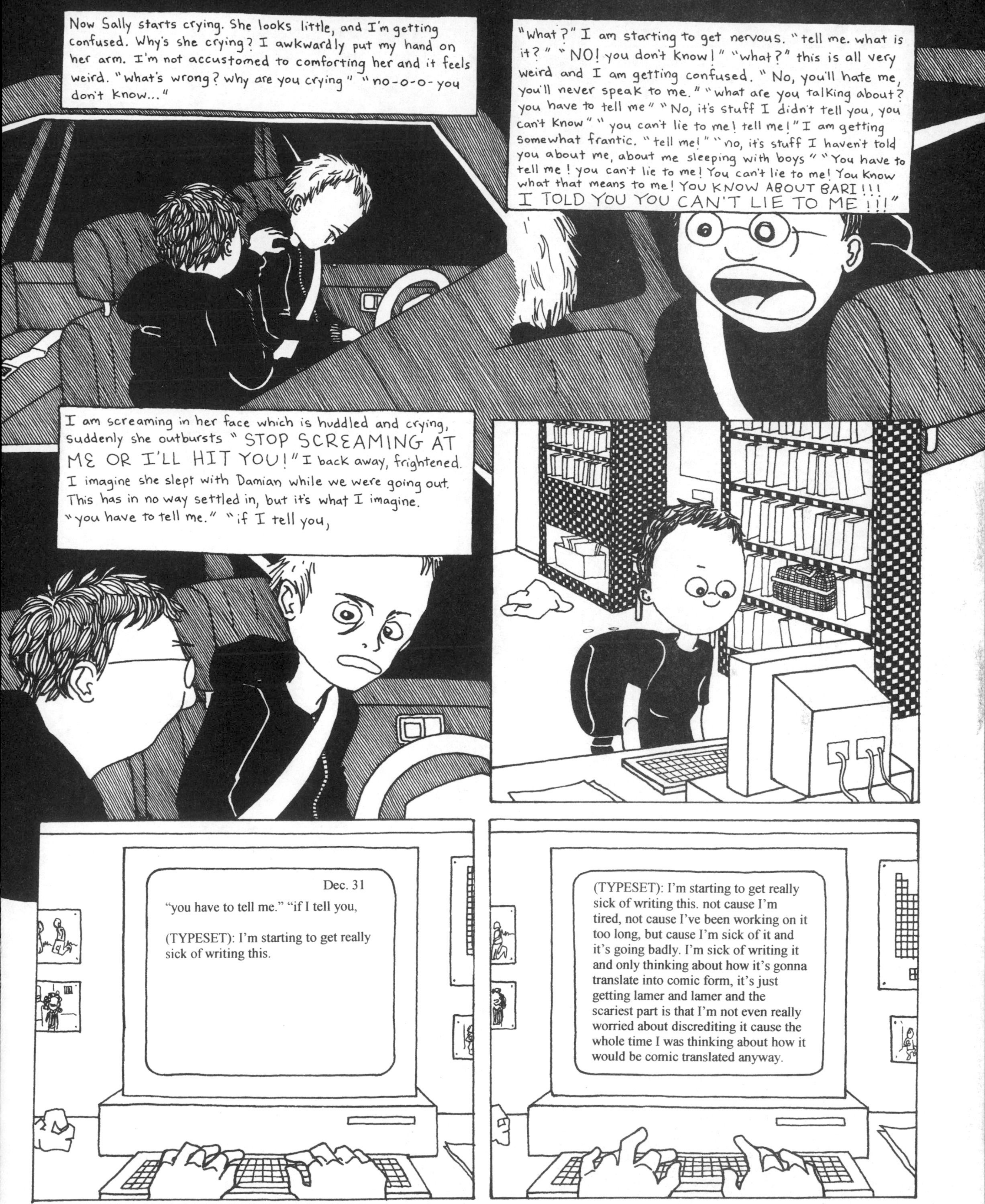

Now Sally starts crying. She looks little, and I'm getting confused. Why's she crying? I awkwardly put my hand on her arm. I'm not accustomed to comforting her and it feels weird. "what's wrong? why are you crying" "no-o-o-you don't know..."
"what?" I am starting to get nervous. "tell me. what is it?" "NO! you don't know!" "what?" this is all very weird and I am getting confused. "No, you'll hate me, you'll never speak to me." "what are you talking about? you have to tell me" "No, it's stuff I didn't tell you, you can't know" "you can't lie to me! tell me!" I am getting somewhat frantic. "tell me!" "no, it's stuff I haven't told you about me, about me sleeping with boys" "You have to tell me! you can't lie to me! You can't lie to me! You know what that means to me! YOU KNOW ABOUT BARI!!! I TOLD YOU YOU CAN'T LIE TO ME!!!"
I am screaming in her face which is huddled and crying, suddenly she outbursts "STOP SCREAMING AT ME OR I'LL HIT YOU!" I back away, frightened. I imagine she slept with Damian while we were going out. This has in no way settled in, but it's what I imagine. "you have to tell me." "if I tell you,
Dec. 31
"you have to tell me." "if I tell you,
(TYPESET): I'm starting to get really sick of writing this.
(TYPESET): I'm starting to get really sick of writing this. not cause I'm tired, not cause I've been working on it too long, but cause I'm sick of it and it's going badly. I'm sick of writing it and only thinking about how it's gonna translate into comic form, it's just getting lamer and lamer and the scariest part is that I'm not even really worried about discrediting it cause the whole time I was thinking about how it would be comic translated anyway.

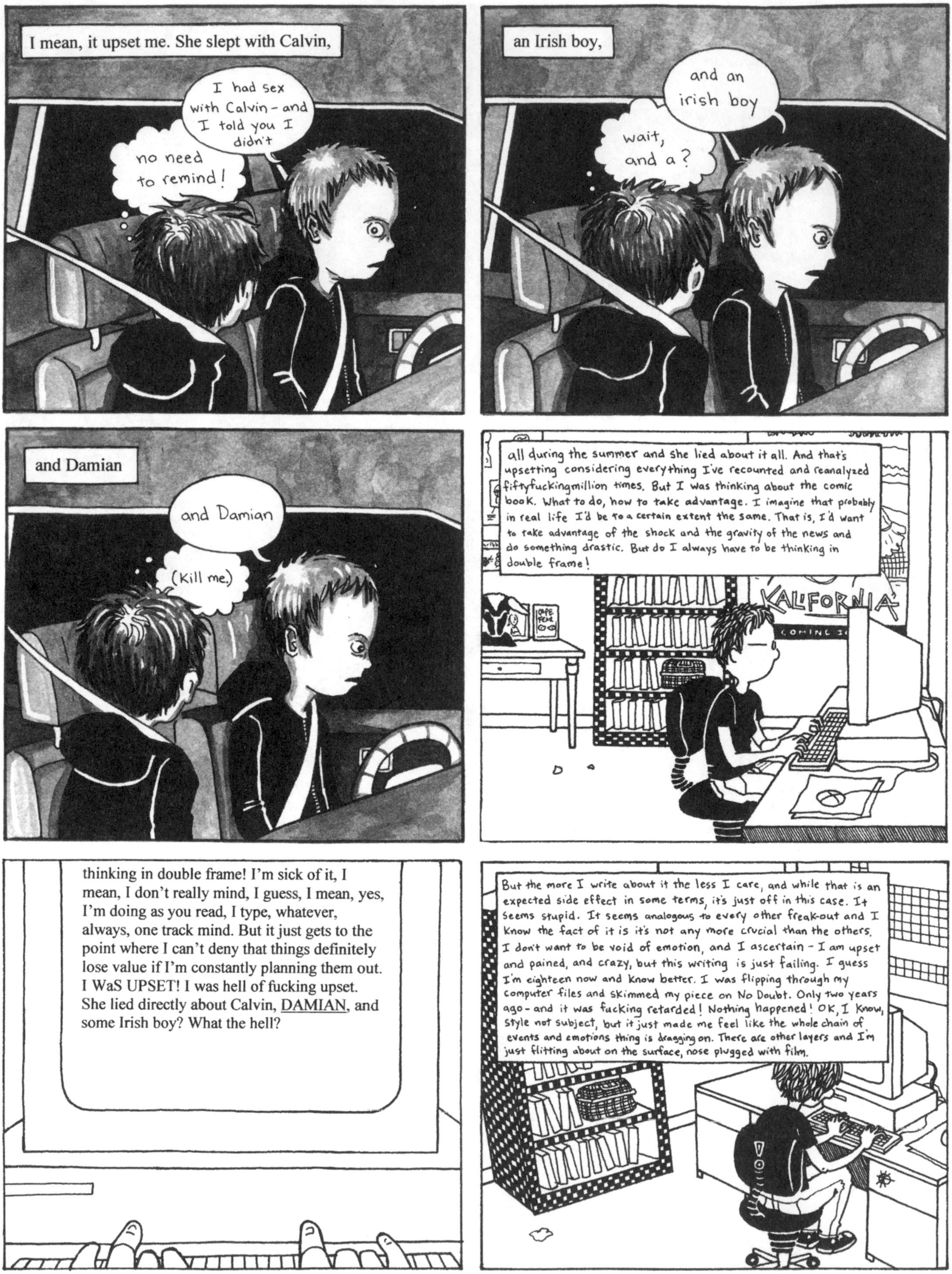
I mean, it upset me. She slept with Calvin,
I had sex with Calvin - and I told you I didn't
no need to remind!
an Irish boy,
and an irish boy
wait, and a ?
and Damian
and Damian
(Kill me.)
all during the summer and she lied about it all. And that's upsetting considering everything I've recounted and reanalyzed fiftyfuckingmillion times. But I was thinking about the comic book. What to do, how to take advantage. I imagine that probably in real life I'd be to a certain extent the same. That is, I'd want to take advantage of the shock and the gravity of the news and do something drastic. But do I always have to be thinking in double frame!
KALIFORNIA
thinking in double frame! I'm sick of it, I mean, I don't really mind, I guess, I mean, yes, I'm doing as you read, I type, whatever, always, one track mind. But it just gets to the point where I can't deny that things definitely lose value if I'm constantly planning them out. I WaS UPSET! I was hell of fucking upset. She lied directly about Calvin, DAMIAN, and some Irish boy? What the hell?
But the more I write about it the less I care, and while that is an expected side effect in some terms, it's just off in this case. It seems stupid. It seems analogous to every other freak-out and I know the fact of it is it's not any more crucial than the others. I don't want to be void of emotion, and I ascertain - I am upset and pained, and crazy, but this writing is just failing. I guess I'm eighteen now and know better. I was flipping through my computer files and skimmed my piece on No Doubt. Only two years ago - and it was fucking retarded! Nothing happened! OK, I know, style not subject, but it just made me feel like the whole chain of events and emotions thing is dragging on. There are other layers and I'm just flitting about on the surface, nose plugged with film.

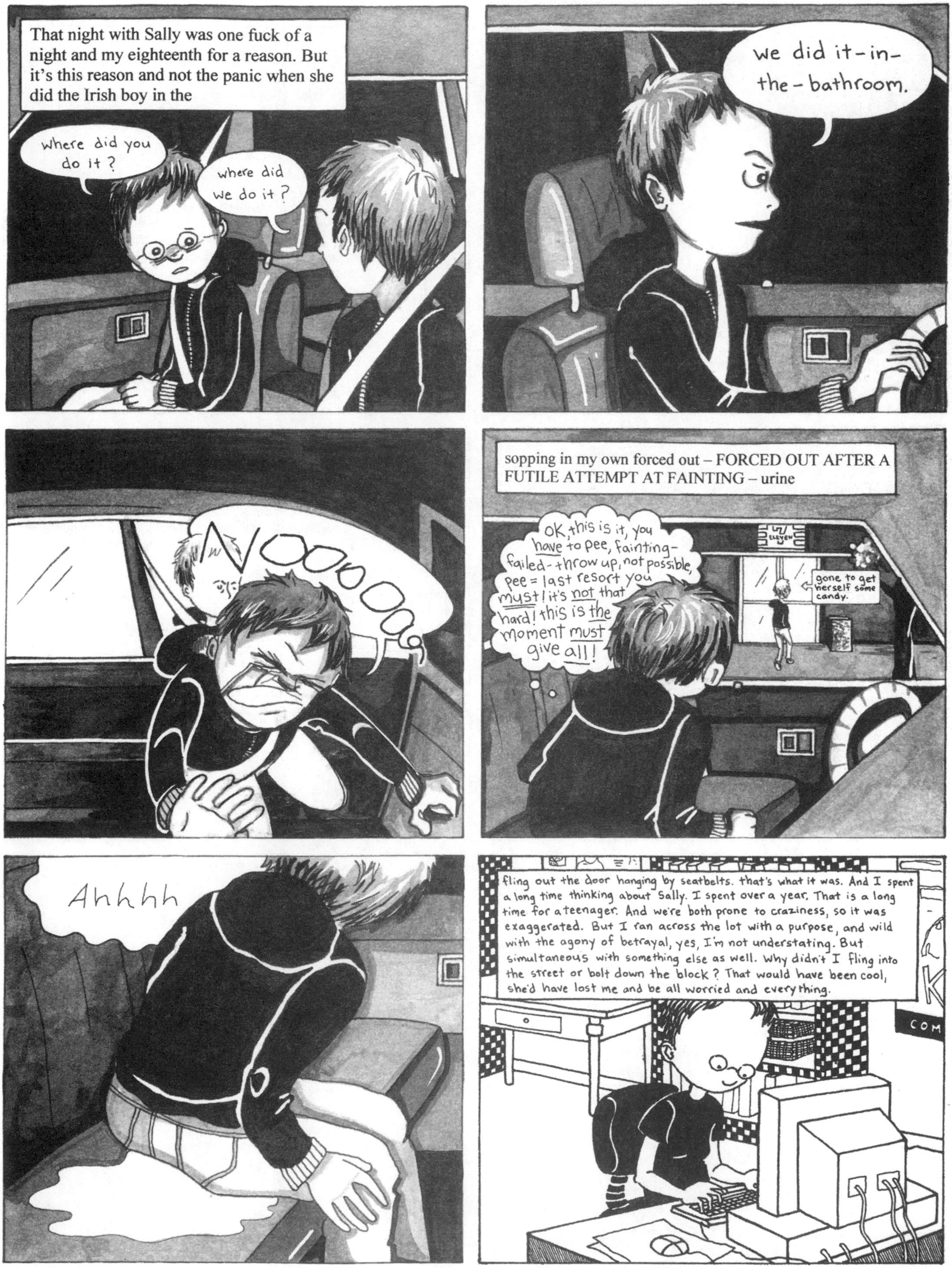

That night with Sally was one fuck of a night and my eighteenth for a reason. But it's this reason and not the panic when she did the Irish boy in the
where did you do it?
where did we do it?
we did it-in-the-bathroom.
NOOOOOOO
sopping in my own forced out – FORCED OUT AFTER A FUTILE ATTEMPT AT FAINTING – urine
OK, this is it, you have to pee, fainting-failed-throw up, not possible, pee = last resort you must! it's not that hard! this is the moment must give all!
ELEVEN
gone to get herself some candy.
Ahhhh
fling out the door hanging by seatbelts. that's what it was. And I spent a long time thinking about Sally. I spent over a year. That is a long time for a teenager. And we're both prone to craziness, so it was exaggerated. But I ran across the lot with a purpose, and wild with the agony of betrayal, yes, I'm not understating. But simultaneous with something else as well. Why didn't I fling into the street or bolt down the block? That would have been cool, she'd have lost me and be all worried and everything.
COM

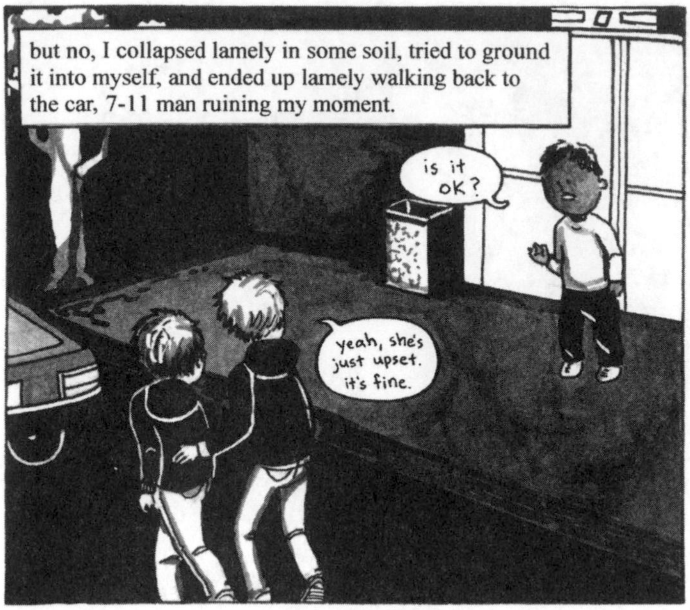
but no, I collapsed lamely in some soil, tried to ground it into myself, and ended up lamely walking back to the car, 7-11 man ruining my moment.
is it OK?
yeah, she's just upset. it's fine.

so what's the rest of the story? I don't feel like dragging it on with all the details of should we talk and I think she's Ronica and oh, she's just like Elisabeth. comic planning comic planning. Now I don't like the idea I spent all that time organizing. The Sally saga, fragments of a school day and Ms. Salt's office and tears. cryingshmying Julia drifting. Then, because that can't hold attention cut to a flashback (inspirited by today's movie) everyone loves flashbacks. Me and Bari, me and Ronica. Cut to Sally's face, make it look like Ronica's. (It really does somewhat!) I think what it is is that I just can't take that seriously when I'm thinking about its form. The book is reality, and that's not reality. I love Sally, I am, oh my no longer in love with her. Not cause she slept with them. We talked about this: I understand completely. I certainly don't blame her for the Irish boy, and the Calvin and Damian stuff was mean, but it's her fucking life and as she put it many times – "who do you think you are!" It's true I set her up like fuck, but here I am analyzing and getting annoyed.

---

pg. 16

and getting annoyed. I'll make it brief: I love Sally because of who she is and how she acts toward me. But she lied and acted like all was fine, and lied some more and said things are settled, and now we're friends, a million times with those lies. More than sad, bad. She's going back to college and going back to fucking that boy and I just don't feel it's really necessary for me to stick around. I – am – tired of writing about Sally. Used to it, but months ago if this incident had happened I would have eaten it up and relished it down, just like my first intention in this piece, but I am eighteen now. I've never felt differently about Sally, so after a year of agony why should I stick around to see if any other option is possible? Maybe I would if she was nice and pure but wasn't in love with me. That could work. But that's not who she is. As much as I understand why she fucked those boys, and why she lied to me about it, I just can't. Maybe I'm scared if I give in and understand I'll just go insane again. stop typing and realize my beautiful epiphany of the pointlessness of it all had transmuted into merely the 1129th Sally analysis.

---

pg. 17

No, I'm not gonna terminate, and I'm not gonna forgive. She was in love with Damian, and she did not know if she was in love with me. Did not know. I told her she had said she wasn't. And she said oh, then she must not have been. I shut the door and walked up to my house in clinging wet pants. See, the problem with it is it's funny, but it's not, and the amount that it's not funny I'm tired of. when something's funny you treasure the experience and just hope you don't play it down or overplay it. And when something's serious, you delve as deep as you can and work it to the fucking bone draining it as you know best. That was Potential. I was in love with Sally all through Potential and that was honest and worked. Tonight, I thought I hated her, but I don't, I don't wanna be friendly with her, and I don't wanna touch her, but I love her, probably the same way she loves me now.
She was there with this comic book interchange. The backdrop mind was present with Alexis, but slight, kind of comical and not very serious. I'm just scared because the conversations I have with myself are so close to the ones with Sally. Anyway, I'm just writing to finish the page in solidity. If anything, I've learned it's hard to come by. Damned to think about Sally for quite some time and time to come. But when you're sick of it you're sick, and I feel like stopping.

---

pg. 18

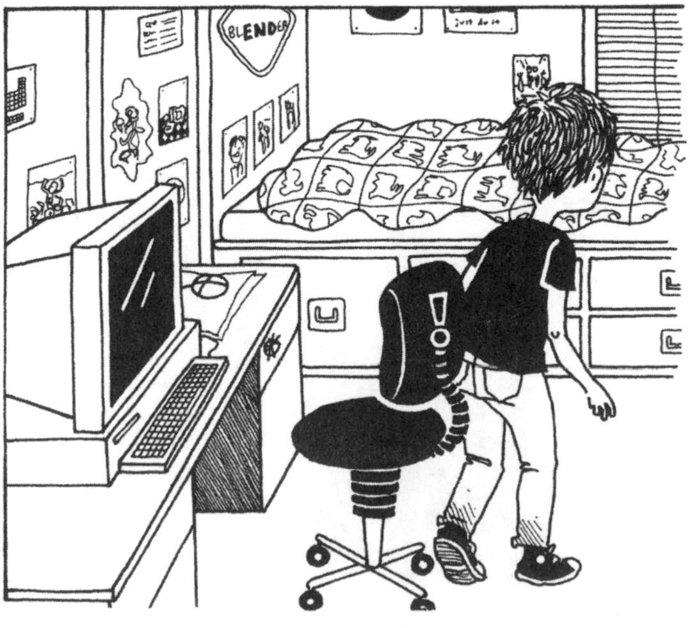
BLENDER

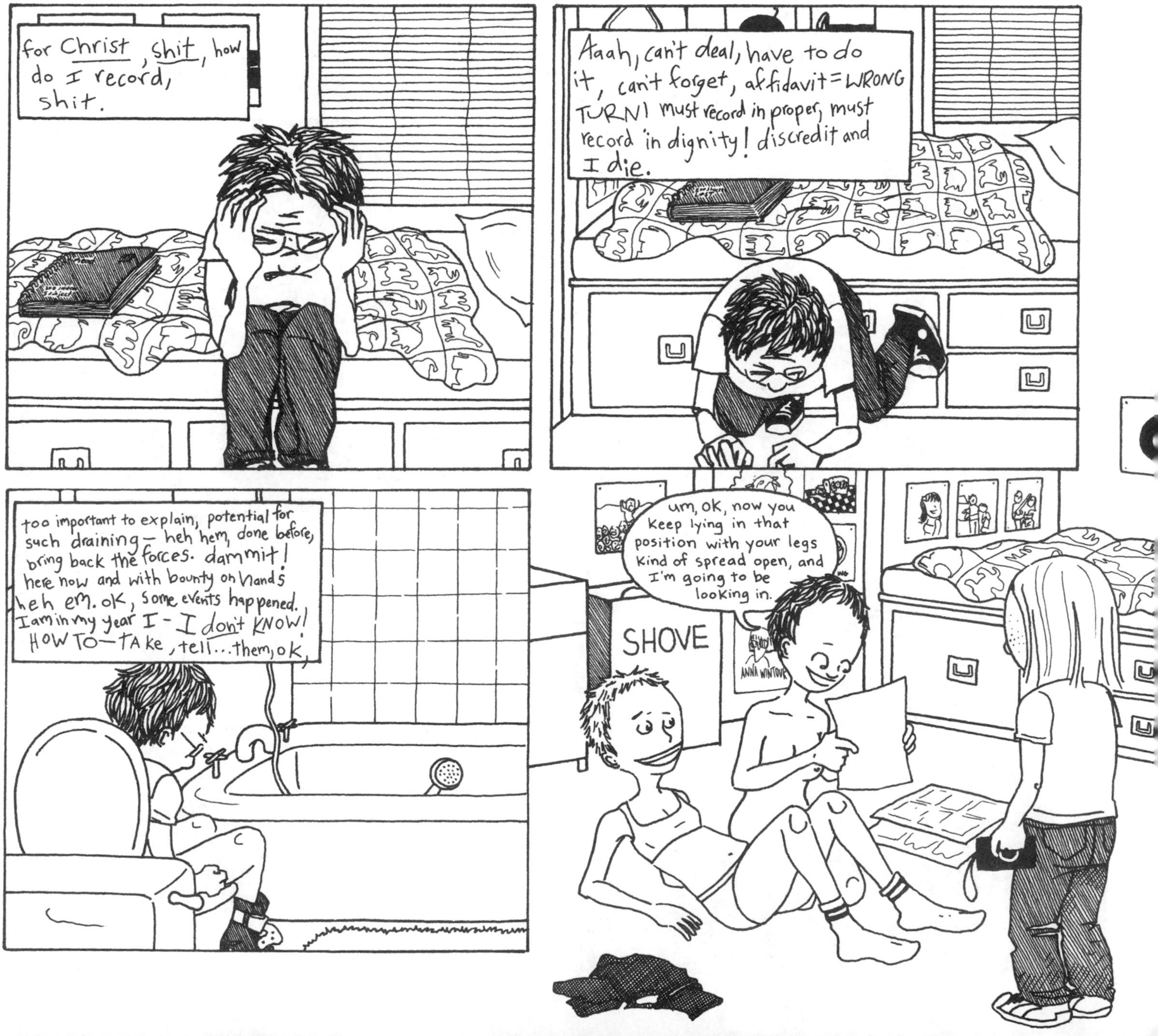
for Christ, shit, how do I record, shit.
Aaah, can't deal, have to do it, can't forget, affidavit = WRONG TURN! must record in proper, must record in dignity! discredit and I die.
too important to explain, potential for such draining— heh hem, done before, bring back the forces. dammit! here now and with bounty on hand's heh em. ok, some events happened. I am in my year I - I don't KNOW! HOW TO—TAKE, tell...them, ok,
um, ok, now you keep lying in that position with your legs kind of spread open, and I'm going to be looking in.
SHOVE
ANNA WINTOUR

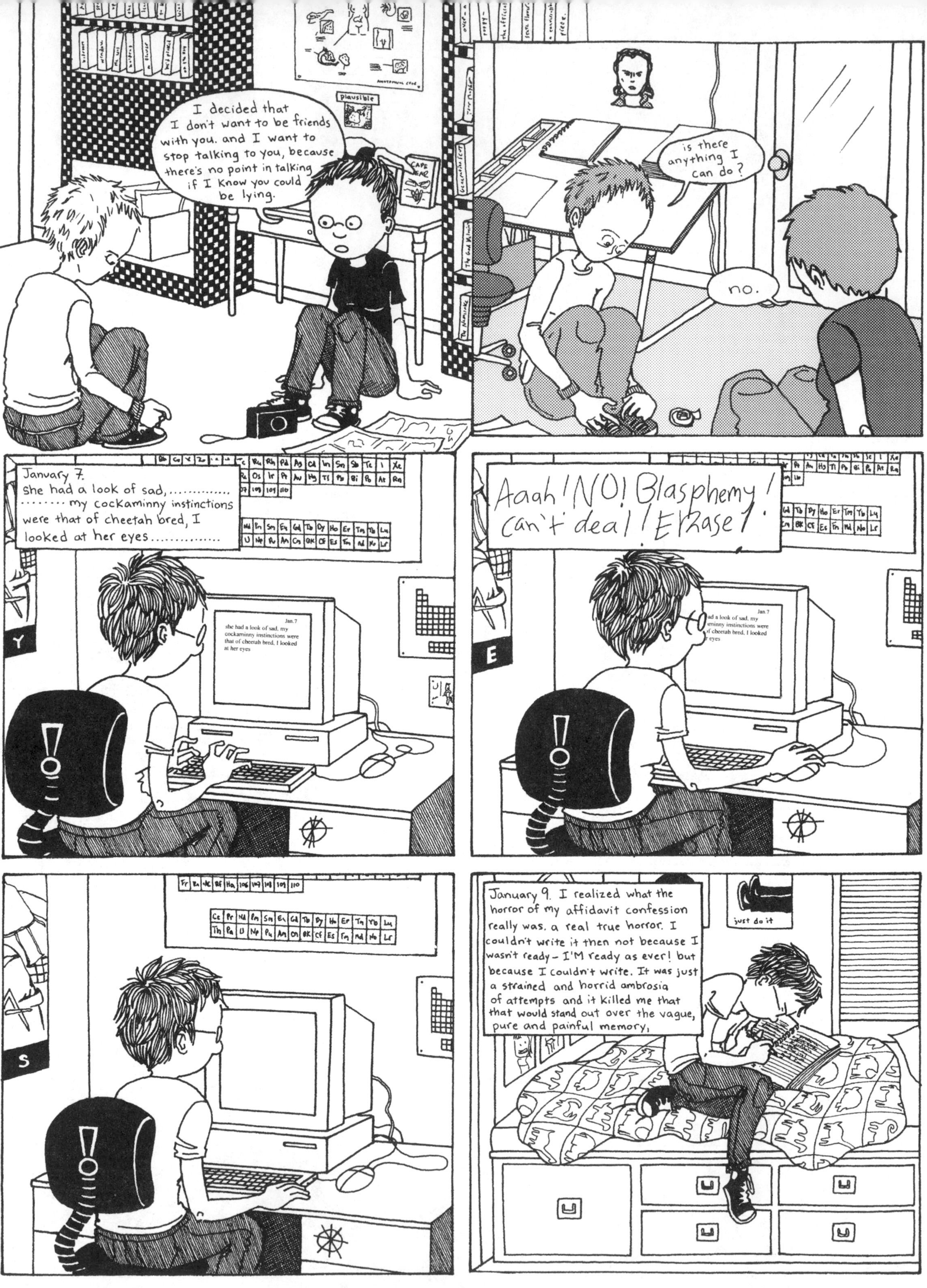
plausible
I decided that I don't want to be friends with you. and I want to stop talking to you, because there's no point in talking if I know you could be lying.
is there anything I can do?
no.
January 7. she had a look of sad, ... my cockaminny instinctions were that of cheetah bred, I looked at her eyes...............
Jan.7 she had a look of sad, my cockaminny instinctions were that of cheetah bred, I looked at her eyes
Y
Aaah! NO! Blasphemy! can't deal! Erase!
E
S
January 9. I realized what the horror of my affidavit confession really was, a real true horror. I couldn't write it then not because I wasn't ready – I'M ready as ever! but because I couldn't write. It was just a strained and horrid ambrosia of attempts and it killed me that that would stand out over the vague, pure and painful memory,
just do it

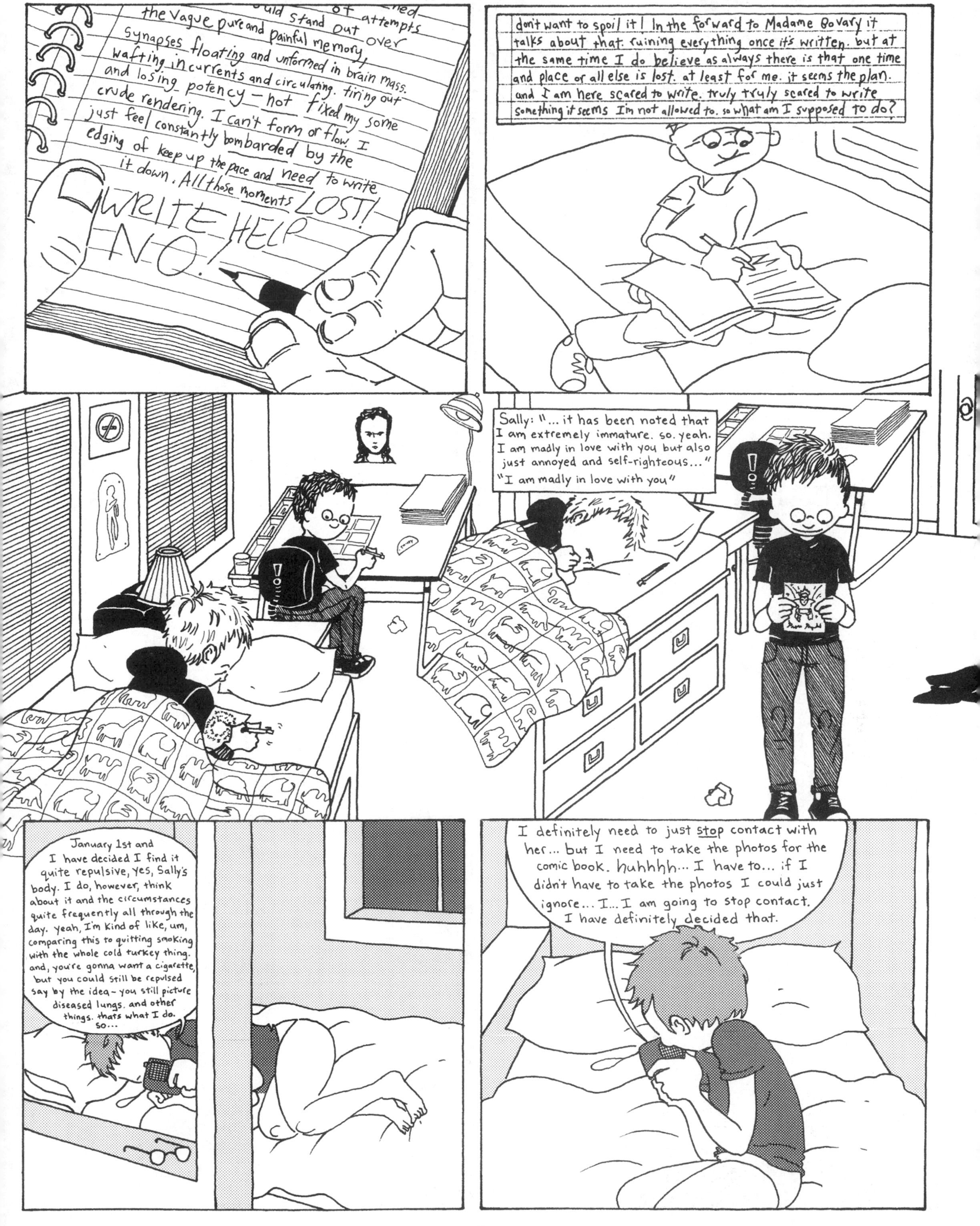

of attempts
uld Stand out over
the vague pure and painful memory,
synapses floating and unformed in brain mass.
wafting in currents and circulating. tiring out
and losing potency — not fixed my some
crude rendering. I can't form or flow. I
just feel constantly bombarded by the
edging of keep up the pace and need to write
it down. All those moments LOST!
WRITE HELP
NO!
don't want to spoil it! In the forward to Madame Bovary it talks about that: ruining everything once it's written. but at the same time I do believe as always there is that one time and place or all else is lost. at least for me. it seems the plan. and I am here scared to write. truly truly scared to write something it seems I'm not allowed to. so what am I supposed to do?
Sally: "... it has been noted that I am extremely immature. so. yeah. I am madly in love with you but also just annoyed and self-righteous..."
"I am madly in love with you"
January 1st and I have decided I find it quite repulsive, yes, Sally's body. I do, however, think about it and the circumstances quite frequently all through the day. yeah, I'm kind of like, um, comparing this to quitting smoking with the whole cold turkey thing. and, you're gonna want a cigarette, but you could still be repulsed say by the idea - you still picture diseased lungs. and other things. thats what I do. so...
I definitely need to just stop contact with her... but I need to take the photos for the comic book. huhhhh... I have to... if I didn't have to take the photos I could just ignore... I... I am going to stop contact. I have definitely decided that.

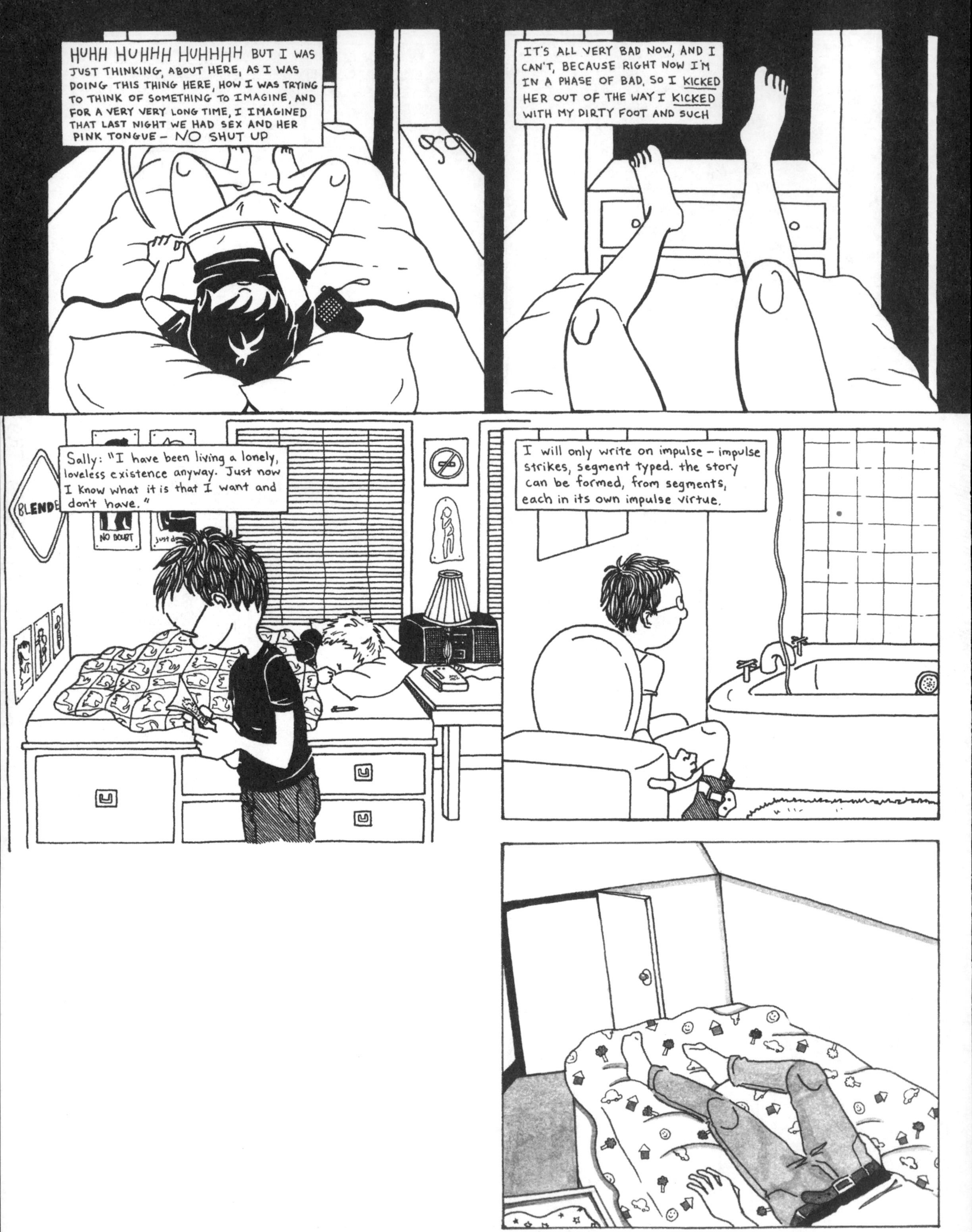
HUHH HUHHH HUHHHH BUT I WAS JUST THINKING, ABOUT HERE, AS I WAS DOING THIS THING HERE, HOW I WAS TRYING TO THINK OF SOMETHING TO IMAGINE, AND FOR A VERY VERY LONG TIME, I IMAGINED THAT LAST NIGHT WE HAD SEX AND HER PINK TONGUE – NO SHUT UP
IT'S ALL VERY BAD NOW, AND I CAN'T, BECAUSE RIGHT NOW I'M IN A PHASE OF BAD. SO I KICKED HER OUT OF THE WAY I KICKED WITH MY DIRTY FOOT AND SUCH
Sally: "I have been living a lonely, loveless existence anyway. Just now I know what it is that I want and don't have."
BLENDE
NO DOUBT
I will only write on impulse – impulse strikes, segment typed. the story can be formed, from segments, each in its own impulse virtue.

you know how when you look at one thing, and it turns into something bad and that leads to another thing, and everything seems evil and against you.

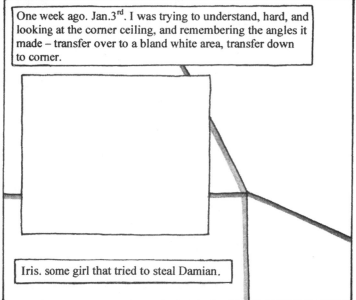

One week ago. Jan.3rd. I was trying to understand, hard, and looking at the corner ceiling, and remembering the angles it made – transfer over to a bland white area, transfer down to corner.

Iris. some girl that tried to steal Damian.

Last year I was front corner and wet and in horrible haircut, easing jealousy, rimming it. brown and smiling, lips spread.

Now, there I was, so clean and slack self proclaimed.

SO

are we in love?

yes

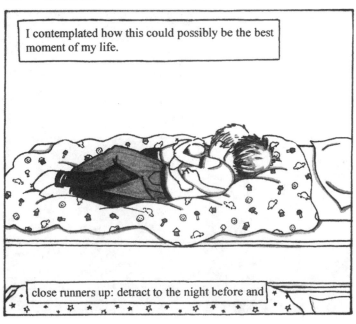

I contemplated how this could possibly be the best moment of my life.

close runners up: detract to the night before and

She had given me clothes to sleep in, a shirt. pants were noted unnecessary.
SOLD
James Dean
James Dean
I'm all my new enderweight and waiting. writhing body next to me, wiggling Sally in her new acquisition is around me. it's black and I think we're talking. Maybe everything that went wrong was that I didn't skip Kindergarten. The implication in general is that we were made for each other.
unclear, and thinking more about her hands which were placed on my fulcrums to her arms bending inward and around.
I think I did that flash thing I'd been repeating ever since we first got in her car after taking the photos and left for one last night at her house.
forward to the future
keep talking
cornered cringe
stop talking
open excised
keep talking
cornered cringe
stop talking
open excised
it's like that and the night ruptures

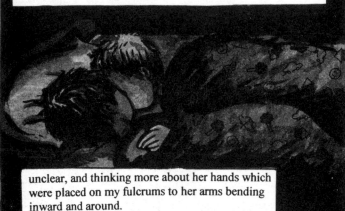

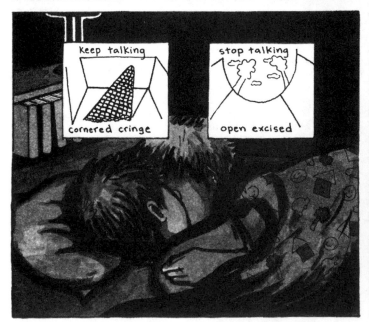

crying. in sounds loud from both of us and rocking and all her desperation pain seems the same as my relief. for all I know it is, locked and riding.

like standing in the womb under the shower and never wanting to leave.

it ends and she starts with sex. I think about how much I should appreciate it, so deprived, all those months! I'm feeling her breasts and thinking about how they've groooown and loving it! She's readily applying hands to mine and surged as ever I feel physical, and detached as I know it.

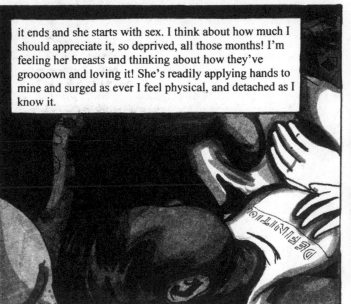

She reaches down and starts rubbing my clit as I press up and pull her on top of me.

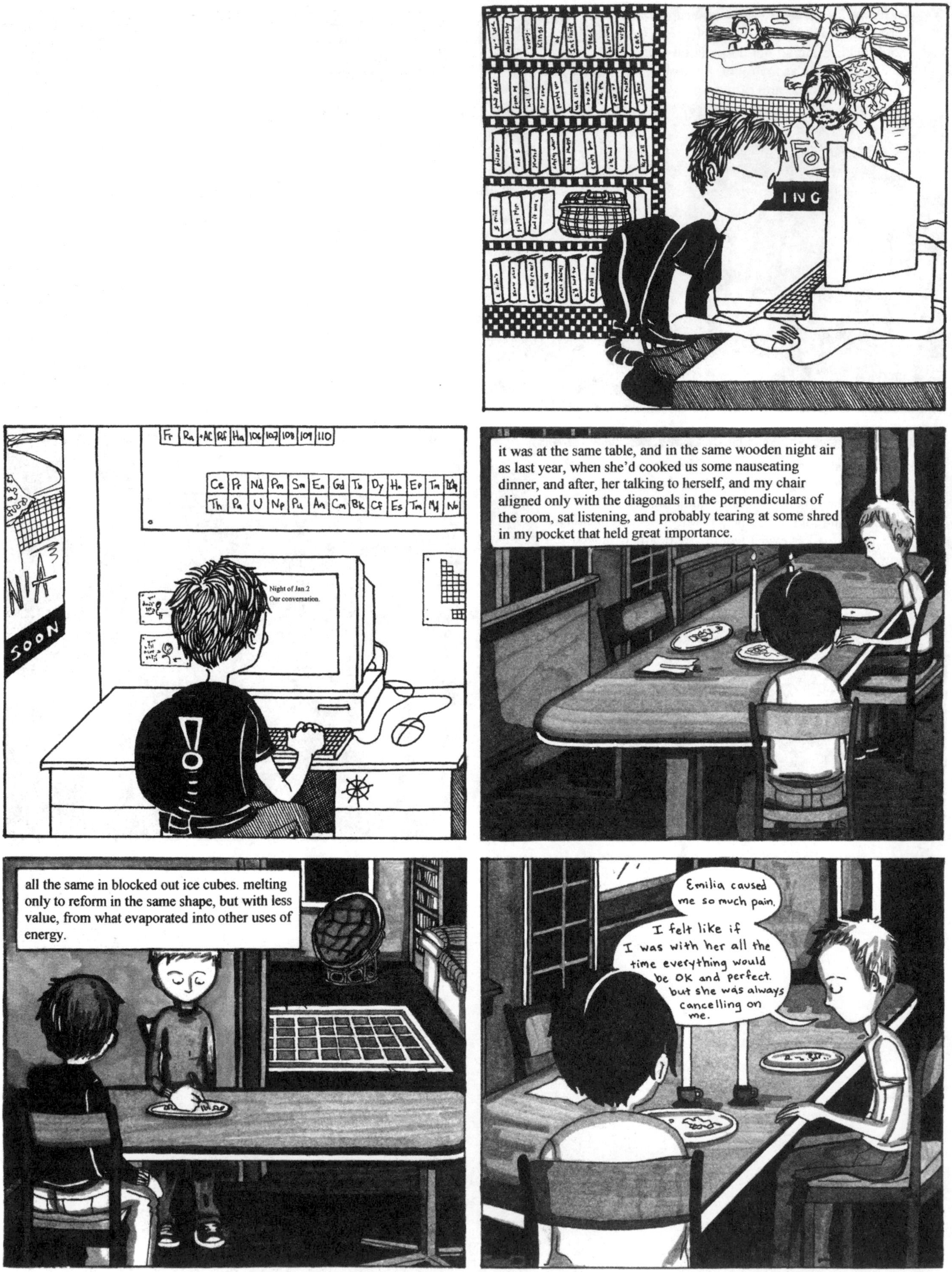
Night of Jan.2
Our conversation.
it was at the same table, and in the same wooden night air as last year, when she'd cooked us some nauseating dinner, and after, her talking to herself, and my chair aligned only with the diagonals in the perpendiculars of the room, sat listening, and probably tearing at some shred in my pocket that held great importance.
all the same in blocked out ice cubes. melting only to reform in the same shape, but with less value, from what evaporated into other uses of energy.
Emilia caused me so much pain.
I felt like if I was with her all the time everything would be OK and perfect. but she was always cancelling on me.

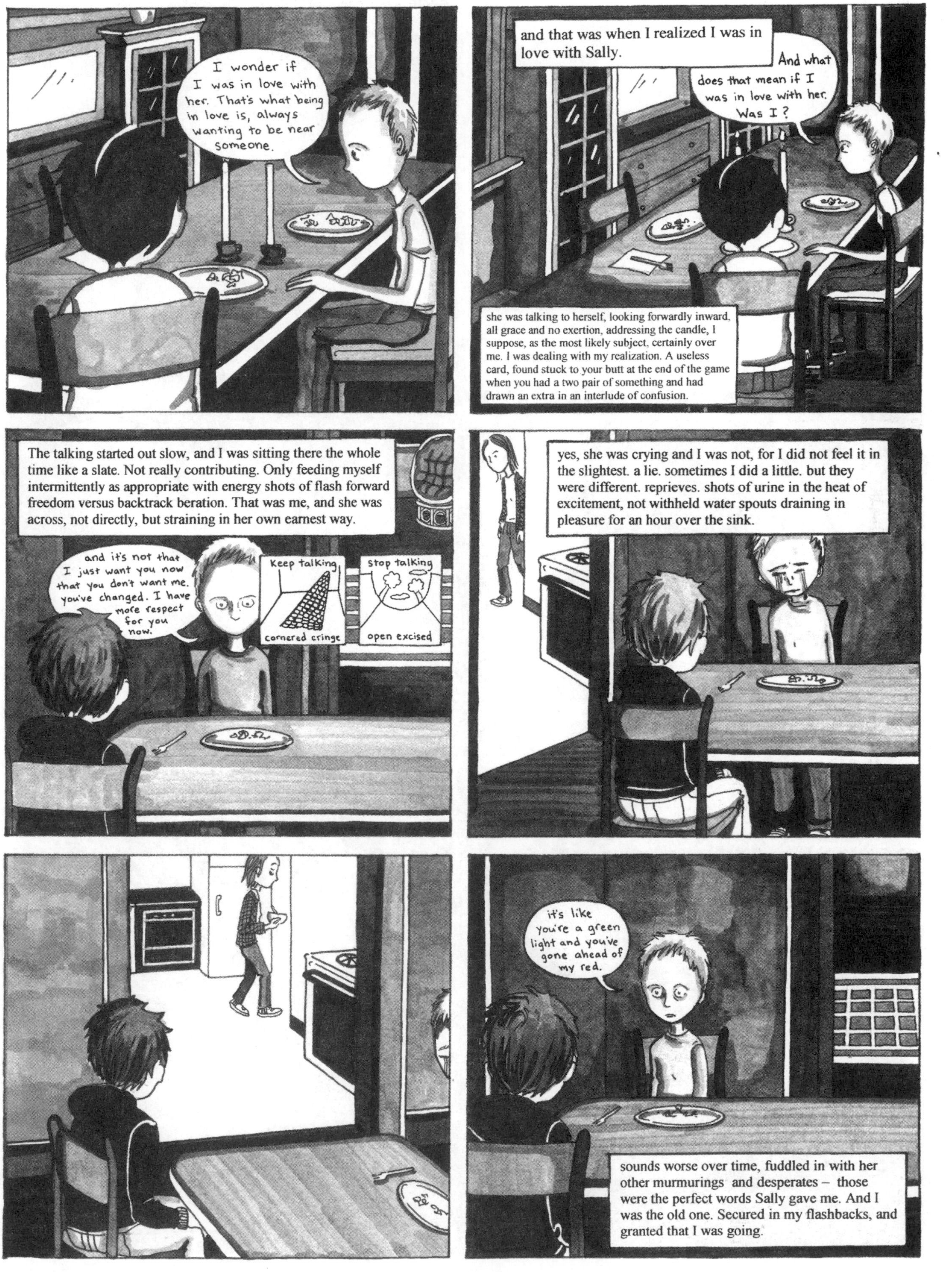
I wonder if I was in love with her. That's what being in love is, always wanting to be near someone.
and that was when I realized I was in love with Sally.
And what does that mean if I was in love with her. Was I?
she was talking to herself, looking forwardly inward, all grace and no exertion, addressing the candle, I suppose, as the most likely subject, certainly over me. I was dealing with my realization. A useless card, found stuck to your butt at the end of the game when you had a two pair of something and had drawn an extra in an interlude of confusion.
The talking started out slow, and I was sitting there the whole time like a slate. Not really contributing. Only feeding myself intermittently as appropriate with energy shots of flash forward freedom versus backtrack beration. That was me, and she was across, not directly, but straining in her own earnest way.
and it's not that I just want you now that you don't want me. you've changed. I have more respect for you now.
Keep talking
cornered cringe
Stop talking
open excised
yes, she was crying and I was not, for I did not feel it in the slightest. a lie. sometimes I did a little. but they were different. reprieves. shots of urine in the heat of excitement, not withheld water spouts draining in pleasure for an hour over the sink.
it's like you're a green light and you've gone ahead of my red.
sounds worse over time, fuddled in with her other murmurings and desperates – those were the perfect words Sally gave me. And I was the old one. Secured in my flashbacks, and granted that I was going.

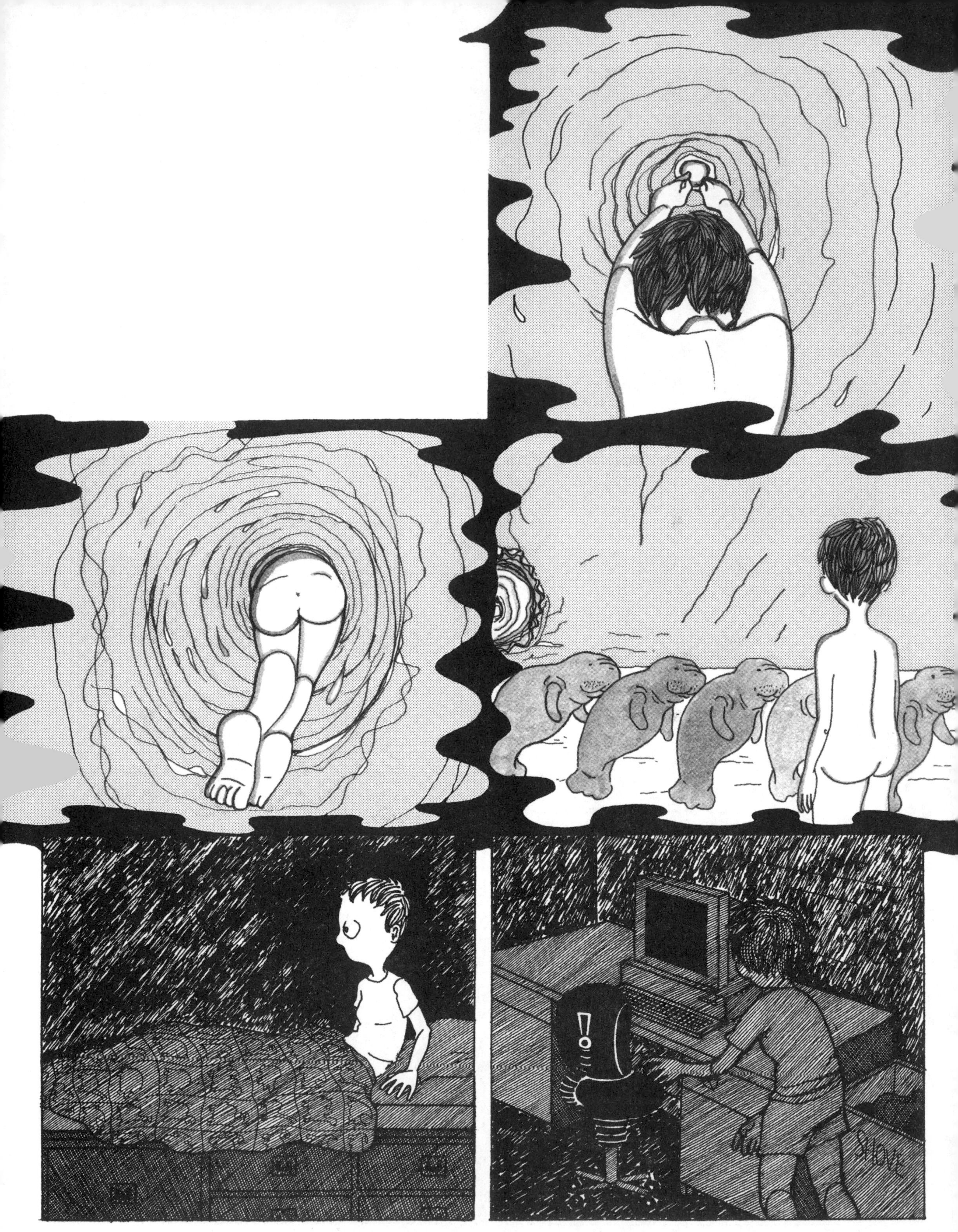

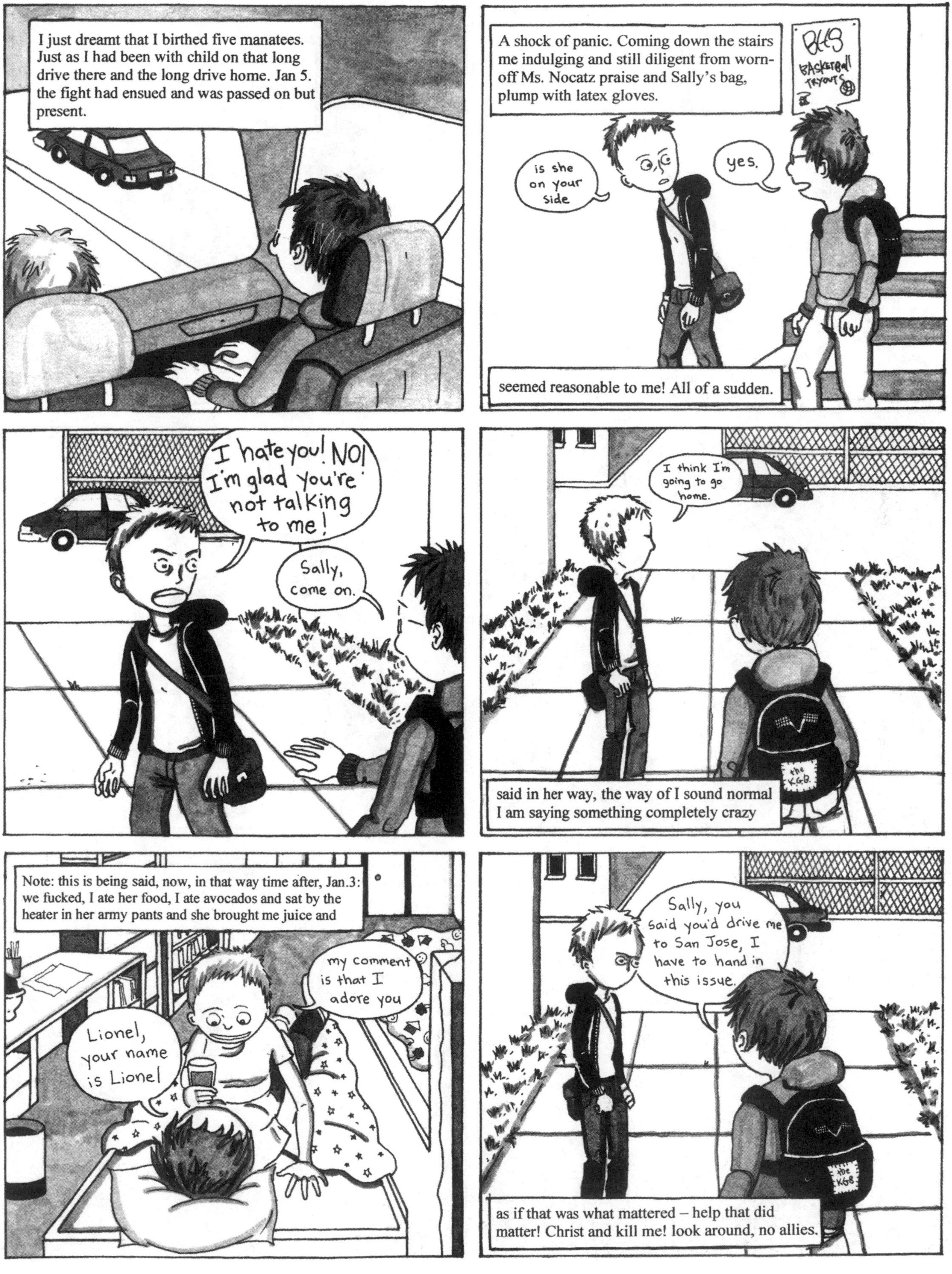
I just dreamt that I birthed five manatees. Just as I had been with child on that long drive there and the long drive home. Jan 5. the fight had ensued and was passed on but present.
A shock of panic. Coming down the stairs me indulging and still diligent from worn-off Ms. Nocatz praise and Sally's bag, plump with latex gloves.
BASKETBALL TRYOUTS
is she on your side
yes.
seemed reasonable to me! All of a sudden.
I hate you! NO! I'm glad you're not talking to me!
Sally, come on.
I think I'm going to go home.
said in her way, the way of I sound normal I am saying something completely crazy
the K.G.B.
Note: this is being said, now, in that way time after, Jan.3: we fucked, I ate her food, I ate avocados and sat by the heater in her army pants and she brought me juice and
my comment is that I adore you
Lionel, your name is Lionel
Sally, you said you'd drive me to San Jose, I have to hand in this issue.
the KGB
as if that was what mattered – help that did matter! Christ and kill me! look around, no allies.

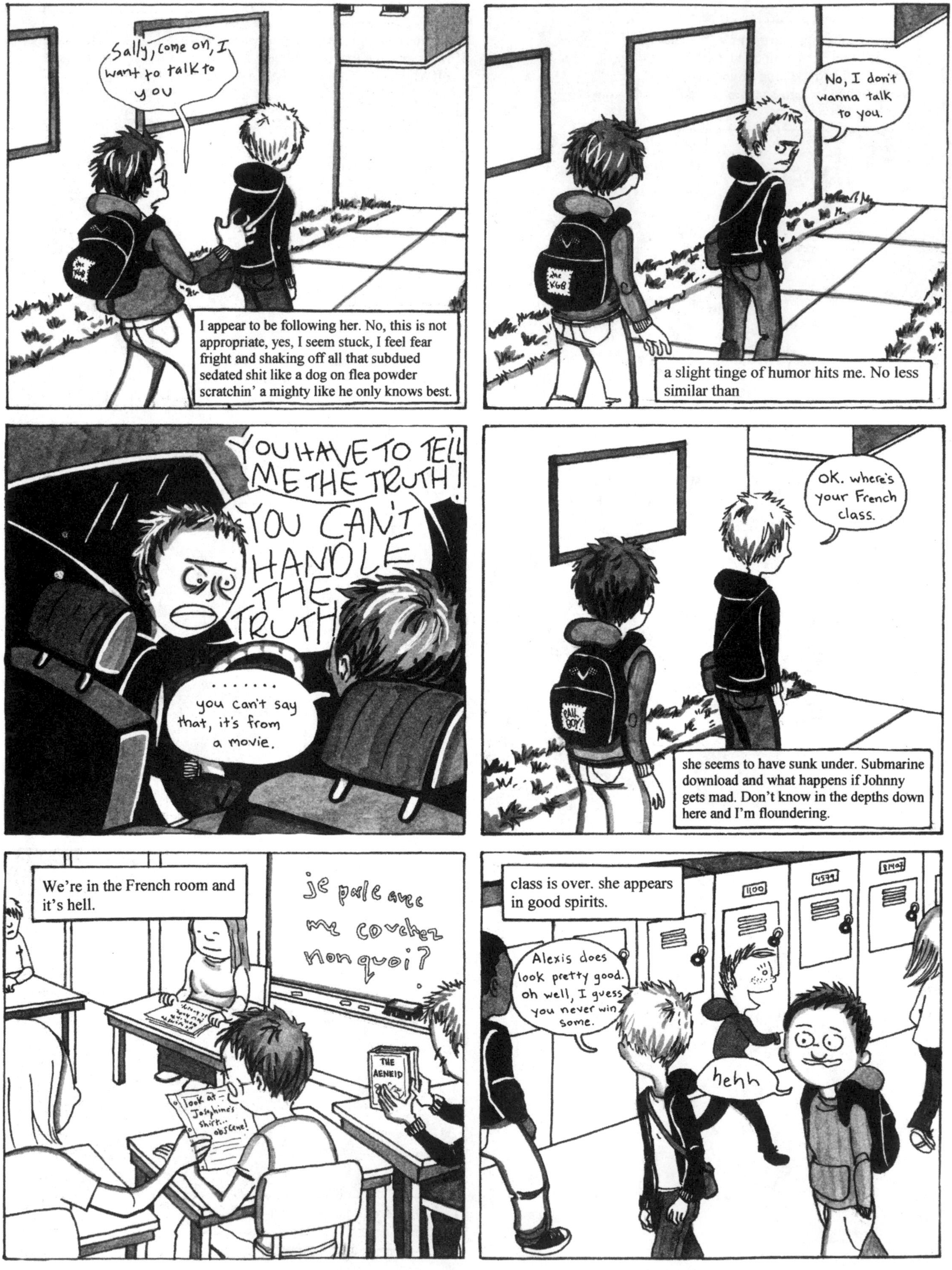
Sally, come on, I want to talk to you
I appear to be following her. No, this is not appropriate, yes, I seem stuck, I feel fear fright and shaking off all that subdued sedated shit like a dog on flea powder scratchin' a mighty like he only knows best.
No, I don't wanna talk to you.
a slight tinge of humor hits me. No less similar than
YOU HAVE TO TELL ME THE TRUTH!
YOU CAN'T HANDLE THE TRUTH
.... you can't say that, it's from a movie.
OK. where's your French class.
she seems to have sunk under. Submarine download and what happens if Johnny gets mad. Don't know in the depths down here and I'm floundering.
We're in the French room and it's hell.
je pale avec me couchez non quoi?
look at Josephine's shirt... obscene!
THE AENEID
class is over. she appears in good spirits.
Alexis does look pretty good. oh well, I guess you never win some.
hehh

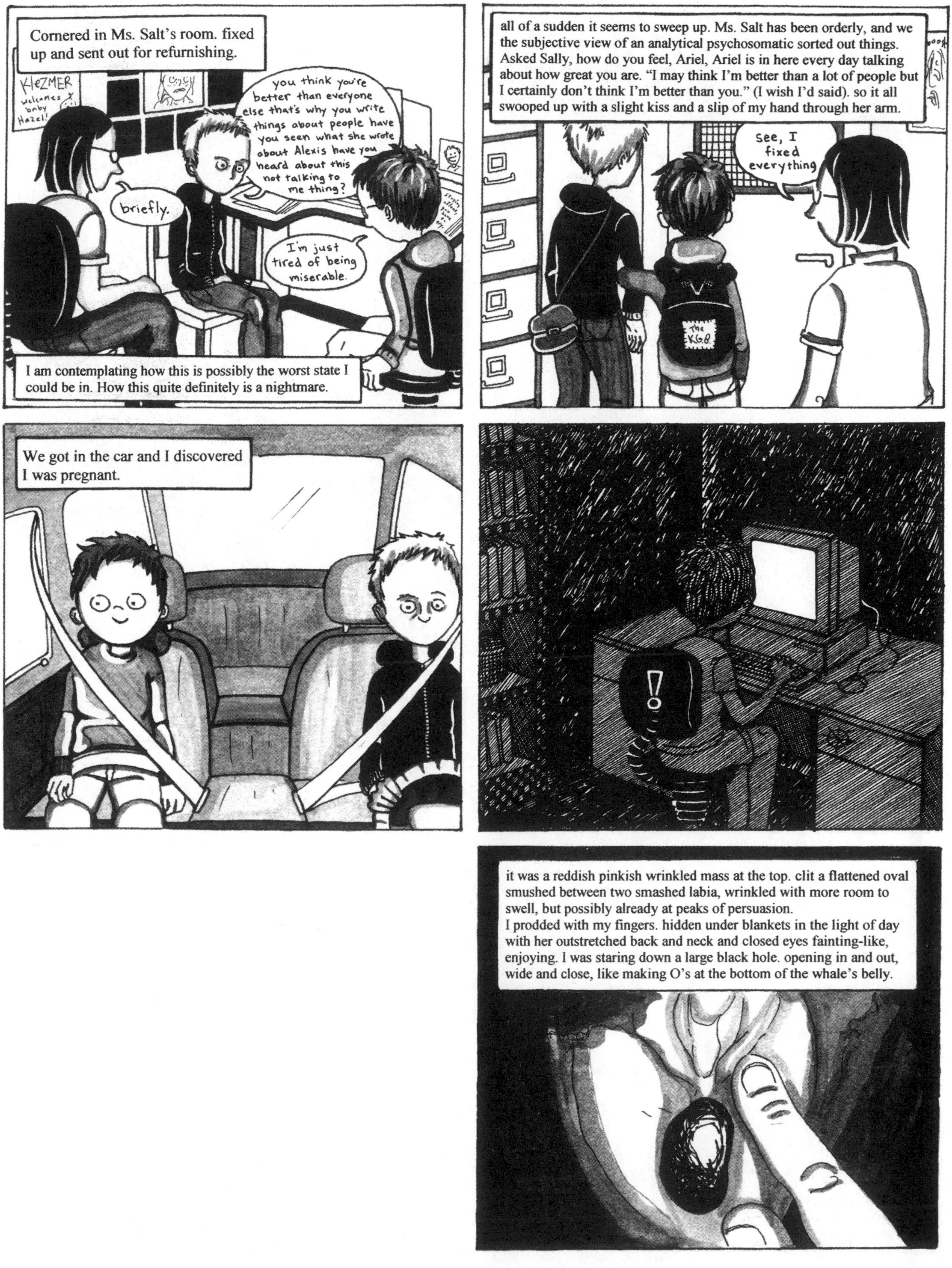

Cornered in Ms. Salt's room. fixed up and sent out for refurnishing.
KlezMER welcomes baby Hazel!
you think you're better than everyone else that's why you write things about people have you seen what she wrote about Alexis have you heard about this not talking to me thing?
briefly.
I'm just tired of being miserable.
I am contemplating how this is possibly the worst state I could be in. How this quite definitely is a nightmare.
all of a sudden it seems to sweep up. Ms. Salt has been orderly, and we the subjective view of an analytical psychosomatic sorted out things. Asked Sally, how do you feel, Ariel, Ariel is in here every day talking about how great you are. "I may think I'm better than a lot of people but I certainly don't think I'm better than you." (I wish I'd said). so it all swooped up with a slight kiss and a slip of my hand through her arm.
see, I fixed everything
The K.G.B.
We got in the car and I discovered I was pregnant.
it was a reddish pinkish wrinkled mass at the top. clit a flattened oval smushed between two smashed labia, wrinkled with more room to swell, but possibly already at peaks of persuasion.
I prodded with my fingers. hidden under blankets in the light of day with her outstretched back and neck and closed eyes fainting-like, enjoying. I was staring down a large black hole. opening in and out, wide and close, like making O's at the bottom of the whale's belly.

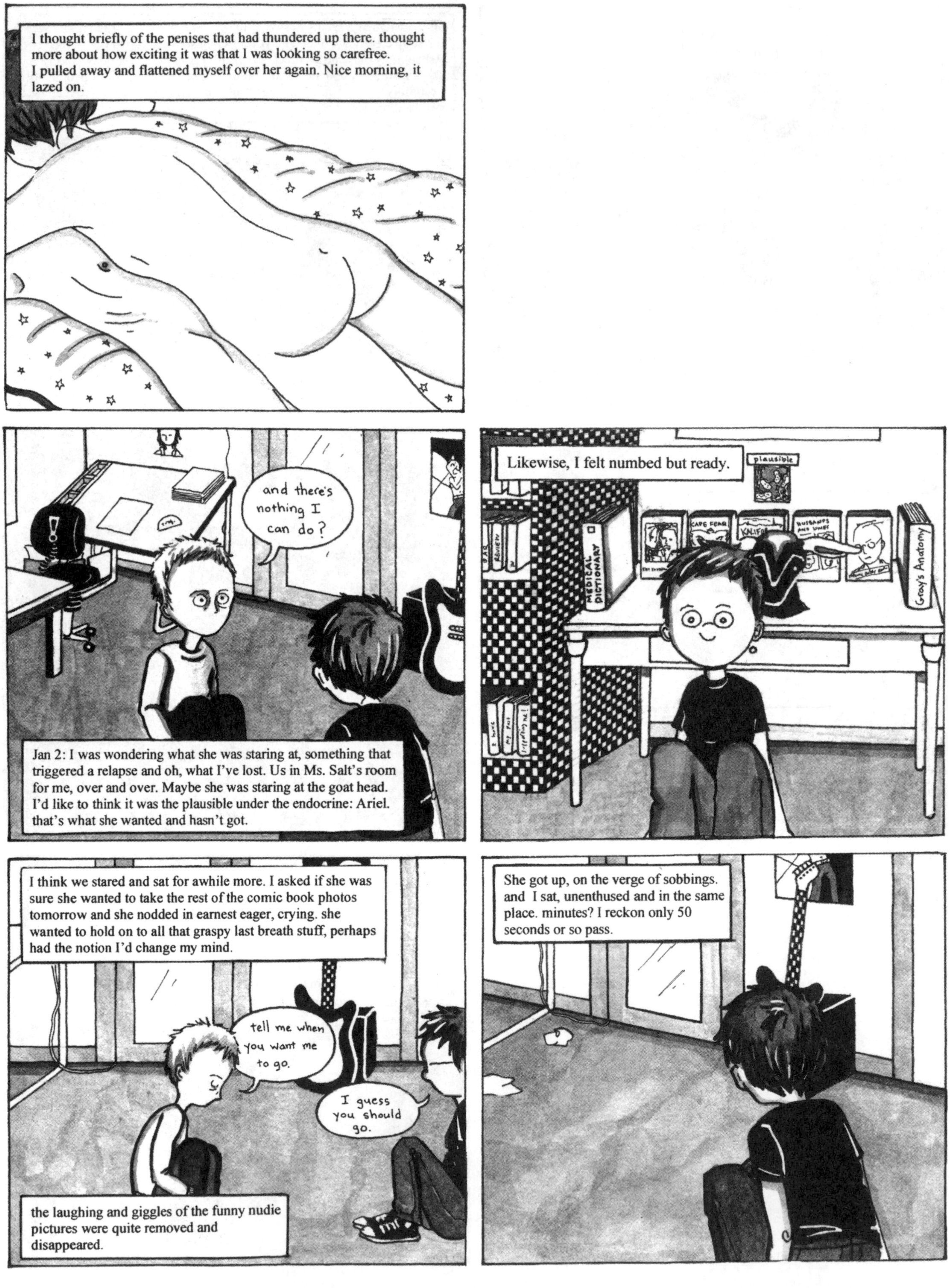
I thought briefly of the penises that had thundered up there. thought more about how exciting it was that I was looking so carefree.
I pulled away and flattened myself over her again. Nice morning, it lazed on.
and there's nothing I can do?
Jan 2: I was wondering what she was staring at, something that triggered a relapse and oh, what I've lost. Us in Ms. Salt's room for me, over and over. Maybe she was staring at the goat head. I'd like to think it was the plausible under the endocrine: Ariel. that's what she wanted and hasn't got.
Likewise, I felt numbed but ready.
plausible
MEDICAL DICTIONARY
I think we stared and sat for awhile more. I asked if she was sure she wanted to take the rest of the comic book photos tomorrow and she nodded in earnest eager, crying. she wanted to hold on to all that graspy last breath stuff, perhaps had the notion I'd change my mind.
tell me when you want me to go.
I guess you should go.
the laughing and giggles of the funny nudie pictures were quite removed and disappeared.
She got up, on the verge of sobbings. and I sat, unenthused and in the same place. minutes? I reckon only 50 seconds or so pass.

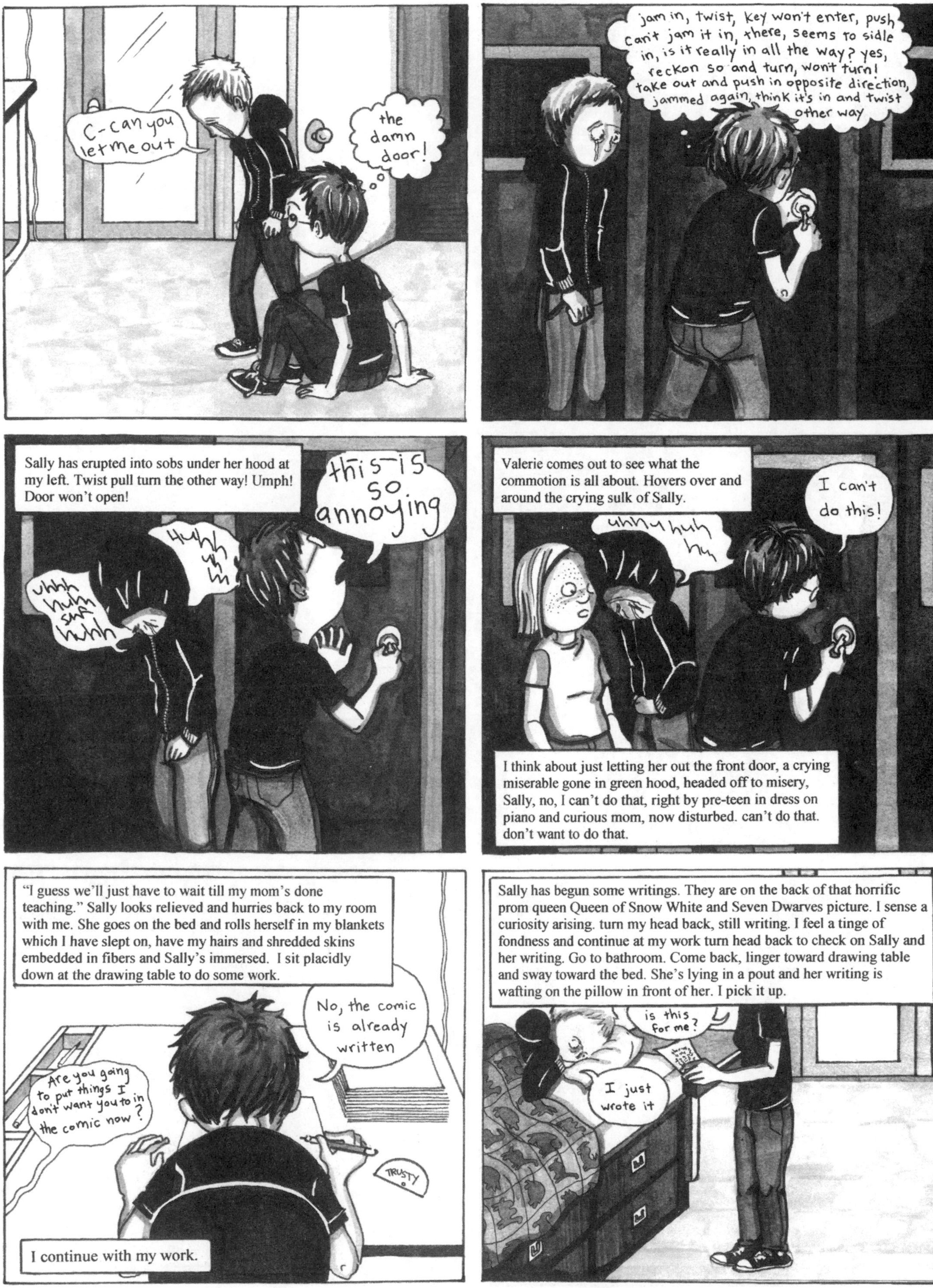
C-can you let me out
the damn door!
jam in, twist, key won't enter, push can't jam it in, there, seems to sidle in, is it really in all the way? yes, reckon so and turn, won't turn! take out and push in opposite direction, jammed again, think it's in and twist other way
Sally has erupted into sobs under her hood at my left. Twist pull turn the other way! Umph! Door won't open!
this is so annoying
uhh uh uh
uhh huh snf uhh
Valerie comes out to see what the commotion is all about. Hovers over and around the crying sulk of Sally.
uhhu huh hu
I can't do this!
I think about just letting her out the front door, a crying miserable gone in green hood, headed off to misery, Sally, no, I can't do that, right by pre-teen in dress on piano and curious mom, now disturbed. can't do that. don't want to do that.
"I guess we'll just have to wait till my mom's done teaching." Sally looks relieved and hurries back to my room with me. She goes on the bed and rolls herself in my blankets which I have slept on, have my hairs and shredded skins embedded in fibers and Sally's immersed. I sit placidly down at the drawing table to do some work.
Are you going to put things I don't want you to in the comic now?
No, the comic is already written
TRUSTY
I continue with my work.
Sally has begun some writings. They are on the back of that horrific prom queen Queen of Snow White and Seven Dwarves picture. I sense a curiosity arising. turn my head back, still writing. I feel a tinge of fondness and continue at my work turn head back to check on Sally and her writing. Go to bathroom. Come back, linger toward drawing table and sway toward the bed. She's lying in a pout and her writing is wafting on the pillow in front of her. I pick it up.
is this for me?
I just wrote it

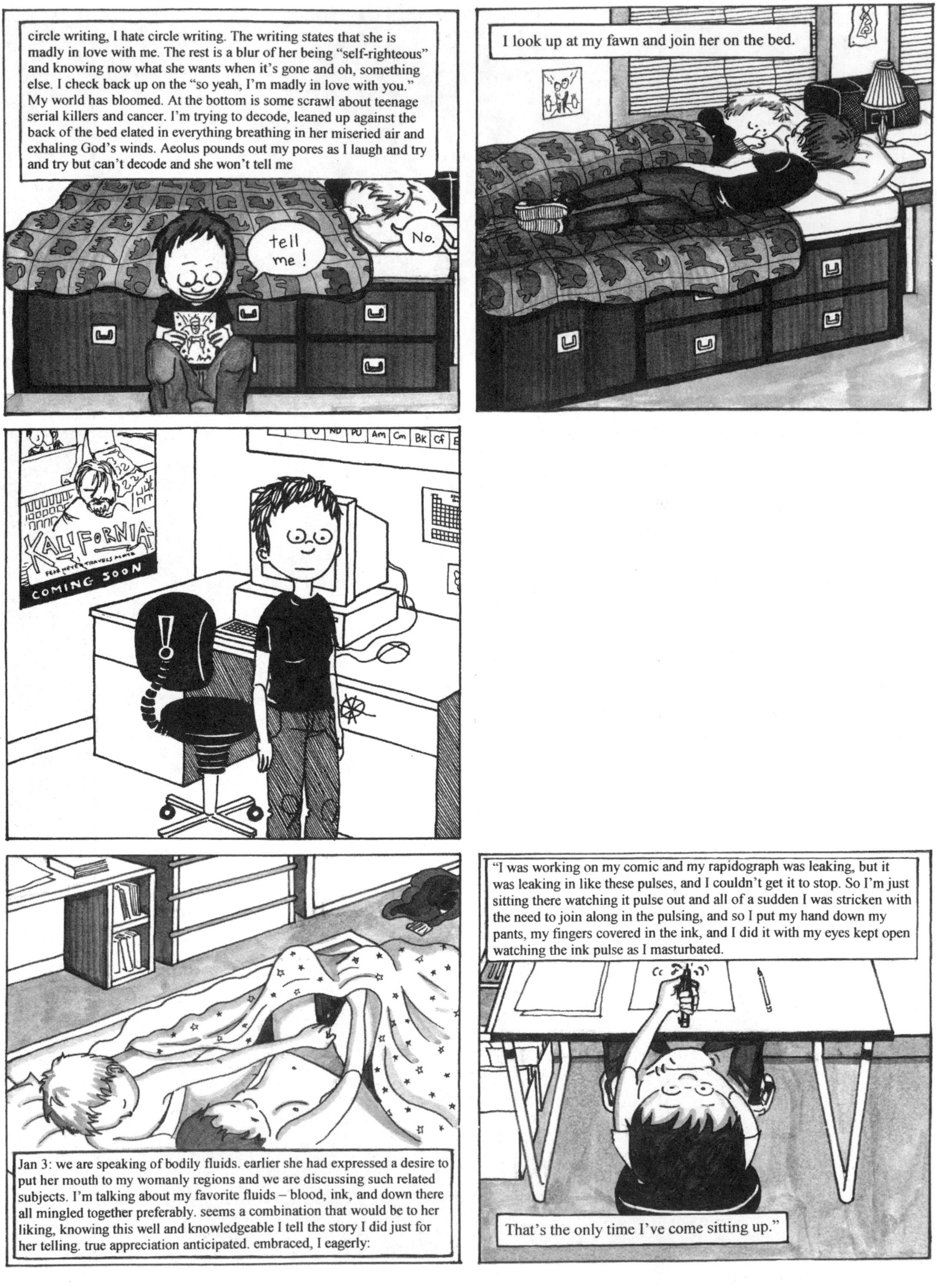
circle writing, I hate circle writing. The writing states that she is madly in love with me. The rest is a blur of her being "self-righteous" and knowing now what she wants when it's gone and oh, something else. I check back up on the "so yeah, I'm madly in love with you." My world has bloomed. At the bottom is some scrawl about teenage serial killers and cancer. I'm trying to decode, leaned up against the back of the bed elated in everything breathing in her miseried air and exhaling God's winds. Aeolus pounds out my pores as I laugh and try and try but can't decode and she won't tell me
tell me!
No.
I look up at my fawn and join her on the bed.
KALIFORNIA
COMING SOON
Jan 3: we are speaking of bodily fluids. earlier she had expressed a desire to put her mouth to my womanly regions and we are discussing such related subjects. I'm talking about my favorite fluids – blood, ink, and down there all mingled together preferably. seems a combination that would be to her liking, knowing this well and knowledgeable I tell the story I did just for her telling. true appreciation anticipated. embraced, I eagerly:
"I was working on my comic and my rapidograph was leaking, but it was leaking in like these pulses, and I couldn't get it to stop. So I'm just sitting there watching it pulse out and all of a sudden I was stricken with the need to join along in the pulsing, and so I put my hand down my pants, my fingers covered in the ink, and I did it with my eyes kept open watching the ink pulse as I masturbated.
That's the only time I've come sitting up."

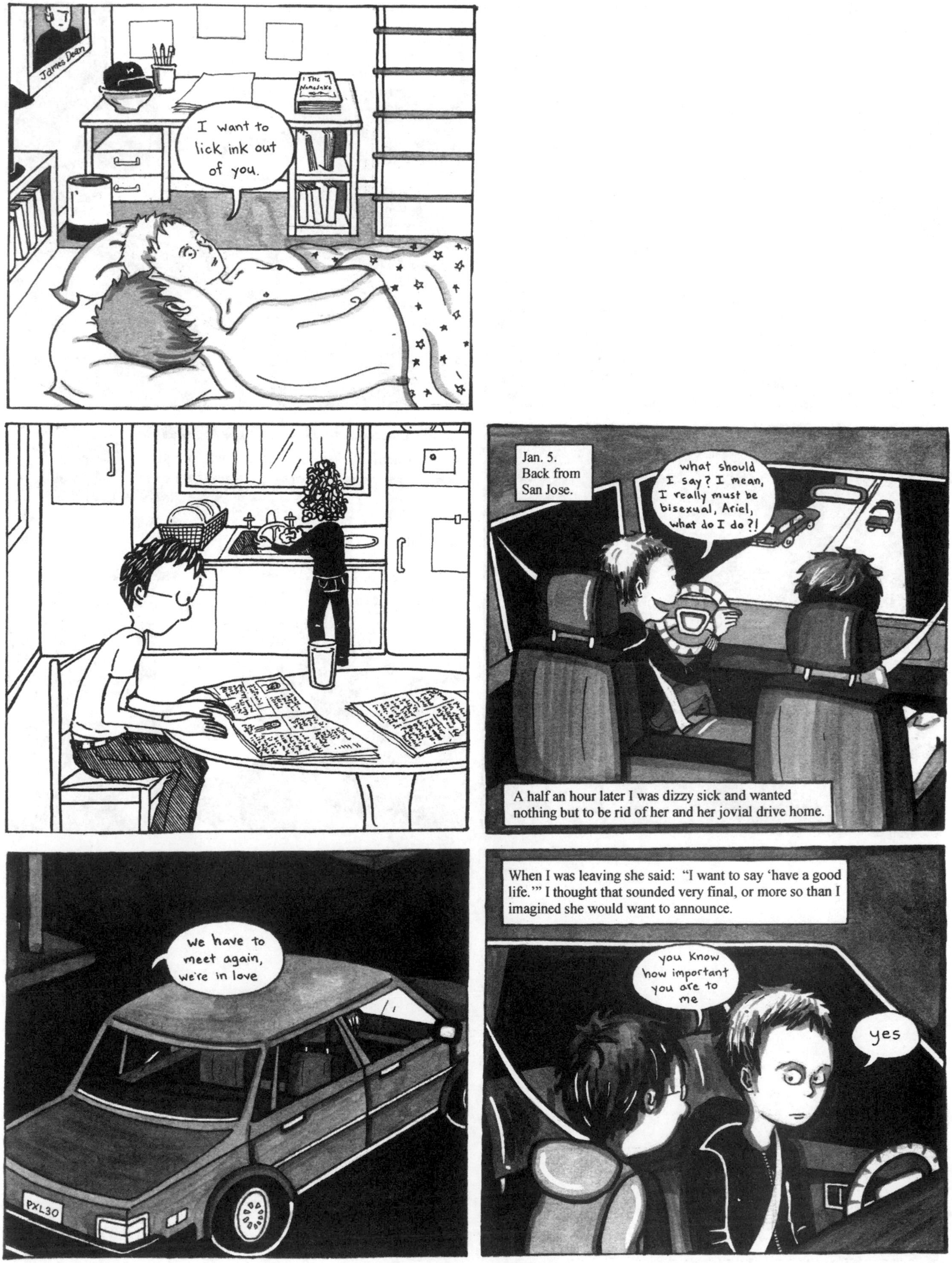
James Dean
The Namesake
I want to lick ink out of you.
Jan. 5. Back from San Jose.
what should I say? I mean, I really must be bisexual, Ariel, what do I do?!
A half an hour later I was dizzy sick and wanted nothing but to be rid of her and her jovial drive home.
we have to meet again, we're in love
PXL30
When I was leaving she said: "I want to say 'have a good life.'" I thought that sounded very final, or more so than I imagined she would want to announce.
you know how important you are to me
yes

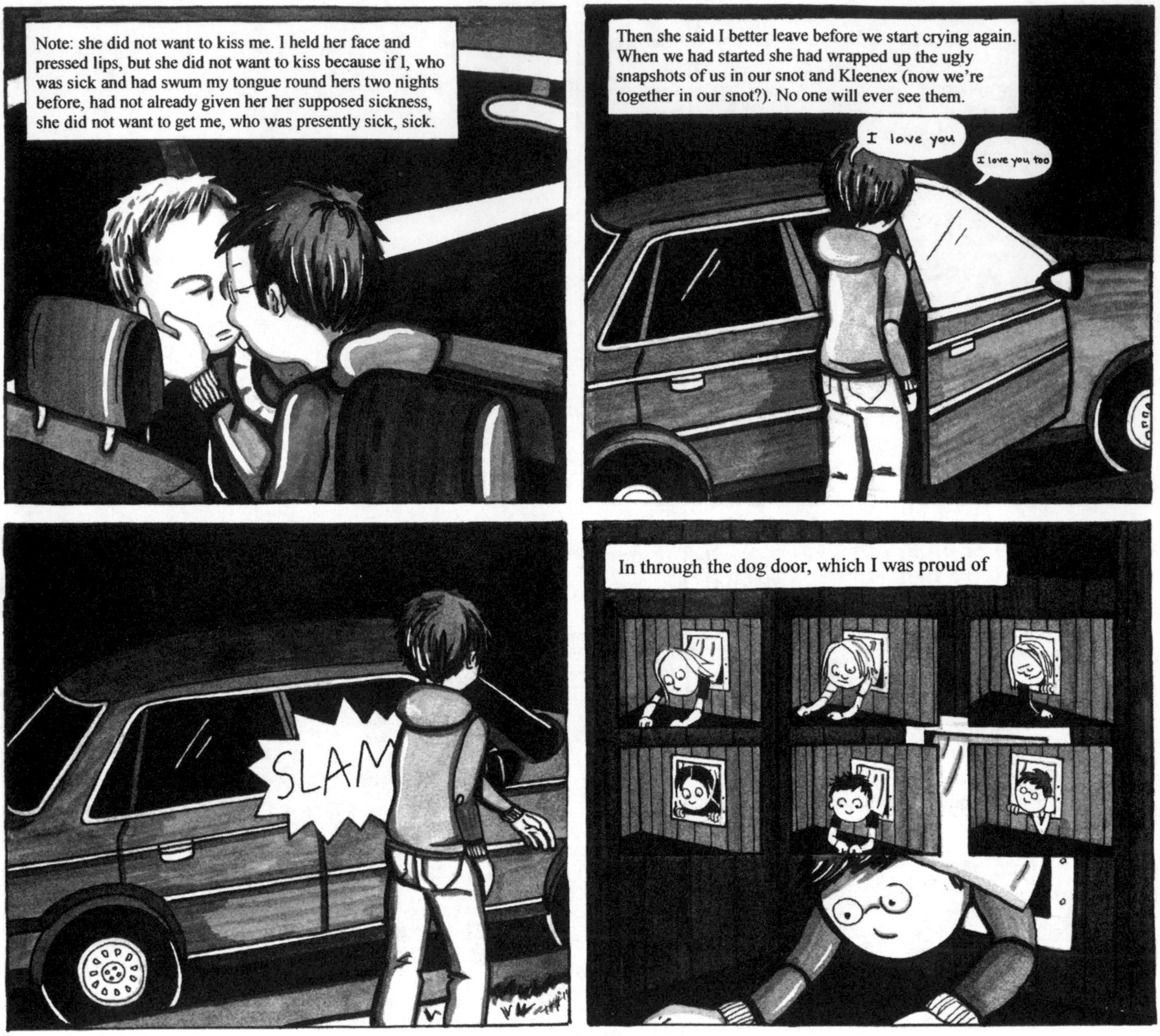
Note: she did not want to kiss me. I held her face and pressed lips, but she did not want to kiss because if I, who was sick and had swum my tongue round hers two nights before, had not already given her her supposed sickness, she did not want to get me, who was presently sick, sick.
Then she said I better leave before we start crying again. When we had started she had wrapped up the ugly snapshots of us in our snot and Kleenex (now we're together in our snot?). No one will ever see them.
I love you
I love you too
SLAM
In through the dog door, which I was proud of

II

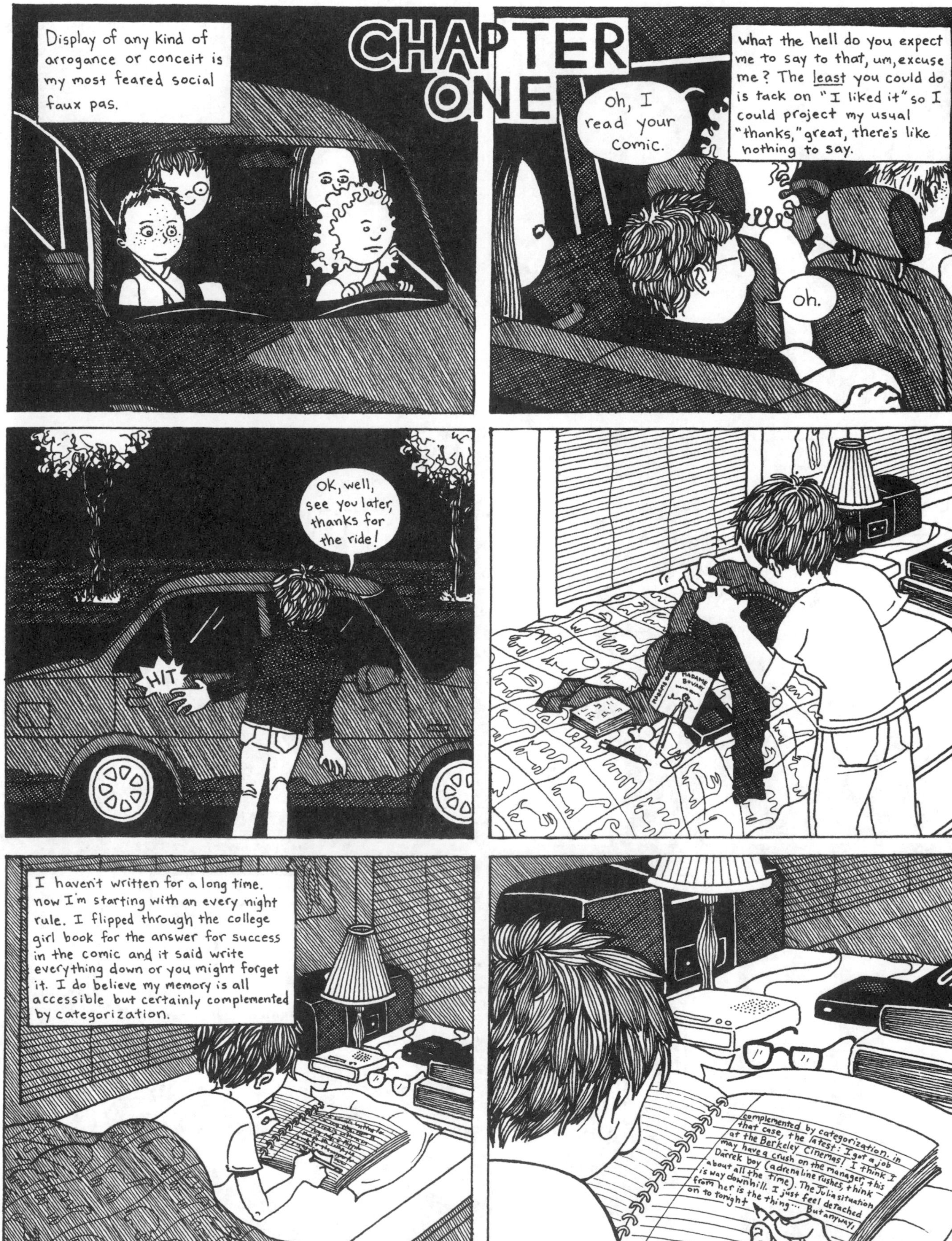
CHAPTER ONE
Display of any kind of arrogance or conceit is my most feared social faux pas.
oh, I read your comic.
what the hell do you expect me to say to that, um, excuse me? The least you could do is tack on "I liked it" so I could project my usual "thanks," great, there's like nothing to say.
oh.
OK, well, see you later, thanks for the ride!
HIT
MADAME BOVARY
I haven't written for a long time. now I'm starting with an every night rule. I flipped through the college girl book for the answer for success in the comic and it said write everything down or you might forget it. I do believe my memory is all accessible but certainly complemented by categorization.
complemented by categorization. in that case, the latest: I got a job at the Berkeley Cinemas! I think I may have a crush on the manager, this Darrek boy (adrenaline rushes, think about all the time). The Julia situation is way downhill. I just feel detached from her is the thing... But anyway, on to tonight

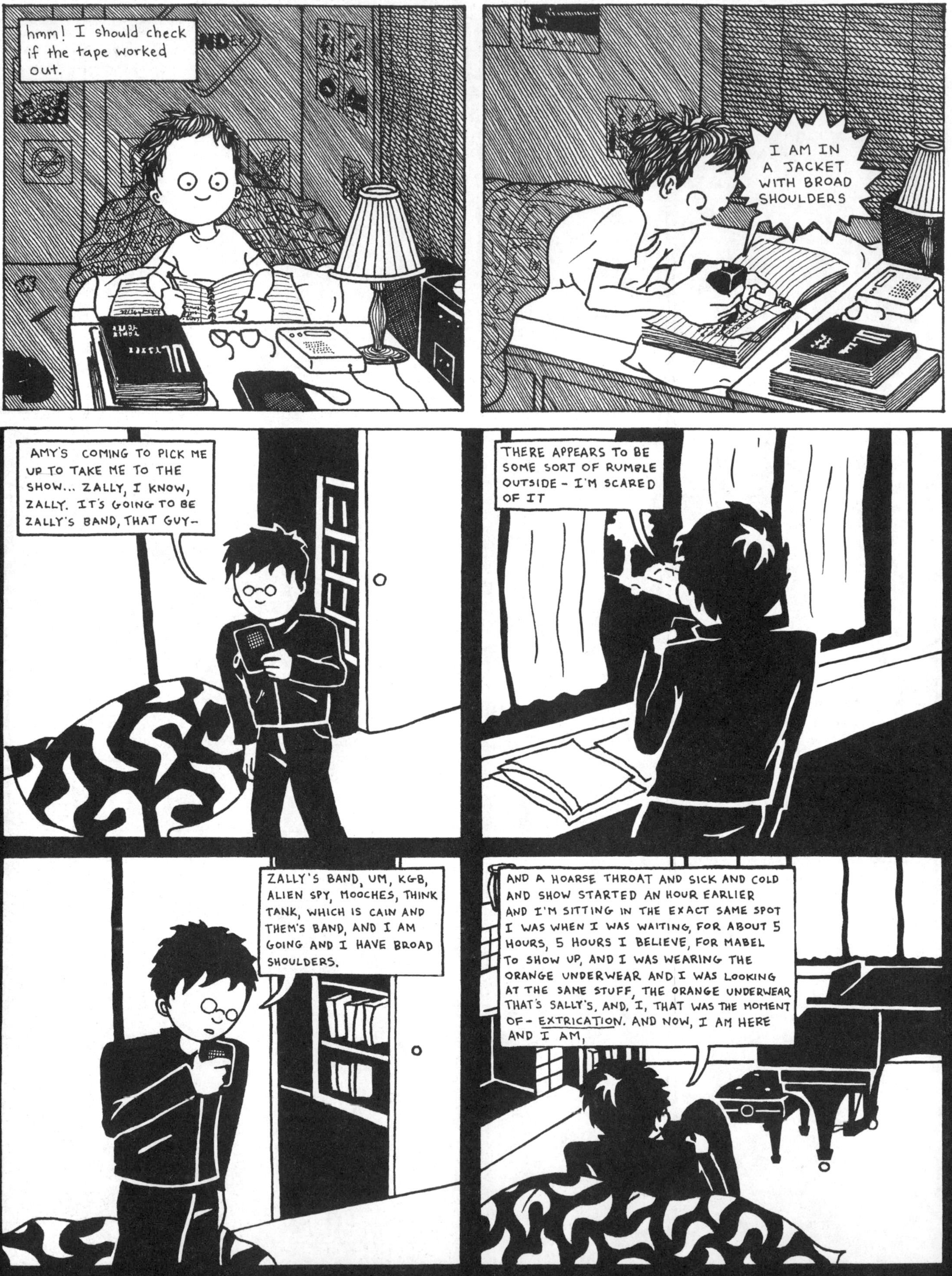
hmm! I should check if the tape worked out.
I AM IN A JACKET WITH BROAD SHOULDERS
AMY'S COMING TO PICK ME UP TO TAKE ME TO THE SHOW... ZALLY, I KNOW, ZALLY. IT'S GOING TO BE ZALLY'S BAND, THAT GUY-
THERE APPEARS TO BE SOME SORT OF RUMBLE OUTSIDE - I'M SCARED OF IT
ZALLY'S BAND, UM, KGB, ALIEN SPY, MOOCHES, THINK TANK, WHICH IS CAIN AND THEM'S BAND, AND I AM GOING AND I HAVE BROAD SHOULDERS.
AND A HOARSE THROAT AND SICK AND COLD AND SHOW STARTED AN HOUR EARLIER AND I'M SITTING IN THE EXACT SAME SPOT I WAS WHEN I WAS WAITING, FOR ABOUT 5 HOURS, 5 HOURS I BELIEVE, FOR MABEL TO SHOW UP, AND I WAS WEARING THE ORANGE UNDERWEAR AND I WAS LOOKING AT THE SAME STUFF, THE ORANGE UNDERWEAR THAT'S SALLY'S, AND, I, THAT WAS THE MOMENT OF- EXTRICATION. AND NOW, I AM HERE AND I AM,

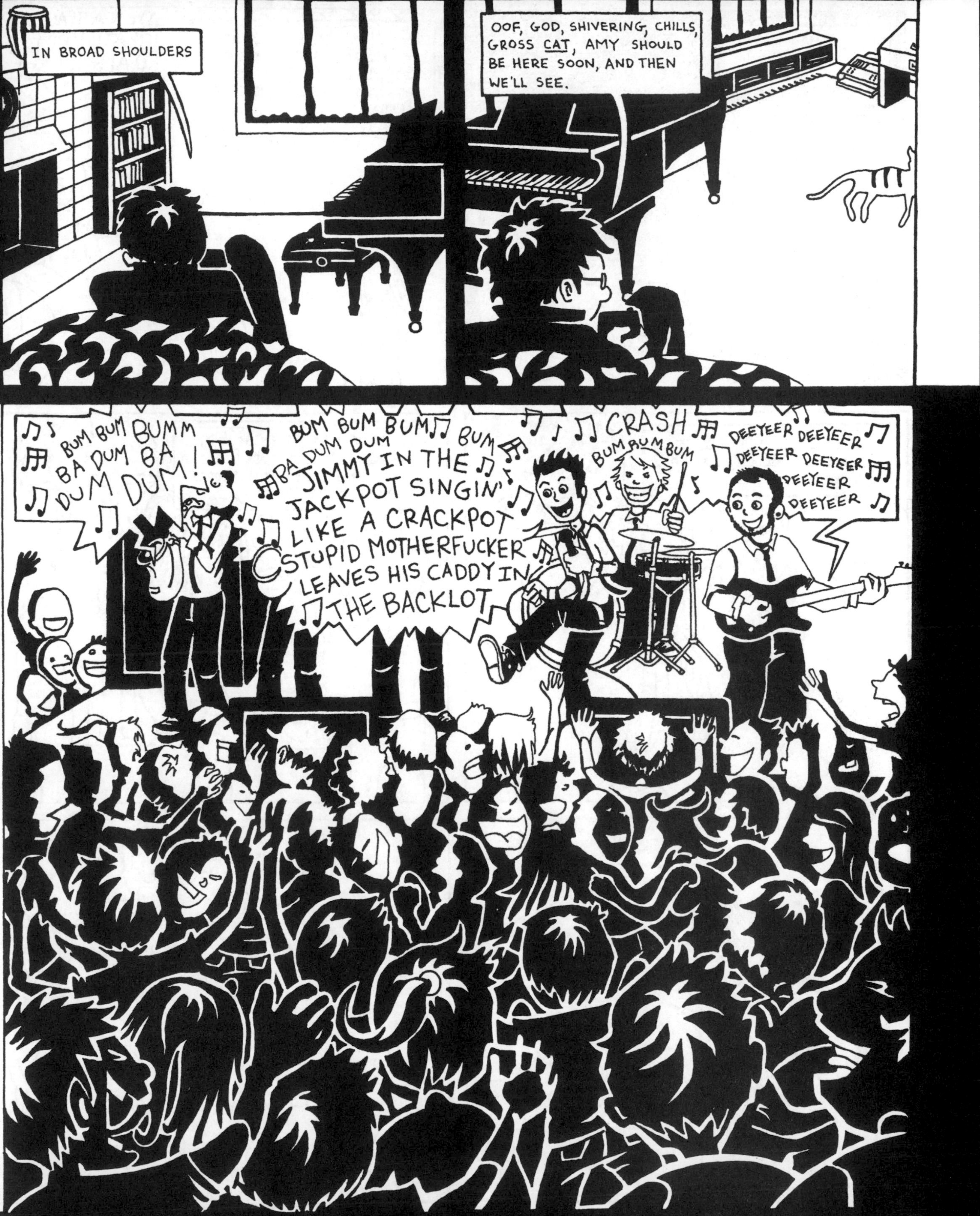
IN BROAD SHOULDERS
OOF, GOD, SHIVERING, CHILLS, GROSS CAT, AMY SHOULD BE HERE SOON, AND THEN WE'LL SEE.
BUM BUM BUMM BA DUM BA DUM DUM!
BUM BUM BUM BA DUM DUM BUM
CRASH
BUM BUM BUM
DEEYEER DEEYEER DEEYEER DEEYEER DEEYEER DEEYEER
JIMMY IN THE JACKPOT SINGIN' LIKE A CRACKPOT STUPID MOTHERFUCKER LEAVES HIS CADDY IN THE BACKLOT

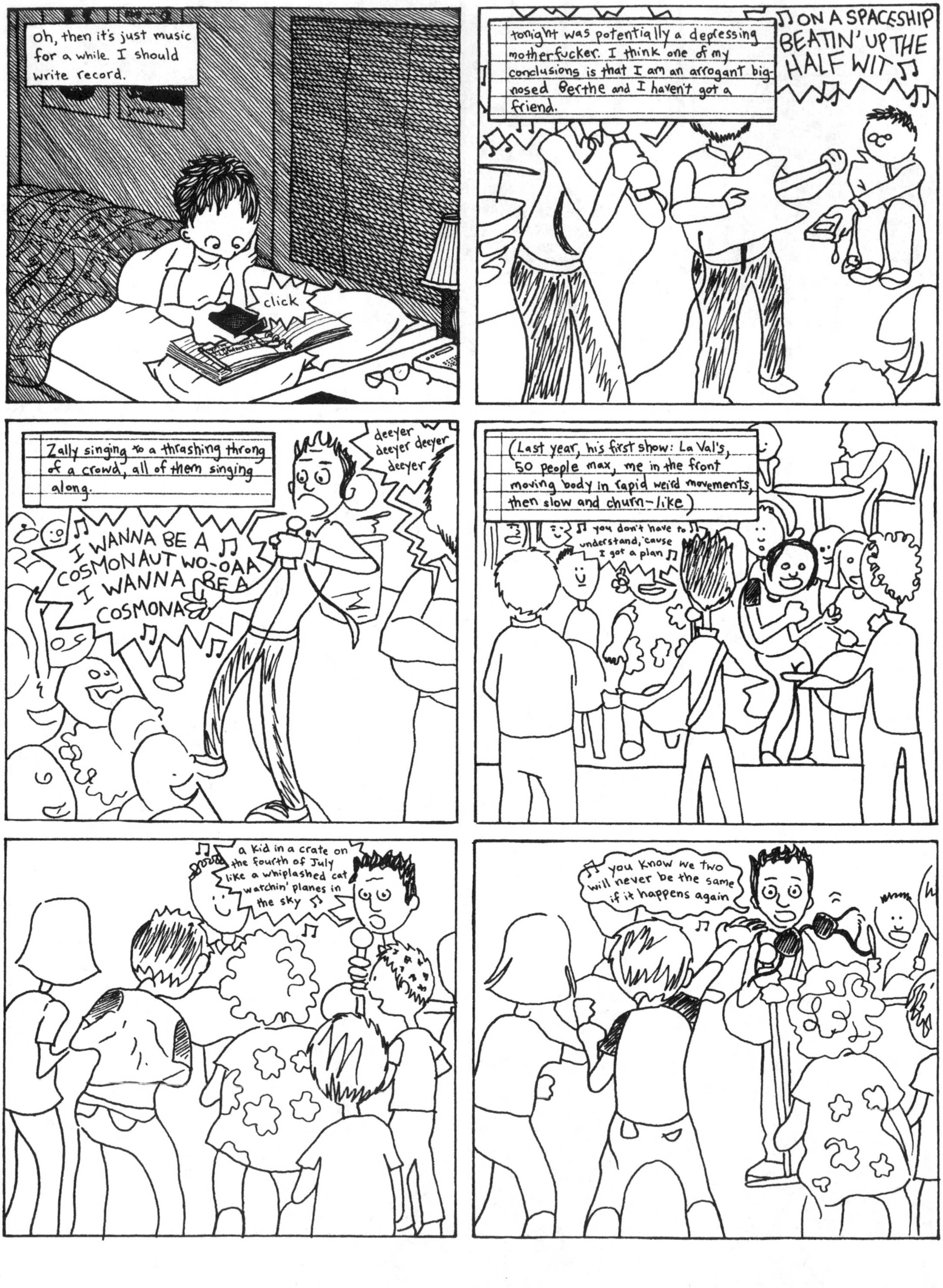

Oh, then it's just music for a while. I should write record.
click
tonight was potentially a depressing motherfucker. I think one of my conclusions is that I am an arrogant big-nosed Berthe and I haven't got a friend.
ON A SPACESHIP BEATIN' UP THE HALF WIT
Zally singing to a thrashing throng of a crowd, all of them singing along.
deeyer deeyer deeyer deeyer
I WANNA BE A COSMONAUT WO-OAA I WANNA BE A COSMONA
(Last year, his first show: La Val's, 50 people max, me in the front moving body in rapid weird movements, then slow and churn-like)
you don't have to understand, 'cause I got a plan
a kid in a crate on the fourth of July like a whiplashed cat watchin' planes in the sky
you know we two will never be the same if it happens again

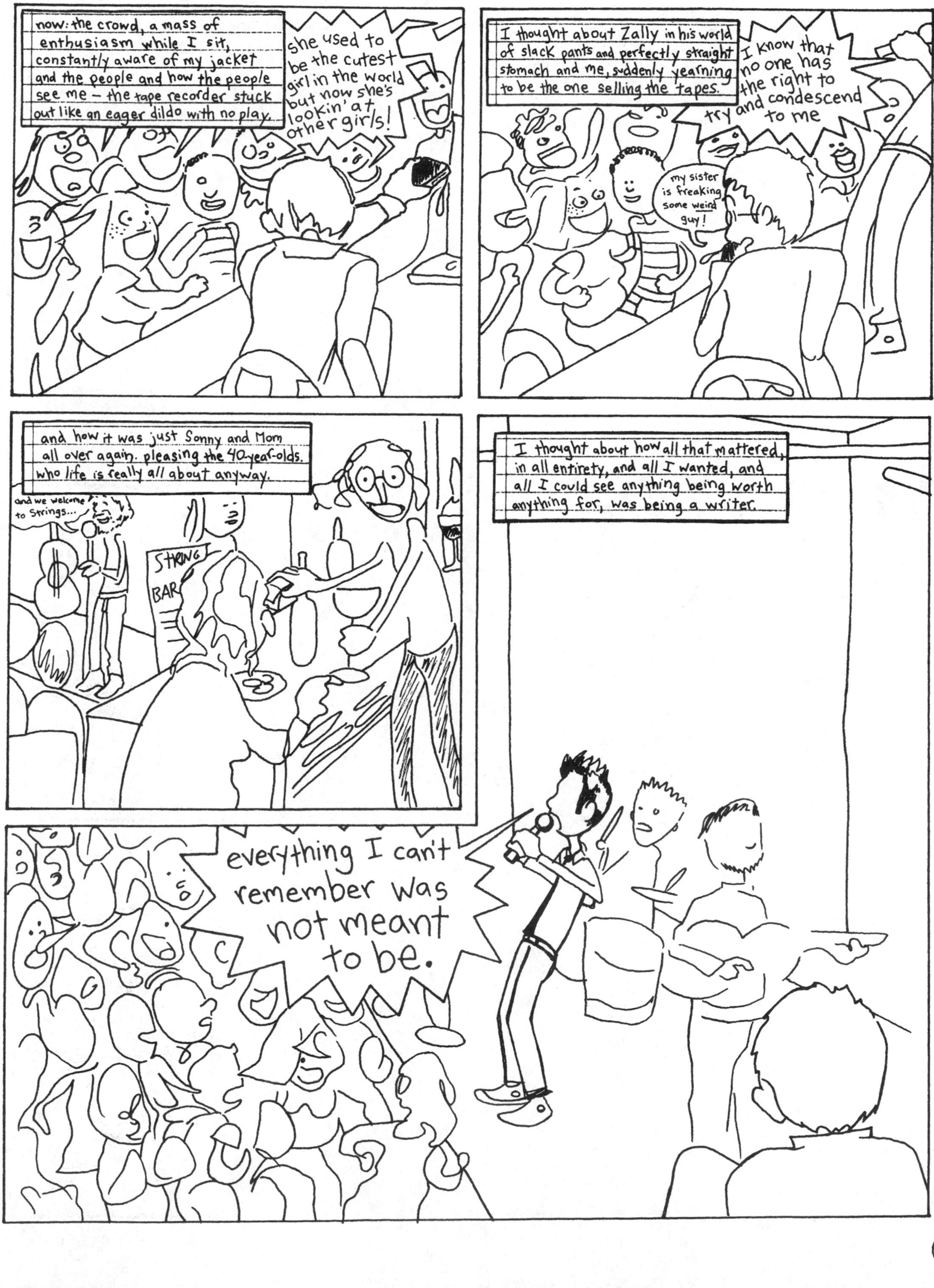

now: the crowd, a mass of enthusiasm while I sit, constantly aware of my jacket and the people and how the people see me — the tape recorder stuck out like an eager dildo with no play.
she used to be the cutest girl in the world but now she's lookin' at other girls!
I thought about Zally in his world of slack pants and perfectly straight stomach and me, suddenly yearning to be the one selling the tapes.
I know that no one has the right to try and condescend to me
my sister is freaking some weird guy!
and how it was just Sonny and Mom all over again. pleasing the 40-year-olds. who life is really all about anyway.
and we welcome to Strings...
STRING
BAR
I thought about how all that mattered, in all entirety, and all I wanted, and all I could see anything being worth anything for, was being a writer.
everything I can't remember was not meant to be.

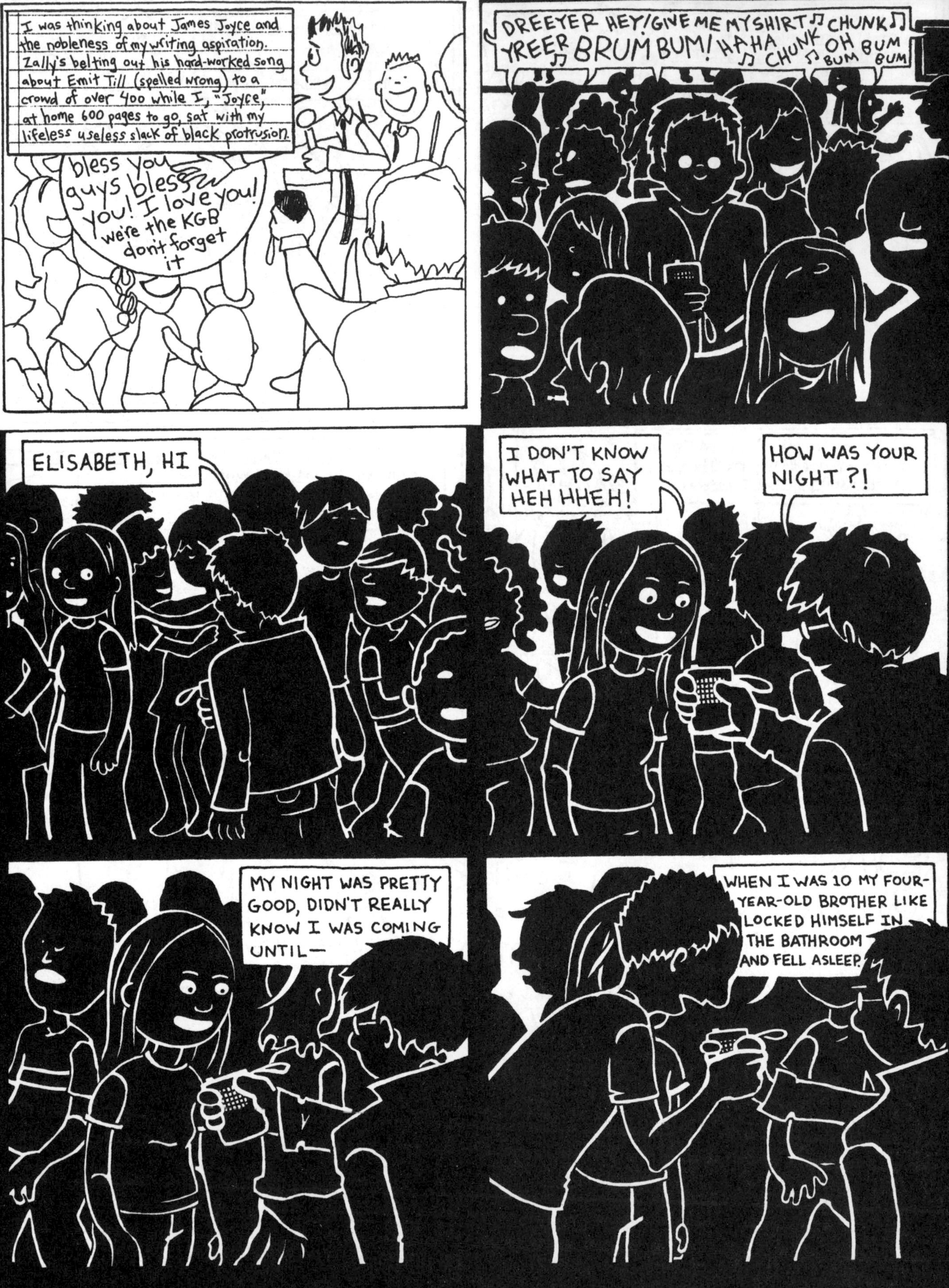
I was thinking about James Joyce and the nobleness of my writing aspiration. Zally's belting out his hard-worked song about Emit Till (spelled wrong) to a crowd of over 400 while I, "Joyce," at home 600 pages to go, sat with my lifeless useless slack of black protrusion.
bless you guys bless you! I love you! we're the KGB don't forget it
DREEYER HEY! GIVE ME MY SHIRT ♫ CHUNK ♫
YREER ♫ BRUM BUM! HAHA ♫ CHUNK ♫ OH BUM BUM BUM BUM
ELISABETH, HI
I DON'T KNOW WHAT TO SAY HEH HHEH!
HOW WAS YOUR NIGHT ?!
MY NIGHT WAS PRETTY GOOD, DIDN'T REALLY KNOW I WAS COMING UNTIL—
WHEN I WAS 10 MY FOUR-YEAR-OLD BROTHER LIKE LOCKED HIMSELF IN THE BATHROOM AND FELL ASLEEP.

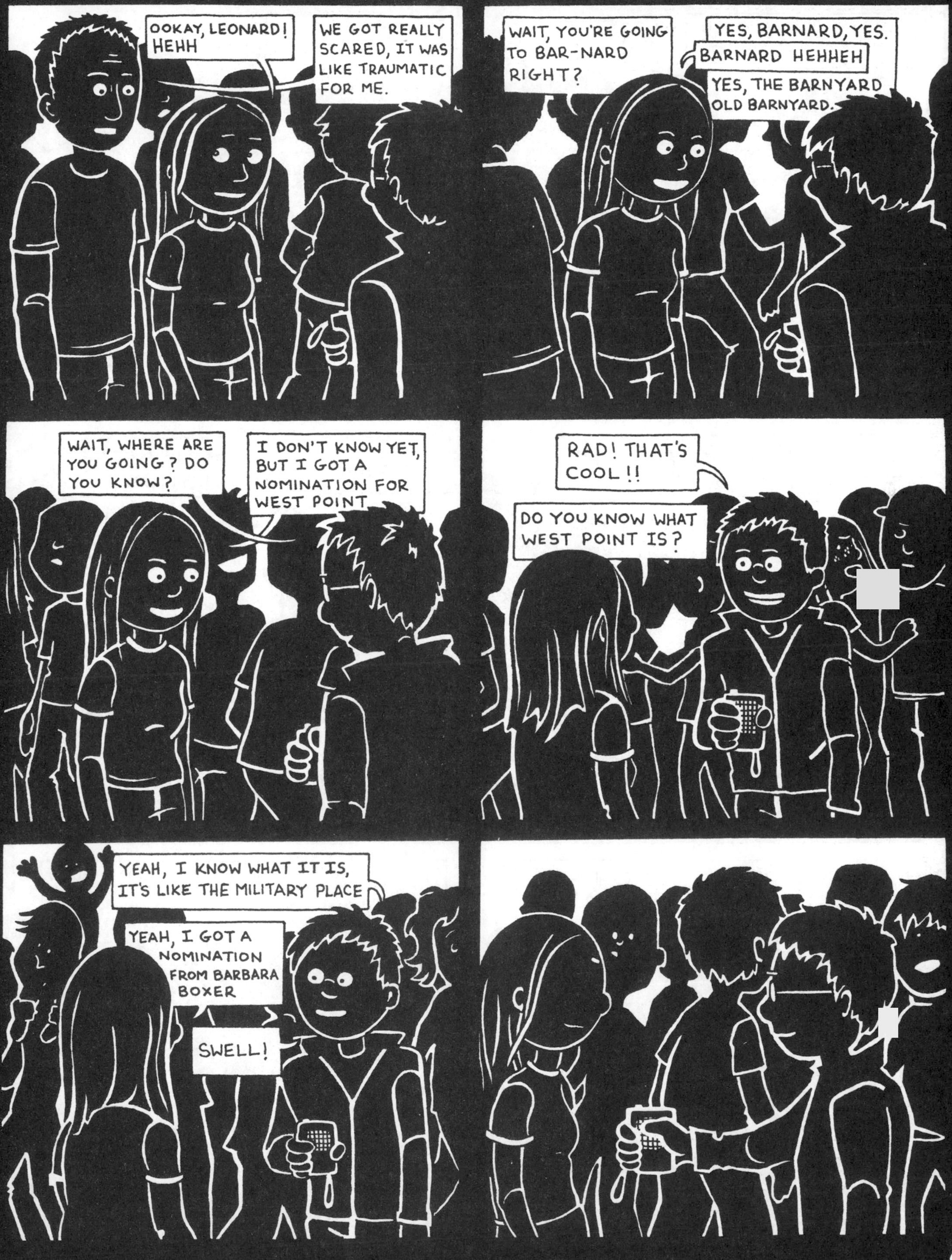
OOKAY, LEONARD! HEHH
WE GOT REALLY SCARED, IT WAS LIKE TRAUMATIC FOR ME.
WAIT, YOU'RE GOING TO BAR-NARD RIGHT?
YES, BARNARD, YES.
BARNARD HEHHEH
YES, THE BARNYARD OLD BARNYARD.
WAIT, WHERE ARE YOU GOING? DO YOU KNOW?
I DON'T KNOW YET, BUT I GOT A NOMINATION FOR WEST POINT
RAD! THAT'S COOL!!
DO YOU KNOW WHAT WEST POINT IS?
YEAH, I KNOW WHAT IT IS, IT'S LIKE THE MILITARY PLACE
YEAH, I GOT A NOMINATION FROM BARBARA BOXER
SWELL!

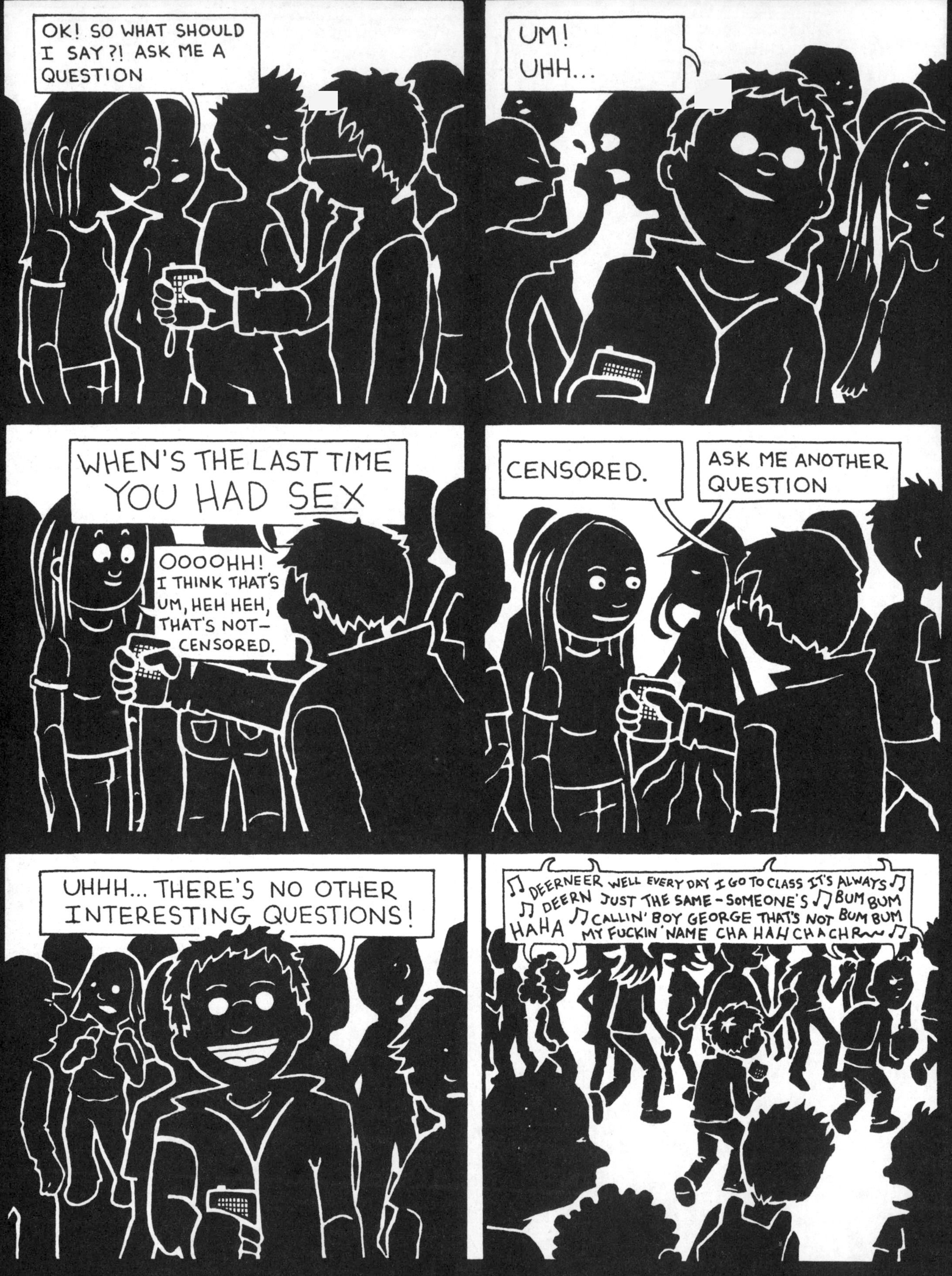
OK! SO WHAT SHOULD I SAY?! ASK ME A QUESTION
UM! UHH...
WHEN'S THE LAST TIME YOU HAD SEX
OOOOHH! I THINK THAT'S UM, HEH HEH, THAT'S NOT— CENSORED.
CENSORED.
ASK ME ANOTHER QUESTION
UHHH... THERE'S NO OTHER INTERESTING QUESTIONS!
♫ DEERNEER
♫ DEERN
HAHA
WELL EVERY DAY I GO TO CLASS IT'S ALWAYS ♫ JUST THE SAME – SOMEONE'S ♫ CALLIN' BOY GEORGE THAT'S NOT MY FUCKIN' NAME CHA HAH CHACHR~~ ♫
BUM BUM BUM BUM

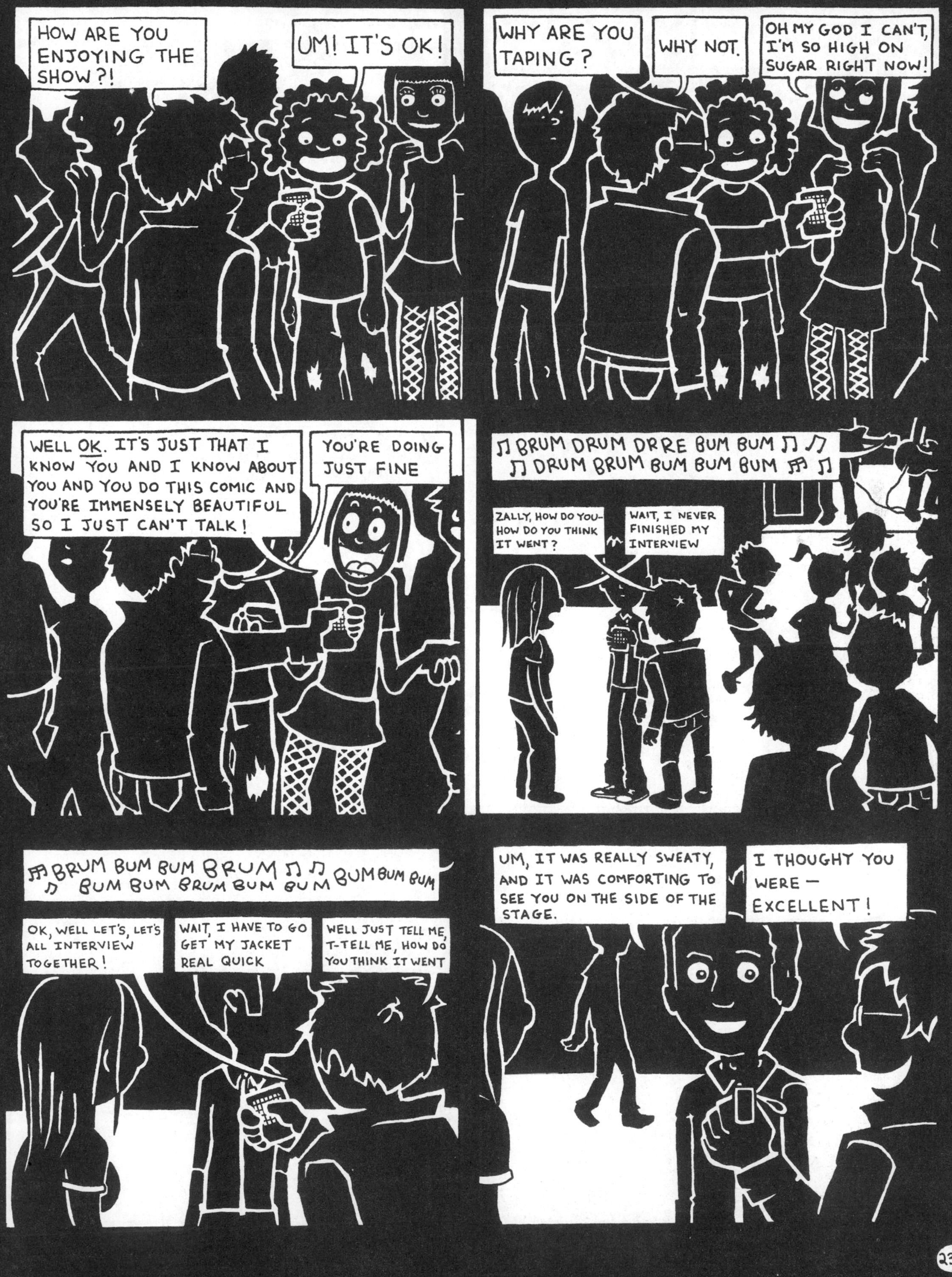
HOW ARE YOU ENJOYING THE SHOW?!
UM! IT'S OK!
WHY ARE YOU TAPING?
WHY NOT.
OH MY GOD I CAN'T, I'M SO HIGH ON SUGAR RIGHT NOW!
WELL OK. IT'S JUST THAT I KNOW YOU AND I KNOW ABOUT YOU AND YOU DO THIS COMIC AND YOU'RE IMMENSELY BEAUTIFUL SO I JUST CAN'T TALK!
YOU'RE DOING JUST FINE
♫ BRUM DRUM DRRE BUM BUM ♫ ♫ ♫ DRUM BRUM BUM BUM BUM ♫ ♫
ZALLY, HOW DO YOU- HOW DO YOU THINK IT WENT?
WAIT, I NEVER FINISHED MY INTERVIEW
♫ BRUM BUM BUM BRUM ♫ ♫ ♫ BUM BUM BRUM BUM BUM BUM BUM BUM
OK, WELL LET'S, LET'S ALL INTERVIEW TOGETHER!
WAIT, I HAVE TO GO GET MY JACKET REAL QUICK
WELL JUST TELL ME, T-TELL ME, HOW DO YOU THINK IT WENT
UM, IT WAS REALLY SWEATY, AND IT WAS COMFORTING TO SEE YOU ON THE SIDE OF THE STAGE.
I THOUGHT YOU WERE — EXCELLENT!

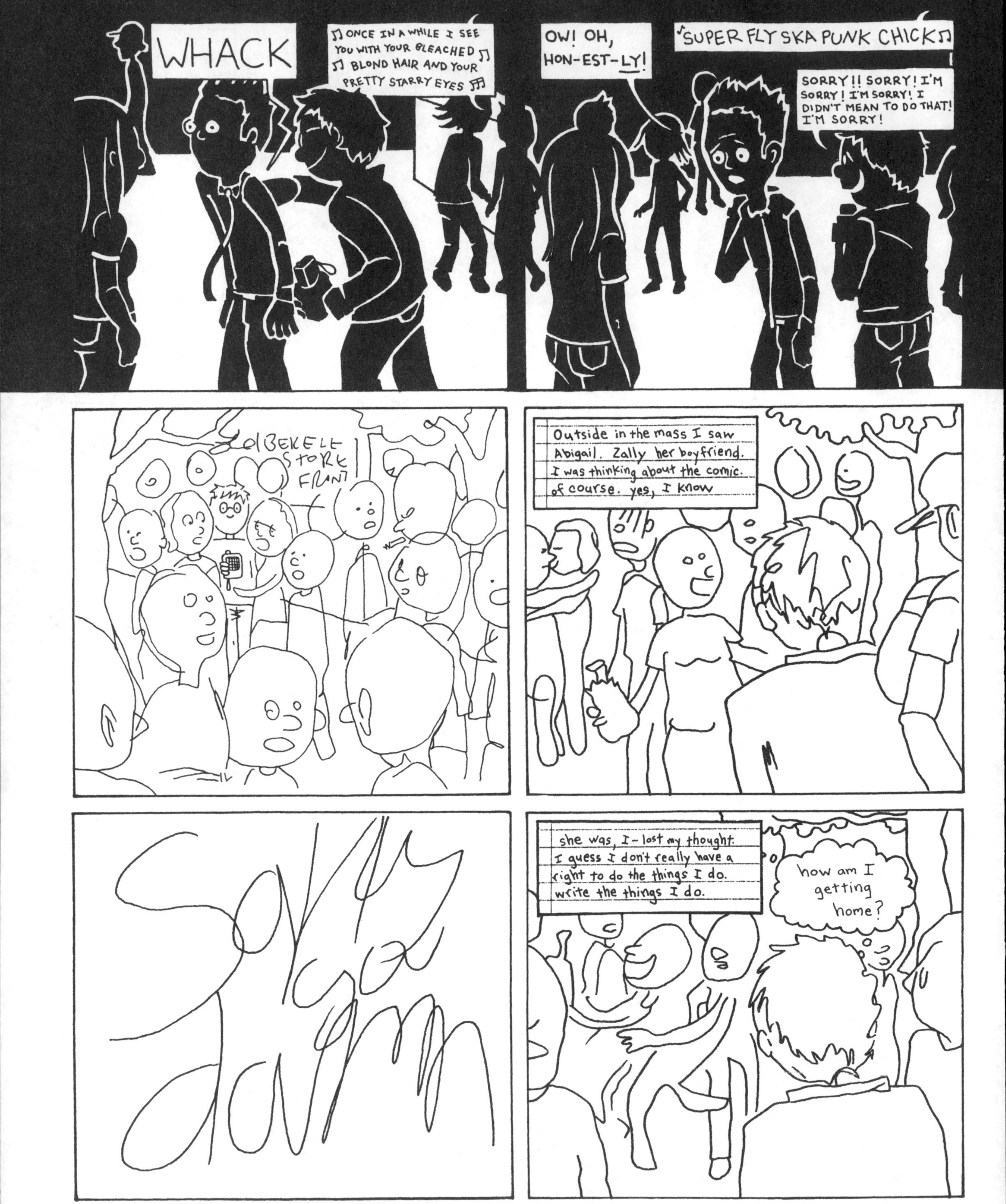
WHACK
ONCE IN A WHILE I SEE YOU WITH YOUR CLEACHED BLOND HAIR AND YOUR PRETTY STARRY EYES
OW! OH, HON-EST-LY!
SUPER FLY SKA PUNK CHICK
SORRY!! SORRY! I'M SORRY! I'M SORRY! I DIDN'T MEAN TO DO THAT! I'M SORRY!
STORE FRONT
Outside in the mass I saw Abigail. Zally her boyfriend. I was thinking about the comic. of course. yes, I know
she was, I- lost my thought. I guess I don't really have a right to do the things I do. write the things I do.
how am I getting home?

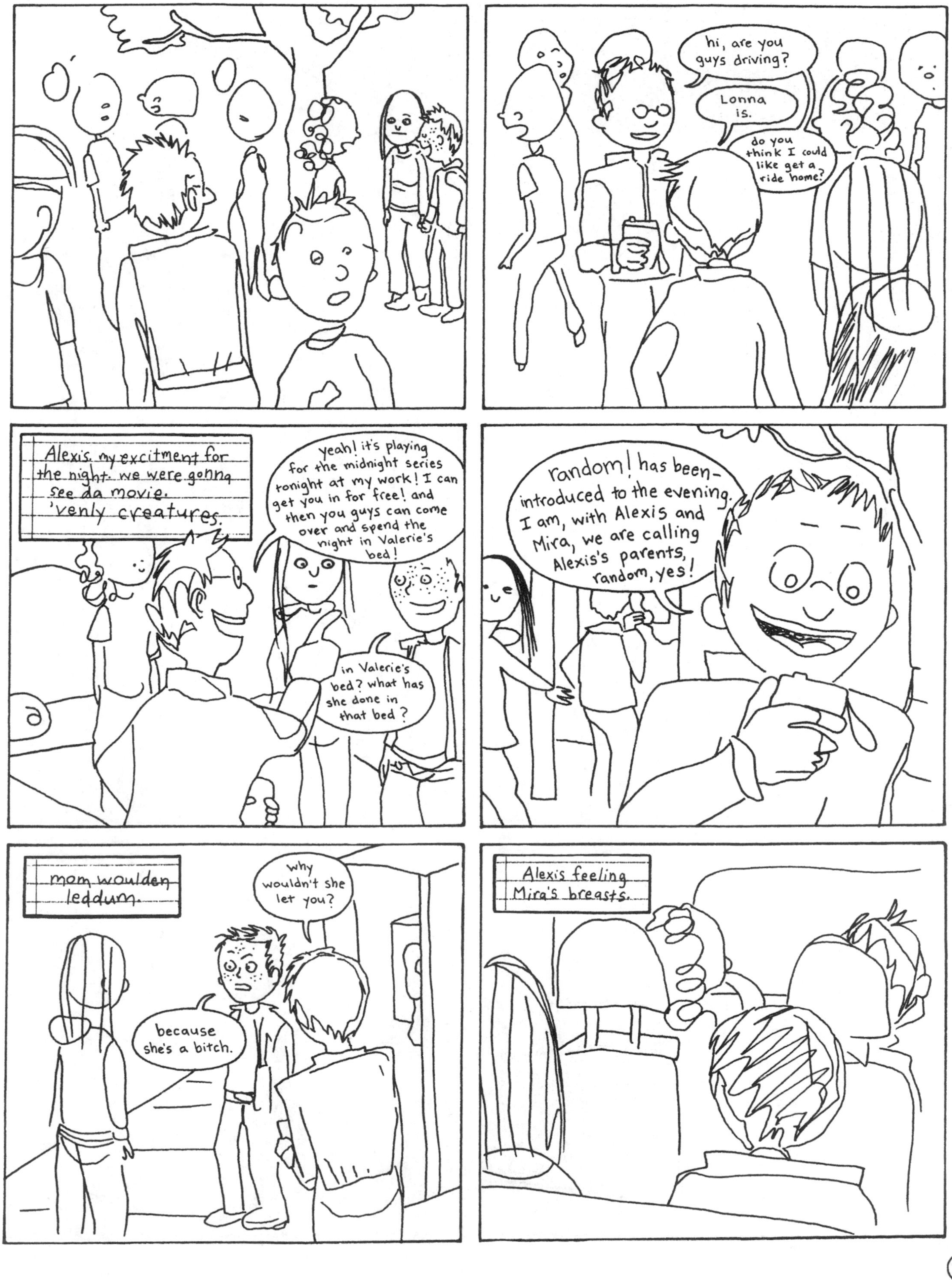
hi, are you guys driving?
Lonna is.
do you think I could like get a ride home?
Alexis. my excitment for the night. we were gonna see da movie. 'venly creatures.
yeah! it's playing for the midnight series tonight at my work! I can get you in for free! and then you guys can come over and spend the night in Valerie's bed!
in Valerie's bed? what has she done in that bed?
random! has been-introduced to the evening. I am, with Alexis and Mira, we are calling Alexis's parents, random, yes!
mom woulden leddum.
why wouldn't she let you?
because she's a bitch.
Alexis feeling Mira's breasts.

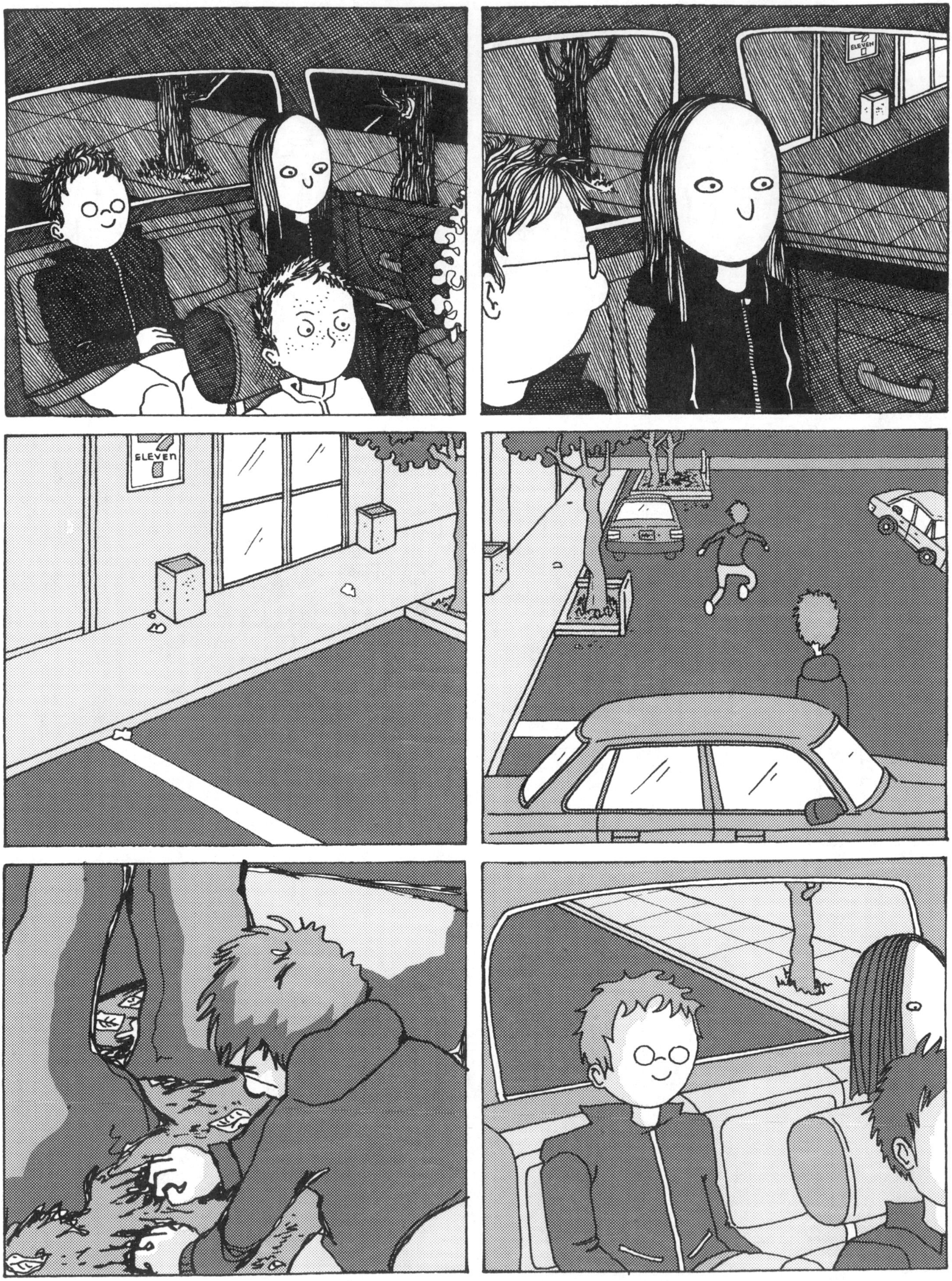
ELEVEN
ELEVEN

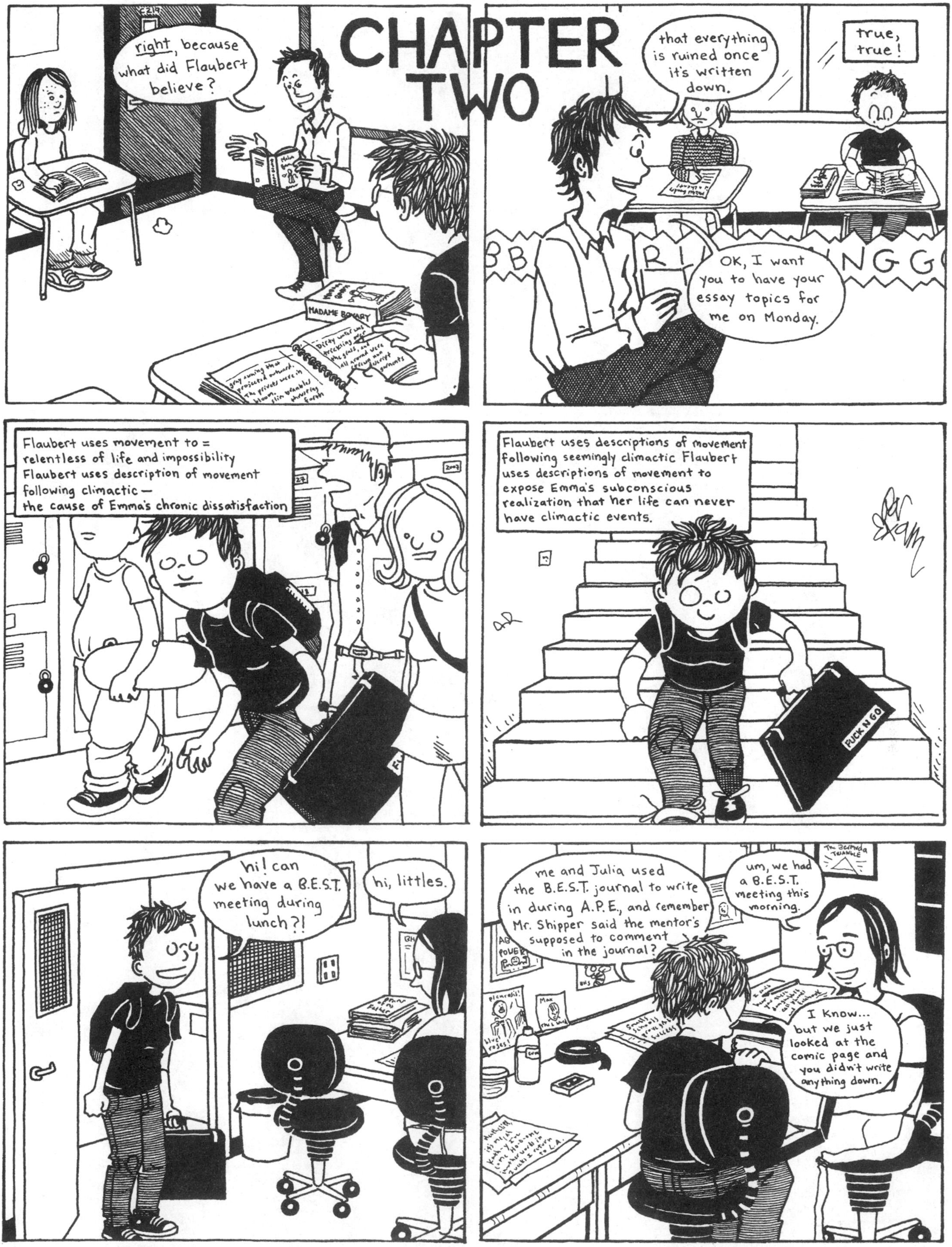
CHAPTER TWO
right, because what did Flaubert believe?
that everything is ruined once it's written down.
true, true!
OK, I want you to have your essay topics for me on Monday.
MADAME BOVARY
Flaubert uses movement to = relentless of life and impossibility Flaubert uses description of movement following climactic — the cause of Emma's chronic dissatisfaction
Flaubert uses descriptions of movement following seemingly climactic Flaubert uses descriptions of movement to expose Emma's subconscious realization that her life can never have climactic events.
PUCK N GO
hi! can we have a B.E.S.T. meeting during lunch?!
hi, littles.
me and Julia used the B.E.S.T. journal to write in during A.P.E., and remember Mr. Shipper said the mentor's supposed to comment in the journal?
um, we had a B.E.S.T. meeting this morning.
I know... but we just looked at the comic page and you didn't write anything down.
The Bermuda Triangle

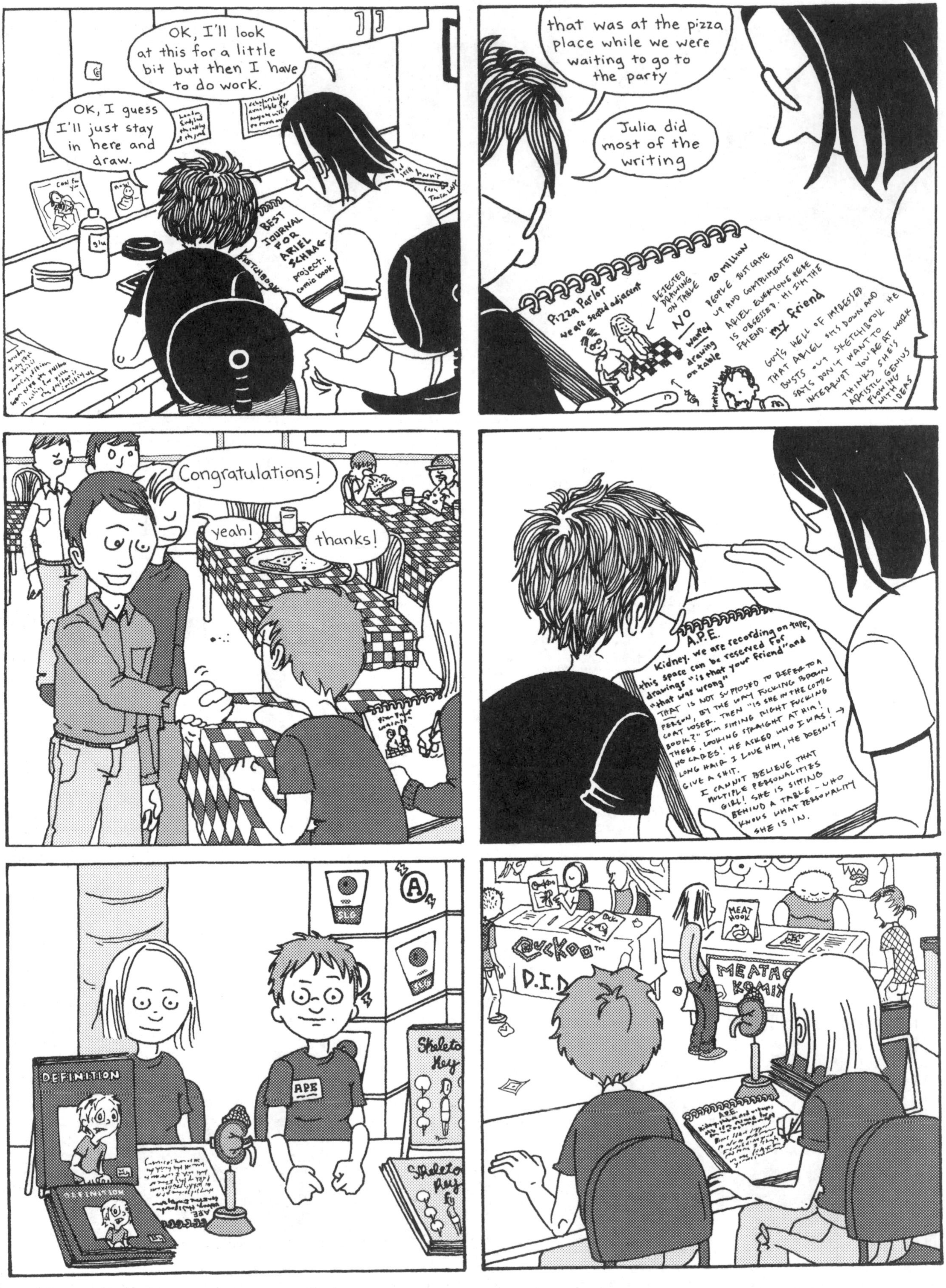
OK, I'll look at this for a little bit but then I have to do work.
OK, I guess I'll just stay in here and draw.
BEST JOURNAL FOR ARIEL SCHRAG project: comic book
SKETCHBOOK
that was at the pizza place while we were waiting to go to the party
Julia did most of the writing
Pizza Parlor
we are seated adjacent
NO
wanted drawing on table
20 MILLION PEOPLE JUST CAME UP AND COMPLIMENTED ARIEL. EVERYONE HERE IS OBSESSED. HI I'M THE FRIEND.
my friend
GUYS HELL OF IMPRESSED THAT ARIEL SITS DOWN AND BUSTS OUT SKETCHBOOK. HE SAYS DON'T WANT TO INTERRUPT YOU'RE AT WORK THINKS SHE'S ARTISTIC GENIUS FLOWING WITH IDEAS
Congratulations!
yeah!
thanks!
A.P.E.
Kidney. we are recording on tape, this space can be reserved for drawings "is that your friend" and "that was wrong"
THAT IS NOT SUPPOSED TO REFER TO A PERSON, BY THE WAY FUCKING BROWN COAT LOSER. THEN "IS SHE IN THE COMIC BOOK?" I'M SITTING RIGHT FUCKING THERE, LOOKING STRAIGHT AT HIM! HE CARES! HE ASKED WHO I WAS! LONG HAIR. I LOVE HIM, HE DOESN'T GIVE A SHIT.
I CANNOT BELIEVE THAT MULTIPLE PERSONALITIES GIRL! SHE IS SITTING BEHIND A TABLE - WHO KNOWS WHAT PERSONALITY SHE IS IN.
SLG
DEFINITION
APE
Skeleton Key
CUCKOO
D.I.
MEAT HOOK
MEATHOOK KOMIX

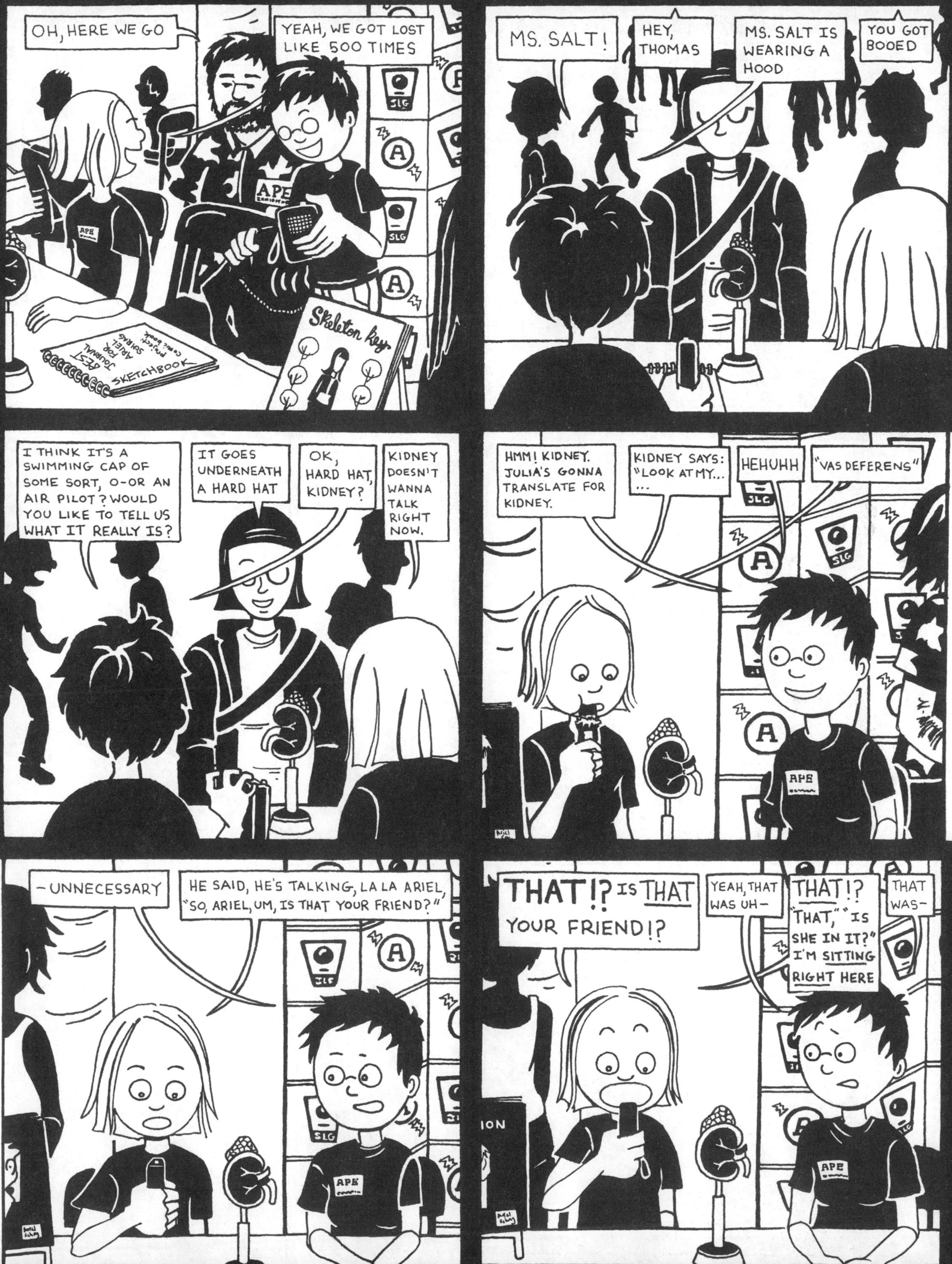
OH, HERE WE GO
YEAH, WE GOT LOST LIKE 500 TIMES
SKETCHBOOK
Skeleton key
MS. SALT!
HEY, THOMAS
MS. SALT IS WEARING A HOOD
YOU GOT BOOED
I THINK IT'S A SWIMMING CAP OF SOME SORT, O-OR AN AIR PILOT? WOULD YOU LIKE TO TELL US WHAT IT REALLY IS?
IT GOES UNDERNEATH A HARD HAT
OK, HARD HAT, KIDNEY?
KIDNEY DOESN'T WANNA TALK RIGHT NOW.
HMM! KIDNEY. JULIA'S GONNA TRANSLATE FOR KIDNEY.
KIDNEY SAYS: "LOOK AT MY... ...
HEHUHH
"VAS DEFERENS"
-UNNECESSARY
HE SAID, HE'S TALKING, LA LA ARIEL, "SO, ARIEL, UM, IS THAT YOUR FRIEND?"
THAT!? IS THAT YOUR FRIEND!?
YEAH, THAT WAS UH-
THAT!? "THAT," "IS SHE IN IT?" I'M SITTING RIGHT HERE
THAT WAS-

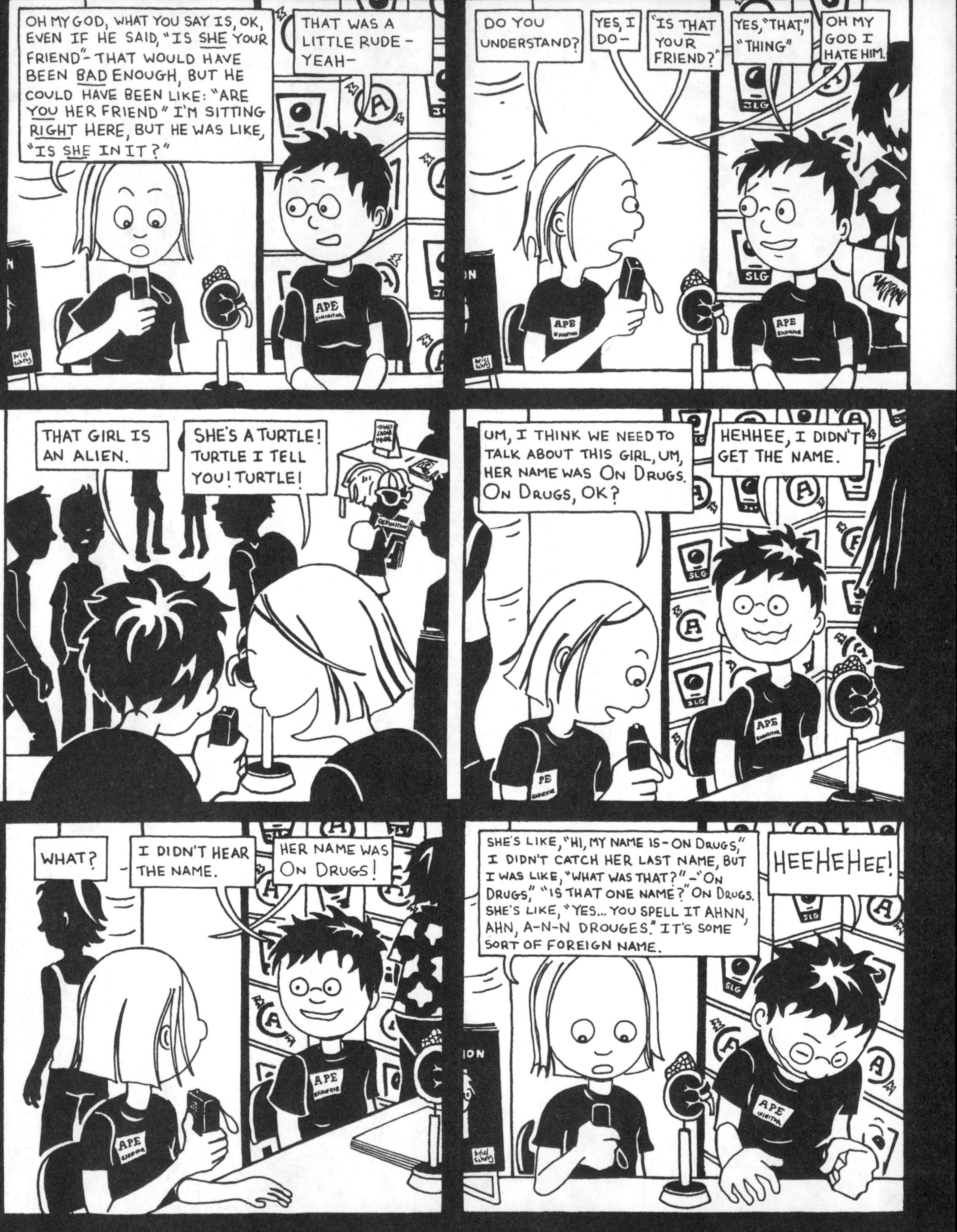
OH MY GOD, WHAT YOU SAY IS, OK, EVEN IF HE SAID, "IS SHE YOUR FRIEND"- THAT WOULD HAVE BEEN BAD ENOUGH, BUT HE COULD HAVE BEEN LIKE: "ARE YOU HER FRIEND" I'M SITTING RIGHT HERE, BUT HE WAS LIKE, "IS SHE IN IT?"
THAT WAS A LITTLE RUDE - YEAH-
DO YOU UNDERSTAND?
YES, I DO-
"IS THAT YOUR FRIEND?"
YES, "THAT," "THING"
OH MY GOD I HATE HIM.
THAT GIRL IS AN ALIEN.
SHE'S A TURTLE! TURTLE I TELL YOU! TURTLE!
UM, I THINK WE NEED TO TALK ABOUT THIS GIRL, UM, HER NAME WAS ON DRUGS. ON DRUGS, OK?
HEHHEE, I DIDN'T GET THE NAME.
WHAT?
I DIDN'T HEAR THE NAME.
HER NAME WAS ON DRUGS!
SHE'S LIKE, "HI, MY NAME IS - ON DRUGS," I DIDN'T CATCH HER LAST NAME, BUT I WAS LIKE, "WHAT WAS THAT?" -"ON DRUGS," "IS THAT ONE NAME?" ON DRUGS. SHE'S LIKE, "YES... YOU SPELL IT AHNN, AHN, A-N-N DROUGES." IT'S SOME SORT OF FOREIGN NAME.
HEEHEHEE!

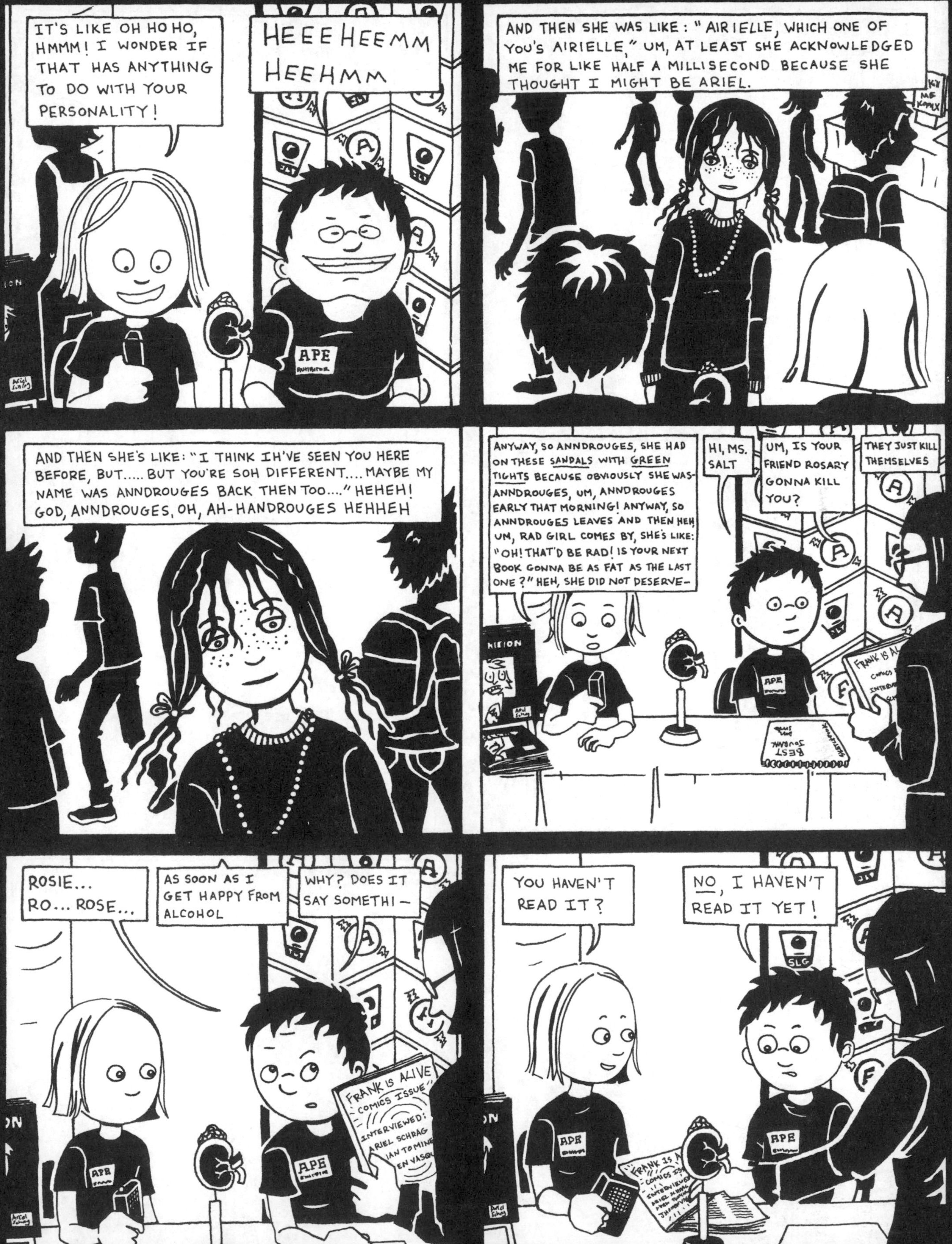
IT'S LIKE OH HO HO, HMMM! I WONDER IF THAT HAS ANYTHING TO DO WITH YOUR PERSONALITY!
HEEEHEEMM HEEHMM
APE
AND THEN SHE WAS LIKE: "AIRIELLE, WHICH ONE OF YOU'S AIRIELLE," UM, AT LEAST SHE ACKNOWLEDGED ME FOR LIKE HALF A MILLISECOND BECAUSE SHE THOUGHT I MIGHT BE ARIEL.
AND THEN SHE'S LIKE: "I THINK IH'VE SEEN YOU HERE BEFORE, BUT..... BUT YOU'RE SOH DIFFERENT.... MAYBE MY NAME WAS ANNDROUGES BACK THEN TOO...." HEHEH! GOD, ANNDROUGES, OH, AH-HANDROUGES HEHHEH
ANYWAY, SO ANNDROUGES, SHE HAD ON THESE SANDALS WITH GREEN TIGHTS BECAUSE OBVIOUSLY SHE WAS-ANNDROUGES, UM, ANNDROUGES EARLY THAT MORNING! ANYWAY, SO ANNDROUGES LEAVES AND THEN HEH UM, RAD GIRL COMES BY, SHE'S LIKE: "OH! THAT'D BE RAD! IS YOUR NEXT BOOK GONNA BE AS FAT AS THE LAST ONE?" HEH, SHE DID NOT DESERVE-
HI, MS. SALT
UM, IS YOUR FRIEND ROSARY GONNA KILL YOU?
THEY JUST KILL THEMSELVES
BEST
ROSIE... RO... ROSE...
AS SOON AS I GET HAPPY FROM ALCOHOL
WHY? DOES IT SAY SOMETHI—
FRANK IS ALIVE
COMICS ISSUE
INTERVIEWED:
ARIEL SCHRAG
APE
YOU HAVEN'T READ IT?
NO, I HAVEN'T READ IT YET!
SLG
APE

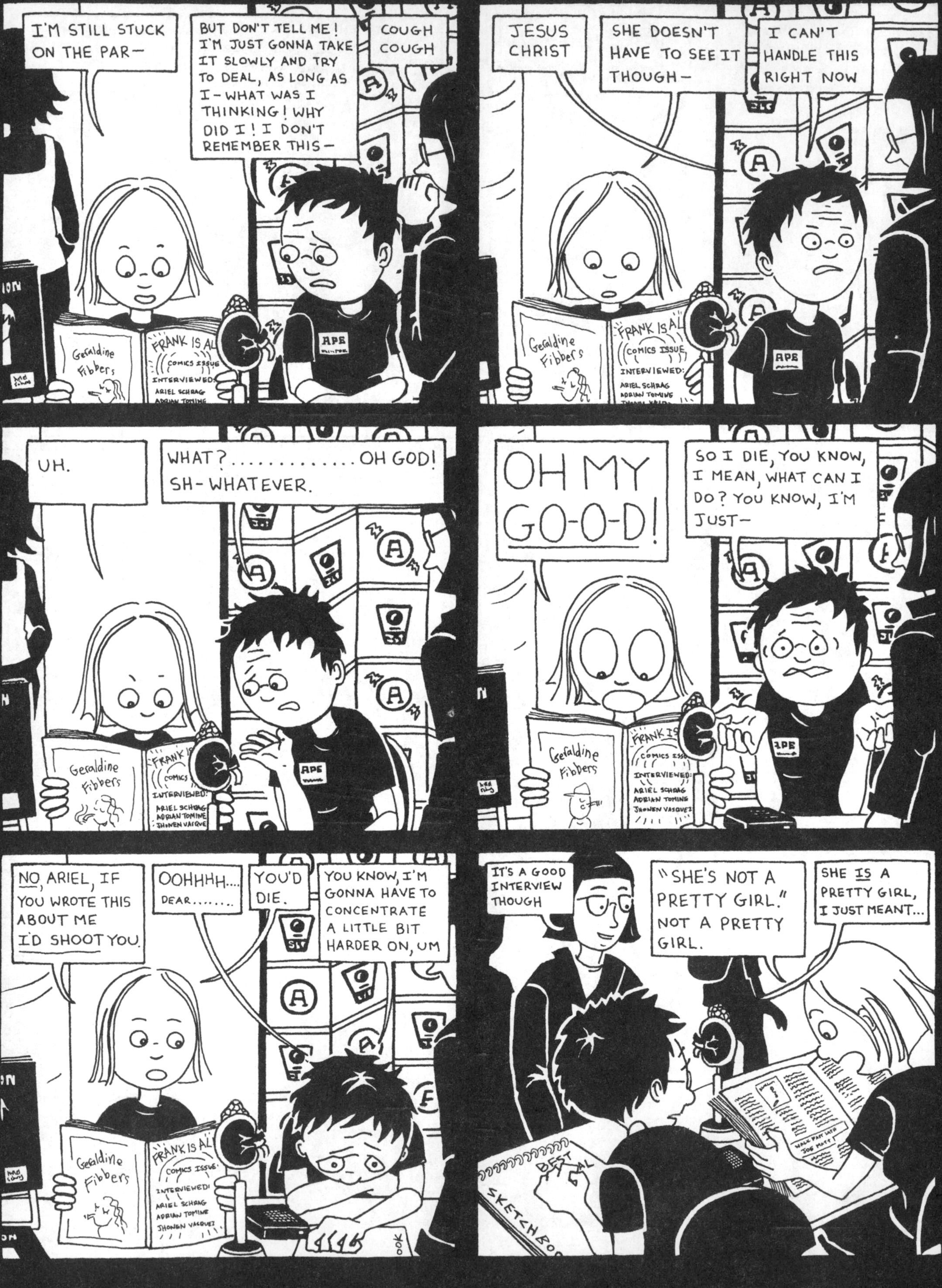
I'M STILL STUCK ON THE PAR—
BUT DON'T TELL ME! I'M JUST GONNA TAKE IT SLOWLY AND TRY TO DEAL, AS LONG AS I— WHAT WAS I THINKING! WHY DID I! I DON'T REMEMBER THIS—
COUGH COUGH
Geraldine Fibbers
FRANK IS AL
COMICS ISSUE
INTERVIEWED:
ARIEL SCHRAG
ADRIAN TOMINE
JESUS CHRIST
SHE DOESN'T HAVE TO SEE IT THOUGH—
I CAN'T HANDLE THIS RIGHT NOW
UH.
WHAT? .... OH GOD! SH- WHATEVER.
OH MY GO-O-D!
SO I DIE, YOU KNOW, I MEAN, WHAT CAN I DO? YOU KNOW, I'M JUST—
JHONEN VASQUEZ
NO, ARIEL, IF YOU WROTE THIS ABOUT ME I'D SHOOT YOU.
OOHHHH.... DEAR........
YOU'D DIE.
YOU KNOW, I'M GONNA HAVE TO CONCENTRATE A LITTLE BIT HARDER ON, UM
IT'S A GOOD INTERVIEW THOUGH
"SHE'S NOT A PRETTY GIRL." NOT A PRETTY GIRL.
SHE IS A PRETTY GIRL, I JUST MEANT...
SKETCHBOO

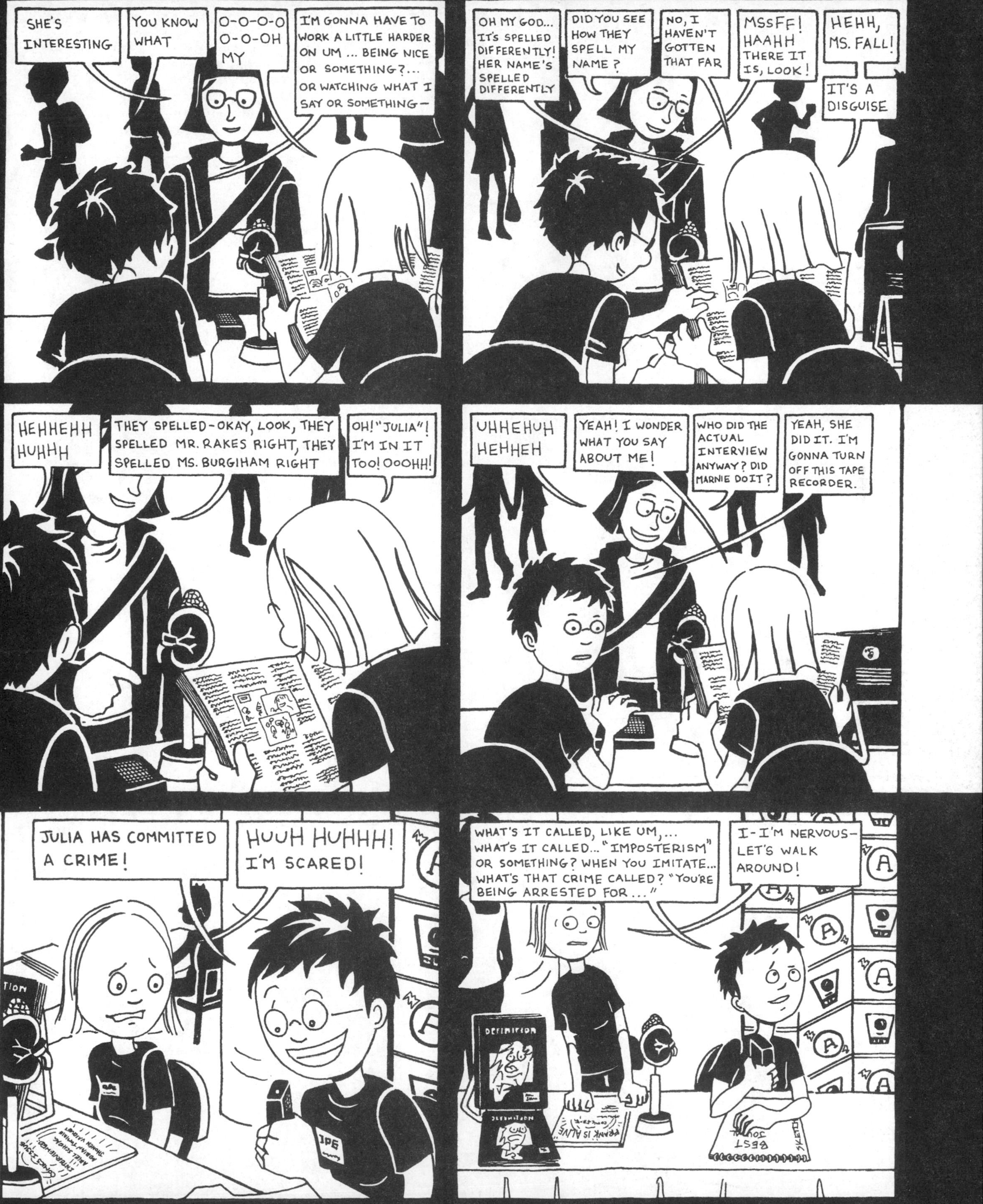
SHE'S INTERESTING
YOU KNOW WHAT
O-O-O-O O-O-OH MY
I'M GONNA HAVE TO WORK A LITTLE HARDER ON UM ... BEING NICE OR SOMETHING?... OR WATCHING WHAT I SAY OR SOMETHING—
OH MY GOD... IT'S SPELLED DIFFERENTLY! HER NAME'S SPELLED DIFFERENTLY
DID YOU SEE HOW THEY SPELL MY NAME?
NO, I HAVEN'T GOTTEN THAT FAR
MSSFF! HAAHH THERE IT IS, LOOK!
HEHH, MS. FALL!
IT'S A DISGUISE
HEHHEHH HUHHH
THEY SPELLED-OKAY, LOOK, THEY SPELLED MR. RAKES RIGHT, THEY SPELLED MS. BURGIHAM RIGHT
OH! "JULIA"! I'M IN IT TOO! OOOHH!
UHHEHUH HEHHEH
YEAH! I WONDER WHAT YOU SAY ABOUT ME!
WHO DID THE ACTUAL INTERVIEW ANYWAY? DID MARNIE DO IT?
YEAH, SHE DID IT. I'M GONNA TURN OFF THIS TAPE RECORDER.
JULIA HAS COMMITTED A CRIME!
HUUH HUHHH! I'M SCARED!
WHAT'S IT CALLED, LIKE UM,... WHAT'S IT CALLED... "IMPOSTERISM" OR SOMETHING? WHEN YOU IMITATE... WHAT'S THAT CRIME CALLED? "YOU'RE BEING ARRESTED FOR..."
I-I'M NERVOUS-LET'S WALK AROUND!

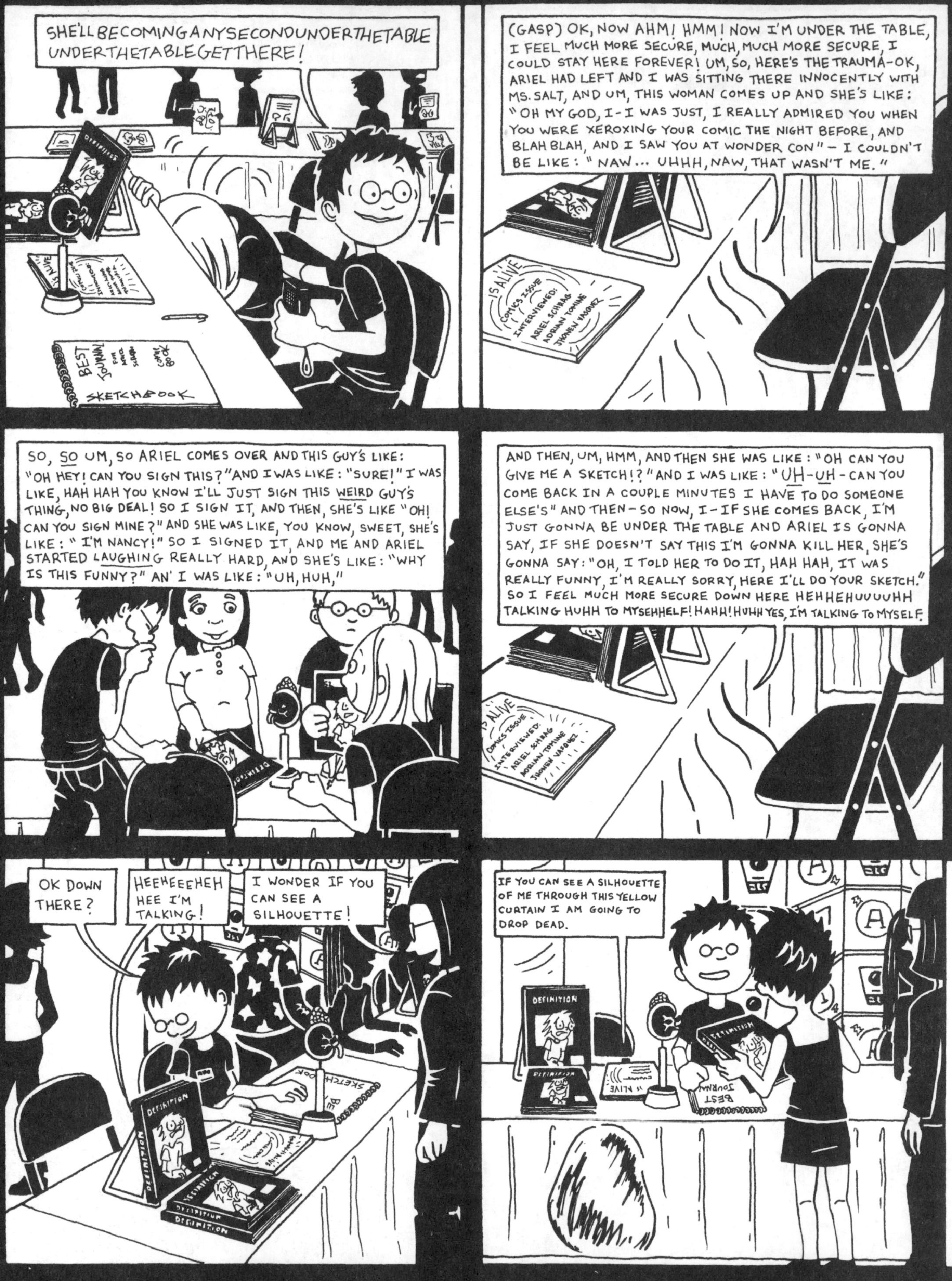
SHE'LLBECOMINGANYSECONDUNDERTHETABLE UNDERTHETABLEGETTHERE!
(GASP) OK, NOW AHM! HMM! NOW I'M UNDER THE TABLE, I FEEL MUCH MORE SECURE, MUCH, MUCH MORE SECURE, I COULD STAY HERE FOREVER! UM, SO, HERE'S THE TRAUMA-OK, ARIEL HAD LEFT AND I WAS SITTING THERE INNOCENTLY WITH MS. SALT, AND UM, THIS WOMAN COMES UP AND SHE'S LIKE: "OH MY GOD, I-I WAS JUST, I REALLY ADMIRED YOU WHEN YOU WERE XEROXING YOUR COMIC THE NIGHT BEFORE, AND BLAH BLAH, AND I SAW YOU AT WONDER CON" — I COULDN'T BE LIKE: "NAW... UHHH, NAW, THAT WASN'T ME."
SO, SO UM, SO ARIEL COMES OVER AND THIS GUY'S LIKE: "OH HEY! CAN YOU SIGN THIS?" AND I WAS LIKE: "SURE!" I WAS LIKE, HAH HAH YOU KNOW I'LL JUST SIGN THIS WEIRD GUY'S THING, NO BIG DEAL! SO I SIGN IT, AND THEN, SHE'S LIKE "OH! CAN YOU SIGN MINE?" AND SHE WAS LIKE, YOU KNOW, SWEET, SHE'S LIKE: "I'M NANCY!" SO I SIGNED IT, AND ME AND ARIEL STARTED LAUGHING REALLY HARD, AND SHE'S LIKE: "WHY IS THIS FUNNY?" AN' I WAS LIKE: "UH, HUH,"
AND THEN, UM, HMM, AND THEN SHE WAS LIKE: "OH CAN YOU GIVE ME A SKETCH!?" AND I WAS LIKE: "UH-UH-CAN YOU COME BACK IN A COUPLE MINUTES I HAVE TO DO SOMEONE ELSE'S" AND THEN—SO NOW, I-IF SHE COMES BACK, I'M JUST GONNA BE UNDER THE TABLE AND ARIEL IS GONNA SAY, IF SHE DOESN'T SAY THIS I'M GONNA KILL HER, SHE'S GONNA SAY: "OH, I TOLD HER TO DO IT, HAH HAH, IT WAS REALLY FUNNY, I'M REALLY SORRY, HERE I'LL DO YOUR SKETCH." SO I FEEL MUCH MORE SECURE DOWN HERE HEHHEHUUUUHH TALKING HUHH TO MYSEHHELF! HAHH! HUHH YES, I'M TALKING TO MYSELF.
OK DOWN THERE?
HEEHEEEHEH HEE I'M TALKING!
I WONDER IF YOU CAN SEE A SILHOUETTE!
IF YOU CAN SEE A SILHOUETTE OF ME THROUGH THIS YELLOW CURTAIN I AM GOING TO DROP DEAD.

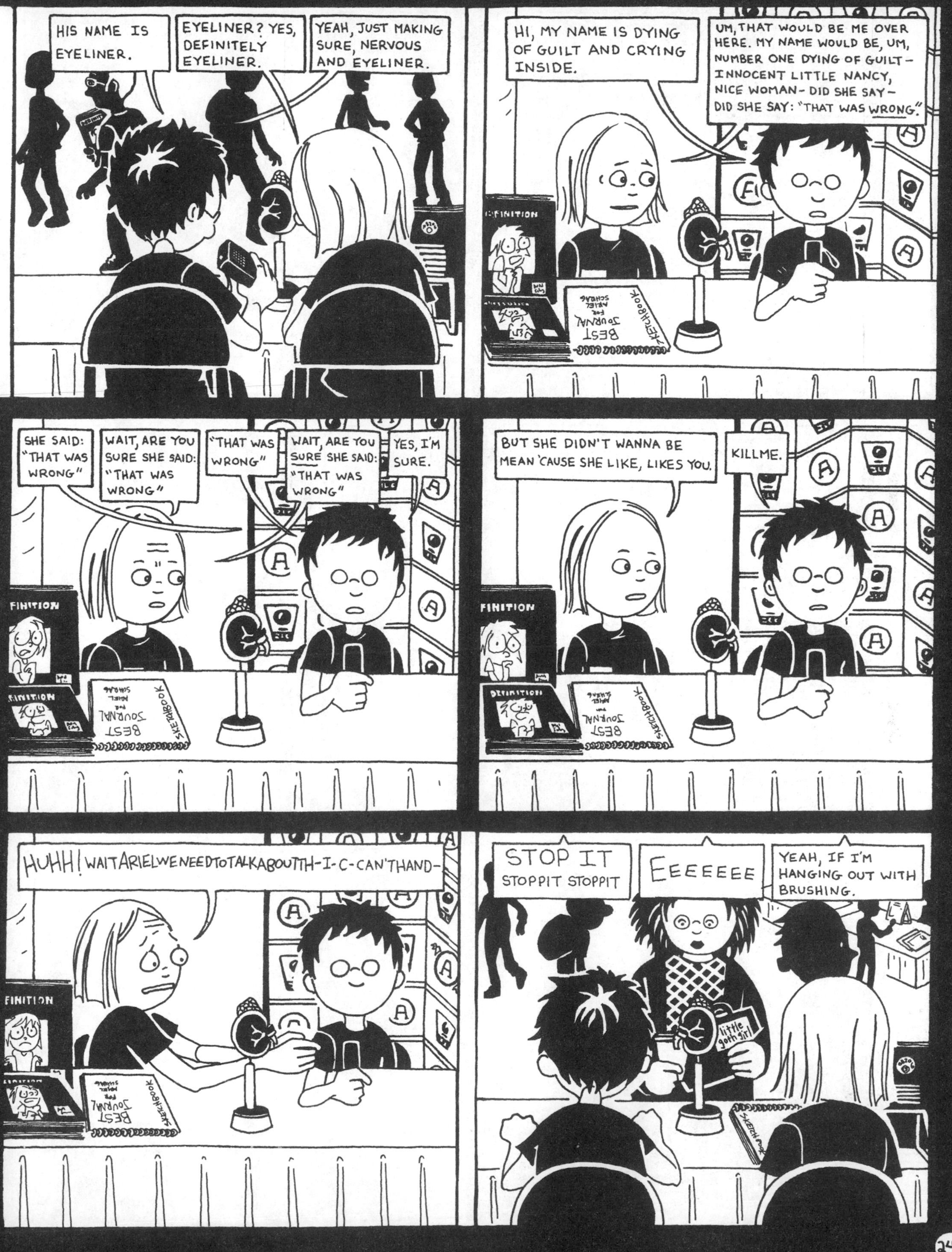

HIS NAME IS EYELINER.
EYELINER? YES, DEFINITELY EYELINER.
YEAH, JUST MAKING SURE, NERVOUS AND EYELINER.
HI, MY NAME IS DYING OF GUILT AND CRYING INSIDE.
UM, THAT WOULD BE ME OVER HERE. MY NAME WOULD BE, UM, NUMBER ONE DYING OF GUILT- INNOCENT LITTLE NANCY, NICE WOMAN- DID SHE SAY- DID SHE SAY: "THAT WAS WRONG."
BEST JOURNAL FOR ARIEL SCHRAG SKETCHBOOK
SHE SAID: "THAT WAS WRONG"
WAIT, ARE YOU SURE SHE SAID: "THAT WAS WRONG"
"THAT WAS WRONG"
WAIT, ARE YOU SURE SHE SAID: "THAT WAS WRONG"
YES, I'M SURE.
BUT SHE DIDN'T WANNA BE MEAN 'CAUSE SHE LIKE, LIKES YOU.
KILLME.
HUHH! WAITARIELWENEEDTOTALKABOUTTH-I-C-CAN'THAND-
STOP IT STOPPIT STOPPIT
EEEEEEE
YEAH, IF I'M HANGING OUT WITH BRUSHING.
little goth girl
SKETCHBOOK

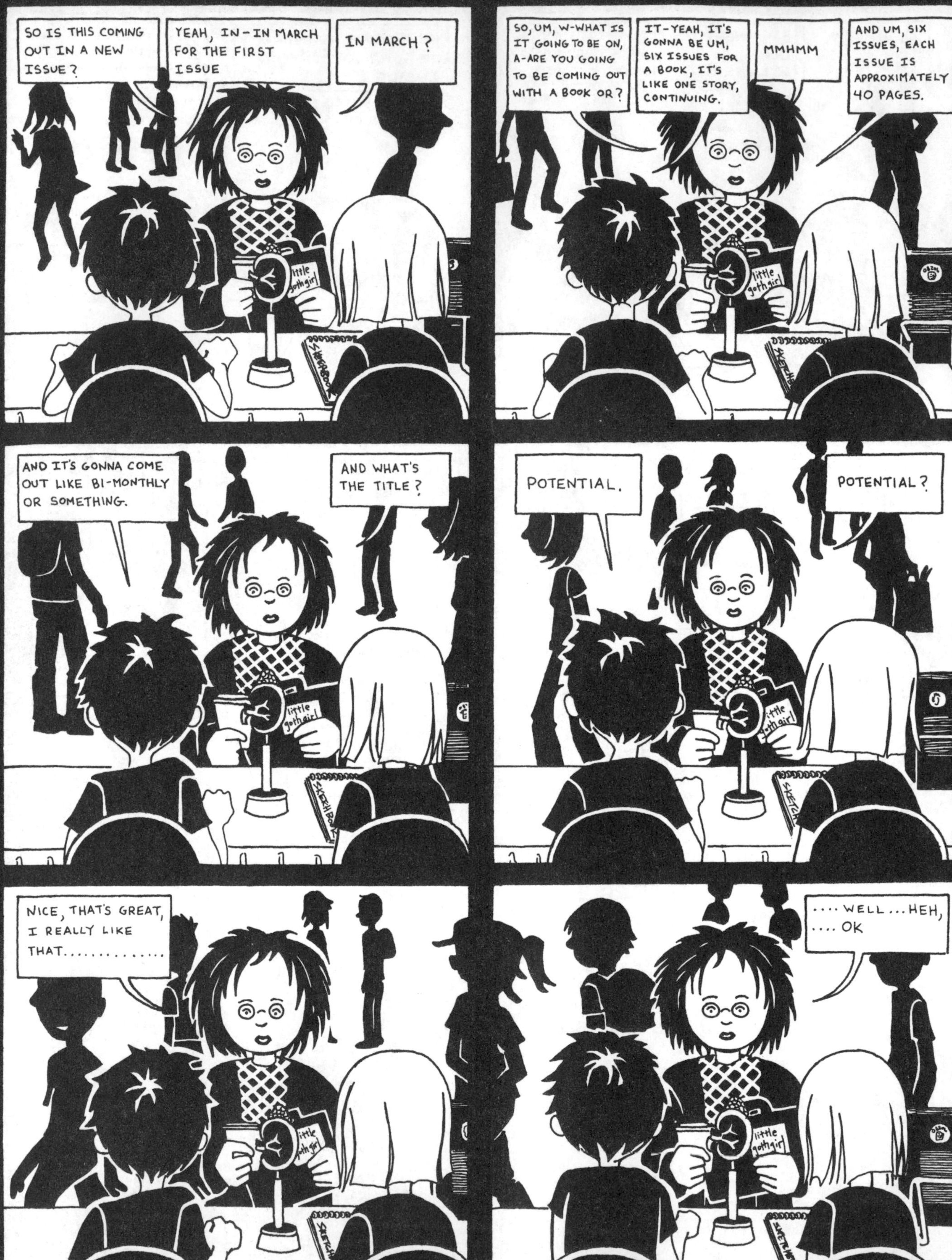
SO IS THIS COMING OUT IN A NEW ISSUE?
YEAH, IN-IN MARCH FOR THE FIRST ISSUE
IN MARCH?
little goth girl
SO, UM, W-WHAT IS IT GOING TO BE ON, A-ARE YOU GOING TO BE COMING OUT WITH A BOOK OR?
IT-YEAH, IT'S GONNA BE UM, SIX ISSUES FOR A BOOK, IT'S LIKE ONE STORY, CONTINUING.
MMHMM
AND UM, SIX ISSUES, EACH ISSUE IS APPROXIMATELY 40 PAGES.
AND IT'S GONNA COME OUT LIKE BI-MONTHLY OR SOMETHING.
AND WHAT'S THE TITLE?
POTENTIAL.
POTENTIAL?
NICE, THAT'S GREAT, I REALLY LIKE THAT..............
....WELL...HEH, ...OK

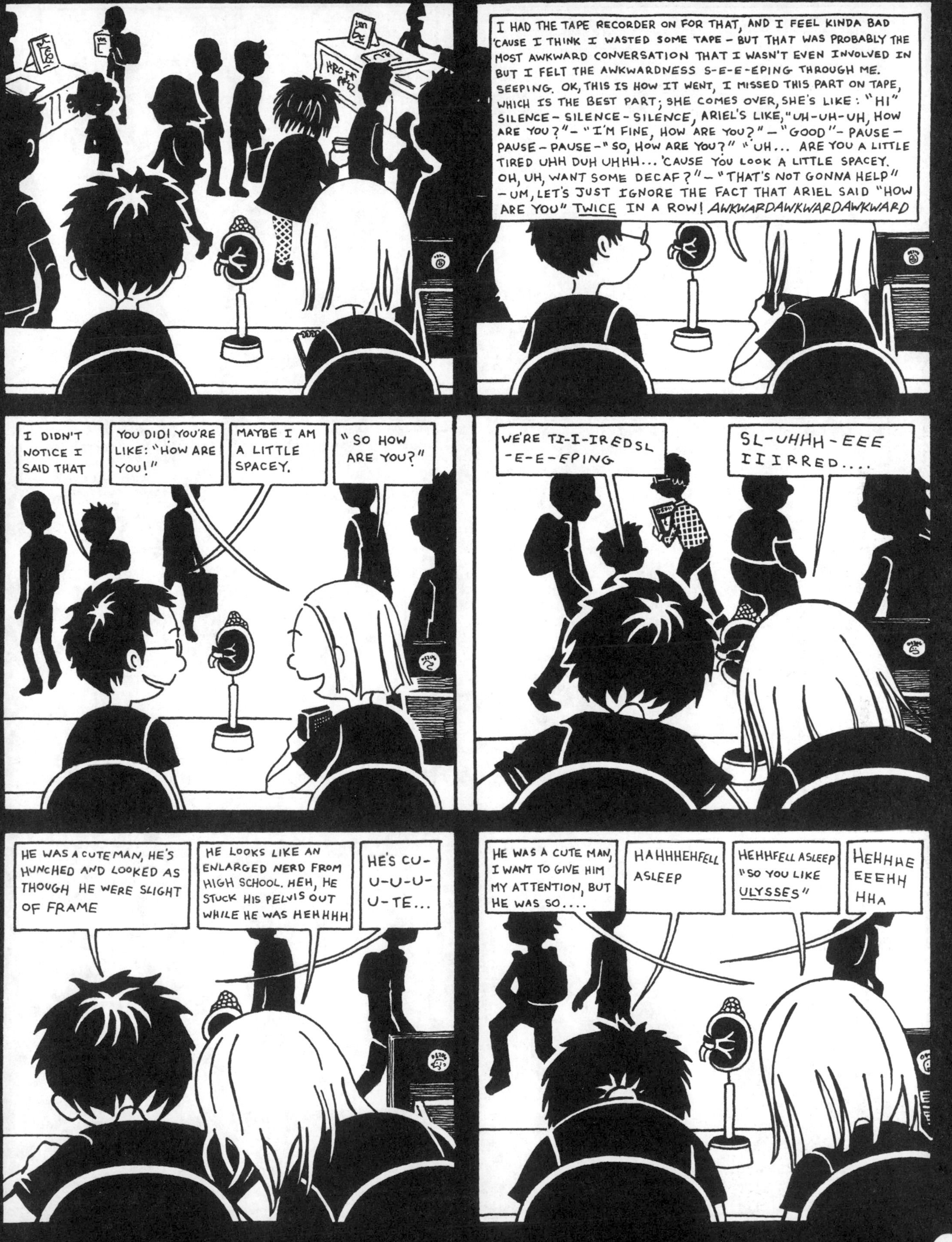
I HAD THE TAPE RECORDER ON FOR THAT, AND I FEEL KINDA BAD 'CAUSE I THINK I WASTED SOME TAPE - BUT THAT WAS PROBABLY THE MOST AWKWARD CONVERSATION THAT I WASN'T EVEN INVOLVED IN BUT I FELT THE AWKWARDNESS S-E-E-EPING THROUGH ME. SEEPING. OK, THIS IS HOW IT WENT, I MISSED THIS PART ON TAPE, WHICH IS THE BEST PART; SHE COMES OVER, SHE'S LIKE: "HI" SILENCE - SILENCE - SILENCE, ARIEL'S LIKE, "UH-UH-UH, HOW ARE YOU?" - "I'M FINE, HOW ARE YOU?" - "GOOD" - PAUSE - PAUSE - PAUSE - "SO, HOW ARE YOU?" "UH... ARE YOU A LITTLE TIRED UHH DUH UHHH... 'CAUSE YOU LOOK A LITTLE SPACEY. OH, UH, WANT SOME DECAF?" - "THAT'S NOT GONNA HELP" - UM, LET'S JUST IGNORE THE FACT THAT ARIEL SAID "HOW ARE YOU" TWICE IN A ROW! AWKWARDAWKWARDAWKWARD
I DIDN'T NOTICE I SAID THAT
YOU DID! YOU'RE LIKE: "HOW ARE YOU!"
MAYBE I AM A LITTLE SPACEY.
"SO HOW ARE YOU?"
WE'RE TI-I-IREDSL-E-E-EPING
SL-UHHH-EEE IIIRRED....
HE WAS A CUTE MAN, HE'S HUNCHED AND LOOKED AS THOUGH HE WERE SLIGHT OF FRAME
HE LOOKS LIKE AN ENLARGED NERD FROM HIGH SCHOOL. HEH, HE STUCK HIS PELVIS OUT WHILE HE WAS HEHHHH
HE'S CU-U-U-U-U-TE...
HE WAS A CUTE MAN, I WANT TO GIVE HIM MY ATTENTION, BUT HE WAS SO....
HAHHHHEHFELL ASLEEP
HEHHFELL ASLEEP "SO YOU LIKE ULYSSES"
HEHHHE EEEHH HHA

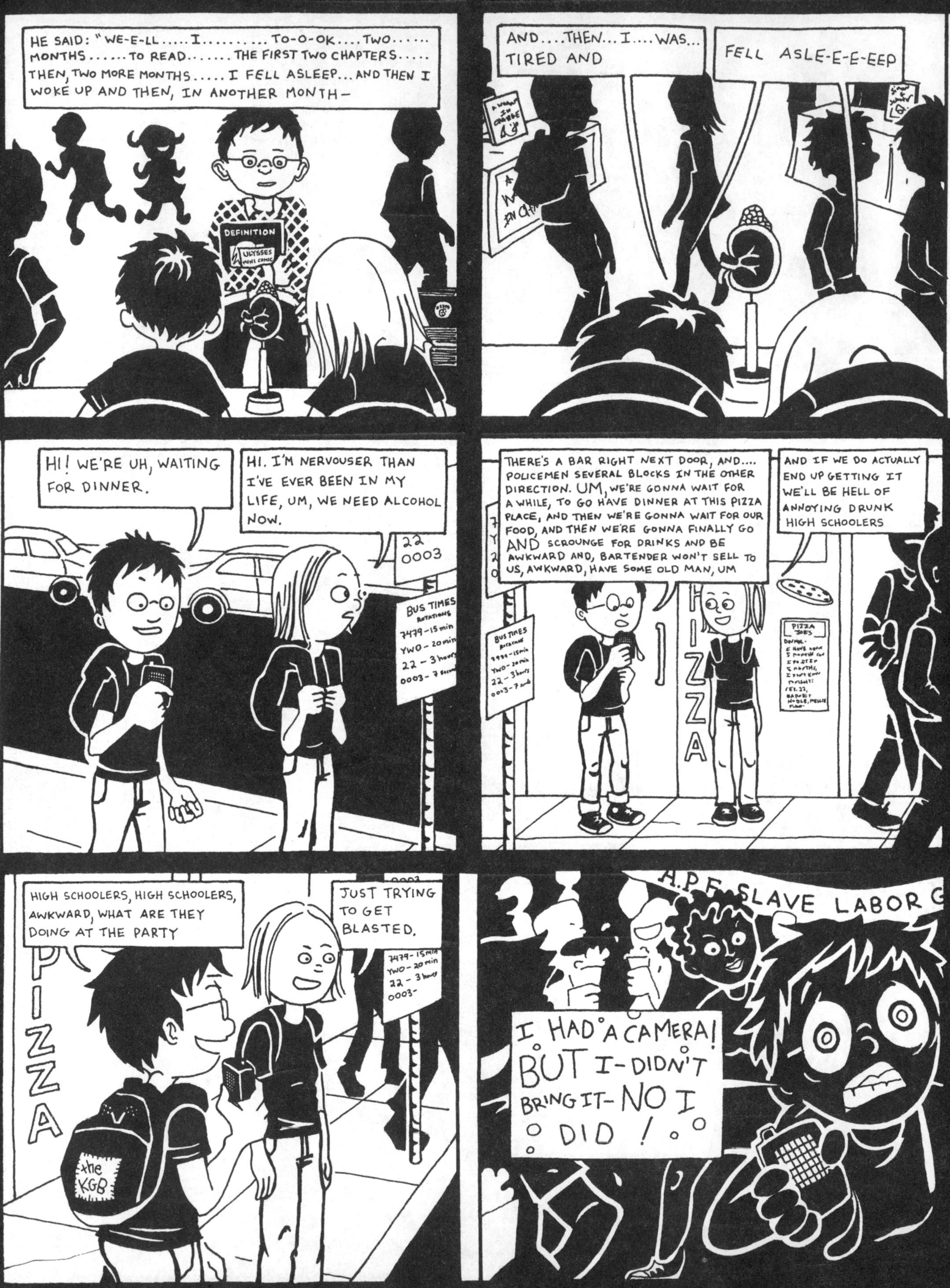
HE SAID: "WE-E-LL..... I.......... TO-O-OK.... TWO...... MONTHS...... TO READ....... THE FIRST TWO CHAPTERS..... THEN, TWO MORE MONTHS..... I FELL ASLEEP... AND THEN I WOKE UP AND THEN, IN ANOTHER MONTH—
DEFINITION
ULYSSES MINI COMIC
AND.... THEN... I.... WAS... TIRED AND
FELL ASLE-E-E-EEP
HI! WE'RE UH, WAITING FOR DINNER.
HI. I'M NERVOUSER THAN I'VE EVER BEEN IN MY LIFE, UM, WE NEED ALCOHOL NOW.
22
0003
BUS TIMES
THERE'S A BAR RIGHT NEXT DOOR, AND.... POLICEMEN SEVERAL BLOCKS IN THE OTHER DIRECTION. UM, WE'RE GONNA WAIT FOR A WHILE, TO GO HAVE DINNER AT THIS PIZZA PLACE, AND THEN WE'RE GONNA WAIT FOR OUR FOOD, AND THEN WE'RE GONNA FINALLY GO AND SCROUNGE FOR DRINKS AND BE AWKWARD AND, BARTENDER WON'T SELL TO US, AWKWARD, HAVE SOME OLD MAN, UM
AND IF WE DO ACTUALLY END UP GETTING IT WE'LL BE HELL OF ANNOYING DRUNK HIGH SCHOOLERS
PIZZA
HIGH SCHOOLERS, HIGH SCHOOLERS, AWKWARD, WHAT ARE THEY DOING AT THE PARTY
JUST TRYING TO GET BLASTED.
PIZZA
the KGB
A.P.F. SLAVE LABOR G
I HAD A CAMERA! BUT I-DIDN'T BRING IT- NO I DID!

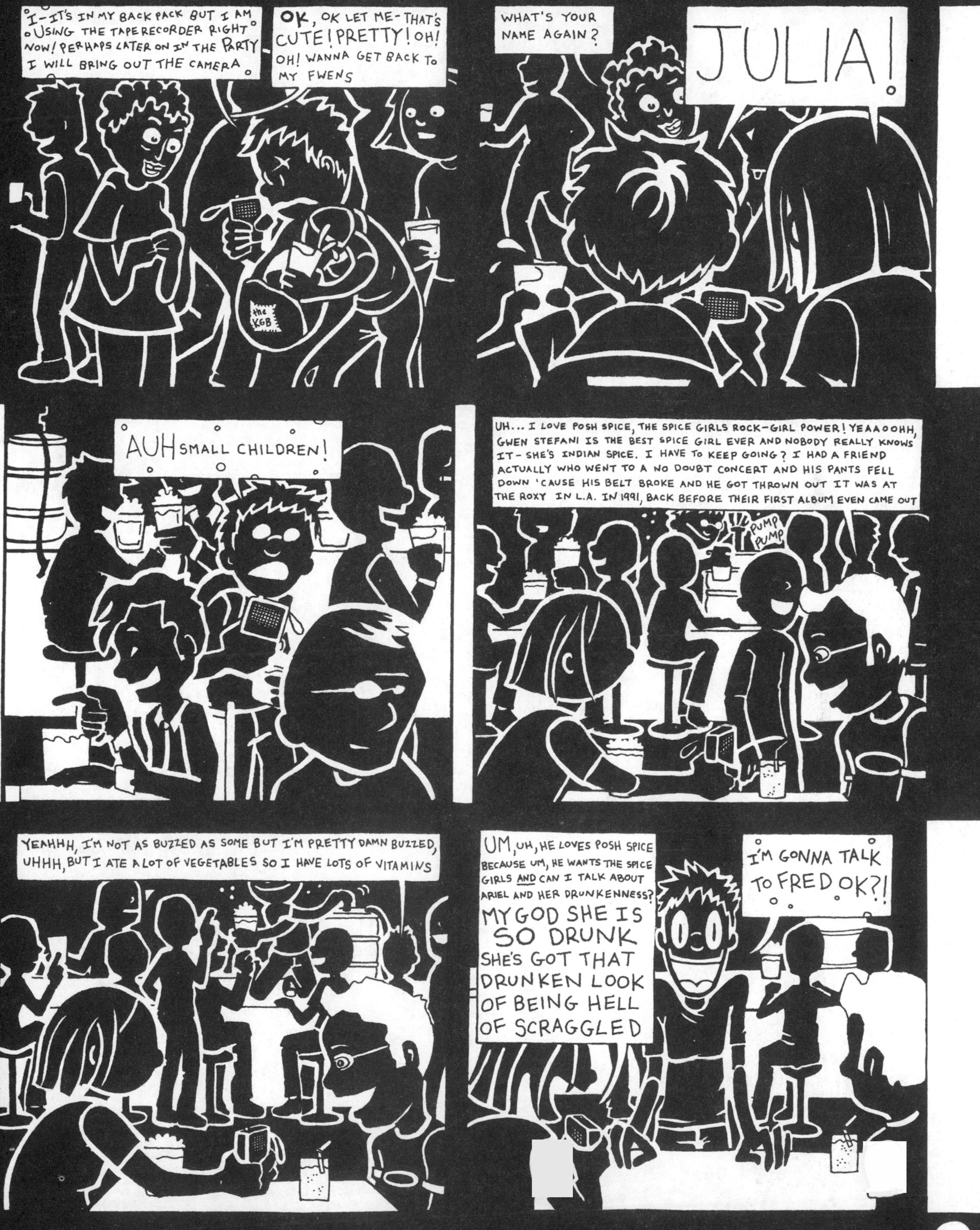
I-IT'S IN MY BACKPACK BUT I AM USING THE TAPE RECORDER RIGHT NOW! PERHAPS LATER ON IN THE PARTY I WILL BRING OUT THE CAMERA
OK, OK LET ME- THAT'S CUTE! PRETTY! OH! OH! WANNA GET BACK TO MY FWENS
the KGB
WHAT'S YOUR NAME AGAIN?
JULIA!
AUH SMALL CHILDREN!
UH... I LOVE POSH SPICE, THE SPICE GIRLS ROCK-GIRL POWER! YEAAOOHH, GWEN STEFANI IS THE BEST SPICE GIRL EVER AND NOBODY REALLY KNOWS IT- SHE'S INDIAN SPICE. I HAVE TO KEEP GOING? I HAD A FRIEND ACTUALLY WHO WENT TO A NO DOUBT CONCERT AND HIS PANTS FELL DOWN 'CAUSE HIS BELT BROKE AND HE GOT THROWN OUT IT WAS AT THE ROXY IN L.A. IN 1991, BACK BEFORE THEIR FIRST ALBUM EVEN CAME OUT
PUMP PUMP
YEAHHH, I'M NOT AS BUZZED AS SOME BUT I'M PRETTY DAMN BUZZED, UHHH, BUT I ATE A LOT OF VEGETABLES SO I HAVE LOTS OF VITAMINS
UM, UH, HE LOVES POSH SPICE BECAUSE UM, HE WANTS THE SPICE GIRLS AND CAN I TALK ABOUT ARIEL AND HER DRUNKENNESS?
MY GOD SHE IS SO DRUNK SHE'S GOT THAT DRUNKEN LOOK OF BEING HELL OF SCRAGGLED
I'M GONNA TALK TO FRED OK?!

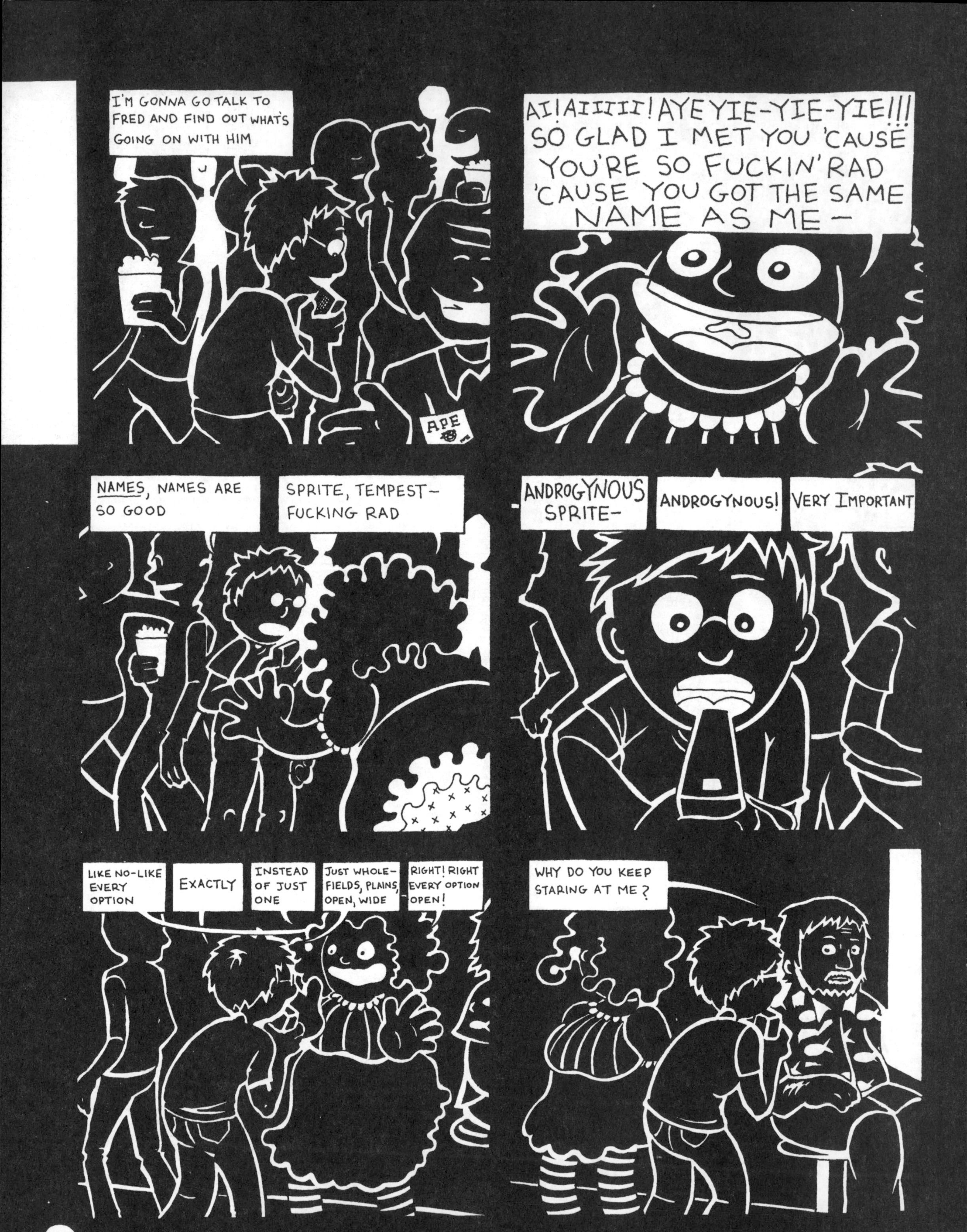
I'M GONNA GO TALK TO FRED AND FIND OUT WHAT'S GOING ON WITH HIM
APE
AI!AIIIII! AYE YIE-YIE-YIE!!! SO GLAD I MET YOU 'CAUSE YOU'RE SO FUCKIN' RAD 'CAUSE YOU GOT THE SAME NAME AS ME-
NAMES, NAMES ARE SO GOOD
SPRITE, TEMPEST-FUCKING RAD
ANDROGYNOUS SPRITE-
ANDROGYNOUS!
VERY IMPORTANT
LIKE NO-LIKE EVERY OPTION
EXACTLY
INSTEAD OF JUST ONE
JUST WHOLE-FIELDS, PLAINS, OPEN, WIDE
RIGHT! RIGHT EVERY OPTION OPEN!
WHY DO YOU KEEP STARING AT ME?

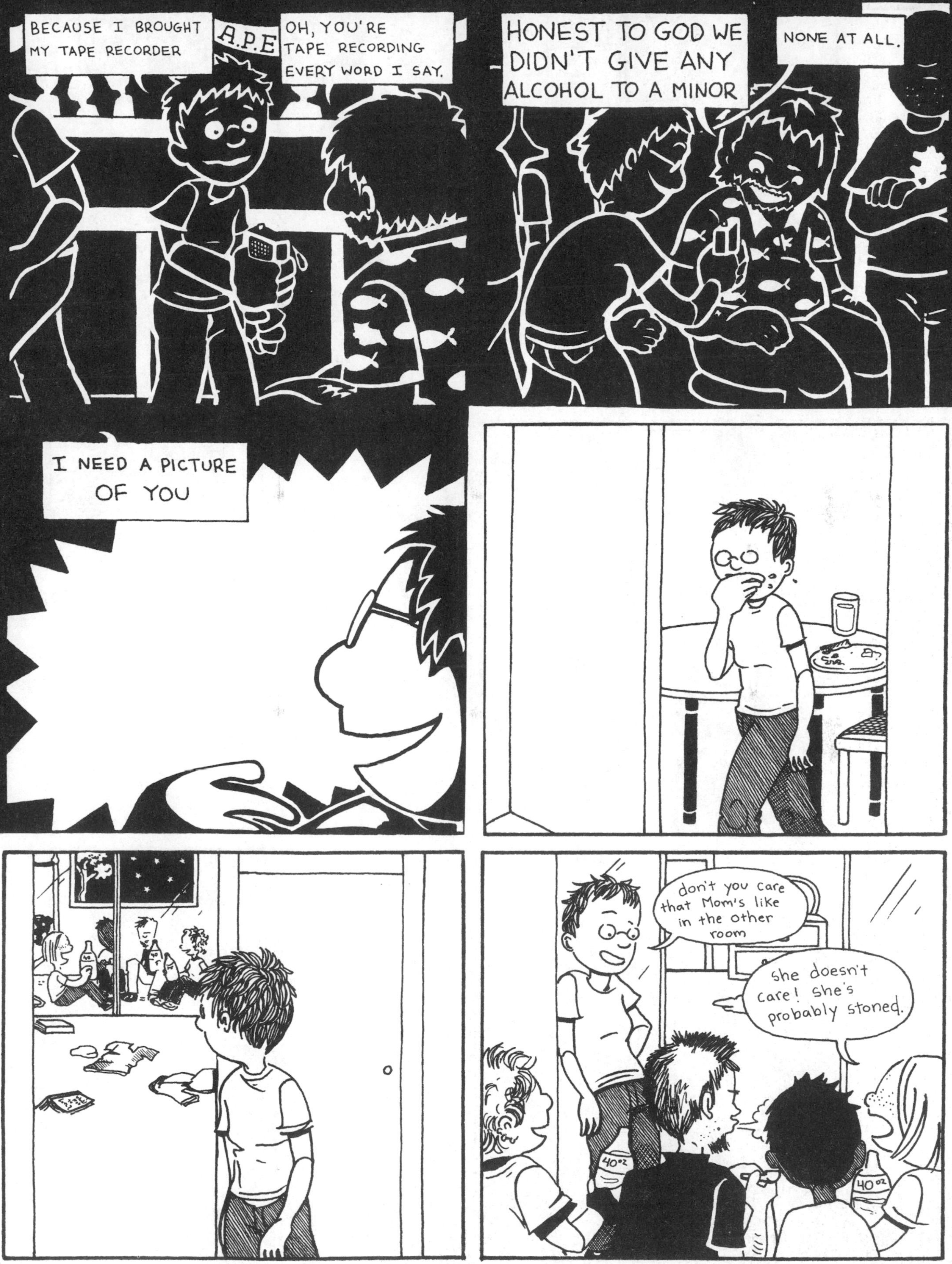
BECAUSE I BROUGHT MY TAPE RECORDER
A.P.E
OH, YOU'RE TAPE RECORDING EVERY WORD I SAY.
HONEST TO GOD WE DIDN'T GIVE ANY ALCOHOL TO A MINOR
NONE AT ALL.
I NEED A PICTURE OF YOU
don't you care that Mom's like in the other room
she doesn't care! she's probably stoned.
40oz
40oz

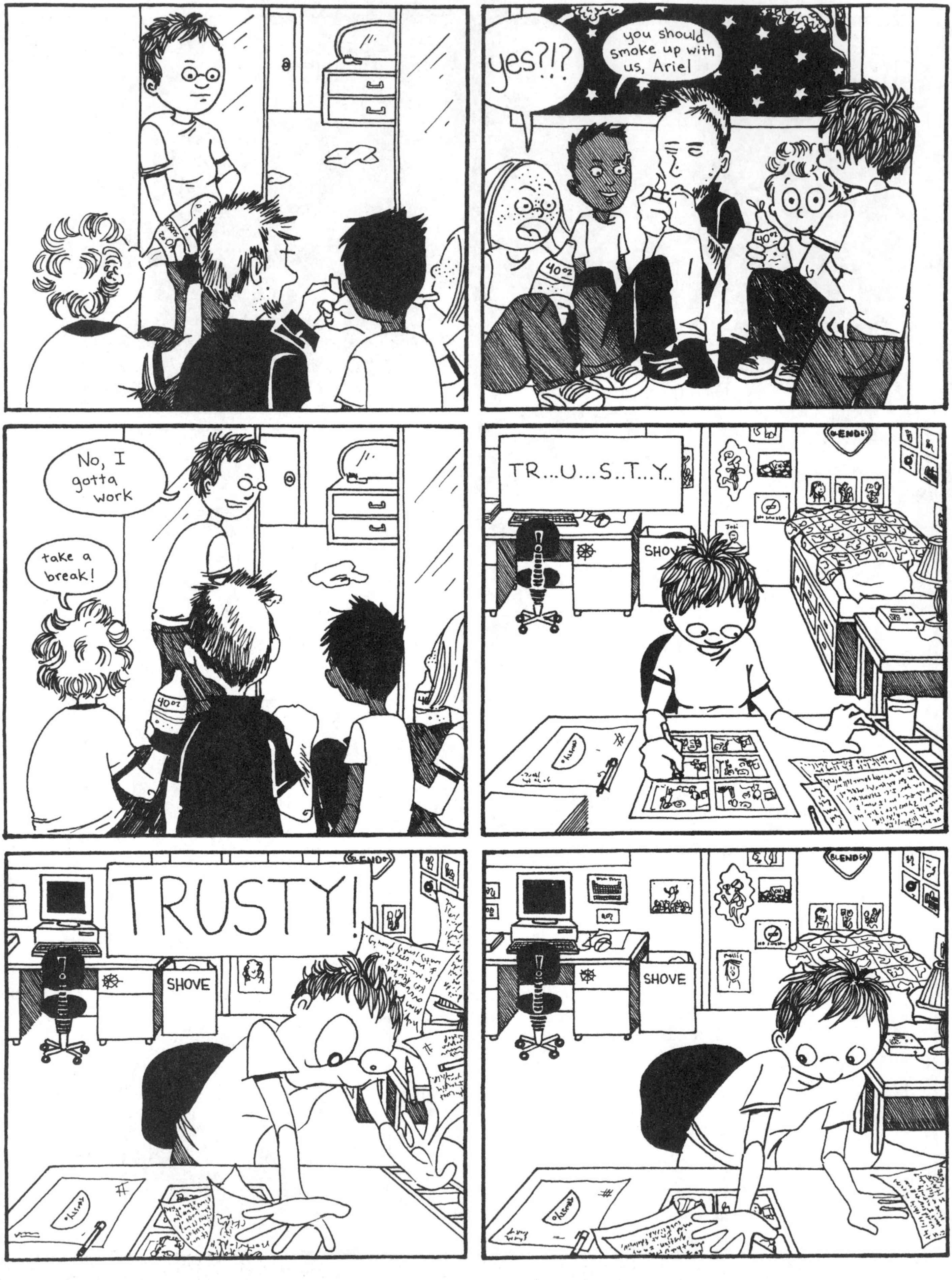
yes?!?
you should smoke up with us, Ariel
No, I gotta work
take a break!
TR...U...S..T...Y..
SHOVE
TRUSTY!
SHOVE
SHOVE

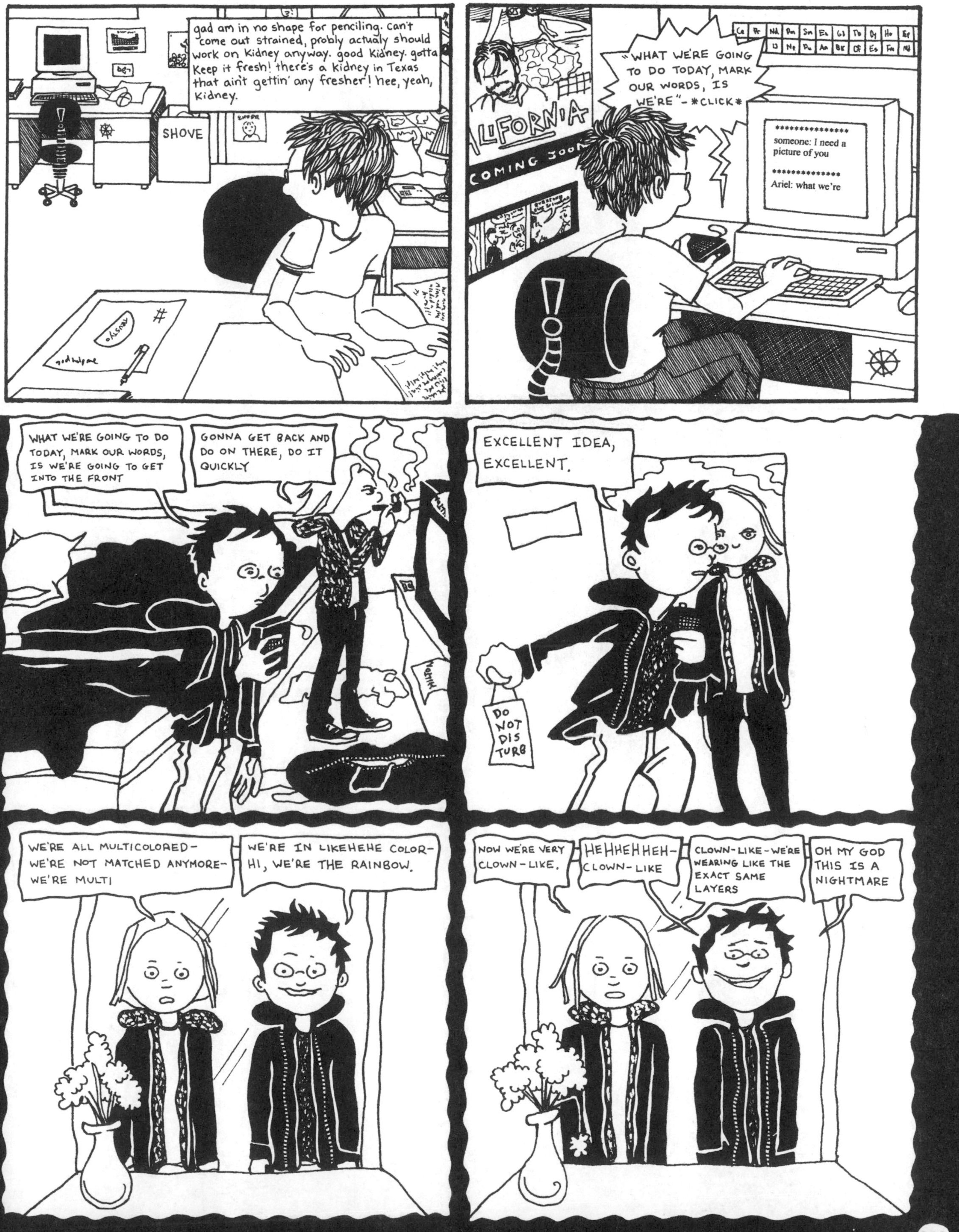

gad am in no shape for penciling. can't come out strained, probly actualy should work on Kidney anyway. good Kidney. gotta Keep it fresh! there's a kidney in Texas that ain't gettin' any fresher! hee, yeah, Kidney.
SHOVE
"WHAT WE'RE GOING TO DO TODAY, MARK OUR WORDS, IS WE'RE"- *CLICK*
someone: I need a picture of you
Ariel: what we're
CALIFORNIA
COMING SOON
WHAT WE'RE GOING TO DO TODAY, MARK OUR WORDS, IS WE'RE GOING TO GET INTO THE FRONT
GONNA GET BACK AND DO ON THERE, DO IT QUICKLY
EXCELLENT IDEA, EXCELLENT.
DO NOT DIS TURB
WE'RE ALL MULTICOLORED- WE'RE NOT MATCHED ANYMORE- WE'RE MULTI
WE'RE IN LIKEHEHE COLOR- HI, WE'RE THE RAINBOW.
NOW WE'RE VERY CLOWN-LIKE.
HEHHEHHEH- CLOWN-LIKE
CLOWN-LIKE-WE'RE WEARING LIKE THE EXACT SAME LAYERS
OH MY GOD THIS IS A NIGHTMARE

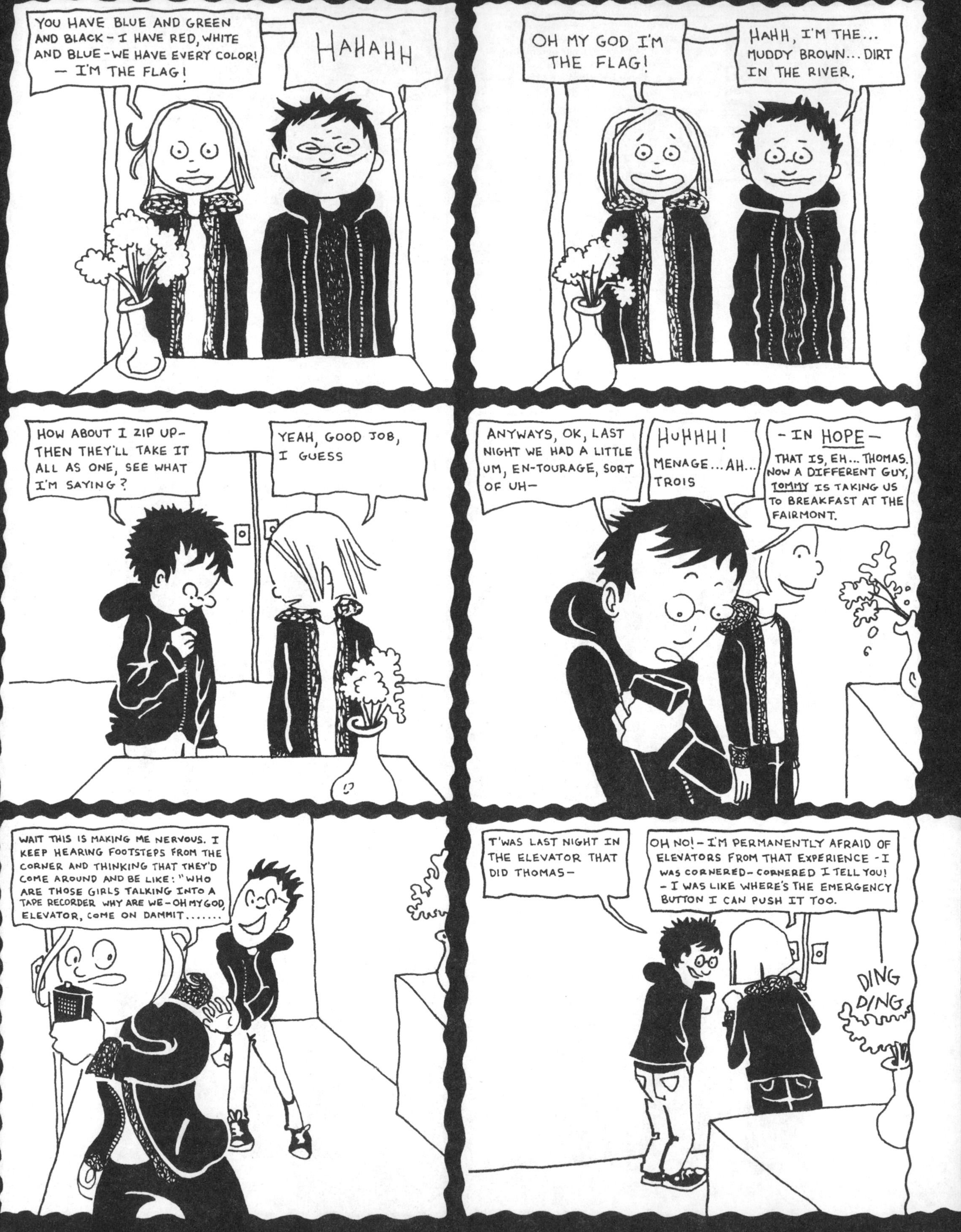
YOU HAVE BLUE AND GREEN AND BLACK - I HAVE RED, WHITE AND BLUE - WE HAVE EVERY COLOR! — I'M THE FLAG!
HAHAHH
OH MY GOD I'M THE FLAG!
HAHH, I'M THE... MUDDY BROWN... DIRT IN THE RIVER.
HOW ABOUT I ZIP UP- THEN THEY'LL TAKE IT ALL AS ONE, SEE WHAT I'M SAYING?
YEAH, GOOD JOB, I GUESS
ANYWAYS, OK, LAST NIGHT WE HAD A LITTLE UM, EN-TOURAGE, SORT OF UH-
HUHHH! MENAGE... AH... TROIS
- IN HOPE - THAT IS, EH... THOMAS. NOW A DIFFERENT GUY, TOMMY IS TAKING US TO BREAKFAST AT THE FAIRMONT.
WAIT THIS IS MAKING ME NERVOUS. I KEEP HEARING FOOTSTEPS FROM THE CORNER AND THINKING THAT THEY'D COME AROUND AND BE LIKE: "WHO ARE THOSE GIRLS TALKING INTO A TAPE RECORDER WHY ARE WE - OH MY GOD, ELEVATOR, COME ON DAMMIT.......
T'WAS LAST NIGHT IN THE ELEVATOR THAT DID THOMAS-
OH NO! - I'M PERMANENTLY AFRAID OF ELEVATORS FROM THAT EXPERIENCE - I WAS CORNERED - CORNERED I TELL YOU! - I WAS LIKE WHERE'S THE EMERGENCY BUTTON I CAN PUSH IT TOO.
DING DING

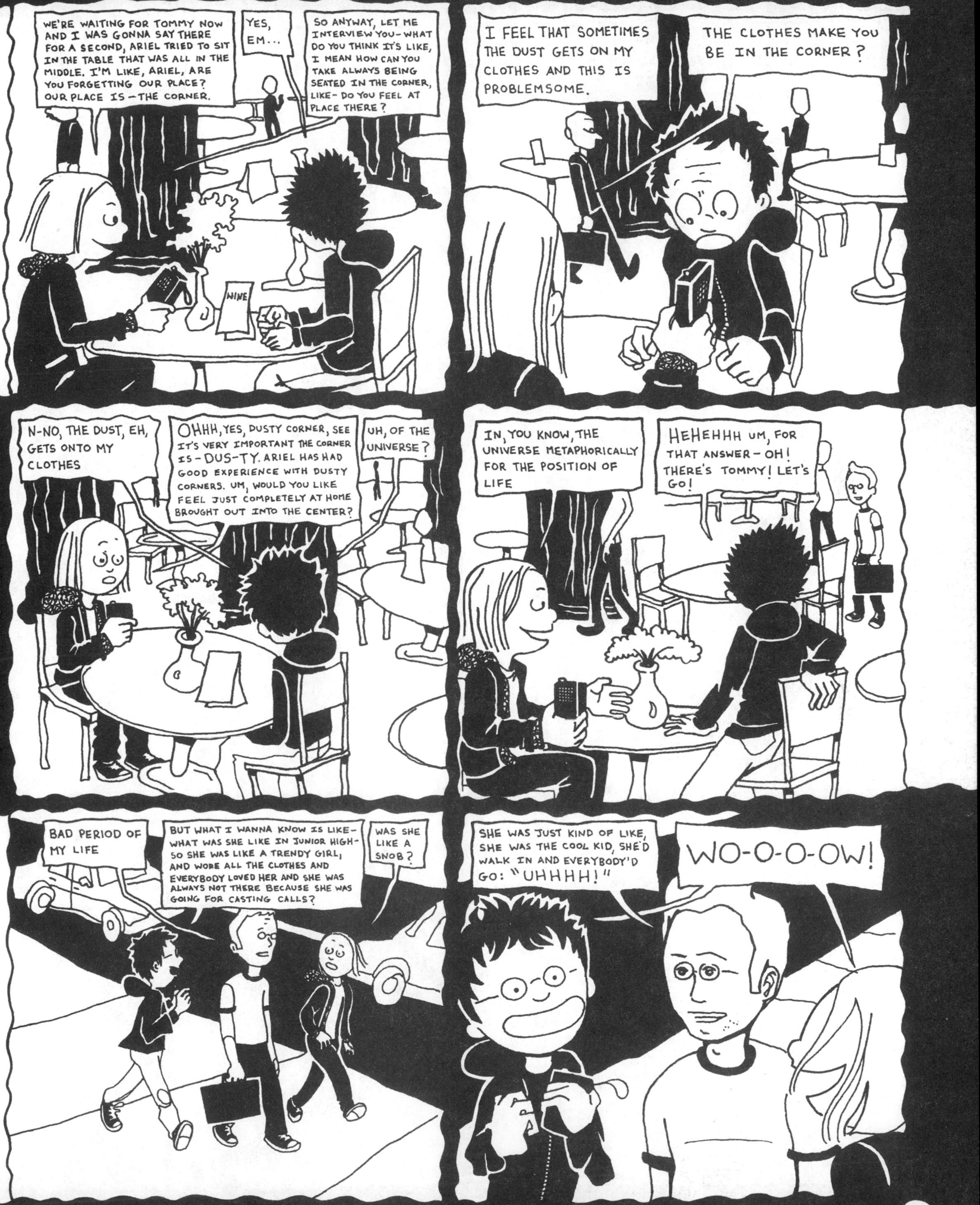
WE'RE WAITING FOR TOMMY NOW AND I WAS GONNA SAY THERE FOR A SECOND, ARIEL TRIED TO SIT IN THE TABLE THAT WAS ALL IN THE MIDDLE. I'M LIKE, ARIEL, ARE YOU FORGETTING OUR PLACE? OUR PLACE IS — THE CORNER.
YES, EM...
SO ANYWAY, LET ME INTERVIEW YOU - WHAT DO YOU THINK IT'S LIKE, I MEAN HOW CAN YOU TAKE ALWAYS BEING SEATED IN THE CORNER, LIKE- DO YOU FEEL AT PLACE THERE?
WINE
I FEEL THAT SOMETIMES THE DUST GETS ON MY CLOTHES AND THIS IS PROBLEMSOME.
THE CLOTHES MAKE YOU BE IN THE CORNER?
N-NO, THE DUST, EH, GETS ONTO MY CLOTHES
OHHH, YES, DUSTY CORNER, SEE IT'S VERY IMPORTANT THE CORNER IS - DUS-TY. ARIEL HAS HAD GOOD EXPERIENCE WITH DUSTY CORNERS. UM, WOULD YOU LIKE FEEL JUST COMPLETELY AT HOME BROUGHT OUT INTO THE CENTER?
UH, OF THE UNIVERSE?
IN, YOU KNOW, THE UNIVERSE METAPHORICALLY FOR THE POSITION OF LIFE
HEHEHHH UM, FOR THAT ANSWER - OH! THERE'S TOMMY! LET'S GO!
BAD PERIOD OF MY LIFE
BUT WHAT I WANNA KNOW IS LIKE- WHAT WAS SHE LIKE IN JUNIOR HIGH- SO SHE WAS LIKE A TRENDY GIRL, AND WORE ALL THE CLOTHES AND EVERYBODY LOVED HER AND SHE WAS ALWAYS NOT THERE BECAUSE SHE WAS GOING FOR CASTING CALLS?
WAS SHE LIKE A SNOB?
SHE WAS JUST KIND OF LIKE, SHE WAS THE COOL KID, SHE'D WALK IN AND EVERYBODY'D GO: "UHHHH!"
WO-O-O-OW!

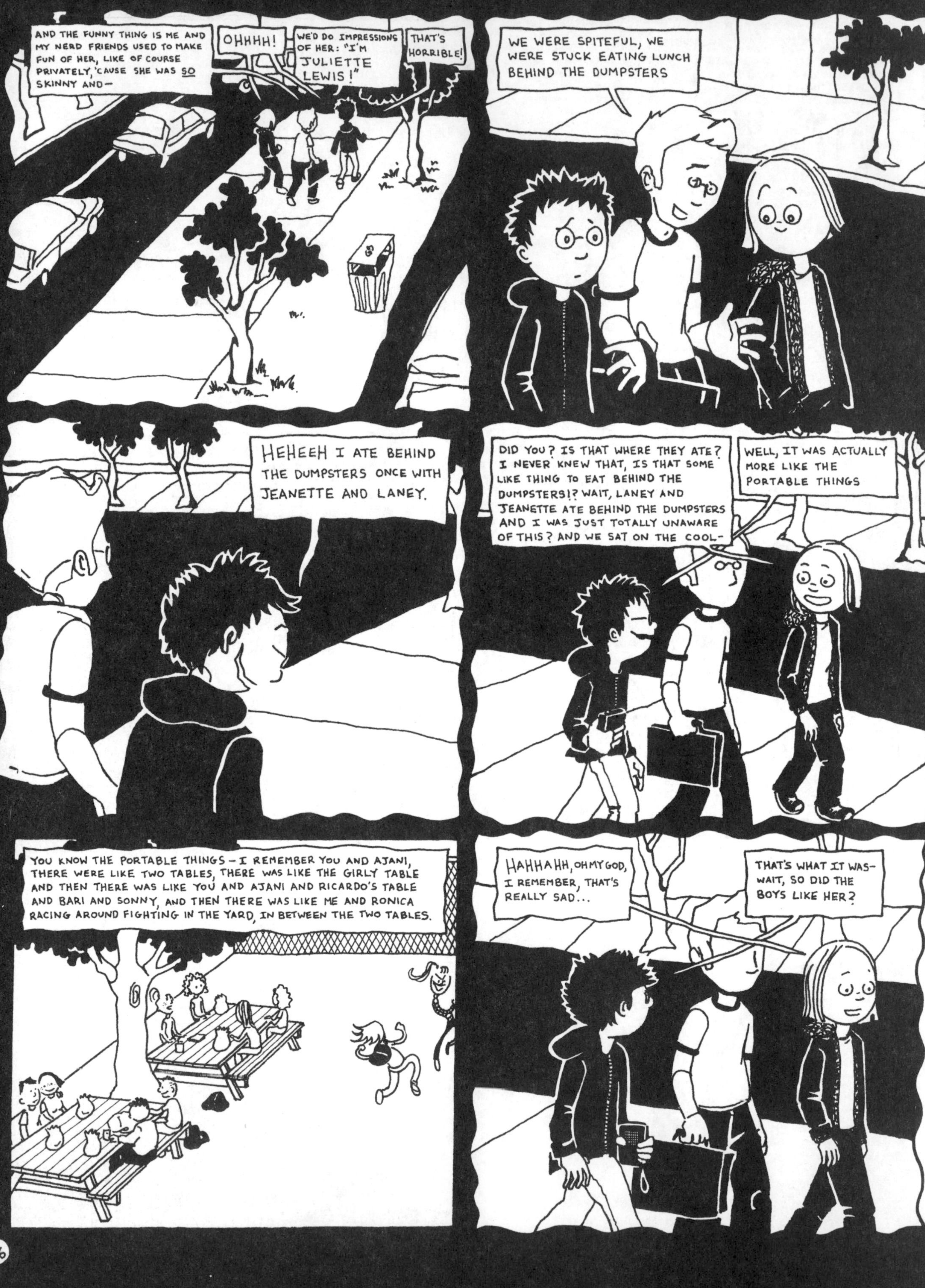

AND THE FUNNY THING IS ME AND MY NERD FRIENDS USED TO MAKE FUN OF HER, LIKE OF COURSE PRIVATELY, 'CAUSE SHE WAS SO SKINNY AND—
OHHHH!
WE'D DO IMPRESSIONS OF HER: "I'M JULIETTE LEWIS!"
THAT'S HORRIBLE!
WE WERE SPITEFUL, WE WERE STUCK EATING LUNCH BEHIND THE DUMPSTERS
HEHEEH I ATE BEHIND THE DUMPSTERS ONCE WITH JEANETTE AND LANEY.
DID YOU? IS THAT WHERE THEY ATE? I NEVER KNEW THAT, IS THAT SOME LIKE THING TO EAT BEHIND THE DUMPSTERS!? WAIT, LANEY AND JEANETTE ATE BEHIND THE DUMPSTERS AND I WAS JUST TOTALLY UNAWARE OF THIS? AND WE SAT ON THE COOL-
WELL, IT WAS ACTUALLY MORE LIKE THE PORTABLE THINGS
YOU KNOW THE PORTABLE THINGS — I REMEMBER YOU AND AJANI, THERE WERE LIKE TWO TABLES, THERE WAS LIKE THE GIRLY TABLE AND THEN THERE WAS LIKE YOU AND AJANI AND RICARDO'S TABLE AND BARI AND SONNY, AND THEN THERE WAS LIKE ME AND RONICA RACING AROUND FIGHTING IN THE YARD, IN BETWEEN THE TWO TABLES.
HAHHAHH, OH MY GOD, I REMEMBER, THAT'S REALLY SAD...
THAT'S WHAT IT WAS- WAIT, SO DID THE BOYS LIKE HER?

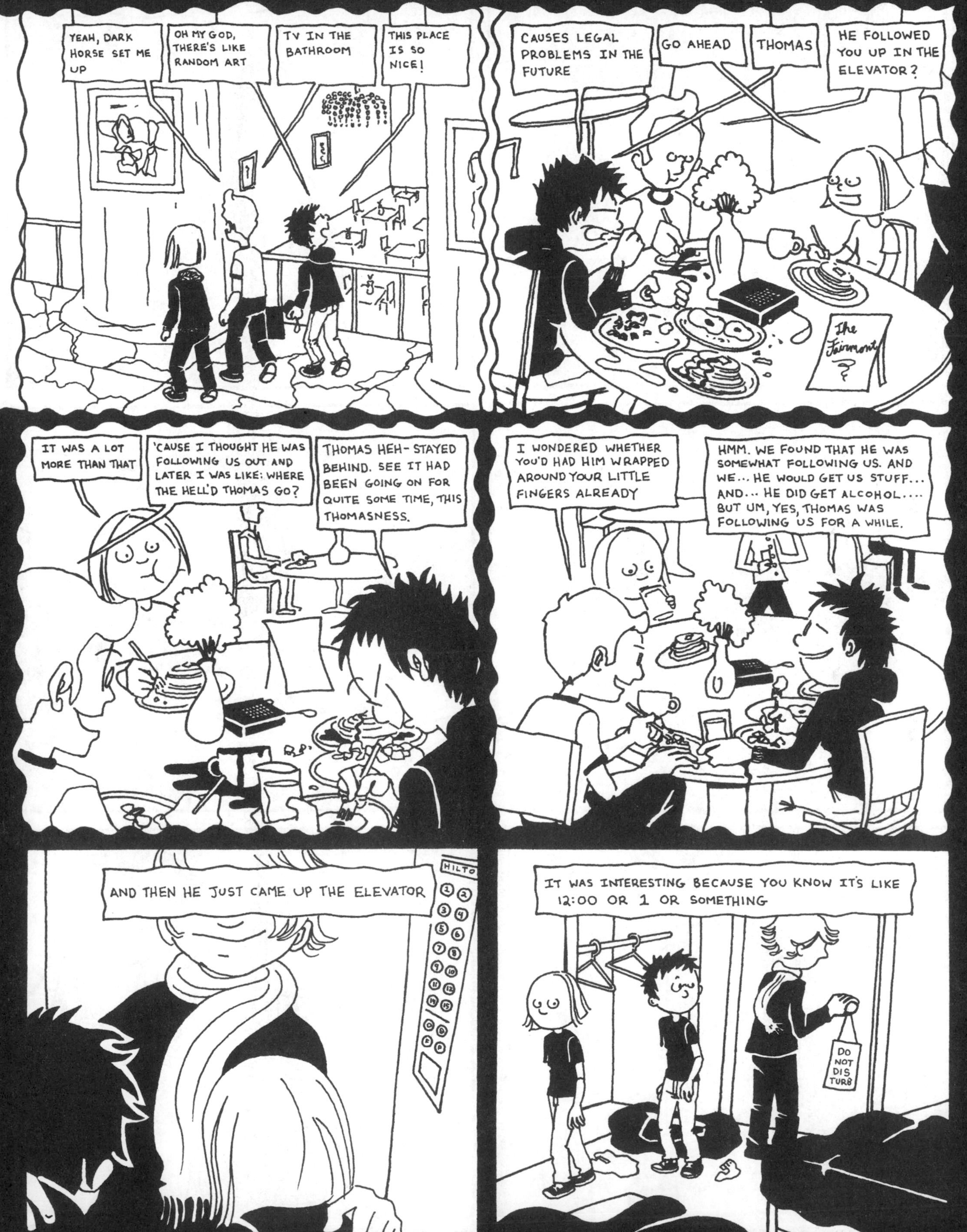
YEAH, DARK HORSE SET ME UP
OH MY GOD, THERE'S LIKE RANDOM ART
TV IN THE BATHROOM
THIS PLACE IS SO NICE!
CAUSES LEGAL PROBLEMS IN THE FUTURE
GO AHEAD
THOMAS
HE FOLLOWED YOU UP IN THE ELEVATOR?
The Fairmont
IT WAS A LOT MORE THAN THAT
'CAUSE I THOUGHT HE WAS FOLLOWING US OUT AND LATER I WAS LIKE: WHERE THE HELL'D THOMAS GO?
THOMAS HEH- STAYED BEHIND. SEE IT HAD BEEN GOING ON FOR QUITE SOME TIME, THIS THOMASNESS.
I WONDERED WHETHER YOU'D HAD HIM WRAPPED AROUND YOUR LITTLE FINGERS ALREADY
HMM. WE FOUND THAT HE WAS SOMEWHAT FOLLOWING US. AND WE... HE WOULD GET US STUFF... AND... HE DID GET ALCOHOL.... BUT UM, YES, THOMAS WAS FOLLOWING US FOR A WHILE.
AND THEN HE JUST CAME UP THE ELEVATOR
HILTO
IT WAS INTERESTING BECAUSE YOU KNOW IT'S LIKE 12:00 OR 1 OR SOMETHING
DO NOT DIS TURB

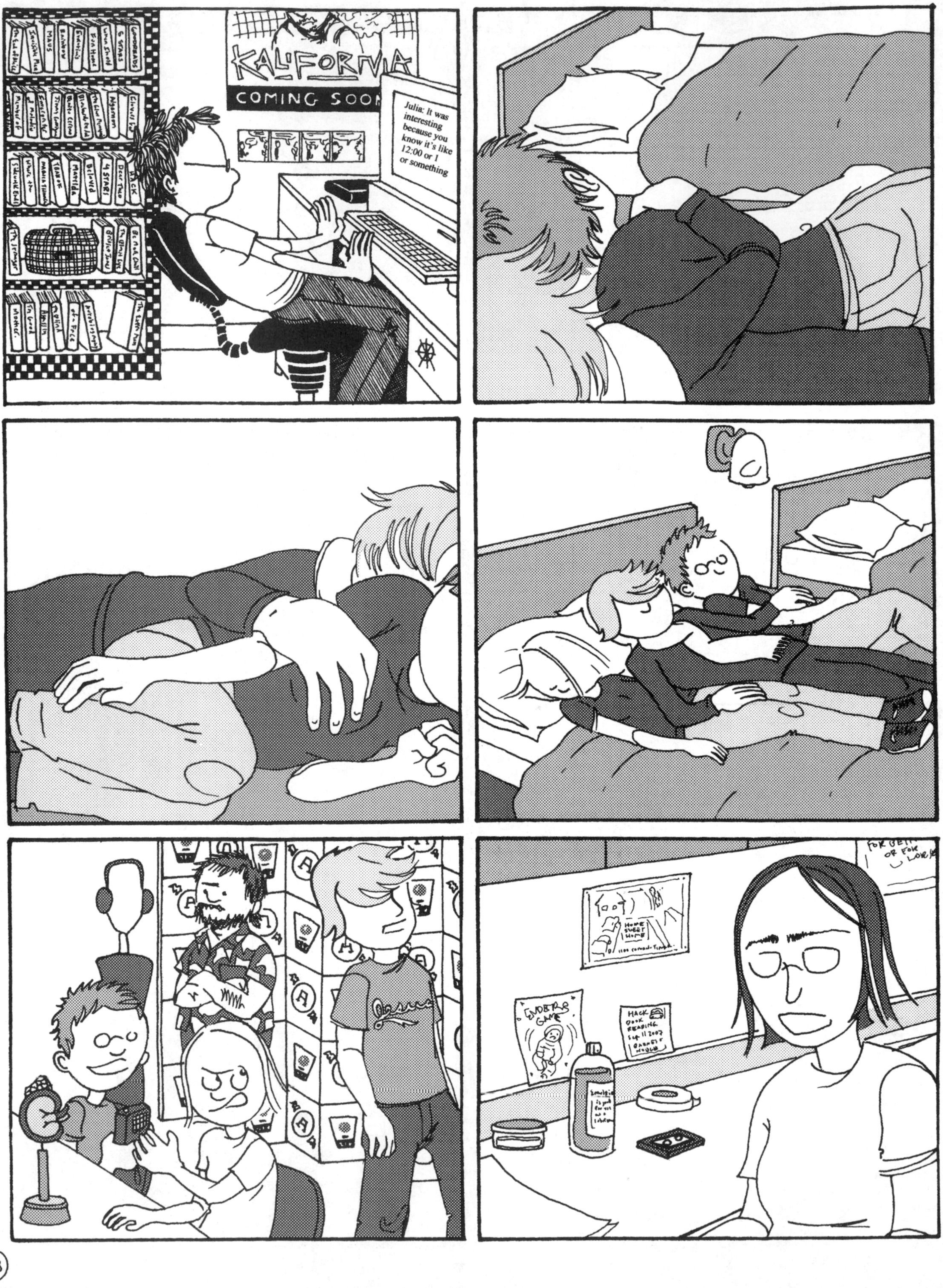
KALIFORNIA
COMING SOON
Julia: It was interesting because you know it's like 12:00 or 1 or something
HOME SWEET HOME
ENDER'S GAME

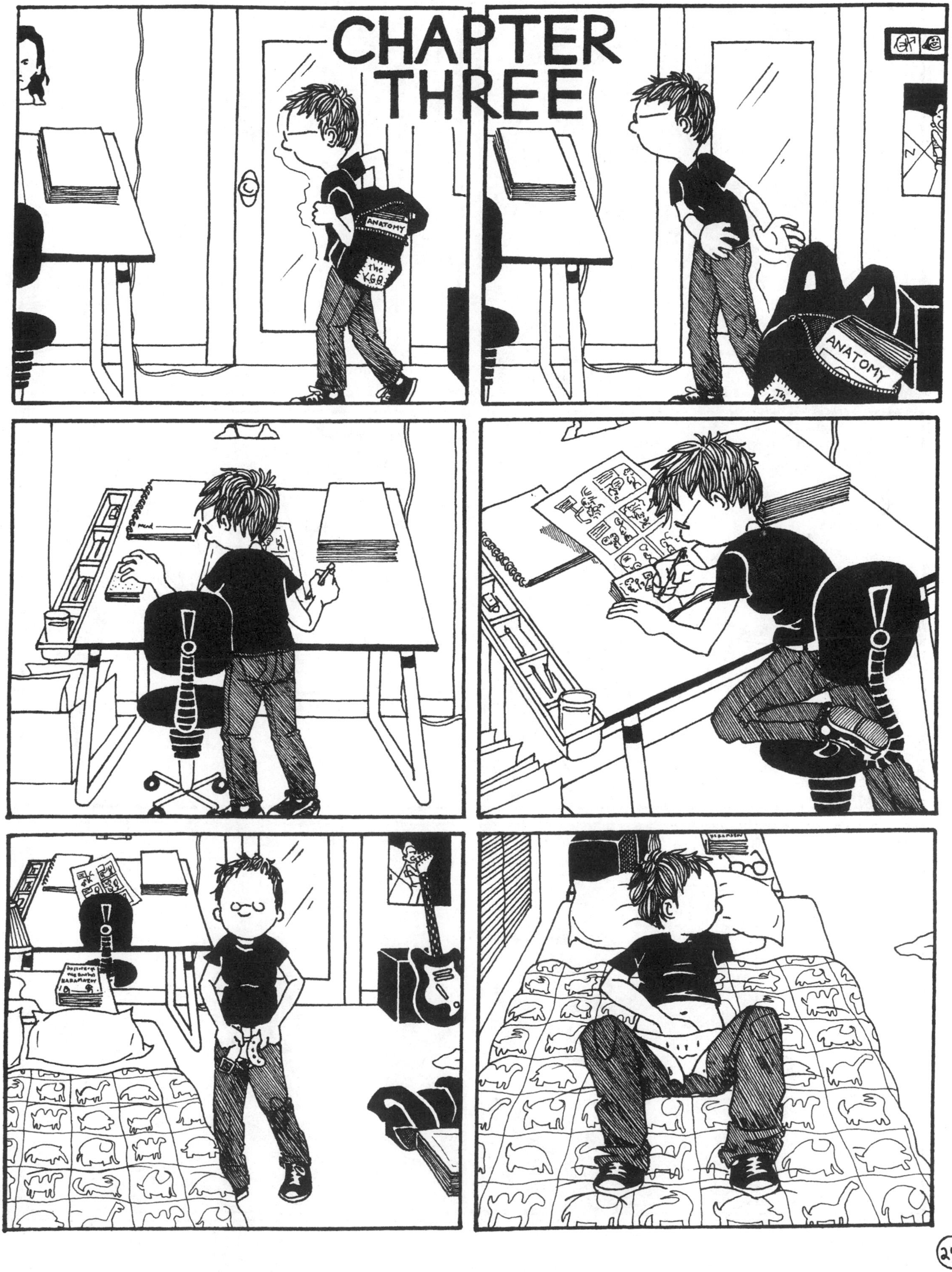
CHAPTER
THREE
ANATOMY
The KGB
ANATOMY

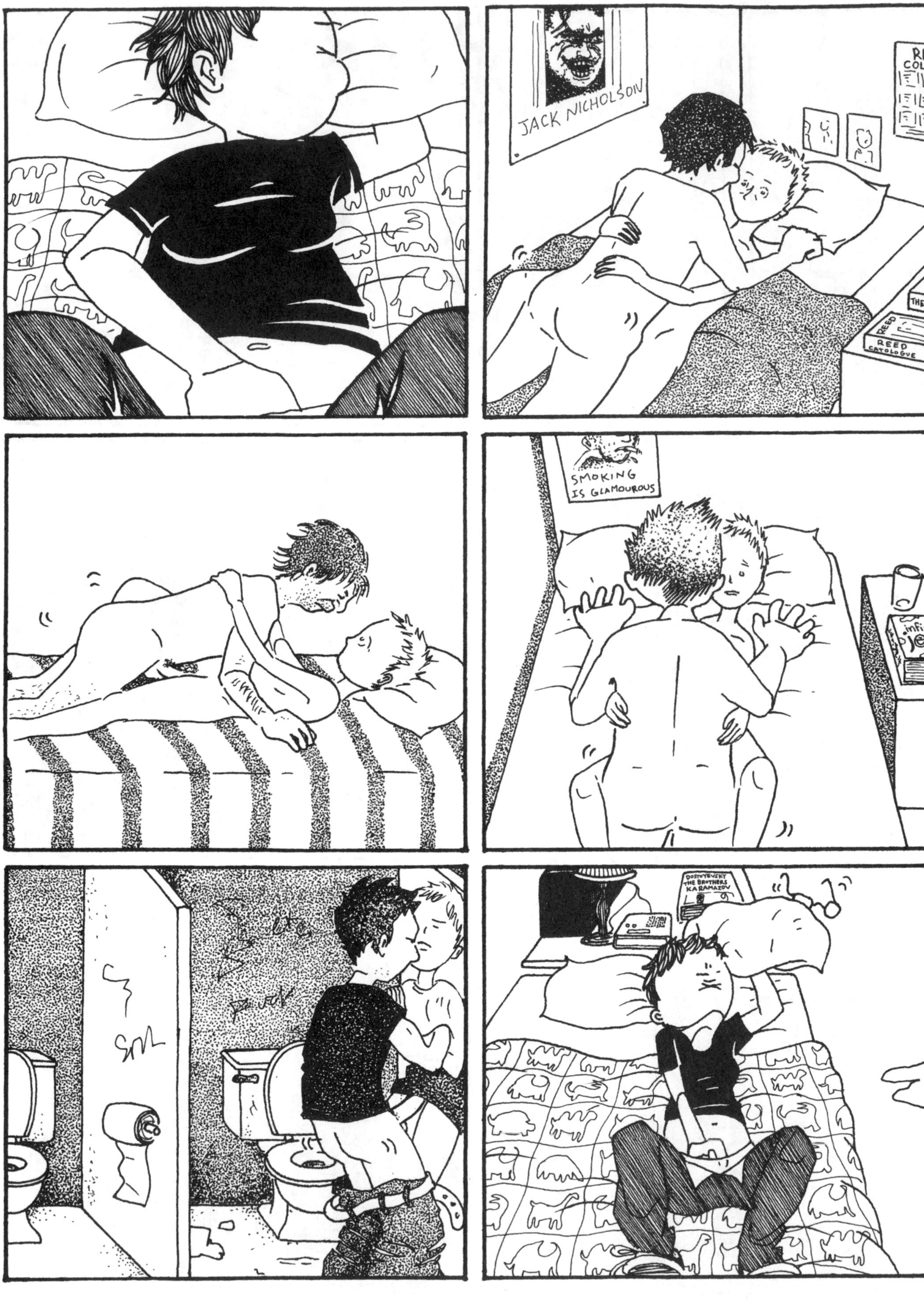
JACK NICHOLSON
REED
THE AENE
REED
REED CATOLOGUE
SMOKING IS GLAMOUROUS
infinite jest
DOSTOYEVSKY THE BROTHERS KARAMAZOV

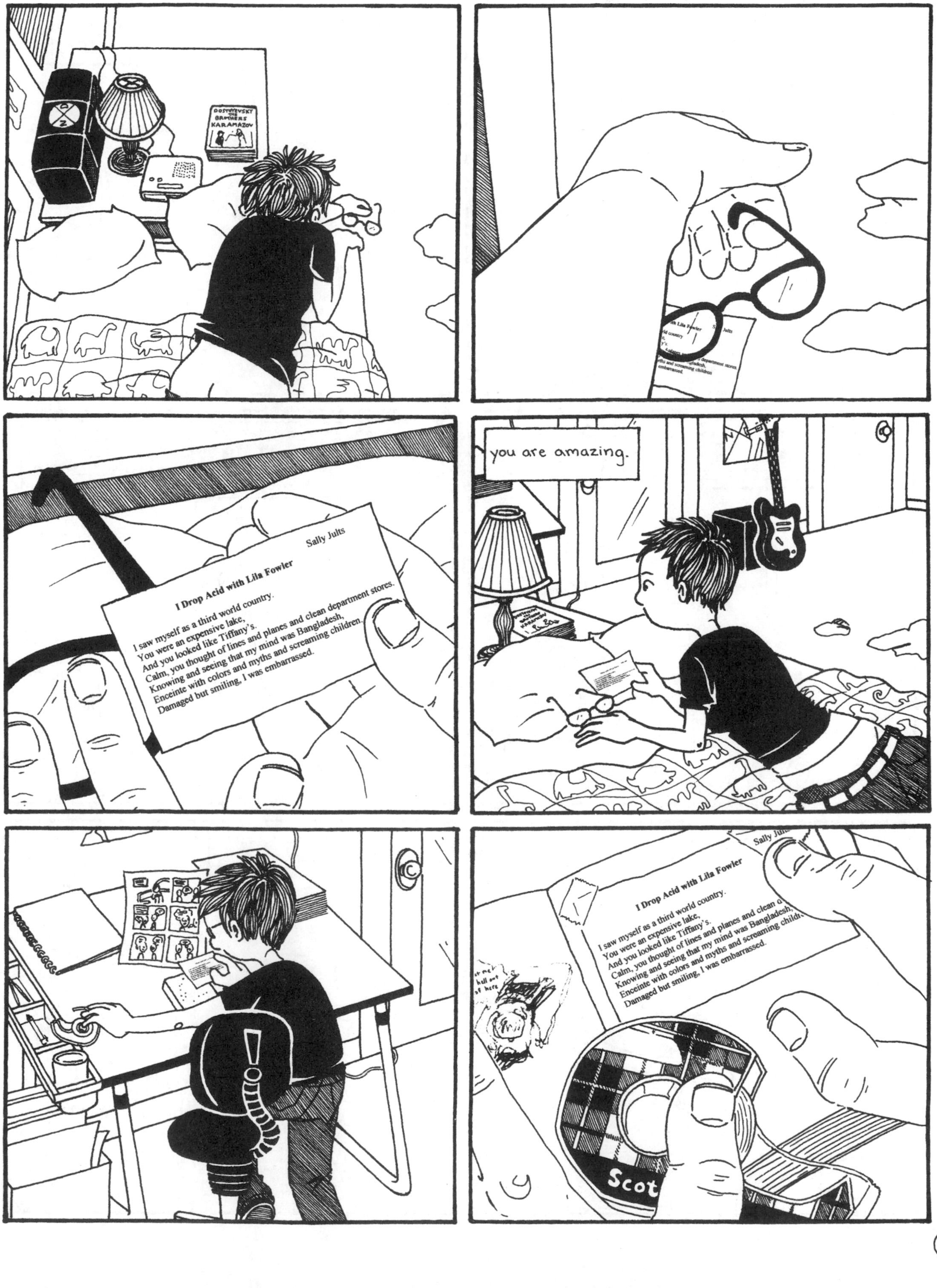
DOSTOYEVSKY THE BROTHERS KARAMAZOV
Sally Jults
I Drop Acid with Lila Fowler
I saw myself as a third world country.
You were an expensive lake,
And you looked like Tiffany's.
Calm, you thought of lines and planes and clean department stores.
Knowing and seeing that my mind was Bangladesh,
Enceinte with colors and myths and screaming children.
Damaged but smiling, I was embarrassed.
you are amazing.
I Drop Acid with Lila Fowler
I saw myself as a third world country.
You were an expensive lake,
And you looked like Tiffany's.
Knowing and seeing that my mind was Bangladesh,
Enceinte with colors and myths and screaming childr
Damaged but smiling, I was embarrassed.
Scot

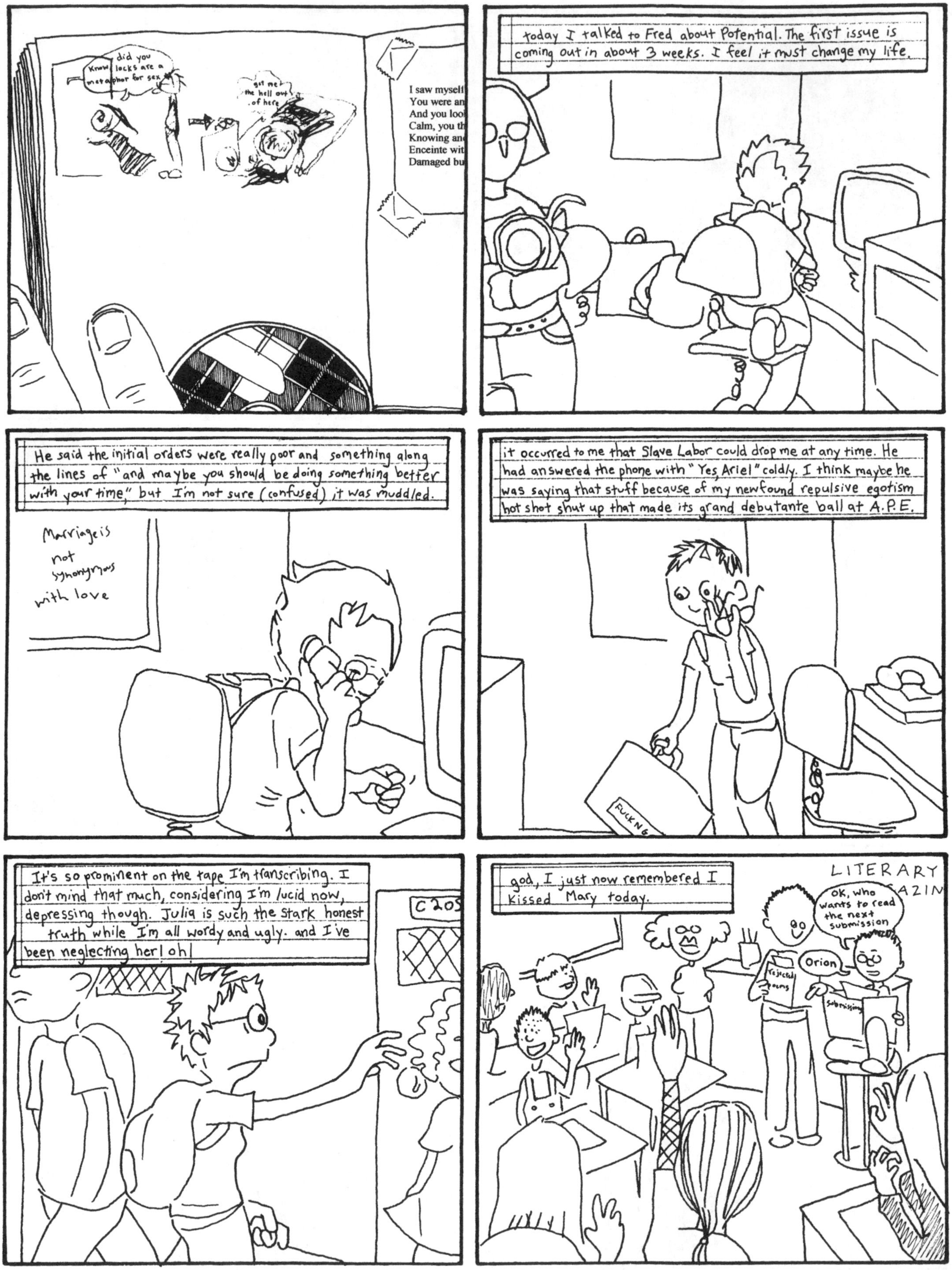
did you know locks are a metaphor for sex
get me the hell out of here
I saw myself
You were an
And you loo
Calm, you th
Knowing an
Enceinte wit
Damaged bu
today I talked to Fred about Potential. The first issue is coming out in about 3 weeks. I feel it must change my life.
He said the initial orders were really poor and something along the lines of "and maybe you should be doing something better with your time," but I'm not sure (confused) it was muddled.
Marriage is not synonymous with love
it occurred to me that Slave Labor could drop me at any time. He had answered the phone with "Yes, Ariel" coldly. I think maybe he was saying that stuff because of my newfound repulsive egotism hot shot shut up that made its grand debutante ball at A.P.E.
FUCKNG
It's so prominent on the tape I'm transcribing. I don't mind that much, considering I'm lucid now, depressing though. Julia is such the stark honest truth while I'm all wordy and ugly. and I've been neglecting her! oh!
C 205
god, I just now remembered I kissed Mary today.
LITERARY
AZIN
OK, who wants to read the next submission
Orion
Rejected poems
Submissions

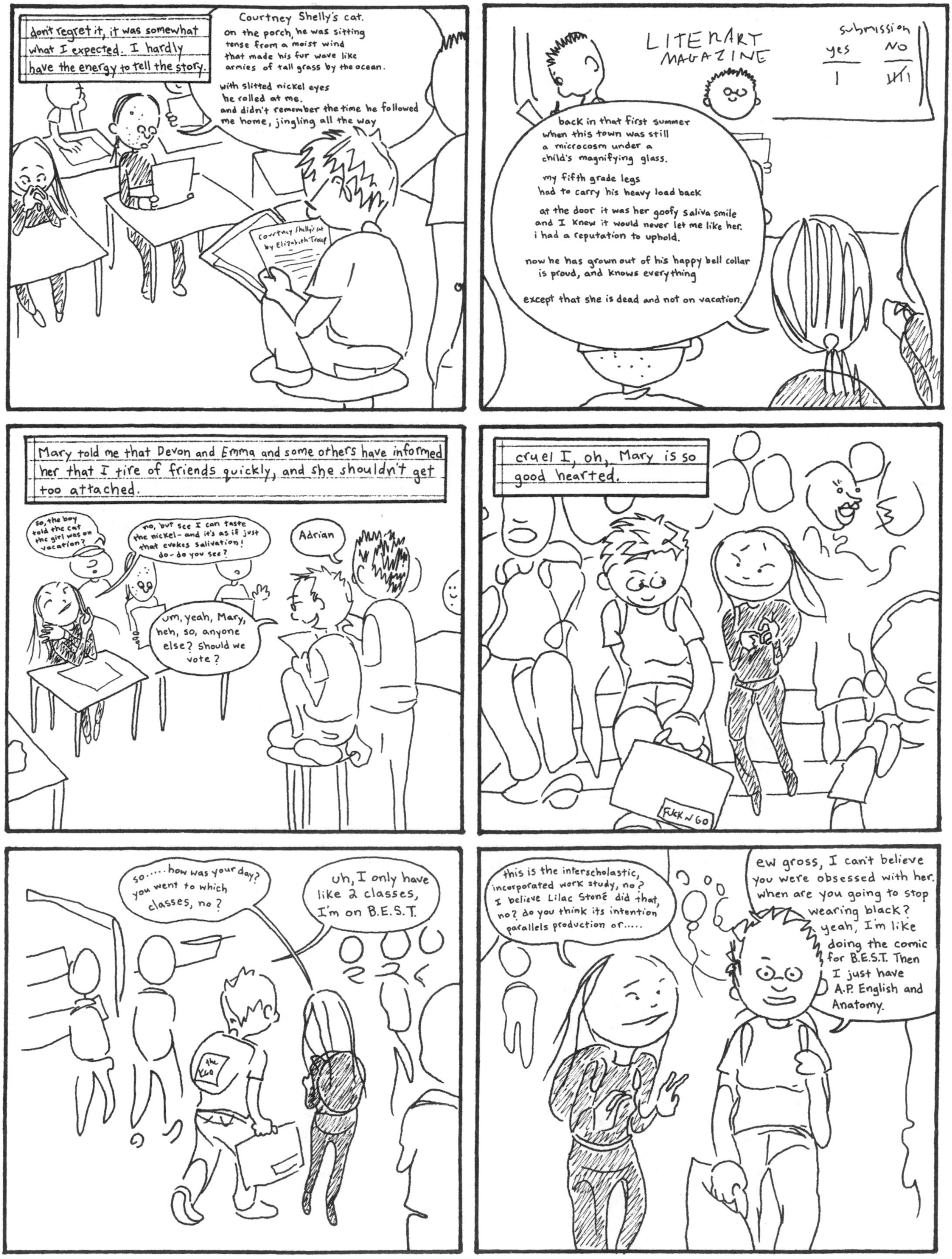

don't regret it, it was somewhat what I expected. I hardly have the energy to tell the story.
Courtney Shelly's cat.
on the porch, he was sitting tense from a moist wind that made his fur wave like armies of tall grass by the ocean.
with slitted nickel eyes he rolled at me. and didn't remember the time he followed me home, jingling all the way
LITERARY MAGAZINE
submission
yes
NO
back in that first summer when this town was still a microcosm under a child's magnifying glass.
my fifth grade legs had to carry his heavy load back
at the door it was her goofy saliva smile and I knew it would never let me like her. i had a reputation to uphold.
now he has grown out of his happy bell collar is proud, and knows everything
except that she is dead and not on vacation.
Mary told me that Devon and Emma and some others have informed her that I tire of friends quickly, and she shouldn't get too attached.
so, the boy told the cat the girl was on vacation?
no, but see I can taste the nickel- and it's as if just that evokes salivation! do- do you see?
Adrian
um, yeah, Mary, heh, so, anyone else? Should we vote?
cruel I, oh, Mary is so good hearted.
FUCK N GO
so..... how was your day? you went to which classes, no?
uh, I only have like 2 classes, I'm on B.E.S.T.
this is the interscholastic, incorporated work study, no? I believe Lilac Stoné did that, no? do you think its intention parallels production or.....
ew gross, I can't believe you were obsessed with her. when are you going to stop wearing black?
yeah, I'm like doing the comic for B.E.S.T. Then I just have A.P. English and Anatomy.

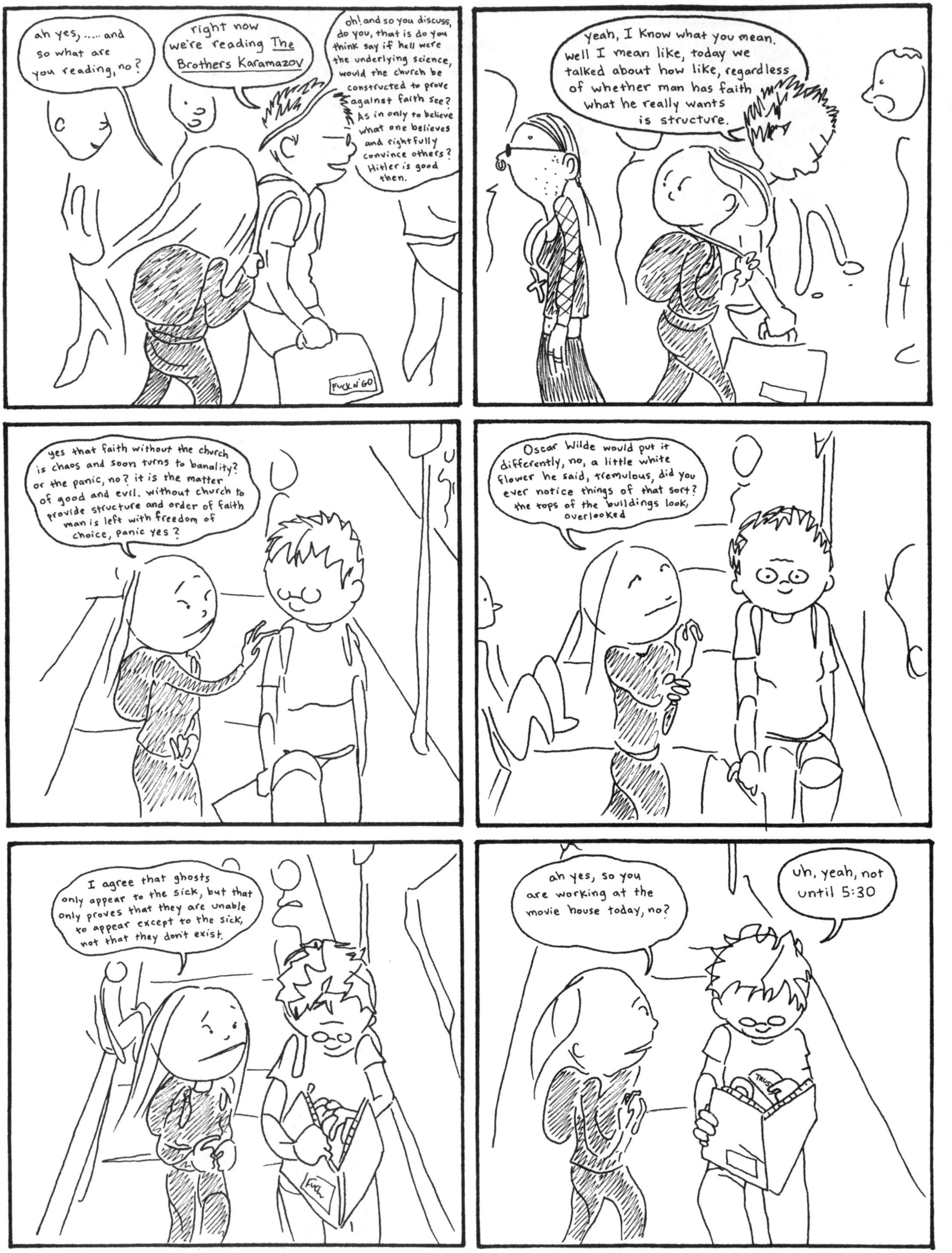
ah yes, ... and so what are you reading, no?
right now we're reading The Brothers Karamazov
oh! and so you discuss, do you, that is do you think say if hell were the underlying science, would the church be constructed to prove against faith see? As in only to believe what one believes and rightfully convince others? Hitler is good then.
FUCK N' GO
Yeah, I Know what you mean. well I mean like, today we talked about how like, regardless of whether man has faith what he really wants is structure.
yes that faith without the church is chaos and soon turns to banality? or the panic, no? it is the matter of good and evil. without church to provide structure and order of faith man is left with freedom of choice, panic yes?
Oscar Wilde would put it differently, no, a little white flower he said, tremulous, did you ever notice things of that sort? the tops of the buildings look, overlooked
I agree that ghosts only appear to the sick, but that only proves that they are unable to appear except to the sick, not that they don't exist.
ah yes, so you are working at the movie house today, no?
uh, yeah, not until 5:30

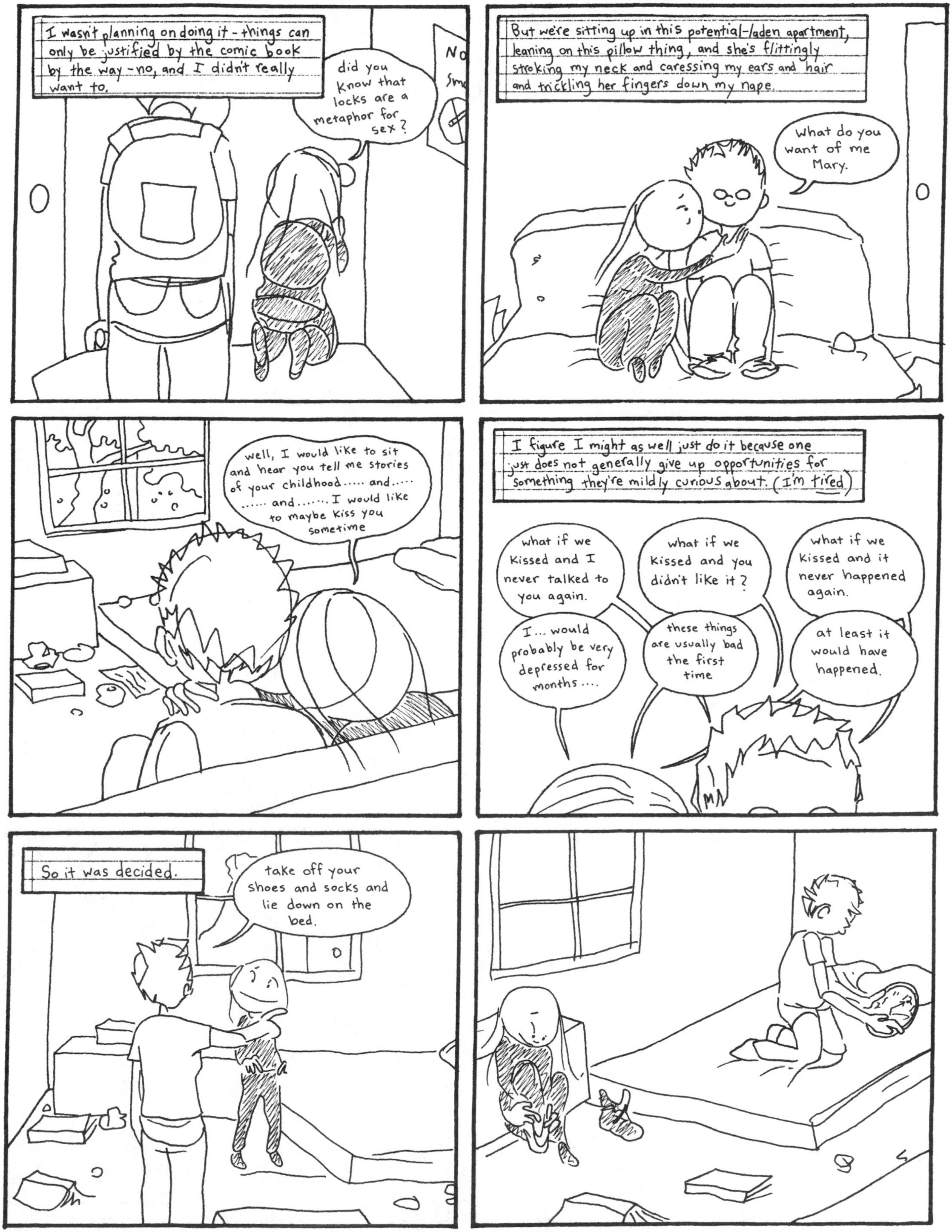
I wasn't planning on doing it - things can only be justified by the comic book by the way - no, and I didn't really want to.
did you know that locks are a metaphor for sex?
But we're sitting up in this potential-laden apartment, leaning on this pillow thing, and she's flittingly stroking my neck and caressing my ears and hair and trickling her fingers down my nape.
What do you want of me Mary.
well, I would like to sit and hear you tell me stories of your childhood..... and..... ...... and....... I would like to maybe kiss you sometime
I figure I might as well just do it because one just does not generally give up opportunities for something they're mildly curious about. (I'm tired)
what if we kissed and I never talked to you again.
I... would probably be very depressed for months....
what if we kissed and you didn't like it?
these things are usually bad the first time
what if we kissed and it never happened again.
at least it would have happened.
So it was decided.
take off your shoes and socks and lie down on the bed.

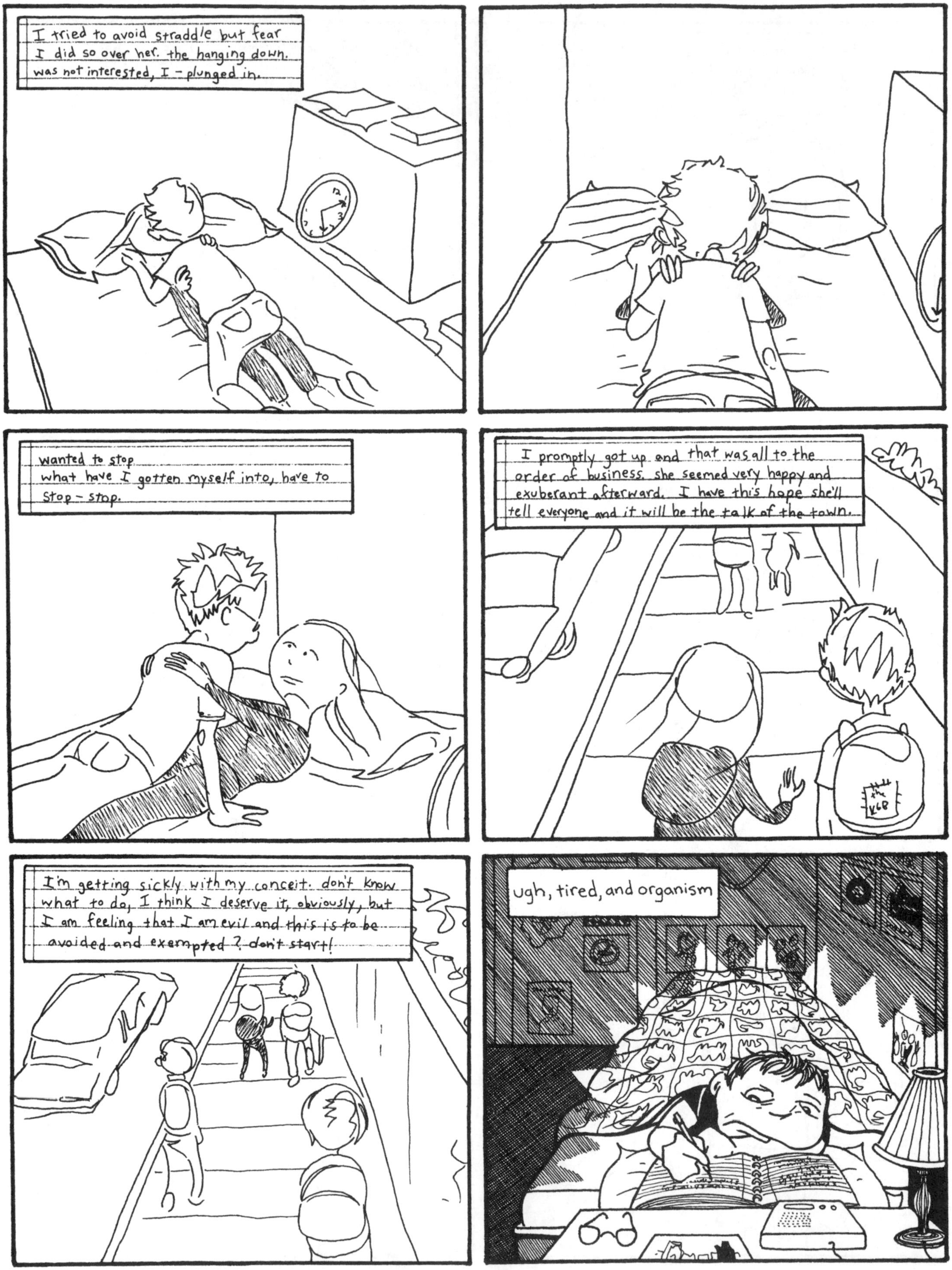
I tried to avoid straddle but fear I did so over her. the hanging down. was not interested, I - plunged in.
wanted to stop what have I gotten myself into, have to stop - stop.
I promptly got up and that was all to the order of business. she seemed very happy and exuberant afterward. I have this hope she'll tell everyone and it will be the talk of the town.
I'm getting sickly with my conceit. don't know what to do, I think I deserve it, obviously, but I am feeling that I am evil and this is to be avoided and exempted? don't start!
ugh, tired, and organism

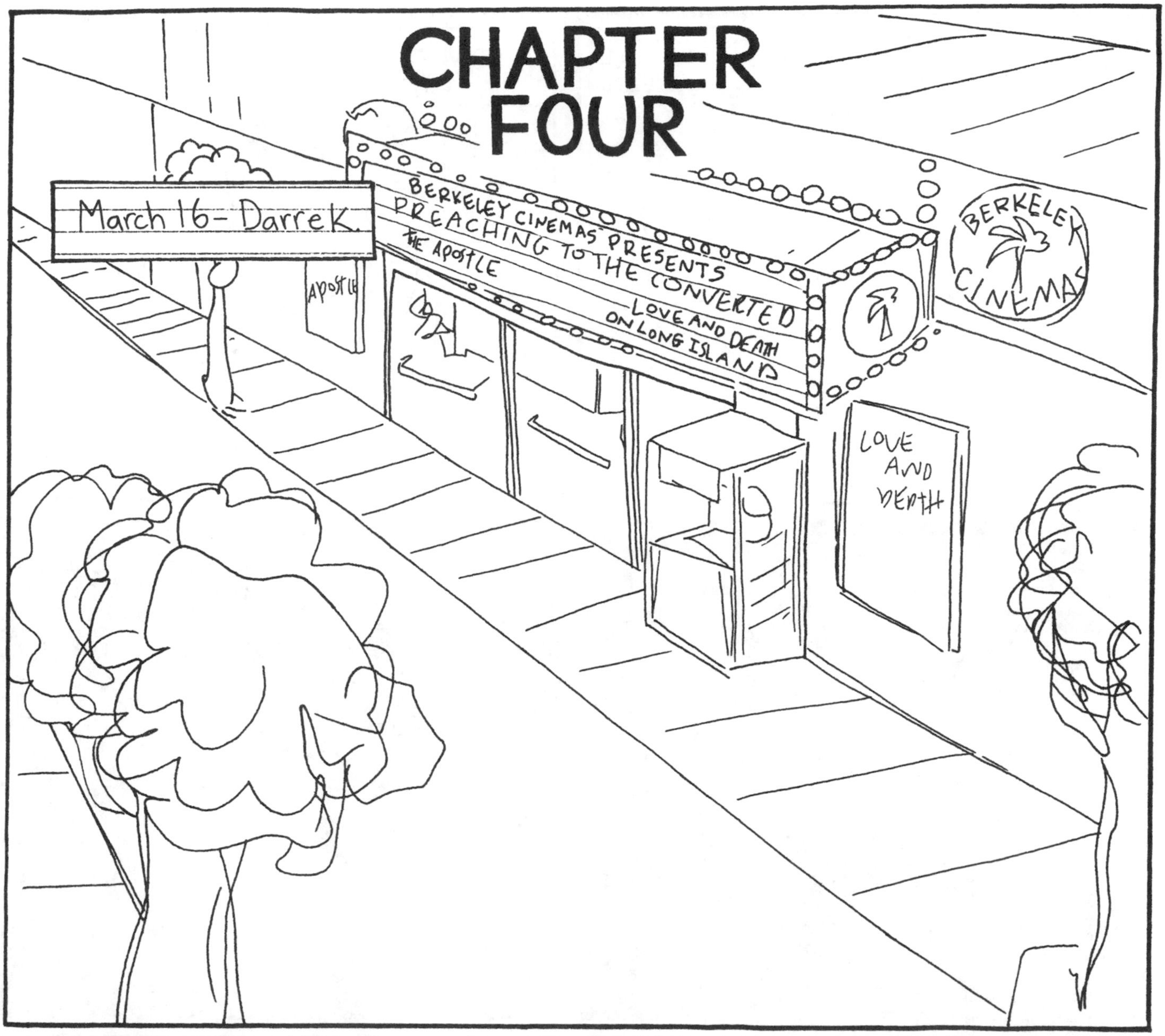
CHAPTER FOUR
March 16- Darrek.
BERKELEY CINEMAS PRESENTS
PREACHING TO THE CONVERTED
THE APOSTLE
LOVE AND DEATH ON LONG ISLAND
APOSTLE
BERKELEY CINEMAS
LOVE AND DEATH

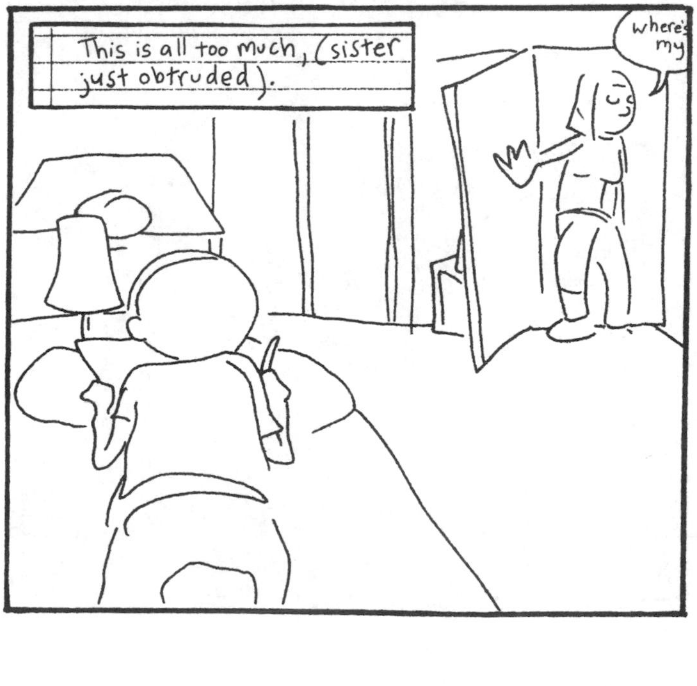
This is all too much, (sister just obtruded).
where's my

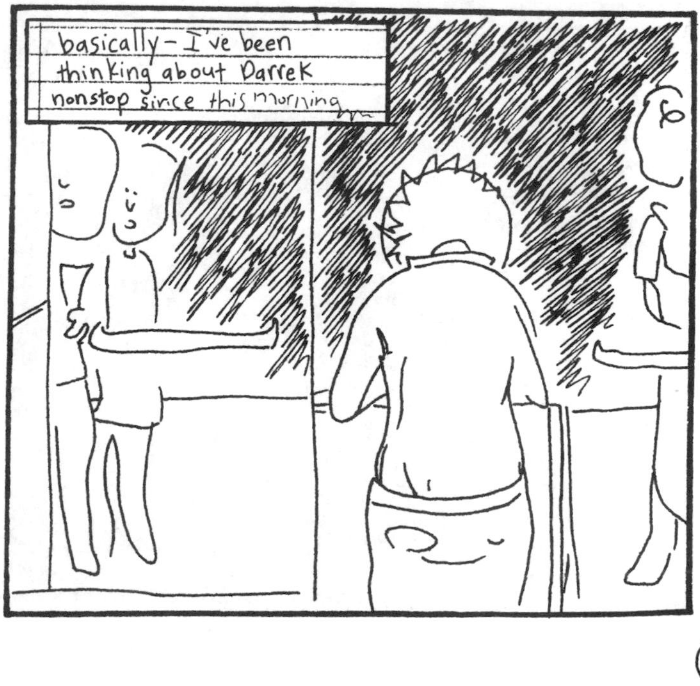
basically- I've been thinking about Darrek nonstop since this morning

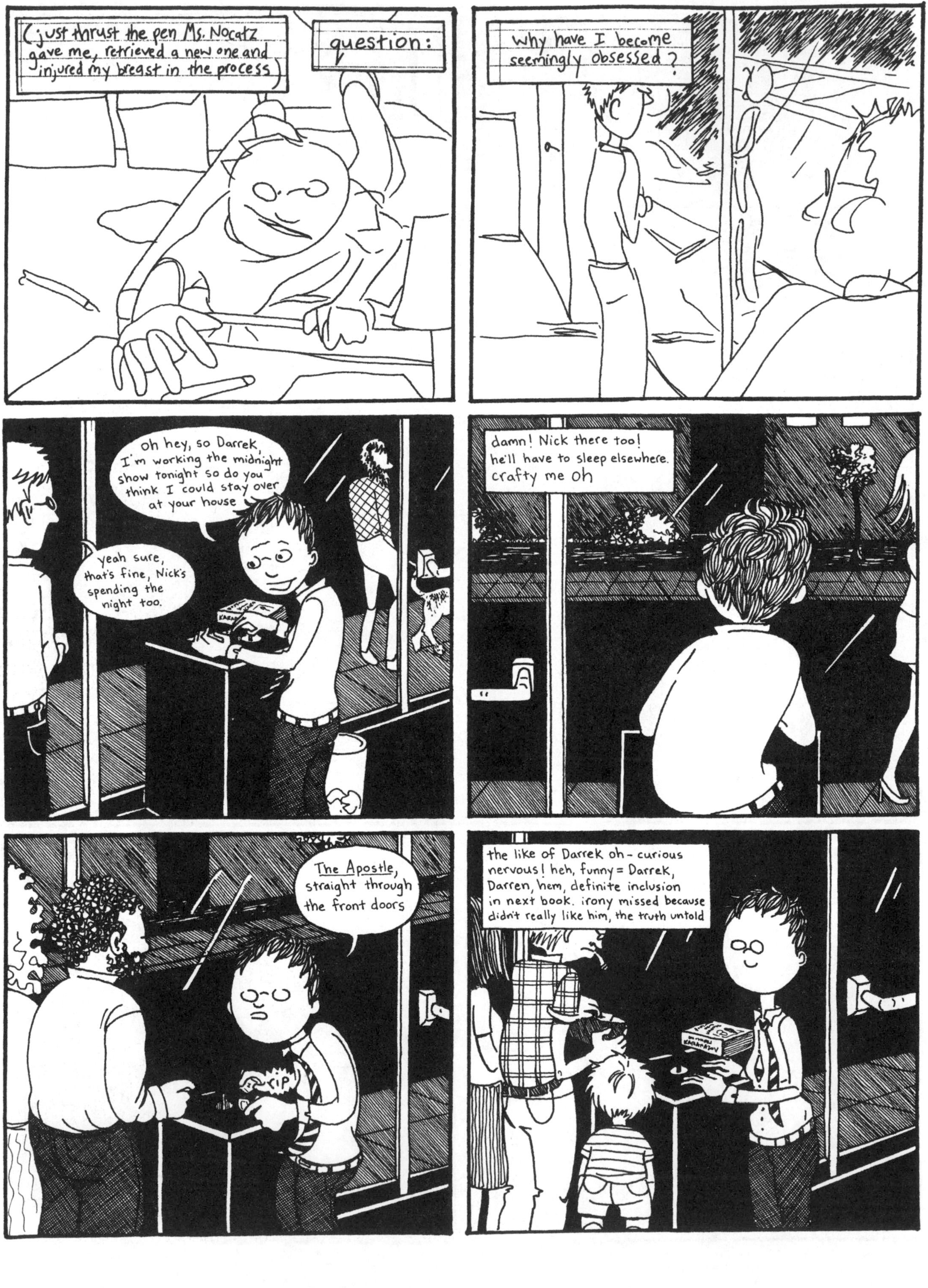
(just thrust the pen Ms. Nocatz gave me, retrieved a new one and injured my breast in the process)
question:
why have I become seemingly obsessed?
oh hey, so Darrek, I'm working the midnight show tonight so do you think I could stay over at your house
yeah sure, that's fine, Nick's spending the night too.
damn! Nick there too! he'll have to sleep elsewhere. crafty me oh
The Apostle, straight through the front doors
rip
the like of Darrek oh - curious nervous! heh, funny = Darrek, Darren, hem, definite inclusion in next book. irony missed because didn't really like him, the truth untold

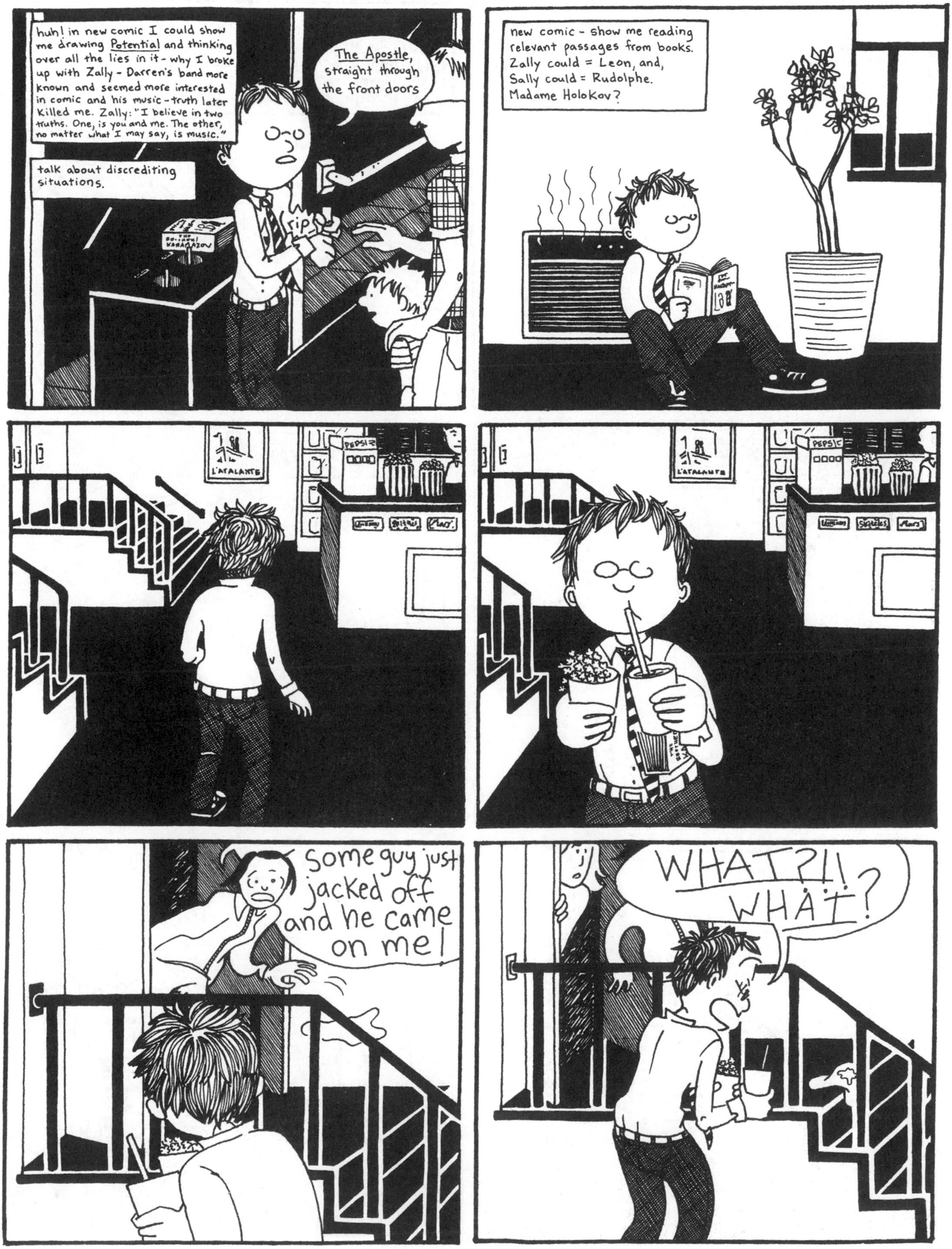
huh! in new comic I could show me drawing Potential and thinking over all the lies in it - why I broke up with Zally - Darren's band more known and seemed more interested in comic and his music - truth later killed me. Zally: "I believe in two truths. One, is you and me. The other, no matter what I may say, is music."
talk about discrediting situations.
The Apostle, straight through the front doors
rip
new comic - show me reading relevant passages from books. Zally could = Leon, and, Sally could = Rudolphe. Madame Holokov?
L'ATALANTE
PEPSI
Some guy just jacked off and he came on me!
WHAT?!! WHAT?

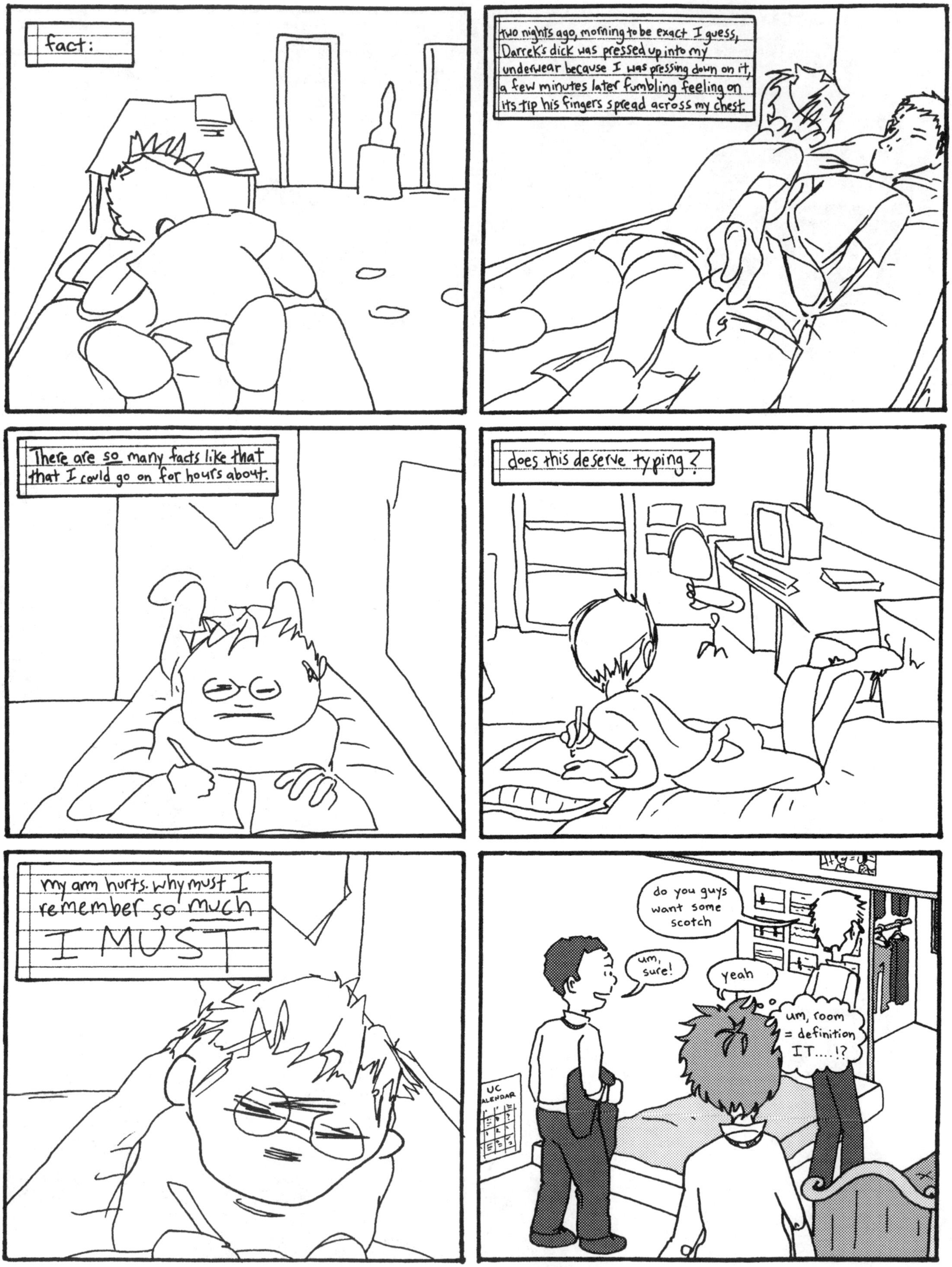
fact:
two nights ago, morning to be exact I guess, Darrek's dick was pressed up into my underwear because I was pressing down on it, a few minutes later fumbling feeling on its tip his fingers spread across my chest.
There are so many facts like that that I could go on for hours about.
does this deserve typing?
my arm hurts. why must I remember so much
I MUST
do you guys want some scotch
um, sure!
yeah
um, room = definition IT....!?
UC CALENDAR

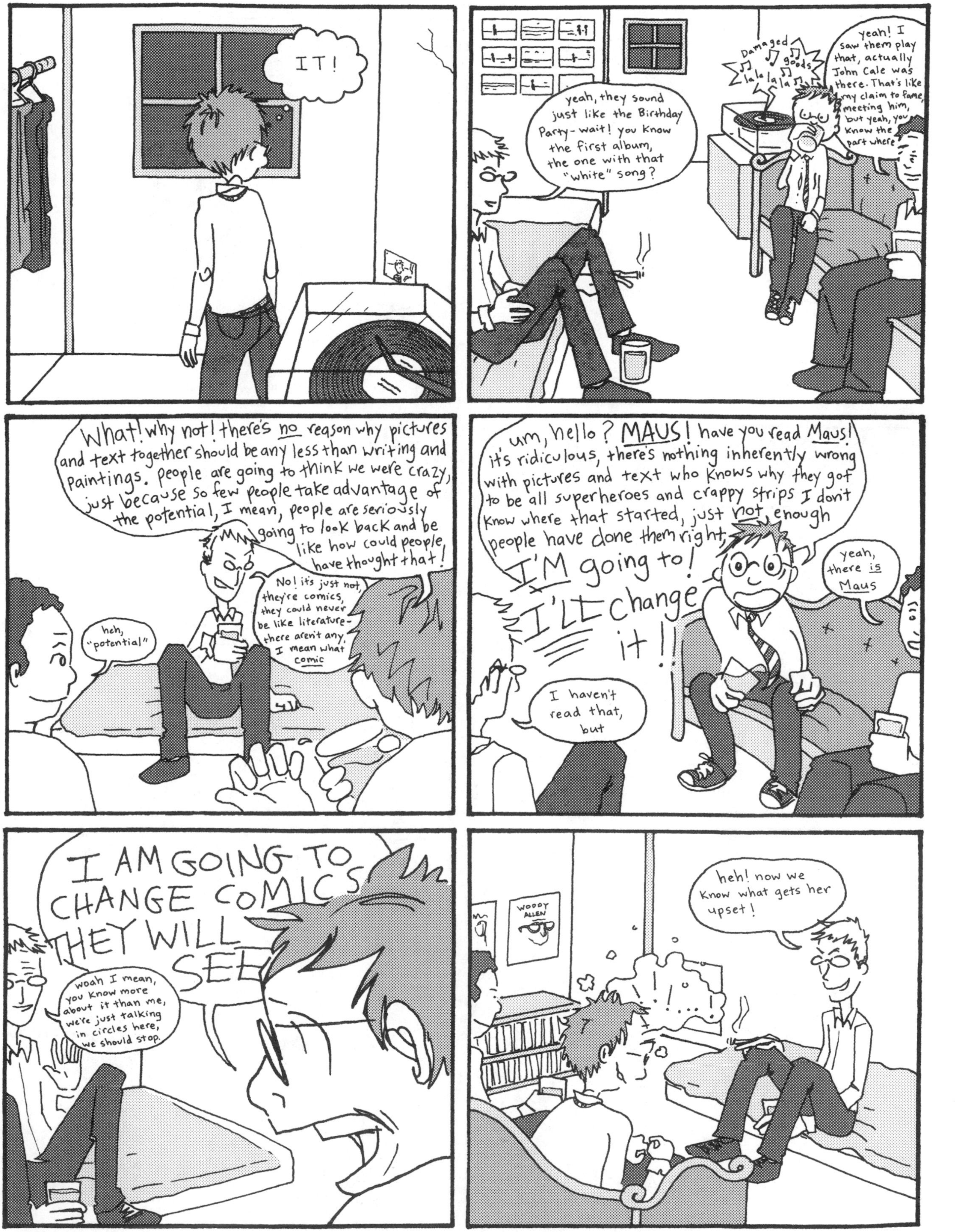
IT!
yeah, they sound just like the Birthday Party - wait! you know the first album, the one with that "white" song?
Damaged goods lalalala
yeah! I saw them play that, actually John Cale was there. That's like my claim to fame, meeting him, but yeah, you know the part where
What! why not! there's no reason why pictures and text together should be any less than writing and paintings. people are going to think we were crazy, just because so few people take advantage of the potential, I mean, people are seriously going to look back and be like how could people have thought that!
No! it's just not, they're comics, they could never be like literature - there aren't any, I mean what comic
heh, "potential"
um, hello? MAUS! have you read Maus! it's ridiculous, there's nothing inherently wrong with pictures and text who knows why they got to be all superheroes and crappy strips I don't know where that started, just not enough people have done them right,
I'M going to! I'LL change it!!
yeah, there is Maus
I haven't read that, but
I AM GOING TO CHANGE COMICS THEY WILL SEE
woah I mean, you know more about it than me, we're just talking in circles here, we should stop.
WOODY ALLEN
!.!...!
heh! now we know what gets her upset!

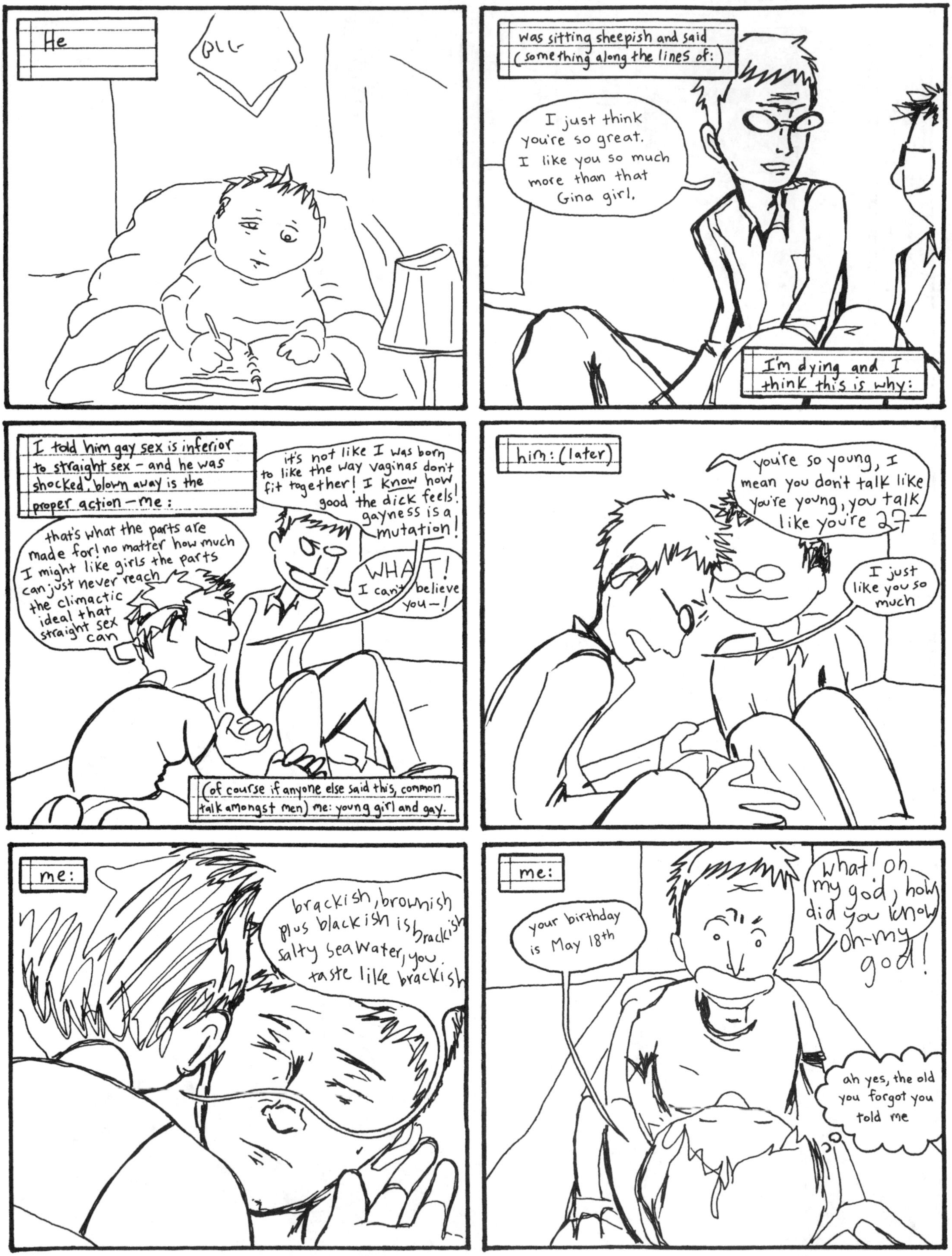
He
was sitting sheepish and said (something along the lines of:)
I just think you're so great. I like you so much more than that Gina girl.
I'm dying and I think this is why:
I told him gay sex is inferior to straight sex - and he was shocked, blown away is the proper action - me:
that's what the parts are made for! no matter how much I might like girls the parts can just never reach the climactic ideal that straight sex can
it's not like I was born to like the way vaginas don't fit together! I know how good the dick feels! gayness is a mutation!
WHAT! I can't believe you-!
(of course if anyone else said this, common talk amongst men) me: young girl and gay.
him: (later)
you're so young, I mean you don't talk like you're young, you talk like you're 27
I just like you so much
me:
brackish, brownish plus blackish is brackish salty seawater, you taste like brackish
me:
your birthday is May 18th
what! oh my god, how did you know oh-my god!
ah yes, the old you forgot you told me

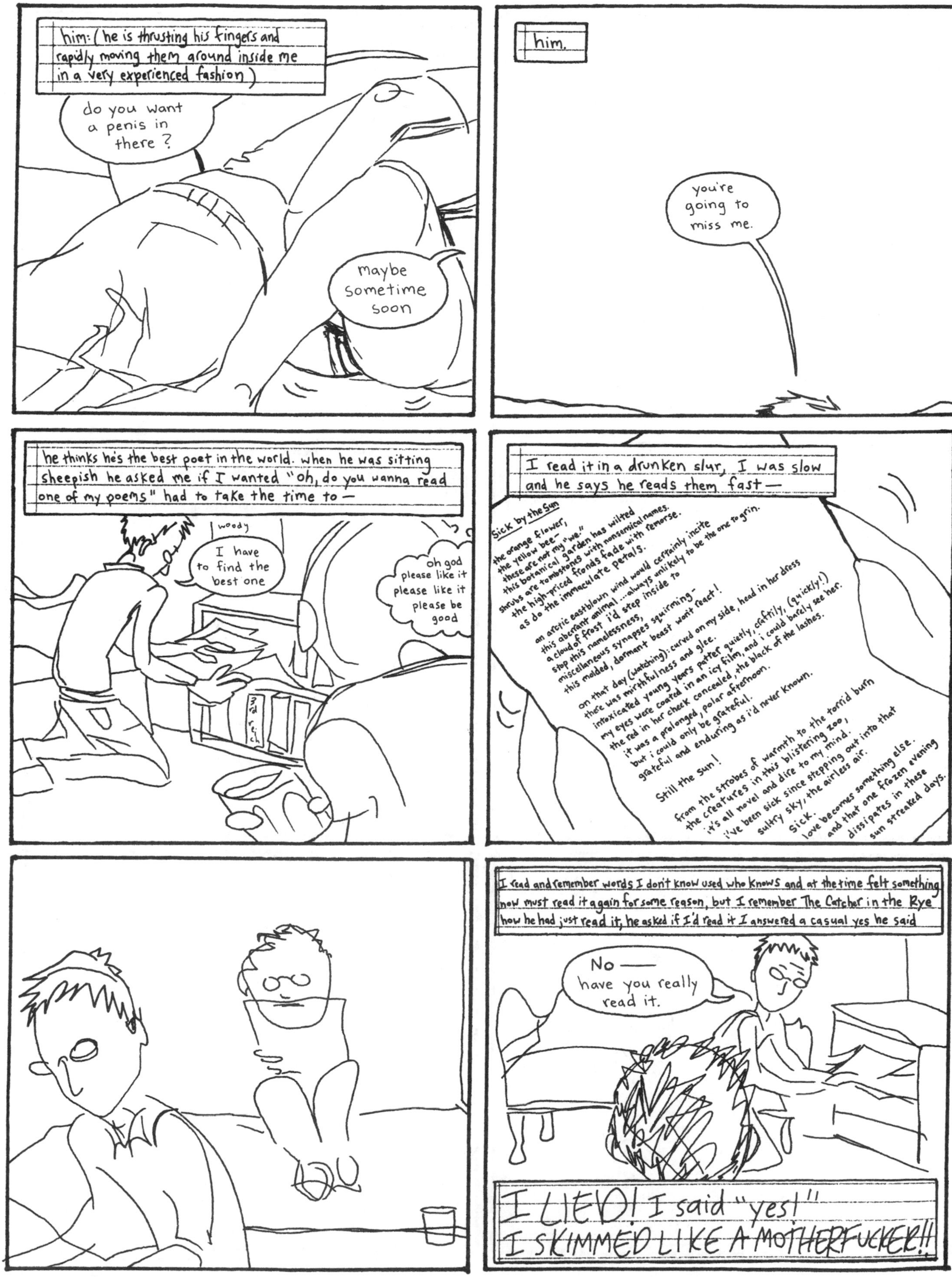

him: (he is thrusting his fingers and rapidly moving them around inside me in a very experienced fashion)
do you want a penis in there?
maybe sometime soon
him.
you're going to miss me.
he thinks he's the best poet in the world. when he was sitting sheepish he asked me if I wanted "oh, do you wanna read one of my poems" had to take the time to —
woody
I have to find the best one
oh god please like it please like it please be good
I read it in a drunken slur, I was slow and he says he reads them fast —
Sick by the Sun
the orange flower,
the yellow bee-
these are not my "we."
this botanical garden has wilted
this botanical garden has wilted
shrubs are tombstones with nonsensical names.
the high-priced fronds fade with remorse.
as do the immaculate petals.
an arctic eastblown wind would certainly incite
this aberrant animal ...always unlikely to be the one to grin.
a cloud of frost i'd step inside to
stop this namelessness,
miscellaneous synapses squirming-
this molded, dormant beast won't react!
on that day (watching): curved on my side, head in her dress
there was mirthfulness and glee.
intoxicated young years patter quietly, craftily, (quickly!)
my eyes were coated in an icy film, and i could barely see her.
the red in her cheek concealed, the black of the lashes.
it was a prolonged, polar afternoon.
but i could only be grateful.
grateful and enduring as i'd never known.
Still the sun!
from the strobes of warmth to the torrid burn
the creatures in this blistering zoo,
it's all novel and dire to my mind.
i've been sick since stepping out into that
sultry sky, the airless air.
Sick.
love becomes something else.
and that one frozen evening
dissipates in these
sun streaked days.
I read and remember words I don't know used who knows and at the time felt something now must read it again for some reason, but I remember The Catcher in the Rye how he had just read it, he asked if I'd read it I answered a casual yes he said
No — have you really read it.
I LIED! I said "yes!" I SKIMMED LIKE A MOTHERFUCKER!!

I know most people read it earlier, but I just finished it, and you know that part where it says "the body meets another body in the rye" — I just started crying, I mean — that part just made me cry.

— remembered today that I think I cried at that part too —

(three days ago I had nothing)

(sister interrupted again)

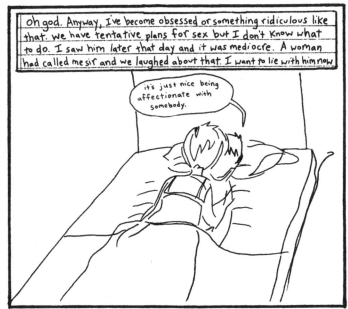

oh god. Anyway, I've become obsessed or something ridiculous like that. we have tentative plans for sex but I don't know what to do. I saw him later that day and it was mediocre. A woman had called me sir and we laughed about that. I want to lie with him now

it's just nice being affectionate with somebody.

me —

there are physical differences, OK, in the brain there are structures that are sexually dimorphic, INAH3 is a cluster of nerve cells larger in men than in women, and a research study, Simon LeVay, shows that INAH3 is 2 to 3 times larger in straight men then in gay men — then there's studies on genes — XQ28 — a gene on the X chromosome, Hamer's study showed that a statistically significant number of gay brothers shared linkage markers in that region

him —

people just say they're gay! they don't read books and talk about XQ28! — all this you going to Columbia stuff is starting to make sense

B-a-a-a-a-ar NARD

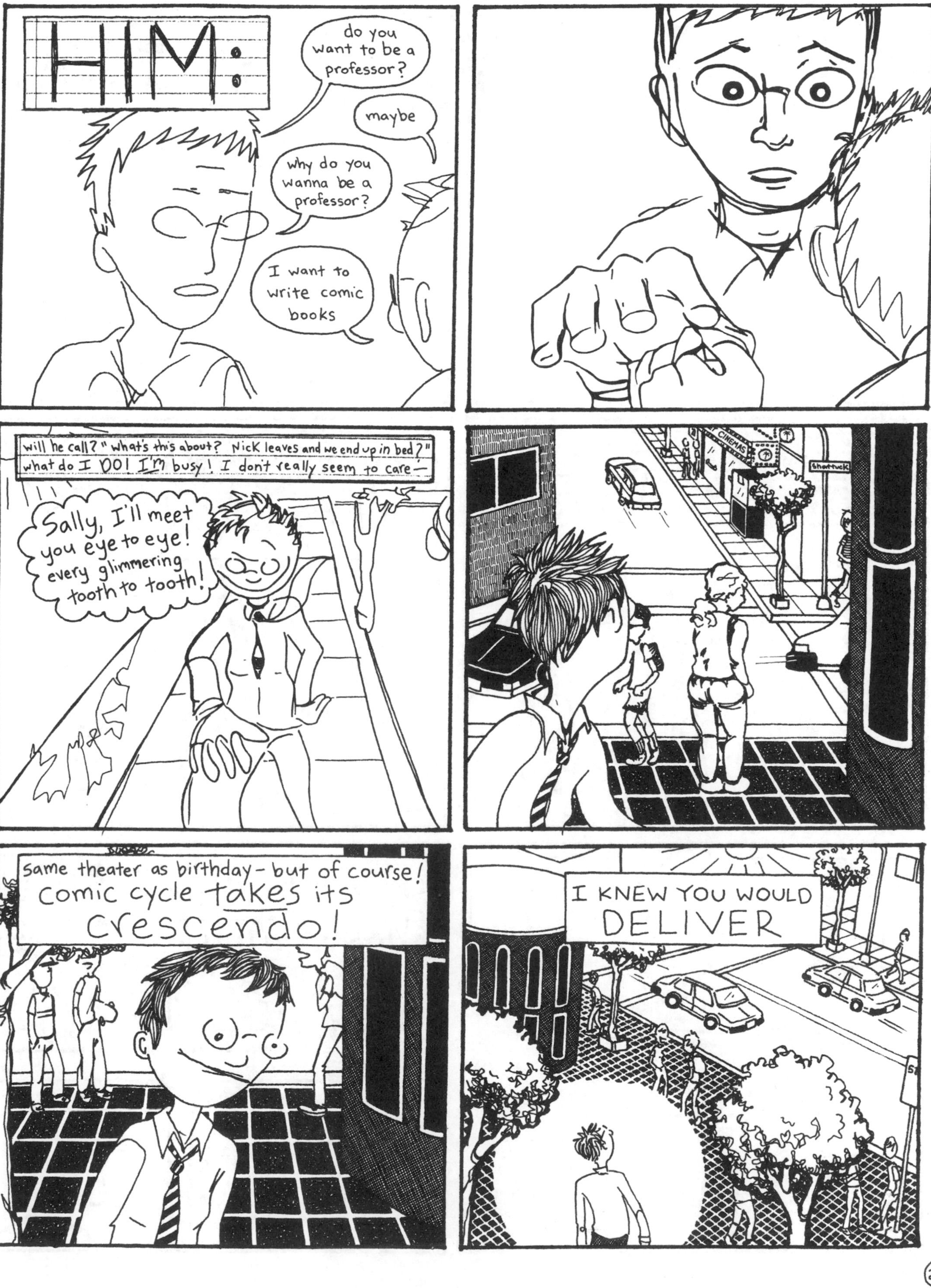
HIM:
do you want to be a professor?
maybe
why do you wanna be a professor?
I want to write comic books
will he call? "what's this about? Nick leaves and we end up in bed?"
what do I DO! I'M busy! I don't really seem to care—
Sally, I'll meet you eye to eye! every glimmering tooth to tooth!
CINEMAS
Shattuck
Same theater as birthday - but of course!
comic cycle takes its crescendo!
I KNEW YOU WOULD DELIVER

CHAPTER FIVE

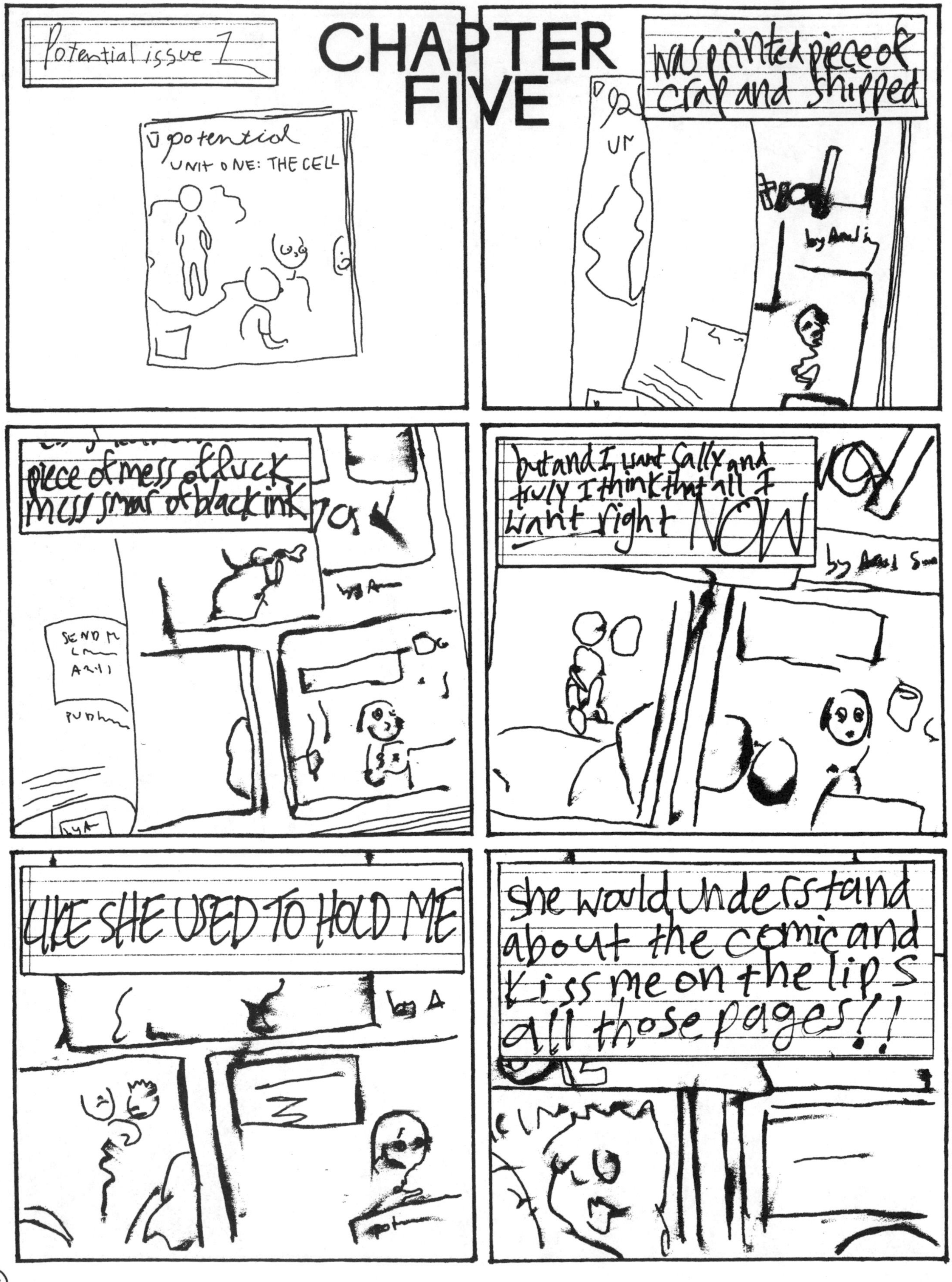

Potential issue 1
potential
UNIT ONE: THE CELL
was printed piece of crap and shipped
piece of mess of luck mess smear of black ink
but and I want Sally and truly I think that all I want right NOW
LIKE SHE USED TO HOLD ME
she would understand about the comic and kiss me on the lips all those pages!!

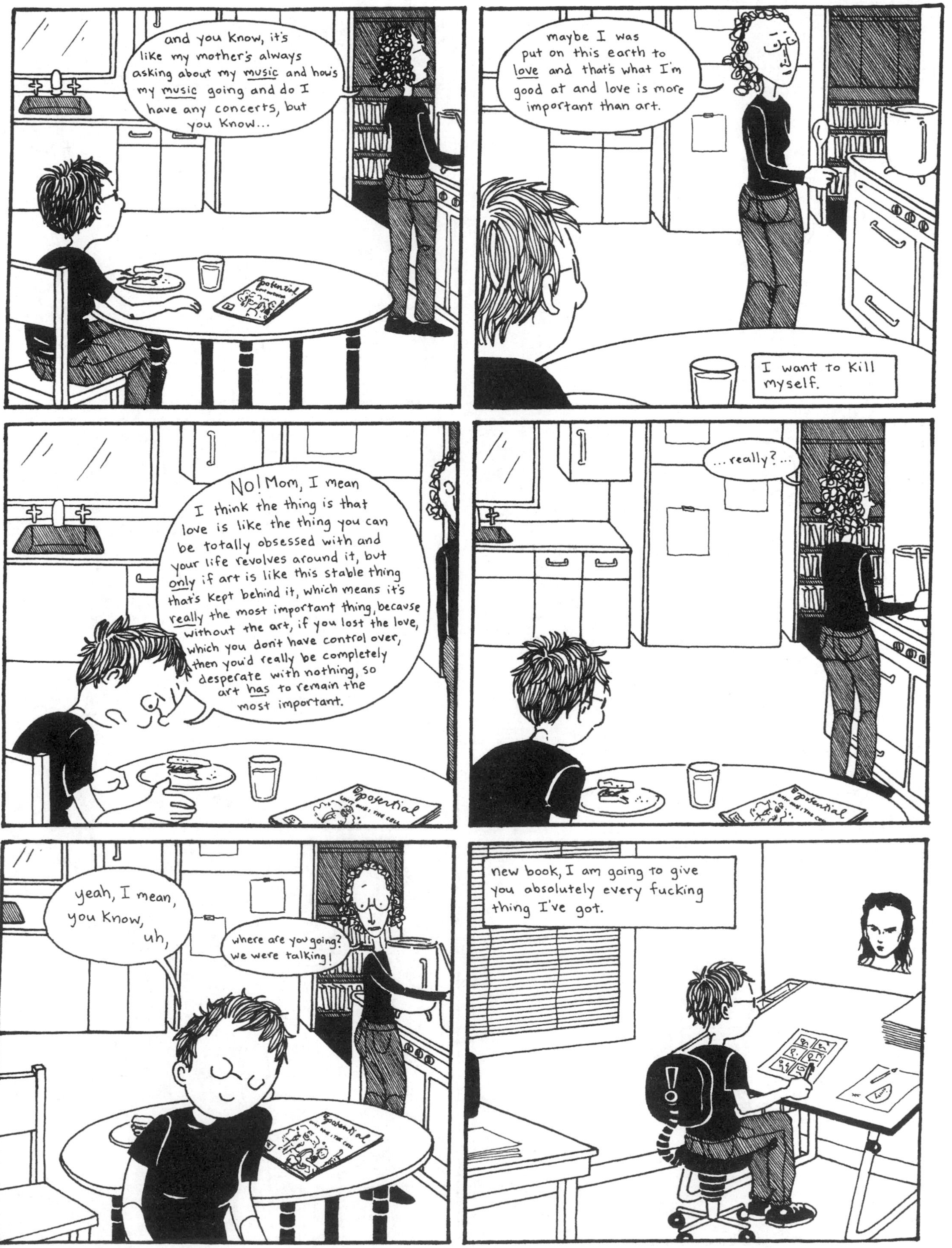
and you know, it's like my mother's always asking about my music and how's my music going and do I have any concerts, but you know...
maybe I was put on this earth to love and that's what I'm good at and love is more important than art.
I want to kill myself.
No! Mom, I mean I think the thing is that love is like the thing you can be totally obsessed with and your life revolves around it, but only if art is like this stable thing that's kept behind it, which means it's really the most important thing, because without the art, if you lost the love, which you don't have control over, then you'd really be completely desperate with nothing, so art has to remain the most important.
...really?...
yeah, I mean, you know, uh,
where are you going? we were talking!
new book, I am going to give you absolutely every fucking thing I've got.

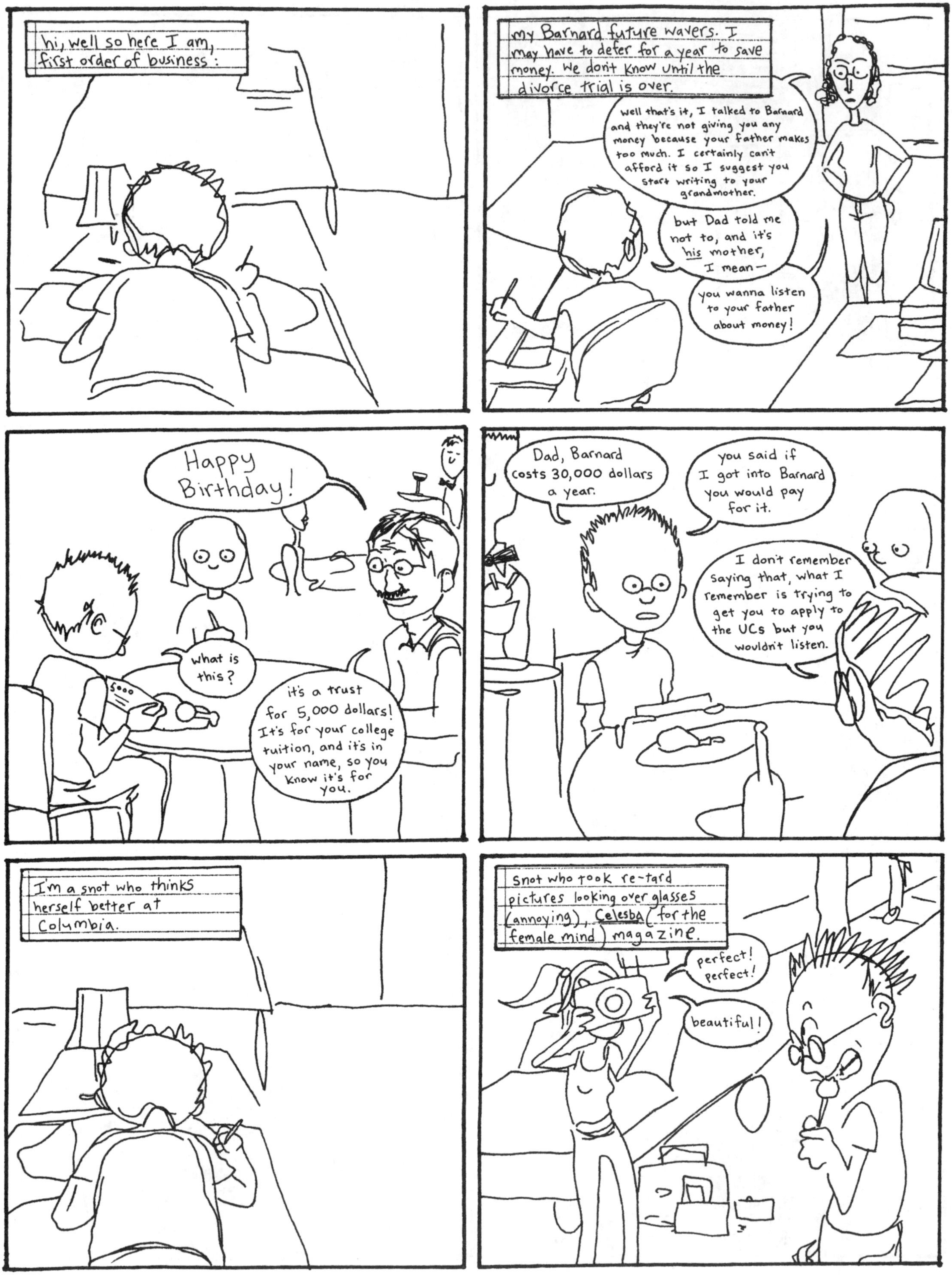
hi, well so here I am, first order of business:
my Barnard future wavers. I may have to defer for a year to save money. We don't know until the divorce trial is over.
well that's it, I talked to Barnard and they're not giving you any money because your father makes too much. I certainly can't afford it so I suggest you start writing to your grandmother.
but Dad told me not to, and it's his mother, I mean—
you wanna listen to your father about money!
Happy Birthday!
5000
what is this?
it's a trust for 5,000 dollars! It's for your college tuition, and it's in your name, so you know it's for you.
Dad, Barnard costs 30,000 dollars a year.
you said if I got into Barnard you would pay for it.
I don't remember saying that, what I remember is trying to get you to apply to the UCs but you wouldn't listen.
I'm a snot who thinks herself better at Columbia.
Snot who took re-tard pictures looking over glasses (annoying), Celesba (for the female mind) magazine.
perfect! perfect!
beautiful!

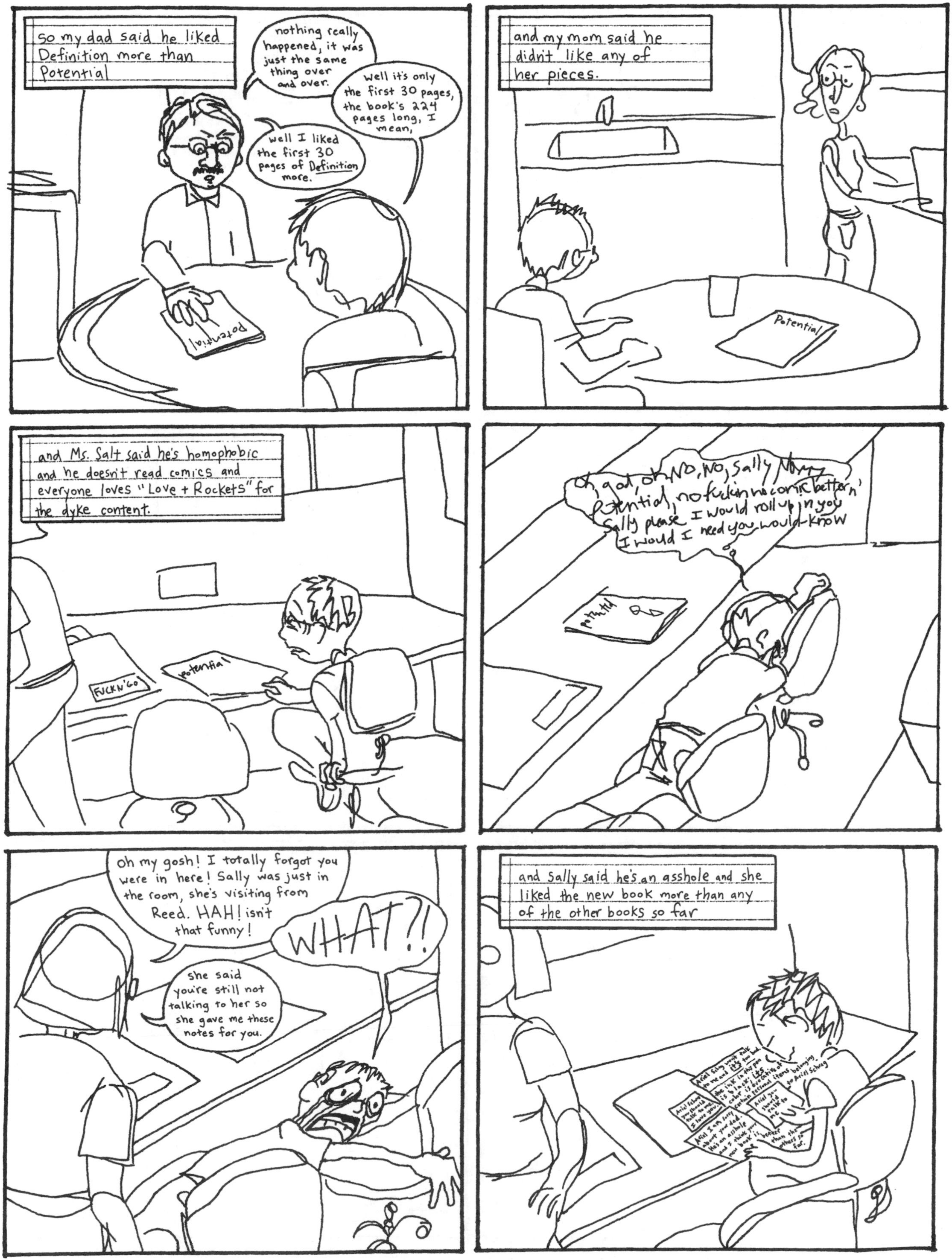

so my dad said he liked Definition more than Potential
nothing really happened, it was just the same thing over and over.
well it's only the first 30 pages, the book's 224 pages long, I mean,
well I liked the first 30 pages of Definition more.
Potential
and my mom said he didn't like any of her pieces.
Potential
and Ms. Salt said he's homophobic and he doesn't read comics and everyone loves "Love + Rockets" for the dyke content.
FUCKN'GO
potential
Oh, god, oh, NO, NO, Sally
Potential, no fuckin no comic better
Sally please I would roll up in you
I would I need you would know
Oh my gosh! I totally forgot you were in here! Sally was just in the room, she's visiting from Reed. HAH! isn't that funny!
WHAT?!
she said you're still not talking to her so she gave me these notes for you.
and Sally said he's an asshole and she liked the new book more than any of the other books so far
Ariel Schrag you should talk to me. I love you.
Ariel Schrag won't talk to me and it's too bad.
the ink in this pen is black, its color is evocative of certain personal items belonging to Ariel Schrag
Ariel you should talk to me
Ariel I am sorry about your dad. He's an asshole and I think your new book is better than the others so far.

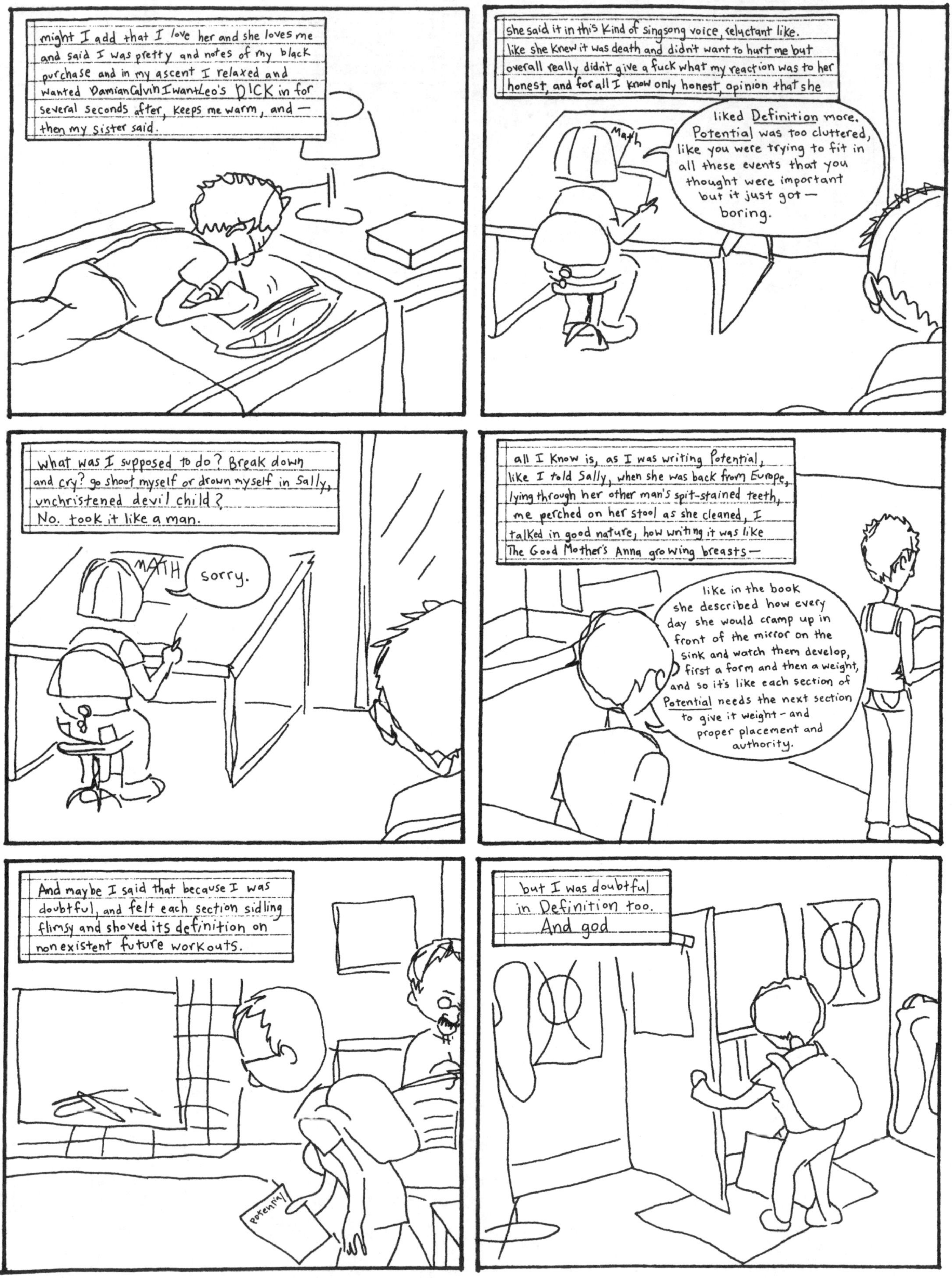
might I add that I love her and she loves me and said I was pretty and notes of my black purchase and in my ascent I relaxed and wanted DamianCalvinIwantLeo's DICK in for several seconds after, keeps me warm, and— then my sister said.
she said it in this kind of singsong voice, reluctant like. like she knew it was death and didn't want to hurt me but overall really didn't give a fuck what my reaction was to her honest, and for all I know only honest, opinion that she
Math
liked Definition more. Potential was too cluttered, like you were trying to fit in all these events that you thought were important but it just got— boring.
what was I supposed to do? Break down and cry? go shoot myself or drown myself in Sally, unchristened devil child? No. took it like a man.
MATH
sorry.
all I know is, as I was writing Potential, like I told Sally, when she was back from Europe, lying through her other man's spit-stained teeth, me perched on her stool as she cleaned, I talked in good nature, how writing it was like The Good Mother's Anna growing breasts—
like in the book she described how every day she would cramp up in front of the mirror on the sink and watch them develop, first a form and then a weight, and so it's like each section of Potential needs the next section to give it weight - and proper placement and authority.
And maybe I said that because I was doubtful, and felt each section sidling flimsy and shoved its definition on nonexistent future workouts.
potential
but I was doubtful in Definition too. And god

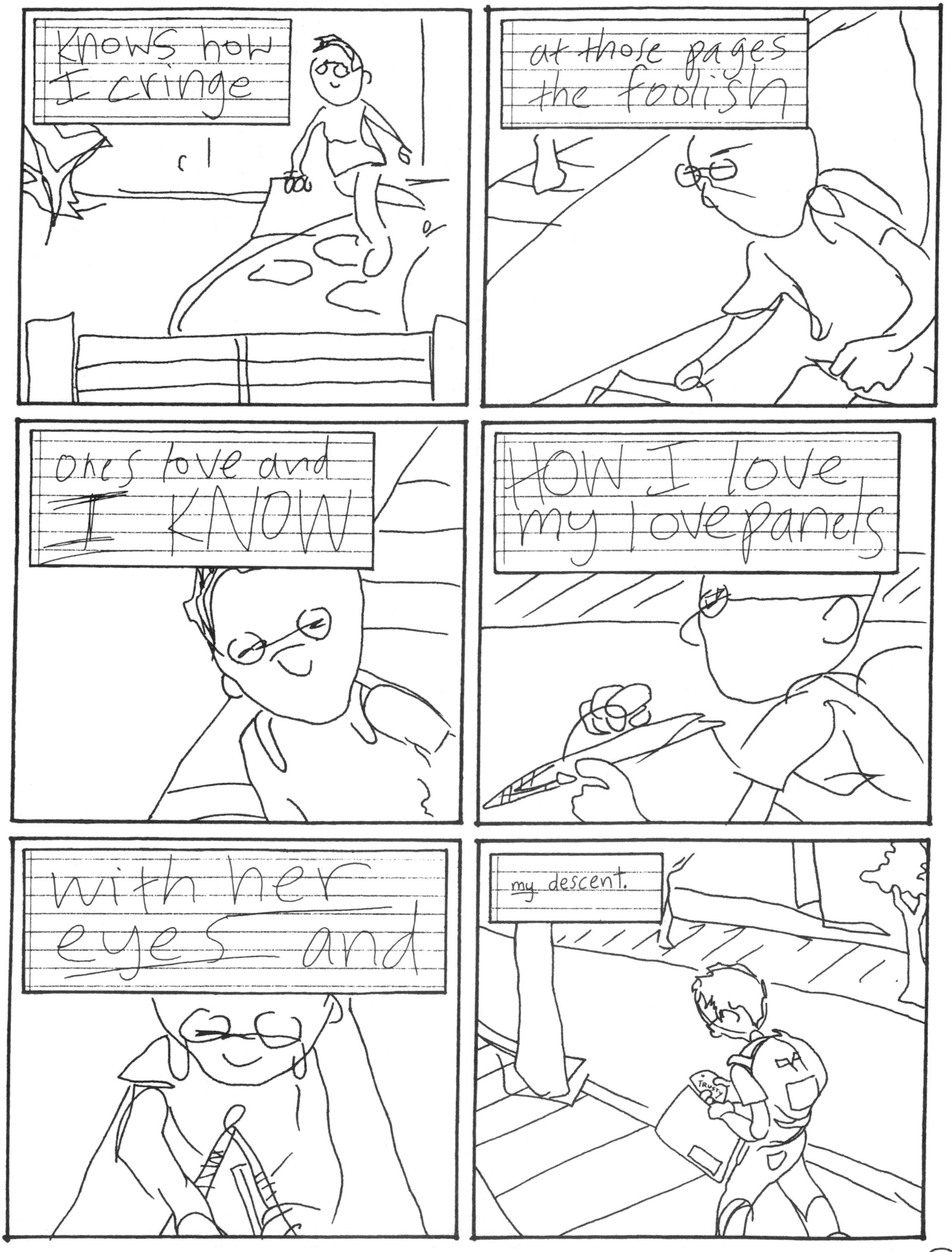
knows how I cringe
at those pages the foolish
ones love and I KNOW
HOW I love my love panels
with her eyes and
my descent.
TRUSTY

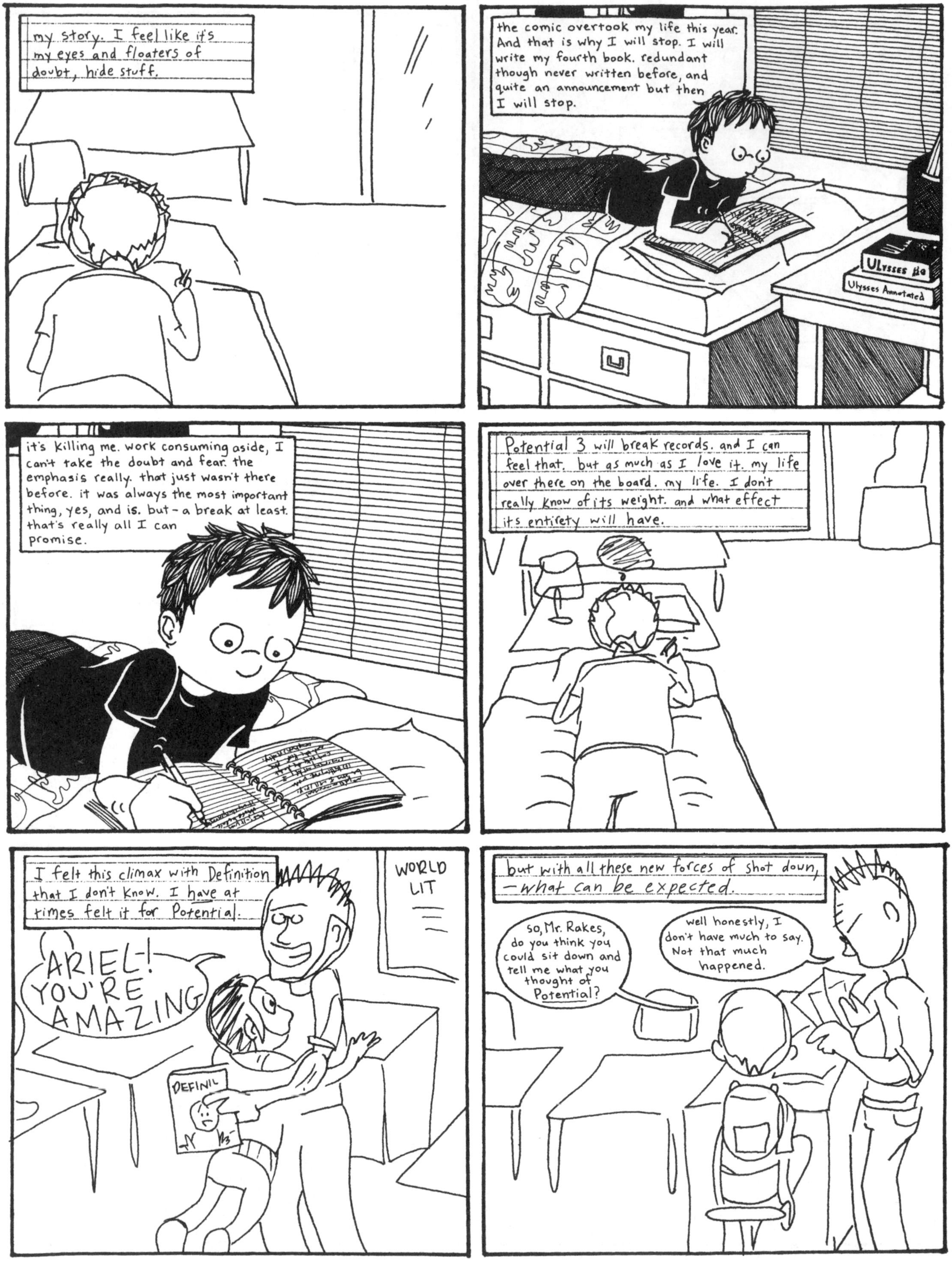
my story. I feel like it's my eyes and floaters of doubt, hide stuff.
the comic overtook my life this year. And that is why I will stop. I will write my fourth book. redundant though never written before, and quite an announcement but then I will stop.
Ulysses
Ulysses Annotated
it's killing me. work consuming aside, I can't take the doubt and fear. the emphasis really. that just wasn't there before. it was always the most important thing, yes, and is. but - a break at least. that's really all I can promise.
Potential 3 will break records. and I can feel that. but as much as I love it. my life over there on the board. my life. I don't really know of its weight. and what effect its entirety will have.
I felt this climax with Definition that I don't know. I have at times felt it for Potential.
WORLD LIT
ARIEL! YOU'RE AMAZING
DEFINIT
but with all these new forces of shot down, —what can be expected.
So, Mr. Rakes, do you think you could sit down and tell me what you thought of Potential?
well honestly, I don't have much to say. Not that much happened.

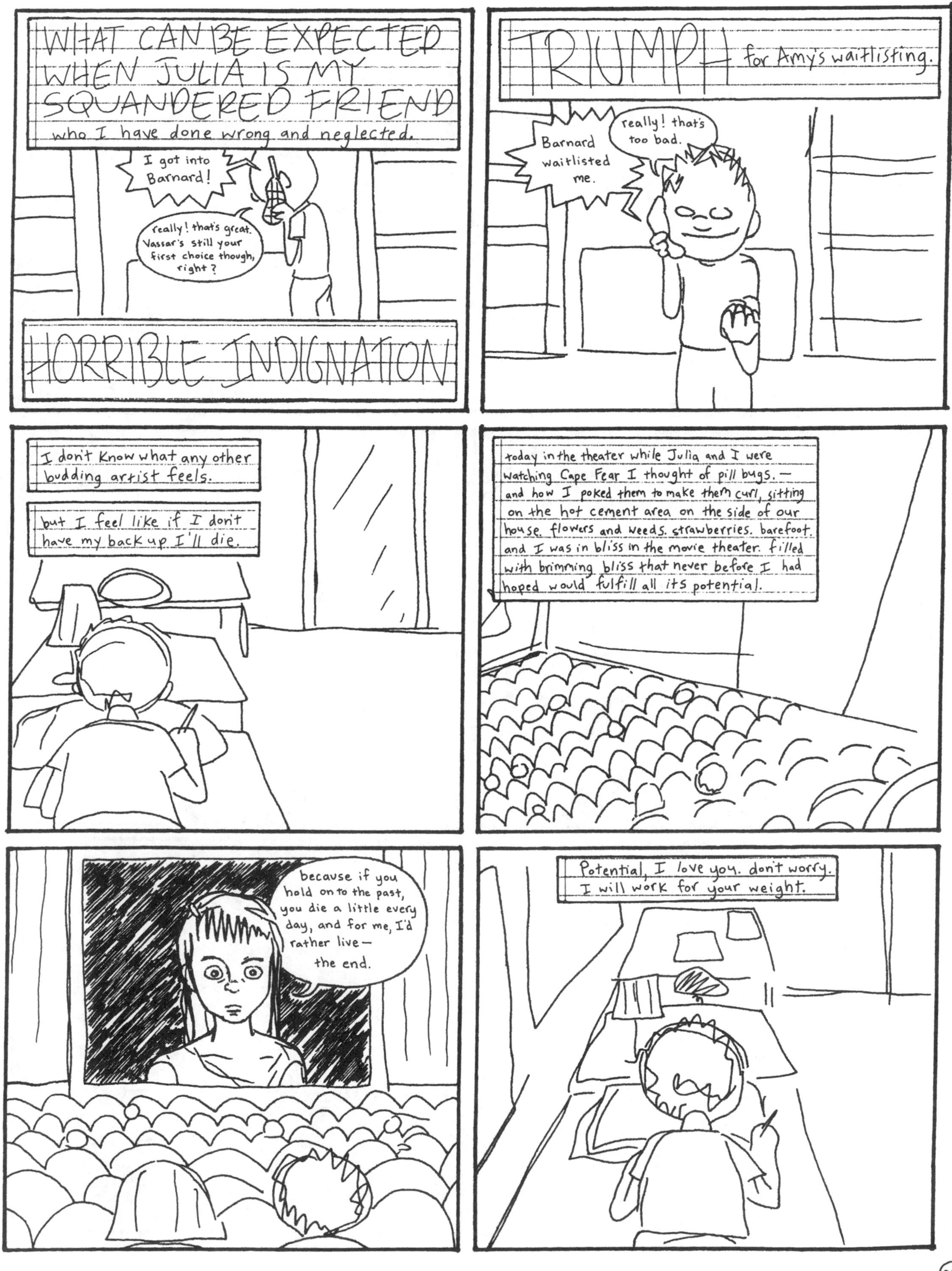
WHAT CAN BE EXPECTED WHEN JULIA IS MY SQUANDERED FRIEND
who I have done wrong and neglected.
I got into Barnard!
really! that's great. Vassar's still your first choice though, right?
HORRIBLE INDIGNATION
TRIUMPH for Amy's waitlisting.
Barnard waitlisted me.
really! that's too bad.
I don't know what any other budding artist feels.
but I feel like if I don't have my back up I'll die.
today in the theater while Julia and I were watching Cape Fear I thought of pill bugs.— and how I poked them to make them curl, sitting on the hot cement area on the side of our house. flowers and weeds. strawberries. barefoot. and I was in bliss in the movie theater. filled with brimming bliss that never before I had hoped would fulfill all its potential.
because if you hold on to the past, you die a little every day, and for me, I'd rather live— the end.
Potential, I love you. don't worry. I will work for your weight.

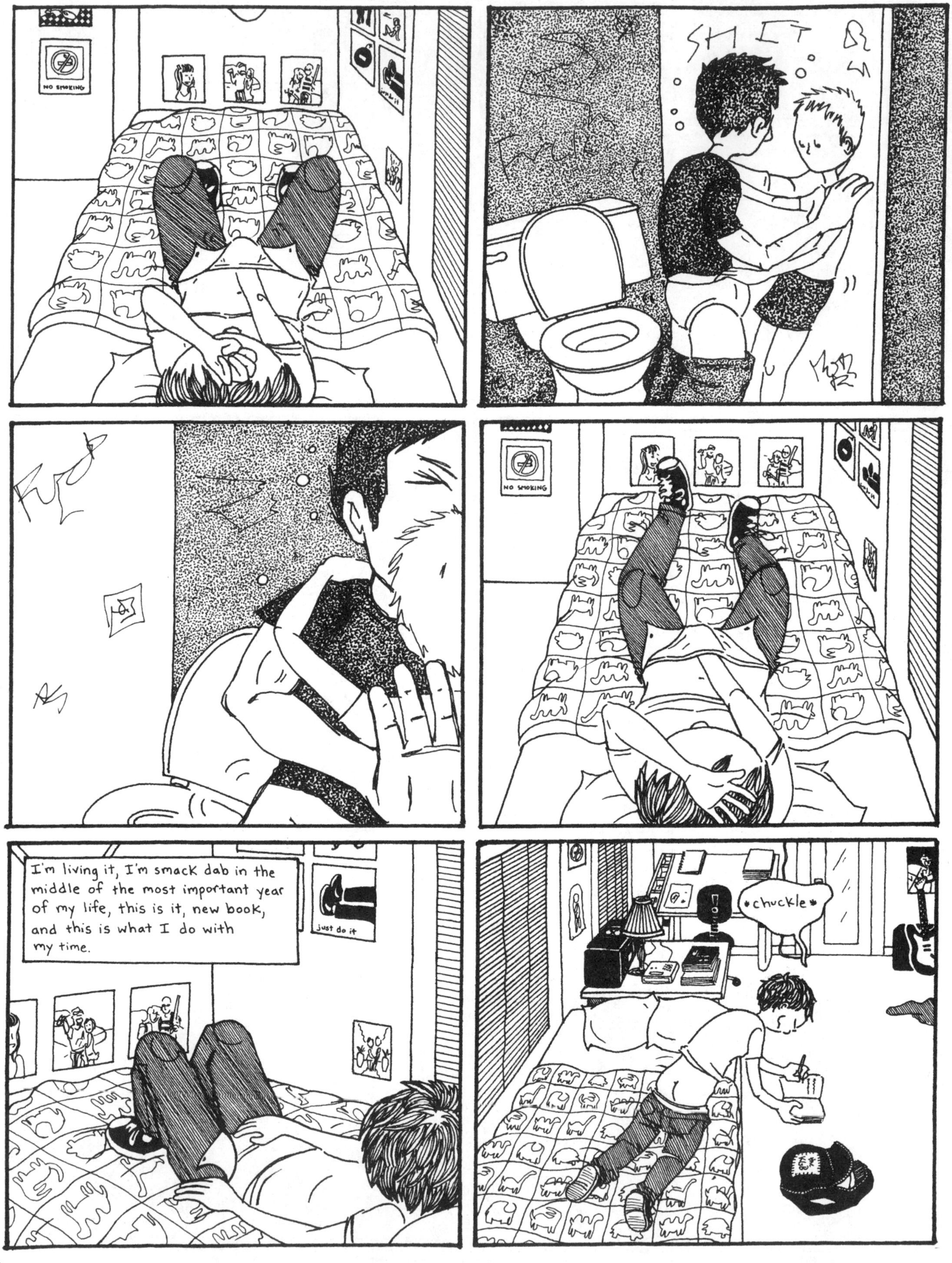
NO SMOKING
NO SMOKING
I'm living it, I'm smack dab in the middle of the most important year of my life, this is it, new book, and this is what I do with my time.
just do it
chuckle

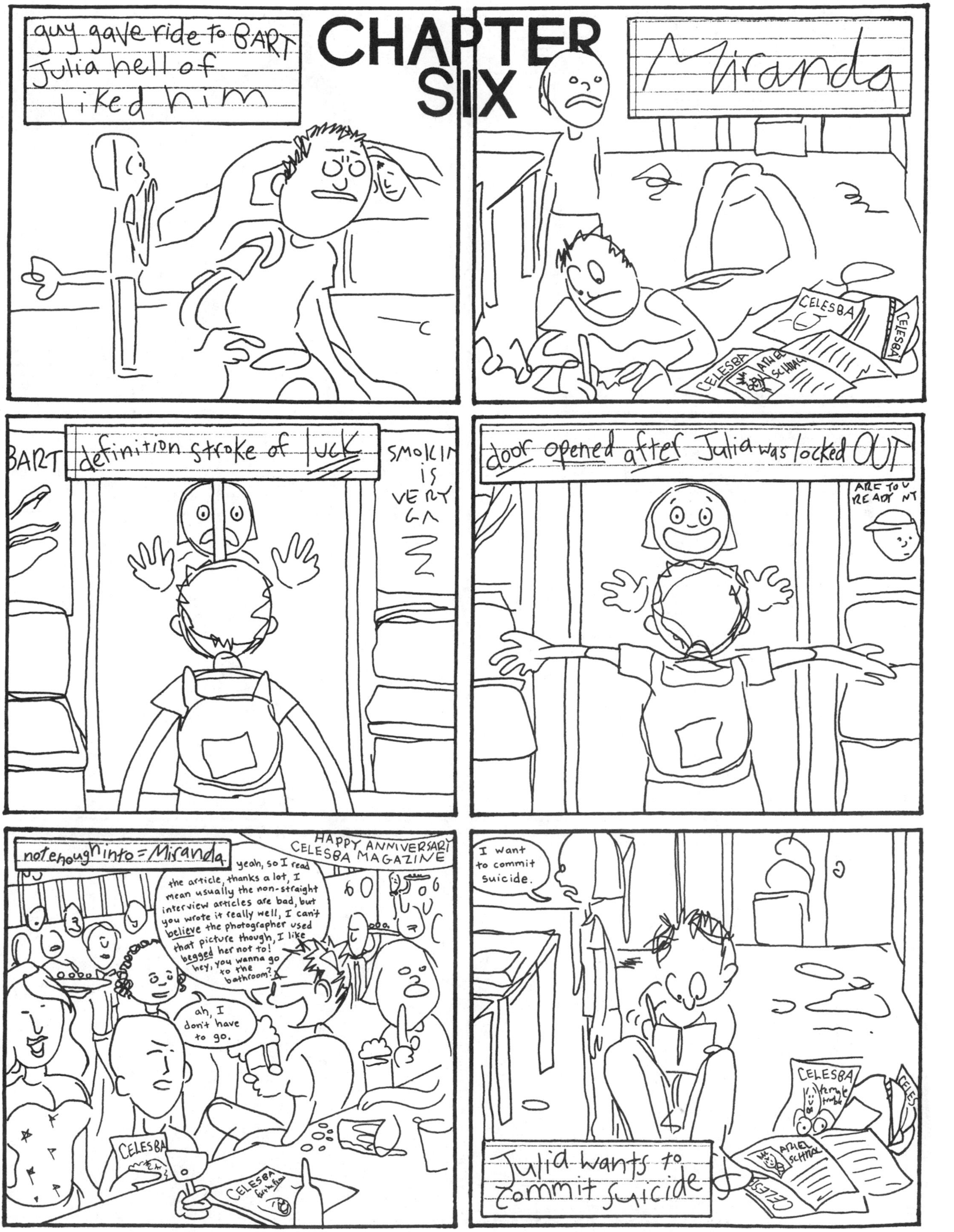
CHAPTER SIX
guy gave ride to BART Julia hell of liked him
Miranda
BART
definition stroke of luck
door opened after Julia was locked OUT
not enough into = Miranda
HAPPY ANNIVERSARI CELESBA MAGAZINE
yeah, so I read the article, thanks a lot, I mean usually the non-straight interview articles are bad, but you wrote it really well, I can't believe the photographer used that picture though, I like begged her not to! hey, you wanna go to the bathroom?
ah, I don't have to go.
CELESBA
I want to commit suicide.
CELESBA
Julia wants to commit suicide

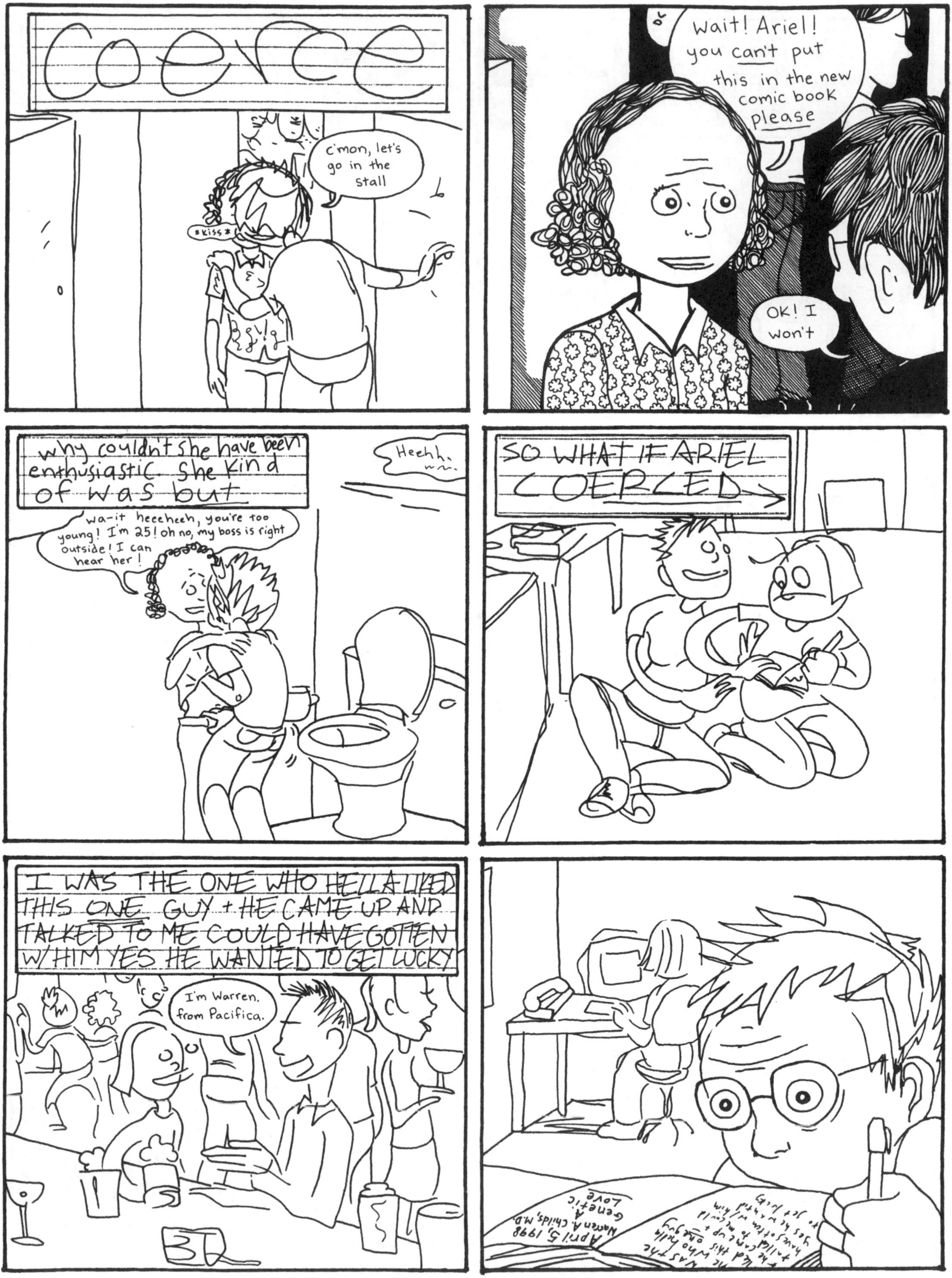
Coerce
c'mon, let's go in the stall
kiss
Wait! Ariel! you can't put this in the new comic book please
OK! I won't
why couldn't she have been enthusiastic. She kind of was but
Heehh.
wa-it heeeheeh, you're too young! I'm 25! oh no, my boss is right outside! I can hear her!
SO WHAT IF ARIEL COERCED
I WAS THE ONE WHO HELLA LIKED THIS ONE GUY + HE CAME UP AND TALKED TO ME COULD HAVE GOTTEN W/HIM YES HE WANTED TO GET LUCKY
I'm Warren. from Pacifica.

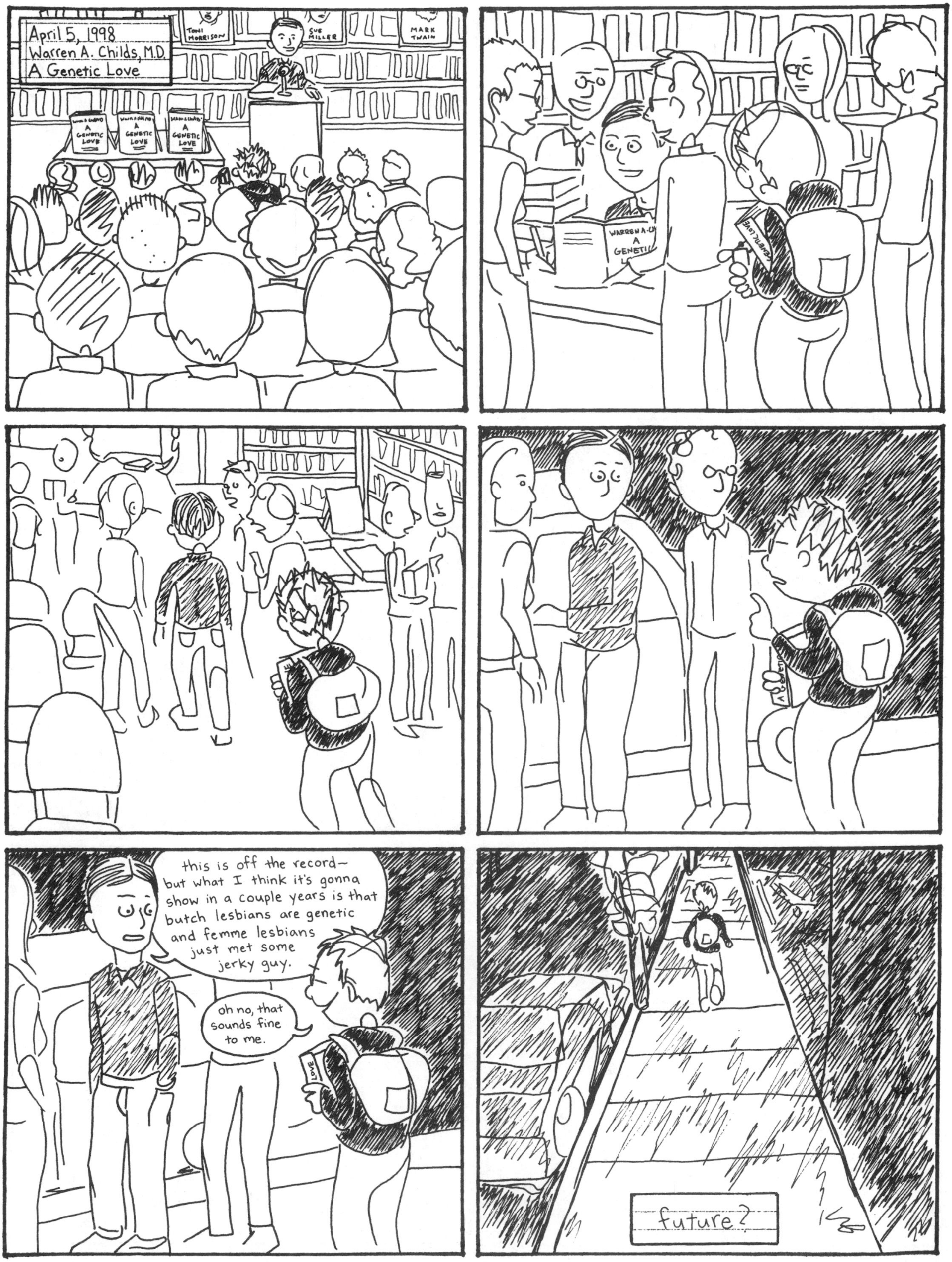
April 5, 1998
Warren A. Childs, M.D.
A Genetic Love
TONI MORRISON
SUE MILLER
MARK TWAIN
A GENETIC LOVE
A GENETIC LOVE
A GENETIC LOVE
this is off the record— but what I think it's gonna show in a couple years is that butch lesbians are genetic and femme lesbians just met some jerky guy.
oh no, that sounds fine to me.
future?

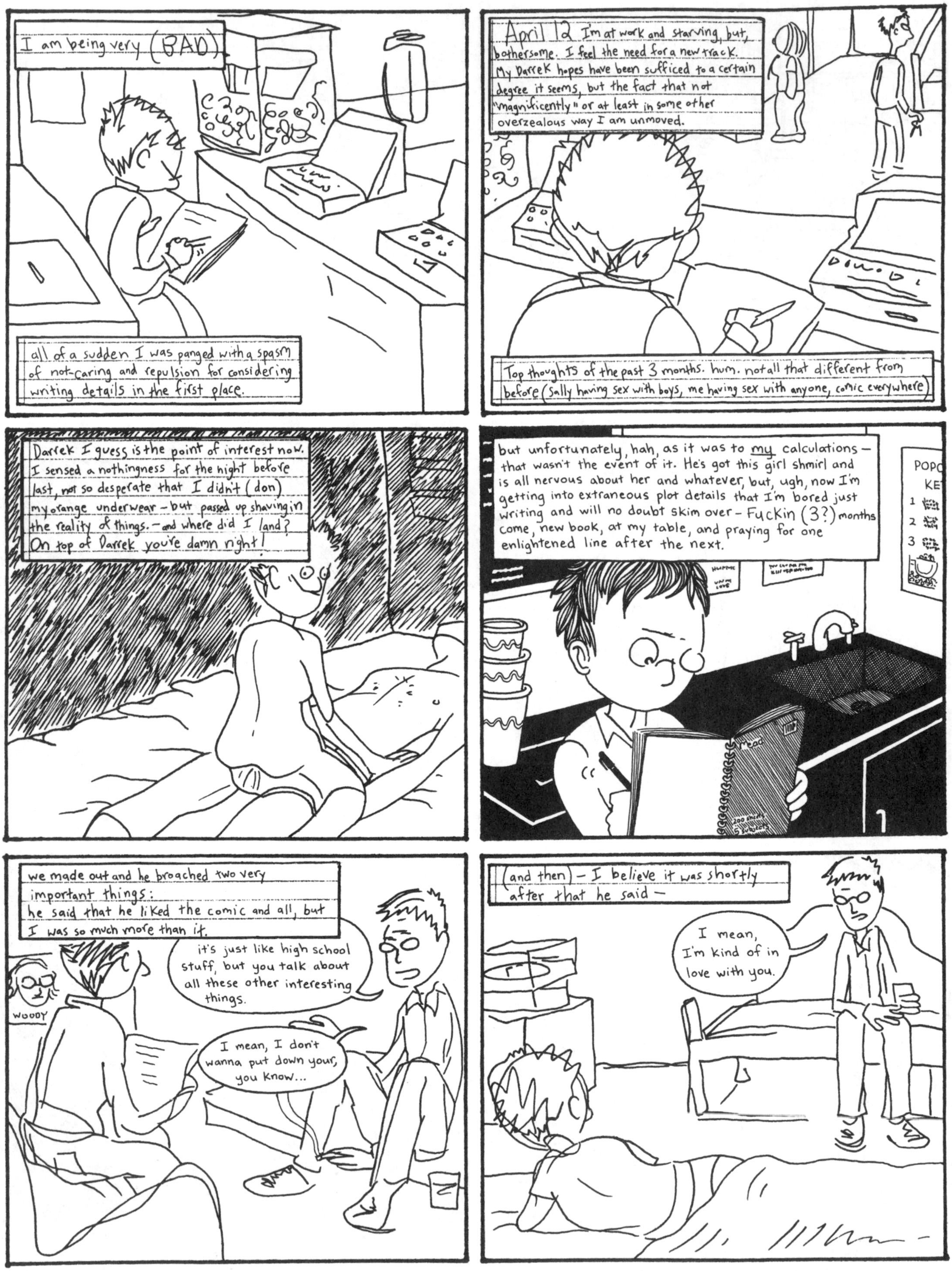
I am being very (BAD)
all of a sudden I was panged with a spasm of not-caring and repulsion for considering writing details in the first place.
April 12 I'm at work and starving, but, bothersome. I feel the need for a new track. My Darrek hopes have been sufficed to a certain degree it seems, but the fact that not "magnificently" or at least in some other overzealous way I am unmoved.
Top thoughts of the past 3 months. hum. not all that different from before (Sally having sex with boys, me having sex with anyone, comic everywhere)
Darrek I guess is the point of interest now. I sensed a nothingness for the night before last, not so desperate that I didn't (don) my orange underwear - but passed up shaving in the reality of things. - and where did I land? On top of Darrek you're damn right!
but unfortunately, hah, as it was to my calculations - that wasn't the event of it. He's got this girl shmirl and is all nervous about her and whatever, but, ugh, now I'm getting into extraneous plot details that I'm bored just writing and will no doubt skim over - FucKin (3?) months come, new book, at my table, and praying for one enlightened line after the next.
we made out and he broached two very important things: he said that he liked the comic and all, but I was so much more than it.
WOODY
it's just like high school stuff, but you talk about all these other interesting things.
I mean, I don't wanna put down your, you know...
(and then) - I believe it was shortly after that he said -
I mean, I'm kind of in love with you.

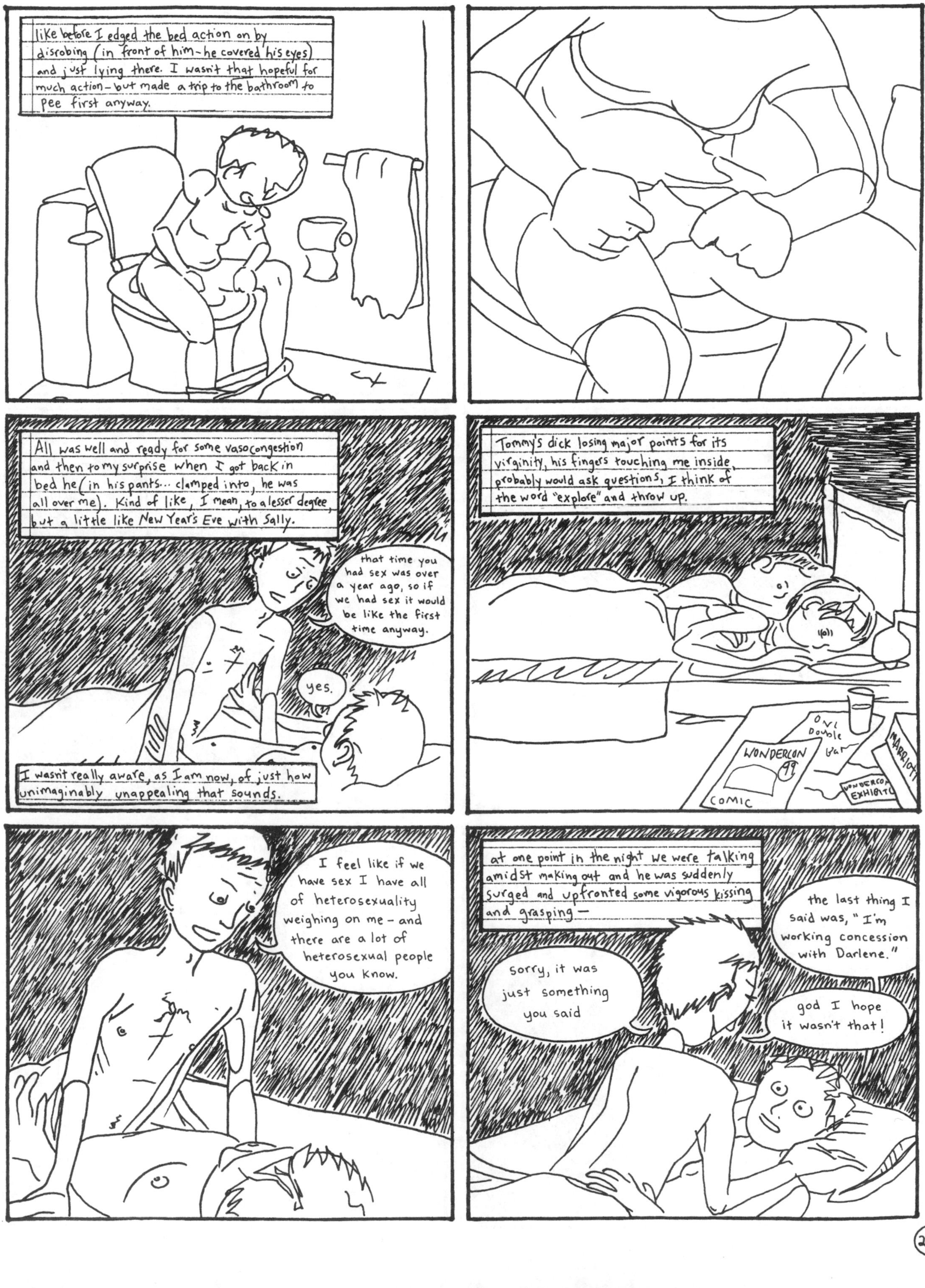
like before I edged the bed action on by disrobing (in front of him - he covered his eyes) and just lying there. I wasn't that hopeful for much action - but made a trip to the bathroom to pee first anyway.
All was well and ready for some vasocongestion and then to my surprise when I got back in bed he (in his pants... clamped into, he was all over me). Kind of like, I mean, to a lesser degree, but a little like New Year's Eve with Sally.
that time you had sex was over a year ago, so if we had sex it would be like the first time anyway.
yes.
I wasn't really aware, as I am now, of just how unimaginably unappealing that sounds.
Tommy's dick losing major points for its virginity, his fingers touching me inside, probably would ask questions, I think of the word "explore" and throw up.
ONI Double
WONDERCON 99
COMIC
MARRIOTT
WONDERCON EXHIBITOR
I feel like if we have sex I have all of heterosexuality weighing on me - and there are a lot of heterosexual people you know.
at one point in the night we were talking amidst making out and he was suddenly surged and upfronted some vigorous kissing and grasping -
the last thing I said was, "I'm working concession with Darlene."
sorry, it was just something you said
god I hope it wasn't that!

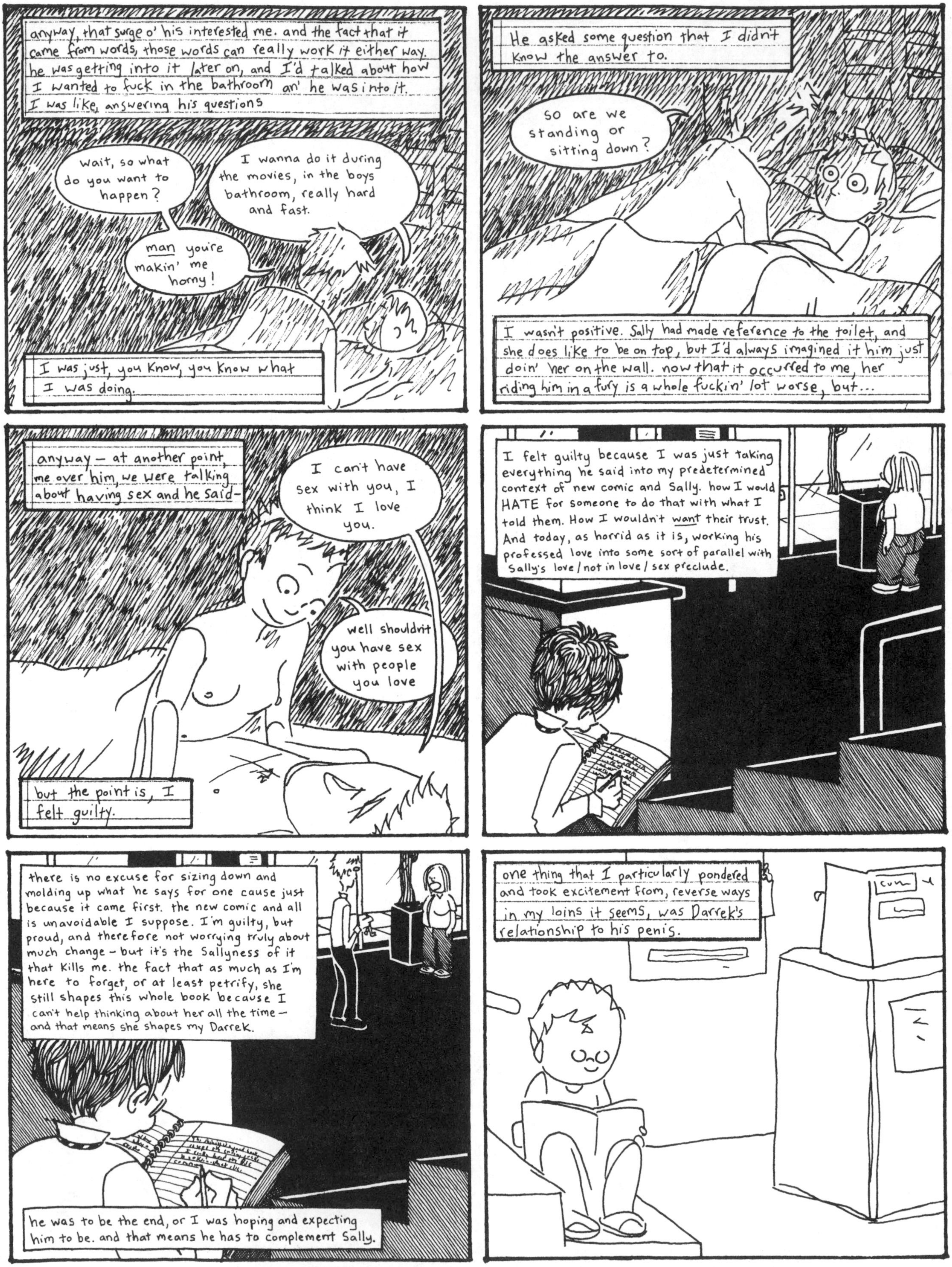

anyway, that surge o' his interested me. and the fact that it came from words, those words can really work it either way. he was getting into it later on, and I'd talked about how I wanted to fuck in the bathroom an' he was into it. I was like, answering his questions
wait, so what do you want to happen?
I wanna do it during the movies, in the boys bathroom, really hard and fast.
man you're makin' me horny!
I was just, you know, you know what I was doing.
He asked some question that I didn't know the answer to.
so are we standing or sitting down?
I wasn't positive. Sally had made reference to the toilet, and she does like to be on top, but I'd always imagined it him just doin' her on the wall. now that it occurred to me, her riding him in a fury is a whole fuckin' lot worse, but...
anyway — at another point, me over him, we were talking about having sex and he said—
I can't have sex with you, I think I love you.
well shouldn't you have sex with people you love
but the point is, I felt guilty.
I felt guilty because I was just taking everything he said into my predetermined context of new comic and Sally. how I would HATE for someone to do that with what I told them. How I wouldn't want their trust. And today, as horrid as it is, working his professed love into some sort of parallel with Sally's love / not in love / sex preclude.
there is no excuse for sizing down and molding up what he says for one cause just because it came first. the new comic and all is unavoidable I suppose. I'm guilty, but proud, and therefore not worrying truly about much change — but it's the Sallyness of it that kills me. the fact that as much as I'm here to forget, or at least petrify, she still shapes this whole book because I can't help thinking about her all the time — and that means she shapes my Darrek.
he was to be the end, or I was hoping and expecting him to be. and that means he has to complement Sally.
one thing that I particularly pondered and took excitement from, reverse ways in my loins it seems, was Darrek's relationship to his penis.

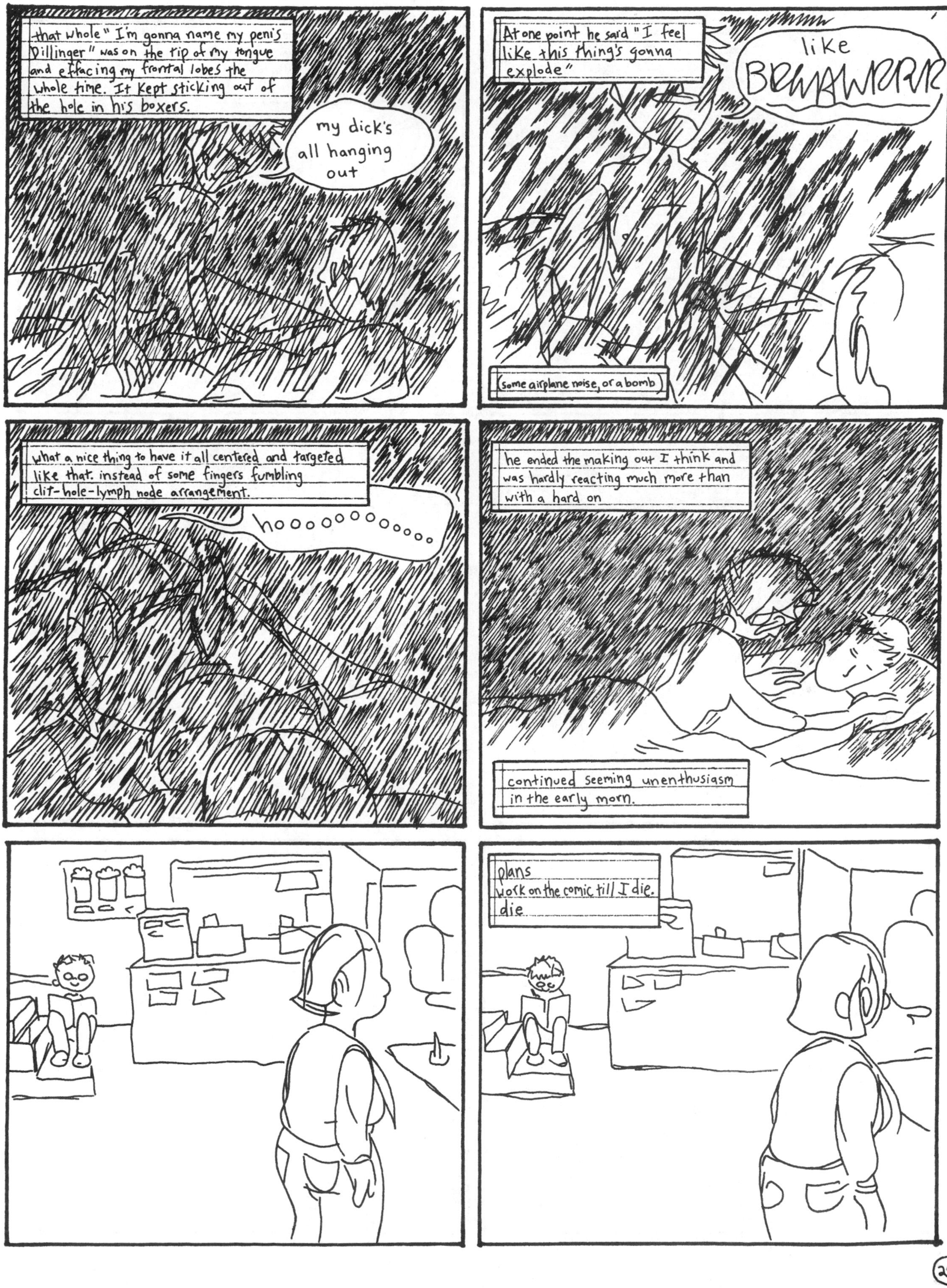
that whole "I'm gonna name my penis Dillinger" was on the tip of my tongue and effacing my frontal lobes the whole time. It kept sticking out of the hole in his boxers.
my dick's all hanging out
At one point he said "I feel like this thing's gonna explode"
like BRWAWRRR
(some airplane noise, or a bomb)
what a nice thing to have it all centered and targeted like that. instead of some fingers fumbling clit-hole-lymph node arrangement.
hoooooooooooo
he ended the making out I think and was hardly reacting much more than with a hard on
continued seeming unenthusiasm in the early morn.
plans
work on the comic till I die.
die

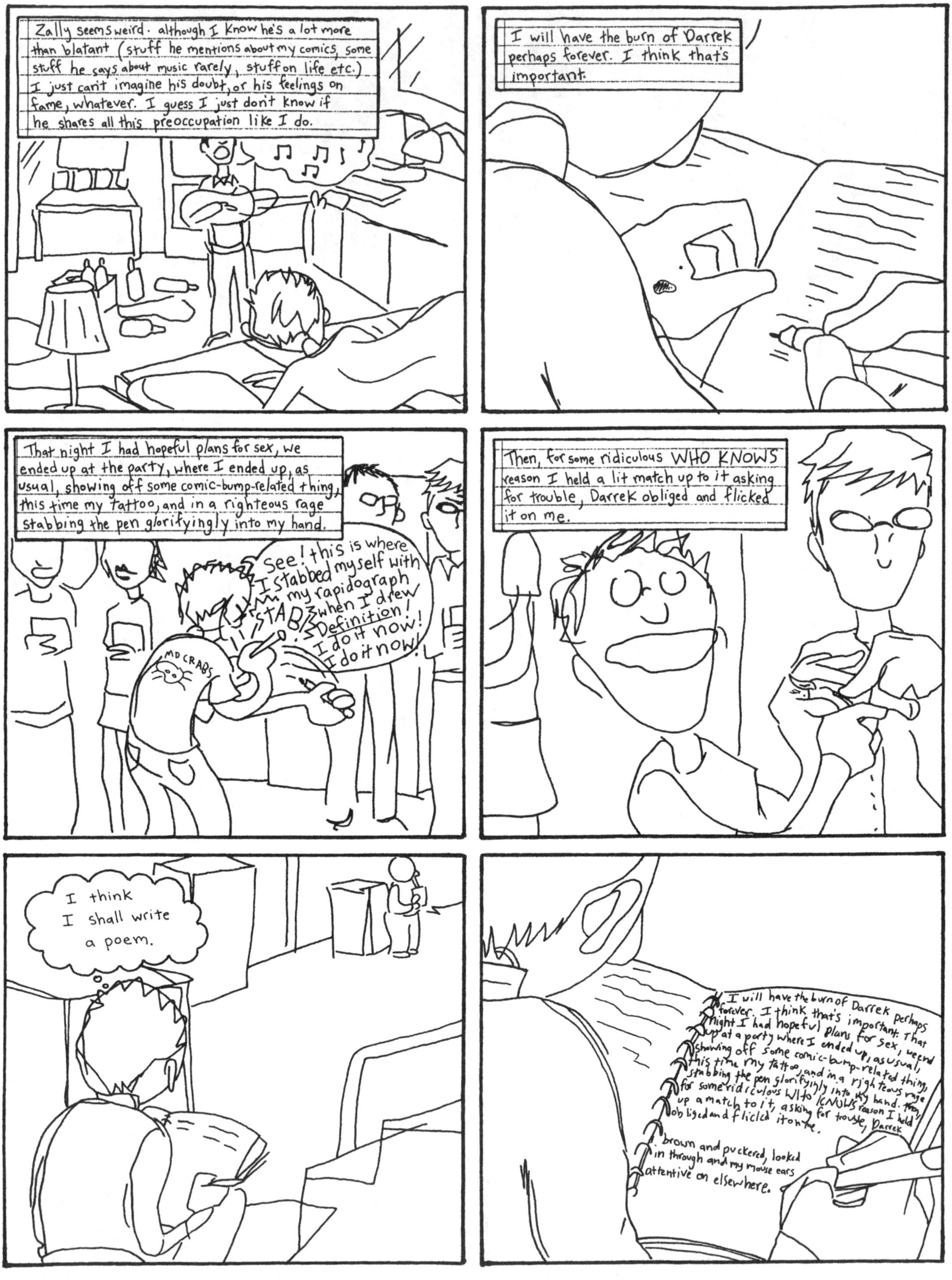
Zally seems weird. although I know he's a lot more than blatant (stuff he mentions about my comics, some stuff he says about music rarely, stuff on life etc.) I just can't imagine his doubt, or his feelings on fame, whatever. I guess I just don't know if he shares all this preoccupation like I do.
I will have the burn of Darrek perhaps forever. I think that's important.
That night I had hopeful plans for sex, we ended up at the party, where I ended up, as usual, showing off some comic-bump-related thing, this time my tattoo, and in a righteous rage stabbing the pen glorifyingly into my hand.
See! this is where I stabbed myself with my rapidograph when I drew Definition! I do it now! I do it now!
STAB!
MD CRABS
Then, for some ridiculous WHO KNOWS reason I held a lit match up to it asking for trouble, Darrek obliged and flicked it on me.
I think I shall write a poem.
I will have the burn of Darrek perhaps forever. I think that's important. That night I had hopeful plans for sex, we end up at a party where I ended up, as usual, showing off some comic-bump-related thing, this time my tattoo, and in a righteous rage stabbing the pen glorifyingly into my hand. Then for some ridiculous WHO KNOWS reason I held up a match to it, asking for trouble, Darrek obliged and flicked it on me.
brown and puckered, looked in through and my mouse ears attentive on elsewhere.

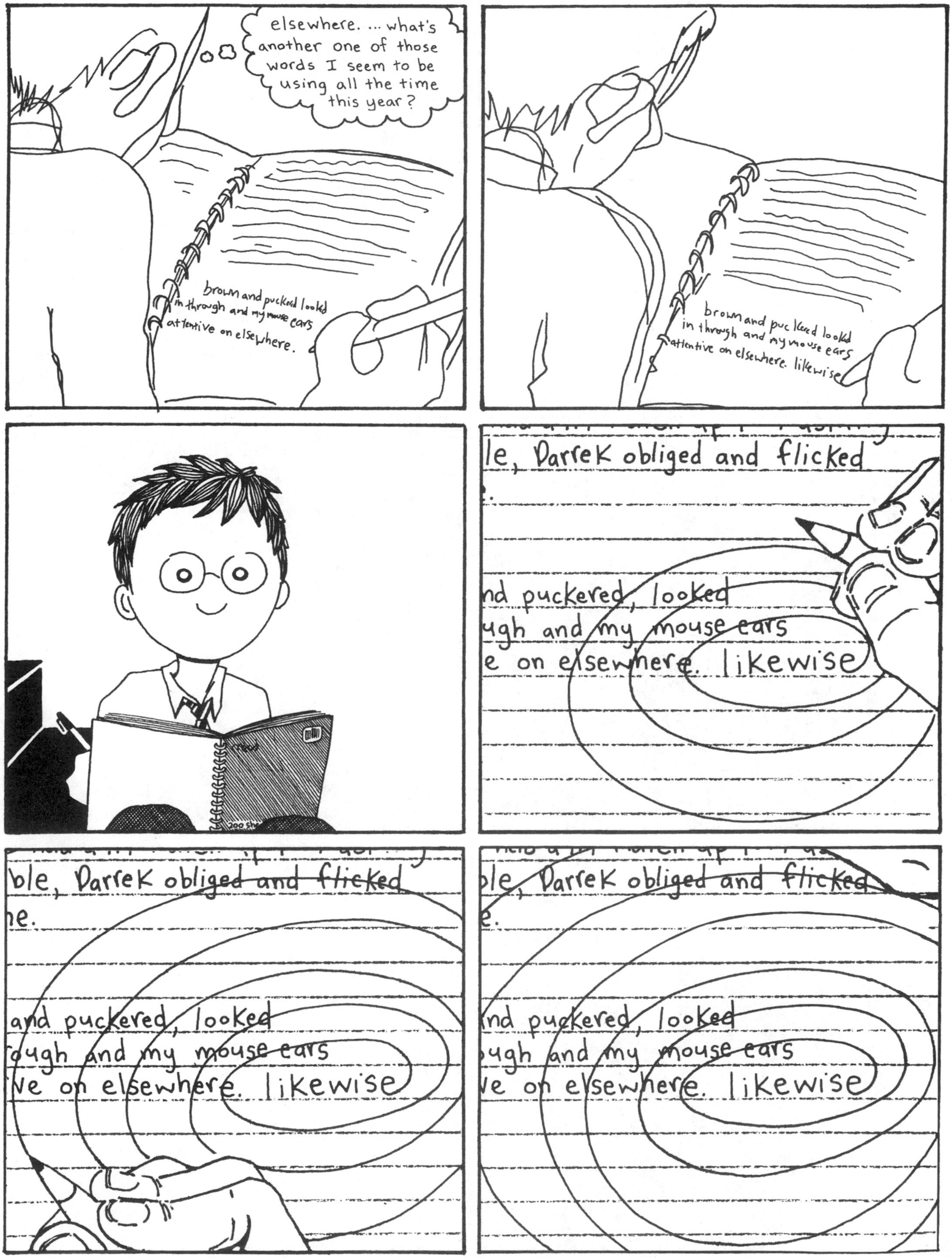
elsewhere. ... what's another one of those words I seem to be using all the time this year?
brown and puckered lookd in through and my mouse ears attentive on elsewhere.
brown and puckered lookd in through and my mouse ears attentive on elsewhere. likewise
le, Darrek obliged and flicked
nd puckered, looked
ugh and my mouse ears
e on elsewhere. likewise
ble, Darrek obliged and flicked
ne.
and puckered, looked
ough and my mouse ears
ve on elsewhere. likewise
ble, Darrek obliged and flicked
and puckered, looked
ugh and my mouse ears
ve on elsewhere. likewise

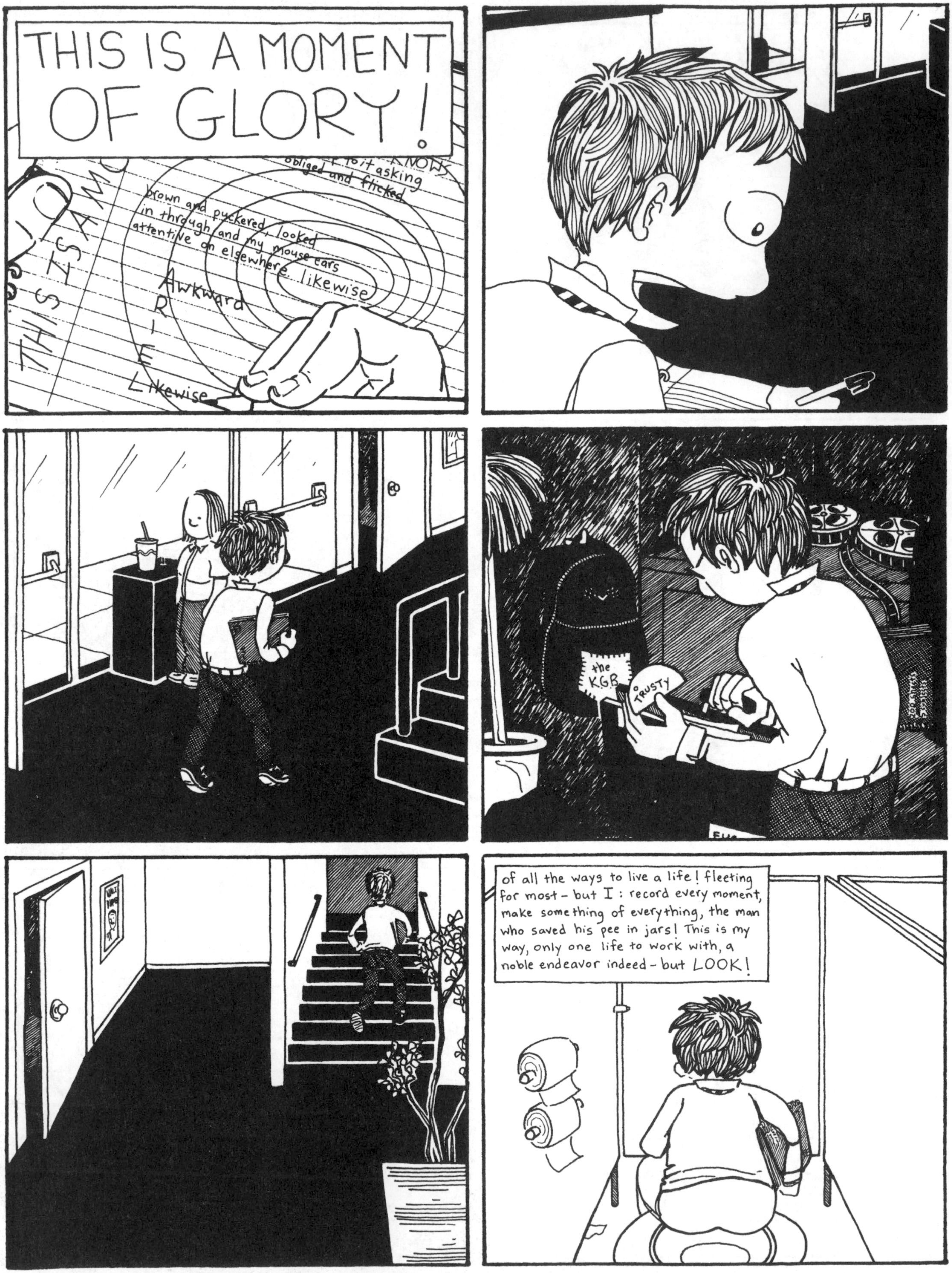
THIS IS A MOMENT OF GLORY!
obliged and flicked
brown and puckered, looked in through and my mouse ears attentive on elsewhere. likewise
Awkward
Likewise
the KGB
TRUSTY
of all the ways to live a life! fleeting for most - but I: record every moment, make something of everything, the man who saved his pee in jars! This is my way, only one life to work with, a noble endeavor indeed - but LOOK!

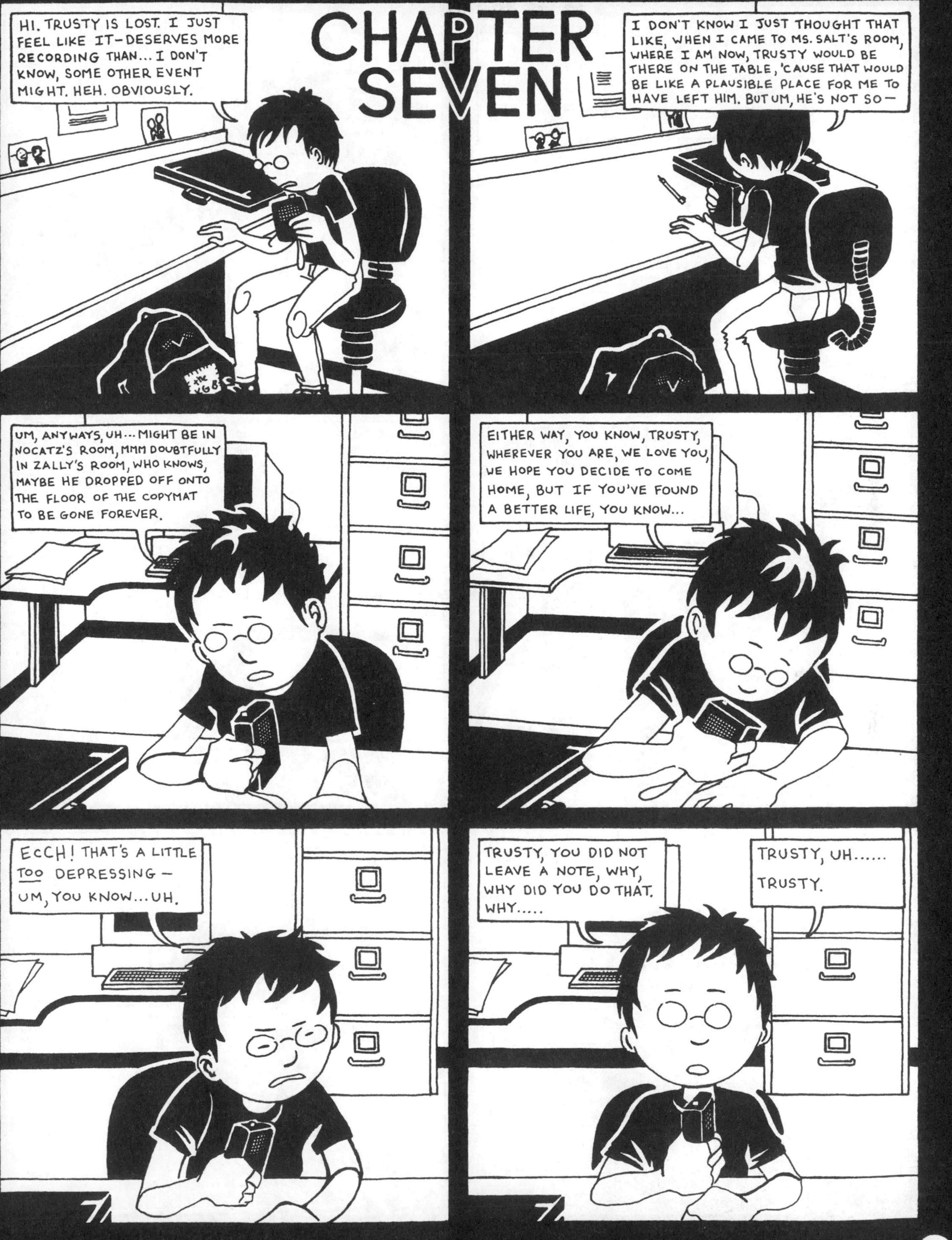
CHAPTER SEVEN
HI. TRUSTY IS LOST. I JUST FEEL LIKE IT–DESERVES MORE RECORDING THAN... I DON'T KNOW, SOME OTHER EVENT MIGHT. HEH. OBVIOUSLY.
I DON'T KNOW I JUST THOUGHT THAT LIKE, WHEN I CAME TO MS. SALT'S ROOM, WHERE I AM NOW, TRUSTY WOULD BE THERE ON THE TABLE, 'CAUSE THAT WOULD BE LIKE A PLAUSIBLE PLACE FOR ME TO HAVE LEFT HIM. BUT UM, HE'S NOT SO—
UM, ANYWAYS, UH... MIGHT BE IN NOCATZ'S ROOM, MMM DOUBTFULLY IN ZALLY'S ROOM, WHO KNOWS, MAYBE HE DROPPED OFF ONTO THE FLOOR OF THE COPYMAT TO BE GONE FOREVER.
EITHER WAY, YOU KNOW, TRUSTY, WHEREVER YOU ARE, WE LOVE YOU, WE HOPE YOU DECIDE TO COME HOME, BUT IF YOU'VE FOUND A BETTER LIFE, YOU KNOW...
ECCH! THAT'S A LITTLE TOO DEPRESSING — UM, YOU KNOW... UH.
TRUSTY, YOU DID NOT LEAVE A NOTE, WHY, WHY DID YOU DO THAT. WHY.....
TRUSTY, UH...... TRUSTY.

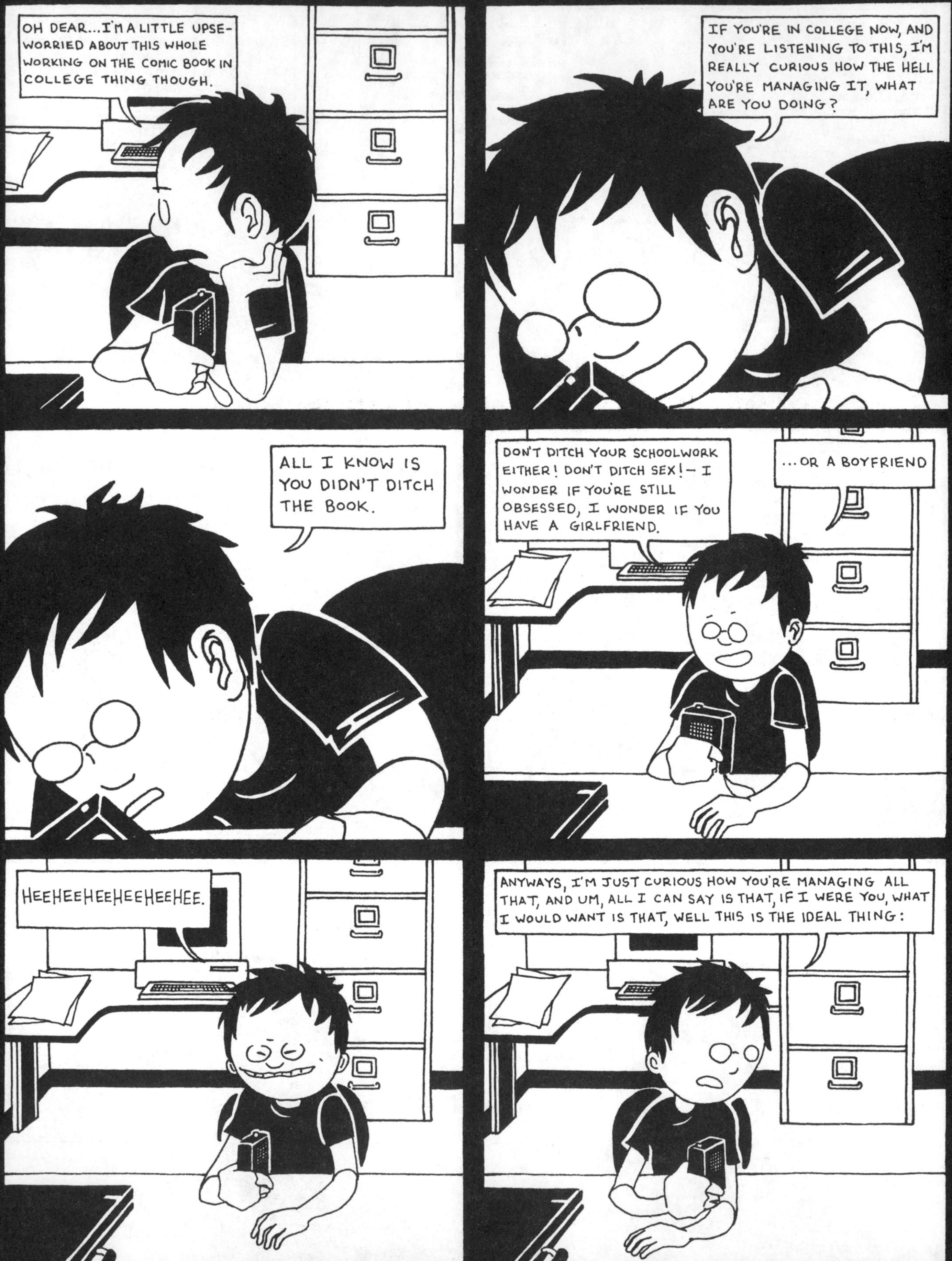
OH DEAR...I'M A LITTLE UPSE- WORRIED ABOUT THIS WHOLE WORKING ON THE COMIC BOOK IN COLLEGE THING THOUGH.
IF YOU'RE IN COLLEGE NOW, AND YOU'RE LISTENING TO THIS, I'M REALLY CURIOUS HOW THE HELL YOU'RE MANAGING IT, WHAT ARE YOU DOING?
ALL I KNOW IS YOU DIDN'T DITCH THE BOOK.
DON'T DITCH YOUR SCHOOLWORK EITHER! DON'T DITCH SEX! — I WONDER IF YOU'RE STILL OBSESSED, I WONDER IF YOU HAVE A GIRLFRIEND.
...OR A BOYFRIEND
HEEHEEHEEHEEHEEHEE.
ANYWAYS, I'M JUST CURIOUS HOW YOU'RE MANAGING ALL THAT, AND UM, ALL I CAN SAY IS THAT, IF I WERE YOU, WHAT I WOULD WANT IS THAT, WELL THIS IS THE IDEAL THING:

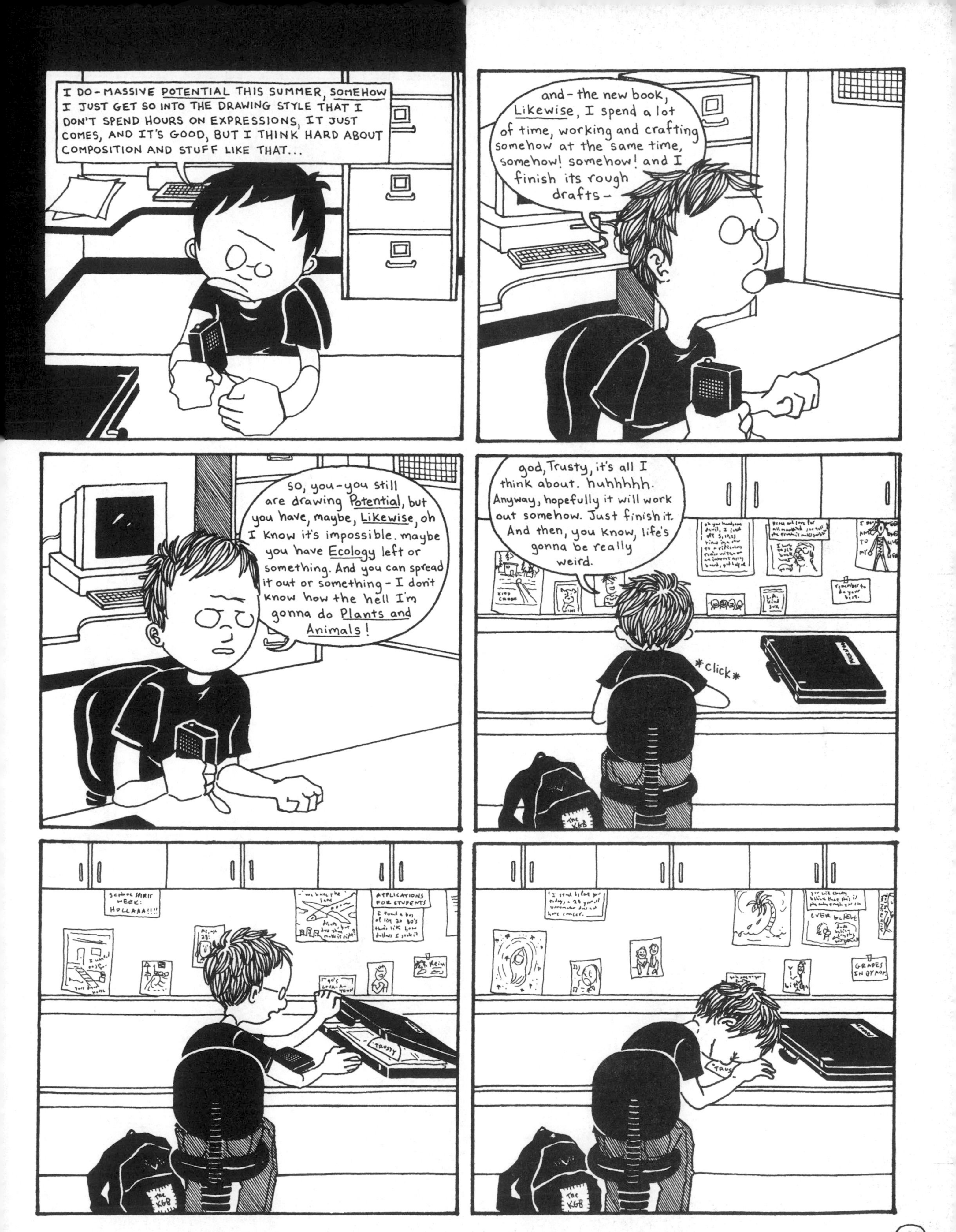
I DO-MASSIVE POTENTIAL THIS SUMMER, SOMEHOW I JUST GET SO INTO THE DRAWING STYLE THAT I DON'T SPEND HOURS ON EXPRESSIONS, IT JUST COMES, AND IT'S GOOD, BUT I THINK HARD ABOUT COMPOSITION AND STUFF LIKE THAT...
and-the new book, Likewise, I spend a lot of time, working and crafting somehow at the same time, somehow! somehow! and I finish its rough drafts-
so, you-you still are drawing Potential, but you have, maybe, Likewise, oh I know it's impossible. maybe you have Ecology left or something. And you can spread it out or something-I don't know how the hell I'm gonna do Plants and Animals!
god, Trusty, it's all I think about. huhhhhh. Anyway, hopefully it will work out somehow. Just finish it. And then, you know, life's gonna be really weird.
click
SCHOOL SPIRIT WEEK: HOLLAAA!!!!
APPLICATIONS FOR STUDENTS
TRUSTY
GRADES
THE KGB

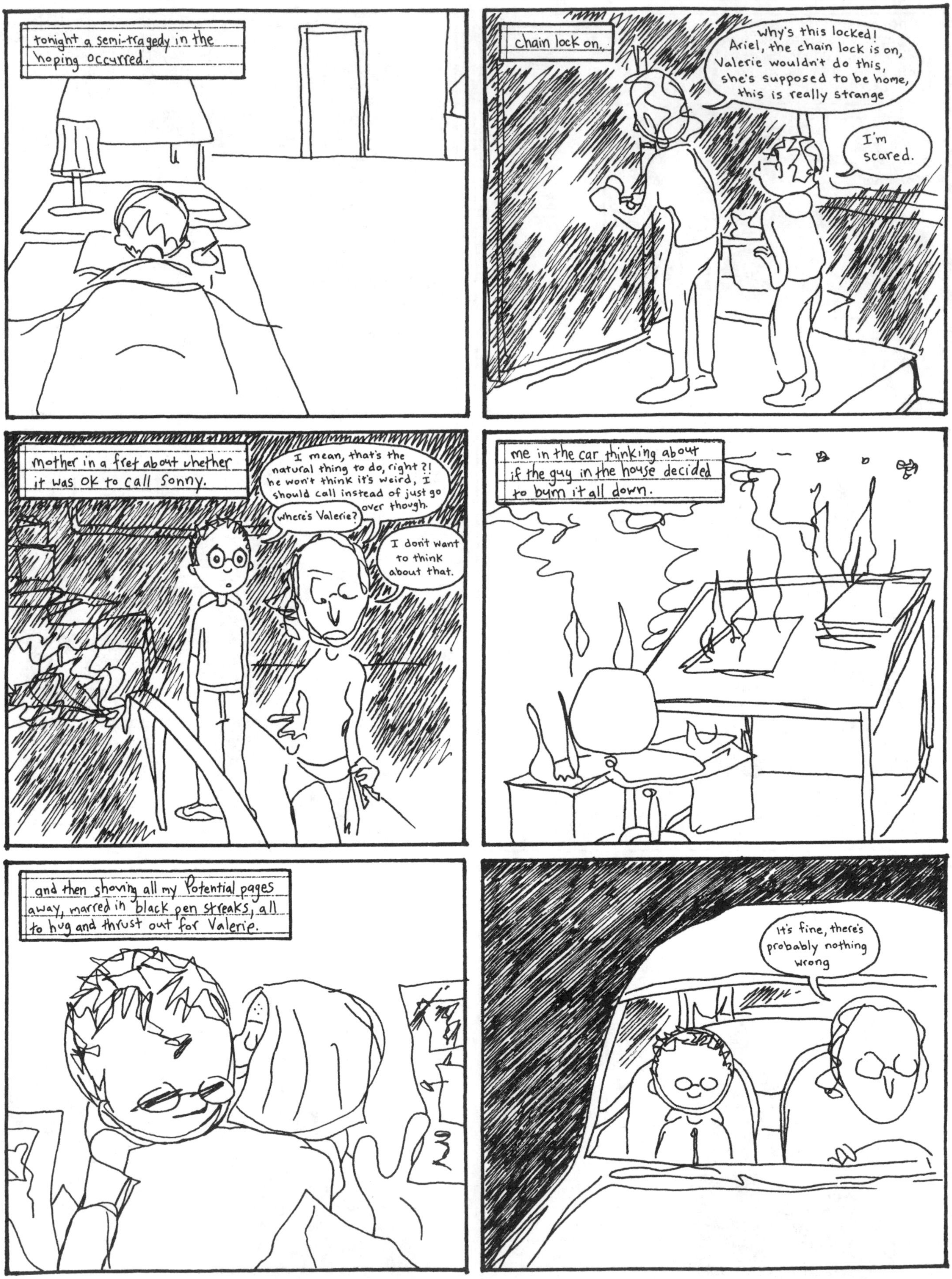
tonight a semi-tragedy in the hoping occurred.
chain lock on.
why's this locked! Ariel, the chain lock is on, Valerie wouldn't do this, she's supposed to be home, this is really strange
I'm scared.
mother in a fret about whether it was OK to call Sonny.
I mean, that's the natural thing to do, right?! he won't think it's weird, I should call instead of just go over though.
where's Valerie?
I don't want to think about that.
me in the car thinking about if the guy in the house decided to burn it all down.
and then shoving all my Potential pages away, marred in black pen streaks, all to hug and thrust out for Valerie.
It's fine, there's probably nothing wrong

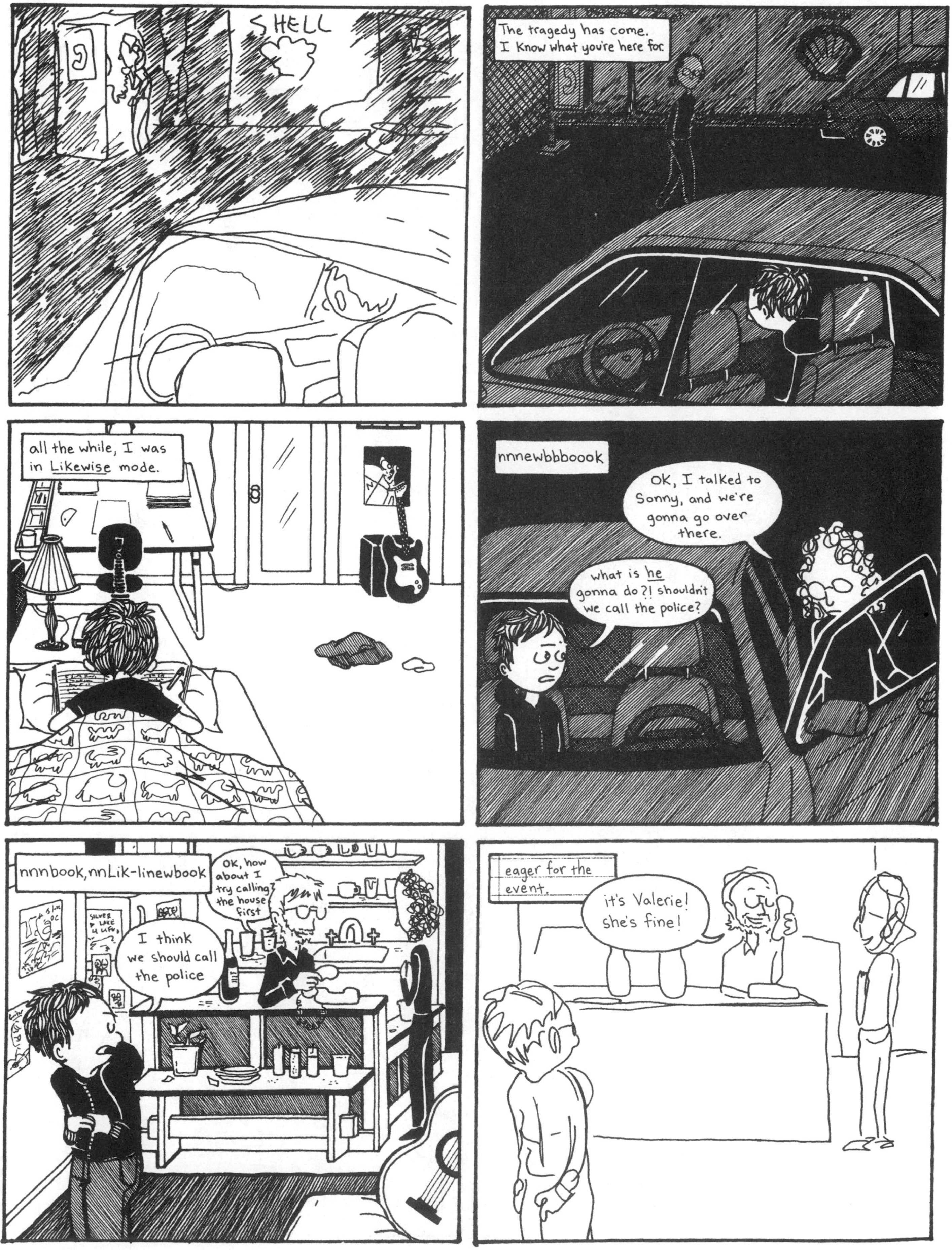

SHELL
The tragedy has come. I know what you're here for.
all the while, I was in Likewise mode.
nnnewbbboook
OK, I talked to Sonny, and we're gonna go over there.
what is he gonna do?! shouldn't we call the police?
nnnbook,nnLik-linewbook
OK, how about I try calling the house first
I think we should call the police
eager for the event.
it's Valerie! she's fine!

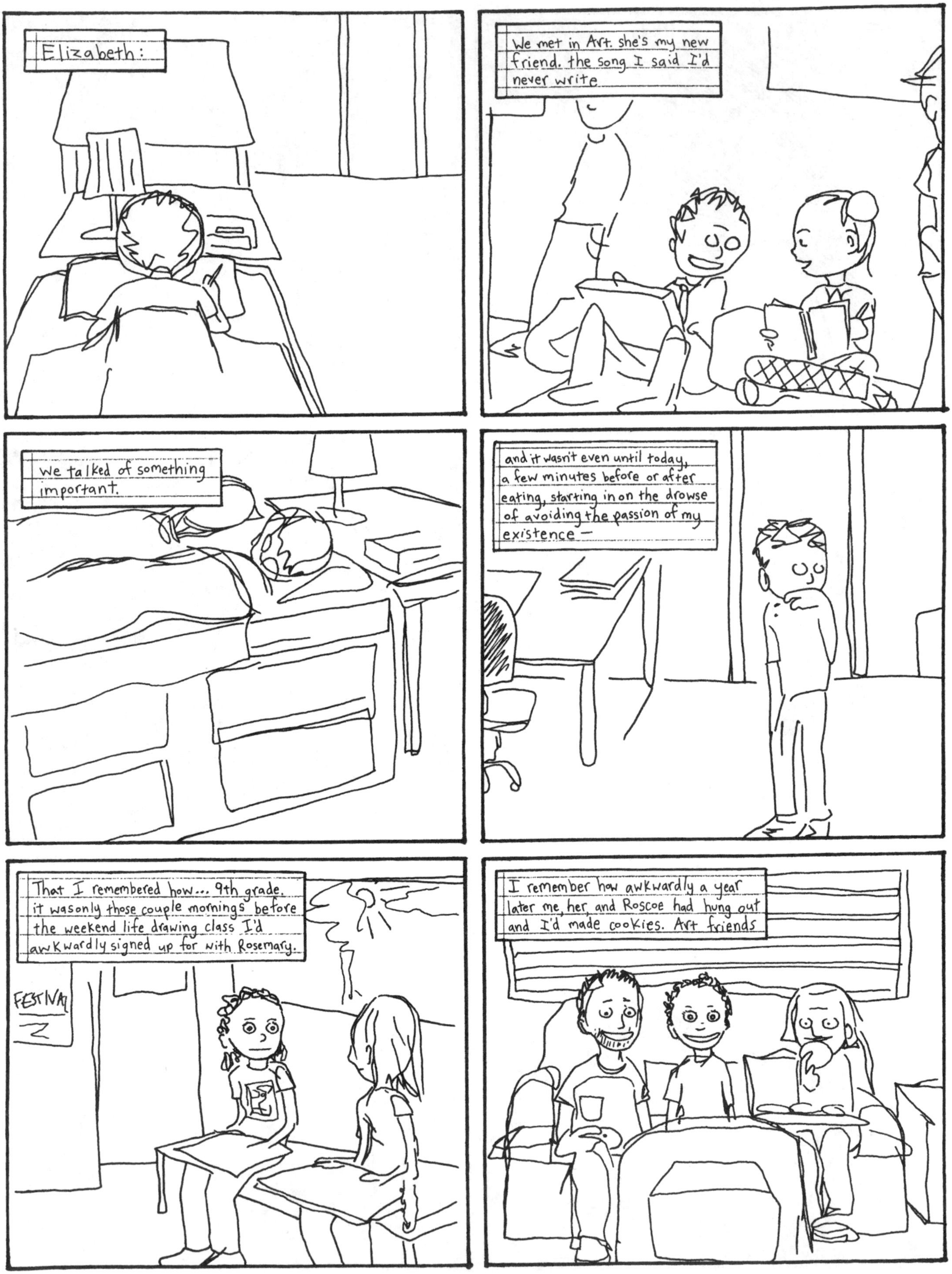
Elizabeth:
We met in Art. she's my new friend. the song I said I'd never write
we talked of something important.
and it wasn't even until today, a few minutes before or after eating, starting in on the drowse of avoiding the passion of my existence —
That I remembered how... 9th grade. it was only those couple mornings before the weekend life drawing class I'd awkwardly signed up for with Rosemary.
FESTIVAL
I remember how awkwardly a year later me, her, and Roscoe had hung out and I'd made cookies. Art friends

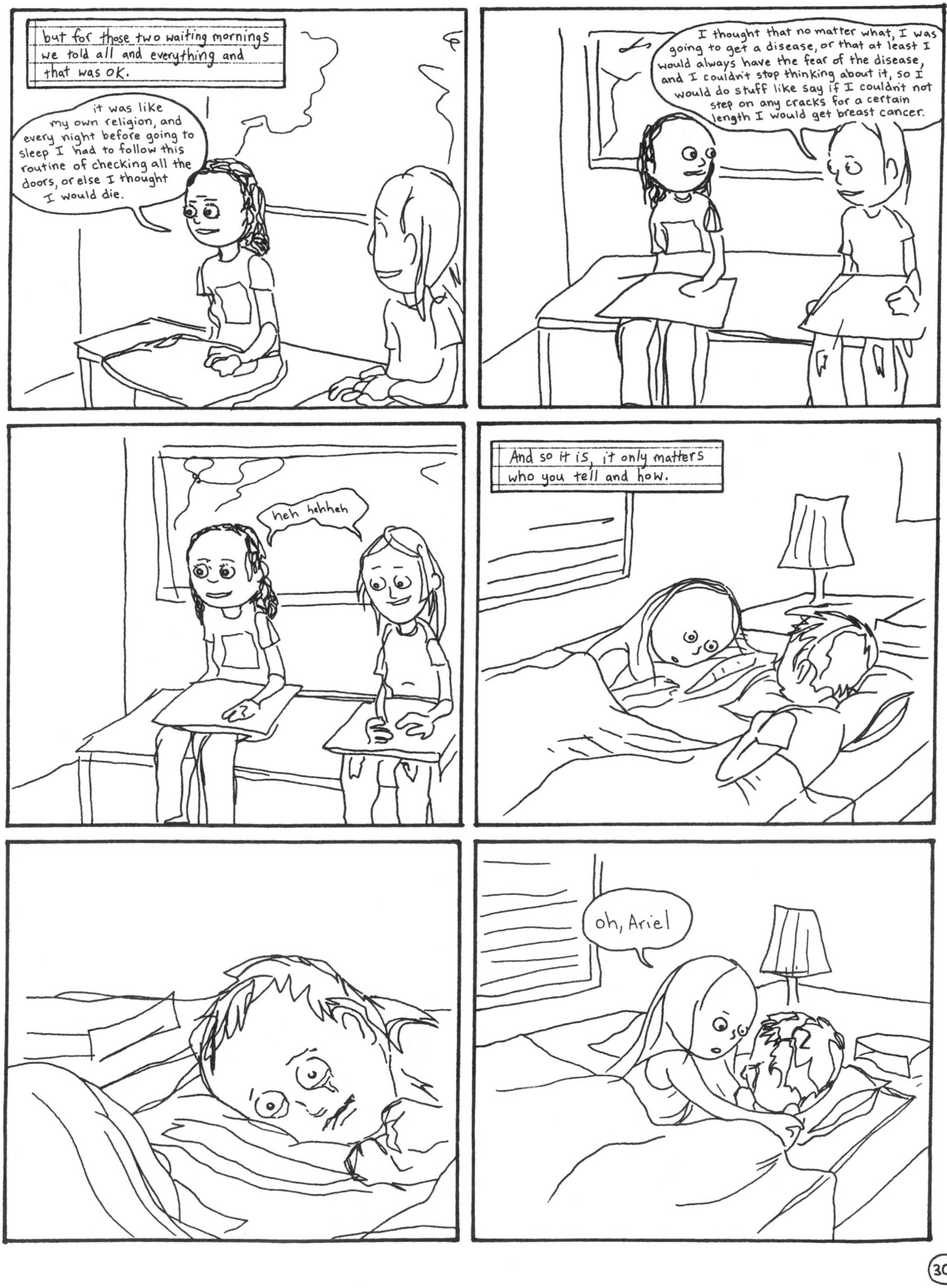
but for those two waiting mornings we told all and everything and that was OK.
it was like my own religion, and every night before going to sleep I had to follow this routine of checking all the doors, or else I thought I would die.
I thought that no matter what, I was going to get a disease, or that at least I would always have the fear of the disease, and I couldn't stop thinking about it, so I would do stuff like say if I couldn't not step on any cracks for a certain length I would get breast cancer.
heh hehheh
And so it is, it only matters who you tell and how.
oh, Ariel

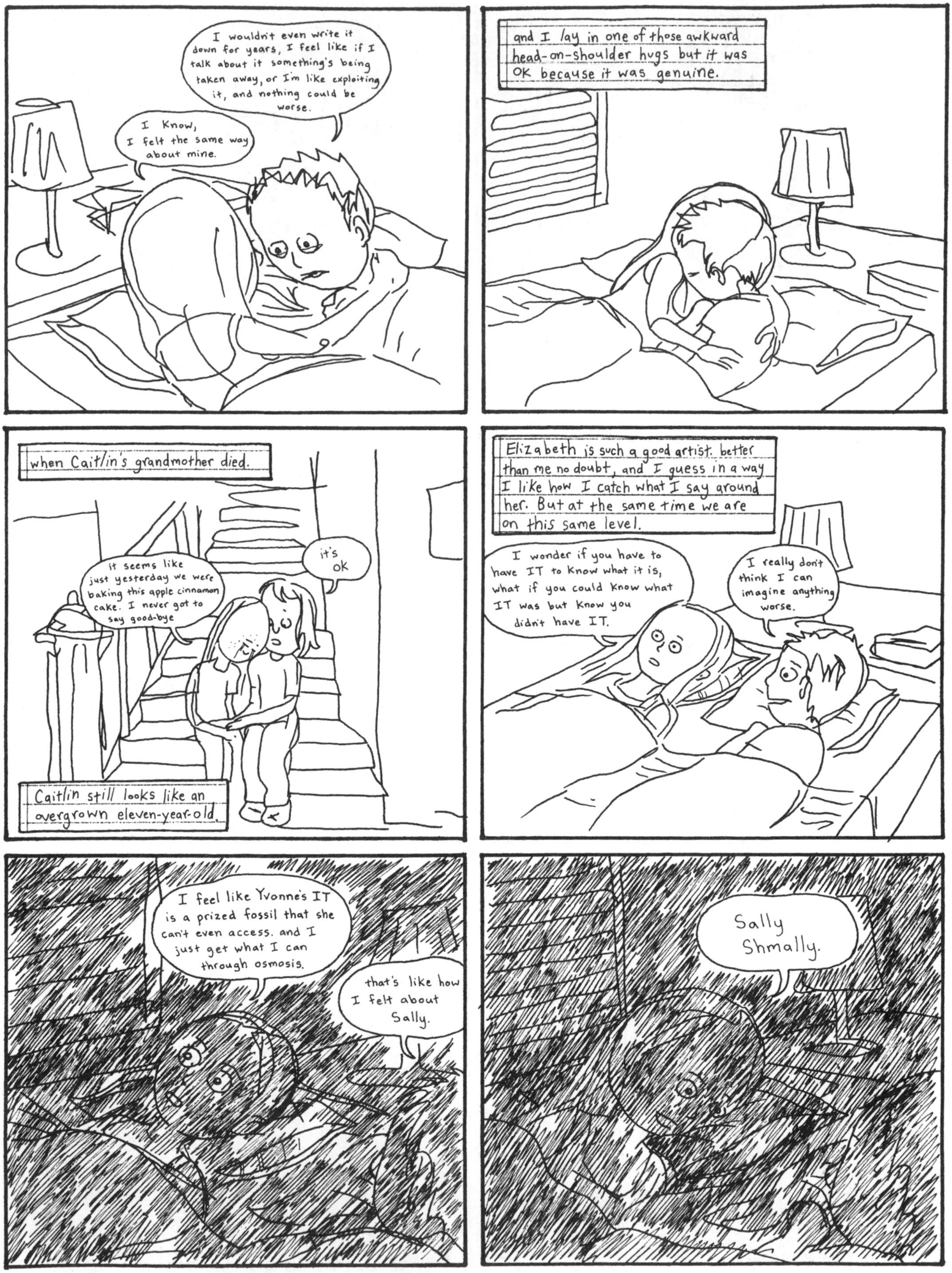
I wouldn't even write it down for years, I feel like if I talk about it something's being taken away, or I'm like exploiting it, and nothing could be worse.
I Know, I felt the same way about mine.
and I lay in one of those awkward head-on-shoulder hugs but it was OK because it was genuine.
when Caitlin's grandmother died.
it seems like just yesterday we were baking this apple cinnamon cake. I never got to say good-bye
it's OK
Caitlin still looks like an overgrown eleven-year-old.
Elizabeth is such a good artist. better than me no doubt, and I guess in a way I like how I catch what I say around her. But at the same time we are on this same level.
I wonder if you have to have IT to Know what it is, what if you could know what IT was but know you didn't have IT.
I really don't think I can imagine anything worse.
I feel like Yvonne's IT is a prized fossil that she can't even access. and I just get what I can through osmosis.
that's like how I felt about Sally.
Sally Shmally.

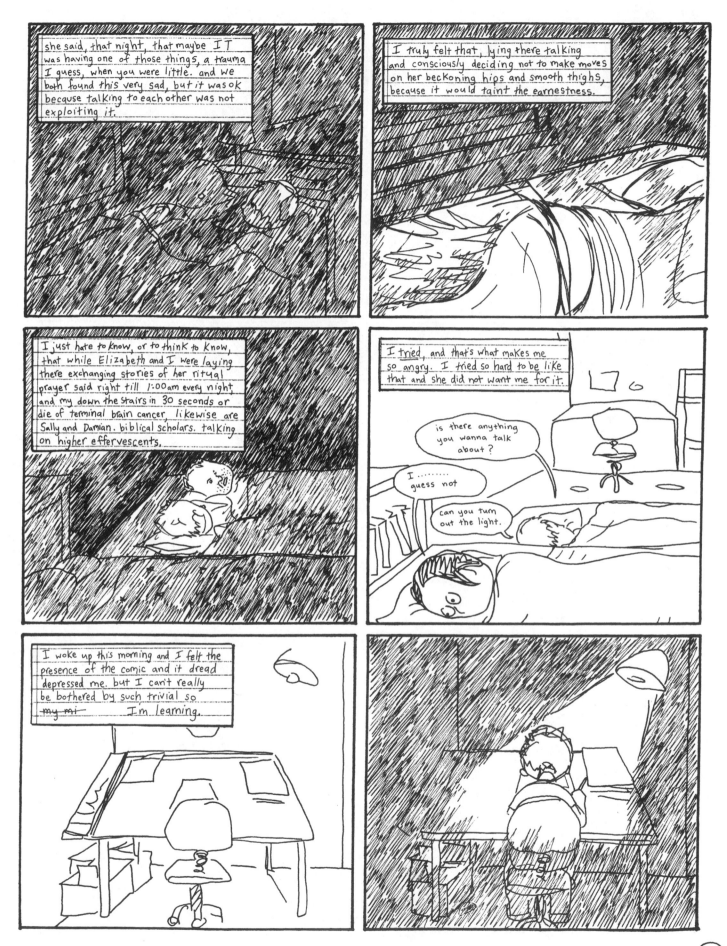

she said, that night, that maybe IT was having one of those things, a trauma I guess, when you were little. and we both found this very sad, but it was ok because talking to each other was not exploiting it.

I truly felt that, lying there talking and consciously deciding not to make moves on her beckoning hips and smooth thighs, because it would taint the earnestness.

I just hate to know, or to think to know, that while Elizabeth and I were laying there exchanging stories of her ritual prayer said right till 1:00am every night and my down the stairs in 30 seconds or die of terminal brain cancer, likewise are Sally and Damian. biblical scholars. talking on higher effervescents.

I tried, and that's what makes me so angry. I tried so hard to be like that and she did not want me for it.

is there anything you wanna talk about?

I .... guess not

can you turn out the light.

I woke up this morning and I felt the presence of the comic and it dread depressed me. but I can't really be bothered by such trivial so my mi   I'm learning.

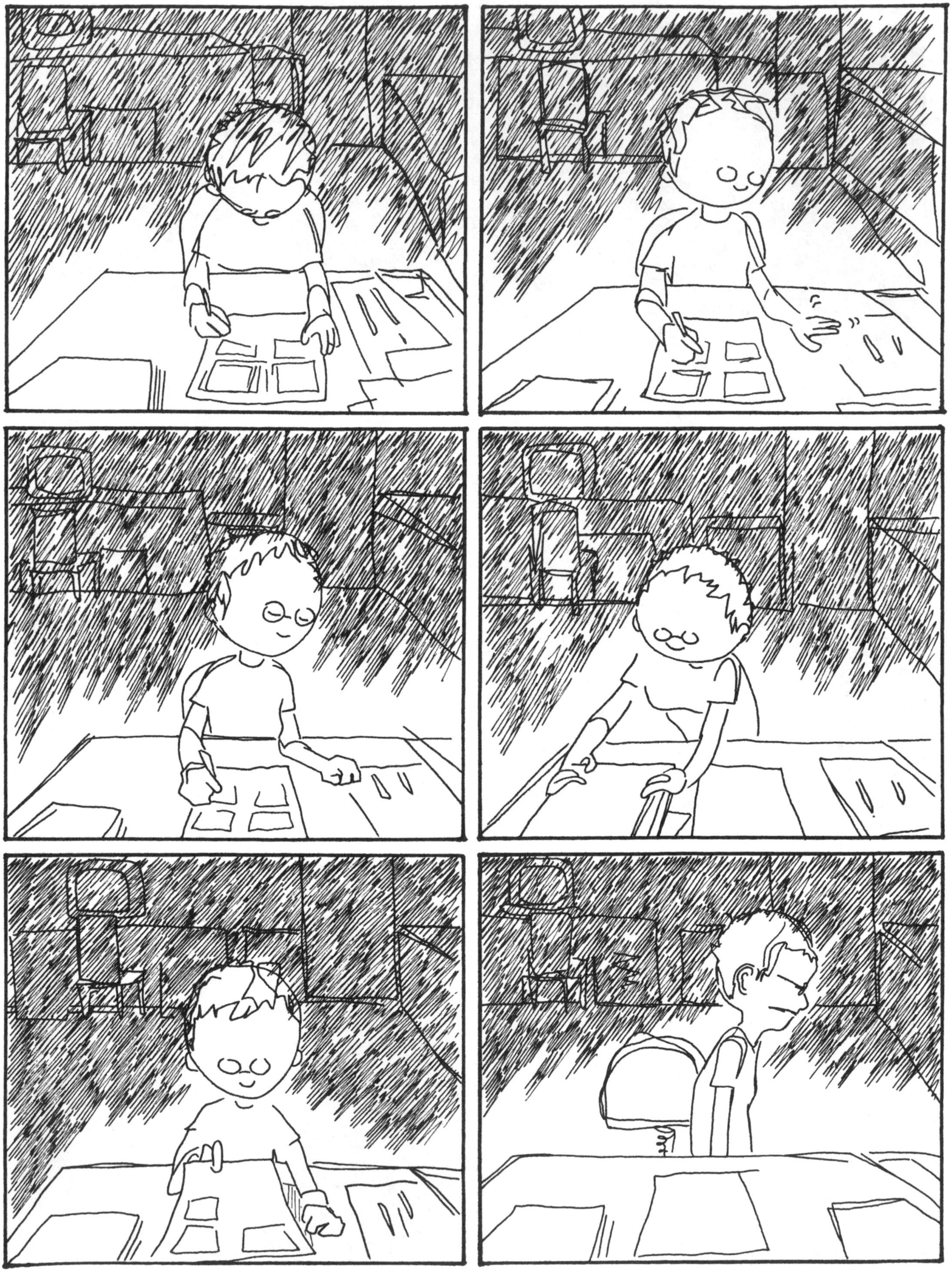

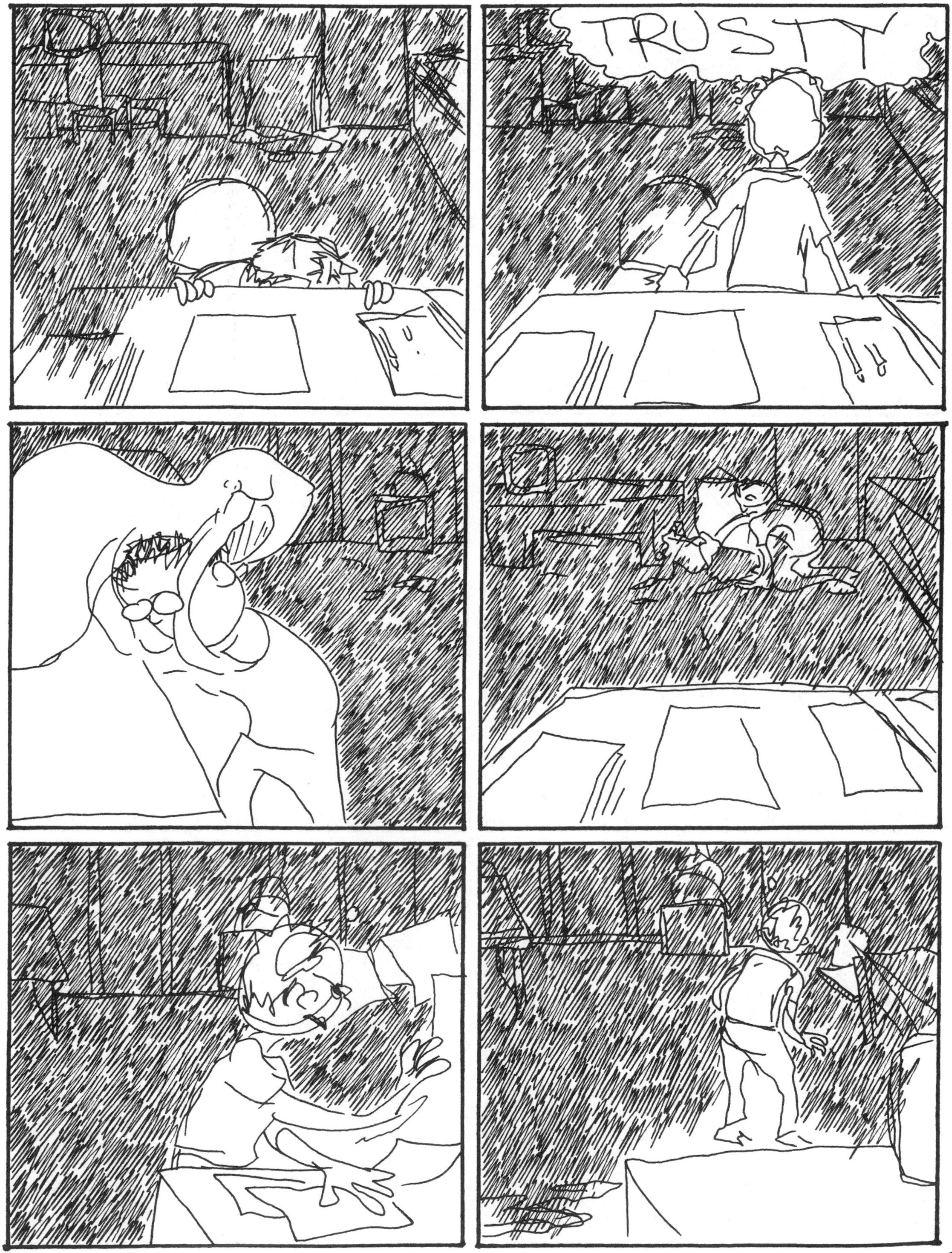
TRUSTY

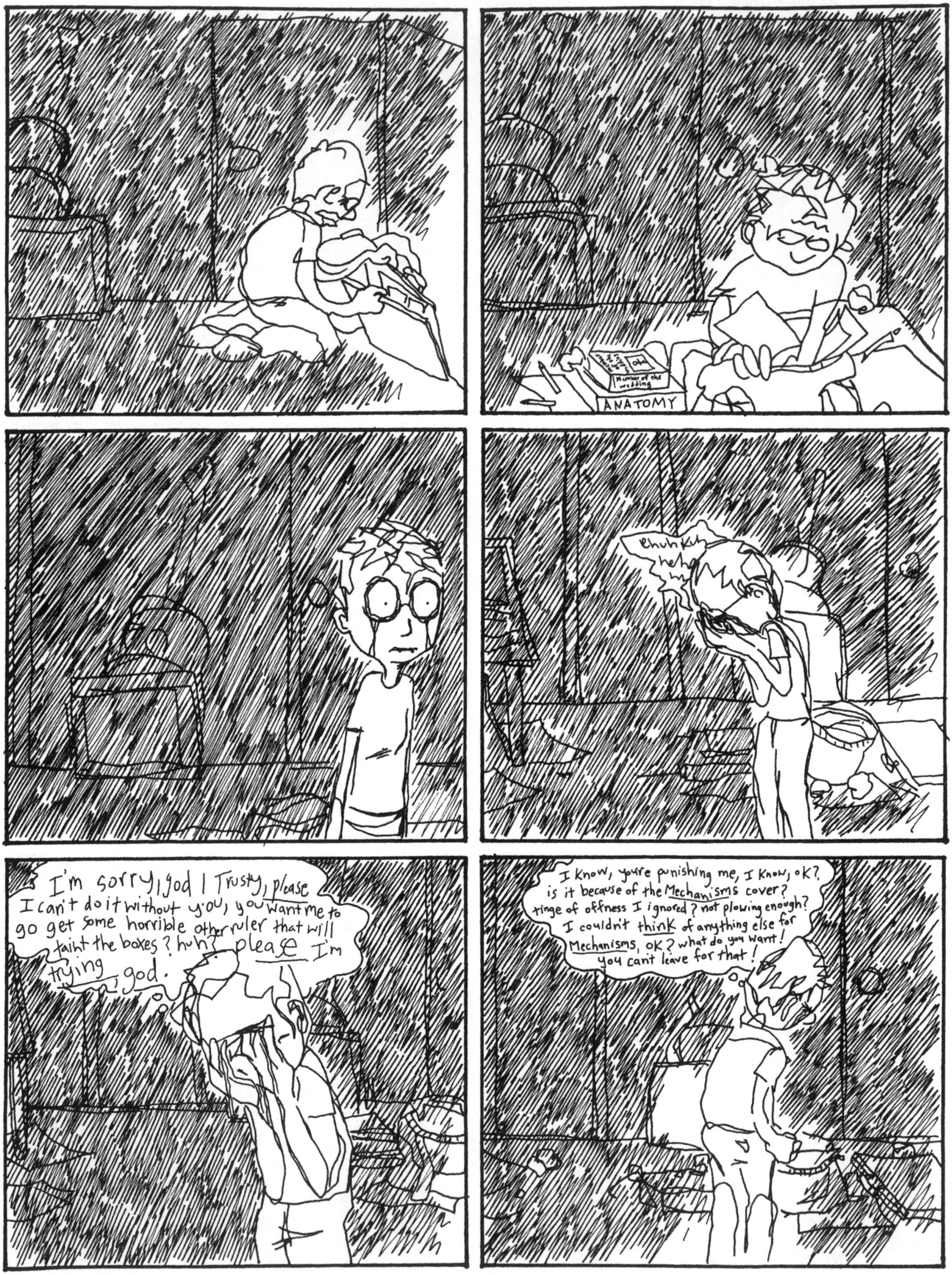
Number of the wedding
ANATOMY
I'm sorry, god / Trusty, please I can't do it without you, you want me to go get some horrible other ruler that will taint the boxes? huh? please I'm trying, god.
I know, you're punishing me, I know, ok? is it because of the Mechanisms cover? tinge of offness I ignored? not plowing enough? I couldn't think of anything else for Mechanisms, ok? what do you want! you can't leave for that!

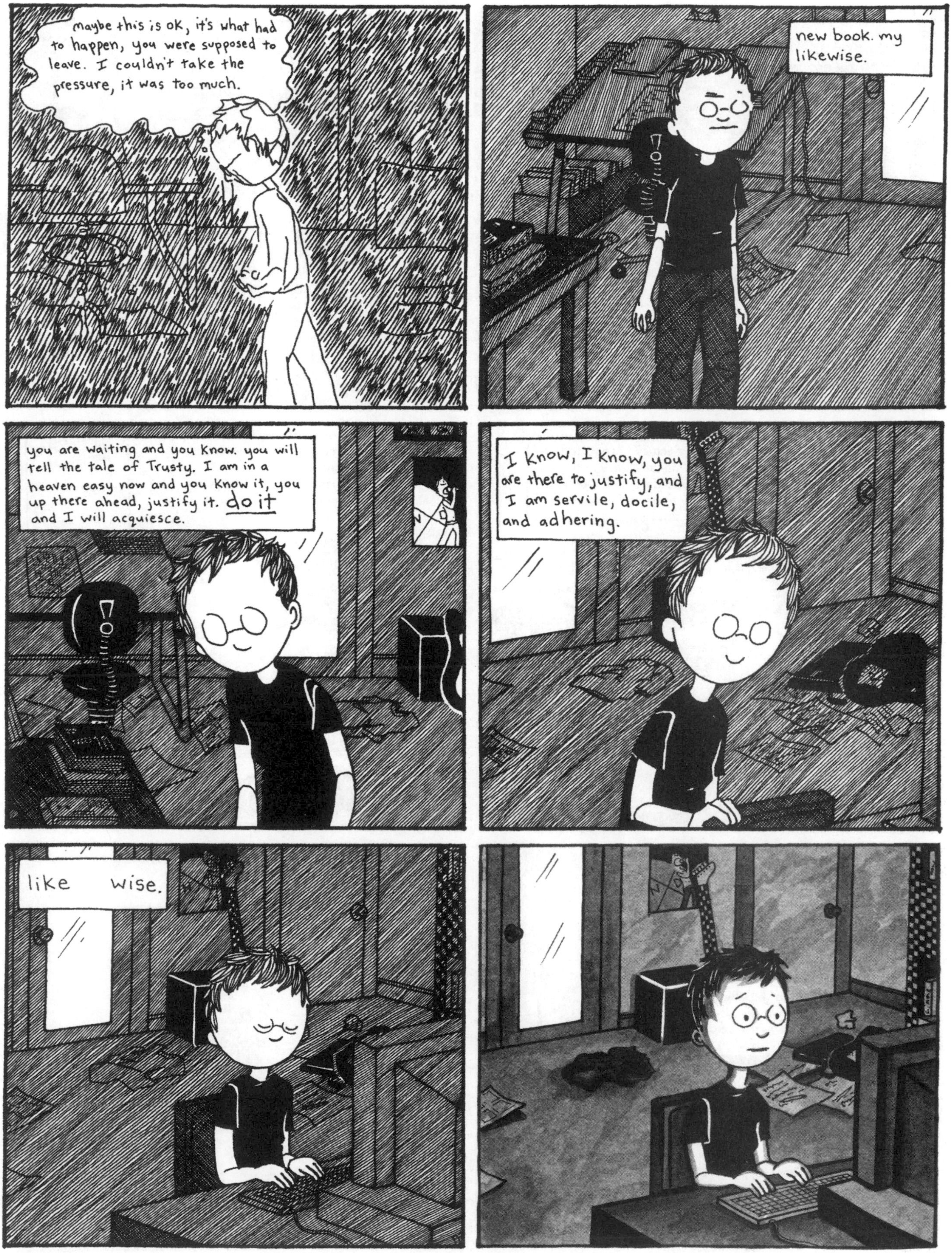
maybe this is ok, it's what had to happen, you were supposed to leave. I couldn't take the pressure, it was too much.
new book. my likewise.
you are waiting and you know. you will tell the tale of Trusty. I am in a heaven easy now and you know it, you up there ahead, justify it. do it and I will acquiesce.
I know, I know, you are there to justify, and I am servile, docile, and adhering.
like wise.

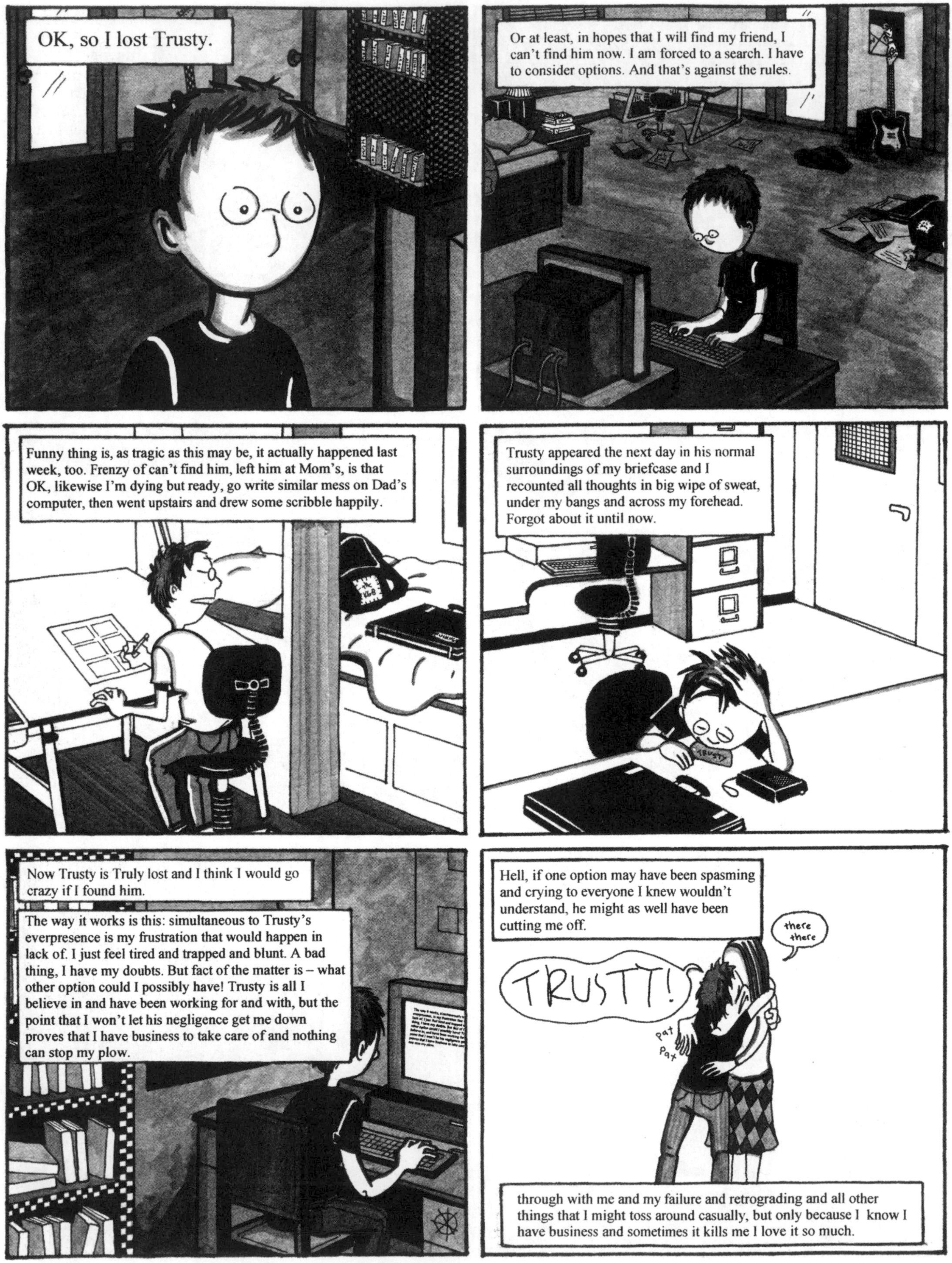
OK, so I lost Trusty.
Or at least, in hopes that I will find my friend, I can't find him now. I am forced to a search. I have to consider options. And that's against the rules.
Funny thing is, as tragic as this may be, it actually happened last week, too. Frenzy of can't find him, left him at Mom's, is that OK, likewise I'm dying but ready, go write similar mess on Dad's computer, then went upstairs and drew some scribble happily.
Trusty appeared the next day in his normal surroundings of my briefcase and I recounted all thoughts in big wipe of sweat, under my bangs and across my forehead. Forgot about it until now.
TRUSTY
Now Trusty is Truly lost and I think I would go crazy if I found him.
The way it works is this: simultaneous to Trusty's everpresence is my frustration that would happen in lack of. I just feel tired and trapped and blunt. A bad thing, I have my doubts. But fact of the matter is – what other option could I possibly have! Trusty is all I believe in and have been working for and with, but the point that I won't let his negligence get me down proves that I have business to take care of and nothing can stop my plow.
Hell, if one option may have been spasming and crying to everyone I knew wouldn't understand, he might as well have been cutting me off.
there there
TRUSTT!
pat
pat
through with me and my failure and retrograding and all other things that I might toss around casually, but only because I know I have business and sometimes it kills me I love it so much.

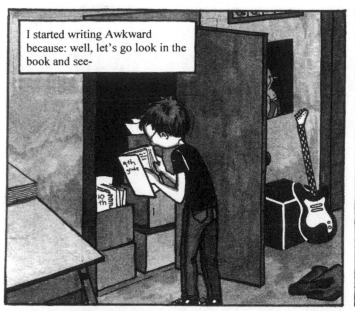

I started writing Awkward because: well, let's go look in the book and see-
"well…This summer is gonna be cool! I'm going I AM GOING to write a comic book (I was inspired by Ariel Bordeaux, cool Deep Girl cartoonist) and it's going to be about my first year of high school with Meg and Michael and cool stuff and cool stuff like that. It's going to be hard. Not as easy and fun as it may seem – I know that but I will do it. And I will be very proud that I didn't spend my summer lazing around with the same 2 other girls smoking a lot."
AIRWALK
AIRWALK
and now? Now I'm ready to bite the bullet because I lost my protractor. Now I worry about exploiting him by drawing him too much in the pages. Now I have to gratuitously kiss him in the presence of others to prove myself for something, honest endeavors at times I'm sure but: it's not like I signed myself on engraved in him.
Now I think of the summer and spasm. Cringe in horror as some teacher smiles that there's only 32 days of school left and five other kids shout out that it's actually 25. I get all hot and have to quickly check in my briefcase for Trusty.
Go home and grimace at the thinness my writings this year have made.
May 2
Darrek don't talk to me anymore
Scold myself for not forcing Darrek into sex.
And imagine jumping in front of a car on the last day of school.

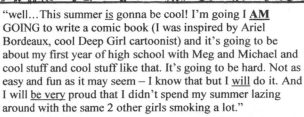

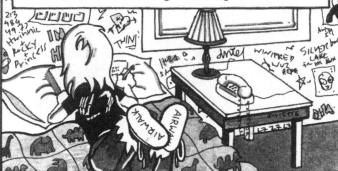

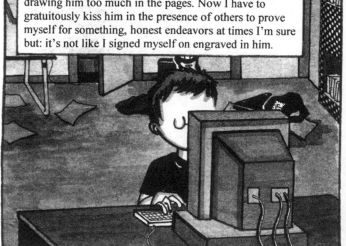

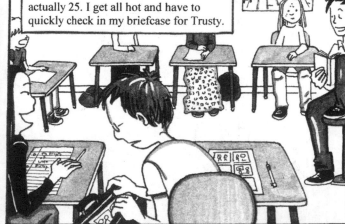

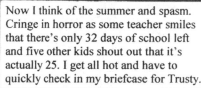

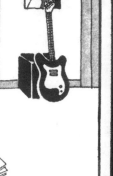

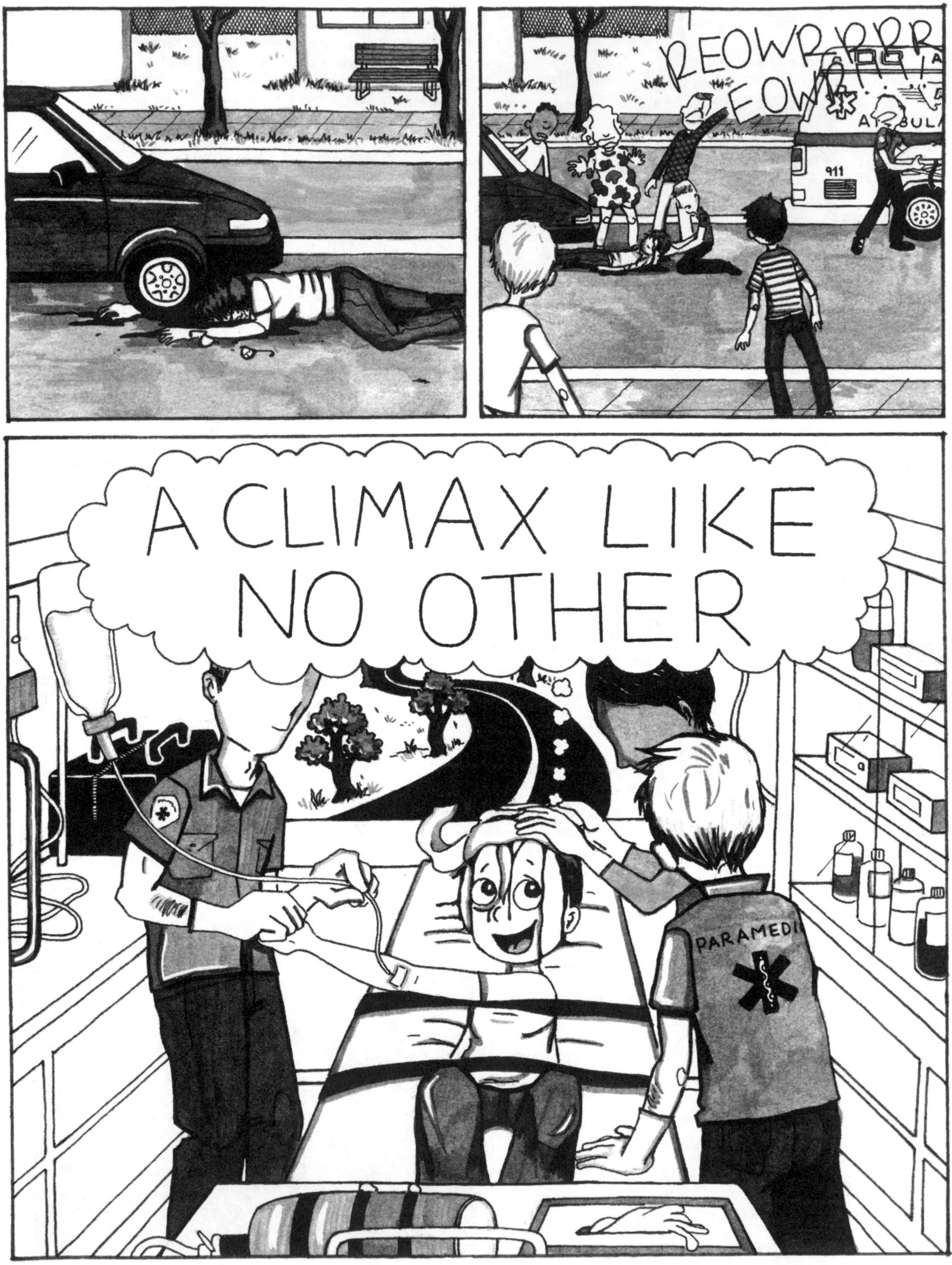
REOWRRRR
EOWRRR!
911
A CLIMAX LIKE
NO OTHER
PARAMEDI

III

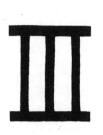

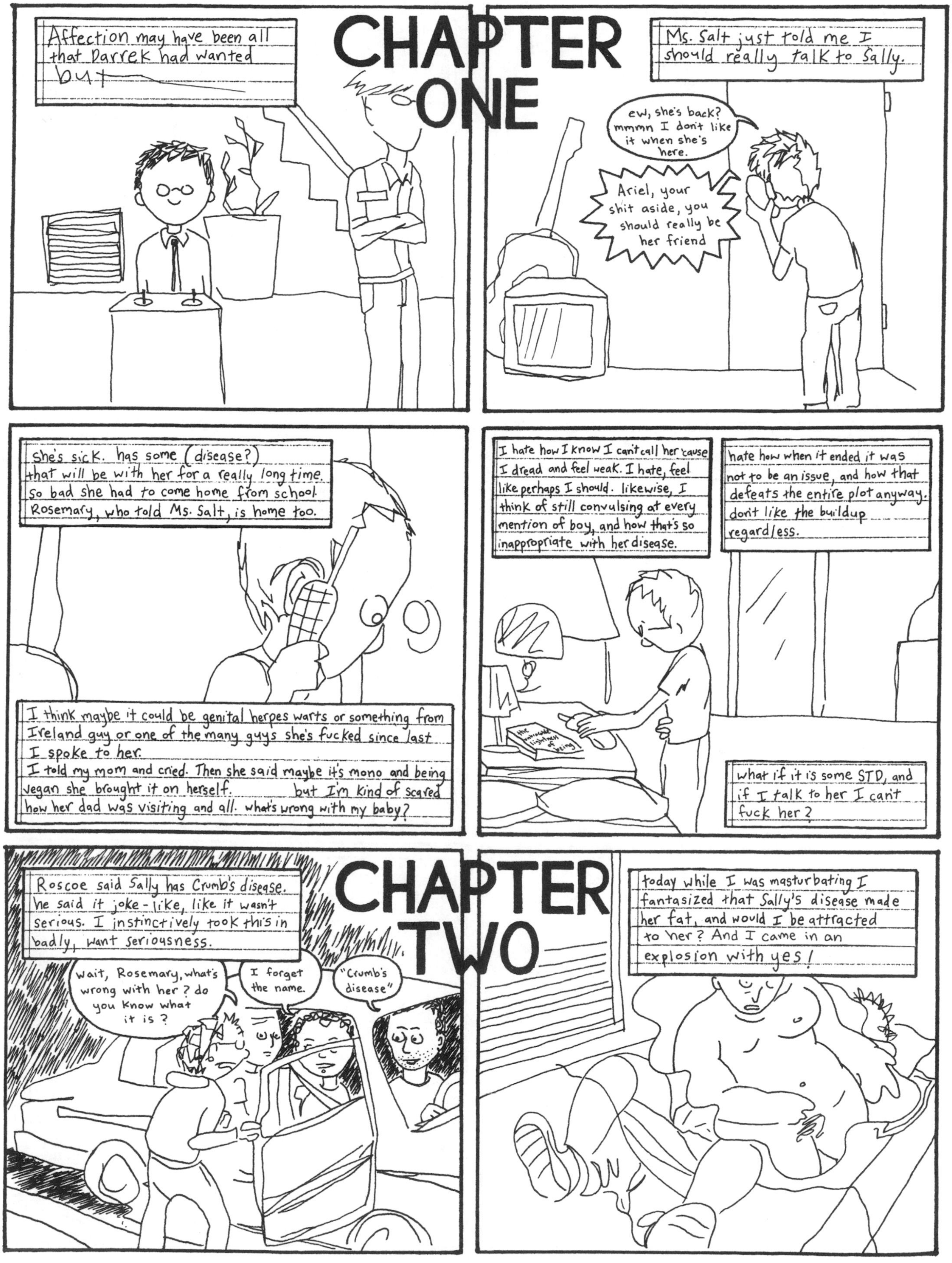
Affection may have been all that Darrek had wanted but
CHAPTER ONE
Ms. Salt just told me I should really talk to Sally.
ew, she's back? mmmn I don't like it when she's here.
Ariel, your shit aside, you should really be her friend
She's sick. has some (disease?) that will be with her for a really long time. so bad she had to come home from school. Rosemary, who told Ms. Salt, is home too.
I think maybe it could be genital herpes warts or something from Ireland guy or one of the many guys she's fucked since last I spoke to her. I told my mom and cried. Then she said maybe it's mono and being vegan she brought it on herself. but I'm kind of scared how her dad was visiting and all. what's wrong with my baby?
I hate how I know I can't call her 'cause I dread and feel weak. I hate, feel like perhaps I should. likewise, I think of still convulsing at every mention of boy, and how that's so inappropriate with her disease.
hate how when it ended it was not to be an issue, and how that defeats the entire plot anyway. don't like the buildup regardless.
what if it is some STD, and if I talk to her I can't fuck her?
CHAPTER TWO
Roscoe said Sally has Crumb's disease. he said it joke-like, like it wasn't serious. I instinctively took this in badly, want seriousness.
wait, Rosemary, what's wrong with her? do you know what it is?
I forget the name.
"Crumb's disease"
today while I was masturbating I fantasized that Sally's disease made her fat, and would I be attracted to her? And I came in an explosion with yes!

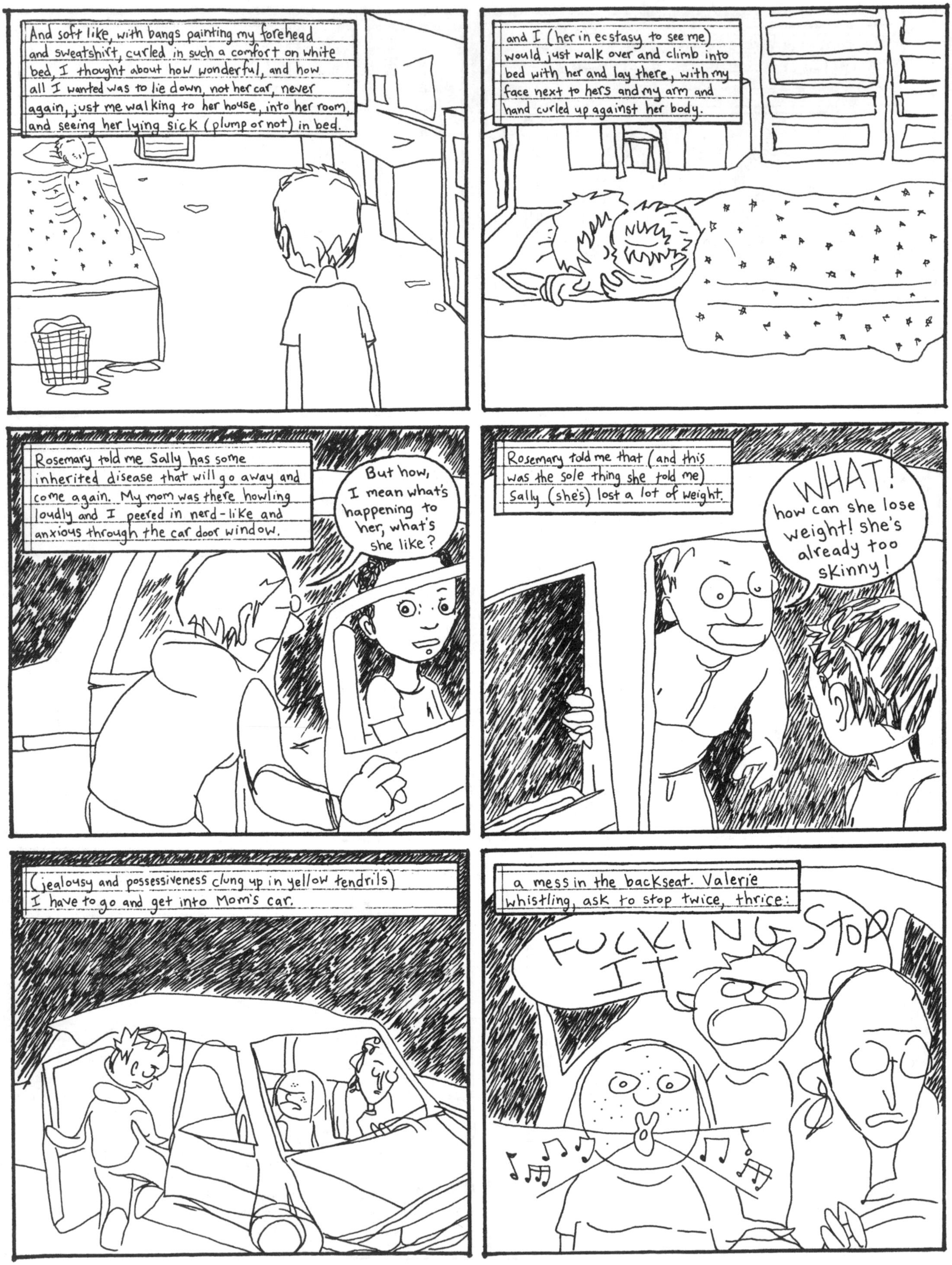
And soft like, with bangs painting my forehead and sweatshirt, curled in such a comfort on white bed, I thought about how wonderful, and how all I wanted was to lie down, not her car, never again, just me walking to her house, into her room, and seeing her lying sick (plump or not) in bed.
and I (her in ecstasy to see me) would just walk over and climb into bed with her and lay there, with my face next to hers and my arm and hand curled up against her body.
Rosemary told me Sally has some inherited disease that will go away and come again. My mom was there howling loudly and I peered in nerd-like and anxious through the car door window.
But how, I mean what's happening to her, what's she like?
Rosemary told me that (and this was the sole thing she told me) Sally (she's) lost a lot of weight.
WHAT! how can she lose weight! she's already too skinny!
(jealousy and possessiveness clung up in yellow tendrils) I have to go and get into Mom's car.
a mess in the backseat. Valerie whistling, ask to stop twice, thrice:
FUCKING STOP IT

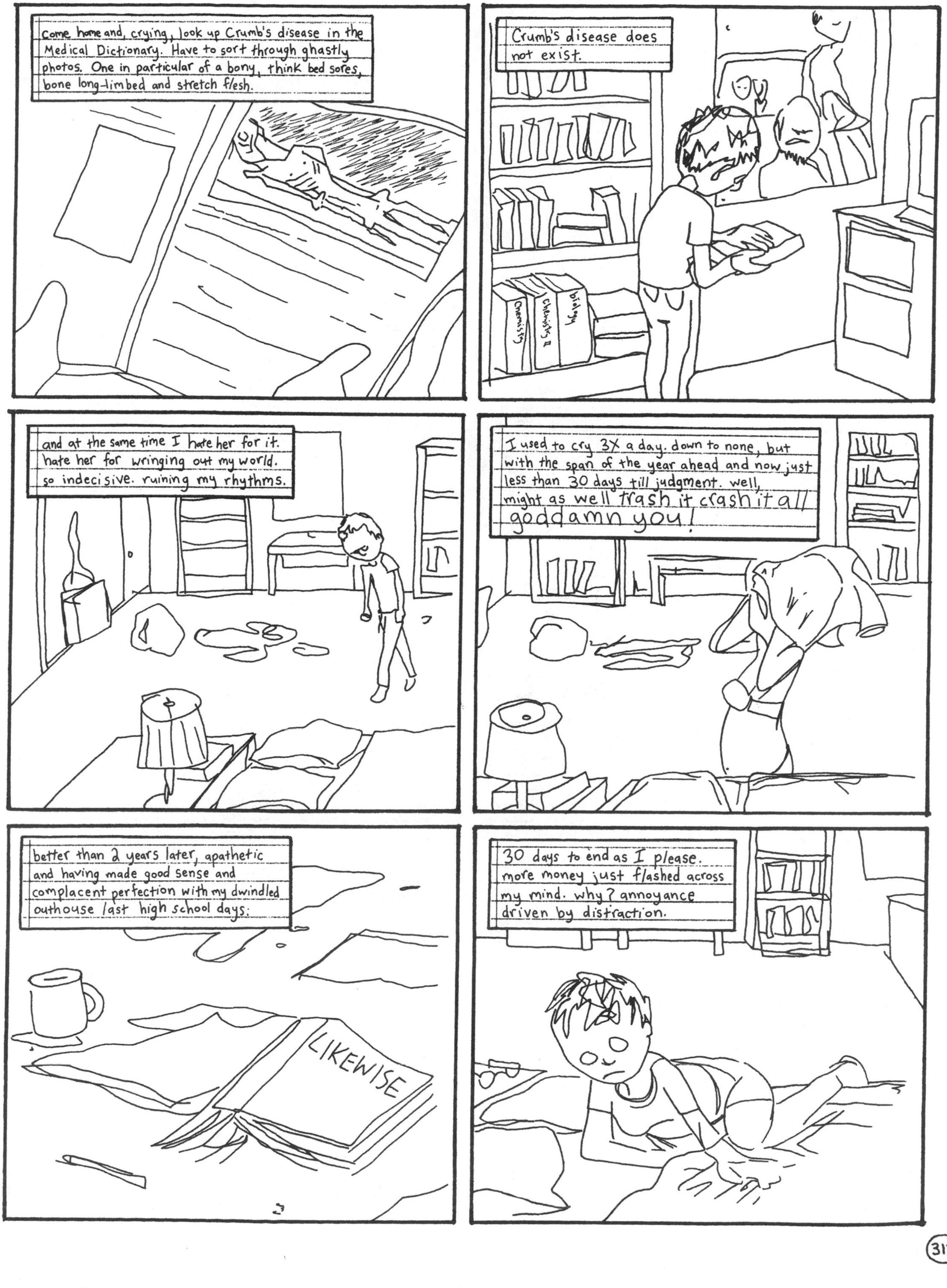
come home and, crying, look up Crumb's disease in the Medical Dictionary. Have to sort through ghastly photos. One in particular of a bony, think bed sores, bone long-limbed and stretch flesh.
Crumb's disease does not exist.
Chemistry
Chemistry II
biology
and at the same time I hate her for it. hate her for wringing out my world. so indecisive. ruining my rhythms.
I used to cry 3X a day. down to none, but with the span of the year ahead and now just less than 30 days till judgment. well, might as well trash it crash it all goddamn you!
better than 2 years later, apathetic and having made good sense and complacent perfection with my dwindled outhouse last high school days.
LIKEWISE
30 days to end as I please. more money just flashed across my mind. why? annoyance driven by distraction.

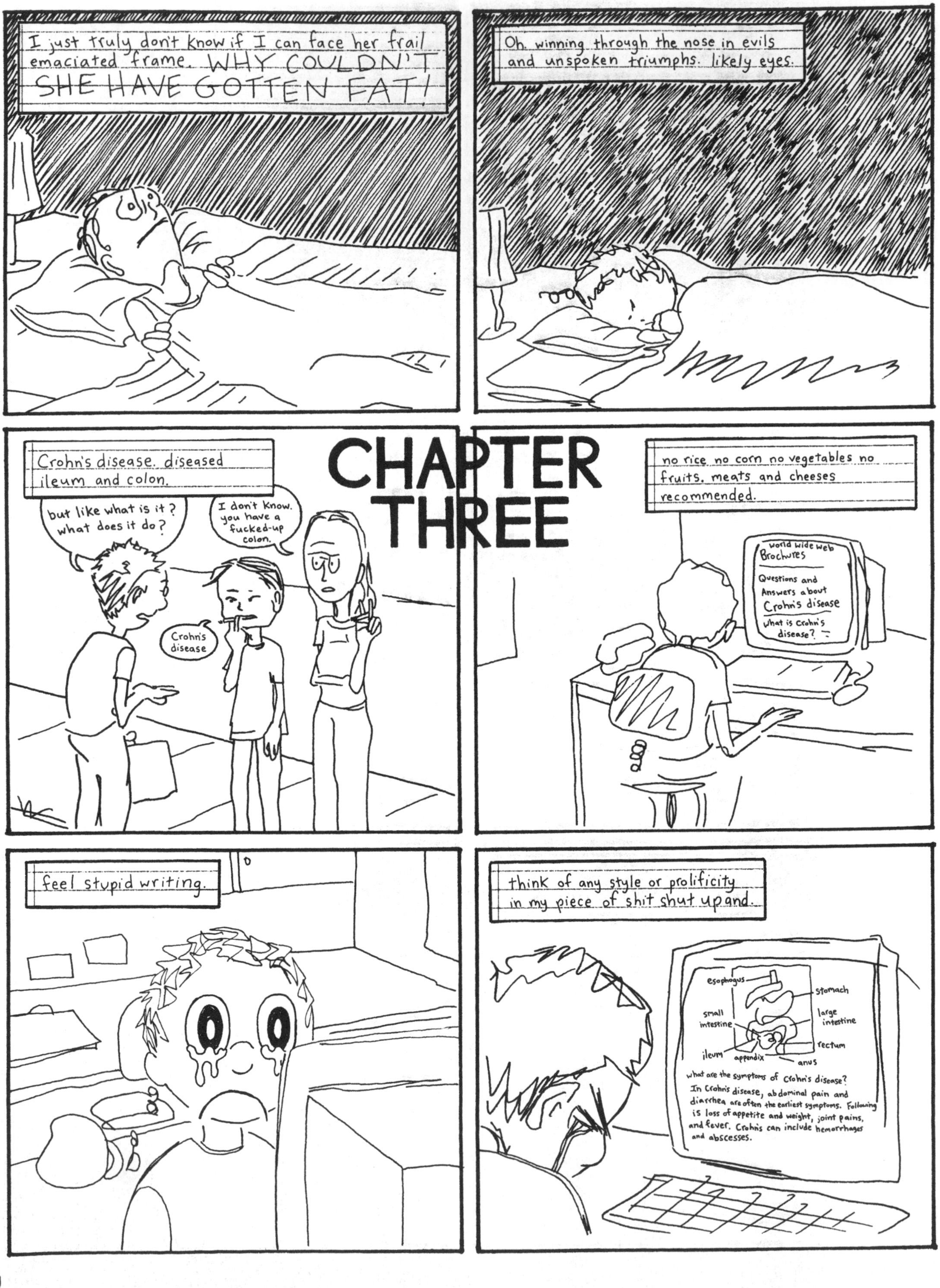

I just truly don't know if I can face her frail emaciated frame. WHY COULDN'T SHE HAVE GOTTEN FAT!
Oh. winning through the nose in evils and unspoken triumphs. likely eyes.
Crohn's disease. diseased ileum and colon.
but like what is it? what does it do?
I don't know. you have a fucked-up colon.
Crohn's disease
CHAPTER THREE
no rice no corn no vegetables no fruits. meats and cheeses recommended.
world wide web
Brochures
Questions and Answers about Crohn's disease
What is Crohn's disease?
feel stupid writing.
think of any style or prolificity in my piece of shit shut up and.
esophagus
stomach
small intestine
large intestine
ileum
appendix
rectum
anus
what are the symptoms of Crohn's disease?
In Crohn's disease, abdominal pain and diarrhea are often the earliest symptoms. Following is loss of appetite and weight, joint pains, and fever. Crohn's can include hemorrhages and abscesses.

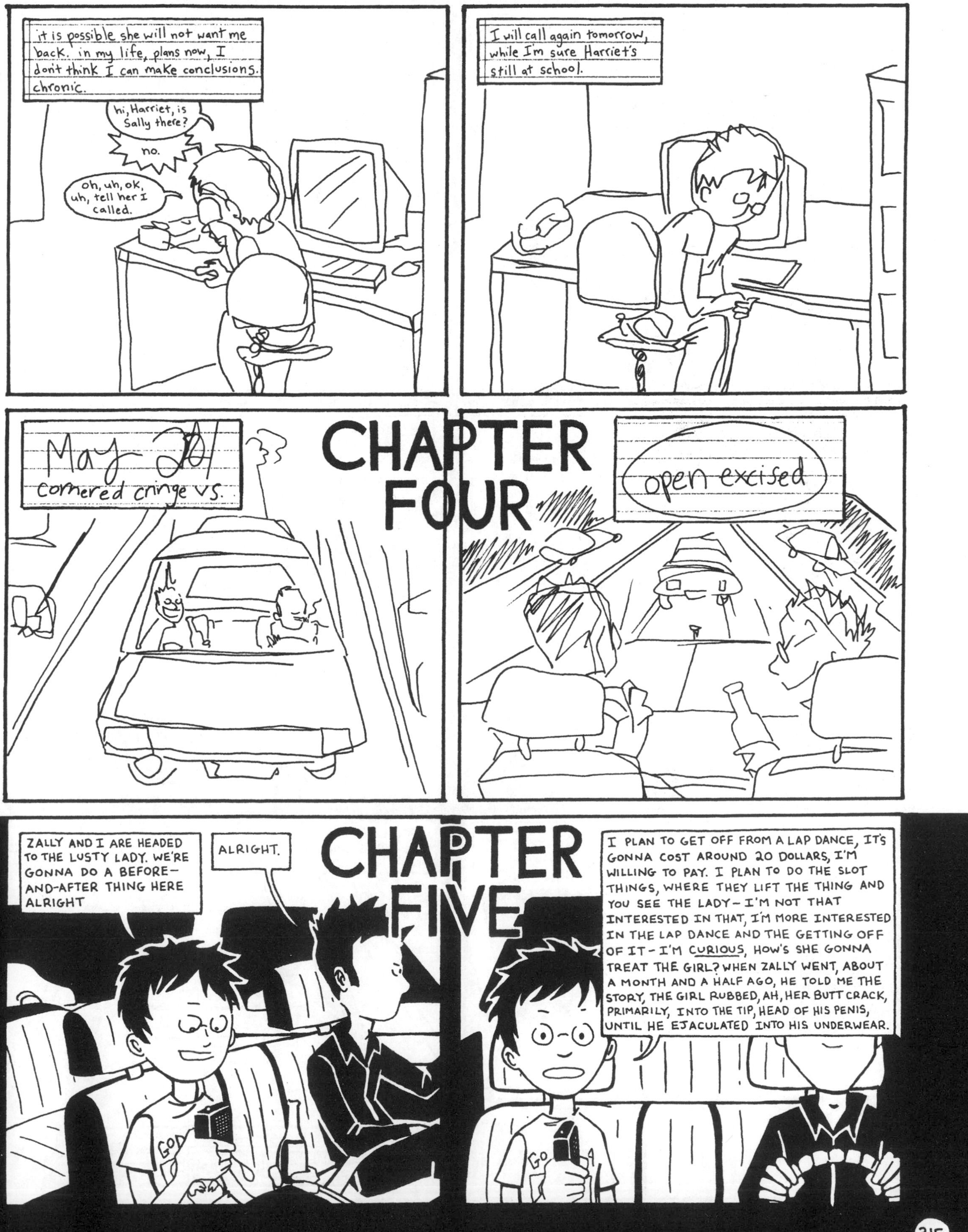

it is possible she will not want me back. in my life, plans now, I don't think I can make conclusions. chronic.
hi, Harriet, is Sally there?
no.
oh, uh, ok, uh, tell her I called.
I will call again tomorrow, while I'm sure Harriet's still at school.
May 20/
cornered cringe vs.
CHAPTER FOUR
open excised
ZALLY AND I ARE HEADED TO THE LUSTY LADY. WE'RE GONNA DO A BEFORE-AND-AFTER THING HERE ALRIGHT
ALRIGHT.
CHAPTER FIVE
I PLAN TO GET OFF FROM A LAP DANCE, IT'S GONNA COST AROUND 20 DOLLARS, I'M WILLING TO PAY. I PLAN TO DO THE SLOT THINGS, WHERE THEY LIFT THE THING AND YOU SEE THE LADY - I'M NOT THAT INTERESTED IN THAT, I'M MORE INTERESTED IN THE LAP DANCE AND THE GETTING OFF OF IT - I'M CURIOUS, HOW'S SHE GONNA TREAT THE GIRL? WHEN ZALLY WENT, ABOUT A MONTH AND A HALF AGO, HE TOLD ME THE STORY, THE GIRL RUBBED, AH, HER BUTT CRACK, PRIMARILY, INTO THE TIP, HEAD OF HIS PENIS, UNTIL HE EJACULATED INTO HIS UNDERWEAR.

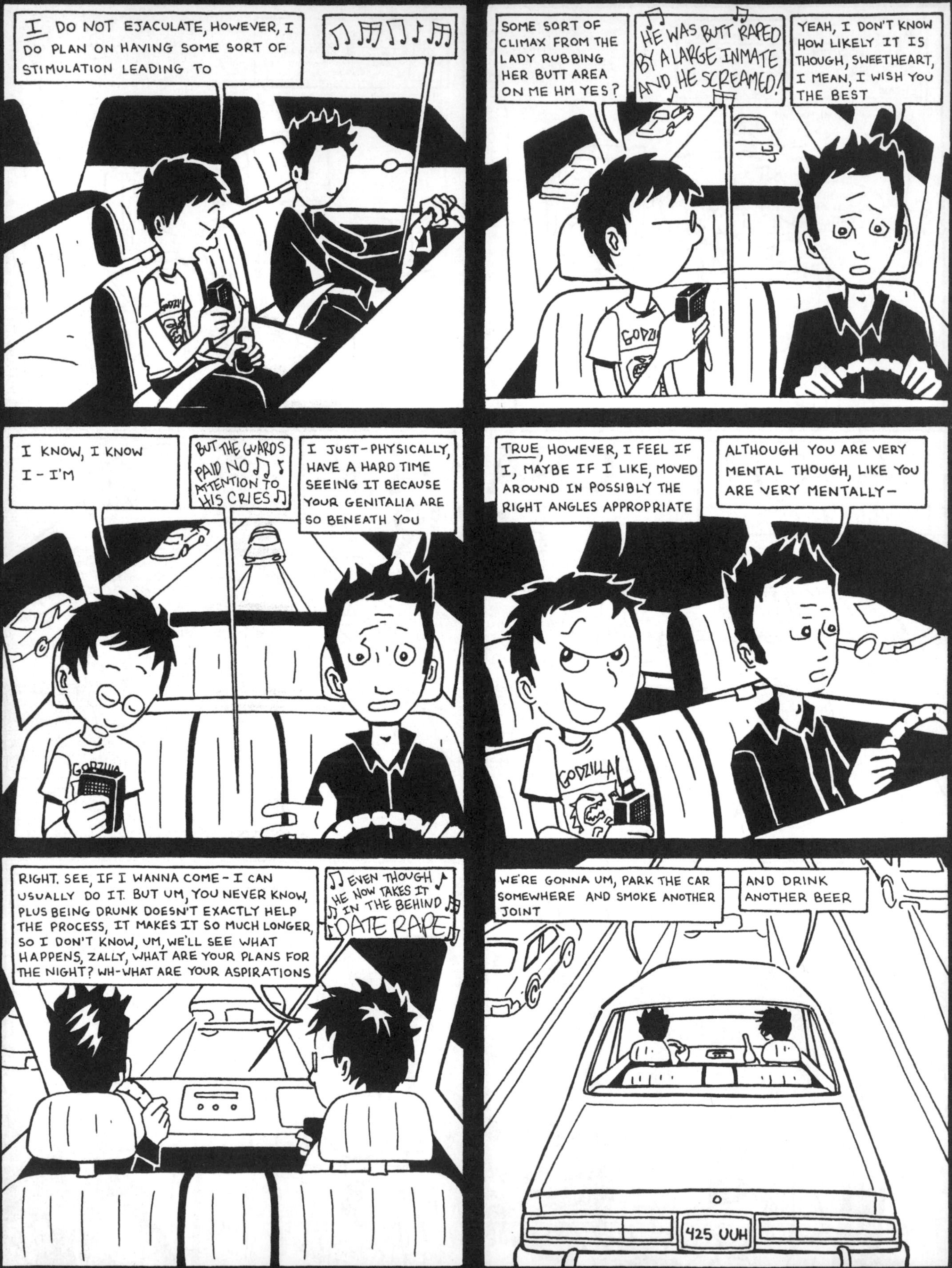
I DO NOT EJACULATE, HOWEVER, I DO PLAN ON HAVING SOME SORT OF STIMULATION LEADING TO
SOME SORT OF CLIMAX FROM THE LADY RUBBING HER BUTT AREA ON ME HM YES?
HE WAS BUTT RAPED BY A LARGE INMATE AND HE SCREAMED!
YEAH, I DON'T KNOW HOW LIKELY IT IS THOUGH, SWEETHEART, I MEAN, I WISH YOU THE BEST
I KNOW, I KNOW I - I'M
BUT THE GUARDS PAID NO ATTENTION TO HIS CRIES
I JUST-PHYSICALLY, HAVE A HARD TIME SEEING IT BECAUSE YOUR GENITALIA ARE SO BENEATH YOU
TRUE, HOWEVER, I FEEL IF I, MAYBE IF I LIKE, MOVED AROUND IN POSSIBLY THE RIGHT ANGLES APPROPRIATE
ALTHOUGH YOU ARE VERY MENTAL THOUGH, LIKE YOU ARE VERY MENTALLY-
RIGHT. SEE, IF I WANNA COME - I CAN USUALLY DO IT. BUT UM, YOU NEVER KNOW, PLUS BEING DRUNK DOESN'T EXACTLY HELP THE PROCESS, IT MAKES IT SO MUCH LONGER, SO I DON'T KNOW, UM, WE'LL SEE WHAT HAPPENS, ZALLY, WHAT ARE YOUR PLANS FOR THE NIGHT? WH-WHAT ARE YOUR ASPIRATIONS
EVEN THOUGH HE NOW TAKES IT IN THE BEHIND
DATE RAPE
WE'RE GONNA UM, PARK THE CAR SOMEWHERE AND SMOKE ANOTHER JOINT
AND DRINK ANOTHER BEER
425 UUH

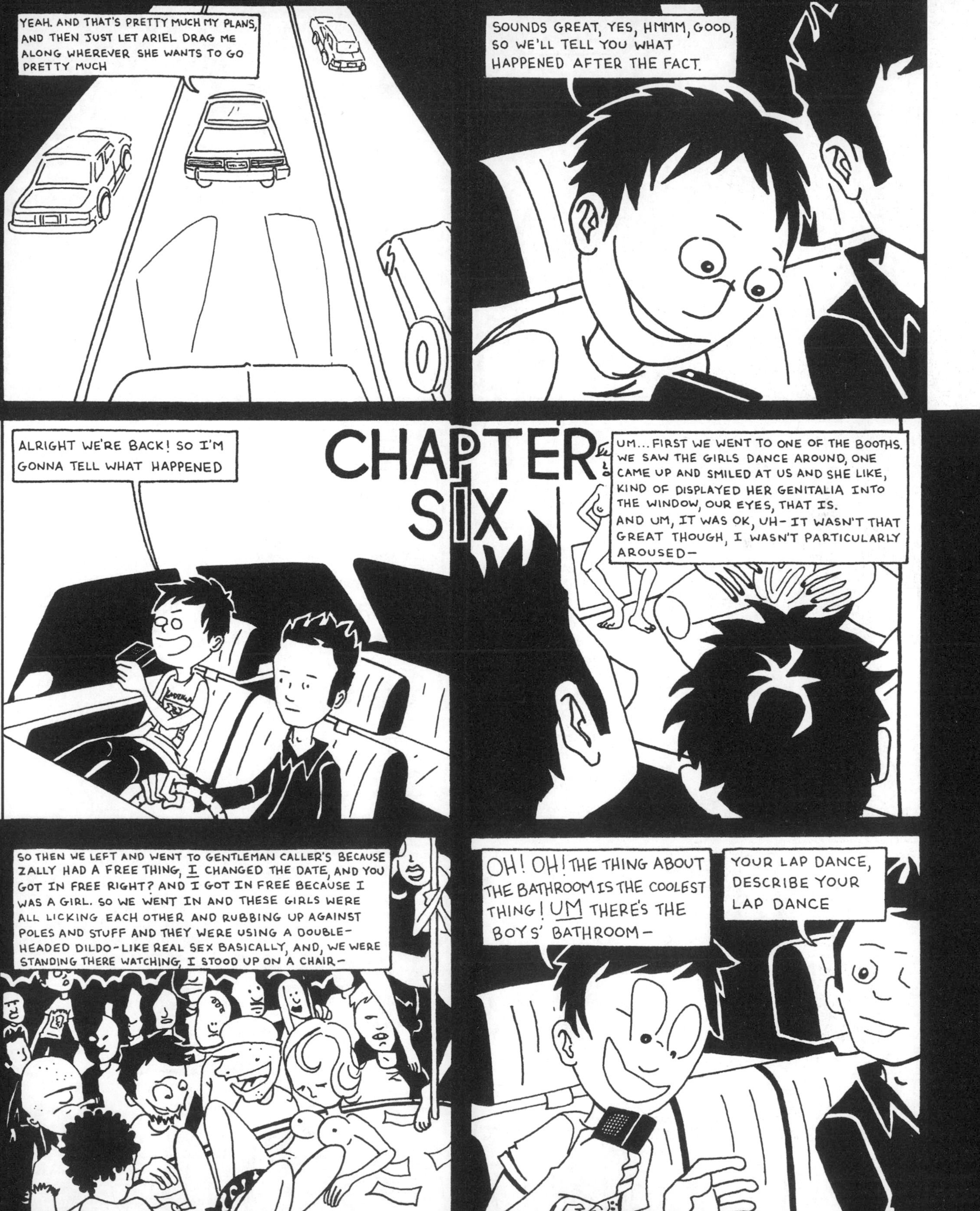
YEAH. AND THAT'S PRETTY MUCH MY PLANS, AND THEN JUST LET ARIEL DRAG ME ALONG WHEREVER SHE WANTS TO GO PRETTY MUCH
SOUNDS GREAT, YES, HMMM, GOOD, SO WE'LL TELL YOU WHAT HAPPENED AFTER THE FACT.
CHAPTER SIX
ALRIGHT WE'RE BACK! SO I'M GONNA TELL WHAT HAPPENED
UM... FIRST WE WENT TO ONE OF THE BOOTHS. WE SAW THE GIRLS DANCE AROUND, ONE CAME UP AND SMILED AT US AND SHE LIKE, KIND OF DISPLAYED HER GENITALIA INTO THE WINDOW, OUR EYES, THAT IS. AND UM, IT WAS OK, UH- IT WASN'T THAT GREAT THOUGH, I WASN'T PARTICULARLY AROUSED-
SO THEN WE LEFT AND WENT TO GENTLEMAN CALLER'S BECAUSE ZALLY HAD A FREE THING, I CHANGED THE DATE, AND YOU GOT IN FREE RIGHT? AND I GOT IN FREE BECAUSE I WAS A GIRL. SO WE WENT IN AND THESE GIRLS WERE ALL LICKING EACH OTHER AND RUBBING UP AGAINST POLES AND STUFF AND THEY WERE USING A DOUBLE-HEADED DILDO-LIKE REAL SEX BASICALLY, AND, WE WERE STANDING THERE WATCHING, I STOOD UP ON A CHAIR-
OH! OH! THE THING ABOUT THE BATHROOM IS THE COOLEST THING! UM THERE'S THE BOYS' BATHROOM-
YOUR LAP DANCE, DESCRIBE YOUR LAP DANCE

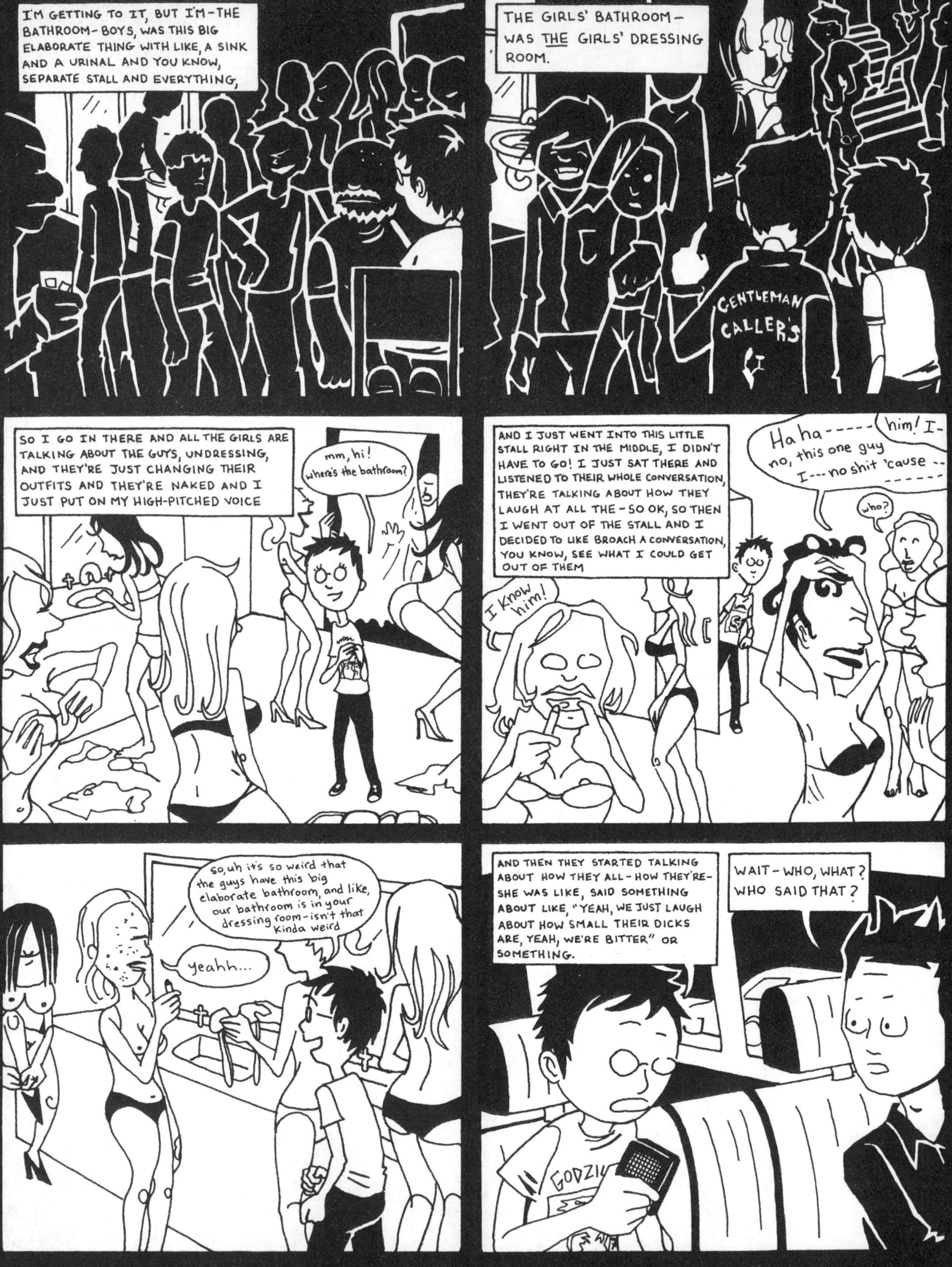
I'M GETTING TO IT, BUT I'M—THE BATHROOM-BOYS, WAS THIS BIG ELABORATE THING WITH LIKE, A SINK AND A URINAL AND YOU KNOW, SEPARATE STALL AND EVERYTHING,
THE GIRLS' BATHROOM—WAS THE GIRLS' DRESSING ROOM.
GENTLEMAN CALLER'S
SO I GO IN THERE AND ALL THE GIRLS ARE TALKING ABOUT THE GUYS, UNDRESSING, AND THEY'RE JUST CHANGING THEIR OUTFITS AND THEY'RE NAKED AND I JUST PUT ON MY HIGH-PITCHED VOICE
mm, hi! where's the bathroom?
AND I JUST WENT INTO THIS LITTLE STALL RIGHT IN THE MIDDLE, I DIDN'T HAVE TO GO! I JUST SAT THERE AND LISTENED TO THEIR WHOLE CONVERSATION, THEY'RE TALKING ABOUT HOW THEY LAUGH AT ALL THE-SO OK, SO THEN I WENT OUT OF THE STALL AND I DECIDED TO LIKE BROACH A CONVERSATION, YOU KNOW, SEE WHAT I COULD GET OUT OF THEM
Ha ha------ no, this one guy I---no shit 'cause ---------
him! I-
who?
I know him!
so, uh it's so weird that the guys have this big elaborate bathroom, and like, our bathroom is in your dressing room-isn't that kinda weird
yeahh...
AND THEN THEY STARTED TALKING ABOUT HOW THEY ALL-HOW THEY'RE-SHE WAS LIKE, SAID SOMETHING ABOUT LIKE, "YEAH, WE JUST LAUGH ABOUT HOW SMALL THEIR DICKS ARE, YEAH, WE'RE BITTER" OR SOMETHING.
WAIT-WHO, WHAT? WHO SAID THAT?
GODZI

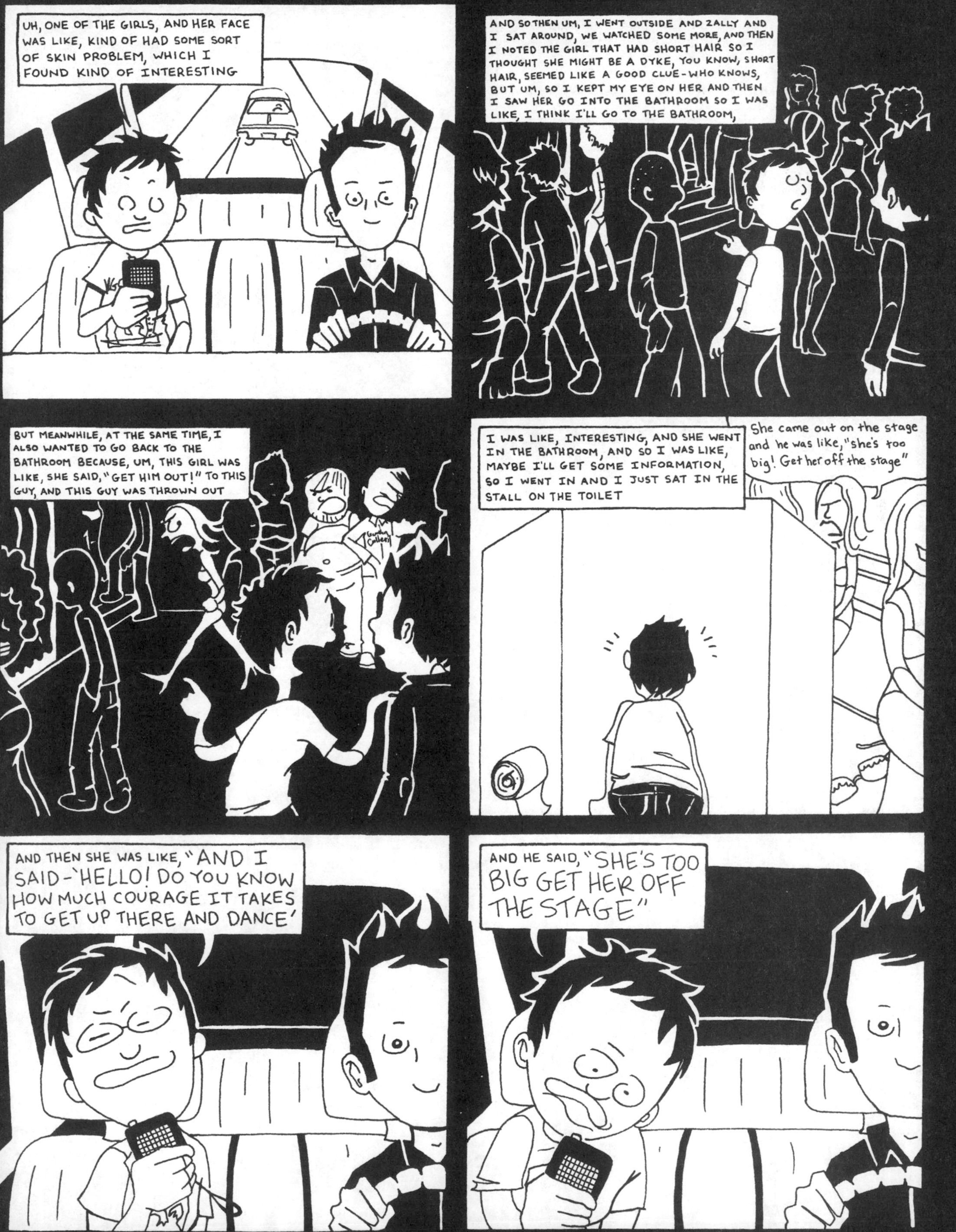
UH, ONE OF THE GIRLS, AND HER FACE WAS LIKE, KIND OF HAD SOME SORT OF SKIN PROBLEM, WHICH I FOUND KIND OF INTERESTING
AND SO THEN UM, I WENT OUTSIDE AND ZALLY AND I SAT AROUND, WE WATCHED SOME MORE, AND THEN I NOTED THE GIRL THAT HAD SHORT HAIR SO I THOUGHT SHE MIGHT BE A DYKE, YOU KNOW, SHORT HAIR, SEEMED LIKE A GOOD CLUE-WHO KNOWS, BUT UM, SO I KEPT MY EYE ON HER AND THEN I SAW HER GO INTO THE BATHROOM SO I WAS LIKE, I THINK I'LL GO TO THE BATHROOM,
BUT MEANWHILE, AT THE SAME TIME, I ALSO WANTED TO GO BACK TO THE BATHROOM BECAUSE, UM, THIS GIRL WAS LIKE, SHE SAID, "GET HIM OUT!" TO THIS GUY, AND THIS GUY WAS THROWN OUT
I WAS LIKE, INTERESTING, AND SHE WENT IN THE BATHROOM, AND SO I WAS LIKE, MAYBE I'LL GET SOME INFORMATION, SO I WENT IN AND I JUST SAT IN THE STALL ON THE TOILET
She came out on the stage and he was like, "she's too big! Get her off the stage"
AND THEN SHE WAS LIKE, "AND I SAID-'HELLO! DO YOU KNOW HOW MUCH COURAGE IT TAKES TO GET UP THERE AND DANCE'
AND HE SAID, "SHE'S TOO BIG GET HER OFF THE STAGE"

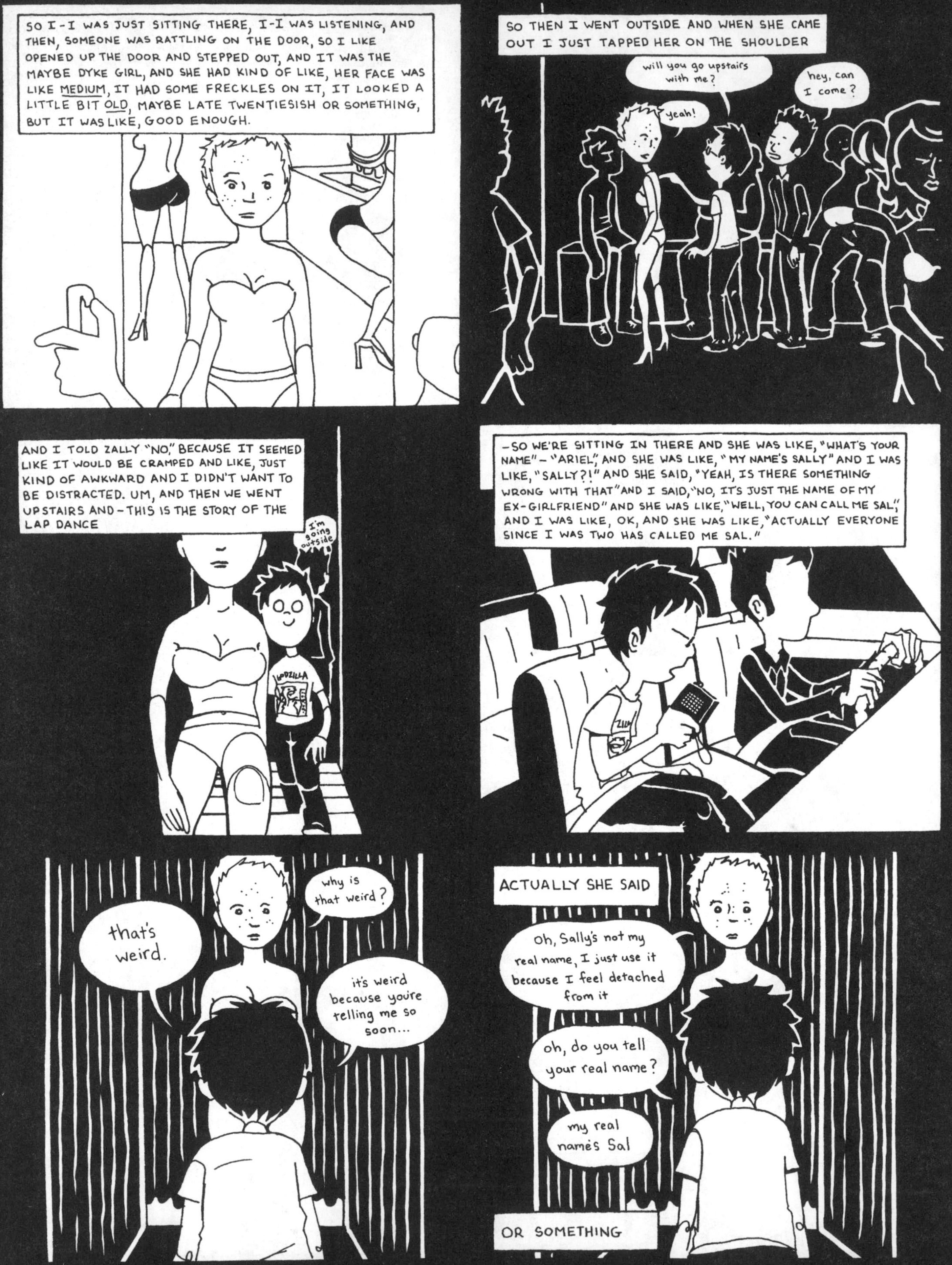
SO I - I WAS JUST SITTING THERE, I-I WAS LISTENING, AND THEN, SOMEONE WAS RATTLING ON THE DOOR, SO I LIKE OPENED UP THE DOOR AND STEPPED OUT, AND IT WAS THE MAYBE DYKE GIRL, AND SHE HAD KIND OF LIKE, HER FACE WAS LIKE MEDIUM, IT HAD SOME FRECKLES ON IT, IT LOOKED A LITTLE BIT OLD, MAYBE LATE TWENTIESISH OR SOMETHING, BUT IT WAS LIKE, GOOD ENOUGH.
SO THEN I WENT OUTSIDE AND WHEN SHE CAME OUT I JUST TAPPED HER ON THE SHOULDER
will you go upstairs with me?
yeah!
hey, can I come?
AND I TOLD ZALLY "NO," BECAUSE IT SEEMED LIKE IT WOULD BE CRAMPED AND LIKE, JUST KIND OF AWKWARD AND I DIDN'T WANT TO BE DISTRACTED. UM, AND THEN WE WENT UPSTAIRS AND - THIS IS THE STORY OF THE LAP DANCE
I'm going outside
- SO WE'RE SITTING IN THERE AND SHE WAS LIKE, "WHAT'S YOUR NAME" - "ARIEL," AND SHE WAS LIKE, "MY NAME'S SALLY" AND I WAS LIKE, "SALLY?!" AND SHE SAID, "YEAH, IS THERE SOMETHING WRONG WITH THAT" AND I SAID, "NO, IT'S JUST THE NAME OF MY EX-GIRLFRIEND" AND SHE WAS LIKE, "WELL, YOU CAN CALL ME SAL," AND I WAS LIKE, OK, AND SHE WAS LIKE, "ACTUALLY EVERYONE SINCE I WAS TWO HAS CALLED ME SAL."
that's weird.
why is that weird?
it's weird because you're telling me so soon...
ACTUALLY SHE SAID
Oh, Sally's not my real name, I just use it because I feel detached from it
oh, do you tell your real name?
my real name's Sal
OR SOMETHING

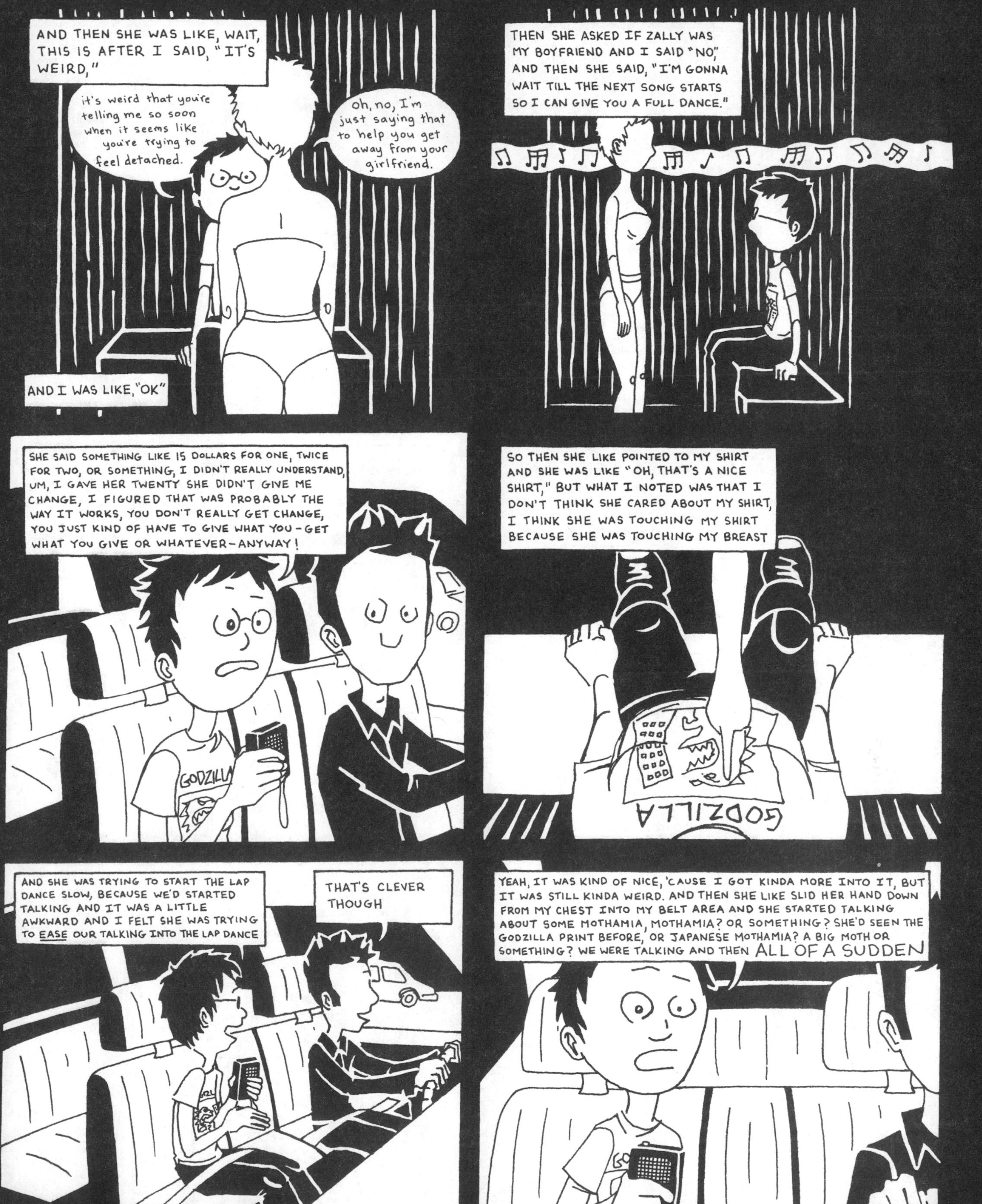
AND THEN SHE WAS LIKE, WAIT, THIS IS AFTER I SAID, "IT'S WEIRD,"
it's weird that you're telling me so soon when it seems like you're trying to feel detached.
oh, no, I'm just saying that to help you get away from your girlfriend.
AND I WAS LIKE, "OK"
THEN SHE ASKED IF ZALLY WAS MY BOYFRIEND AND I SAID "NO," AND THEN SHE SAID, "I'M GONNA WAIT TILL THE NEXT SONG STARTS SO I CAN GIVE YOU A FULL DANCE."
SHE SAID SOMETHING LIKE 15 DOLLARS FOR ONE, TWICE FOR TWO, OR SOMETHING, I DIDN'T REALLY UNDERSTAND, UM, I GAVE HER TWENTY SHE DIDN'T GIVE ME CHANGE, I FIGURED THAT WAS PROBABLY THE WAY IT WORKS, YOU DON'T REALLY GET CHANGE, YOU JUST KIND OF HAVE TO GIVE WHAT YOU - GET WHAT YOU GIVE OR WHATEVER - ANYWAY!
GODZILLA
SO THEN SHE LIKE POINTED TO MY SHIRT AND SHE WAS LIKE "OH, THAT'S A NICE SHIRT," BUT WHAT I NOTED WAS THAT I DON'T THINK SHE CARED ABOUT MY SHIRT, I THINK SHE WAS TOUCHING MY SHIRT BECAUSE SHE WAS TOUCHING MY BREAST
GODZILLA
AND SHE WAS TRYING TO START THE LAP DANCE SLOW, BECAUSE WE'D STARTED TALKING AND IT WAS A LITTLE AWKWARD AND I FELT SHE WAS TRYING TO EASE OUR TALKING INTO THE LAP DANCE
THAT'S CLEVER THOUGH
YEAH, IT WAS KIND OF NICE, 'CAUSE I GOT KINDA MORE INTO IT, BUT IT WAS STILL KINDA WEIRD. AND THEN SHE LIKE SLID HER HAND DOWN FROM MY CHEST INTO MY BELT AREA AND SHE STARTED TALKING ABOUT SOME MOTHAMIA, MOTHAMIA? OR SOMETHING? SHE'D SEEN THE GODZILLA PRINT BEFORE, OR JAPANESE MOTHAMIA? A BIG MOTH OR SOMETHING? WE WERE TALKING AND THEN ALL OF A SUDDEN

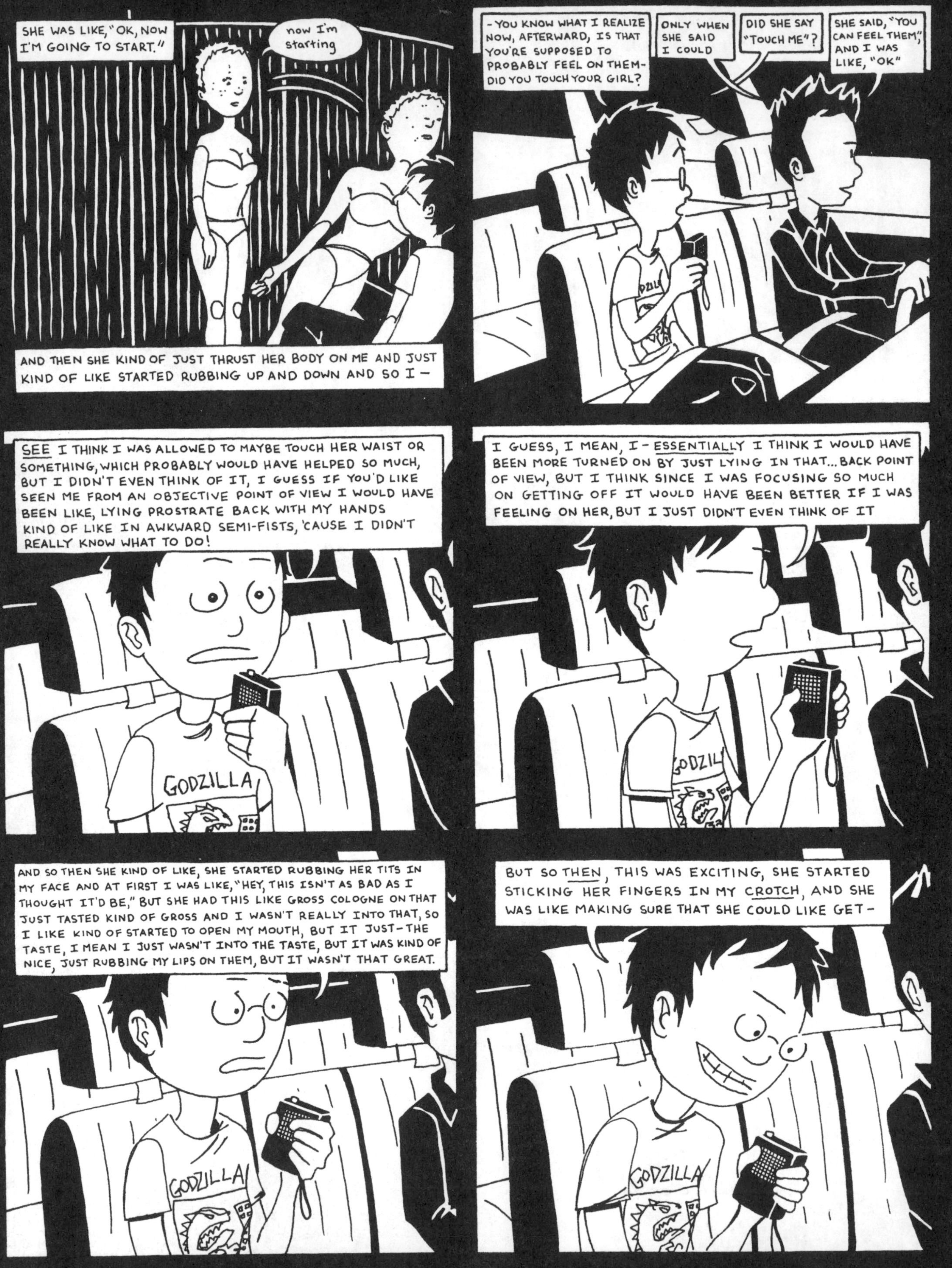
SHE WAS LIKE, "OK, NOW I'M GOING TO START."
now I'm starting
AND THEN SHE KIND OF JUST THRUST HER BODY ON ME AND JUST KIND OF LIKE STARTED RUBBING UP AND DOWN AND SO I —
- YOU KNOW WHAT I REALIZE NOW, AFTERWARD, IS THAT YOU'RE SUPPOSED TO PROBABLY FEEL ON THEM - DID YOU TOUCH YOUR GIRL?
ONLY WHEN SHE SAID I COULD
DID SHE SAY "TOUCH ME"?
SHE SAID, "YOU CAN FEEL THEM," AND I WAS LIKE, "OK"
SEE I THINK I WAS ALLOWED TO MAYBE TOUCH HER WAIST OR SOMETHING, WHICH PROBABLY WOULD HAVE HELPED SO MUCH, BUT I DIDN'T EVEN THINK OF IT, I GUESS IF YOU'D LIKE SEEN ME FROM AN OBJECTIVE POINT OF VIEW I WOULD HAVE BEEN LIKE, LYING PROSTRATE BACK WITH MY HANDS KIND OF LIKE IN AWKWARD SEMI-FISTS, 'CAUSE I DIDN'T REALLY KNOW WHAT TO DO!
GODZILLA
I GUESS, I MEAN, I - ESSENTIALLY I THINK I WOULD HAVE BEEN MORE TURNED ON BY JUST LYING IN THAT... BACK POINT OF VIEW, BUT I THINK SINCE I WAS FOCUSING SO MUCH ON GETTING OFF IT WOULD HAVE BEEN BETTER IF I WAS FEELING ON HER, BUT I JUST DIDN'T EVEN THINK OF IT
AND SO THEN SHE KIND OF LIKE, SHE STARTED RUBBING HER TITS IN MY FACE AND AT FIRST I WAS LIKE, "HEY, THIS ISN'T AS BAD AS I THOUGHT IT'D BE," BUT SHE HAD THIS LIKE GROSS COLOGNE ON THAT JUST TASTED KIND OF GROSS AND I WASN'T REALLY INTO THAT, SO I LIKE KIND OF STARTED TO OPEN MY MOUTH, BUT IT JUST - THE TASTE, I MEAN I JUST WASN'T INTO THE TASTE, BUT IT WAS KIND OF NICE, JUST RUBBING MY LIPS ON THEM, BUT IT WASN'T THAT GREAT.
GODZILLA
BUT SO THEN, THIS WAS EXCITING, SHE STARTED STICKING HER FINGERS IN MY CROTCH, AND SHE WAS LIKE MAKING SURE THAT SHE COULD LIKE GET -
GODZILLA

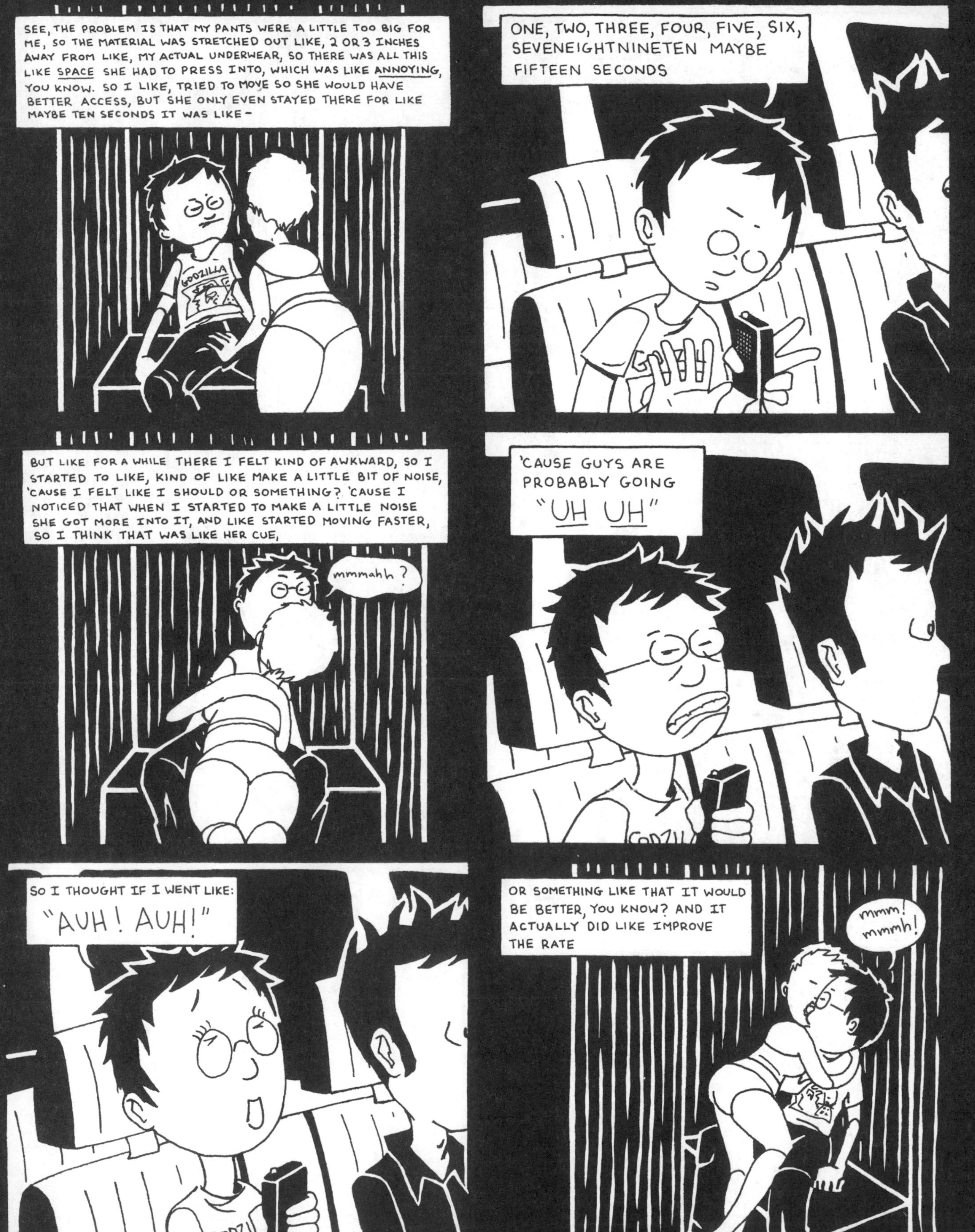

SEE, THE PROBLEM IS THAT MY PANTS WERE A LITTLE TOO BIG FOR ME, SO THE MATERIAL WAS STRETCHED OUT LIKE, 2 OR 3 INCHES AWAY FROM LIKE, MY ACTUAL UNDERWEAR, SO THERE WAS ALL THIS LIKE SPACE SHE HAD TO PRESS INTO, WHICH WAS LIKE ANNOYING, YOU KNOW. SO I LIKE, TRIED TO MOVE SO SHE WOULD HAVE BETTER ACCESS, BUT SHE ONLY EVEN STAYED THERE FOR LIKE MAYBE TEN SECONDS IT WAS LIKE-
GODZILLA
ONE, TWO, THREE, FOUR, FIVE, SIX, SEVENEIGHTNINETEN MAYBE FIFTEEN SECONDS
BUT LIKE FOR A WHILE THERE I FELT KIND OF AWKWARD, SO I STARTED TO LIKE, KIND OF LIKE MAKE A LITTLE BIT OF NOISE, 'CAUSE I FELT LIKE I SHOULD OR SOMETHING? 'CAUSE I NOTICED THAT WHEN I STARTED TO MAKE A LITTLE NOISE SHE GOT MORE INTO IT, AND LIKE STARTED MOVING FASTER, SO I THINK THAT WAS LIKE HER CUE,
mmmahh?
'CAUSE GUYS ARE PROBABLY GOING "UH UH"
SO I THOUGHT IF I WENT LIKE: "AUH! AUH!"
OR SOMETHING LIKE THAT IT WOULD BE BETTER, YOU KNOW? AND IT ACTUALLY DID LIKE IMPROVE THE RATE
mmm! mmmh!

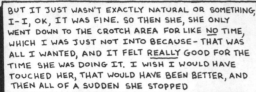

BUT IT JUST WASN'T EXACTLY NATURAL OR SOMETHING, I- I, OK, IT WAS FINE. SO THEN SHE, SHE ONLY WENT DOWN TO THE CROTCH AREA FOR LIKE NO TIME, WHICH I WAS JUST NOT INTO BECAUSE- THAT WAS ALL I WANTED, AND IT FELT REALLY GOOD FOR THE TIME SHE WAS DOING IT. I WISH I WOULD HAVE TOUCHED HER, THAT WOULD HAVE BEEN BETTER, AND THEN ALL OF A SUDDEN SHE STOPPED

GODZILLA

that's it

OK.

did you enjoy it?

yes

GODZILLA

BUT I ACTUALLY WASN'T DONE AT ALL, SO THEN ZALLY AND I WENT BACK TO THE LUSTY LADY AND WE JACKED OFF IN THE BOOTH.

10:44
May 27 a day of nothingness.

CHAPTER SEVEN

I had a semi-breakdown today. reconciled quickly by hanging out with Ms. Salt and making cookies. But in its prime moments I was in the tub and realized I could barely move.

ew! Elizabeth! this room is a nothingness we can't work in here

Well the other room is more of a nothingness

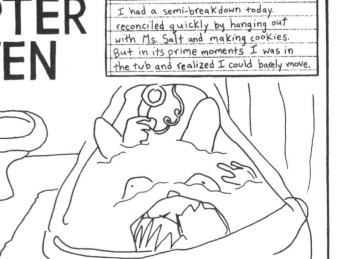

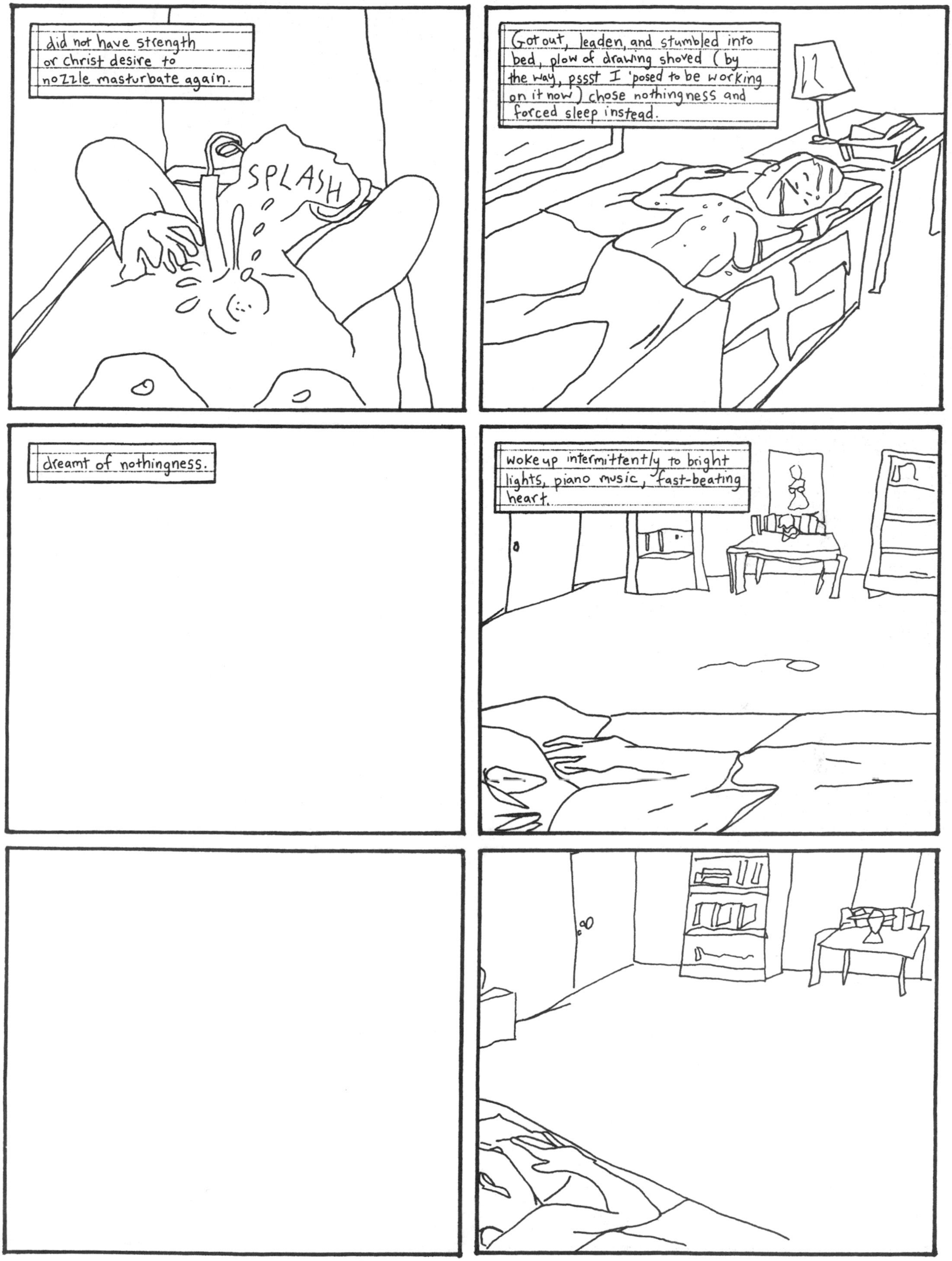
did not have strength or christ desire to nozzle masturbate again.
SPLASH
Got out, leaden, and stumbled into bed, plow of drawing shoved (by the way, pssst I 'posed to be working on it now) chose nothingness and forced sleep instead.
dreamt of nothingness.
wokeup intermittently to bright lights, piano music, fast-beating heart.

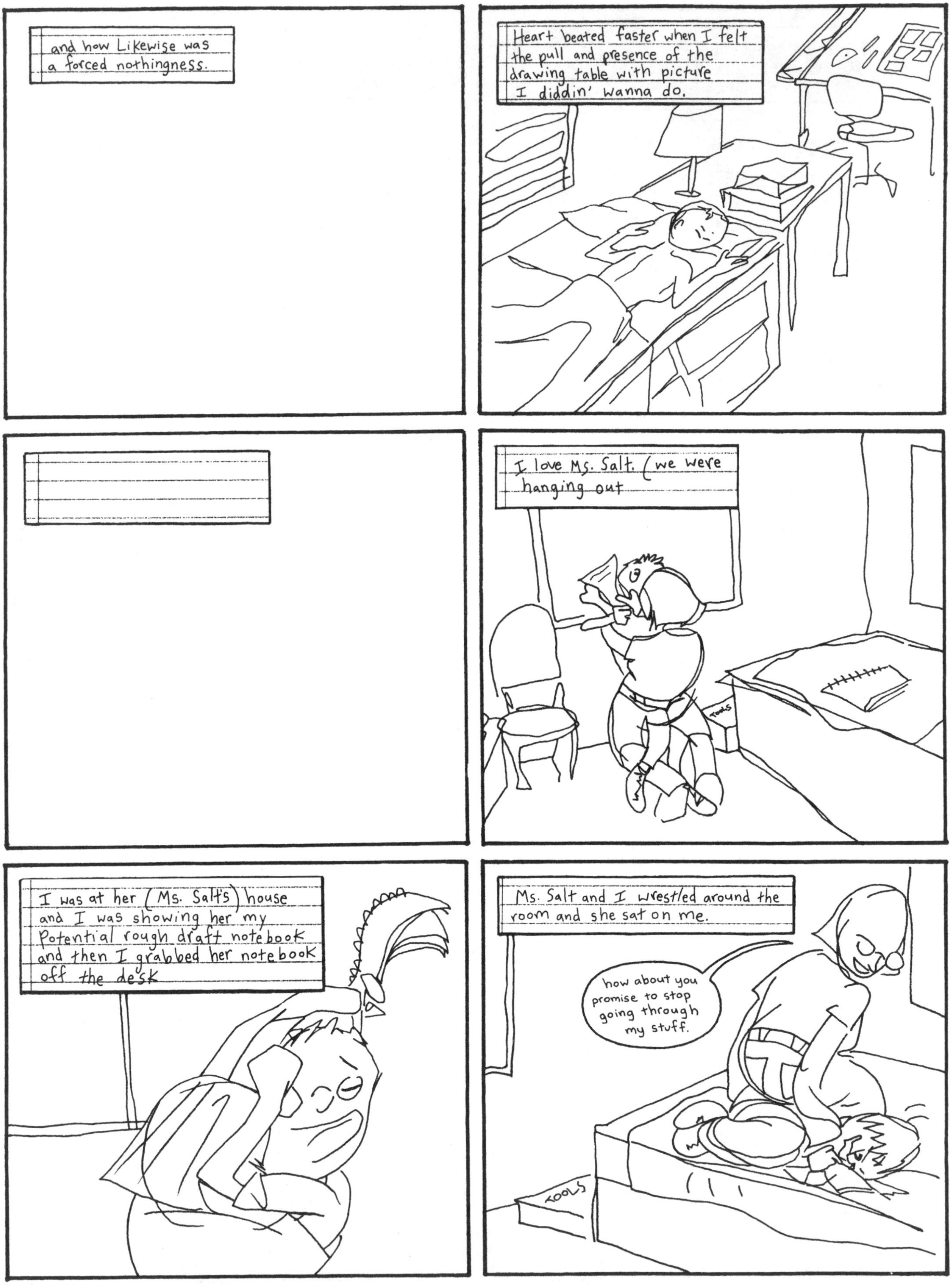
and how Likewise was a forced nothingness.
Heart beated faster when I felt the pull and presence of the drawing table with picture I diddin' wanna do.
I love Ms. Salt. (we were hanging out
TOOLS
I was at her (Ms. Salt's) house and I was showing her my Potential rough draft notebook and then I grabbed her notebook off the desk
Ms. Salt and I wrestled around the room and she sat on me.
how about you promise to stop going through my stuff.
TOOLS

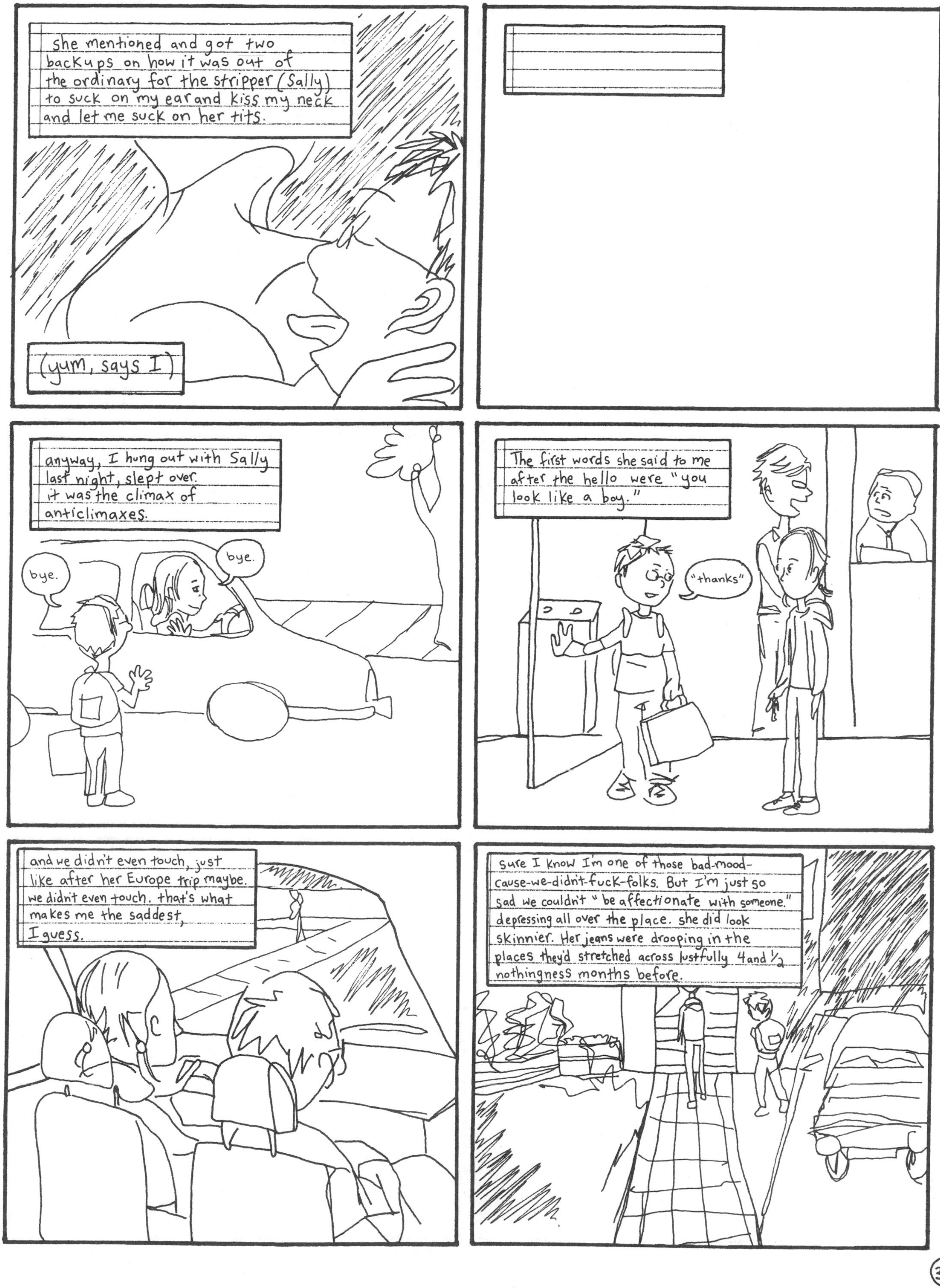
she mentioned and got two backups on how it was out of the ordinary for the stripper (Sally) to suck on my ear and kiss my neck and let me suck on her tits.
(yum, says I)
anyway, I hung out with Sally last night, slept over. it was the climax of anticlimaxes.
bye.
bye.
The first words she said to me after the hello were "you look like a boy."
"thanks"
and we didn't even touch, just like after her Europe trip maybe. we didn't even touch. that's what makes me the saddest, I guess.
sure I know I'm one of those bad-mood-cause-we-didn't-fuck-folks. But I'm just so sad we couldn't "be affectionate with someone." depressing all over the place. she did look skinnier. Her jeans were drooping in the places they'd stretched across lustfully 4 and 1/2 nothingness months before.

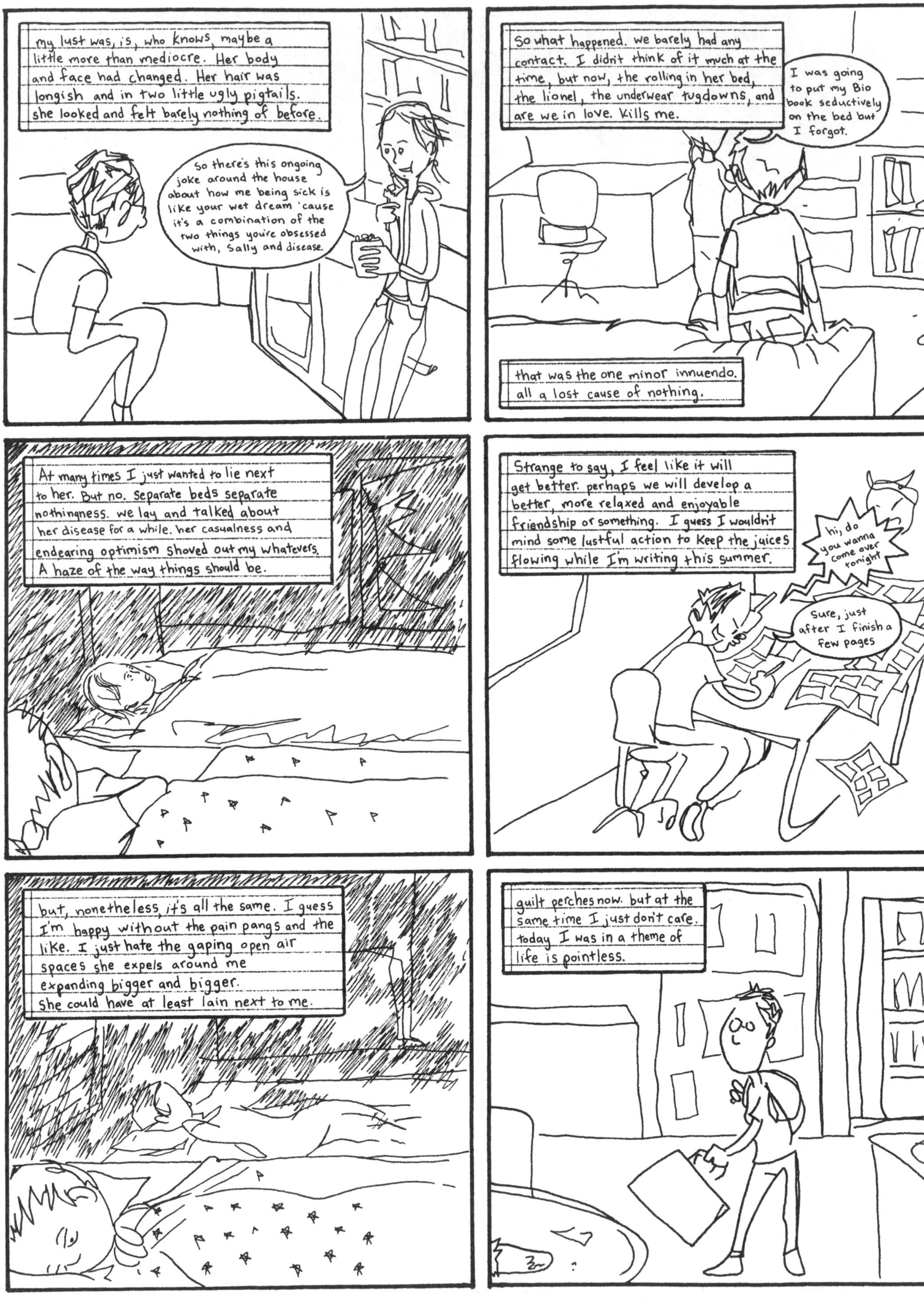
my lust was, is, who knows, maybe a little more than mediocre. Her body and face had changed. Her hair was longish and in two little ugly pigtails. she looked and felt barely nothing of before.
So there's this ongoing joke around the house about how me being sick is like your wet dream 'cause it's a combination of the two things you're obsessed with, Sally and disease.
So what happened. we barely had any contact. I didn't think of it much at the time, but now, the rolling in her bed, the lionel, the underwear tugdowns, and are we in love. Kills me.
I was going to put my Bio book seductively on the bed but I forgot.
that was the one minor innuendo. all a lost cause of nothing.
At many times I just wanted to lie next to her. But no. separate beds separate nothingness. we lay and talked about her disease for a while. her casualness and endearing optimism shoved out my whatevers. A haze of the way things should be.
Strange to say, I feel like it will get better. perhaps we will develop a better, more relaxed and enjoyable friendship or something. I guess I wouldn't mind some lustful action to keep the juices flowing while I'm writing this summer.
hi, do you wanna come over tonight
Sure, just after I finish a few pages
but, nonetheless, it's all the same. I guess I'm happy without the pain pangs and the like. I just hate the gaping open air spaces she expels around me expanding bigger and bigger. She could have at least lain next to me.
guilt perches now. but at the same time I just don't care. today I was in a theme of life is pointless.

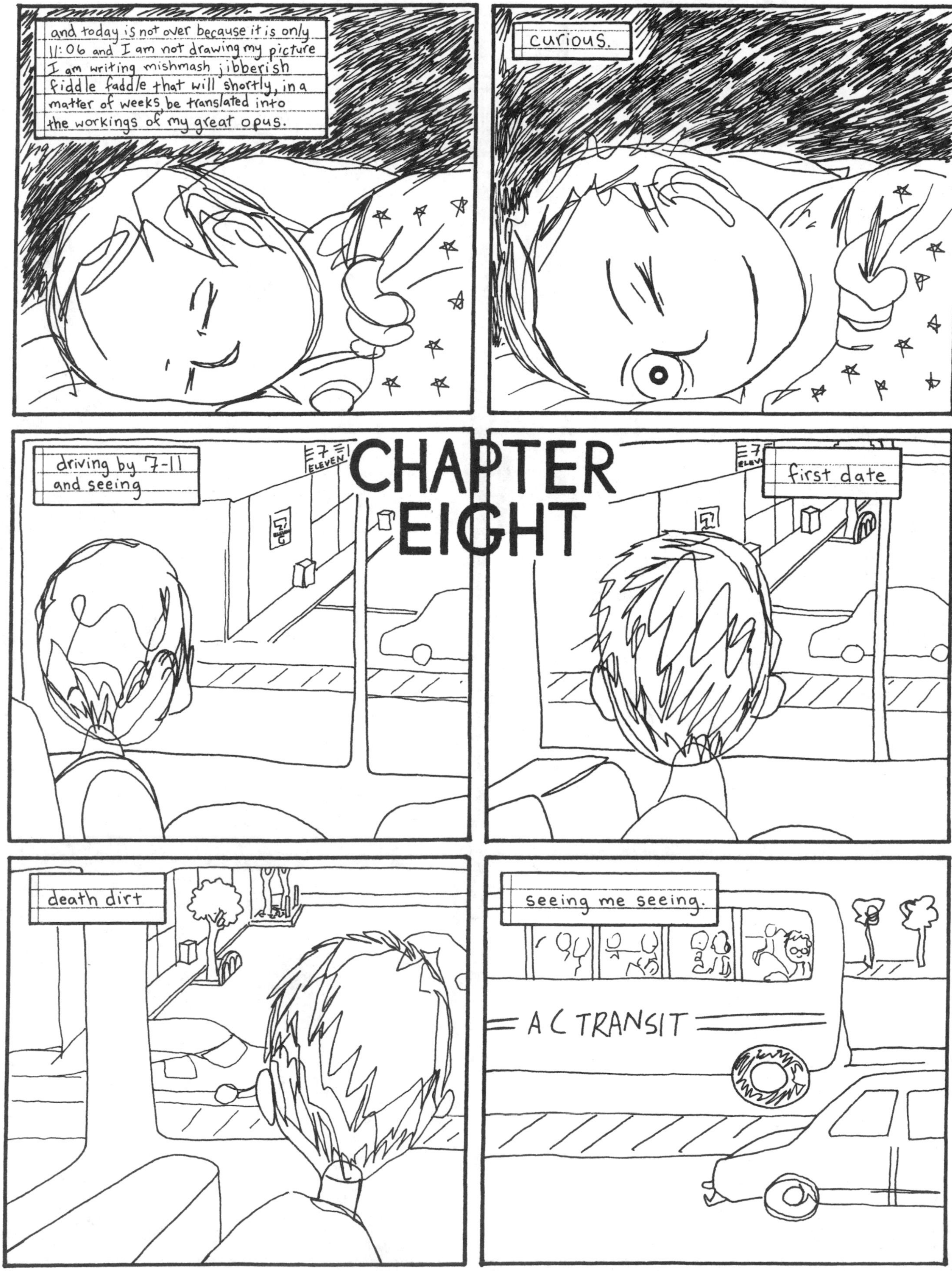
and today is not over because it is only 11:06 and I am not drawing my picture I am writing mishmash jibberish fiddle faddle that will shortly, in a matter of weeks be translated into the workings of my great opus.
curious.
CHAPTER EIGHT
driving by 7-11 and seeing
7 ELEVEN
first date
death dirt
seeing me seeing.
A C TRANSIT

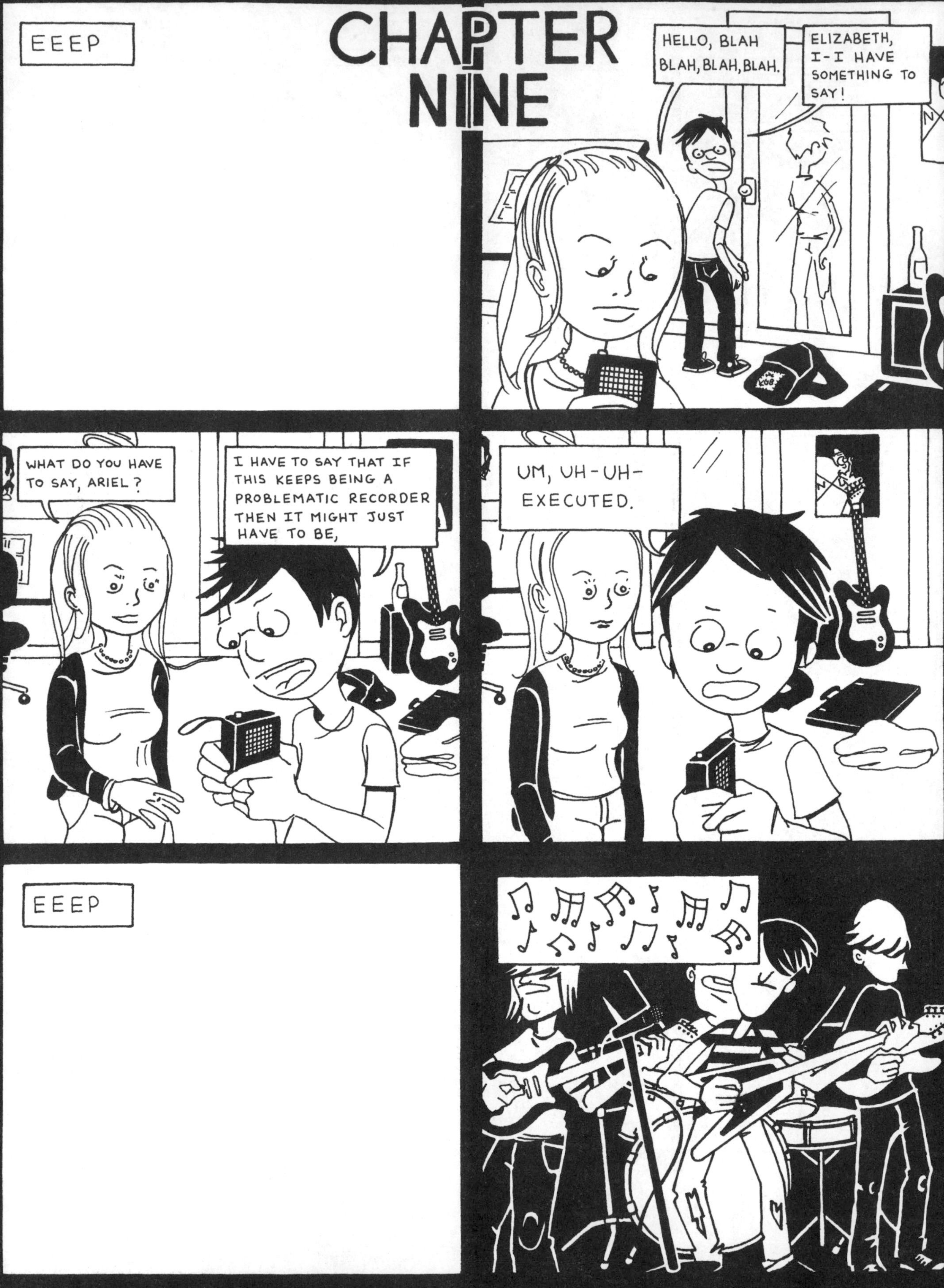
EEEP
CHAPTER NINE
HELLO, BLAH BLAH, BLAH, BLAH.
ELIZABETH, I-I HAVE SOMETHING TO SAY!
WHAT DO YOU HAVE TO SAY, ARIEL?
I HAVE TO SAY THAT IF THIS KEEPS BEING A PROBLEMATIC RECORDER THEN IT MIGHT JUST HAVE TO BE,
UM, UH-UH-EXECUTED.
EEEP

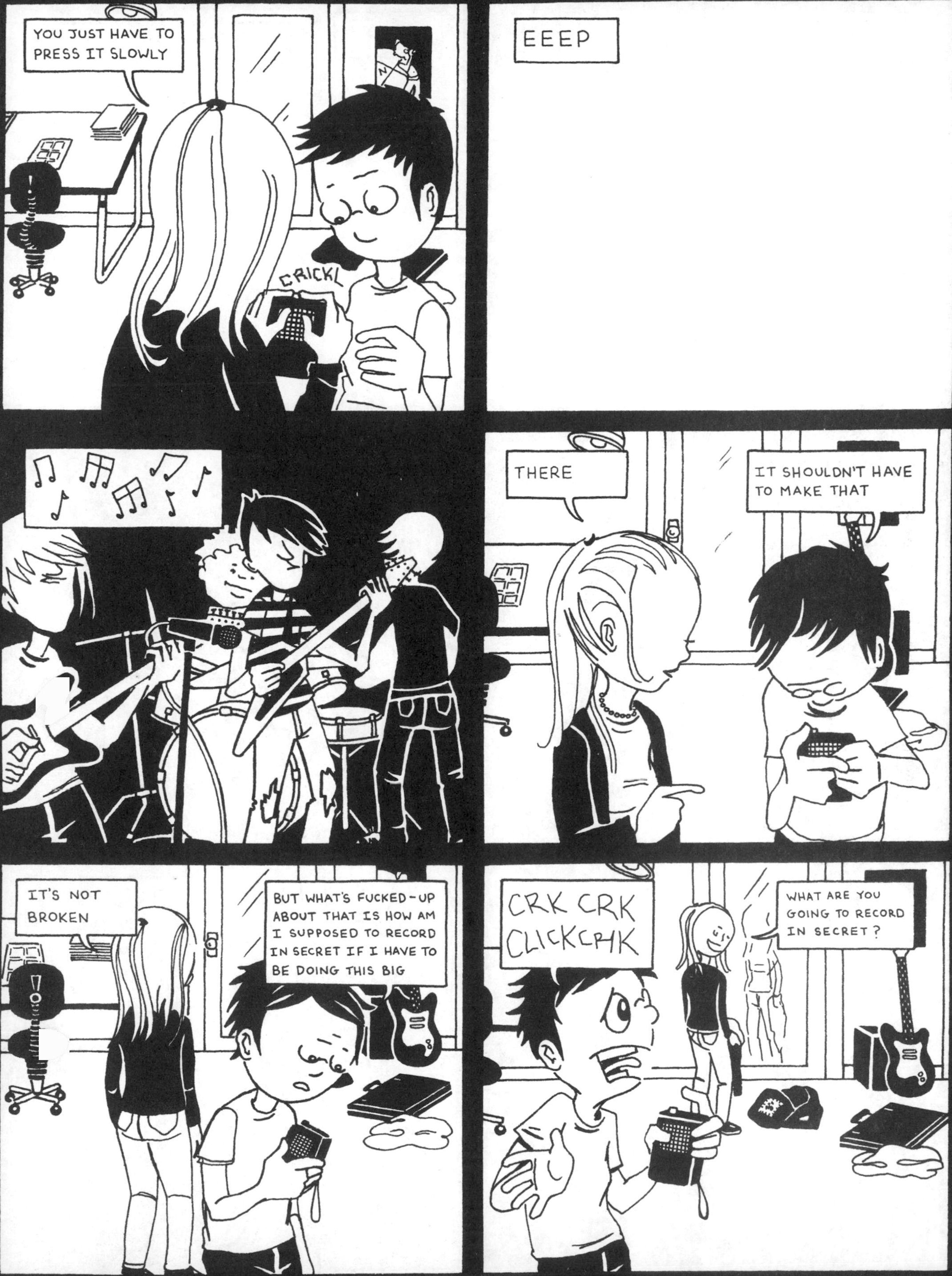
YOU JUST HAVE TO PRESS IT SLOWLY
CRICKL
EEEP
THERE
IT SHOULDN'T HAVE TO MAKE THAT
IT'S NOT BROKEN
BUT WHAT'S FUCKED-UP ABOUT THAT IS HOW AM I SUPPOSED TO RECORD IN SECRET IF I HAVE TO BE DOING THIS BIG
CRK CRK CLICKCRK
WHAT ARE YOU GOING TO RECORD IN SECRET?

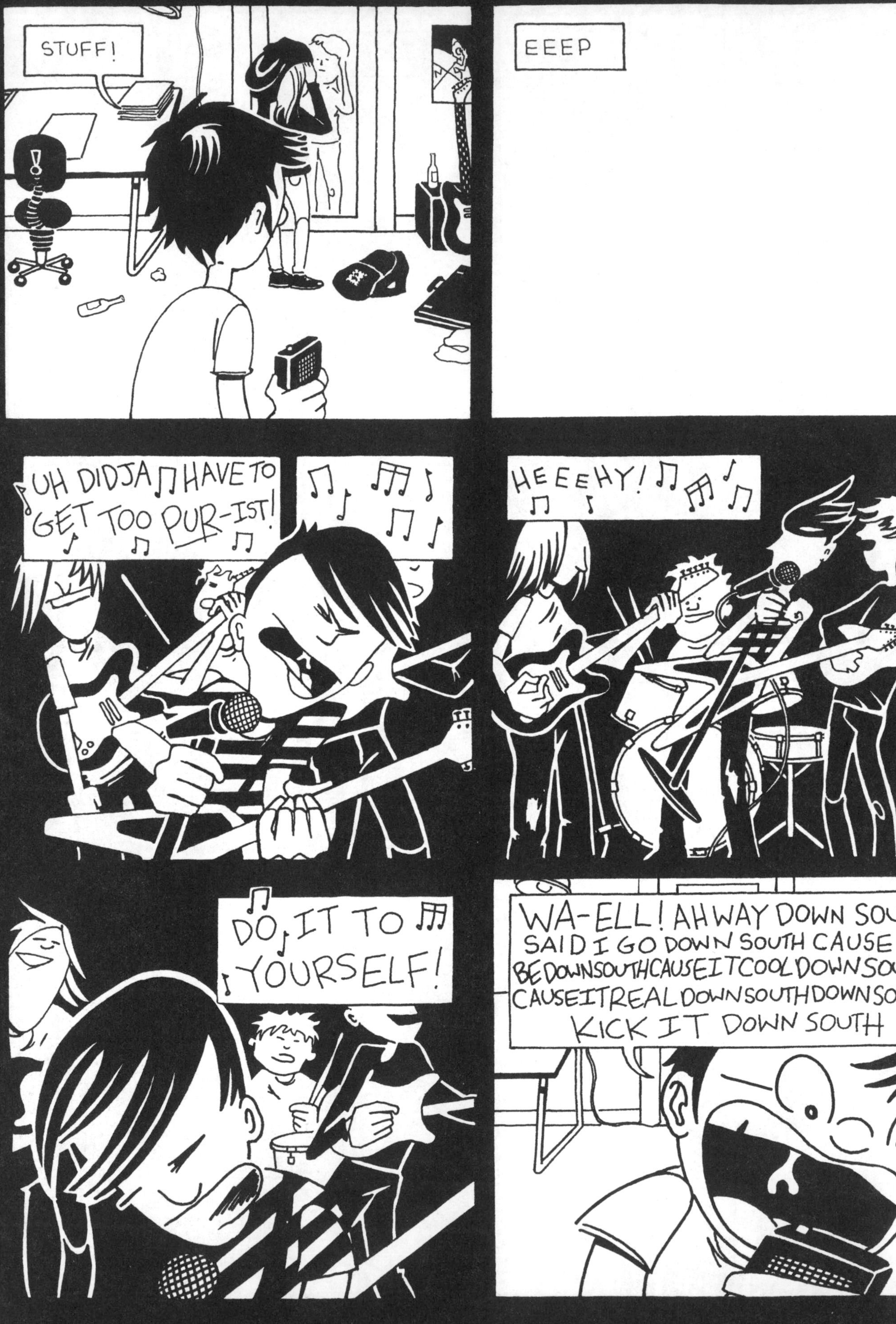
STUFF!
EEEP
UH DIDJA HAVE TO GET TOO PUR-IST!
HEEEHY!
DO IT TO YOURSELF!
WA-ELL! AH WAY DOWN SOUTH SAID I GO DOWN SOUTH CAUSE I BE DOWN SOUTH CAUSE IT COOL DOWN SOUTH CAUSE IT REAL DOWN SOUTH DOWN SOUTH KICK IT DOWN SOUTH

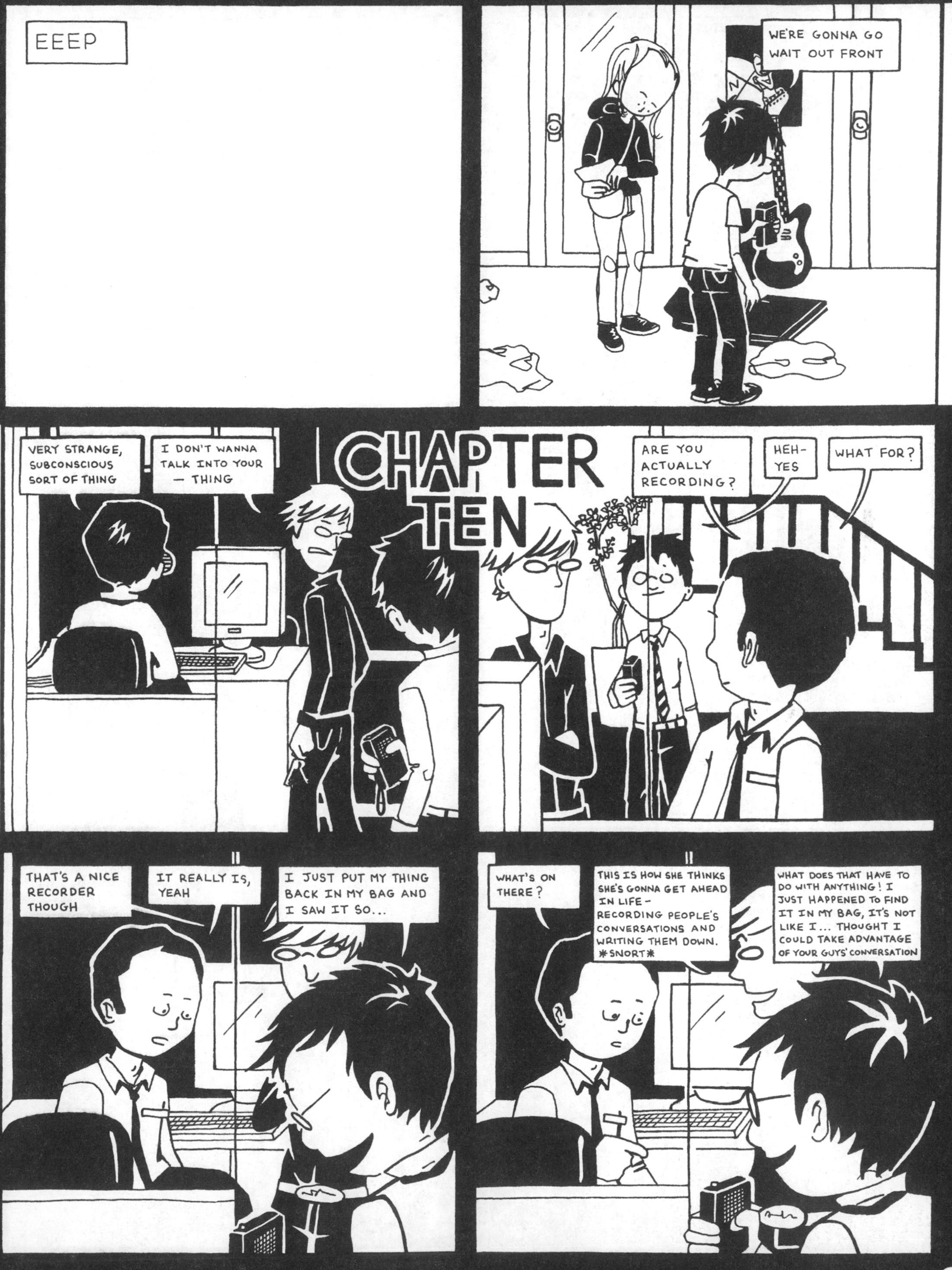
EEEP
WE'RE GONNA GO WAIT OUT FRONT
VERY STRANGE, SUBCONSCIOUS SORT OF THING
I DON'T WANNA TALK INTO YOUR — THING
CHAPTER TEN
ARE YOU ACTUALLY RECORDING?
HEH- YES
WHAT FOR?
THAT'S A NICE RECORDER THOUGH
IT REALLY IS, YEAH
I JUST PUT MY THING BACK IN MY BAG AND I SAW IT SO...
WHAT'S ON THERE?
THIS IS HOW SHE THINKS SHE'S GONNA GET AHEAD IN LIFE - RECORDING PEOPLE'S CONVERSATIONS AND WRITING THEM DOWN. *SNORT*
WHAT DOES THAT HAVE TO DO WITH ANYTHING! I JUST HAPPENED TO FIND IT IN MY BAG, IT'S NOT LIKE I... THOUGHT I COULD TAKE ADVANTAGE OF YOUR GUYS' CONVERSATION

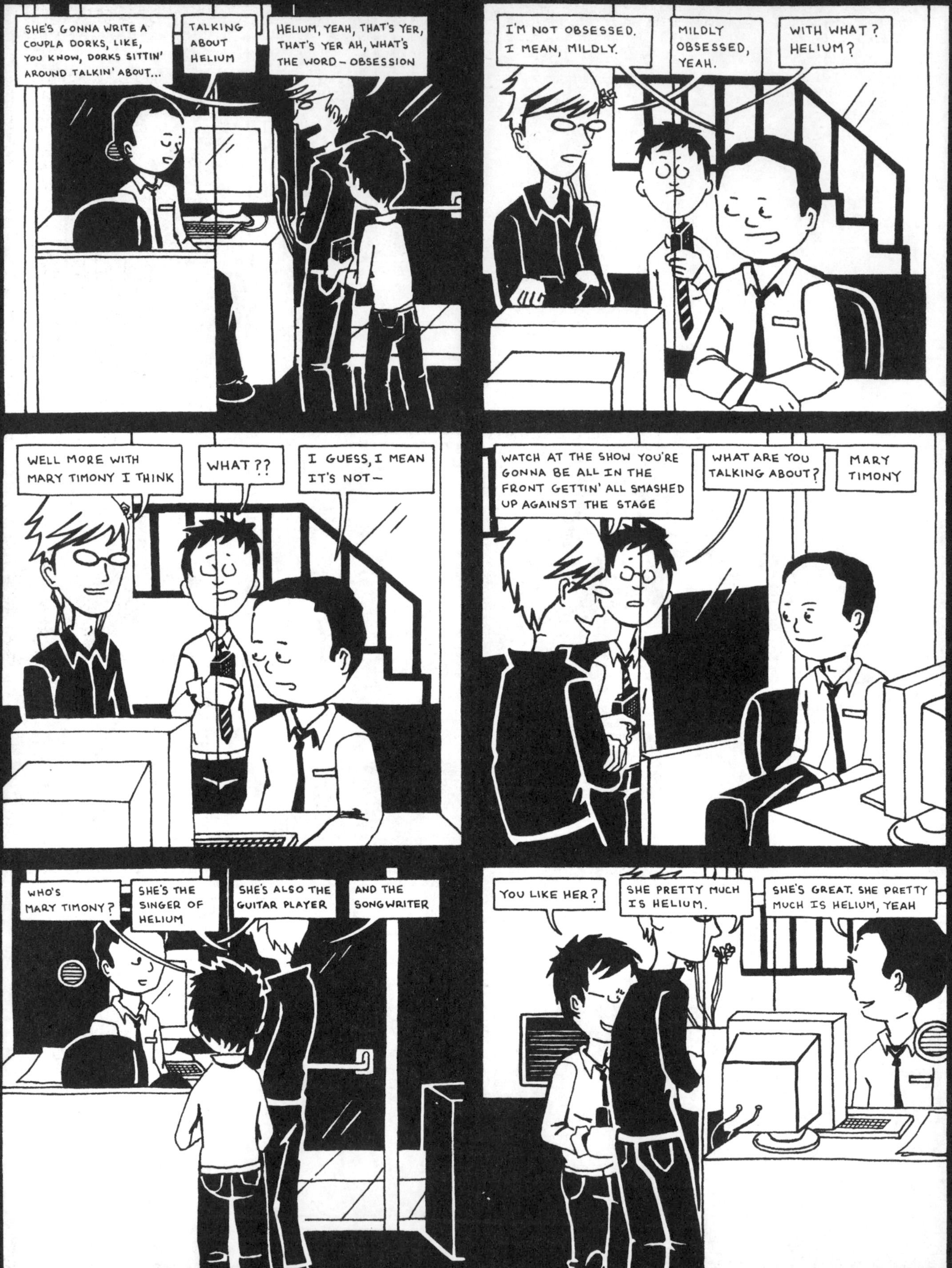
SHE'S GONNA WRITE A COUPLA DORKS, LIKE, YOU KNOW, DORKS SITTIN' AROUND TALKIN' ABOUT...
TALKING ABOUT HELIUM
HELIUM, YEAH, THAT'S YER, THAT'S YER AH, WHAT'S THE WORD – OBSESSION
I'M NOT OBSESSED. I MEAN, MILDLY.
MILDLY OBSESSED, YEAH.
WITH WHAT? HELIUM?
WELL MORE WITH MARY TIMONY I THINK
WHAT??
I GUESS, I MEAN IT'S NOT–
WATCH AT THE SHOW YOU'RE GONNA BE ALL IN THE FRONT GETTIN' ALL SMASHED UP AGAINST THE STAGE
WHAT ARE YOU TALKING ABOUT?
MARY TIMONY
WHO'S MARY TIMONY?
SHE'S THE SINGER OF HELIUM
SHE'S ALSO THE GUITAR PLAYER
AND THE SONGWRITER
YOU LIKE HER?
SHE PRETTY MUCH IS HELIUM.
SHE'S GREAT. SHE PRETTY MUCH IS HELIUM, YEAH

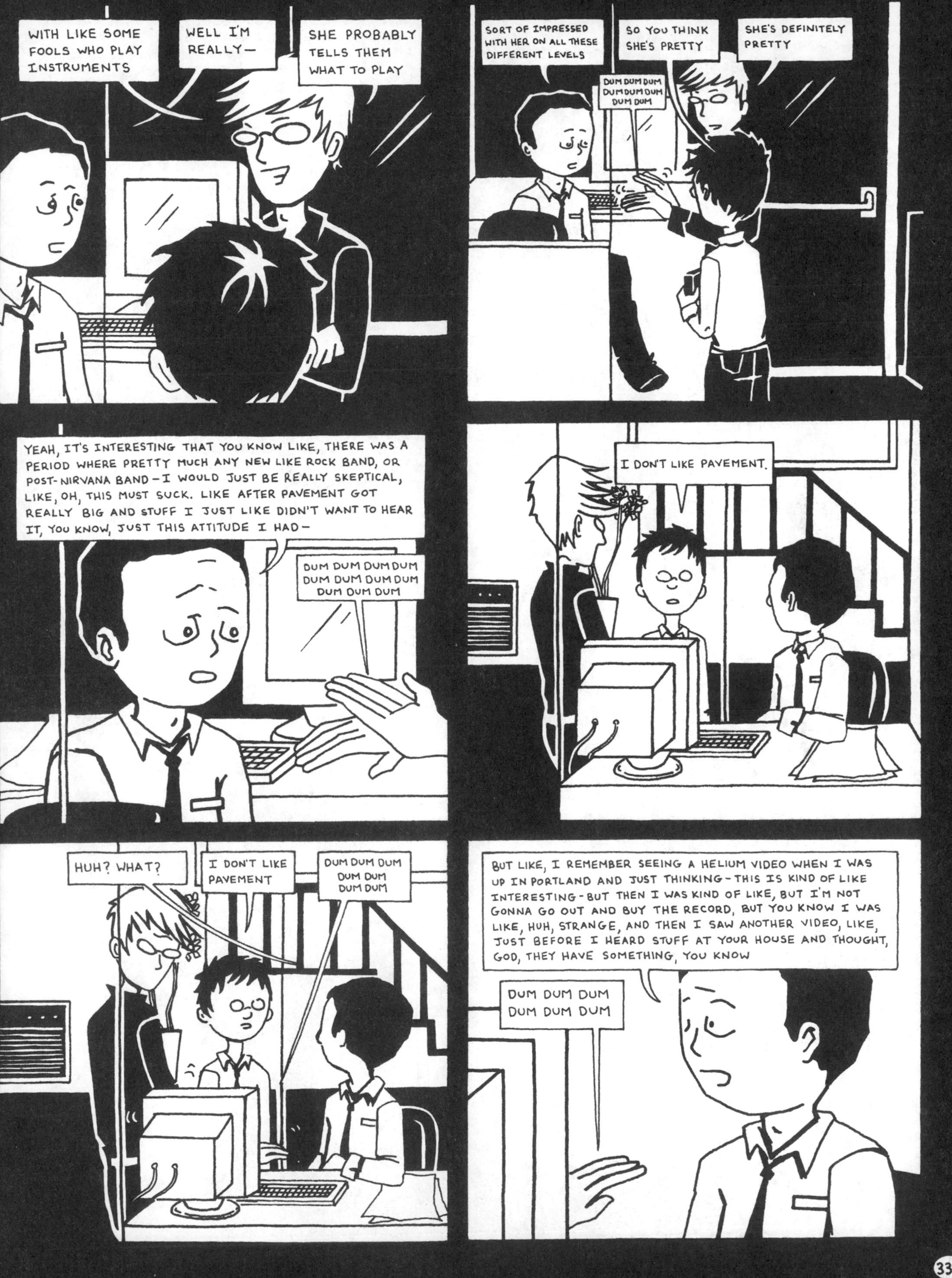
WITH LIKE SOME FOOLS WHO PLAY INSTRUMENTS
WELL I'M REALLY—
SHE PROBABLY TELLS THEM WHAT TO PLAY
SORT OF IMPRESSED WITH HER ON ALL THESE DIFFERENT LEVELS
DUM DUM DUM DUM DUM DUM DUM DUM
SO YOU THINK SHE'S PRETTY
SHE'S DEFINITELY PRETTY
YEAH, IT'S INTERESTING THAT YOU KNOW LIKE, THERE WAS A PERIOD WHERE PRETTY MUCH ANY NEW LIKE ROCK BAND, OR POST-NIRVANA BAND – I WOULD JUST BE REALLY SKEPTICAL, LIKE, OH, THIS MUST SUCK. LIKE AFTER PAVEMENT GOT REALLY BIG AND STUFF I JUST LIKE DIDN'T WANT TO HEAR IT, YOU KNOW, JUST THIS ATTITUDE I HAD–
DUM DUM DUM DUM DUM DUM DUM DUM DUM DUM DUM
I DON'T LIKE PAVEMENT.
HUH? WHAT?
I DON'T LIKE PAVEMENT
DUM DUM DUM DUM DUM DUM DUM
BUT LIKE, I REMEMBER SEEING A HELIUM VIDEO WHEN I WAS UP IN PORTLAND AND JUST THINKING – THIS IS KIND OF LIKE INTERESTING – BUT THEN I WAS KIND OF LIKE, BUT I'M NOT GONNA GO OUT AND BUY THE RECORD, BUT YOU KNOW I WAS LIKE, HUH, STRANGE, AND THEN I SAW ANOTHER VIDEO, LIKE, JUST BEFORE I HEARD STUFF AT YOUR HOUSE AND THOUGHT, GOD, THEY HAVE SOMETHING, YOU KNOW
DUM DUM DUM DUM DUM DUM

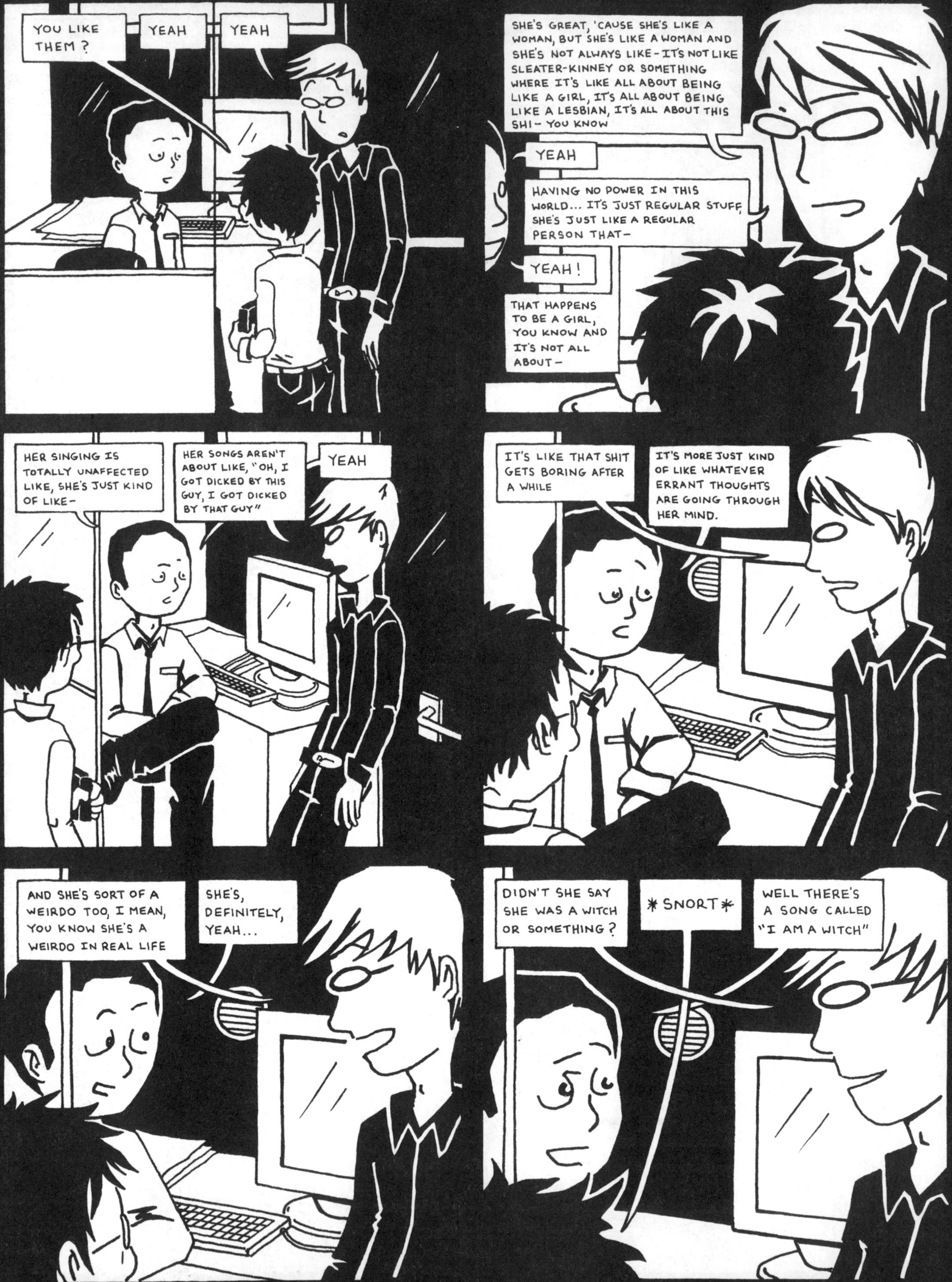
YOU LIKE THEM ?
YEAH
YEAH
SHE'S GREAT, 'CAUSE SHE'S LIKE A WOMAN, BUT SHE'S LIKE A WOMAN AND SHE'S NOT ALWAYS LIKE - IT'S NOT LIKE SLEATER-KINNEY OR SOMETHING WHERE IT'S LIKE ALL ABOUT BEING LIKE A GIRL, IT'S ALL ABOUT BEING LIKE A LESBIAN, IT'S ALL ABOUT THIS SHI- YOU KNOW
YEAH
HAVING NO POWER IN THIS WORLD... IT'S JUST REGULAR STUFF, SHE'S JUST LIKE A REGULAR PERSON THAT-
YEAH!
THAT HAPPENS TO BE A GIRL, YOU KNOW AND IT'S NOT ALL ABOUT-
HER SINGING IS TOTALLY UNAFFECTED LIKE, SHE'S JUST KIND OF LIKE-
HER SONGS AREN'T ABOUT LIKE, "OH, I GOT DICKED BY THIS GUY, I GOT DICKED BY THAT GUY"
YEAH
IT'S LIKE THAT SHIT GETS BORING AFTER A WHILE
IT'S MORE JUST KIND OF LIKE WHATEVER ERRANT THOUGHTS ARE GOING THROUGH HER MIND.
AND SHE'S SORT OF A WEIRDO TOO, I MEAN, YOU KNOW SHE'S A WEIRDO IN REAL LIFE
SHE'S, DEFINITELY, YEAH...
DIDN'T SHE SAY SHE WAS A WITCH OR SOMETHING?
SNORT
WELL THERE'S A SONG CALLED "I AM A WITCH"

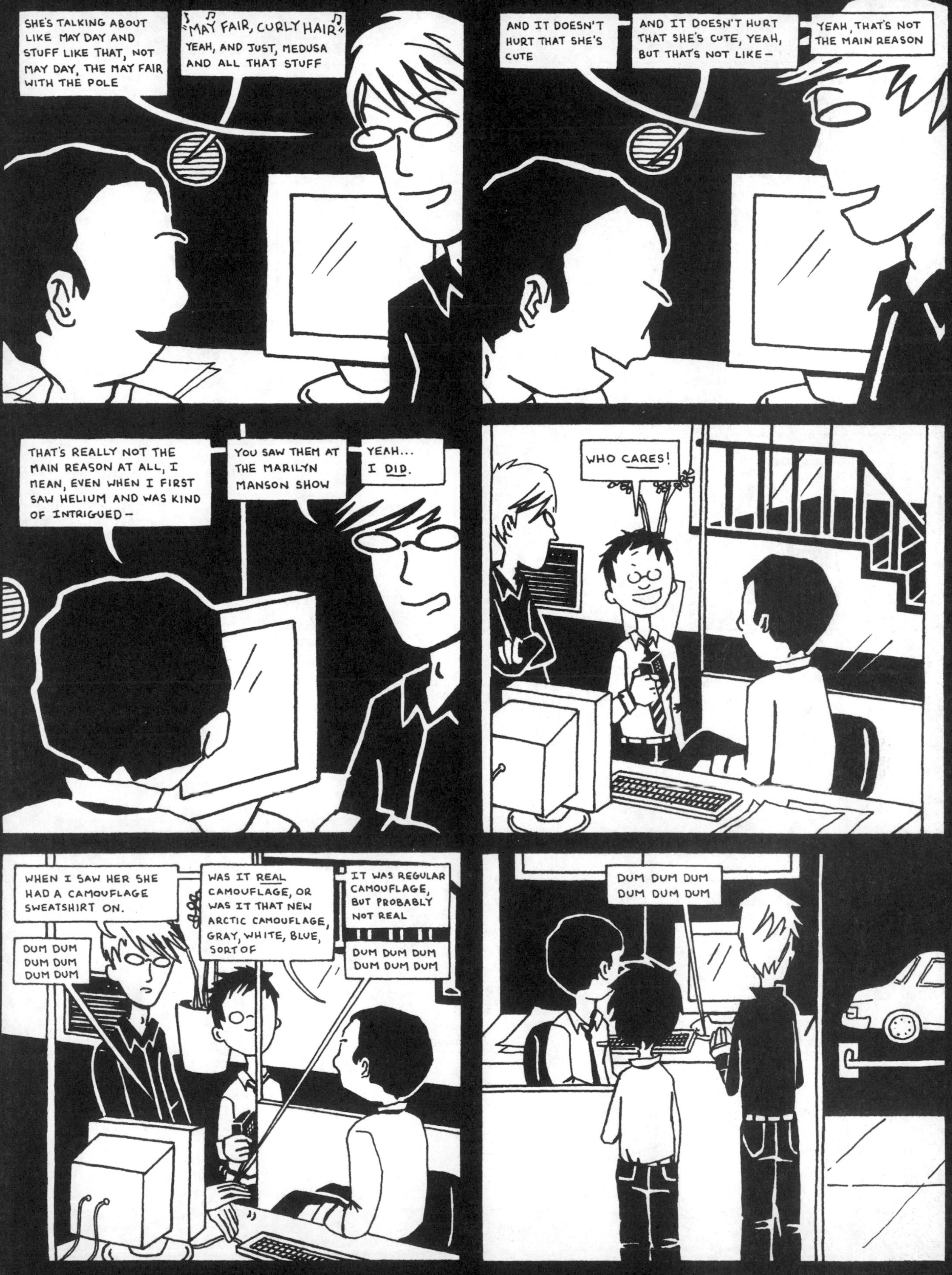
SHE'S TALKING ABOUT LIKE MAY DAY AND STUFF LIKE THAT, NOT MAY DAY, THE MAY FAIR WITH THE POLE
"MAY FAIR, CURLY HAIR"
YEAH, AND JUST, MEDUSA AND ALL THAT STUFF
AND IT DOESN'T HURT THAT SHE'S CUTE
AND IT DOESN'T HURT THAT SHE'S CUTE, YEAH, BUT THAT'S NOT LIKE—
YEAH, THAT'S NOT THE MAIN REASON
THAT'S REALLY NOT THE MAIN REASON AT ALL, I MEAN, EVEN WHEN I FIRST SAW HELIUM AND WAS KIND OF INTRIGUED—
YOU SAW THEM AT THE MARILYN MANSON SHOW
YEAH... I DID.
WHO CARES!
WHEN I SAW HER SHE HAD A CAMOUFLAGE SWEATSHIRT ON.
WAS IT REAL CAMOUFLAGE, OR WAS IT THAT NEW ARCTIC CAMOUFLAGE, GRAY, WHITE, BLUE, SORT OF
IT WAS REGULAR CAMOUFLAGE, BUT PROBABLY NOT REAL
DUM DUM DUM DUM DUM DUM
DUM DUM DUM DUM DUM DUM
DUM DUM DUM DUM DUM DUM

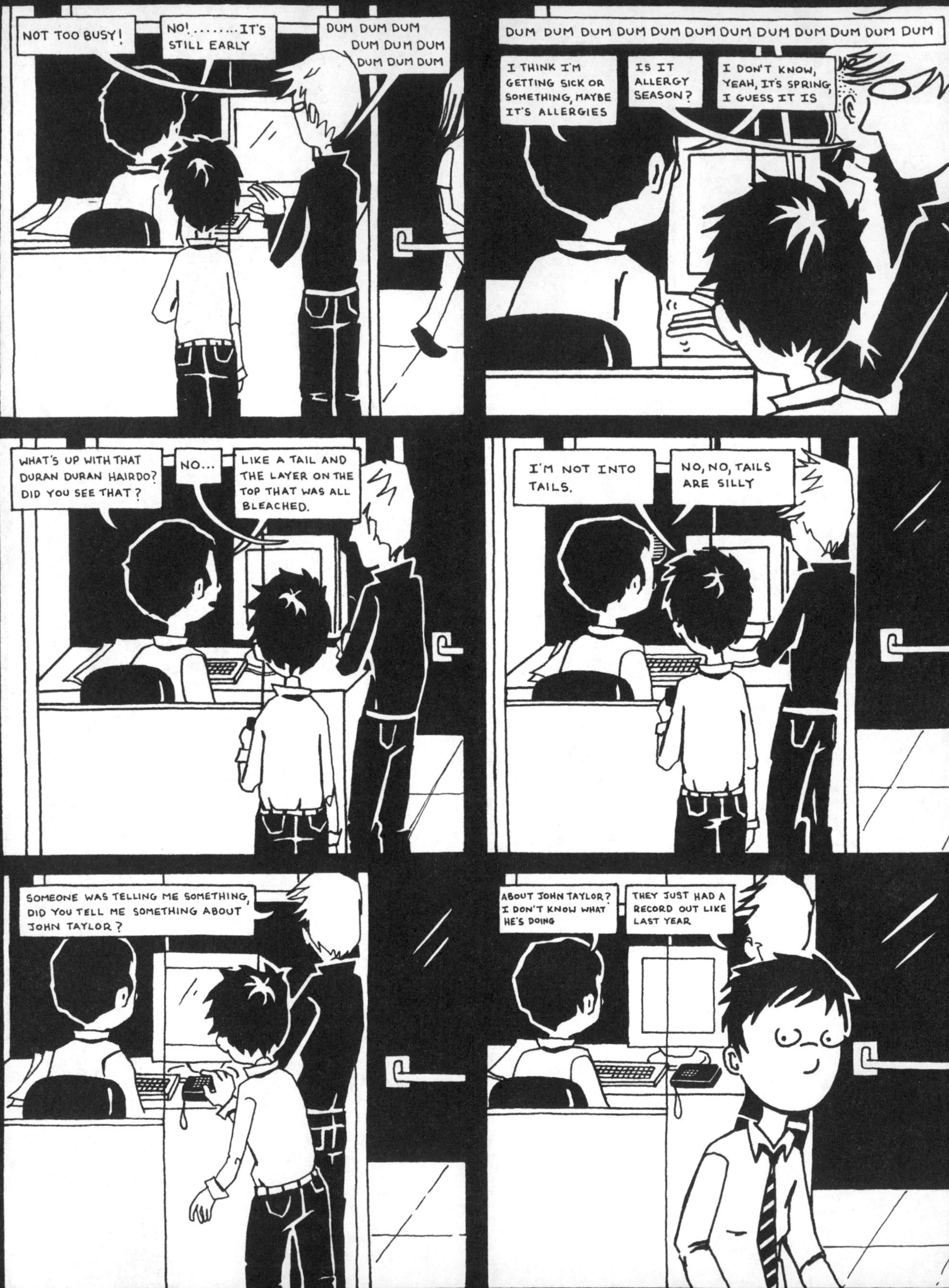
NOT TOO BUSY!
NO!........IT'S STILL EARLY
DUM DUM DUM DUM DUM DUM DUM DUM DUM
DUM DUM DUM DUM DUM DUM DUM DUM DUM DUM DUM DUM
I THINK I'M GETTING SICK OR SOMETHING, MAYBE IT'S ALLERGIES
IS IT ALLERGY SEASON?
I DON'T KNOW, YEAH, IT'S SPRING, I GUESS IT IS
WHAT'S UP WITH THAT DURAN DURAN HAIRDO? DID YOU SEE THAT?
NO...
LIKE A TAIL AND THE LAYER ON THE TOP THAT WAS ALL BLEACHED.
I'M NOT INTO TAILS.
NO, NO, TAILS ARE SILLY
SOMEONE WAS TELLING ME SOMETHING, DID YOU TELL ME SOMETHING ABOUT JOHN TAYLOR?
ABOUT JOHN TAYLOR? I DON'T KNOW WHAT HE'S DOING
THEY JUST HAD A RECORD OUT LIKE LAST YEAR

OH, WELL, HE'S DOING THAT, I GUESS,
THAT SONG LIKE, ELECTRIC BARBARELLA OR SOMETHING
YEAH,
TRYIN' TO LIKE, COP OFF THEIR OWN NA-
CLICK
"I just feel like I could die and no one would care."
"Well that's reality, that is reality."
CHAPTER ELEVEN
"yep."
I I had sex with Elizabeth
CHAPTER TWELVE

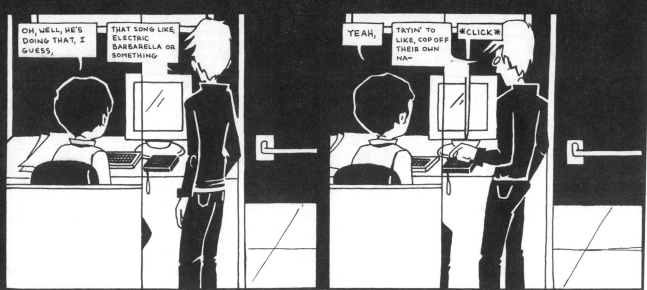

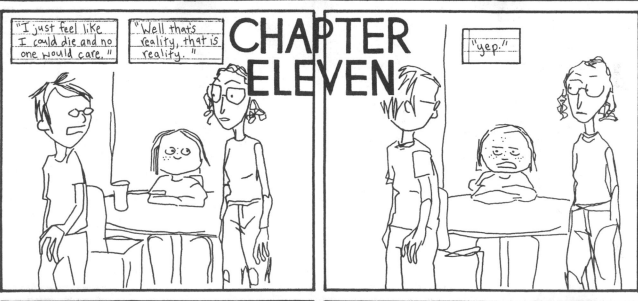

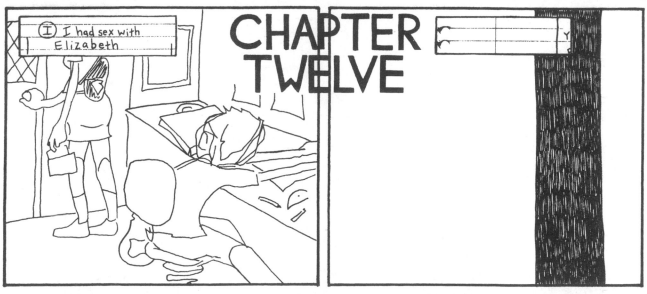

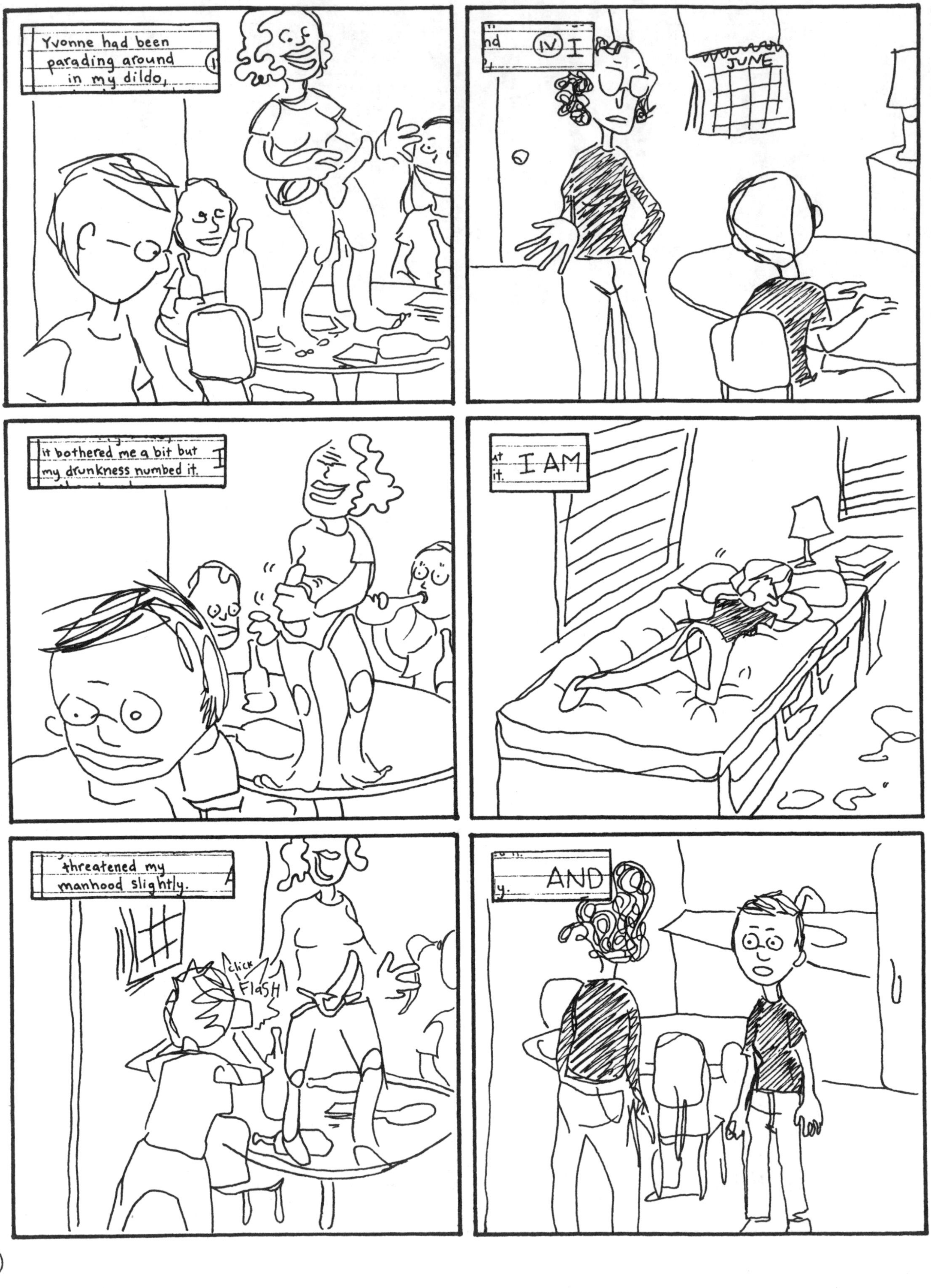

Yvonne had been parading around in my dildo,
I
JUNE
it bothered me a bit but my drunkness numbed it.
I AM
threatened my manhood slightly.
click
FLASH
AND

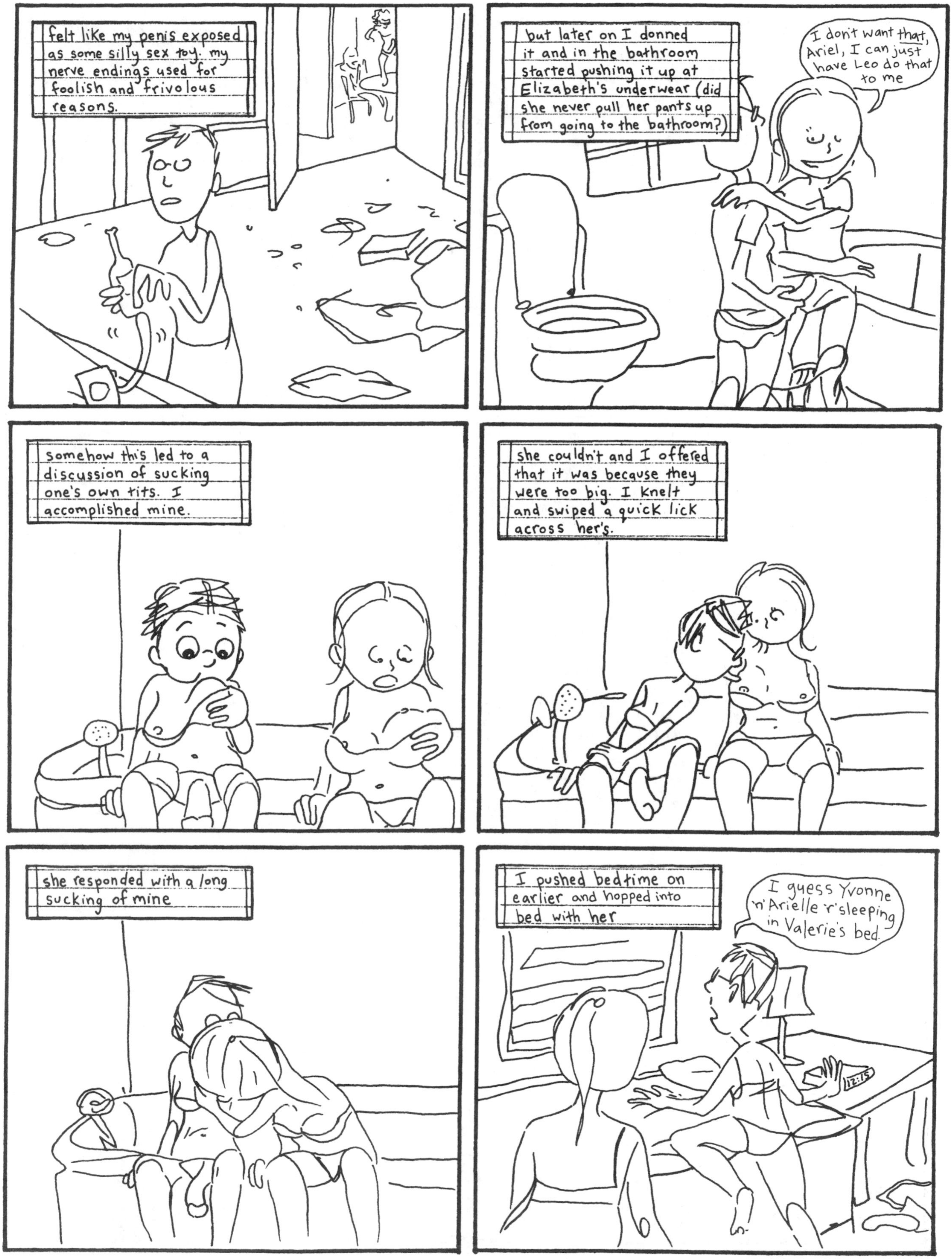
felt like my penis exposed as some silly sex toy. my nerve endings used for foolish and frivolous reasons.
but later on I donned it and in the bathroom started pushing it up at Elizabeth's underwear (did she never pull her pants up from going to the bathroom?)
I don't want that, Ariel, I can just have Leo do that to me
somehow this led to a discussion of sucking one's own tits. I accomplished mine.
she couldn't and I offered that it was because they were too big. I knelt and swiped a quick lick across her's.
she responded with a long sucking of mine
I pushed bedtime on earlier and hopped into bed with her
I guess Yvonne 'n' Arielle 'r' sleeping in Valerie's bed.
12:15

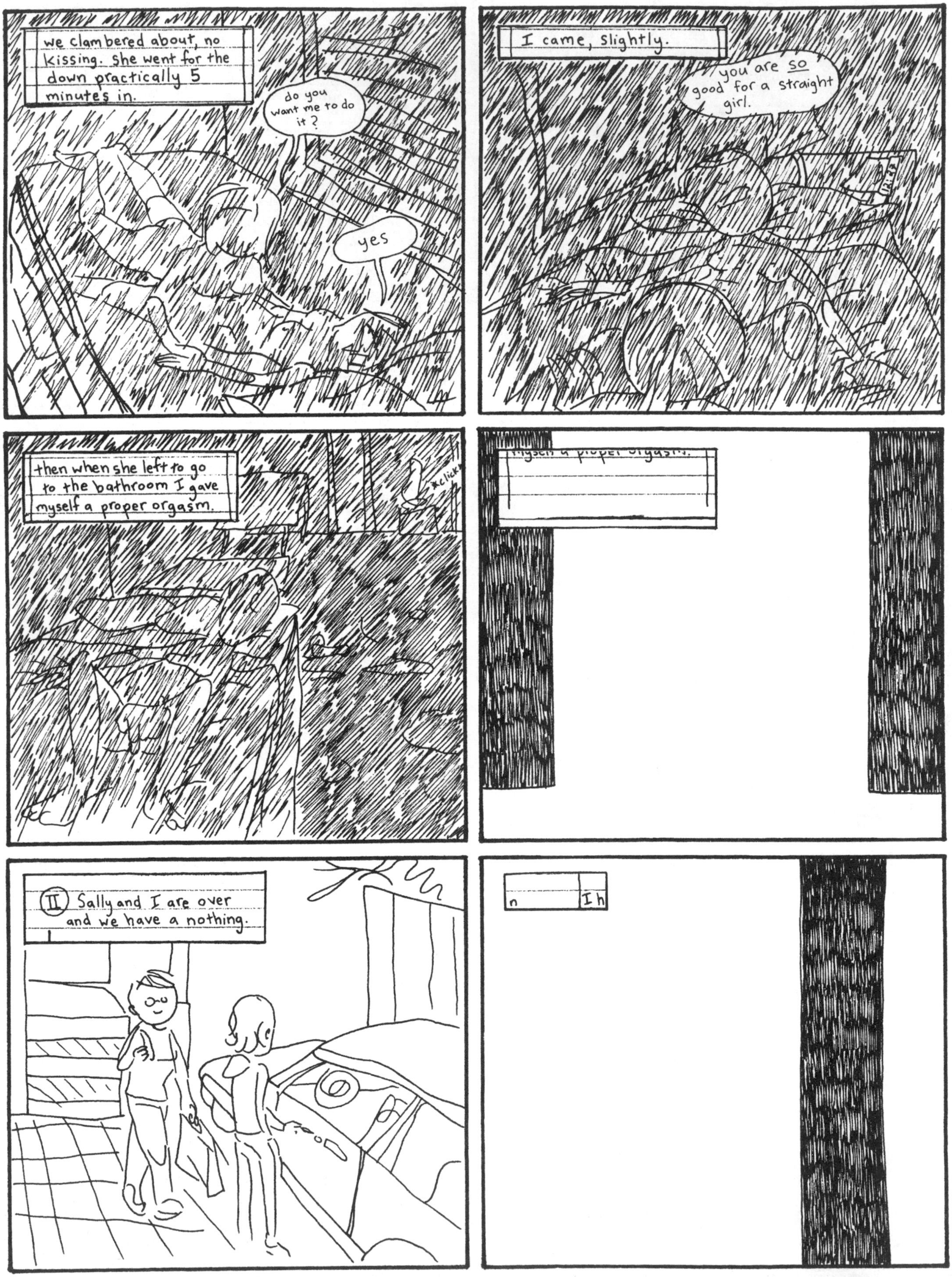
we clambered about, no kissing. she went for the down practically 5 minutes in.
do you want me to do it?
yes
I came, slightly.
you are so good for a straight girl.
then when she left to go to the bathroom I gave myself a proper orgasm.
click
II Sally and I are over and we have a nothing.

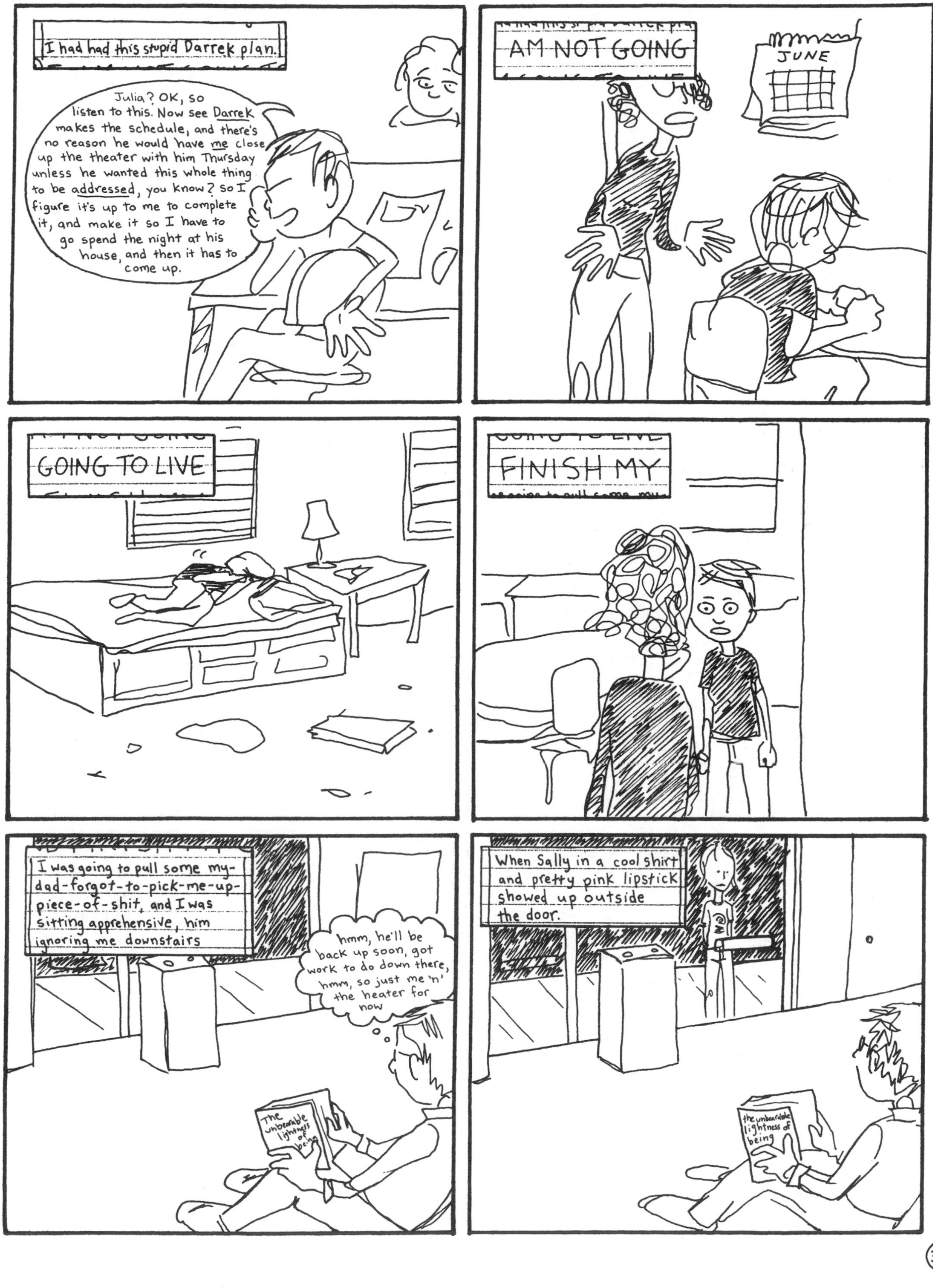

I had had this stupid Darrek plan.
Julia? OK, so listen to this. Now see Darrek makes the schedule, and there's no reason he would have me close up the theater with him Thursday unless he wanted this whole thing to be addressed, you know? So I figure it's up to me to complete it, and make it so I have to go spend the night at his house, and then it has to come up.
AM NOT GOING
JUNE
GOING TO LIVE
FINISH MY
I was going to pull some my-dad-forgot-to-pick-me-up-piece-of-shit, and I was sitting apprehensive, him ignoring me downstairs
hmm, he'll be back up soon, got work to do down there, hmm, so just me 'n' the heater for now
The unbearable lightness of being
When Sally in a cool shirt and pretty pink lipstick showed up outside the door.
the unbearable lightness of being

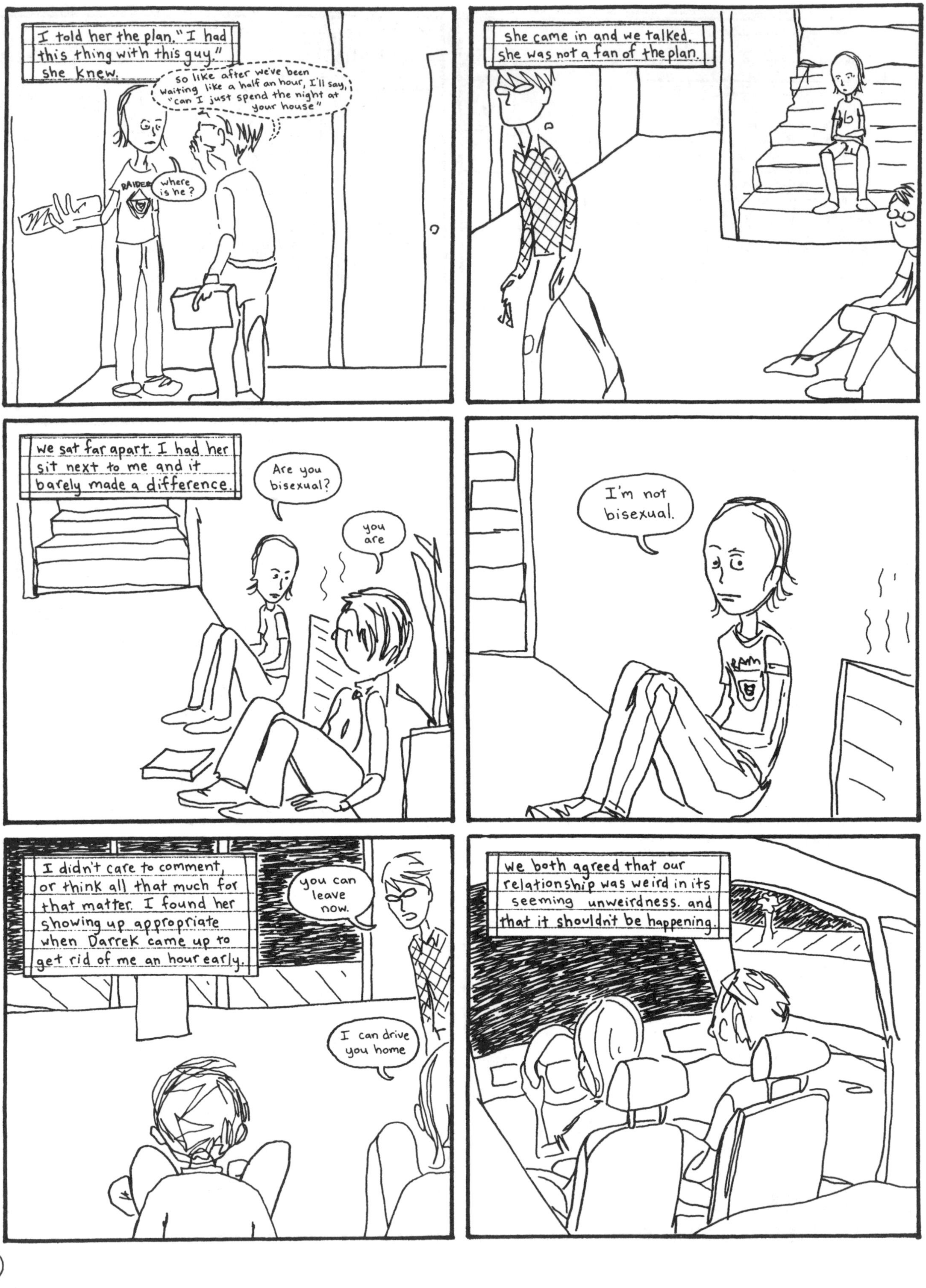
I told her the plan. "I had this thing with this guy." she knew.
so like after we've been waiting like a half an hour, I'll say, "can I just spend the night at your house"
RAIDERS
where is he?
she came in and we talked. she was not a fan of the plan.
we sat far apart. I had her sit next to me and it barely made a difference.
Are you bisexual?
you are
I'm not bisexual.
I didn't care to comment, or think all that much for that matter. I found her showing up appropriate when Darrek came up to get rid of me an hour early.
you can leave now.
I can drive you home
we both agreed that our relationship was weird in its seeming unweirdness. and that it shouldn't be happening.

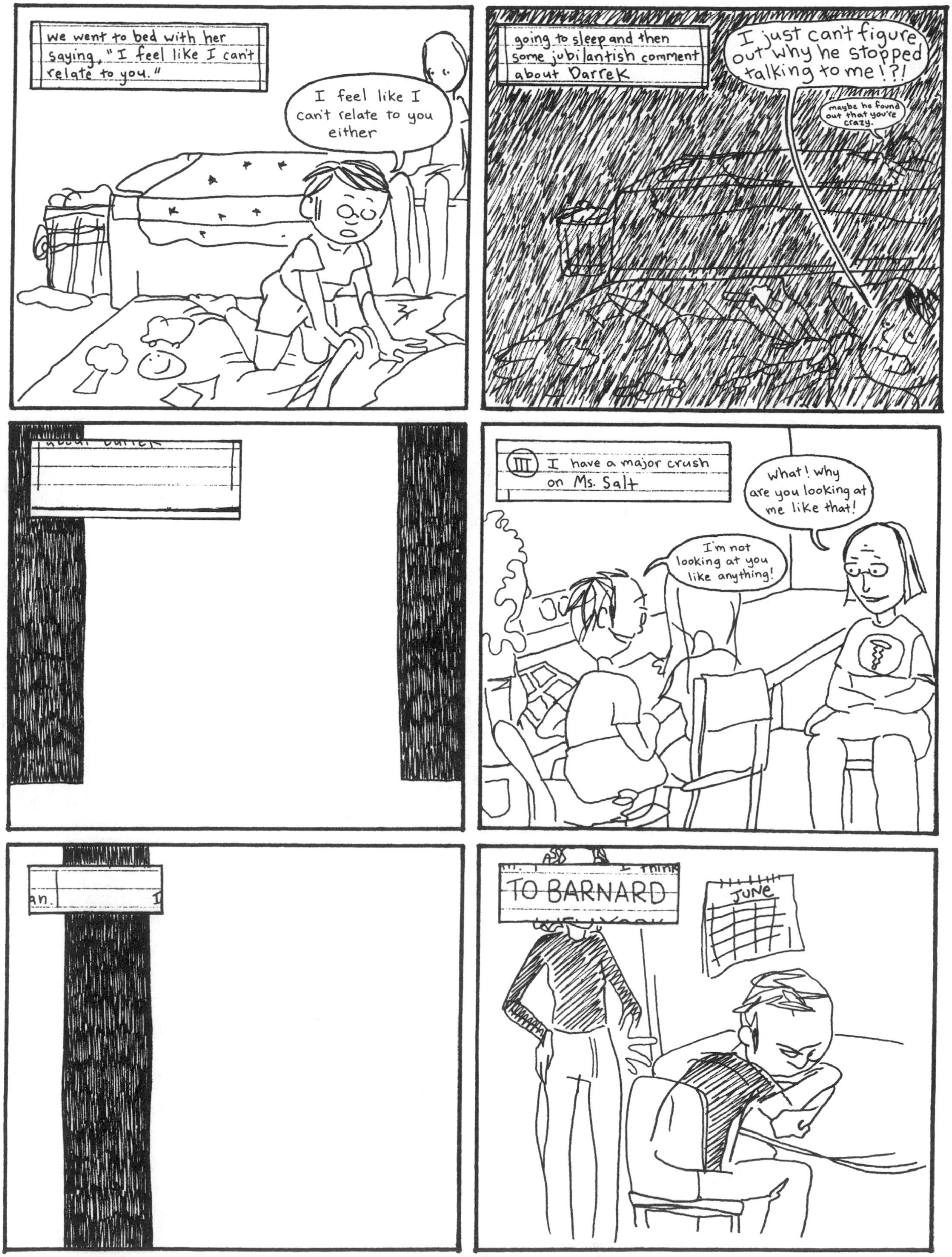

we went to bed with her saying, "I feel like I can't relate to you."
I feel like I can't relate to you either
going to sleep and then some jubilantish comment about Darrek
I just can't figure out why he stopped talking to me!?!
maybe he found out that you're crazy.
III I have a major crush on Ms. Salt
What! why are you looking at me like that!
I'm not looking at you like anything!
TO BARNARD
June

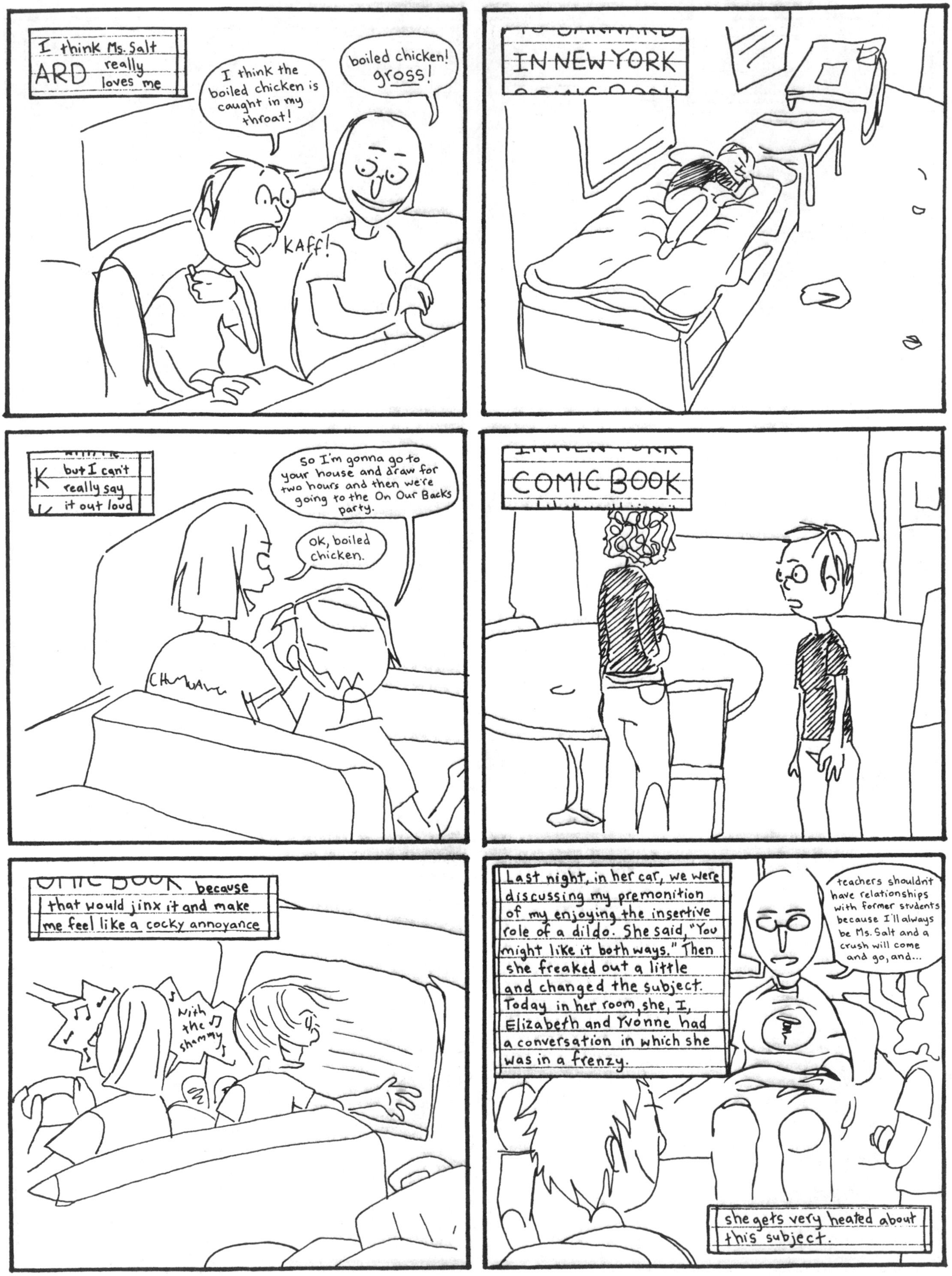
I think Ms. Salt
ARD really loves me
I think the boiled chicken is caught in my throat!
boiled chicken! gross!
KAFF!
IN NEW YORK
K but I can't really say it out loud
So I'm gonna go to your house and draw for two hours and then we're going to the On Our Backs party.
Ok, boiled chicken.
COMIC BOOK
because that would jinx it and make me feel like a cocky annoyance
With the shammy
Last night, in her car, we were discussing my premonition of my enjoying the insertive role of a dildo. She said, "You might like it both ways." Then she freaked out a little and changed the subject. Today in her room, she, I, Elizabeth and Yvonne had a conversation in which she was in a frenzy.
teachers shouldn't have relationships with former students because I'll always be Ms. Salt and a crush will come and go, and...
she gets very heated about this subject.

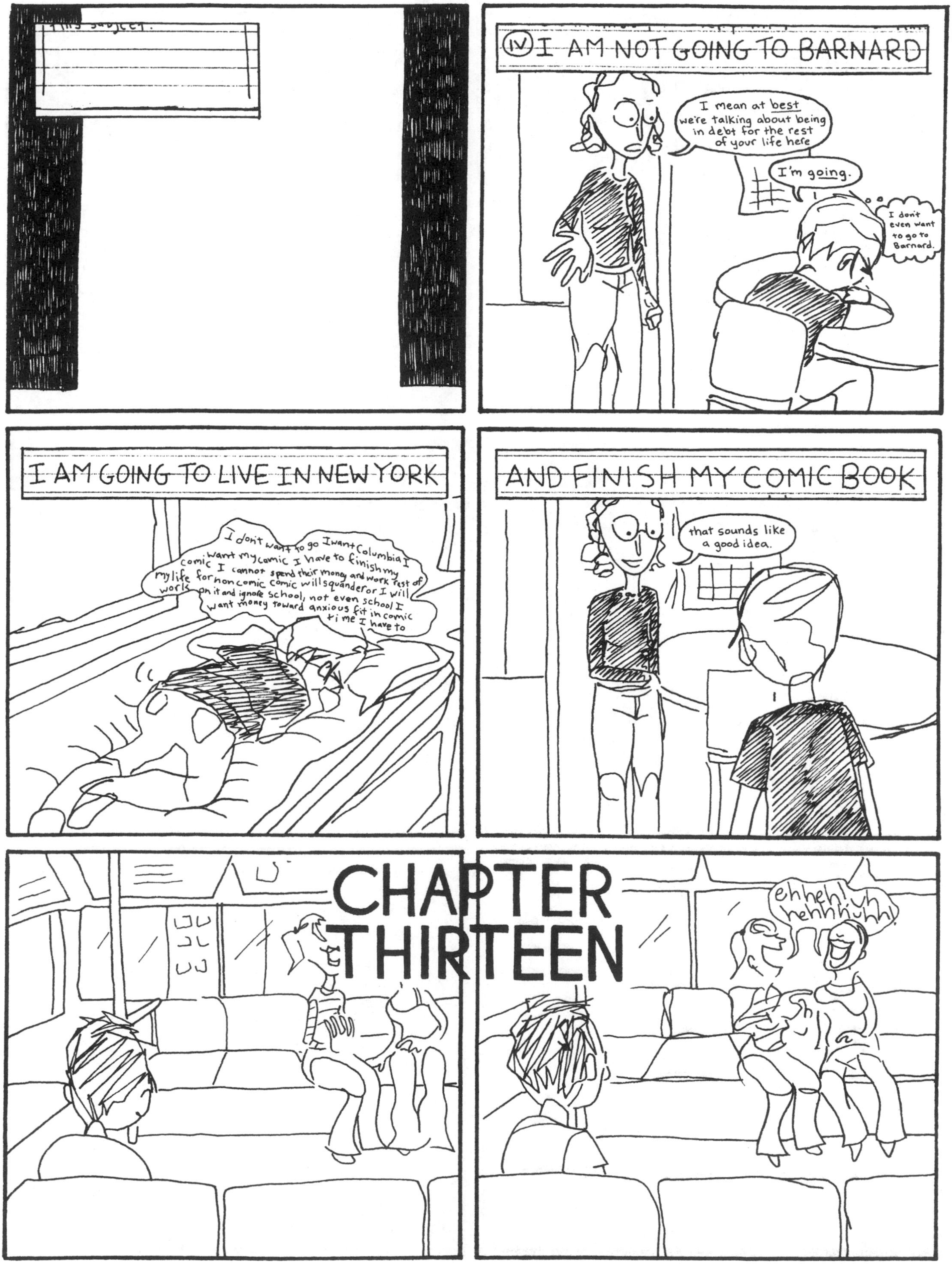
IV I AM NOT GOING TO BARNARD
I mean at best we're talking about being in debt for the rest of your life here
I'm going.
I don't even want to go to Barnard.
I AM GOING TO LIVE IN NEW YORK
I don't want to go I want Columbia I want my comic I have to finish my comic I cannot spend their money and work rest of my life for non comic comic will squander or I will work on it and ignore school, not even school I want money toward anxious fit in comic time I have to
AND FINISH MY COMIC BOOK
that sounds like a good idea.
CHAPTER THIRTEEN
ehheh! uh hehhhuhh!

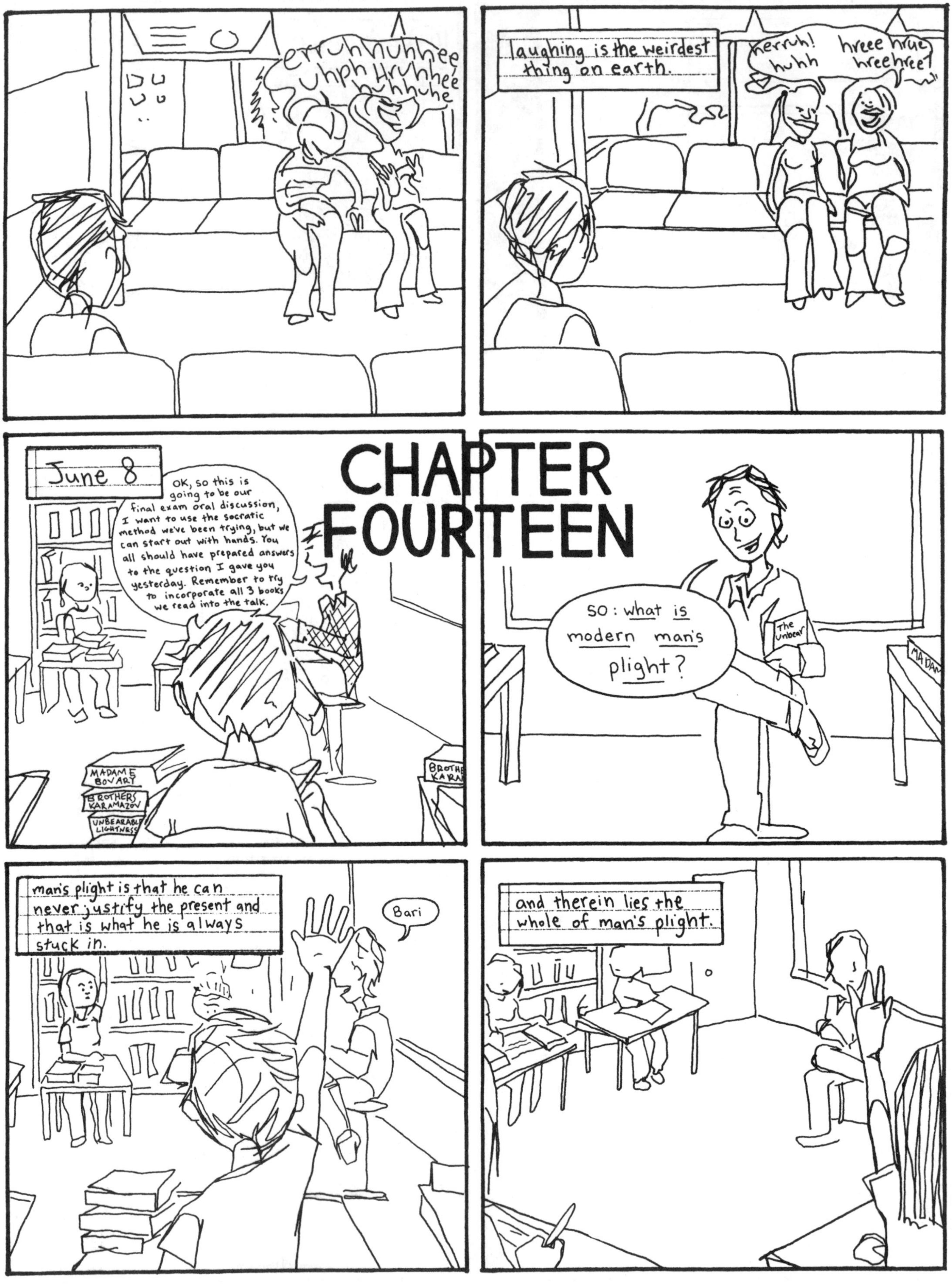
errruhnuhhee
uhph hruhhee
huhhuhe
laughing is the weirdest thing on earth.
herruh! huhh
hreee hrue hreehree!
June 8
CHAPTER FOURTEEN
OK, so this is going to be our final exam oral discussion, I want to use the socratic method we've been trying, but we can start out with hands. You all should have prepared answers to the question I gave you yesterday. Remember to try to incorporate all 3 books we read into the talk.
MADAME BOVARY
BROTHERS KARAMAZOV
UNBEARABLE LIGHTNESS
SO: what is modern man's plight?
The Unbear
man's plight is that he can never justify the present and that is what he is always stuck in.
Bari
and therein lies the whole of man's plight.

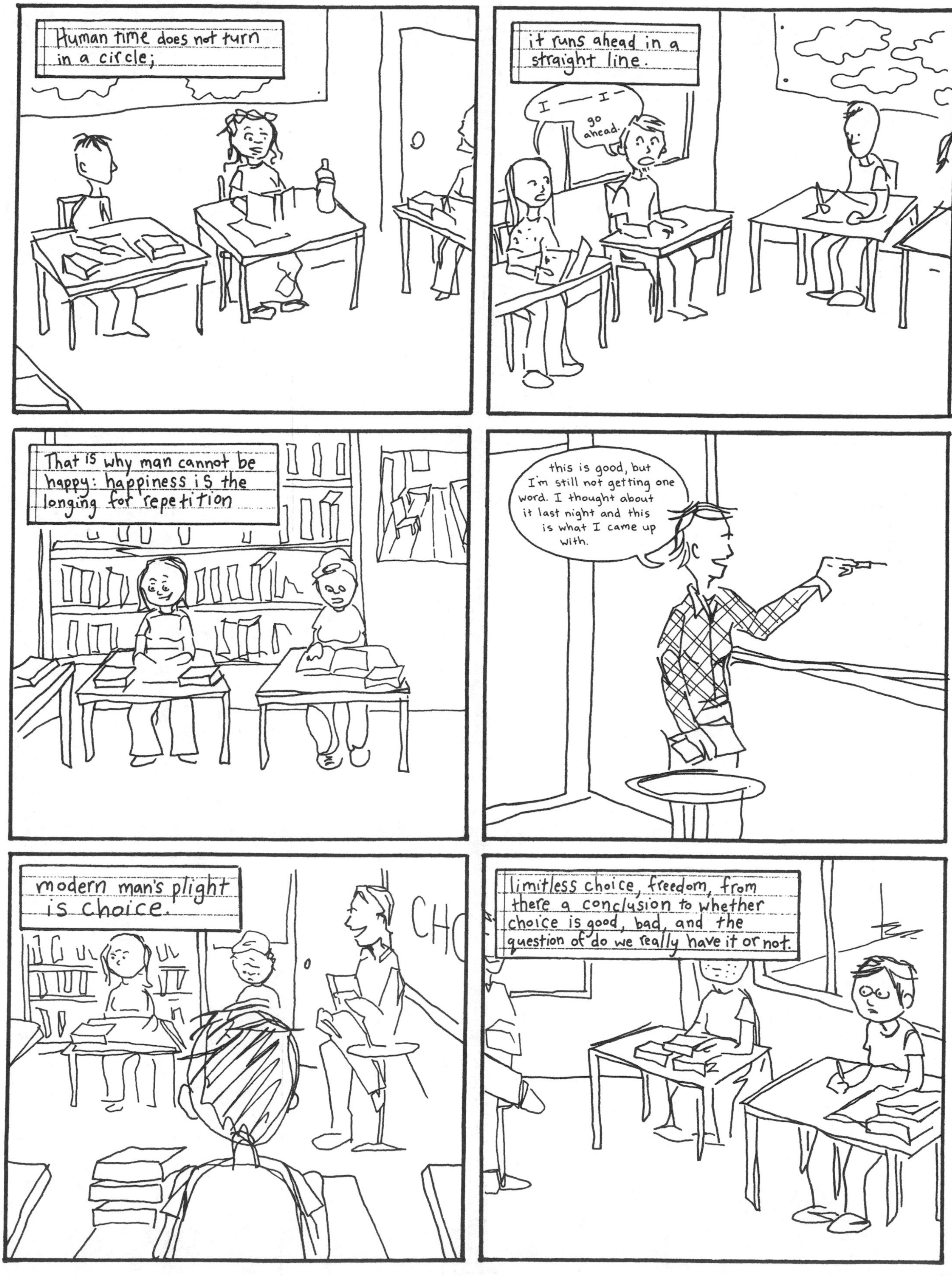
Human time does not turn in a circle;
it runs ahead in a straight line.
I — I —
go ahead.
That is why man cannot be happy: happiness is the longing for repetition
this is good, but I'm still not getting one word. I thought about it last night and this is what I came up with.
modern man's plight is choice.
limitless choice, freedom, from there a conclusion to whether choice is good, bad, and the question of do we really have it or not.

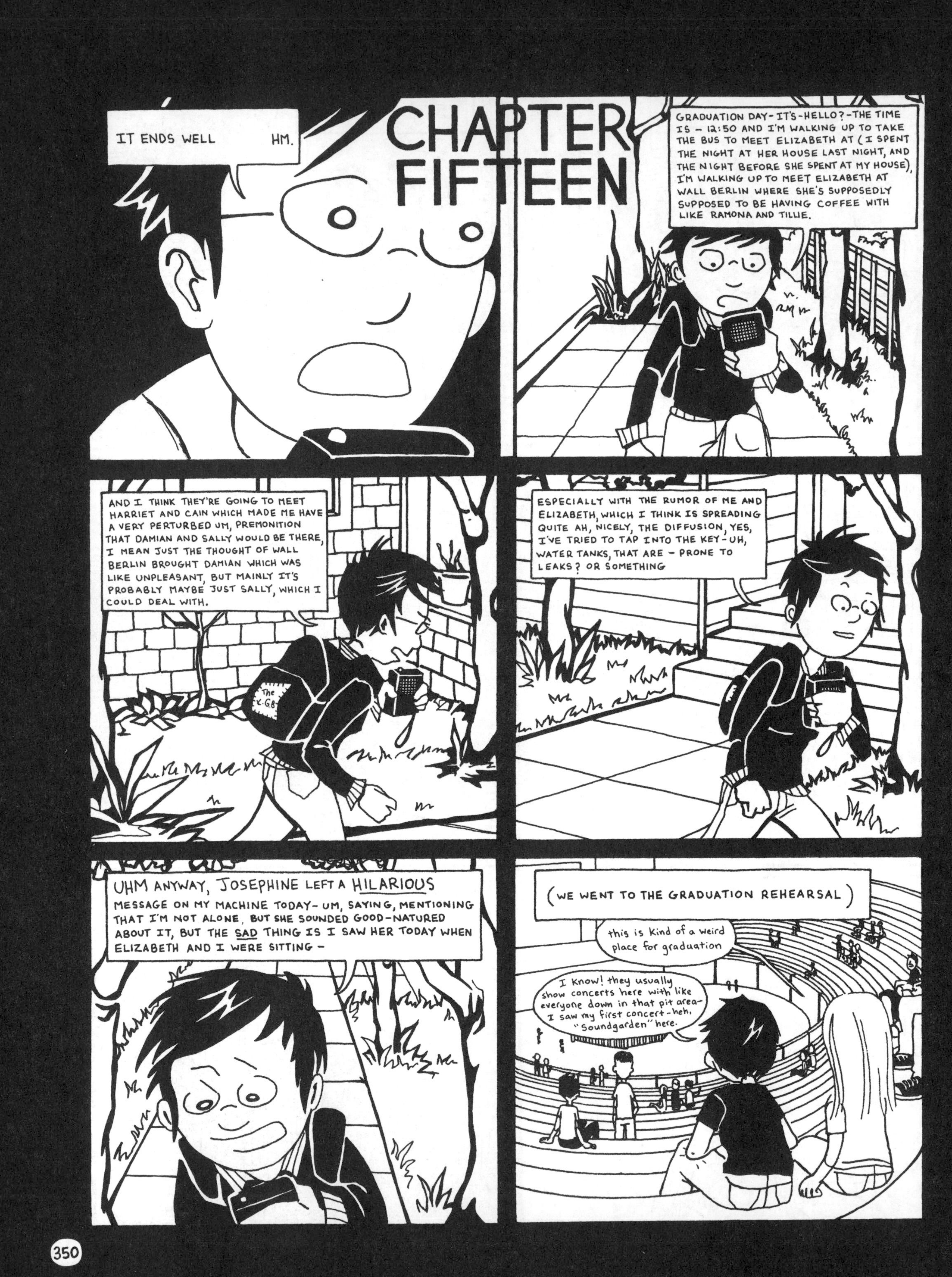
CHAPTER FIFTEEN
IT ENDS WELL HM.
GRADUATION DAY- IT'S-HELLO?-THE TIME IS - 12:50 AND I'M WALKING UP TO TAKE THE BUS TO MEET ELIZABETH AT (I SPENT THE NIGHT AT HER HOUSE LAST NIGHT, AND THE NIGHT BEFORE SHE SPENT AT MY HOUSE), I'M WALKING UP TO MEET ELIZABETH AT WALL BERLIN WHERE SHE'S SUPPOSEDLY SUPPOSED TO BE HAVING COFFEE WITH LIKE RAMONA AND TILLIE.
AND I THINK THEY'RE GOING TO MEET HARRIET AND CAIN WHICH MADE ME HAVE A VERY PERTURBED UM, PREMONITION THAT DAMIAN AND SALLY WOULD BE THERE, I MEAN JUST THE THOUGHT OF WALL BERLIN BROUGHT DAMIAN WHICH WAS LIKE UNPLEASANT, BUT MAINLY IT'S PROBABLY MAYBE JUST SALLY, WHICH I COULD DEAL WITH.
The K.G.B
ESPECIALLY WITH THE RUMOR OF ME AND ELIZABETH, WHICH I THINK IS SPREADING QUITE AH, NICELY, THE DIFFUSION, YES, I'VE TRIED TO TAP INTO THE KEY-UH, WATER TANKS, THAT ARE - PRONE TO LEAKS? OR SOMETHING
UHM ANYWAY, JOSEPHINE LEFT A HILARIOUS MESSAGE ON MY MACHINE TODAY- UM, SAYING, MENTIONING THAT I'M NOT ALONE, BUT SHE SOUNDED GOOD-NATURED ABOUT IT, BUT THE SAD THING IS I SAW HER TODAY WHEN ELIZABETH AND I WERE SITTING -
(WE WENT TO THE GRADUATION REHEARSAL)
this is kind of a weird place for graduation
I know! they usually show concerts here with like everyone down in that pit area- I saw my first concert-heh, "Soundgarden" here.

WHEN ELIZABETH AND I WERE SITTING UP ON THE LIKE SEATS AND I SAI— AND I TOLD HER THAT JOSEPHINE DEPRESSED ME

She like died of awkwardness. She fell into the pit and never came out. plus I think she has mono.

AND YOU KNOW HOW LIKE I'M SAYING THAT PEOPLE DEPRESS ME ALL THE TIME? — IT'S SUCH A HORRIBLE THING BECAUSE LIKE, I DON'T THINK THERE'S ANYTHING WORSE THAN FOR SOMEBODY ELSE TO REFER TO YOU AS DEPRESSING THEM. AND I WOULD REALLY NOT LIKE TO TAKE PART IN THAT ANYMORE.

ANYWAY, PLANS FOR LATER, I'M GOING TO EAT SOMETHING UP ON TELEGRAPH BECAUSE I DIDN'T WANT TO, OH MY GOD, MY MOM WAS DRIVING ME CRAZY, LIKE, "LEAVE ME ALONE, MA" UM, I WAS LIKE, AUNT SUZANNA HAD LEFT SOME LIKE NOTE OR SOMETHING AND IN THE MAIL WAS SOME OTHER THING FROM TWO GIRLS WHO ARE IN SOME BAND CALLED THE CHUBBIES, LIKE SOMEONE GAVE THEM POTENTIAL 1 AND THEY WANTED POTENTIAL 2 WHICH WAS REALLY NICE BECAUSE THEY SENT ME THEIR RECORD, IT'S LIKE SOME GIRL THING, UM, BUT LIKE ANYWAY, SO LIKE, SUZANNA HAD WRITTEN THIS LETTER, I MEAN IT WAS NICE, IT WAS A LITTLE WEIRD, "HAVE A COLLEGE EDUCATION OFFERED TO YOU AND THEN PULLED AWAY" AND IT SAID, "I WISH IT COULD BE MORE ABOUT YOUR CHOICES," BUT IT IS ABOUT MY CHOICES, I WANT TO MOVE TO NEW YORK AND FINISH MY COMIC, WHICH IS ANOTHER THING,

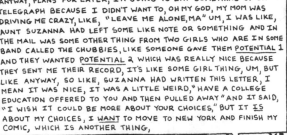

TOTALLY ANNOYING, BARNARD, SOME DUMB-ASS LEAVES LIKE SOME MESSAGE ON MY MACHINE ABOUT HOW I HAVEN'T SENT MY HOUSING APPLICATION — THEY DON'T KNOW ANYTHING! MEANWHILE I'M LIKE TALKING TO THE DEAN AND THE DEAN OF ADMISSIONS ABOUT HOW I'M NOT GOING TO BE GOING THERE,

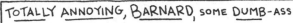

ARE YOU RETARDED

ah, hello, I'm trying to reach Are-ielle, this is Barnard Housing at Barnard College, we,

AND IT'S LIKE, SUCH A MESS, YOU KNOW I TOTALLY REMEMBER WHEN I WAS LIKE, HAD JUST GOTTEN INTO BARNARD, AND I WAS LIKE WALKING UP THIS STREET, LISTENING TO LIZ PHAIR BECAUSE I WAS LIKE, YOU KNOW, RELISHING, AND THERE WAS THIS TINGE OF OFFNESS, AND I THINK THAT LIKE, IT'S KIND OF SCARY TO LIKE THINK ABOUT HOW LIKE, THAT CAN BE A CLUE-IN MORE THAN ONE WOULD NORMALLY EXPECT HUHH, I MEAN THERE HAVE BEEN SITUATIONS WHERE LIKE THEY HAVEN'T BEEN RESOLVED SIMILARLY... BUT I THOUGHT THAT WAS KIND OF INTERESTING.

BUT, I GOT KIND OF OFF TRACK, SO LIKE, AND ALSO IN THE LETTER SHE WAS LIKE, "WHY WE HAVE A BAD RELATIONSHIP" OR, "NOT A VERY DEVELOPED RELATIONSHIP" IS BECAUSE LIKE, "ON LACK OF" MY PARENTS, AND MY MOM WAS TALKING ABOUT HOW THAT WAS BECAUSE SUZANNA HATED HER OR SOMETHING, BECAUSE OF LIKE, AND THEN SHE WENT INTO THIS LONG THING THAT OF COURSE INCLUDED SONNY, ABOUT LIKE, HOW, UM, I HAD TO DO WITH LIKE SOME ART SHOW THAT LIKE DIDN'T WORK OUT BECAUSE THE SLIDES — AND I DIDN'T WANT TO HEAR IT, AND SHE GAVE ME 30 DOLLARS AND MY MOM GRABBED THE CHECK TO SEE IF IT WAS TO HER — VALERIE, MEANWHILE, HAD OPENED UP THE CHECK FROM GRANDMA WHICH WAS FOR 300 DOLLARS

yeah, I know what this is about

um, can I please have my stuff?

WHAT!!

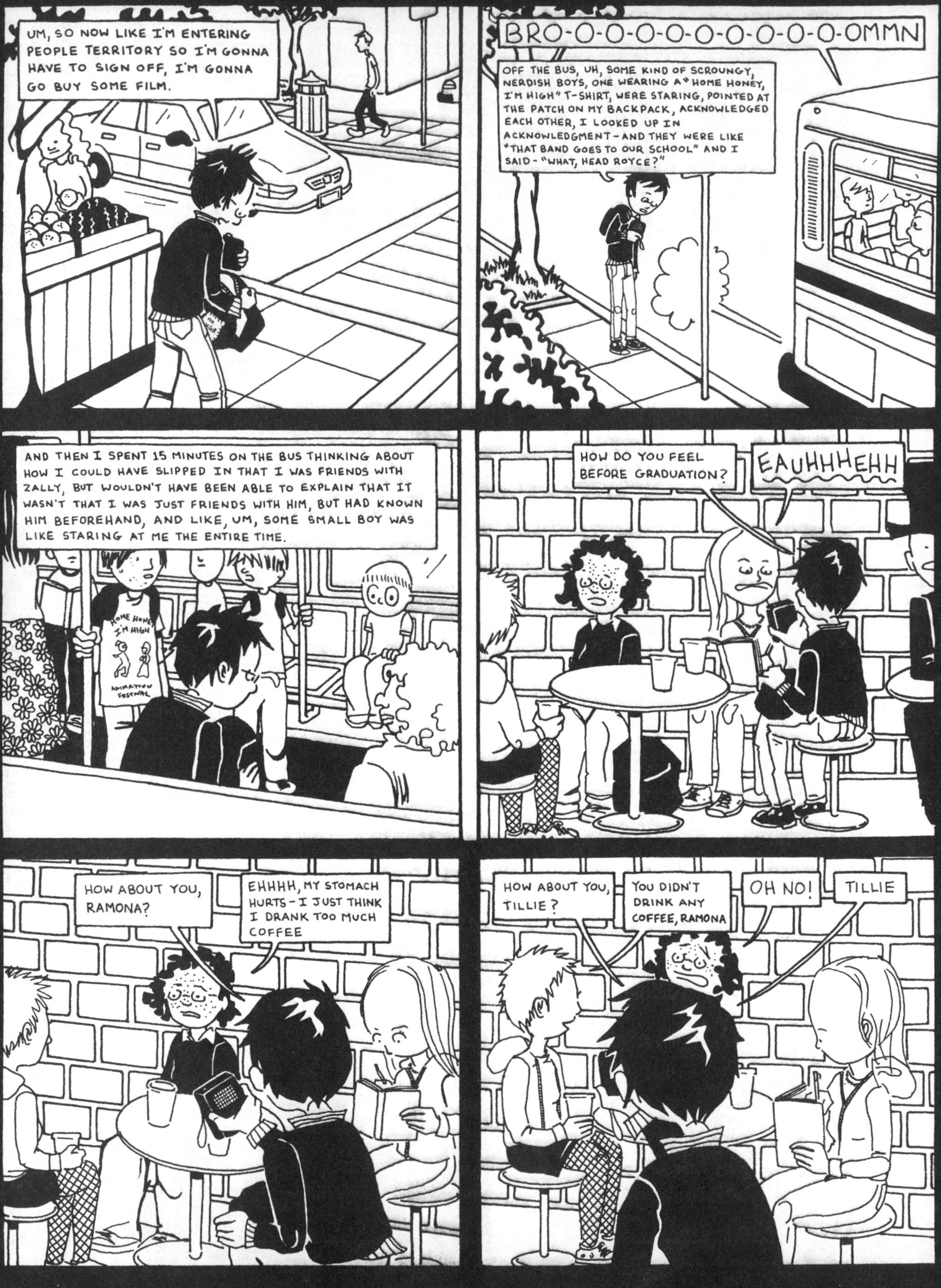
UM, SO NOW LIKE I'M ENTERING PEOPLE TERRITORY SO I'M GONNA HAVE TO SIGN OFF, I'M GONNA GO BUY SOME FILM.
BRO-O-O-O-O-O-O-O-O-O-O-OMMN
OFF THE BUS, UH, SOME KIND OF SCROUNGY, NERDISH BOYS, ONE WEARING A "HOME HONEY, I'M HIGH" T-SHIRT, WERE STARING, POINTED AT THE PATCH ON MY BACKPACK, ACKNOWLEDGED EACH OTHER, I LOOKED UP IN ACKNOWLEDGMENT - AND THEY WERE LIKE "THAT BAND GOES TO OUR SCHOOL" AND I SAID - "WHAT, HEAD ROYCE?"
AND THEN I SPENT 15 MINUTES ON THE BUS THINKING ABOUT HOW I COULD HAVE SLIPPED IN THAT I WAS FRIENDS WITH ZALLY, BUT WOULDN'T HAVE BEEN ABLE TO EXPLAIN THAT IT WASN'T THAT I WAS JUST FRIENDS WITH HIM, BUT HAD KNOWN HIM BEFOREHAND, AND LIKE, UM, SOME SMALL BOY WAS LIKE STARING AT ME THE ENTIRE TIME.
HOME HONEY I'M HIGH
ANIMATION FESTIVAL
HOW DO YOU FEEL BEFORE GRADUATION?
EAUHHHEHH
HOW ABOUT YOU, RAMONA?
EHHHH, MY STOMACH HURTS - I JUST THINK I DRANK TOO MUCH COFFEE
HOW ABOUT YOU, TILLIE?
YOU DIDN'T DRINK ANY COFFEE, RAMONA
OH NO!
TILLIE

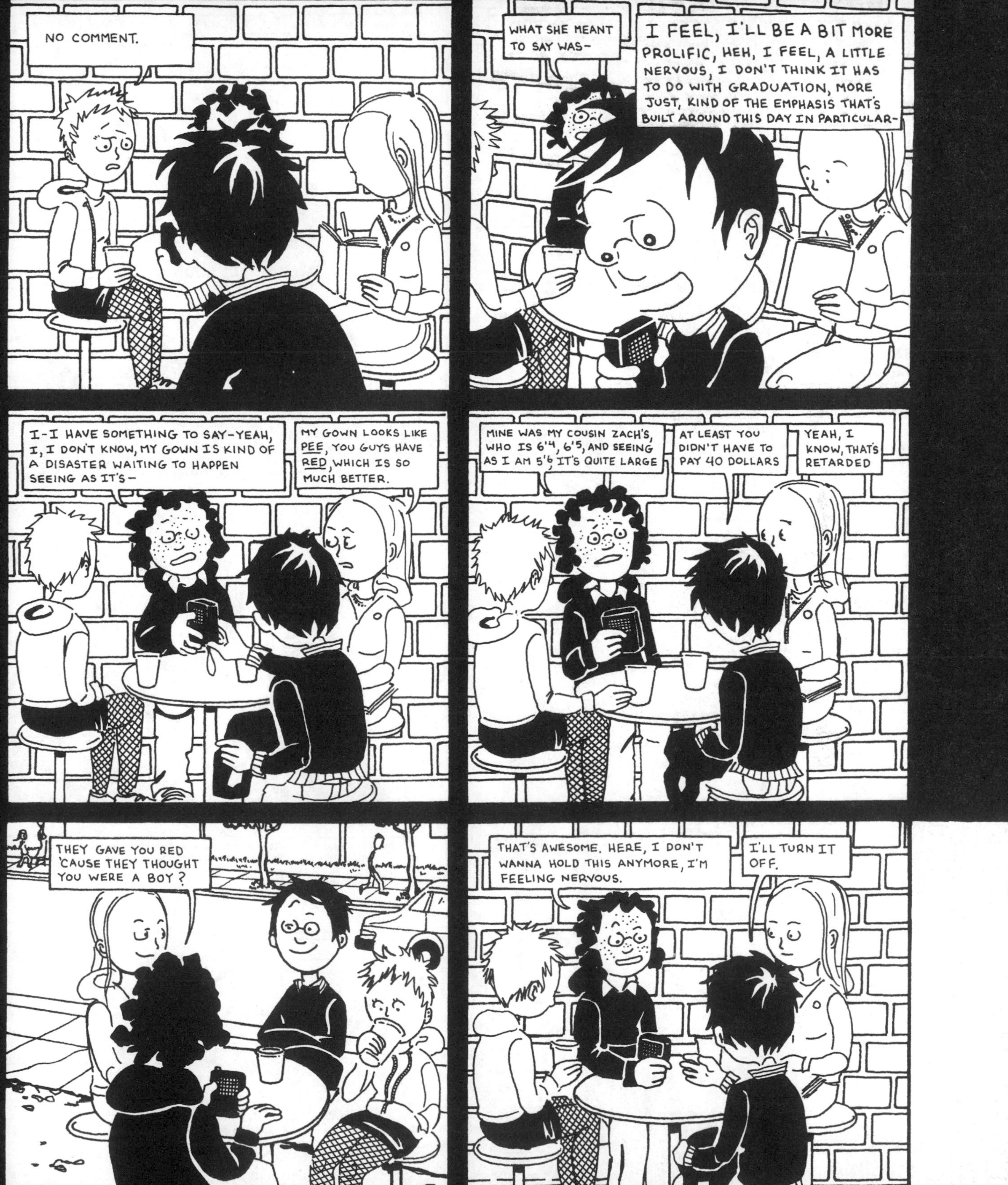
NO COMMENT.
WHAT SHE MEANT TO SAY WAS-
I FEEL, I'LL BE A BIT MORE PROLIFIC, HEH, I FEEL, A LITTLE NERVOUS, I DON'T THINK IT HAS TO DO WITH GRADUATION, MORE JUST, KIND OF THE EMPHASIS THAT'S BUILT AROUND THIS DAY IN PARTICULAR-
I-I HAVE SOMETHING TO SAY-YEAH, I, I DON'T KNOW, MY GOWN IS KIND OF A DISASTER WAITING TO HAPPEN SEEING AS IT'S-
MY GOWN LOOKS LIKE PEE, YOU GUYS HAVE RED, WHICH IS SO MUCH BETTER.
MINE WAS MY COUSIN ZACH'S, WHO IS 6'4, 6'5, AND SEEING AS I AM 5'6, IT'S QUITE LARGE
AT LEAST YOU DIDN'T HAVE TO PAY 40 DOLLARS
YEAH, I KNOW, THAT'S RETARDED
THEY GAVE YOU RED 'CAUSE THEY THOUGHT YOU WERE A BOY?
THAT'S AWESOME. HERE, I DON'T WANNA HOLD THIS ANYMORE, I'M FEELING NERVOUS.
I'LL TURN IT OFF.

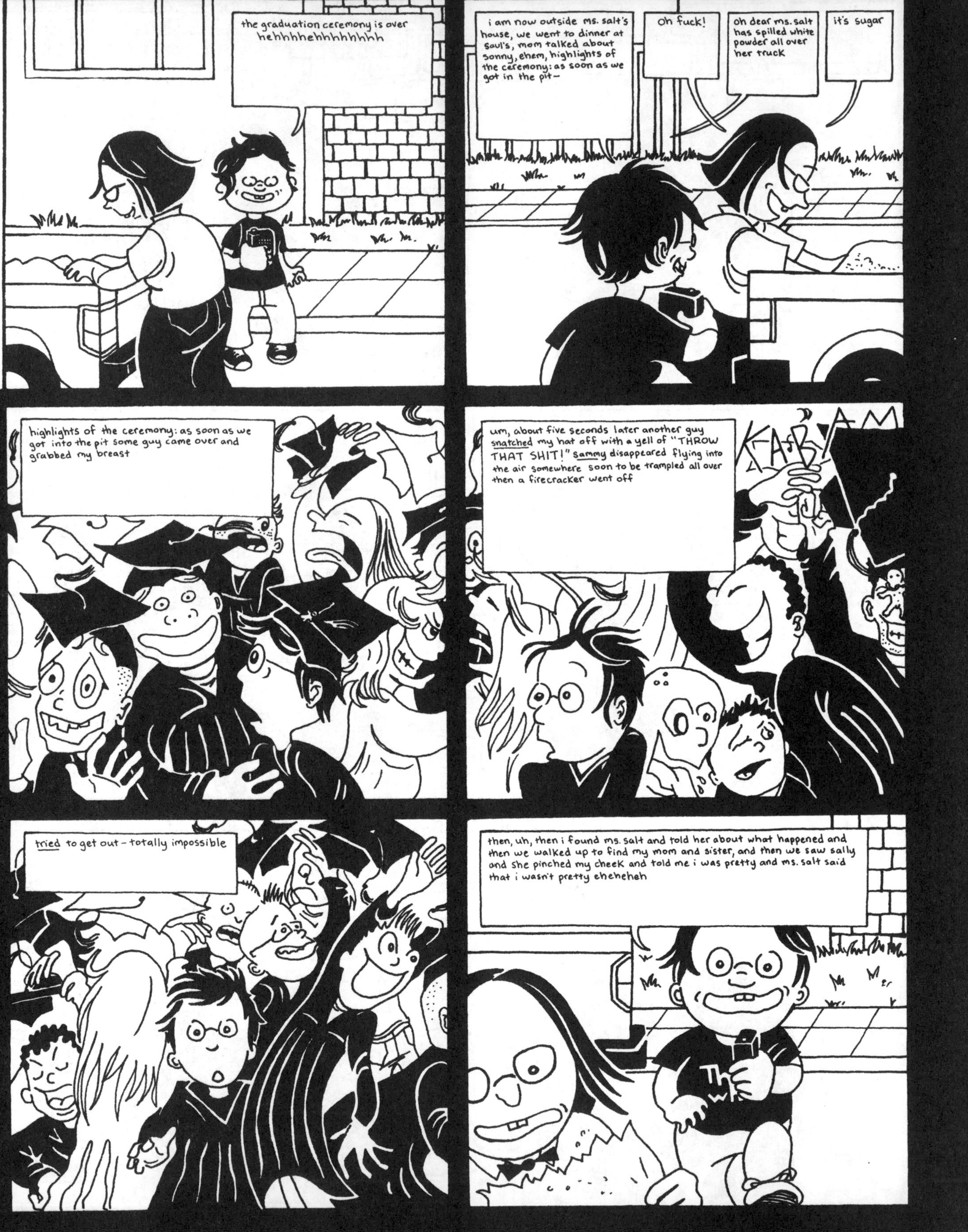
the graduation ceremony is over hehhhhehhhhhhhh
i am now outside ms. salt's house, we went to dinner at saul's, mom talked about sonny, ehem, highlights of the ceremony: as soon as we got in the pit—
oh fuck!
oh dear ms. salt has spilled white powder all over her truck
it's sugar
highlights of the ceremony: as soon as we got into the pit some guy came over and grabbed my breast
um, about five seconds later another guy snatched my hat off with a yell of "THROW THAT SHIT!" sammy disappeared flying into the air somewhere soon to be trampled all over then a firecracker went off
KABAM
tried to get out — totally impossible
then, uh, then i found ms. salt and told her about what happened and then we walked up to find my mom and sister, and then we saw sally and she pinched my cheek and told me i was pretty and ms. salt said that i wasn't pretty eheheheh

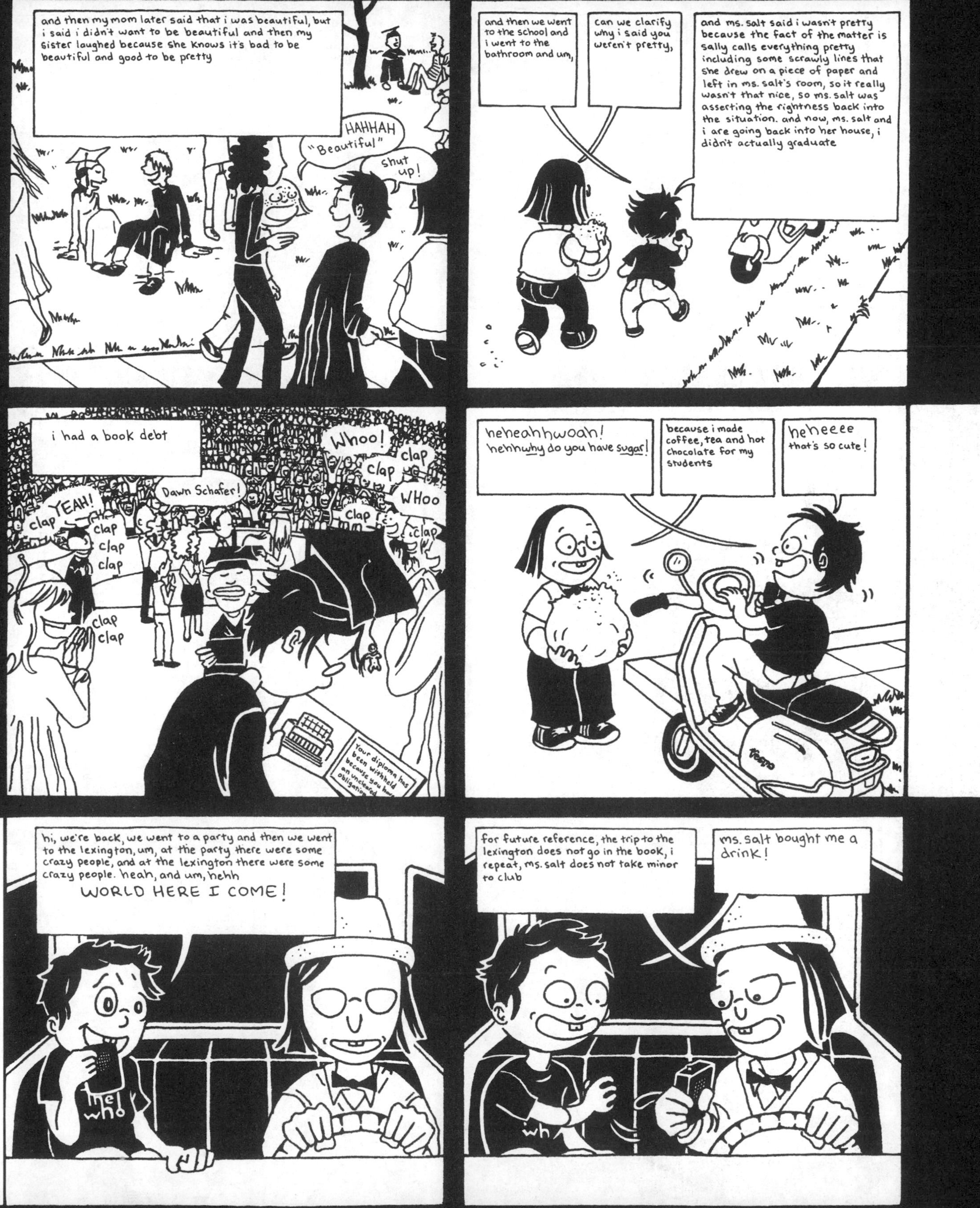
and then my mom later said that i was beautiful, but i said i didn't want to be beautiful and then my sister laughed because she knows it's bad to be beautiful and good to be pretty
HAHHAH
"Beautiful"
shut up!
and then we went to the school and i went to the bathroom and um,
can we clarify why i said you weren't pretty,
and ms. salt said i wasn't pretty because the fact of the matter is sally calls everything pretty including some scrawly lines that she drew on a piece of paper and left in ms. salt's room, so it really wasn't that nice, so ms. salt was asserting the rightness back into the situation. and now, ms. salt and i are going back into her house, i didn't actually graduate
i had a book debt
Whoo!
clap
clap
Dawn Schafer!
YEAH!
clap
clap
clap
clap
WHoo
clap
clap
clap
clap
Your diploma has been withheld because you hav an uncleared obligation
heheahhwoah! hehhwhy do you have sugar!
because i made coffee, tea and hot chocolate for my students
heheeee that's so cute!
hi, we're back, we went to a party and then we went to the lexington, um, at the party there were some crazy people, and at the lexington there were some crazy people. heah, and um, hehh
WORLD HERE I COME!
for future reference, the trip to the lexington does not go in the book, i repeat, ms. salt does not take minor to club
ms. salt bought me a drink!

for the record, salt bought — eh, nobody a drink

it was a bass ale, except bob actually bought it

um, so there was like this crazy girl there with like arched eyebrows and um, _crazy_ written all over her face, she was there with a poor young butch girlfriend that was so proud to be showing off her hot young femme at the bar and, but she was left with an open arm the entire night – just left there open and, oh, sprawled against the seat while girl, crazy, was like hugging this other – "woman" (butch) that uh, brought this lady that ms. salt had, uh, some past problems with, um, later that night when we were leaving i saw a glare coming from them and a crazy wave from crazy

and um, oooh, i like sunflower seeds and um, kissable girls were not the forté of the night but um, you know...mnch, chmp... .....you win some you lose some, but, the main point being, that uh, that um,

i'm keeping the window open so i can _spit_!

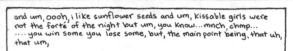

What to say about my graduation?

CHAPTER SIXTEEN

I can say that I imagined it, or at least assumed it to have a larger impact than it ended up with. It was just the whole swarm of the ceremony idea that made me think something writable and conclusive had to happen.

At the same time, of course I knew that no matter what happened it would fill the space regardless, and I imagined myself smiling after a night of nothingness, beautifully appropriate.

But despite all that mishmash I can't deny the fragment of hope that something grand would still happen, something that would catapult me into summer, diving down in enthusiasm to the writing of the book. Something that would send a domino stream down all past events, till they lay, fours up all around, proclaiming me winner.

Ms. Salt and I were in the truck and I was sitting opposite her. This was the end, and – in my forced drunk state, I felt as much the Fact as anything. A moment that meant something. Comic aside, an earnest thank-you.

you really were my best friend this year

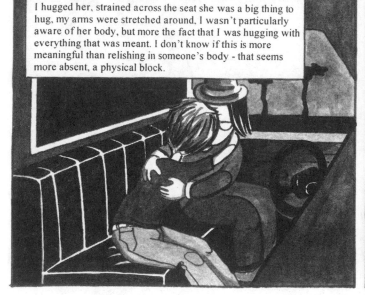

I hugged her, strained across the seat she was a big thing to hug, my arms were stretched around, I wasn't particularly aware of her body, but more the fact that I was hugging with everything that was meant. I don't know if this is more meaningful than relishing in someone's body - that seems more absent, a physical block.

I love you

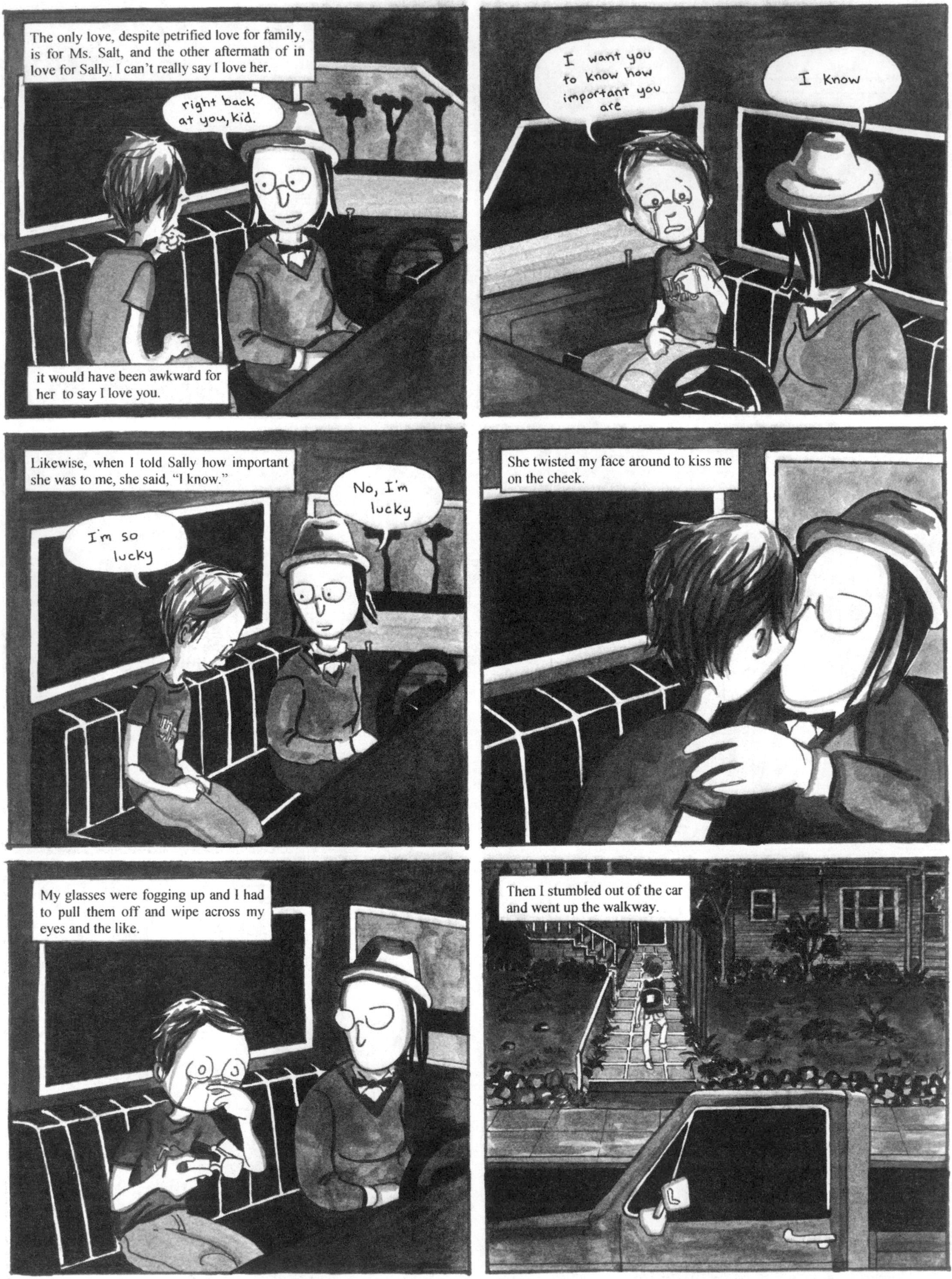
The only love, despite petrified love for family, is for Ms. Salt, and the other aftermath of in love for Sally. I can't really say I love her.
right back at you, kid.
it would have been awkward for her to say I love you.
I want you to know how important you are
I Know
Likewise, when I told Sally how important she was to me, she said, "I know."
I'm so lucky
No, I'm lucky
She twisted my face around to kiss me on the cheek.
My glasses were fogging up and I had to pull them off and wipe across my eyes and the like.
Then I stumbled out of the car and went up the walkway.

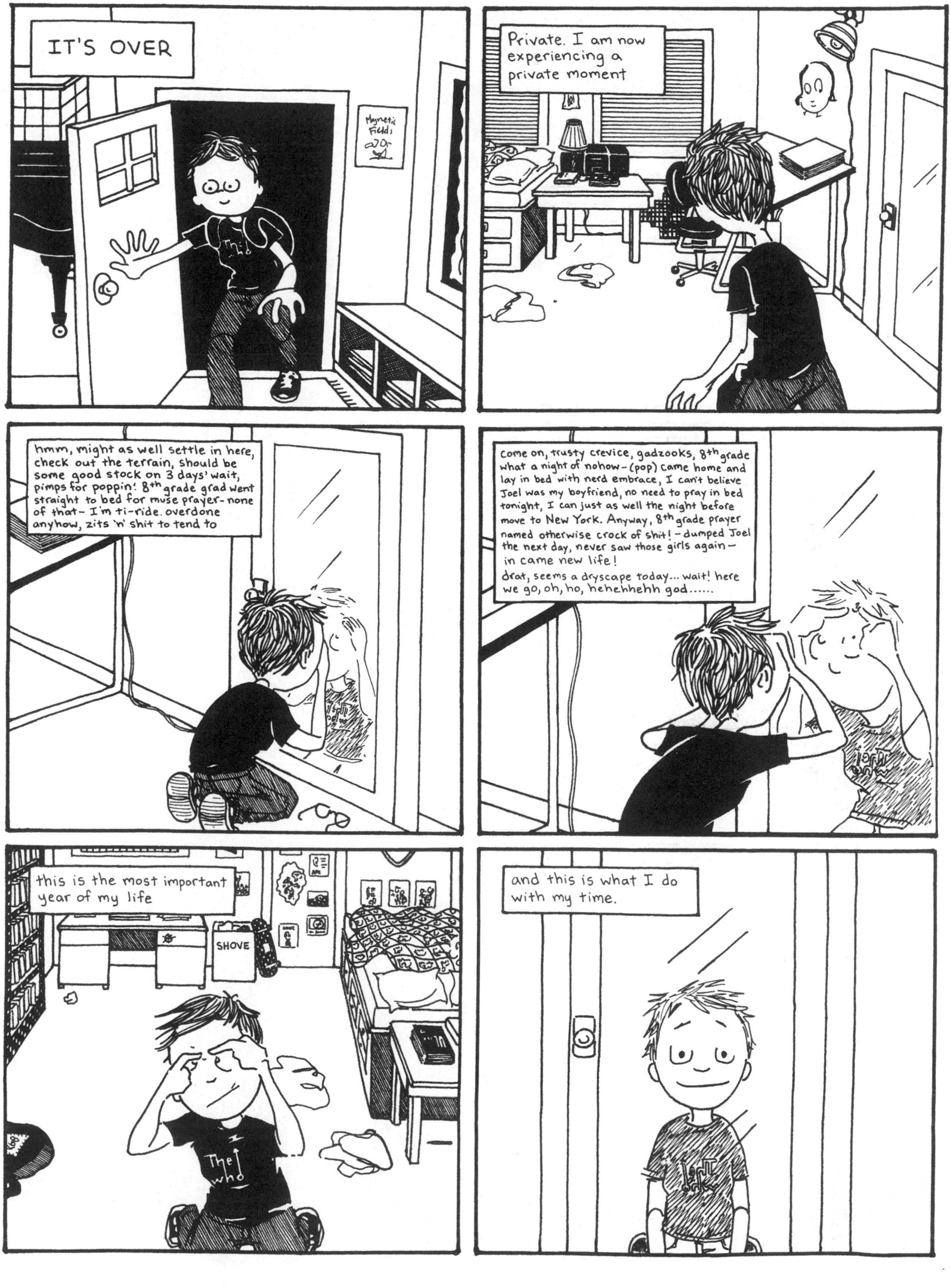
IT'S OVER
Magnetic Fields
Private. I am now experiencing a private moment
hmm, might as well settle in here, check out the terrain, should be some good stock on 3 days' wait, pimps for poppin'. 8th grade grad went straight to bed for muse prayer- none of that- I'm ti-ride. overdone anyhow, zits 'n' shit to tend to
come on, trusty crevice, gadzooks, 8th grade what a night of nohow-(pop) came home and lay in bed with nerd embrace, I can't believe Joel was my boyfriend, no need to pray in bed tonight, I can just as well the night before move to New York. Anyway, 8th grade prayer named otherwise crock of shit! - dumped Joel the next day, never saw those girls again - in came new life!
drat, seems a dryscape today... wait! here we go, oh, ho, hehehhehh god......
this is the most important year of my life
SHOVE
The who
and this is what I do with my time.

THANK YOU

Julia, Tania, Jessica, Toby, Dad.

Sasha W., Nick d., Kirsten L., Bekka, Celeste, Anna, Jessy, Jake, Kerry, Tanya, Lisa Q., Carrie, Heather, Ehren, Katharine, Lisa O., Nick Y., Erin, Rachel, Sasha S., Brian, Sarah, Mike, Sharon, Joey, Bryan, Jamie, Kirsten D.

Amanda Patten!
Lauren Spiegel, Mike Kwan, Cherlynne Li, Marcia Burch, Jamie MacDonald, Ellen Silberman, Stacy Lasner, Elisa Rivlin, and everyone at Simon & Schuster.

Jay Mandel! Renee Kurtz, and everyone at William Morris Agency.

Jodi Peikoff and everyone at Peikoff Law Office.

Amy Hanson, Miriam Klein Stahl, Beau Valtz, Jamie Marantz.

Dan Vado and everyone at Slave Labor Graphics. Jocelyn Hayes Simpson, Christine Vachon, Katie Roumel, and everyone at Killer Films. Rose Troche. Ilene Chaiken and everyone at The L Word.

Ariel Bordeaux, Megan Kelso, Alison Bechdel.

Mitch Cutler at Saint Mark's Comics. Sharon Barnes. Angela Cheng. Joy Peskin. Noah Berlatsky. Jennifer Camper. Deborah Landau. Lindsay Webster and everyone at OurChart. Michelle Tea. Dan Wolf. Patty Jeres, Ted Abenheim, and everyone at Prism Comics. Gigi Nicolas. Angela Cheng Caplan. Mary Gibbons and Alex Cox at Rocketship.

Melissa Plaut!
Kris Peterson ♡
Anna Sochynsky
Gabrielle Bell

Liz Brown, Melissa Anderson, Nico Muhly, Anne Simmons.

Uncle Philip, Aunt Lisa, Cousin Sarah, Cousin Sam, Grandma Lala, Cousin David and Rhoda, Cousin Zachary and Rebecca, Grandma Annette, Aunt Joanna, Uncle Peter, Cousin Isaac, Aunt Ann, Cousin Thor.

Adrian Tomine, Sasha Rossman, Kristin Hultgren, Chloe Aftel, Kristin Poor, Alex Klein, Sadie Robson Crabtree, Tony Groutsis, Stella Robertson, Peggy and Warren Wincorn, Joshua Lyon, A.M. Homes, Jeffrey Witte, Ned Vizzini, Karen Sneider, Rikki Grubb, Angela Robinson, Alex Kondracke, Leigh Spader, Joe Matt, Aimee Mann, Kevin Seccia.

And most of all, my mom, Molly Axtmann.

The High School Comic Chronicles of
Ariel Schrag

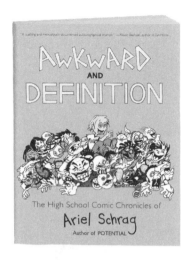

9th Grade

10th Grade

11th Grade

12th Grade